Mastering
VMware vSphere® 5

Mastering

VMware vSphere® 5

Scott Lowe

WILEY

John Wiley & Sons, Inc.

Acquisitions Editor: Agatha Kim
Development Editor: Jennifer Leland
Technical Editor: Duncan Epping
Production Editor: Liz Britten
Copy Editor: Linda Recktenwald
Editorial Manager: Pete Gaughan
Production Manager: Tim Tate
Vice President and Executive Group Publisher: Richard Swadley
Vice President and Publisher: Neil Edde
Book Designer: Maureen Forys, Happenstance Type-O-Rama; Judy Fung
Proofreader: Kristy Eldredge; Word One, New York
Indexer: Ted Laux
Project Coordinator, Cover: Katherine Crocker
Cover Designer: Ryan Sneed

Cover Image: © Pete Gardner/DigitalVision/Getty Images
Copyright © 2011 by John Wiley & Sons, Inc., Indianapolis, Indiana
Published simultaneously in Canada

ISBN: 978-0-470-89080-6
ISBN: 978-1-118-18010-5 (ebk.)
ISBN: 978-1-118-18012-9 (ebk.)
ISBN: 978-1-118-18011-2 (ebk.)

Dear Reader,

Thank you for choosing Mastering *VMware vSphere 5*. This book is part of a family of premium-quality Sybex books, all of which are written by outstanding authors who combine practical experience with a gift for teaching.

Sybex was founded in 1976. More than 30 years later, we're still committed to producing consistently exceptional books. With each of our titles, we're working hard to set a new standard for the industry. From the paper we print on, to the authors we work with, our goal is to bring you the best books available.

I hope you see all that reflected in these pages. I'd be very interested to hear your comments and get your feedback on how we're doing. Feel free to let me know what you think about this or any other Sybex book by sending me an email at nedde@wiley.com. If you think you've found a technical error in this book, please visit http://sybex.custhelp.com. Customer feedback is critical to our efforts at Sybex.

Best regards,

Neil Edde
Vice President and Publisher
Sybex, an Imprint of Wiley

Acknowledgments

One thing I've learned now after writing three other books is that more people are involved than most folks ever realize. Unfortunately, there just isn't enough room on the cover to include everyone's name, even though they all deserve it.

I'll start by thanking my contributing authors, who pitched in and helped me get this book done in a timely fashion. Forbes, it was great working with you again after *VMware vSphere Design*. Gabe, thanks for your contributions and your attention to detail. Glenn, your expertise is much appreciated and it shows in your work. To each of you, thank you. Your help is greatly valued.

The technical accuracy of a book like this is of paramount importance, and I can't think of a better person to help in that area than my technical editor, Duncan Epping. Duncan, thank you for your time and effort. This book is a better work for your involvement, and I hope that we have the opportunity to work together again in the future.

Next, I'd like to thank the entire Sybex team: Agatha Kim, the acquisitions editor; Jennifer Leland, the developmental editor; Liz Britten, the production editor; Linda Recktenwald, the copyeditor; proofreader, Kristy Eldredge; Pete Gaughan, the editorial manager; and Neil Edde, the publisher. I cannot adequately describe just how important each of you was in producing this book and making it what it is. Thank you, each and every one of you.

Thank you, Matt Portnoy, for reviewing the content and providing an objective opinion on what could be done to improve it. I appreciate your time and your candor.

Thank you, EMC Corporation, for your cooperation in getting this book published.

Finally, thanks to the vendors who supplied equipment to use while I was writing the book (in alphabetical order): Brocade, Cisco, Dell, EMC, Intel, and NetApp. I sincerely appreciate the support of all of these vendors. I'd particularly like to thank Cisco, which was gracious enough to host the entire lab environment for this book in one of their labs.

About the Author

Scott Lowe is an author, consultant, speaker, and blogger focusing on virtualization, storage, and other enterprise technologies. Scott is currently the CTO for the vSpecialist team at EMC Corporation. In this role, Scott provides technical leadership, support, and training to the vSpecialist team worldwide.

Scott's technical expertise extends into several areas. He holds industry certifications from Cisco, EMC, Microsoft, NetApp, VMware, and others. He also holds the premier VMware Certified Design Expert (VCDX) certification; Scott is VCDX #39. For Scott's leadership and involvement in the VMware community, he was awarded a VMware vExpert award by VMware three years in a row: 2009, 2010, and 2011.

As an author, Scott has contributed to numerous online magazines focused on VMware and related virtualization technologies. He is regularly quoted as a virtualization expert in virtualization news stories. He has three other published books: *Mastering VMware vSphere 4*, *VMware vSphere 4 Administration Instant Reference* (with Jase McCarty and Matthew Johnson), and *VMware vSphere Design* (with Forbes Guthrie and Maish Saidel-Keesing), all by Sybex.

Scott has spoken at several VMworld conferences as well as other virtualization conferences. He regularly speaks at VMware user group meetings, both locally and abroad.

Scott is perhaps best known for his acclaimed virtualization blog at `http://blog` `.scottlowe.org`, where he regularly posts technical articles on a wide variety of topics. VMware, Microsoft, and other virtualization industry leaders regularly refer to content on his site, and it is regularly voted among the top five virtualization weblogs worldwide. Scott's weblog is one of the oldest virtualization-centric weblogs that is still active; he's been blogging since early 2005, and his weblog was among the very first blogs to be aggregated on VMware's Planet V12n website.

About the Contributors

The following individuals also contributed to this book.

Forbes Guthrie is a systems engineer and infrastructure architect who specializes in virtualization and storage. He has worked in a variety of technical roles for over 12 years and achieved several industry certifications including VMware's VCP2, VCP3, VCP4, and VCP5. His experience spans many different industries, and he has worked in Europe, Asia-Pacific, and North America. He holds a bachelor's degree in mathematics and business analysis and is a former captain in the British army.

Forbes is the lead author of the acclaimed *VMware vSphere Design* (co-authored by Scott Lowe, along with Maish Saidel-Keesing), also published by Sybex.

Forbes's blog, `http://www.vReference.com`, is well regarded in the virtualization field and is aggregated on VMware's Planet V12n website. He is perhaps best known for his collection of free reference cards, long revered by those studying for their VMware qualifications.

Forbes was awarded the luminary designation of vExpert by VMware for his contribution to the virtualization community. His passion and knowledge have also been rewarded with the peer-reviewed top virtualization bloggers listing for the last two years.

Gabrie van Zanten is a virtualization specialist. As a consultant, he designs and implements virtual infrastructures for customers. Besides being a consultant, Gabrie runs one of the top-10–ranked blogs on VMware at `http://www.GabesVirtualWorld.com`. He writes about VMware and helps his readers get in-depth understanding on how VMware products work. His blogging activities, the presentations he gives, and the effort he puts into helping members of the VMware community have earned him the VMware vExpert award in 2009, 2010, and 2011.

Glenn Sizemore has held just about every position one could hold in IT—everything from cable dog to enterprise architect. He started scripting early in his IT career and had mastered VBScript by the time PowerShell first shipped. As a scripter, he was an early adopter and had conquered PowerShell when the VMware Toolkit for Windows (PowerCLI) first shipped. Curiosity carried Glenn to an internal team-testing virtualization. Three years later, he was attending his third VMworld and had just been awarded the status of VMware vExpert. Along the way, Glenn started a blog, `http://www.Get-Admin.com`, to share scripts and automation techniques. Outside of work, Glenn is the proud father of two beautiful children and an avid PowerShell evangelist.

Contents at a Glance

Contents

Introduction

I remember in 2004 (or was it 2003?) when I first started describing the use of server virtualization to a colleague of mine. VMware was pretty much the only vendor in the server virtualization space at the time, and I was describing to him how you could use virtualization to run multiple instances of an operating system on the same physical hardware. I was so excited. He merely asked, "Why in the world would you want to do that?"

The times have changed quite a bit since that time, and now virtualization—especially server virtualization—is readily embraced in corporate datacenters worldwide. VMware has gone from a relatively small vendor to one of the corporate heavyweights, garnering a commanding share of the server virtualization market with their top-notch virtualization products. Even now, when other companies such as Microsoft and Citrix have jumped into the server virtualization space, it's still VMware that's almost synonymous with virtualization. For all intents and purposes, VMware invented the market.

If you're reading this, though, there's a chance you're just now starting to learn about virtualization. What is virtualization, and why is it important to you?

I define *virtualization* as *the abstraction of one computing resource from another computing resource*. Consider storage virtualization; in this case, you are abstracting servers (one computing resource) from the storage to which they are connected (another computing resource). This holds true for other forms of virtualization, too, like application virtualization (abstracting applications from the operating system). When most information technology professionals think of virtualization, they think of hardware (or server) virtualization: abstracting the operating system from the underlying hardware on which it runs and thus enabling multiple operating systems to run simultaneously on the same physical server. That is the technology on which VMware has built its market share.

Almost singlehandedly, VMware's enterprise-grade virtualization solution has revolutionized how organizations manage their datacenters. Prior to the introduction of VMware's powerful virtualization solution, organizations bought a new server every time a new application needed to be provisioned. Over time, datacenters became filled with servers that were all using only a fraction of their overall capacity. Even though these servers were operating at only a fraction of their total capacity, organizations still had to pay to power them and to dissipate the heat they generated.

Now, using VMware's server virtualization products, organizations can run multiple operating systems and applications on their existing hardware, and new hardware needs to be purchased only when capacity needs dictate. No longer do organizations need to purchase a new physical server whenever a new application needs to be deployed. By stacking workloads together using virtualization, organizations derive greater value from their hardware investments. They also reduce operational costs by reducing the number of physical servers and associated hardware in the datacenter, in turn reducing power usage and cooling needs in the datacenter. In some cases these operational cost savings can be quite significant.

But consolidation is only one benefit of virtualization; companies also realize greater work-load mobility, increased uptime, streamlined disaster-recovery options, and a bevy of other benefits from adopting virtualization. And virtualization, specifically server virtualization, has created the foundation for a new way of approaching the computing model: cloud computing.

Cloud computing is built on the tenets of broad network access, resource pooling, rapid elasticity, on-demand self service, and measured service. Virtualization, such as that provided by VMware's products, enables the IT industry to embrace this new operational model of more efficiently providing services to their customers, whether those customers are internal (their employees) or external (partners, end users, or consumers). That ability to efficiently provide services is the reason why virtualization is important to you.

This book provides all the information you, as an information technology professional, need to design, deploy, configure, manage, and monitor a dynamic virtualized environment built on VMware's fifth-generation enterprise-class server virtualization product, vSphere 5.

What Is Covered in This Book

This book is written with a start-to-finish approach to installing, configuring, managing, and monitoring a virtual environment using the VMware vSphere 5 product suite. The book begins by introducing the vSphere product suite and all of its great features. After introducing all of the bells and whistles, this book details an installation of the product and then moves into con-figuration. This includes configuring vSphere's extensive networking and storage functionality. I wrap up the configuration section with sections on high availability, redundancy, and resource utilization. Upon completion of the installation and configuration, I move into virtual machine creation and management and then into monitoring and troubleshooting. This book can be read from cover to cover to gain an understanding of the vSphere product suite in preparation for a new virtual environment. Or it can also be used as a reference for IT professionals who have begun their virtualization and want to complement their skills with real-world tips, tricks, and best practices as found in each chapter.

This book, geared toward the aspiring as well as the practicing virtualization professional, provides information to help implement, manage, maintain, and troubleshoot an enterprise vir-tualization scenario.

Here is a glance at what's in each chapter:

Chapter 1: Introducing VMware vSphere 5   I begin with a general overview of all the products that make up the vSphere 5 product suite. This chapter also covers vSphere licens-ing and provides some examples of benefits that an organization might see from adopting vSphere as its virtualization solution.

Chapter 2: Planning and Installing VMware ESXi   This chapter looks at selecting the physical hardware, choosing your version of VMware ESXi, planning your installation, and actually installing VMware ESXi, both manually and in an unattended fashion.

Chapter 3: Installing and Configuring vCenter Server   In this chapter, I dive deep into planning your vCenter Server environment. vCenter Server is a critical management compo-nent of vSphere, and so this chapter discusses the proper design, planning, installation, and configuration for vCenter Server.

Chapter 4: Installing and Configuring vSphere Update Manager   This chapter describes what is involved in planning, designing, installing and configuring vSphere Update Manager. You'll use vCenter Update Manager to keep your vSphere environment patched and up to date.

Chapter 5: Creating and Configuring Virtual Networks   The virtual networking chapter covers the design, management, and optimization of virtual networks, including new features like the vSphere Distributed Switch and the Cisco Nexus 1000V. In addition, it initiates discussions and provides solutions on how to integrate the virtual networking architecture with the physical network architecture while maintaining network security.

Chapter 6: Creating and Configuring Storage Devices   This in-depth chapter provides an extensive overview of the various storage architectures available for vSphere. This chapter discusses Fibre Channel, iSCSI, and NAS storage design and optimization techniques as well as storage features like thin provisioning, multipathing, and round-robin load balancing.

Chapter 7: Ensuring High Availability and Business Continuity   This exciting chapter covers the hot topics regarding business continuity and disaster recovery. I provide details on building highly available server clusters in virtual machines. In addition, this chapter discusses the use of vSphere High Availability (HA) and vSphere Fault Tolerance (FT) as ways of providing failover for virtual machines running in a vSphere environment. I also discuss backup options using vSphere's Storage APIs—Data Protection and Data Recovery.

Chapter 8: Securing VMware vSphere   Security is an important part of any implementation, and in this chapter I cover different security management aspects, including managing direct ESXi host access and integrating vSphere with Active Directory. This chapter also covers how to manage user access for environments with multiple levels of system administration and how to employ Windows users and groups in conjunction with the vSphere security model to ease the administrative delegation that comes with enterprise-level deployments. I also touch on the VMware vShield family of products and discuss some techniques for incorporating security through the vSphere environment.

Chapter 9: Creating and Managing Virtual Machines   This chapter introduces the practices and procedures involved in provisioning virtual machines through vCenter Server. In addition, you're introduced to timesaving techniques, virtual machine optimization, and best practices that will ensure simplified management as the number of virtual machines grows larger over time.

Chapter 10: Using Templates and vApps   Chapter 10 introduces the idea of templates, a mechanism for more rapidly deploying standardized VM images. I also discuss cloning and the concept of a vApp—a specialized container used by vSphere for the distribution of multi-VM environments. I also discuss the OVF standard used by VMware and other vendors for distributing VMs.

Chapter 11: Managing Resource Allocation   In this chapter I provide a comprehensive look at managing resource allocation. From individual virtual machines to resource pools to clusters of ESXi hosts, this chapter explores how resources are consumed in vSphere and addresses the mechanisms you can use—reservations, limits, and shares—to manage and modify that resource allocation.

Chapter 12: Balancing Resource Utilization   Resource allocation isn't the same as resource utilization, and this chapter follows up the discussion of resource allocation in Chapter 11 with a look at some of the ways vSphere offers to balance resource utilization. In this chapter, you'll learn about vSphere vMotion, Enhanced vMotion Compatibility, vSphere Distributed Resource Scheduler (DRS), Storage vMotion, and Storage DRS.

Chapter 13: Monitoring VMware vSphere Performance   In Chapter 13 I look at some of the native tools in vSphere that give virtual infrastructure administrators the ability to track and troubleshoot performance issues. The chapter focuses on monitoring CPU, memory, disk, and network adapter performance across ESXi hosts, resource pools, and clusters in vCenter Server.

Chapter 14: Automating VMware vSphere   Many tasks VMware vSphere administrators face are repetitive, and here automation can help. In Chapter 14 I discuss several different ways to bring automation to your vSphere environment, including vCenter Orchestrator and PowerCLI.

Appendix A: Solutions to the Master It Problems   This appendix offers solutions to the Master It problems at the end of each chapter.

The Mastering Series

The *Mastering* series from Sybex provides outstanding instruction for readers with intermediate and advanced skills, in the form of top-notch training and development for those already working in their field and clear, serious education for those aspiring to become pros. Every *Mastering* book includes the following:

◆ Real-World Scenarios, ranging from case studies to interviews, that show how the tool, technique, or knowledge presented is applied in actual practice

◆ Skill-based instruction, with chapters organized around real tasks rather than abstract concepts or subjects

◆ Self-review test questions, so you can be certain you're equipped to do the job right

The Hardware behind the Book

Because of the specificity of the hardware for installing VMware vSphere 5, it can be difficult to build an environment in which you can learn by implementing the exercises and practices detailed in this book. It is possible to build a practice lab to follow along with the book; however, the lab will require specific hardware and might be quite costly. Be sure to read Chapter 2 and Chapter 3 before you attempt to construct any type of environment for development purposes.

For the purpose of writing this book, I used the following hardware configuration:

◆ Four Cisco UCS B200 blade servers connected to a pair of UCS 6120 fabric interconnects

◆ Four Dell PowerEdge R610 servers

◆ Several models of Fibre Channel host bus adapters (HBAs) and Fibre Channel over Ethernet (FCoE) converged network adapters (CNAs), including adapters from both QLogic and Emulex

◆ Intel X520 10 Gigabit Ethernet network adapters

- A number of different storage arrays, including

  - NetApp FAS6080

  - EMC Symmetrix VMAX

  - EMC VNX7500

- Several models of Fibre Channel switches, including Cisco MDS 9134 and MDS 9148, Brocade 200e, and Brocade Silkworm 3800 Fibre Channel switches

- Several models of Ethernet switches, including Cisco Nexus 5010 and Dell PowerConnect 6248

Clearly, this is not the sort of environment to which most people have access. For entry-level NFS and iSCSI testing, a number of vendors including EMC, HP, and NetApp offer virtual storage appliances or simulators that you can use to gain some familiarity with shared storage concepts and that specific vendor's products. I encourage you to use these sorts of tools where applicable in your learning process.

Special thanks go to Brocade, Cisco, Dell, EMC, Intel, and NetApp for their help in supplying the equipment used during the writing of this book.

Who Should Buy This Book

This book is for IT professionals looking to strengthen their knowledge of constructing and managing a virtual infrastructure on vSphere 5. While the book can also be helpful for those new to IT, a strong set of assumptions is made about the target reader:

- A basic understanding of networking architecture

- Experience working in a Microsoft Windows environment

- Experience managing DNS and DHCP

- A basic understanding of how virtualization differs from traditional physical infrastructures

- A basic understanding of hardware and software components in standard x86 and x64 computing

How to Contact the Author

I welcome feedback from you about this book or about books you'd like to see from me in the future. You can reach me by writing to scott.lowe@scottlowe.org or by visiting my blog at http://blog.scottlowe.org.

## Chapter 1

Introducing VMware vSphere 5

Now in its fifth generation, VMware vSphere 5 builds on previous generations of VMware's enterprise-grade virtualization products. vSphere 5 extends fine-grained resource allocation controls to more types of resources, enabling VMware administrators to have even greater control over how resources are allocated to and used by virtual workloads. With dynamic resource controls, high availability, unprecedented fault-tolerance features, distributed resource management, and backup tools included as part of the suite, IT administrators have all the tools they need to run an enterprise environment ranging from a few servers up to thousands of servers.

In this chapter, you will learn to

- ◆ Identify the role of each product in the vSphere product suite

- ◆ Recognize the interaction and dependencies between the products in the vSphere suite

- ◆ Understand how vSphere differs from other virtualization products

Exploring VMware vSphere 5

The VMware vSphere product suite is a comprehensive collection of products and features that together provide a full array of enterprise virtualization functionality. The vSphere product suite includes the following products and features:

- ◆ VMware ESXi

- ◆ VMware vCenter Server

- ◆ vSphere Update Manager

- ◆ VMware vSphere Client and vSphere Web Client

- ◆ VMware vShield Zones

- ◆ VMware vCenter Orchestrator

- ◆ vSphere Virtual Symmetric Multi-Processing

- ◆ vSphere vMotion and Storage vMotion

- ◆ vSphere Distributed Resource Scheduler

- ◆ vSphere Storage DRS

- ◆ Storage I/O Control and Network I/O Control

◆ Profile-Driven Storage

◆ vSphere High Availability

◆ vSphere Fault Tolerance

◆ vSphere Storage APIs for Data Protection and VMware Data Recovery

Rather than waiting to introduce these products and features in their own chapters, I'll introduce each product or feature in the following sections. This will allow me to explain how each product or feature affects the design, installation, and configuration of your virtual infrastructure. After I cover the features and products in the vSphere suite, you'll have a better grasp of how each of them fits into the design and the big picture of virtualization.

Certain products outside the vSphere product suite extend the vSphere product line with new functionality. Examples of these additional products include VMware View, VMware vCloud Director, VMware vCloud Request Manager, VMware vCenter AppSpeed, and VMware vCenter Site Recovery Manager, just to name a few. Because of the size and scope of these products and because they are developed and released on a schedule separate from VMware vSphere, they are not covered in this book.

As of the writing of this book, VMware vSphere 5 is the latest release of the VMware vSphere product family. This book covers functionality found in version 5. Where possible, I've tried to note differences between 4.*x* and 5. For detailed information on VMware vSphere 4.0, refer to *Mastering VMware vSphere 4*, also published by Sybex.

To help simplify navigation and to help you find information on the breadth of products and features in the vSphere product suite, I've prepared Table 1.1, which contains cross-references to where you can find more information about that particular product or feature elsewhere in the book.

Table 1.1:   Product and feature cross-references

VMWARE VSPHERE PRODUCT OR FEATURE	MORE INFORMATION FOUND IN THIS CHAPTER
VMware ESXi	Installation – Chapter 2
	Networking – Chapter 5
	Storage – Chapter 6
VMware vCenter Server	Installation – Chapter 3
	Networking – Chapter 5
	Storage – Chapter 6
	Security – Chapter 8
vSphere Update Manager	Chapter 4
vSphere Client and vSphere Web Client	Installation – Chapter 2
	Usage – Chapters 3–14
VMware vShield Zones	Chapter 8

TABLE 1.1: Product and feature cross-references *(CONTINUED)*

VMWARE VSPHERE PRODUCT OR FEATURE	MORE INFORMATION FOUND IN THIS CHAPTER
VMware vCenter Orchestrator	Chapter 14
vSphere Virtual Symmetric Multi-Processing	Chapter 9
vSphere vMotion and Storage vMotion	Chapter 12
vSphere Distributed Resource Scheduler	Chapter 12
vSphere Storage DRS	Chapter 12
Storage I/O Control and Network I/O Control	Chapter 11
Profile-Driven Storage	Chapter 6
vSphere High Availability	Chapter 7
vSphere Fault Tolerance	Chapter 7
vSphere Storage APIs for Data Protection	Chapter 7
VMware Data Recovery	Chapter 7

First I look at the actual products that make up the VMware vSphere product suite, and then I examine the major features. Let's start with the products in the suite; in particular, let's start with VMware ESXi.

Examining the Products in the vSphere Suite

In this section, I'll describe and review the products found in the vSphere product suite.

VMWARE ESXI

The core of the vSphere product suite is the hypervisor, which is the virtualization layer that serves as the foundation for the rest of the product line. In vSphere 5, the hypervisor comes in the form of VMware ESXi.

This is a significant difference from earlier versions of the VMware vSphere product suite. In earlier versions of VMware vSphere, the hypervisor was available in two forms: VMware ESX and VMware ESXi. Although both products shared the same core virtualization engine, supported the same set of virtualization features, leveraged the same licenses, and were both considered bare-metal installations, there were still notable architectural differences. In VMware ESX, VMware used a Linux-derived Service Console to provide an interactive environment through which users could interact with the hypervisor. The Linux-based Service Console also included services found in traditional operating systems, such as a firewall, Simple Network Management Protocol (SNMP) agents, and a web server.

TYPE 1 AND TYPE 2 HYPERVISORS

Hypervisors are generally grouped into two classes: type 1 hypervisors and type 2 hypervisors. Type 1 hypervisors run directly on the system hardware and thus are often referred to as *bare-metal* hypervisors. Type 2 hypervisors require a host operating system, and the host operating system provides I/O device support and memory management. VMware ESXi is a type 1 bare-metal hypervisor. (In earlier versions of vSphere, VMware ESX was also considered a type 1 bare-metal hypervisor.) Other type 1 bare-metal hypervisors include Microsoft Hyper-V and products based on the open source Xen hypervisor like Citrix XenServer and Oracle VM.

VMware ESXi, on the other hand, is the next generation of the VMware virtualization foundation. Unlike VMware ESX, ESXi installs and runs without the Linux-based Service Console. This gives ESXi an ultralight footprint of approximately 70 MB. Despite the lack of the Service Console, ESXi provides all the same virtualization features that VMware ESX supported in earlier versions. Of course, ESXi 5 has been enhanced from earlier versions to support even more functionality, as you'll see in this chapter and in future chapters.

The key reason that VMware ESXi is able to support the same extensive set of virtualization functionality as VMware ESX without the Service Console is that the core of the virtualization functionality wasn't (and still isn't) found in the Service Console. It's the *VMkernel* that is the foundation of the virtualization process. It's the VMkernel that manages the VMs' access to the underlying physical hardware by providing CPU scheduling, memory management, and virtual switch data processing. Figure 1.1 shows the structure of VMware ESXi.

FIGURE 1.1
The VMkernel is the foundation of the virtualization functionality found in VMware ESXi.

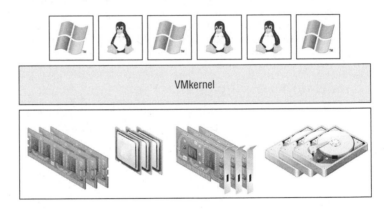

I mentioned earlier that VMware ESXi 5 is enhanced over earlier releases. One such area of enhancement is in the limits of what the hypervisor is capable of supporting. Table 1.2 shows the configuration maximums for the last few versions of VMware ESX/ESXi.

These are just some of the configuration maximums. Where appropriate, future chapters will include additional values for VMware ESXi maximums for network interface cards (NICs), storage, VMs and so forth.

Given that VMware ESXi is the foundation of virtualization within the vSphere product suite, you'll see content for VMware ESXi throughout the book. Table 1.1, earlier in this section, tells you where you can find more information about specific features of VMware ESXi elsewhere in the book.

Table 1.2:   VMware ESXi Maximums

COMPONENT	VMWARE ESXI 5 MAXIMUM	VMWARE ESX/ ESXI 4.0 MAXIMUM	VMWARE ESX 3.5 MAXIMUM
Number of virtual CPUs per host	2048	512	128
Number of cores per host	160	64	32
Number of logical CPUs (hyperthreading enabled)	160	64	32
Number of virtual CPUs per core	25	20 (increased to 25 in Update 1)	8 (increased to 20 in Update 3)
Amount of RAM per host	2 TB	1 TB	128 GB (increased to 256 GB in Update 3)

I'M ONLY TALKING VMWARE ESXI 5 HERE

Throughout this book, I'll refer only to ESXi. It's true that some of the information I present in this book could apply to earlier versions of the product and thus could potentially apply to VMware ESX as well as VMware ESXi. However, I will refer only to ESXi throughout this book, and the information presented will have been tested only with VMware ESXi 5.

VMWARE vCENTER SERVER

Stop for a moment to think about your current network. Does it include Active Directory? There is a good chance it does. Now imagine your network without Active Directory, without the ease of a centralized management database, without the single sign-on capabilities, and without the simplicity of groups. That is what managing VMware ESXi hosts would be like without using VMware vCenter Server. Not a very pleasant thought, is it? Now calm yourself down, take a deep breath, and know that vCenter Server, like Active Directory, is meant to provide a centralized management utility for all ESXi hosts and their respective VMs. vCenter Server allows IT administrators to deploy, manage, monitor, automate, and secure a virtual infrastructure in a centralized fashion. To help provide scalability, vCenter Server leverages a backend database (Microsoft SQL Server and Oracle are both supported, among others) that stores all the data about the hosts and VMs.

In previous versions of VMware vSphere, vCenter Server was a Windows-only application. Version 5 of vSphere still offers this Windows-based installation of vCenter Server. However, in this version VMware adds a prebuilt vCenter Server appliance (a virtual appliance, in fact, something you'll learn about in Chapter 10, "Using Templates and vApps" that is based on Linux. The delivery of a Linux-based vCenter Server is a deliverable that VMware has been discussing for quite some time, and it's nice to see it finally arrive in vSphere 5!

In addition to vCenter Server's configuration and management capabilities—which include features such as VM templates, VM customization, rapid provisioning and deployment of VMs, role-based access controls, and fine-grained resource allocation controls—vCenter Server provides the tools for the more advanced features of vSphere vMotion, vSphere Distributed Resource Scheduler, vSphere High Availability, and vSphere Fault Tolerance. All of these features are described briefly in this chapter and in more detail in later chapters.

In addition to vSphere vMotion, vSphere Distributed Resource Scheduler, vSphere High Availability, and vSphere Fault Tolerance, using vCenter Server to manage ESXi hosts enables a number of other features:

◆ Enhanced vMotion Compatibility (EVC), which leverages hardware functionality from Intel and AMD to enable greater CPU compatibility between servers grouped into vSphere DRS clusters

◆ Host profiles, which allow administrators to bring greater consistency to host configurations across larger environments and to identify missing or incorrect configurations

◆ Storage I/O Control, which provides cluster-wide quality of service (QoS) controls so that administrators can ensure that critical applications receive sufficient I/O resources even during times of congestion

◆ vSphere Distributed Switches, which provide the foundation for cluster-wide networking settings and third-party virtual switches

◆ Network I/O Control, which allows administrators to flexibly partition physical NIC bandwidth for different types of traffic

◆ vSphere Storage DRS, which enables VMware vSphere to dynamically migrate storage resources to meet demand, much in the same way that DRS balances CPU and memory utilization

vCenter Server plays a central role in any sizable VMware vSphere implementation. In Chapter 3, "Installing and Configuring vCenter Server," I discuss planning and installing vCenter Server as well as look at ways to ensure its availability. Chapter 3 will also examine the differences between the Windows-based version of vCenter Server and the Linux-based vCenter Server virtual appliance. Because of vCenter Server's central role in a VMware vSphere deployment, I'll touch on vCenter Server in almost every chapter throughout the rest of the book. Refer to Table 1.1 previously in this chapter for specific cross-references.

vCenter Server is available in three packages:

◆ vCenter Server Essentials is integrated into the vSphere Essentials kits for small office deployment.

◆ vCenter Server Standard provides all the functionality of vCenter Server, including provisioning, management, monitoring, and automation.

◆ vCenter Server Foundation is like vCenter Server Standard but is limited to managing three ESXi hosts and does not include vCenter Orchestrator or support for linked-mode operation.

You can find more information on licensing and product editions for VMware vSphere in the section "Licensing VMware vSphere."

vSphere Update Manager

vSphere Update Manager is a plug-in for vCenter Server that helps users keep their ESXi hosts and select VMs patched with the latest updates. vSphere Update Manager provides the following functionality:

♦ Scans to identify systems that are not compliant with the latest updates

♦ User-defined rules for identifying out-of-date systems

♦ Automated installation of patches for ESXi hosts

♦ Full integration with other vSphere features like Distributed Resource Scheduler

vSphere Update Manager works with both the Windows-based installation of vCenter Server as well as the prepackaged vCenter Server virtual appliance. Refer to Table 1.1 for more information on where vSphere Update Manager is described in this book.

VMware vSphere Client and vSphere Web Client

vCenter Server provides a centralized management framework for VMware ESXi hosts, but it's the vSphere Client where vSphere administrators will spend most of their time.

The vSphere Client is a Windows-based application that allows you to manage ESXi hosts, either directly or through an instance of vCenter Server. You can install the vSphere Client by browsing to the URL of an ESXi host or vCenter Server and selecting the appropriate installation link (although keep in mind that Internet access might be required in order to download the client in some instances). The vSphere Client provides a rich graphical user interface (GUI) for all day-to-day management tasks and for the advanced configuration of a virtual infrastructure. While you can connect the vSphere Client either directly to an ESXi host or to an instance of vCenter Server, the full set of management capabilities are only available when connecting the vSphere Client to vCenter Server.

With the release of vSphere 5, VMware also adds a robust new vSphere Web Client as well. The vSphere Web Client provides a dynamic, web-based user interface for managing a virtual infrastructure, and enables vSphere administrators to manage their infrastructure without first needing to install the full vSphere Client on a system. However, the vSphere Web Client in its current form only provides a subset of the functionality available to the "full" vSphere Client.

Because the vSphere Web Client currently only provides a subset of the functionality, I focus primarily on how to use the vSphere Client throughout this book. Tasks in the vSphere Web Client should be similar.

VMware vShield Zones

VMware vSphere offers some compelling virtual networking functionality, and vShield Zones builds on vSphere's virtual networking functionality to add virtual firewall functionality. vShield Zones allows vSphere administrators to see and manage the network traffic flows occurring on the virtual network switches. You can apply network security policies across entire groups of machines, ensuring that these policies are maintained properly even though VMs may move from host to host using vSphere vMotion and vSphere DRS.

OTHER MEMBERS OF THE VSHIELD FAMILY

vShield Zones is not the only member of the vShield family of products. VMware also offers vShield App, a guest-level firewall that operates at a virtual NIC level and enforces access control policies even between VMs in the same port group; vShield Edge, which provides network edge security and gateway services such as DHCP, NAT, site-to-site VPN, and load balancing; and vShield Endpoint, which enables an introspection-based antivirus solution that third-party antivirus vendors can leverage for more efficient antivirus protection. Because these products aren't part of the VMware vSphere suite, I don't discuss them in great detail in this book.

VMWARE VCENTER ORCHESTRATOR

VMware vCenter Orchestrator is a workflow automation engine that is automatically installed with every instance of vCenter Server. Using vCenter Orchestrator, vSphere administrators can build automated workflows for a wide variety of tasks available within vCenter Server. The automated workflows you build using vCenter Orchestrator range from simple to complex. VMware also makes vCenter Orchestrator plug-ins to extend the functionality to include manipulating Microsoft Active Directory, Cisco's Unified Computing System (UCS), and VMware vCloud Director. This makes vCenter Orchestrator a powerful tool to use in building automated workflows in the virtualized data center.

Now that I've discussed the specific products in the VMware vSphere product suite, I'd like to take a closer look at some of the significant features.

Examining the Features in VMware vSphere

In this section, I'll take a closer look at some of the features that are available in the vSphere product suite. I'll start with Virtual SMP.

VSPHERE VIRTUAL SYMMETRIC MULTI-PROCESSING

The vSphere Virtual Symmetric Multi-Processing (vSMP or Virtual SMP) product allows virtual infrastructure administrators to construct VMs with multiple virtual processors. vSphere Virtual SMP is *not* the licensing product that allows ESXi to be installed on servers with multiple processors; it is the technology that allows the use of multiple processors *inside* a VM. Figure 1.2 identifies the differences between multiple processors in the ESXi host system and multiple virtual processors.

With vSphere Virtual SMP, applications that require and can actually use multiple CPUs can be run in VMs configured with multiple virtual CPUs. This allows organizations to virtualize even more applications without negatively impacting performance or being unable to meet service-level agreements (SLAs).

vSphere 5 expands this functionality by also allowing users to specify multiple virtual cores per virtual CPU. Using this feature, a user could provision a dual "socket" VM with two cores per "socket" for a total of four virtual cores. This gives users tremendous flexibility in carving up CPU processing power among the VMs.

FIGURE 1.2
vSphere Virtual
SMP allows VMs
to be created with
more than one
virtual CPU.

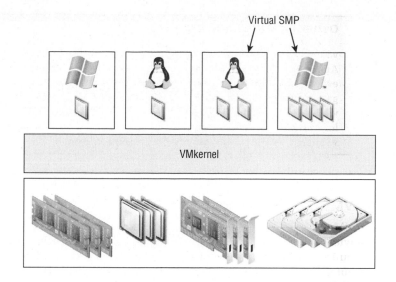

vSphere vMotion and vSphere Storage vMotion

If you have read anything about VMware, you have most likely read about the extremely
useful feature called vMotion. vSphere vMotion, also known as *live migration*, is a feature of
ESXi and vCenter Server that allows an administrator to move a running VM from one physical
host to another physical host without having to power off the VM. This migration between two
physical hosts occurs with no downtime and with no loss of network connectivity to the VM.
The ability to manually move a running VM between physical hosts on an as-needed basis is a
powerful feature that has a number of use cases in today's datacenters.

Suppose a physical machine has experienced a non-fatal hardware failure and needs to be
repaired. Administrators can easily initiate a series of vMotion operations to remove all VMs
from an ESXi host that is to undergo scheduled maintenance. After the maintenance is complete
and the server is brought back online, administrators can utilize vMotion to return the VMs to
the original server.

Alternately, consider a situation in which you are migrating from one set of physical servers to a new set of physical servers. Assuming that the details have been addressed—and I'll
discuss the details around vMotion in Chapter 12, "Balancing Resource Utilization"—you can
use vMotion to move the VMs from the old servers to the newer servers, making quick work of a
server migration with no interruption of service.

Even in normal day-to-day operations, vMotion can be used when multiple VMs on the same
host are in contention for the same resource (which ultimately is causing poor performance
across all the VMs). vMotion can solve the problem by allowing an administrator to migrate any
VMs that are facing contention to another ESXi host with greater availability for the resource in
demand. For example, when two VMs are in contention with each other for CPU resources, an
administrator can eliminate the contention by using vMotion to move of one of the VMs to an
ESXi host that has more available CPU resources.

---

vMotion Enhancements

vSphere 5 enhances vMotion's functionality, making VM migrations faster and enabling more concurrent VM migrations than were supported in previous versions of vSphere or VMware Infrastructure 3. vSphere 5 also enhances vMotion to take advantage of multiple network interfaces, further improving live migration performance.

---

vMotion moves the execution of a VM, relocating the CPU and memory footprint between physical servers but leaving the storage untouched. Storage vMotion builds on the idea and principle of vMotion by providing the ability to leave the CPU and memory footprint untouched on a physical server but migrating a VM's storage while the VM is still running.

Deploying vSphere in your environment generally means that lots of shared storage—Fibre Channel or iSCSI SAN or NFS—is needed. What happens when you need to migrate from an older storage array to a newer storage array? What kind of downtime would be required? Or what about a situation where you need to rebalance utilization of the array, either from a capacity or performance perspective?

vSphere Storage vMotion directly addresses these situations. By providing the ability to move the storage for a running VM between datastores, Storage vMotion enables administrators to address all of these situations without downtime. This feature ensures that outgrowing datastores or moving to a new SAN does not force an outage for the affected VMs and provides administrators with yet another tool to increase their flexibility in responding to changing business needs.

vSphere Distributed Resource Scheduler

vMotion is a manual operation, meaning that an administrator must initiate the vMotion operation. What if VMware vSphere could perform vMotion operations automatically? That is the basic idea behind vSphere Distributed Resource Scheduler (DRS). If you think that vMotion sounds exciting, your anticipation will only grow after learning about DRS. DRS, simply put, leverages vMotion to provide automatic distribution of resource utilization across multiple ESXi hosts that are configured in a cluster.

Given the prevalence of Microsoft Windows Server in today's datacenters, the use of the term *cluster* often draws IT professionals into thoughts of Microsoft Windows Server clusters. Windows Server clusters are often active-passive or active-active-passive clusters. However, ESXi clusters are fundamentally different, operating in an active-active mode to aggregate and combine resources into a shared pool. Although the underlying concept of aggregating physical hardware to serve a common goal is the same, the technology, configuration, and feature sets are quite different between VMware ESXi clusters and Windows Server clusters.

Aggregate Capacity and Single Host Capacity

Although I say that a DRS cluster is an implicit aggregation of CPU and memory capacity, it's important to keep in mind that a VM is limited to using the CPU and RAM of a single physical host at any given time. If you have two ESXi servers with 32 GB of RAM each in a DRS cluster, the cluster will correctly report 64 GB of aggregate RAM available, but any given VM will not be able to use more than approximately 32 GB of RAM at a time.

An ESXi cluster is an implicit aggregation of the CPU power and memory of all hosts involved in the cluster. After two or more hosts have been assigned to a cluster, they work in unison to provide CPU and memory to the VMs assigned to the cluster. The goal of DRS is twofold:

◆ At startup, DRS attempts to place each VM on the host that is best suited to run that VM at that time.

◆ While a VM is running, DRS seeks to provide that VM with the required hardware resources while minimizing the amount of contention for those resources in an effort to maintain balanced utilization levels.

The first part of DRS is often referred to as *intelligent placement*. DRS can automate the placement of each VM as it is powered on within a cluster, placing it on the host in the cluster that it deems to be best suited to run that VM at that moment.

DRS isn't limited to operating only at VM startup, though. DRS also manages the VM's location while it is running. For example, let's say three servers have been configured in an ESXi cluster with DRS enabled. When one of those servers begins to experience a high contention for CPU utilization, DRS detects that the cluster is imbalanced in its resource usage and uses an internal algorithm to determine which VM(s) should be moved in order to create the least imbalanced cluster. For every VM, DRS will simulate a migration to each host and the results will be compared. The migrations that create the least imbalanced cluster will be recommended or automatically performed, depending upon DRS's configuration.

DRS performs these on-the-fly migrations without any downtime or loss of network connectivity to the VMs by leveraging vMotion, the live migration functionality I described earlier. This makes DRS extremely powerful because it allows clusters of ESXi hosts to dynamically rebalance their resource utilization based on the changing demands of the VMs running on that cluster.

FEWER BIGGER SERVERS OR MORE SMALLER SERVERS?

Remember from Table 1.2 that VMware ESXi supports servers with up to 160 CPU cores (64 CPU cores in vSphere 4.0) and up to 2 TB of RAM. With vSphere DRS, though, you can combine multiple smaller servers for the purpose of managing aggregate capacity. This means that bigger, more powerful servers might not be better servers for virtualization projects. These larger servers, in general, are significantly more expensive than smaller servers, and using a greater number of smaller servers (often referred to as "scaling out") may provide greater flexibility than a smaller number of larger servers (often referred to as "scaling up"). The new vRAM licensing model for vSphere 5, discussed in the "Licensing VMware vSphere" section, would also affect this decision. The key thing to remember is that a bigger server isn't necessarily a better server.

---

vSphere Storage DRS

vSphere Storage DRS, a major new feature of VMware vSphere 5, takes the idea of vSphere DRS and applies it to storage. Just as vSphere DRS helps to balance CPU and memory utilization across a cluster of ESXi hosts, Storage DRS helps balance storage capacity and storage performance across a cluster of datastores using mechanisms that echo those used by vSphere DRS.

I described vSphere DRS's feature called intelligent placement, which automates the placement of new VMs based on resource usage within an ESXi cluster. In the same fashion, Storage DRS has an intelligent placement function that automates the placement of VM virtual disks based on storage utilization. Storage DRS does this through the use of datastore clusters. When you create a new VM, you simply point it to a datastore cluster, and Storage DRS automatically places the VM's virtual disks on an appropriate datastore within that datastore cluster.

Likewise, just as vSphere DRS uses vMotion to balance resource utilization dynamically, Storage DRS uses Storage vMotion to rebalance storage utilization. Because Storage vMotion operations are typically much more resource intensive than vMotion operations, vSphere provides extensive controls over the thresholds, timing, and other guidelines that will trigger a Storage DRS automatic migration via Storage vMotion.

STORAGE I/O CONTROL AND NETWORK I/O CONTROL

VMware vSphere has always had extensive controls for modifying or controlling the allocation of CPU and memory resources to VMs. What vSphere didn't have prior to the release of vSphere 4.1 was a way to apply these same sort of extensive controls to storage I/O and network I/O. Storage I/O Control and Network I/O Control address that shortcoming.

Storage I/O Control allows vSphere administrators to assign relative priority to storage I/O as well as assign storage I/O limits to VMs. These settings are enforced cluster-wide; when an ESXi host detects storage congestion through an increase of latency beyond a user-configured threshold, it will apply the settings configured for that VM. The result is that VMware administrators can ensure that the VMs that need priority access to storage resources get the resources they need. In vSphere 4.1, Storage I/O Control applied only to VMFS storage; vSphere 5 extends that functionality to NFS datastores.

The same goes for Network I/O Control, but for network traffic on the physical NICs. As the widespread adoption of 10 Gigabit Ethernet continues, Network I/O Control provides VMware administrators a way to more reliably ensure that network bandwidth is properly allocated to VMs based on priority and limits.

PROFILE-DRIVEN STORAGE

With profile-driven storage, a new feature found in vSphere 5, vSphere administrators are able to use storage capabilities and VM storage profiles to ensure that VMs are residing on storage that is able to provide the necessary levels of capacity, performance, availability, and redundancy. Profile-driven storage is built on two key components:

◆ Storage capabilities, leveraging vSphere's storage awareness APIs

◆ VM storage profiles

Storage capabilities are either provided by the storage array itself (if the array is capable of using vSphere's storage awareness APIs) and/or defined by a vSphere administrator. These storage capabilities represent various attributes of the storage solution.

VM storage profiles define the storage requirements for a VM and its virtual disks. You create VM storage profiles by selecting the storage capabilities that must be present in order for the VM to run. Datastores that have all the capabilities defined in the VM storage profile are compliant with the VM storage profile and represent possible locations where the VM could be stored.

This functionality gives vSphere administrators much greater control over the placement of VMs on shared storage and helps ensure that the appropriate functionality for each VM is indeed being provided by the underlying storage.

Refer to Table 1.1 to find out which chapter discusses profile-driven storage in more detail.

vSphere High Availability

In many cases, high availability (HA)—or the lack of high availability—is the key argument used against virtualization. The most common form of this argument more or less sounds like this: "Before virtualization, the failure of a physical server affected only one application or workload. After virtualization, the failure of a physical server will affect many more applications or workloads running on that server at the same time." We can't put all our eggs in one basket!

VMware addresses this concern with another feature present in ESXi clusters called vSphere HA. Once again, by nature of the naming conventions (clusters, high availability), many traditional Windows administrators will have preconceived notions about this feature. Those notions, however, are incorrect in that vSphere HA does not function like a high-availability configuration in Windows. The vSphere HA feature provides an automated process for restarting VMs that were running on an ESXi host at a time of complete server failure. Figure 1.3 depicts the VM migration that occurs when an ESXi host that is part of an HA-enabled cluster experiences failure.

FIGURE 1.3
The vSphere HA feature will restart any VMs that were previously running on an ESXi host that experiences server failure.

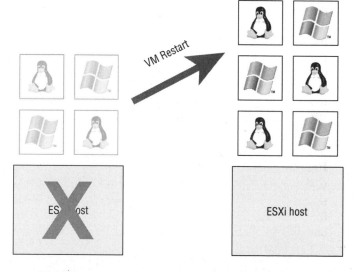

The vSphere HA feature, unlike DRS, does not use the vMotion technology as a means of migrating servers to another host. vMotion is applicable only for planned migrations, where both the source and destination ESXi host are running and functioning properly. In a vSphere HA failover situation, there is no anticipation of failure; it is not a planned outage, and therefore there is no time to perform a vMotion operation. vSphere HA is intended to address unplanned downtime because of the failure of a physical ESXi host.

vSphere HA Improvements in vSphere 5

vSphere HA has received a couple of notable improvements since vSphere 4.0. First, the scalability of vSphere HA has been significantly improved; you can now run up to 512 VMs per host (up from 100 in earlier versions) and 3,000 VMs per cluster (up from 1,280 in earlier versions). Second, vSphere HA now integrates more closely with vSphere DRS's intelligent placement functionality, giving vSphere HA greater ability to restart VMs in the event of a host failure. The third and perhaps most significant improvement is the complete rewrite of the underlying architecture for vSphere HA; this entirely new architecture, known as Fault Domain Manager (FDM), eliminates many of the constraints found in earlier versions of VMware vSphere.

By default, vSphere HA does not provide failover in the event of a guest OS failure, although you can configure vSphere HA to monitor VMs and restart them automatically if they fail to respond to an internal heartbeat. This feature is called VM Failure Monitoring, and it uses a combination of internal heartbeats and I/O activity to attempt to detect if the guest OS inside a VM has stopped functioning. If the guest OS has stopped functioning, the VM can be restarted automatically.

With vSphere HA, it's important to understand that there will be an interruption of service. If a physical host fails, vSphere HA restarts the VM, and during that period of time while the VM is restarting, the applications or services provided by that VM are unavailable. For users who need even higher levels of availability than can be provided using vSphere HA, vSphere Fault Tolerance (FT), which is described in the next section, can help.

vSphere Fault Tolerance

For users who require even greater levels of high availability than vSphere HA can provide, VMware vSphere has a feature known as vSphere Fault Tolerance (FT).

As I described in the previous section, vSphere HA protects against unplanned physical server failure by providing a way to automatically restart VMs upon physical host failure. This need to restart a VM in the event of a physical host failure means that some downtime—generally less than three minutes—is incurred. vSphere FT goes even further and eliminates any downtime in the event of a physical host failure. Using vLockstep technology that is based on VMware's earlier "record and replay" functionality, vSphere FT maintains a mirrored secondary VM on a separate physical host that is kept in lockstep with the primary VM. Everything that occurs on the primary (protected) VM also occurs simultaneously on the secondary (mirrored) VM, so that if the physical host on which the primary VM is running fails, the secondary VM can immediately step in and take over without any loss of connectivity. vSphere FT will also automatically re-create the secondary (mirrored) VM on another host if the physical host on which the secondary VM is running fails, as illustrated in Figure 1.4. This ensures protection for the primary VM at all times.

FIGURE 1.4
vSphere FT
provides protection
against host failures
with no downtime
experienced by the
VMs.

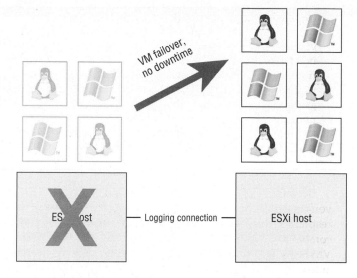

In the event of multiple host failures—say, the hosts running both the primary and secondary VMs failed—vSphere HA will reboot the primary VM on another available server, and vSphere FT will automatically create a new secondary VM. Again, this ensures protection for the primary VM at all times.

vSphere FT can work in conjunction with vMotion, but in vSphere 4.0 it could not work with DRS; DRS had to be manually disabled on VMs that were protected with vSphere FT. In vSphere 5, FT is now integrated with vSphere DRS, although this feature does require Enhanced vMotion Compatibility (EVC).

vSphere Storage APIs for Data Protection and VMware Data Recovery

One of the most critical aspects to any network, not just a virtualized infrastructure, is a solid backup strategy as defined by a company's disaster recovery and business continuity plan. To help address the needs of organizations for backup, VMware vSphere 5 has two key components: the vSphere Storage APIs for Data Protection (VADP) and VMware Data Recovery (VDR).

VADP is a set of application programming interfaces (APIs) that backup vendors leverage in order to provide enhanced backup functionality of virtualized environments. VADP enables functionality like file-level backup and restore; support for incremental, differential, and full-image backups; native integration with backup software; and support for multiple storage protocols.

On its own, though, VADP is just a set of interfaces, like a framework for making backups possible. You can't actually back up VMs with VADP. You'll need a VADP-enabled backup application. There are a growing number of third-party backup applications that are designed to work with VADP, and VMware also offers its own backup tool, VMware Data Recovery (VDR). VDR leverages VADP to provide a full backup solution for smaller VMware vSphere environments.

 **Real World Scenario**

VMWARE VSPHERE COMPARED TO HYPER-V AND XENSERVER

It's not really possible to compare some virtualization solutions to other virtualization solutions because they are fundamentally different in approach and purpose. Such is the case with VMware ESXi and some of the other virtualization solutions on the market.

To make accurate comparisons between vSphere and other virtualization solutions, you must include only type 1 ("bare-metal") virtualization solutions. This would include ESXi, of course, and Microsoft Hyper-V and Citrix XenServer. It would not include products such as VMware Server or Microsoft Virtual Server, both of which are type 2 ("hosted") virtualization products. Even within the type 1 hypervisors, there are architectural differences that make direct comparisons difficult.

For example, both Microsoft Hyper-V and Citrix XenServer route all the VM I/O through the "parent partition" or "dom0." This typically provides greater hardware compatibility with a wider range of products. In the case of Hyper-V, for example, as soon as Windows Server 2008—the general-purpose operating system running in the parent partition—supports a particular type of hardware, then Hyper-V supports it also. Hyper-V "piggybacks" on Windows' hardware drivers and the I/O stack. The same can be said for XenServer, although its "dom0" runs Linux and not Windows.

VMware ESXi, on the other hand, handles I/O within the hypervisor itself. This typically provides greater throughput and lower overhead at the expense of slightly more limited hardware compatibility. In order to add more hardware support or updated drivers, the hypervisor must be updated because the I/O stack and device drivers are in the hypervisor.

This architectural difference is fundamental. Nowhere is this architectural difference more greatly demonstrated than in ESXi, which has a small footprint yet provides a full-featured virtualization solution. Both Citrix XenServer and Microsoft Hyper-V require a full installation of a general-purpose operating system (Windows Server 2008 for Hyper-V, Linux for XenServer) in the parent partition/dom0 in order to operate.

In the end, each of the virtualization products has its own set of advantages and disadvantages, and large organizations may end up using multiple products. For example, VMware vSphere might be best suited in the large corporate datacenter, while Microsoft Hyper-V or Citrix XenServer might be acceptable for test, development, or branch-office deployment. Organizations that don't require VMware vSphere's advanced features like vSphere DRS, vSphere FT, or Storage vMotion may also find that Microsoft Hyper-V or Citrix XenServer is a better fit for their needs.

As you can see, VMware vSphere offers some pretty powerful features that will change the way you view the resources in your datacenter. The latest release of vSphere, version 5, expands existing features and adds powerful new features like Storage I/O Control. Some of these features, though, might not be applicable to all organizations, which is why VMware has crafted a flexible licensing scheme for organizations of all sizes.

LICENSING VMWARE VSPHERE

With the introduction of VMware vSphere 4, VMware introduced new licensing tiers and bundles that were intended to provide a good fit for every market segment. VMware has refined this licensing arrangement with the release of VMware vSphere 5. In this section, I'll explain how the various features that I've discussed so far fit into vSphere's licensing model.

You've already seen how VMware packages and licenses VMware vCenter Server, but here's a quick review:

◆ VMware vCenter Server for Essentials kits, which is bundled with the vSphere Essentials kits (more on the kits in just a moment).

◆ VMware vCenter Server Foundation supports the management of up to three vSphere hosts.

◆ VMware vCenter Server Standard, which includes all functionality and does not have a preset limit on the number of vSphere hosts it can manage (although normal sizing limits do apply). vCenter Orchestrator is only included in the Standard edition of vCenter Server.

In addition to the three editions of vCenter Server, VMware also offers three editions of VMware vSphere:

◆ vSphere Standard Edition

◆ vSphere Enterprise Edition

◆ vSphere Enterprise Plus Edition

NO MORE VSPHERE ADVANCED

If you were familiar with the editions of VMware vSphere 4, you'll note that the Advanced Edition no longer exists in vSphere 5. Users who purchased Advanced Edition are entitled to use the Enterprise Edition in vSphere 5.

These three editions are differentiated by two things: the features each edition supports and the vRAM entitlement. Before I get to the features supported by each edition, I'd like to first discuss vRAM entitlements.

Starting with vSphere 5.0, VMware now uses vRAM entitlements as a part of the licensing scheme. Prior to vSphere 5, VMware's licensing was per-processor but included restrictions on the number of physical cores and the amount of the physical RAM in the server. For example, the Enterprise Edition of VMware vSphere 4 limited users to 6 cores per CPU socket and a maximum of 256GB of RAM in the server. The idea of limits on physical CPU cores and physical RAM goes away in vSphere 5. Servers licensed with VMware vSphere 5 can have as many cores per CPU socket and as much physical memory installed as the user would like. The licensing is still per-processor, but instead of using CPU core or memory limits, VMware has introduced the concept of *vRAM entitlements*.

vRAM is the term used to describe the amount of RAM configured for a VM. For example, a VM configured to use 8 GB of RAM is configured for 8 GB of vRAM. (You'll see more on how to configure VMs and memory assigned to VMs in Chapter 9.) In vSphere 5, each edition has an associated vRAM entitlement—a soft limit on the amount of vRAM configured for your VMs—associated with the license. Here are the vRAM entitlements for the different editions:

◆ vSphere Standard Edition: vRAM entitlement of 32 GB

◆ vSphere Enterprise Edition: vRAM entitlement of 64 GB

◆ vSphere Enterprise Plus Edition: vRAM entitlement of 96 GB

These vRAM entitlements are per license of vSphere 5, and vSphere 5 continues to be licensed on a per-processor basis. So, a physical server with two physical CPUs would need two licenses, and there is no limit on the number of cores or the amount of RAM that can be physically installed in the server. If you were to license that server with two licenses of vSphere Enterprise Plus, you would have a vRAM entitlement of 192 GB. This means that you can have up to 192 GB of vRAM allocated to running VMs. (The vRAM entitlement only applies to powered-on VMs.) If you were to license the server with Standard Edition, you would have a vRAM entitlement of 64 GB, and you could have up to 64 GB of vRAM allocated to running VMs on that server.

Further, vRAM entitlements can be pooled across all the hosts being managed by vCenter Server. So, if you had five dual-socket hosts, you'd need ten vSphere 5 licenses (one each for the ten CPUs across the five dual-socket hosts). Depending on which edition you used, you would have a pooled vRAM entitlement *for the entire pool of servers* of 320 GB (for Standard Edition), 640 GB (for Enterprise Edition), or 960 GB (for Enterprise Plus Edition). vRAM entitlements that aren't being used by one server can be used on another server, as long as the total across the entire pool falls below the limit. This gives administrators greater flexibility in managing vRAM entitlements.

The basic idea behind vRAM entitlements is to help organizations move closer to usage-based cost and chargeback models that are more typical of cloud computing environments and Infrastructure as a Service (IaaS) models.

Let's now summarize the features that are supported for each edition of VMware vSphere 5, along with the associated vRAM entitlements for each edition. This information is presented in Table 1.3.

TABLE 1.3: Overview of VMware vSphere product editions

	ESSENTIALS	ESSENTIALS PLUS	STANDARD	ENTERPRISE	ENTERPRISE PLUS
vCenter Server compatibility	vCenter Server for Essentials	vCenter Server for Essentials	vCenter Server Foundation and Standard	vCenter Server Foundation and Standard	vCenter Server Foundation and Standard
vRAM Entitlement	32 GB	32 GB	32 GB	64 GB	96 GB
vCPUs per VM	8	8	8	8	32
High Availability		X	X	X	X
Data Recovery		X	X	X	X
vMotion		X	X	X	X
Virtual Serial Port Concentrator				X	X
Hot Add				X	X
vShield Zones				X	X

TABLE 1.3:   Overview of VMware vSphere product editions   *(CONTINUED)*

	ESSENTIALS	ESSENTIALS PLUS	STANDARD	ENTERPRISE	ENTERPRISE PLUS
Fault Tolerance				X	X
Storage APIs for Array Integration, Multipathing				X	X
Storage vMotion				X	X
Distributed Resource Scheduler and Distributed Power Management				X	X
Distributed Switch					X
I/O Controls (Network and Storage)					X
Host Profiles					X
Auto Deploy					X
Policy-Driven Storage					X
Storage DRS					X

Source: "VMware vSphere 5.0 Licensing, Pricing and Packaging" white paper published by VMware, available at `www.vmware.com`.

It's important to note that all editions of VMware vSphere 5 include support for thin provisioning, vSphere Update Manager, and the vSphere Storage APIs for Data Protection. I did not include them in Table 1.3 because these features are supported in all editions. Because prices change and vary depending on partner, region, and other factors, I have not included any pricing information here.

On all editions of vSphere, VMware requires at least one year of Support and Subscription (SnS). The only exception is the Essential Kits, as I'll explain in a moment.

In addition to the different editions described above, VMware also offers some bundles, referred to as kits. VMware offers both Essentials Kits as well as Acceleration Kits.

Essentials Kits are all-in-one solutions for small environments (up to three vSphere hosts with two CPUs each and a 32 GB vRAM entitlement). To support three hosts with two CPUs each, the Essentials Kits come with 6 licenses and a total pooled vRAM entitlement of 192 GB. All these limits are product-enforced. There are three Essentials Kits available:

◆ VMware vSphere Essentials

◆ VMware vSphere Essentials Plus

◆ VMware vSphere Essentials for Retail and Branch Offices

You can't buy these kits on a per-CPU basis; these are bundled solutions for three servers. vSphere Essentials includes one year of subscription; support is optional and available on a per-incident basis. Like other editions, vSphere Essentials Plus requires at least one year of SnS; this must be purchased separately and is not included in the bundle.

The Retail and Branch Offices (RBO) kits are differentiated from the "normal" Essentials and Essentials Plus kits only by the licensing guidelines. These kits are licensed per site (10 sites minimum, with a maximum of three hosts per site), and customers can add additional sites as required.

VMware also has Acceleration Kits, which combine the different components of the vSphere product suite together. There are three Acceleration Kits:

◆ Standard Acceleration Kit: This kit includes one license of vCenter Server Standard plus licenses for vSphere Standard Edition.

◆ Enterprise Acceleration Kit: The Enterprise Acceleration Kit includes one license of vCenter Server Standard and licenses for vSphere Enterprise Edition.

◆ Enteprise Plus Acceleration Kit: This kit includes both licenses for vSphere Enterprise Plus Edition and a single license for vCenter Server Standard.

While the Essentials Kits are bundled and treated as a single unit, the Acceleration Kits merely offer customers an easier way to purchase the necessary licenses in one step.

Now that you have an idea of how VMware licenses vSphere, I'll review why an organization might choose to use vSphere and what benefits that organization could see as a result.

Why Choose vSphere?

Much has been said and written about the total cost of ownership (TCO) and return on investment (ROI) for virtualization projects involving VMware virtualization solutions. Rather than rehashing that material here, I'll instead focus, briefly, on why an organization should choose VMware vSphere as their virtualization platform.

ONLINE TCO CALCULATOR

VMware offers a web-based TCO calculator that helps you calculate the TCO and ROI for a virtualization project using VMware virtualization solutions. This calculator is available online at www.vmware.com/go/calculator.

You've already read about the various features that VMware vSphere offers. To help you understand how these features can benefit your organization, I'll apply them to the fictional XYZ Corporation. I'll walk through several different scenarios and look at how vSphere helps in these scenarios:

Scenario 1 XYZ Corporation's IT team has been asked by senior management to rapidly provision six new servers to support a new business initiative. In the past, this meant ordering hardware, waiting on the hardware to arrive, racking and cabling the equipment once it arrived, installing the operating system and patching it with the latest updates, and then installing the application. The time frame for all these steps ranged anywhere from a few days to a few months and was typically a couple of weeks. Now, with VMware vSphere in place, the IT team can use vCenter Server's templates functionality to build a VM, install the operating system, and apply the latest updates, and then rapidly clone—or copy—this VM to create additional VMs. Now their provisioning time is down to hours, likely even minutes. Chapter 10 discusses this functionality in detail.

Scenario 2 Empowered by the IT team's ability to quickly respond to the needs of this new business initiative, XYZ Corporation is moving ahead with deploying updated versions of a line-of-business application. However, the business leaders are a bit concerned about upgrading the current version. Using the snapshot functionality present in ESXi and vCenter Server, the IT team can take a "point-in-time picture" of the VM so that if something goes wrong during the upgrade, it's a simple rollback to the snapshot for recovery. Chapter 9 discusses snapshots.

Scenario 3 XYZ Corporation is impressed with the IT team and vSphere's functionality and is now interested in expanding their use of virtualization. In order to do so, however, a hardware upgrade is needed on the servers currently running ESXi. The business is worried about the downtime that will be necessary to perform the hardware upgrades. The IT team uses vMotion to move VMs off one host at a time, upgrading each host in turn without incurring any downtime to the company's end users. Chapter 12 discusses vMotion in more depth.

Scenario 4 After the great success it has had virtualizing its infrastructure with vSphere, XYZ Corporation now finds itself in need of a new, larger shared storage array. vSphere's support for Fibre Channel, iSCSI, and NFS gives XYZ room to choose the most cost-effective storage solution available, and the IT team uses Storage vMotion to migrate the VMs without any downtime. Chapter 12 discusses Storage vMotion.

These scenarios begin to provide some idea of the benefits that organizations see when virtualizing with an enterprise-class virtualization solution like VMware vSphere.

WHAT DO I VIRTUALIZE WITH VMWARE VSPHERE?

Virtualization, by its very nature, means that you are going to take multiple operating systems—such as Microsoft Windows, Linux, Solaris, or Novell NetWare—and run them on a single physical server. While VMware vSphere offers broad support for virtualizing a wide range of operating systems, it would be almost impossible for me to discuss how virtualization impacts all the different versions of all the different operating systems that vSphere supports.

Because the majority of organizations that adopt vSphere are primarily virtualizing Microsoft Windows, that operating system will receive the majority of attention when it comes to describing procedures that must occur within a virtualized operating system. You will also see coverage of tasks for a virtualized installation of Linux as well, but the majority of the coverage will be for Microsoft Windows.

If you are primarily virtualizing something other than Microsoft Windows, VMware provides more in-depth information on all the operating systems it supports and how vSphere interacts with those operating systems on its website at www.vmware.com.

The Bottom Line

Identify the role of each product in the vSphere product suite.   The VMware vSphere product suite contains VMware ESXi and vCenter Server. ESXi provides the base virtualization functionality and enables features like Virtual SMP. vCenter Server provides management for ESXi and enables functionality like vMotion, Storage vMotion, vSphere Distributed Resource Scheduler (DRS), vSphere High Availability (HA), and vSphere Fault Tolerance (FT). Storage I/O Control (SIOC) and Network I/O Control (NetIOC) provide granular resource controls for VMs. The vSphere Storage APIs for Data Protection (VADP) provide a backup framework that allows for the integration of third-party backup solutions into a vSphere implementation.

Master It   Which products are licensed features within the VMware vSphere suite?

Master It   Which two features of VMware ESXi and VMware vCenter Server together aim to reduce or eliminate downtime due to unplanned hardware failures?

Recognize the interaction and dependencies between the products in the vSphere suite   VMware ESXi forms the foundation of the vSphere product suite, but some features require the presence of vCenter Server. Features like vMotion, Storage vMotion, vSphere DRS, vSphere HA, vSphere FT, SIOC, and NetIOC require both ESXi as well as vCenter Server.

Master It   Name three features that are supported only when using vCenter Server along with ESXi.

Master It   Name two features that are supported without vCenter Server but with a licensed installation of ESXi.

Understand how vSphere differs from other virtualization products.   VMware vSphere's hypervisor, ESXi, uses a type 1 bare-metal hypervisor that handles I/O directly within the hypervisor. This means that a host operating system, like Windows or Linux, is not required in order for ESXi to function. Although other virtualization solutions are listed as "type 1 bare-metal hypervisors," most other type 1 hypervisors on the market today require the presence of a "parent partition" or "dom0," through which all VM I/O must travel.

Master It   One of the administrators on your team asked whether he should install Windows Server on the new servers you purchased for ESXi. What should you tell him, and why?

## Chapter 2

Planning and Installing VMware ESXi

Now that you've taken a closer look at VMware vSphere and its suite of applications in Chapter 1, "Introducing VMware vSphere 5," it's easy to see that VMware ESXi is the foundation of vSphere. The deployment, installation, and configuration of VMware ESXi require adequate planning for a successful, VMware-supported implementation.

In this chapter, you will learn to

- Understand the differences between ESXi Installable and ESXi Embedded

- Understand ESXi compatibility requirements

- Plan an ESXi deployment

- Deploy ESXi

- Perform post-installation configuration of ESXi

- Install the vSphere Client

Planning a VMware vSphere Deployment

Deploying VMware vSphere is more than just virtualizing servers. A vSphere deployment affects storage, networking, and security in as equally significant ways as the physical servers themselves. As a result of this broad impact on numerous facets of your organization's IT, the process of planning the vSphere deployment becomes even more important. Without the appropriate planning, your vSphere implementation runs the risk of configuration problems, instability, incompatibilities, and diminished financial impact.

Your planning process for a vSphere deployment involves answering a number of questions (please note that this list is far from comprehensive):

- What form of ESXi will I use: Installable or Embedded?

- What types of servers will I use for the underlying physical hardware?

- What kinds of storage will I use, and how will I connect that storage to my servers?

- How will the networking be configured?

In some cases, the answers to these questions will determine the answers to other questions. After you have answered these questions, you can then move on to more difficult issues. These center on how the vSphere deployment will impact your staff, your business processes, and your operational procedures. I'm not going to help you answer those sorts of questions here; instead, let's just focus on the technical issues.

---

vSphere Design Is a Topic on Its Own

The first section of this chapter barely scratches the surface of what is involved in planning and designing a vSphere deployment. vSphere design is significant enough a topic that it warranted its own book: *VMware vSphere Design*, published in March 2011 by Sybex. If you are interested in a more detailed discussion of design decisions and design impacts, that's the book for you.

In the next few sections, I'll discuss the four major questions that I outlined previously that are a key part of planning your vSphere deployment.

Selecting ESXi Installable or ESXi Embedded

As of the 5.0 release, vSphere no longer includes ESX. In previous versions of vSphere, users had to choose between using ESX—with the full Linux-based Service Console—or ESXi. Now, with this release of vSphere, ESXi is the only form of the VMware hypervisor available.

Even though users no longer need to choose between ESX and ESXi, they do need to choose which variant of ESXi they will use: ESXi Installable or ESXi Embedded.

ESXi Installable (which I'll refer to hereafter as just ESXi) is the "traditional" form of the vSphere hypervisor. Users have the option of installing ESXi onto local hard drives within the server or installing ESXi in a boot from a SAN configuration, and you can either interactively install ESXi or perform an unattended (or scripted) installation. You also have the option of provisioning ESXi in a stateless fashion. Each of these approaches has its own advantages and disadvantages. I'll discuss some of the specifics of each approach later in this chapter in the section "Deploying VMware ESXi."

ESXi Embedded refers to the original equipment manufacturer (OEM) installation of the vSphere hypervisor onto a persistent storage device inside qualified hardware. This is an exciting option that saves administrators the time of performing any type of installation. The embedded hypervisor truly allows for the Plug and Play hardware-type atmosphere. You can see that major server manufacturers are banking on this idea because their server designs include an internal USB port or SD card slot. Perhaps eventually the ESXi hypervisor will move from the USB flash drive on an internal port to some type of flash memory built right onto the motherboard, but until that time ESXi Embedded is as close as you can get. Very little is involved to deploy ESXi Embedded, but I'll discuss what is involved in the section "Deploying VMware ESXi Embedded."

After you've decided between ESXi and ESXi Embedded, you'll need to select a server platform upon which you'll deploy vSphere.

Choosing a Server Platform

The second major decision to make when planning to deploy vSphere is choosing a hardware platform. Compared to traditional operating systems like Windows or Linux, ESXi has more stringent hardware restrictions. ESXi won't necessarily support every storage controller or every network adapter chipset available on the market. ESXi Embedded, in particular, has a strict list of supported hardware platforms. Although these hardware restrictions do limit the options for deploying a supported virtual infrastructure, they also ensure the hardware has been tested and will work as expected when used with ESXi. Although not every vendor or white-box configuration can play host to ESXi, the list of supported hardware platforms continues to grow and change as VMware tests newer models from more vendors.

You can check for hardware compatibility using the searchable Hardware Compatibility List (HCL) available on VMware's website at www.vmware.com/resources/compatibility/ search.php. A quick search returns dozens of systems from major vendors such as Hewlett-Packard, Cisco, IBM, and Dell. For example, at the time of this writing, searching the HCL for *HP* returned 163 results, including blades and traditional rack-mount servers supported across several different versions of vSphere 4.0 and 4.1. Within the major vendors, it is generally not too difficult to find a tested and supported platform on which to run ESXi. When you expand the list to include other vendors, it's clear that there is a substantial base of compatible servers that are supported by vSphere from which to choose.

THE RIGHT SERVER FOR THE JOB

Selecting the appropriate server is undoubtedly the first step in ensuring a successful vSphere deployment. In addition, it is the only way to ensure VMware will provide the necessary support. Remember the discussion from Chapter 1, though—a bigger server isn't necessarily a better server!

Finding a supported server is only the first step. It's also important to find the right server—the server that strikes the correct balance of capacity and affordability. Do you use larger servers, such as servers that support up to four physical CPUs and 128 GB of RAM? Or would smaller servers, such as servers that support dual physical CPUs and 64 GB of RAM, be a better choice? There is a point of diminishing returns when it comes to adding more physical CPUs and more RAM to a server. Once you pass that point, the servers get more expensive to acquire and support, but the number of VMs the servers can host doesn't increase enough to offset the increase in cost. The challenge, therefore, is finding server models that provide enough expansion for growth and then fitting them with the right amount of resources to meet your needs.

Fortunately, a deeper look into the server models available from a specific vendor, such as HP, reveals server models of all types and sizes (see Figure 2.1), including the following:

- Half-height C-class blades, such as the BL460c and BL465c
- Full-height C-class blades, such as the BL685c
- Dual-socket 1U servers, such as the DL360
- Dual-socket 2U servers, such as the DL380 and the DL385
- Quad-socket 4U servers, such as the DL580 and DL585

FIGURE 2.1
Servers on the HCL come in various sizes and models.

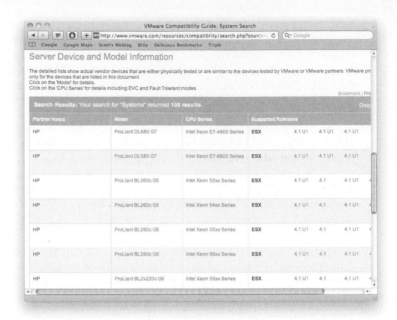

You'll note that Figure 2.1 doesn't show vSphere 5 in the list; at the time of this writing, VMware's HCL hadn't yet been updated to include information on vSphere 5. However, once VMware updates their HCL and vendors complete their testing, you'll be able to easily view compatibility with vSphere 5 using VMware's online HCL.

Which server is the right server? The answer to that question depends on many factors. The number of CPU cores is often used as a determining factor, but you should also consider the total number of RAM slots. A higher number of RAM slots means that you can use lower-cost, lower-density RAM modules and still reach high memory configurations. You should also consider server expansion options, such as the number of available Peripheral Component Interconnect (PCI) or Peripheral Component Interconnect Express (PCIe) buses, expansion slots, and the types of expansion cards supported in the server. Finally, be sure to consider the server form factor; blade servers have advantages and disadvantages versus rack-mount servers.

Determining a Storage Architecture

Selecting the right storage solution is the third major decision that you must make before you proceed with your vSphere deployment. The lion's share of advanced features within vSphere—features like vMotion, vSphere DRS, vSphere HA, and vSphere FT—depend on the presence of a shared storage architecture, making it equally as critical a decision as the choice of the server hardware on which to run ESXi.

THE HCL ISN'T JUST FOR SERVERS

VMware's HCL isn't just for servers. The searchable HCL also provides compatibility information on storage arrays and other storage components. Be sure to use the searchable HCL to verify the compatibility of your host bus adapters (HBAs) and storage arrays to ensure the appropriate level of support from VMware.

Fortunately, vSphere supports a number of storage architectures out of the box and has implemented a modular, plug-in architecture that will make supporting future storage technologies easier. vSphere supports Fibre Channel- and Fibre Channel over Ethernet (FCoE)-based storage, iSCSI-based storage, and storage accessed via Network File System (NFS). In addition, vSphere supports the use of multiple storage protocols within a single solution so that one portion of the vSphere implementation might run over Fibre Channel, while another portion runs over NFS. This provides a great deal of flexibility in choosing your storage solution. Finally, vSphere provides support for software-based initiators as well as hardware initiators (also referred to as host bus adapters or converged network adapters), so this is another option you must consider when selecting your storage solution.

WHAT IS REQUIRED FOR FIBRE CHANNEL OVER ETHERNET SUPPORT?

Fibre Channel over Ethernet (FCoE) is a relatively new storage protocol. However, because FCoE was designed to be compatible with Fibre Channel, it looks, acts, and behaves like Fibre Channel to ESXi. As long as drivers for the FCoE Converged Network Adapter (CNA) are available—and this is where you would go back to the VMware HCL again—support for FCoE should not be an issue.

When determining the correct storage solution, you must consider the following questions:

◆ What type of storage will best integrate with your existing storage or network infrastructure?

◆ Do you have experience or expertise with some types of storage?

◆ Can the storage solution provide the necessary performance to support your environment?

◆ Does the storage solution offer any form of advanced integration with vSphere?

The procedures involved in creating and managing storage devices are discussed in detail in Chapter 6, "Creating and Configuring Storage Devices."

Integrating with the Network Infrastructure

The fourth major decision that you need to make during the planning process is how your vSphere deployment will integrate with the existing network infrastructure. In part, this decision is driven by the choice of server hardware and the storage protocol.

For example, an organization selecting a blade form factor may run into limitations on the number of network interface cards (NICs) that can be supported in a given blade model. This affects how the vSphere implementation will integrate with the network. Similarly, organizations choosing to use iSCSI or NFS instead of Fibre Channel will typically have to deploy more NICs in their ESXi hosts to accommodate the additional network traffic or use 10 Gigabit Ethernet. Organizations also need to account for network interfaces for vMotion and vSphere FT.

Until 10 Gigabit Ethernet becomes more common, the ESXi hosts in many vSphere deployments will have a minimum of 6 NICs and often will have 8, 10, or even 12 NICs. So, how do you decide how many NICs to use? We'll discuss some of this in greater detail in Chapter 5, "Creating and Configuring Virtual Networks," but here are some general guidelines:

◆ The ESXi management network needs at least one NIC. I strongly recommend adding a second NIC for redundancy. In fact, some features of vSphere, such as vSphere

HA, will note warnings if the hosts do not have redundant network connections for the management network.

◆ vMotion needs a NIC. Again, I heartily recommend a second NIC for redundancy. These NICs should be at least Gigabit Ethernet. In some cases, this traffic can be safely combined with ESXi management traffic, so I'll assume that two NICs will handle both ESXi management and vMotion.

◆ vSphere FT, if you will be utilizing that feature, needs an NIC. A second NIC would provide redundancy and is recommended. This should be at least a Gigabit Ethernet NIC, preferably a 10 Gigabit Ethernet NIC.

◆ For deployments using iSCSI or NFS, at least one more NIC, preferably two, is needed. Gigabit Ethernet or 10 Gigabit Ethernet is necessary here. Although you can get by with a single NIC, I strongly recommend at least two.

◆ Finally, at least two NICs would be needed for traffic originating from the VMs themselves. Gigabit Ethernet or faster is strongly recommended for VM traffic.

This adds up to eight NICs per server (again, assuming management and vMotion share a pair of NICs). For this sort of deployment, you'll want to ensure that you have enough network ports available, at the appropriate speeds, to accommodate the needs of the vSphere deployment. This is, of course, only a rudimentary discussion of networking design for vSphere and doesn't incorporate any discussion on the use of 10 Gigabit Ethernet, FCoE (which, while a storage protocol, impacts the network design), or what type of virtual switching infrastructure you will use. All of these other factors would affect your networking setup.

HOW ABOUT 18 NICS?

Lots of factors go into designing how a vSphere deployment will integrate with the existing network infrastructure. For example, I was involved in a deployment of ESX 4 in a manufacturing environment that had 7 subnets—one for each department within the manufacturing facility. Normally in a situation like that, I recommend using VLANs and VLAN tagging so that the ESX hosts can easily support all the current subnets as well as any future subnets. This sort of configuration is discussed in more detail in Chapter 5.

In this particular case, though, the physical switches into which these ESX hosts would be connected were configured in such a way that each subnet had a separate physical switch. The switch into which we plugged our Ethernet cable determined which subnet we used. Additionally, the core network switches didn't have the necessary available ports for us to connect the ESX hosts directly to them. These factors, taken together, meant that we would need to design the ESX hosts to have enough NICs to physically connect them to each of the different switches.

With 7 subnets, plus connections for the Service Console and vMotion, the final design ended up with 18 NICs connected in pairs to 9 different physical switches. Fortunately, the servers that had been selected to host this environment had 2 onboard NICs and enough expansion slots to hold the 4 quad-port NICs and two Fibre Channel HBAs that were necessary to support the required network connectivity.

With these four questions answered, you at least have the basics of a vSphere deployment established. As I mentioned previously, this section is far from a comprehensive or complete discussion on designing a vSphere solution. I do recommend that you find a good resource on vSphere design and consider going through a comprehensive design exercise before actually deploying vSphere.

Deploying VMware ESXi

Once you've established the basics of your vSphere design and you've settled on ESXi (as opposed to ESXi Embedded, which I'll discuss later in the section "Deploying VMware ESXi Embedded"), you have to decide exactly how you are going to deploy ESXi.

There are three primary ways to deploy ESXi:

◆ Interactive installation of ESXi

◆ Unattended (scripted) installation of ESXi

◆ Stateless provisioning of ESXi

Of these, the simplest is an interactive installation of ESXi. The most complex—but perhaps the most powerful, depending on your needs and your environment—is stateless provisioning of ESXi. In this section, I'll describe all three of these methods for deploying ESXi in your environment.

Let's start with the simplest method first: interactively installing ESXi.

Installing VMware ESXi Interactively

VMware has done a great job of making the interactive installation of ESXi as simple and straightforward as possible. Let's walk through the process.

Perform the following steps to interactively install ESXi:

1. Ensure that your server hardware is configured to boot from the CD-ROM drive.

This will vary from manufacturer to manufacturer and will also depend on whether you are installing locally or remotely via an IP-based KVM or other remote management facility.

2. Ensure that VMware ESXi installation media are available to the server.

Again, this will vary based on a local installation (which involves simply inserting the VMware ESXi installation CD into the optical drive) or a remote installation (which typically involves mapping an image of the installation media, known as an ISO image, to a virtual optical drive).

OBTAINING VMWARE ESXI INSTALLATION MEDIA

You can download the installation files from VMware's website at www.vmware.com/downloads.

---

3. Power on the server.

Once it boots from the installation media, the initial boot menu screen displays, as shown in Figure 2.2.

FIGURE 2.2
The initial ESXi installation routine has options for booting the installer or booting from the local disk.

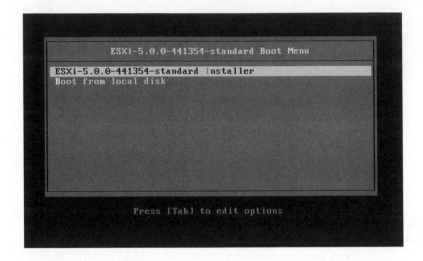

4. Press Enter to boot the ESXi installer.

The installer will boot the vSphere hypervisor and eventually stop at a welcome message. Press Enter to continue.

5. At the End User License Agreement (EULA) screen, press F11 to accept the EULA and continue with the installation.

6. Next, the installer will display a list of available disks on which you can install or upgrade ESXi.

Potential devices are identified as either local devices or remote devices. Figure 2.3 and Figure 2.4 show two different views of this screen: one with a local device and one with remote devices.

FIGURE 2.3
The installer offers options for both local and remote devices; in this case, only a local device was detected.

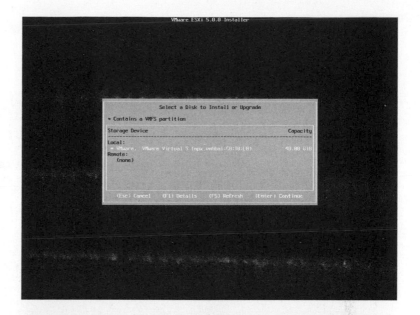

FIGURE 2.4
Although local SAS devices are supported, they are listed as remote devices.

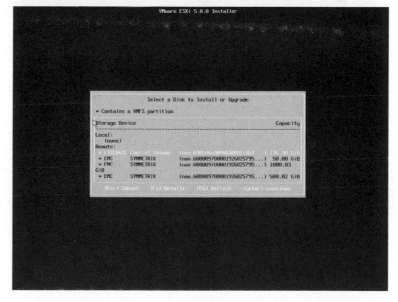

> **RUNNING ESXI AS A VM**
>
> You might be able to deduce from the screenshot in Figure 2.3 that I'm actually running ESXi 5 as a VM. Yes, that's right—you can virtualize ESXi (as well as ESX 4.*X*)! In this particular case, I'm using VMware's desktop virtualization solution for Mac OS X, VMware Fusion, to run an instance of ESXi as a VM. As of this writing, the latest version of VMware Fusion is 3.1, and it includes ESX Server 4.0 as an officially supported guest OS. ESXi 5 is not listed as an officially supported version, but it does run.

SAN LUNs are listed as remote devices, as you can see in Figure 2.4. Local SAS devices are also listed as remote devices. Figure 2.4 shows a SAS drive connected to an LSI Logic controller; although this device is physically local to the server on which we are installing ESXi, the installation routine marks it as remote.

If you want to create a boot-from-SAN environment, where each ESXi host boots from a SAN LUN, then you'd select the appropriate SAN LUN here. You can also install directly to your own USB or Secure Digital (SD) device—simply select the appropriate device from the list.

> **WHICH DESTINATION IS BEST?**
>
> Local device, SAN LUN, or USB? Which destination is the best when you're installing ESXi? Those questions truly depend on the overall vSphere design you are implementing, and there is no simple answer. Many variables affect this decision. Are you using an iSCSI SAN and you don't have iSCSI hardware initiators in your servers? That would prevent you from using a boot-from-SAN setup. Are you installing into an environment like Cisco UCS, where booting from SAN is highly recommended? Be sure to consider all the factors when deciding where to install ESXi.

7. To get more information about a device, highlight the device and press F1.

This will display more information about the device, including whether it detected an installation of ESXi and what VMFS datastores, if any, are present on that device, as shown in Figure 2.5. Press Enter to return to the device-selection screen when you have finished reviewing the information for the selected device.

FIGURE 2.5
Checking a device to see if there are any VMFS datastores on the device can help prevent accidentally overwriting data.

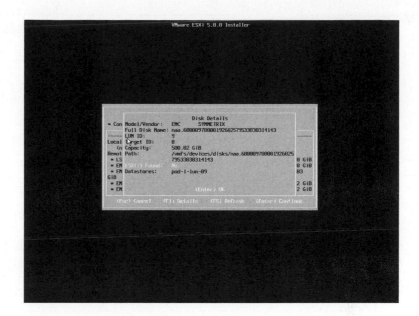

8. Use the arrow keys to select the device on which you are going to install ESXi, and press Enter.

9. If the selected device includes a VMFS datastore or an installation of ESXi, you'll be prompted to choose what action you want to take, as illustrated in Figure 2.6. Select the desired action and press Enter.

The available actions are these:

◆ Upgrade ESXi, Preserve VMFS Datastore: This option upgrades to ESXi 5 and preserves the existing VMFS datastore.

◆ Install ESXi, Preserve VMFS Datastore: This option installs a fresh copy of ESXi 5 and preserves the existing VMFS datastore.

◆ Install ESXi, Overwrite VMFS Datastore: This option overwrites the existing VMFS datastore with a new one and installs a fresh installation of ESXi 5.

FIGURE 2.6
You can upgrade or install ESXi as well as choose to pre-serve or overwrite an existing VMFS datastore.

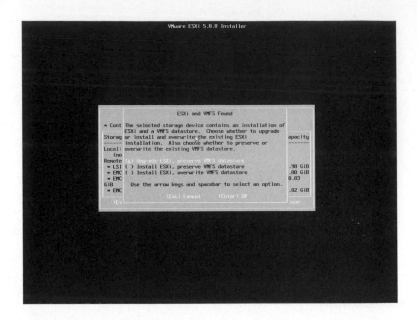

10. Select the desired keyboard layout and press Enter.

11. Enter (and confirm) a password for the root account. Press Enter when you are ready to continue with the installation. Be sure to make note of this password—you'll need it later.

12. At the final confirmation screen, press F11 to proceed with the installation of ESXi.

After the installation process begins, it takes only a few minutes to install ESXi onto the selected storage device.

13. Press Enter to reboot the host at the Installation Complete screen.

After the server reboots, ESXi is installed. ESXi is configured by default to obtain an IP address via Dynamic Host Configuration Protocol (DHCP). Depending on the network configuration, you might find that ESXi will not be able to obtain an IP address via DHCP. Later in this chapter in the section "Reconfiguring the Management Network," I'll discuss how to correct networking problems after installing ESXi by using the Direct Console User Interface (DCUI).

VMware also provides support for scripted installations of ESXi. As you've already seen, there isn't a lot of interaction required to install ESXi, but support for scripting the installation of ESXi reduces the time to deploy even further.

INTERACTIVELY INSTALLING ESXi FROM USB OR ACROSS THE NETWORK

As an alternative to launching the ESXi installer from the installation CD/DVD, you can install ESXi from a USB flash drive or across the network via Preboot Execution Environment (PXE). More details on how to use a USB flash drive or to PXE boot the ESXi installer are found in the *vSphere Installation and Setup Guide*, available from www.vmware.com. Note that PXE booting the installer is not the same as PXE booting ESXi itself, something that I'll discuss later in the section "Deploying VMware ESXi with Auto Deploy."

Performing an Unattended Installation of VMware ESXi

ESXi supports the use of an installation script (often referred to as a kickstart script) that automates the installation routine. By using an installation script, users can create unattended installation routines that make it easy to quickly deploy multiple instances of ESXi.

ESXi comes with a default installation script on the installation media. Listing 2.1 shows the default installation script.

LISTING 2.1:   ESXi provides a default installation script

```
#
# Sample scripted installation file
#
# Accept the VMware End User License Agreement
vmaccepteula
# Set the root password for the DCUI and Tech Support Mode
rootpw mypassword
# Install on the first local disk available on machine
install --firstdisk --overwritevmfs
# Set the network to DHCP on the first network adapater
network --bootproto=dhcp --device=vmnic0
# A sample post-install script
%post --interpreter=python --ignorefailure=true
import time
stampFile = open('/finished.stamp', mode='w')
stampFile.write( time.asctime() )
```

If you want to use this default install script to install ESXi, you can specify it when booting the VMware ESXi installer by adding the ks=file://etc/vmware/weasel/ks.cfg boot option. I'll show you how to specify that boot option shortly.

Of course, the default installation script is useful only if the settings work for your environment. Otherwise, you'll need to create a custom installation script. The installation script commands are much the same as those supported in previous versions of vSphere. Here's a breakdown of some of the commands supported in the ESXi installation script:

accepteula or vmaccepteula These commands accept the ESXi license agreement. They function the same way they did for ESXi 4.1.

install The install command specifies that this is a fresh installation of ESXi, not an upgrade. This replaces the autopart command used in ESXi 4.1 scripted installations. You must also specify the following parameters:

--firstdisk Specifies the disk on which ESXi should be installed. By default, the ESXi installer chooses local disks first, then remote disks, and then USB disks. You can change the order by appending a comma-separated list to the --firstdisk command, like this:

--firstdisk=remote,local

This would install to the first available remote disk and then to the first available local disk. Be careful here—you don't want to inadvertently overwrite something (see the next set of commands).

--overwritevmfs or --preservevmfs These commands specify how the installer will handle existing VMFS datastores. The commands are pretty self-explanatory.

keyboard This command specifies the keyboard type. It's an optional component in the installation script.

network This command provides the network configuration for the ESXi host being installed. It is optional but generally recommended. Depending on your configuration, some of the additional parameters are required:

--bootproto This parameter is set to dhcp for assigning a network address via DHCP or to static for manual assignment of an IP address.

--ip This sets the IP address and is required with --bootproto=static. The IP address should be specified in standard dotted-decimal format.

--gateway This command specifies the IP address of the default gateway in standard dotted-decimal format. It's required if you specified --bootproto=static.

--netmask The network mask, in standard dotted-decimal format, is specified with this command. If you specify --bootproto=static, you must include this value.

--hostname Specifies the hostname for the installed system.

--vlanid If you need the system to use a VLAN ID, specify it with this command. Without a VLAN ID specified, the system will respond only to untagged traffic.

--addvmportgroup This parameter is set to either 0 or 1 and controls whether a default VM Network port group is created. 0 does not create the port group; 1 does create the port group.

reboot   This command is optional and, if specified, will automatically reboot the system at the end of installation. If you add the --noeject parameter, the CD is not ejected.

rootpw   This is a required parameter and sets the root password for the system. If you don't want the root password displayed in the clear, generate an encrypted password and use the --iscrypted parameter.

upgrade   This specifies an upgrade to ESXi 5. The upgrade command uses many of the same parameters as install and also supports a parameter for deleting the ESX Service Console VMDK for upgrades from ESX to ESXi. This parameter is the --deletecosvmdk parameter.

This is by no means a comprehensive list of all the commands available in the ESXi installation script, but it does cover the majority of the commands you'll see in use.

Looking back at Listing 2.1, you'll see that the default installation script incorporates a %post section, where additional scripting can be added using either the Python interpreter or the Busybox interpreter. What you don't see in Listing 2.1 is the %firstboot section, which also allows you to add Python or Busybox commands for customizing the ESXi installation. This section comes after the installation script commands but before the %post section. Any command supported in the ESXi shell can be executed in the %firstboot section, so commands such as vim-cmd, esxcfg-vswitch, esxcfg-vmknic, and others can be combined in the %firstboot section of the installation script.

A number of commands that were supported in previous versions of vSphere (by ESX or ESXi) are no longer supported in installation scripts for ESXi 5, such as these:

◆ autopart (replaced by install, upgrade, or installorupgrade)

◆ auth or authconfig

◆ bootloader

◆ esxlocation

◆ firewall

◆ firewallport

◆ serialnum or vmserialnum

◆ timezone

◆ virtualdisk

◆ zerombr

◆ The --level option of %firstboot

Once you have created the installation script you will use, you need to specify that script as part of the installation routine.

Specifying the location of the installation script as a boot option is not only how you would tell the installer to use the default script but also how you tell the installer to use a custom installation script that you've created. This installation script can be located on a USB flash drive or in a network location accessible via NFS, HTTP, HTTPS, or FTP. Table 2.1 summarizes some of the supported boot options for use with an unattended installation of ESXi.

Table 2.1: Boot options for an unattended ESXi installation

BOOT OPTION	BRIEF DESCRIPTION
ks=cdrom:/*path*	Uses the installation script found at *path* on the CD-ROM. The installer will check all CD-ROM drives until the file matching the specified path is found.
ks=usb	Uses the installation script named ks.cfg found in the root directory of an attached USB device. All USB devices are searched as long as they have a FAT16 or FAT32 filesystem.
ks=usb:/*path*	Uses the installation script at the specified *path* on an attached USB device. This allows you to use a different filename or location for the installation script.
ks=*protocol:/serverpath*	Uses the installation script found at the specified network location. The protocol can be NFS, HTTP, HTTPS, or FTP.
ip=*XX.XX.XX.XX*	Specifies a static IP address for downloading the installation script and the installation media.
nameserver=*XX.XX.XX.XX*	Provides the IP address of a Domain Naming System (DNS) server to use for name resolution when downloading the installation script or the installation media.
gateway=*XX.XX.XX.XX*	Provides the network gateway to be used as the default gateway for downloading the installation script and the installation media.
netmask=*XX.XX.XX.XX*	Specifies the network mask for the network interface used to download the installation script or the installation media.
vlanid=*XX*	Configures the network interface to be on the specified VLAN when downloading the installation script or the installation media.

NOT A COMPREHENSIVE LIST OF BOOT OPTIONS

The list found in Table 2.1 includes only some of the more commonly used boot options when performing a scripted installation of ESXi. For the complete list of supported boot options, refer to the *vSphere Installation and Setup Guide*, available from www.vmware.com.

To use one or more of these boot options during the installation, you'll need to specify them at the boot screen for the ESXi installer. Figure 2.7 shows the ESXi Installer boot screen; note the bottom of the screen, where it states that you can press Shift+O to edit the boot options.

FIGURE 2.7
Press Shift+O
to edit the boot
options and specify
an installation
script.

Figure 2.8 shows a series of boot options added to retrieve the installation script from an HTTP URL.

FIGURE 2.8
Installation scripts
can be stored and
retrieved across the
network.

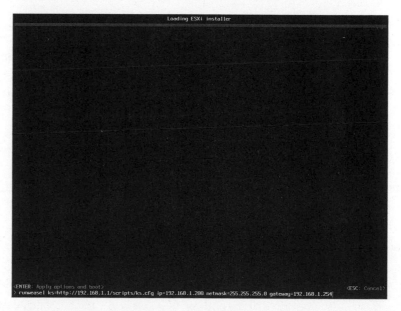

Using an installation script to install ESXi not only speeds up the installation process but also helps to ensure the consistent configuration of all your ESXi hosts.

The final method for deploying ESXi—using vSphere Auto Deploy—is the most complex, but it also offers administrators a great deal of flexibility.

Deploying VMware ESXi with vSphere Auto Deploy

When you deploy ESXi using vSphere Auto Deploy, you aren't actually installing ESXi. That's why I titled this section "Deploying VMware ESXi" instead of "Installing VMware ESXi." Instead of actually installing ESXi onto a local disk or a SAN boot LUN, you are instead building an environment where ESXi is directly loaded into memory on a physical host as it boots. vSphere Auto Deploy uses a set of rules (called *deployment rules*) to control which hosts are assigned a particular ESXi image (called an *image profile*). Because ESXi isn't actually installed on the local disks, this means that deploying a new ESXi image is as simple as modifying the deployment rule to point that physical host to a new image profile and then rebooting. When the host boots up, it will receive a new image profile.

Sounds easy, right? In theory, it is—but there are several steps you have to accomplish before you're ready to actually deploy ESXi in this fashion:

1. You must set up a vSphere Auto Deploy server. This is the server that stores the image profiles.

2. You must set up and configure a Trivial File Transfer Protocol (TFTP) server on your network.

3. You must configure a DHCP server on your network to pass the correct information to hosts booting up.

4. You must create an image profile using PowerCLI.

5. Still using PowerCLI, you must create a deployment rule that assigns the image profile to a particular subset of hosts.

Once you've completed these five steps, you're ready to start provisioning physical hosts with ESXi. When everything is configured and in place, the process looks something like this:

1. When the physical server boots, the server starts a PXE boot sequence. The DHCP server assigns an IP address to the host and provides the IP address of the TFTP server as well as a boot filename to download.

2. The host contacts the TFTP server and downloads the specified filename, which contains the gPXE boot file and a gPXE configuration file.

3. gPXE executes; this causes the host to make an HTTP boot request to the Auto Deploy server. This request includes information about the host, the host hardware, and host network information. This information is written to the server console when gPXE is executing, as you can see in Figure 2.9.

4. Based on the information passed to it from gPXE (the host information shown in Figure 2.9), the Auto Deploy server matches the server against a deployment rule and assigns the correct image profile. The Auto Deploy server then streams the assigned ESXi image across the network to the physical host.

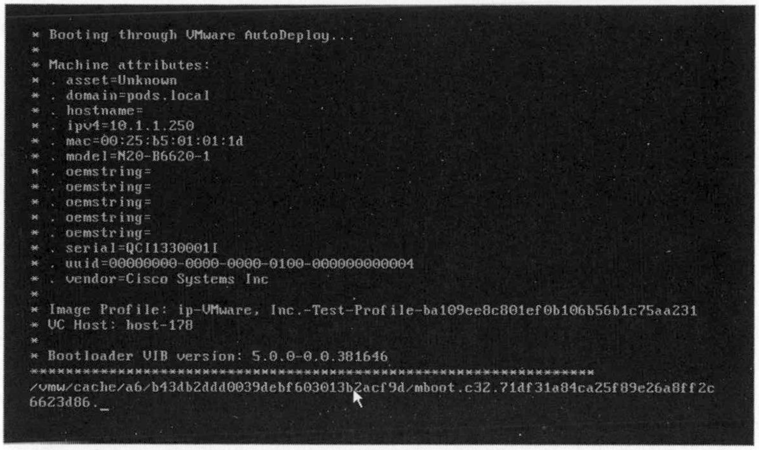

FIGURE 2.9
Host information is echoed to the server console when it performs a network boot.

When the host has finished executing, you have a physical system running ESXi. The Auto Deploy server also has the ability to automatically join the ESXi host to vCenter Server and assign a host profile (which I'll discuss in a bit more detail in Chapter 3, "Installing and Configuring vCenter Server") for further configuration. As you can see, this system potentially offers administrators tremendous flexibility and power.

Ready to get started with provisioning ESXi hosts using Auto Deploy? Let's start with setting up the vSphere Auto Deploy server.

INSTALLING THE vSPHERE AUTO DEPLOY SERVER

The vSphere Auto Deploy server is where the various ESXi image profiles are stored. The image profile is transferred from this server via HTTP to a physical host when it boots. The image profile is the actual ESXi image, and it comprises multiple VIB files. VIBs are ESXi software packages; these could be drivers, Common Information Management (CIM) providers, or other applications that extend or enhance the ESXi platform. Both VMware and VMware's partners could distribute software as VIBs.

You can install vSphere Auto Deploy on the same system as vCenter Server or on a separate Windows Server–based system (this could certainly be a VM). In addition, the vCenter virtual appliance comes preloaded with the Auto Deploy server installed. If you want to use the vCenter virtual appliance, you need only deploy the appliance and configure the service from the web-based administrative interface. I'll describe the process for deploying the vCenter virtual appliance in more detail in Chapter 3. In this section, I'll walk you through installing the Auto Deploy server on a separate Windows-based system.

Perform the following steps to install the vSphere Auto Deploy server:

1. Make the vCenter Server installation media available to the Windows Server–based system where you will be installing Auto Deploy.

If this is a VM, you can map the vCenter Server installation ISO to the VM's CD/DVD drive.

2. From the VMware vCenter Installer screen, select VMware Auto Deploy and click Install.

3. Choose the language for the installer and click OK.

This will launch the vSphere Auto Deploy installation wizard.

4. Click Next at the first screen of the installation wizard.

5. Click Next to acknowledge the VMware patents.

6. Select I Accept The Terms In The License Agreement, and click Next to continue.

7. Click Next to accept the default installation location, the default repository location, and the default maximum repository size.

If you need to change locations, use either of the Change buttons; if you need to change the repository size, specify a new value in gigabytes (GB).

8. If you are installing on a system separate from vCenter Server, specify the IP address or name of the vCenter Server with which this Auto Deploy server should register.

You'll also need to provide a username and password. Click Next when you have finished entering this information.

9. Click Next to accept the default Auto Deploy server port.

10. Click Next to accept the Auto Deploy server identifying itself on the network via its IP address.

11. Click Install to install the Auto Deploy server.

12. Click Finish to complete the installation.

If you now go back to the vSphere Client (if you haven't installed it yet, skip ahead to the section "Installing the vSphere Client" and then come back) and connect to vCenter Server, you'll see a new Auto Deploy icon on the vSphere Client's home page. Click it to see information about the registered Auto Deploy server. Figure 2.10 shows the Auto Deploy screen after I've installed and registered an Auto Deploy server with vCenter Server.

That's it for the Auto Deploy server itself; once it's been installed and is up and running, there's very little additional work or configuration required, except configuring TFTP and DHCP on your network to support vSphere Auto Deploy. The next section provides an overview of the required configurations for TFTP and DHCP.

CONFIGURING TFTP AND DHCP FOR AUTO DEPLOY

The exact procedures for configuring TFTP and DHCP are going to vary based on the specific TFTP and DHCP servers you are using on your network. For example, configuring the ISC DHCP server to support vSphere Auto Deploy is dramatically different from configuring the DHCP Server service provided with Windows Server. As a matter of necessity, then, I can only provide high-level information in this section. Refer to your specific vendor's documentation for details on how the configuration is carried out.

Configuring TFTP

For TFTP, you only need to upload the appropriate TFTP boot files to the TFTP directory. The Download TFTP Boot Zip hyperlink shown in Figure 2.10 provides the necessary files. Simply download the Zip file using that link, unzip the file, and place the contents of the unzipped file in the TFTP directory on the TFTP server.

FIGURE 2.10
This screen pro-
vides information
about the Auto
Deploy server that
is registered with
vCenter Server.

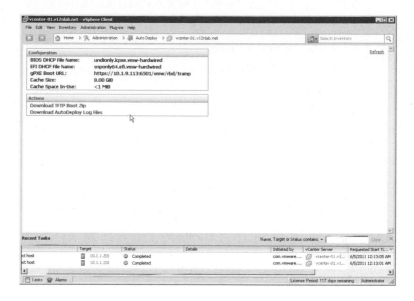

Configuring DHCP

For DHCP, you need to specify two additional DHCP options:

◆ Option 66, referred to as `next-server` or as Boot Server Host Name, must specify the IP address of the TFTP server.

◆ Option 67, called `boot-filename` or Bootfile Name, should contain the value `undionly.kpxe.vmw-hardwired`.

If you want to identify hosts by IP address in the deployment rules, then you'll need a way to ensure that the host gets the IP address you expect. You can certainly use DHCP reservations to accomplish this, if you like; just be sure that options 66 and 67 apply to the reservation as well.

Once you've configured TFTP and DHCP, you're ready to create the image profile.

CREATING AN IMAGE PROFILE

The process for creating an image profile may seem counterintuitive at first; it did for me. Creating an image profile involves first adding at least one *software depot*. A software depot could be a directory structure of files and folders on an HTTP server, or (more commonly) it could be an offline depot in the form of a Zip file. You can add multiple software depots.

Some software depots will already have one or more image profiles defined, and you can define additional image profiles (usually by cloning an existing image profile). You'll then have the ability to add software packages (in the form of VIBs) to the image profile you've created. Once you've finished adding or removing software packages or drivers from the image profile, you can export the image profile (either to an ISO or as a Zip file for use as an offline depot).

All image profile tasks are accomplished using PowerCLI, so you'll need to ensure that you have a system with PowerCLI installed in order to perform these tasks. I'll describe PowerCLI, along with other automation tools, in more detail in Chapter 14, "Automating VMware vSphere." In the next part of this section, I'll walk you through creating an image profile based on the ESXi 5.0.0 offline depot Zip file available for downloading by registered customers.

Perform the following steps to create an image profile:

1. At a PowerCLI prompt, use the `Connect-VIServer` cmdlet to connect to vCenter Server.

2. Use the `Add-EsxSoftwareDepot` command to add the ESXi 5.0.0 offline depot file:

   ```
   Add-EsxSoftwareDepot -DepotURL C:\vmware-ESXi-5.0.0-XXXXXX-depot.zip
   ```

3. Repeat the `Add-EsxSoftwareDepot` command to add other software depots as necessary.

4. Use the `Get-EsxImageProfile` command to list all image profiles in all currently visible depots.

5. To create a new image profile, clone an existing profile (existing profiles are typically read-only) using the `New-EsxImageProfile` command:

   ```
   New-EsxImageProfile -CloneProfile "ESXi-5.0.0-XXXXXX-standard" -Name "My_Custom_Profile"
   ```

Once you have an image profile established, you can customize the image profile by adding VIBs or you can export the image profile. You might want to export the image profile, because once you exit a PowerCLI session where you've created image profiles, the image profiles will not be available when you start a new session. Exporting the image profile as a Zip file offline depot, you can easily add the image profile back in when you start a new session.

To export an image profile as a Zip file offline depot, run this command:

```
Export-EsxImageProfile -ImageProfile "My_Custom_Profile" -ExportToBundle -
FilePath "C:\path\to\ZIP-file-offline-depot.zip"
```

When you start a new PowerCLI session to work with an image profile, simply add this offline depot with the `Add-EsxSoftwareDepot` command.

The final step is establishing deployment rules that link image profiles to servers in order to provision ESXi to them at boot time. I'll describe how to do this in the next section.

ESTABLISHING DEPLOYMENT RULES

The deployment rules are where the "rubber meets the road" for vSphere Auto Deploy. When you define a deployment rule, you are linking an image profile to one or more physical hosts. It's at this point that vSphere Auto Deploy will copy all the VIBs defined in the specified image profile up to the Auto Deploy server so that they are accessible from the hosts. Once a deployment rule is in place, you can actually begin provisioning hosts via Auto Deploy (assuming all the other pieces are in place and functioning correctly, of course).

As with image profiles, deployment rules are managed via PowerCLI. You'll use the `New-DeployRule` and `Add-DeployRule` commands to define new deployment rules and add them to the working rule set, respectively.

Perform the following steps to define a new deployment rule:

1. In a PowerCLI session where you've previously connected to vCenter Server and defined an image profile, use the `New-DeployRule` command to define a new deployment rule that matches an image profile to a physical host:

```
New-DeployRule -Name "Img_Rule " -Item "My_Custom_Profile" -Pattern
"vendor=Cisco", "ipv4=10.1.1.225,10.1.1.250"
```

This rule assigns the image profile named My_Custom_Profile to all hosts with "Cisco" in the vendor string and having either the IP address 10.1.1.225 or 10.1.1.250. You could also specify an IP range like 10.1.1.225-10.1.1.250 (using a hyphen to separate the start and end of the IP address range).

2. Next, create a deployment rule that assigns the ESXi host to a cluster within vCenter Server:

```
New-DeployRule -Name "Default_Cluster" -Item "Cluster-1" -AllHosts
```

This rule puts all hosts into the cluster named Cluster-1 in the vCenter Server with which the Auto Deploy server is registered. (Recall that an Auto Deploy server must be registered with a vCenter Server instance.)

3. Add these rules to the working rule set:
```
Add-DeployRule Img_Rule
Add-DeployRule Default_Cluster
```

As soon as you add the deployment rules to the working rule set, vSphere Auto Deploy will, if necessary, start uploading VIBs to the Auto Deploy server in order to satisfy the rules you've defined.

4. Verify that these rules have been added to the working rule set with the `Get-DeployRuleSet` command.

Now that a deployment rule is in place, you're ready to provision via Auto Deploy. Boot the physical host that matches the patterns you defined in the deployment rule, and it should follow the boot sequence I described at the start of this section. Figure 2.11 shows what it looks like when a host is booting ESXi via vSphere Auto Deploy.

By now, you should be starting to see the flexibility that Auto Deploy offers. If you need to deploy a new ESXi image, you need only define a new image profile (using a new software depot, if necessary), assign that image profile with a deployment rule, and reboot the physical servers. When the physical servers come up, they will boot the newly assigned ESXi image via PXE.

FIGURE 2.11
Note the differences
in the ESXi boot
process when using
Auto Deploy versus
a traditional instal-
lation of ESXi.

Of course, there are some additional concerns that you'll need to address should you decide to go this route:

◆ The image profile doesn't contain any ESXi configuration state information, such as virtual switches, security settings, advanced parameters, and so forth. Host profiles are used to store this configuration state information in vCenter Server and pass that configuration information down to a host automatically. You can use a deployment rule to assign a host profile, or you can assign a host profile to a cluster and then use a deployment rule to join hosts to a cluster. I'll describe host profiles in greater detail in Chapter 3.

◆ State information such as log files, generated private keys, and so forth is stored in host memory and is lost during a reboot. Therefore, you must configure additional settings such as setting up syslog for capturing the ESXi logs. Otherwise, this vital operational information is lost every time the host is rebooted. The configuration for capturing this state information can be included in a host profile that is assigned to a host or cluster.

Because the ESXi image doesn't contain configuration state and doesn't maintain dynamic state information, ESXi hosts provisioned via Auto Deploy would be considered *stateless ESXi hosts*. All the state information is stored elsewhere instead of on the host itself.

vSphere Auto Deploy offers some great advantages, especially for environments with lots of ESXi hosts to manage. However, if you'd prefer to have the OEM worry about the installation of ESXi and you have compatible OEM hardware, then you could choose to deploy ESXi Embedded, as described in the next section.

Deploying VMware ESXi Embedded

When you purchase a system with ESXi Embedded, you only need to rack the server, connect the networking cables, and power on. The ESXi Embedded on the persistent storage will obtain an IP address from a DHCP server to provide immediate access via the console, vSphere Client, or vCenter Server.

The server set to run ESXi Embedded must be configured to boot from the appropriate device. Take, for example, an HP server with a USB flash drive with ESXi Embedded connected to an internal (or external) USB port. To run the thin hypervisor, the server must be configured to boot from the USB device. Figure 2.12 shows the BIOS of an HP ProLiant DL385 G2 server.

FIGURE 2.12
To run ESXi Embedded, you must configure the server to boot from the persistent storage device.

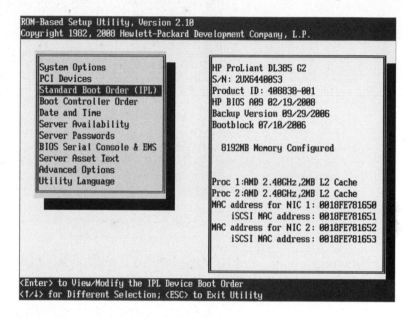

Because ESXi Embedded is installed on and running from the internal USB device, no local hard drives are necessary in this sort of configuration. Customers deploying ESXi Embedded can use servers without hard drives, further reducing power consumption and heat generation. Additionally, because ESXi Embedded is already "installed" on the USB device, there is no installation of which to speak. Once the server is configured to boot from the persistent storage device and ESXi Embedded is up and running, it is managed and configured in the same fashion as ESXi Installable. This makes it incredibly easy to deploy additional servers in rapid fashion.

Although ESXi Embedded is intended for use by OEMs, it's possible to create your own "ESXi Embedded" edition by putting ESXi (the Installable version) onto a USB drive and then booting from this USB drive. This is a great way to test ESXi, but keep in mind that VMware might not support this sort of configuration.

Performing Post-installation Configuration

Whether you are installing from a CD/DVD or performing an unattended installation of ESXi, once the installation is complete, there are several post-installation steps that are necessary or might be necessary, depending on your specific configuration. I'll discuss these tasks in the following sections.

Installing the vSphere Client

This might come as a bit of shock for IT professionals who have grown accustomed to managing Microsoft Windows–based servers from the server's console (even via Remote Desktop), but

ESXi wasn't designed for you to manage it from the server's console. Instead, you should use the vSphere Client.

The vSphere Client is a Windows-only application that allows for connecting directly to an ESXi host or to a vCenter Server installation. The only difference in the tools used is that connecting directly to an ESXi host requires authentication with a user account that exists on that specific host, while connecting to a vCenter Server installation relies on Windows users for authentication. Additionally, some features of the vSphere Client—such as initiating vMotion, for example—are available only when connecting to a vCenter Server installation.

AN ALTERNATIVE TO THE VSPHERE CLIENT

In vSphere 5, VMware added a new web-based client, called the vSphere Web Client, as a potential alternative to the Windows-based vSphere Client. The vSphere Web Client provides a subset of the functionality offered by the vSphere Client, focusing on daily tasks like VM provisioning. Because not all tasks can be completed with the vSphere Web Client, I'll focus primarily on the vSphere Client in this book.

You can install the vSphere Client with the vCenter Server installation media. Figure 2.13 shows the VMware vCenter Installer with the vSphere Client option selected.

FIGURE 2.13
You can install the vSphere Client directly from the vCenter Server installation media.

In previous versions of VMware vSphere, one of the easiest installation methods was to simply connect to an ESX/ESXi host or a vCenter Server instance using your web browser. From there, you clicked a link to download the vSphere Client right from the web page. In vSphere 5, the vSphere Client download link for ESXi hosts doesn't point to a local copy of the installation files; it redirects you to a VMware-hosted website to download the files. The vSphere Client download link for vCenter Server 5, though, still points to a local copy of the vSphere Client installer.

Because you might not have installed vCenter Server yet—that is the focus of the next chapter, Chapter 3—I'll walk you through installing the vSphere Client from the vCenter Server installation media. Regardless of how you obtain the installer, once the installation wizard starts, the process is the same.

Perform the following steps to install the vSphere Client from the vCenter Server installation media:

1. Make the vCenter Server installation media available via CD/DVD to the system where you want to install the vSphere Client.

If you are installing the vSphere Client on a Windows VM, you can mount the vCenter Server installation ISO image as a virtual CD/DVD image. Refer to Chapter 7, "Ensuring High Availability and Business Continuity," for more details if you are unsure how to attach a virtual CD/DVD image.

2. If AutoRun doesn't automatically launch the VMware vCenter Installer (shown previously in Figure 2.13), navigate to the CD/DVD and double-click `Autorun.exe`.

3. From the VMware vCenter Installer main screen, click vSphere Client under VMware Product Installers, and then click Install.

4. Select the language for the installer and click OK.

5. Click the Next button on the welcome page of the Virtual Infrastructure Client Wizard.

6. Click Next at the End User Patent Agreement screen.

7. Click the radio button labeled I Accept The Terms In The License Agreement, and then click the Next button.

8. Specify a username and organization name, and then click the Next button.

9. Configure the destination folder, and then click the Next button.

10. Click the Install button to begin the installation.

11. If prompted, select I Have Read And Accept The Terms Of The License Agreement, and then click Install to install the Microsoft .NET Framework, which is a prerequisite for the vSphere Client.

12. When the .NET Framework installation completes (if applicable), click Exit to continue with the rest of the vSphere Client installation.

13. Click the Finish button to complete the installation. Restart the computer if prompted.

64-Bit vs. 32-Bit

Although the vSphere Client can be installed and is supported on 64-bit Windows operating systems, the vSphere Client itself remains a 32-bit application and runs in 32-bit compatibility mode.

Reconfiguring the Management Network

During the installation of ESXi, the installer creates a virtual switch—also known as a *vSwitch*—bound to a physical NIC. The tricky part, depending on your server hardware, is that the installer might select a different physical NIC than the one you need for correct network connectivity. Consider the scenario depicted in Figure 2.14. If, for whatever reason, the ESXi installer doesn't link the correct physical NIC to the vSwitch it creates, then you won't have network connectivity to that host. I'll talk more about why ESXi's network connectivity must be configured with the correct NIC in Chapter 5, but for now just understand that this is a requirement for connectivity. Since you need network connectivity to manage the host from the vSphere Client, how do you fix this?

FIGURE 2.14

Network connectivity won't be established if the ESXi installer links the wrong NIC to the management network.

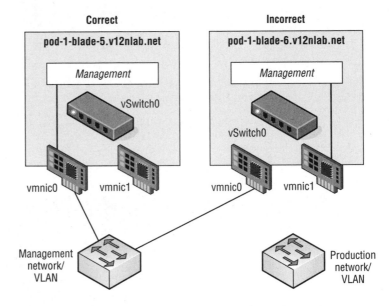

The simplest fix for this problem is to unplug the network cable from the current Ethernet port in the back of the server and continue trying the remaining ports until the host is accessible, but that's not always possible or desirable. The better way is to use the DCUI to reconfigure the management network so that it is converted the way you need it to be configured.

Perform the following steps to fix the management NIC in ESXi using the DCUI:

1. Access the console of the ESXi host, either physically or via a remote console solution such as an IP-based KVM.

2. On the ESXi home screen, shown in Figure 2.15, press F2 for Customize System/View Logs. If a root password has been set, enter that root password.

3. From the System Customization menu, select Configure Management Network, and press Enter.

4. From the Configure Management Network menu, select Network Adapters, and press Enter.

5. Use the spacebar to toggle which network adapter or adapters will be used for the system's management network, as shown in Figure 2.16. Press Enter when finished.

FIGURE 2.15
The ESXi home screen provides options for customizing the system and restarting or shutting down the server.

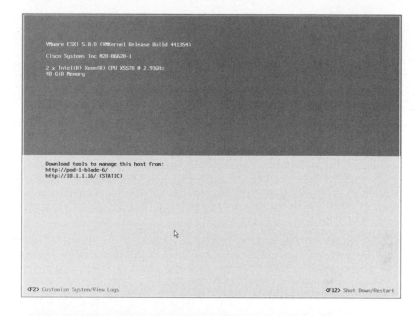

FIGURE 2.16
In the event the incorrect NIC is assigned to ESXi's management network, you can select a different NIC.

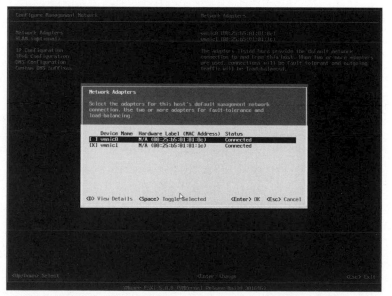

6. Press Esc to exit the Configure Management Network menu. When prompted to apply changes and restart the management network, press Y.

After the correct NIC has been assigned to the ESXi management network, the System Customization menu provides a Test Management Network option to verify network connectivity.

7. Press Esc to log out of the System Customization menu and return to the ESXi home screen.

At this point, you should have management network connectivity to the ESXi host, and from here forward you can use the vSphere Client to perform other configuration tasks, such as configuring time synchronization.

Configuring Time Synchronization

Time synchronization in ESXi is an important configuration because the ramifications of incorrect time run deep. While ensuring that ESXi has the correct time seems trivial, time-synchronization issues can affect features such as performance charting, SSH key expirations, NFS access, backup jobs, authentication, and more. After the installation of ESXi Installable or during an unattended installation of ESXi using an installation script, the host should be configured to perform time synchronization with a reliable time source. This source could be another server on your network or a time source located on the Internet. For the sake of managing time synchronization, it is easiest to synchronize all your servers against one reliable internal time server and then synchronize the internal time server with a reliable Internet time server. ESXi provides a Network Time Protocol (NTP) implementation to provide this functionality.

The simplest way to configure time synchronization for ESXi involves the vSphere Client. Perform the following steps to enable NTP using the vSphere Client:

1. Use the vSphere Client to connect directly to the ESXi host (or to a vCenter Server installation, if you have vCenter Server running at this point).

2. Select the hostname from the inventory tree on the left, and then click the Configuration tab in the details pane on the right.

3. Select Time Configuration from the Software menu.

4. Click the Properties link.

5. In the Time Configuration dialog box, select NTP Client Enabled.

6. Still in the Time Configuration dialog box, click the Options button.

7. Select the NTP Settings option in the left side of the NTP Daemon (ntpd) Options dialog box, and add one or more NTP servers to the list, as shown in Figure 2.17.

8. Check the box marked Restart NTP Service To Apply Changes; then click OK.

9. Click OK to return to the vSphere Client. The Time Configuration area will update to show the new NTP servers.

You'll note that using the vSphere Client to enable NTP this way also automatically enables NTP traffic through the firewall. You can verify this by noting an "Open Firewall Ports" entry in the Tasks pane or by clicking Security Profile under the Software menu and seeing an entry for NTP Client listed under Outgoing Connections.

FIGURE 2.17
Specifying NTP servers allows ESXi to automatically keep time synchronized.

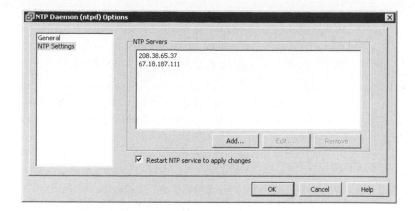

WINDOWS AS A RELIABLE TIME SERVER

You can configure an existing Windows Server as a reliable time server by performing these steps:

1. Use the Group Policy Object editor to navigate to Administrative Templates ➤ System ➤ Windows Time Service ➤ Time Providers.

2. Enable the Enable Windows NTP Server Group Policy option.

3. Navigate to Administrative Templates ➤ System ➤ Windows Time Service.

4. Double-click the Global Configuration Settings option, and select the Enabled radio button.

5. Set the AnnounceFlags option to 4.

6. Click the OK button.

In this chapter I've discussed some of the decisions that you'll have to make as you deploy ESXi in your datacenter, and I've shown you how to deploy these products using both interactive and unattended methods. In the next chapter, I'll show you how to deploy VMware vCenter Server, a key component in your virtualization environment.

The Bottom Line

Understand the differences between ESXi Installable and ESXi Embedded. Although ESXi Installable and ESXi Embedded share the same core hypervisor technology and the same functionality, ESXi Embedded is an OEM solution that is designed to be preinstalled and integrated by equipment manufacturers; ESXi Installable (referred to just as ESXi in this chapter) is designed to be deployed and installed by customers.

Master It You're evaluating ESXi Installable and ESXi Embedded and trying to decide which to use for the vSphere deployment within your company. What are some of the factors that might lead you to choose ESXi Installable over ESXi Embedded or vice versa?

Understand ESXi compatibility requirements. Unlike traditional operating systems like Windows or Linux, ESXi has much stricter hardware compatibility requirements. This helps ensure a stable, well-tested product line that is able to support even the most mission-critical applications.

Master It You'd like to run ESXi Embedded, but your hardware vendor doesn't have a model that includes it. Should you go ahead and buy the servers anyway, even though the hardware vendor doesn't have a model with ESXi Embedded?

Master It You have some older servers onto which you'd like to deploy ESXi. They aren't on the Hardware Compatibility List. Will they work with ESXi?

Plan an ESXi deployment. Deploying ESXi will affect many different areas of your organization—not only the server team but also the networking team, the storage team, and the security team. There are many issues to consider, including server hardware, storage hardware, storage protocols or connection types, network topology, and network connections. Failing to plan properly could result in an unstable and unsupported implementation.

Master It Name three areas of networking that must be considered in a vSphere design.

Deploy ESXi. ESXi can be installed onto any supported and compatible hardware platform. You have three different ways to deploy ESXi: you can install it interactively, you can perform an unattended installation, or you can use vSphere Auto Deploy to provision ESXi directly to the host memory of a server as it boots up. This last method is also referred to as a stateless configuration.

Master It Your manager asks you to provide him with a copy of the unattended installation script that you will be using when you roll out ESXi using vSphere Auto Deploy. Is this something you can give him?

Master It Name two advantages and two disadvantages of using vSphere Auto Deploy to provision ESXi hosts.

Perform post-installation configuration of ESXi. Following the installation of ESXi, some additional configuration steps may be required. For example, if the wrong NIC is assigned to the management network, then the server won't be accessible across the network. You'll also need to configure time synchronization.

Master It You've installed ESXi on your server, but the welcome web page is inaccessible, and the server doesn't respond to a ping. What could be the problem?

Install the vSphere Client. ESXi is managed using the vSphere Client, a Windows-only application that provides the functionality to manage the virtualization platform. There are a couple of different ways to obtain the vSphere Client installer, including running it directly from the VMware vCenter Installer or by downloading it using a web browser connected to the IP address of a vCenter Server instance.

Master It List two ways by which you can install the vSphere Client.

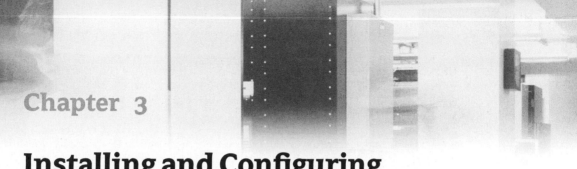

Chapter 3

Installing and Configuring vCenter Server

In the majority of today's information systems, the client-server architecture is king. This emphasis is because the client-server architecture has the ability to centralize management of resources and to provide end users and client systems with access to those resources in a simplified manner. Information systems used to exist in a flat, peer-to-peer model, when user accounts were required on every system where resource access was needed and when significant administrative overhead was needed simply to make things work. That is how managing a large infrastructure with many ESXi hosts feels without vCenter Server. vCenter Server brings the advantages of the client-server architecture to the ESXi host and to VM management.

In this chapter, you will learn to

♦ Understand the features and role of vCenter Server

♦ Plan a vCenter Server deployment

♦ Install and configure a vCenter Server database

♦ Install and configure vCenter Server

♦ Use vCenter Server's management features

Introducing vCenter Server

As the size of a virtual infrastructure grows, the ability to manage the infrastructure from a central location becomes significantly more important. vCenter Server is a Windows-based application that serves as a centralized management tool for ESXi hosts and their respective VMs. vCenter Server acts as a proxy that performs tasks on the individual ESXi hosts that have been added as members of a vCenter Server installation. As I discussed in Chapter 1, "Introducing VMware vSphere 5," VMware includes vCenter Server licensing in every kit and every edition of vSphere, underscoring the importance of vCenter Server. Although VMware does offer a couple of different editions of vCenter Server (vCenter Server Essentials, vCenter Server Foundation, and vCenter Server Standard), I'll focus only on vCenter Server Standard in this book.

As you will see throughout this book, much of the advanced functionality that vSphere offers comes only when vCenter Server is present. Specifically, vCenter Server offers core services in the following areas:

◆ Resource management for ESXi hosts and VMs

◆ Template management

◆ VM deployment

◆ VM management

◆ Scheduled tasks

◆ Statistics and logging

◆ Alarms and event management

◆ ESXi host management

Figure 3.1 outlines the core services available through vCenter Server.

FIGURE 3.1
vCenter Server provides a full spectrum of virtualization management functions.

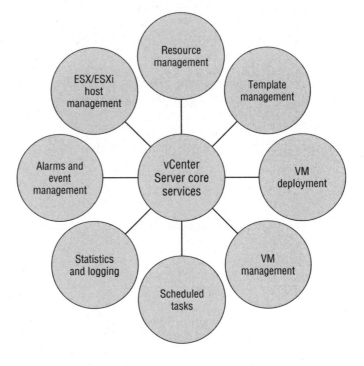

WHY IS ESX/ESXi HOST MANAGEMENT LISTED FOR VCENTER SERVER?

Although this book primarily focuses on vSphere 5, there are areas where you'll see references to ESX, which is no longer included with vSphere 5. For example, in Chapter 4, "Installing and Configuring vSphere Update Manager," you'll see references to ESX because vSphere Update Manager supports updating and upgrading ESX 4.x hosts to ESXi 5. In this chapter, any references to ESX are because vCenter Server 5 is capable of managing ESX/ESXi 4.x hosts as well as ESXi 5 hosts.

New to vSphere 5 is the inclusion of vCenter Server in an entirely new format: as a Linux-based virtual appliance. You'll learn more about virtual appliances in Chapter 10, "Using Templates and vApps," but for now suffice it to say that the vCenter Server virtual appliance (which you may see referred to as VCVA) offers an option to quickly and easily deploy a full installation of vCenter Server on SuSE Linux.

Because of the breadth of features included in vCenter Server, most of these core services are discussed in later chapters. For example, Chapter 9, "Creating and Managing Virtual Machines," discusses VM deployment, VM management, and template management. Chapter 11, "Managing Resource Allocation," and Chapter 12, "Balancing Resource Utilization," deal with resource management for ESXi hosts and VMs, and Chapter 13, "Monitoring VMware vSphere Performance," discusses alarms. In this chapter, I'll focus primarily on ESXi host management, but I'll also discuss scheduled tasks, statistics and logging, and event management.

There are two other key items about vCenter Server that you can't really consider core services. Instead, these underlying features support the core services provided by vCenter Server. In order to help you more fully understand the value of vCenter Server in a vSphere deployment, I need to provide a closer look at the centralized user authentication and extensible framework that vCenter Server provides.

Centralizing User Authentication Using vCenter Server

Centralized user authentication is not listed as a core service of vCenter Server, but it is essential to how vCenter Server operates, and it is essential to the reduction of management overhead that vCenter Server brings to a vSphere implementation. In Chapter 2, "Planning and Installing VMware ESXi," I discussed a user's authentication to an ESXi host under the context of a user account created and stored locally on that host. Generally speaking, without vCenter Server you would need a separate user account on each ESXi host for each administrator who needed access to the server. As the number of ESXi hosts and the number of administrators who need access to these hosts grows, the number of accounts to manage grows exponentially. There are workarounds for this overhead; one such workaround is integrating your ESXi hosts into Active Directory, a topic that I discuss in more detail in Chapter 8, "Securing VMware vSphere." In this chapter, I'll assume the use of local accounts, but be aware that using Active Directory integration with your ESXi hosts does change the picture somewhat. In general, though, the centralized user authentication vCenter Server offers is significantly simpler and easier to manage than other available methods.

In a virtualized infrastructure with only one or two ESXi hosts, administrative effort is not a major concern. Administration of one or two servers would not incur incredible effort on the part of the administrator, and the creation of user accounts for administrators would not be too much of a burden.

In situations like this, vCenter Server might not be missed from a management perspective, but it will certainly be missed from a feature set viewpoint. In addition to its management capabilities, vCenter Server provides the ability to perform vMotion, configure vSphere Distributed Resource Scheduler (DRS), establish vSphere High Availability (HA), and use vSphere Fault Tolerance (FT). These features are not accessible using ESXi hosts without vCenter Server. Without vCenter Server, you also lose key functionality such as vSphere Distributed Switches, host profiles, profile-driven storage, and vSphere Update Manager. vCenter Server is a requirement for any enterprise-level virtualization project.

VCENTER SERVER REQUIREMENT

Strictly speaking, vCenter Server is not a requirement for a vSphere deployment. You can create and run VMs without vCenter Server. However, to utilize the advanced features of the vSphere product suite—features such as vSphere Update Manager, vMotion, vSphere DRS, vSphere HA, vSphere Distributed Switches, host profiles, or vSphere FT—vCenter Server must be licensed, installed, and configured accordingly.

But what happens when the environment grows? What happens when there are 10 ESXi hosts and five administrators? Now, the administrative effort of maintaining all these local accounts on the ESXi hosts becomes a significant burden. If a new account is needed to manage the ESXi hosts, you must create the account on 10 different hosts. If the password to an account needs to change, you must change the password on 10 different hosts.

vCenter Server addresses this problem. When you install vCenter Server on a Windows Server–based OS, it uses standard Windows user accounts and groups for authentication. These users and groups can reside in the local security accounts manager (SAM) database for that specific Windows-based server, or the users and groups can belong to the Active Directory domain to which the vCenter Server computer belongs. Alternately, when you deploy the Linux-based vCenter Server virtual appliance, it integrates into Active Directory to provide access to Active Directory–based users and groups. Either way, with vCenter Server in place, you can use the vSphere Client to connect to vCenter Server using a Windows-based account or to connect to an ESXi host using a local account. Further, vCenter Server enables this centralized authentication without any extensive changes on the ESXi host itself; it's just built into the way vCenter Server and ESXi interact.

Although the vSphere Client supports authentication of both vCenter Server and ESXi hosts, organizations should use a consistent method for provisioning user accounts to manage their vSphere infrastructure because local user accounts created on an ESXi host are not reconciled or synchronized with the Windows or Active Directory accounts that vCenter Server uses.

For example, if a user account named Shane is created locally on an ESXi host named `pod-1 -blade-5.v12nlab.net` and the user account is granted the permissions necessary to manage the host, Shane will not be able to utilize the vSphere Client connected to vCenter Server to perform his management capabilities. The inverse is also true. If a Windows user account named Elaine is granted permission through vCenter Server to manage an ESXi host named `pod-1-blade-6.v12nlab.net`, then Elaine will not be able to manage the host by using the vSphere Client to connect directly to that ESXi host.

AUTHENTICATION WITH THE VSPHERE CLIENT

Generally speaking, logging on to an ESXi host using the vSphere Client requires the use of an account created and stored locally on that host. Using the same vSphere Client to connect to vCenter Server requires the use of a Windows user account. Keep in mind that vCenter Server and ESXi hosts do not make any attempt to reconcile the user accounts in their respective account databases.

Using the vSphere Client to connect directly to an ESXi host that is currently being managed by vCenter Server can cause negative effects in vCenter Server. A successful logon to a managed host results in a pop-up box that warns you of this potential problem.

Providing an Extensible Framework

Just as centralized authentication is not a core vCenter Server service, I don't include vCenter Server's extensible framework as a core service. Rather, this extensible framework provides the foundation for vCenter Server's core services and enables third-party developers to create applications built around vCenter Server. Figure 3.2 shows some of the components that revolve around the core services of vCenter Server.

FIGURE 3.2
Other applications can extend vCenter Server's core services to provide additional management functionality.

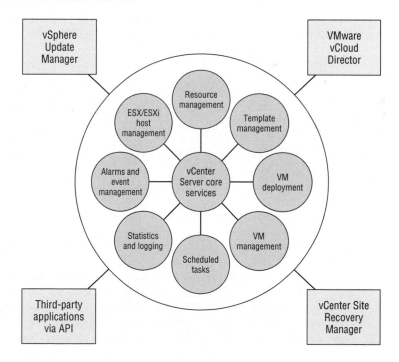

A key aspect for the success of virtualization is the ability to allow third-party companies to provide additional products that add value, ease, and functionality to existing products. By building vCenter Server in an extensible fashion and providing an application programming interface (API) to vCenter Server, VMware has shown its interest in allowing third-party software developers to play an integral part in virtualization. The vCenter Server API allows companies to develop custom applications that can take advantage of the virtual infrastructure created in vCenter Server. For example, numerous companies have created backup utilities that work off the exact inventory created inside vCenter Server to allow for advanced backup options of VMs. Storage vendors use the vCenter API to create plug-ins that expose storage details, and other third-party applications use the vCenter Server APIs to provide management, monitoring, life cycle management, or automation functionality.

You can find more information on vCenter Server functionality in Chapter 10, which provides a detailed look at templates along with VM deployment and management, and Chapter 8, which goes deeper into vCenter Server's access controls. Chapter 11 discusses resource management, while Chapter 13 offers an in-depth look at ESXi host and VM monitoring, as well as alarms.

You're almost ready to take a closer look at installing, configuring, and managing vCenter Server. First, however, I'll discuss choosing which version of vCenter Server you should deploy in your environment.

Choosing the Version of vCenter Server

I mentioned in the previous section that in vSphere 5 vCenter Server now comes not only as a Windows-based application but also as SuSE Linux-based virtual appliance. As a result, one of the primary decisions that you must make as you prepare to deploy vCenter Server is which version of vCenter Server you will use. Will you use the Windows Server–based version or use the virtual appliance?

There are some advantages and disadvantages to each approach:

◆ The Linux-based virtual appliance comes preloaded with additional services like Auto Deploy (which I covered in Chapter 2), Dynamic Host Configuration Protocol (DHCP), Trivial File Transfer Protocol (TFTP), and Syslog. If you need these services on your network, you can provide these services with a single deployment of the vCenter virtual appliance. With the Windows Server–based version, these services are separate installations or possibly even separate VMs (or, worse yet, separate physical servers!).

◆ If your experience is primarily with Windows Server, the Linux underpinnings of the vCenter virtual appliance are something with which you may not be familiar. This introduces a learning curve that you should consider.

◆ Conversely, if your experience is primarily with Linux, then deploying a Windows Server–based application will require some learning and acclimation for you and/or your staff.

◆ If you need support for Microsoft SQL Server, the Linux-based vCenter virtual appliance won't work; you'll need to deploy the Windows Server–based version of vCenter Server. However, if you are using Oracle or DB2, or if you are a small installation without a separate database server, the vCenter Server virtual appliance will work just fine (it has its own embedded database if you don't have or don't need a separate database server).

◆ If you need to use linked mode, you must deploy the Windows Server–based version of vCenter Server. The vCenter Server virtual appliance does not support linked mode.

◆ If you need support for IPv6, the vCenter Server virtual appliance does not provide that support; you must deploy the Windows Server–based version.

◆ Because the vCenter Server virtual appliance naturally runs only as a VM, you are constrained to that particular design decision. If you want or need to run vCenter Server on a physical system, you cannot use the vCenter Server virtual appliance.

◆ If you want to use vCenter Heartbeat to protect vCenter Server from downtime, you'll need to use the Windows Server–based version of vCenter Server.

As you can see, there are a number of considerations that will affect your decision to deploy vCenter Server as a Windows Server–based installation or as a Linux-based virtual appliance.

MY VIEW ON THE VCENTER VIRTUAL APPLIANCE

Because of some of the support limitations around the SuSE Linux-based vCenter Server virtual appliance, I'm inclined to position this solution as more appropriate for smaller installations. This is not because the virtual appliance is in some way not capable of handling the larger environments but simply because the idea of deploying a virtual appliance that handles all the various services that are required would appeal more to a smaller implementation. Deploying the vCenter Server virtual appliance is a one-step solution that would work for many smaller vSphere environments or perhaps is an ideal solution for test/development environments.

In the next section, I'll discuss some of the planning and design considerations that have to be addressed if you are planning on deploying the Windows Server–based version of vCenter Server. Most of these apply to the Windows Server–based version of vCenter Server, but some of these considerations may also apply to the virtual appliance; I'll point those out where applicable.

Planning and Designing a vCenter Server Deployment

vCenter Server is a critical application for managing your virtual infrastructure. Its implementation should be carefully designed and executed to ensure availability and data protection. When discussing the deployment of vCenter Server, some of the most common questions include the following:

◆ How much hardware do I need to power vCenter Server?

◆ Which database server should I use with vCenter Server?

◆ How do I prepare vCenter Server for disaster recovery?

◆ Should I run vCenter Server in a VM?

A lot of the answers to these questions are dependent on each other, but I have to start somewhere, so I'll start with the first topic: figuring out how much hardware you need for vCenter Server.

Sizing Hardware for vCenter Server

The amount of hardware that vCenter Server requires is directly related to the number of hosts and VMs it will be managing. This planning and design consideration applies only to the Windows Server–based version of vCenter Server, because—by the nature of the fact that it is a prepackaged virtual appliance—the virtual hardware of the vCenter Server virtual appliance is predefined and established before it is deployed.

As a starting point, the minimum hardware requirements for the Windows Server–based version of vCenter Server are as follows:

- ◆ Two 64-bit CPUs or a single dual-core 64-bit CPU.

- ◆ 2 GHz processor or faster.

- ◆ 3 GB of RAM or more.

- ◆ 3 GB of free disk space.

- ◆ A network adapter (Gigabit Ethernet strongly recommended).

- ◆ A supported version of Windows (Windows Server 2003, Windows Server 2003 R2, Windows Server 2008, or Windows Server 2008 R2); vCenter Server 5 requires a 64-bit version of Windows.

Keep in mind these are *minimum* system requirements. Large enterprise environments with many ESXi hosts and VMs must scale the vCenter Server system accordingly.

LOCAL DISKS ON VCENTER SERVER

Disk storage allocation is of minimal concern when planning a vCenter Server installation because the data is generally stored in an SQL Server, Oracle, or DB2 database on a remote server.

In addition, the requirements for the Windows Server–based edition of vCenter Server do not account for running a database server, which vCenter Server requires. Although vCenter Server is the application that performs the management of your ESXi hosts and VMs, vCenter Server uses a database for storing all of its configuration, permissions, statistics, and other data. Figure 3.3 shows the relationship between vCenter Server and the separate database server.

FIGURE 3.3
vCenter Server acts as a proxy for managing ESXi hosts, but all of the data for vCenter Server is stored in a database.

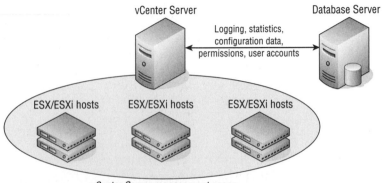

vCenter Server management scope

When answering the question of how much hardware vCenter Server requires, you have to address not only the computer running vCenter Server but also the computer running the database server. Although you can run vCenter Server and the database server on the same machine, it's usually not recommended because it creates a single point of failure for two key aspects of your virtual infrastructure.

Throughout this chapter, I'll use the term *separate database server* to refer to a database server application that is separately installed and managed. Although it might reside on the same computer, it is still considered a separate database server because it is managed independently of vCenter Server. You'll also see the term *backend database*, which refers to the actual database that vCenter Server uses on the separate database server.

Without considering the separate database server for vCenter Server, VMware suggests a system configured with two CPU cores and 4 GB of RAM to support up to 50 ESXi hosts and 500 powered-on VMs. For environments up to 300 ESXi hosts and up to 3,000 powered-on VMs, VMware recommends four CPU cores and 8 GB of RAM. Finally, for environments scaling all the way up to 1,000 ESXi hosts and up to 10,000 powered-on VMs, vCenter Server should have eight CPU cores and 16 GB of RAM.

CPU CORES

Most modern physical servers ship by default with quad-core CPUs. As you can see based on VMware's recommendations, vCenter Server will leverage multiple CPU cores when necessary.

Should you choose to run the separate database server on the same physical computer as vCenter Server, you'll need to consult the documentation for whatever database server you choose to use. Without doubt, the database server requires additional CPU capacity, RAM, and disk storage, and you will need to plan accordingly. That brings me to the next topic: choosing which database server to use.

Choosing a Database Server for vCenter Server

In light of the sensitive and critical nature of the data in the vCenter Server database, VMware supports vCenter Server issues only with backend databases on enterprise-level database servers. Both the Windows Server–based version and the virtual appliance version of vCenter Server use a backend database, so deciding which backend database to use is a decision you'll need to make either way. vCenter Server officially supports the following database servers:

◆ IBM DB2 9.5 (fix pack 5 required; fix pack 7 recommended)

◆ IBM DB2 9.7 (fix pack 2 required; fix pack 3a recommended)

◆ Microsoft SQL Server 2008 R2 Express (bundled with vCenter Server)

◆ Microsoft SQL Server 2005 (32-bit or 64-bit; SP3 is required, and SP4 is recommended)

◆ Microsoft SQL Server 2008 (32-bit or 64-bit; SP1 is required, and SP2 is recommended)

◆ Microsoft SQL Server 2008 R2

◆ Oracle 10*g* R2 (10.2.0.4 required)

◆ Oracle 11*g* R1 (11.1.0.7 required)

◆ Oracle 11*g* R2 (11.2.0.1 with patch 5 required)

Note that although a database might be supported for use with vCenter Server, that same database might not be supported for use with other components of vSphere such as vSphere Update Manager or other plug-ins that require database support. For up-to-date compatibility information, refer to the vSphere Compatibility Matrixes available from VMware's website (www.vmware.com). In addition, note that Microsoft SQL Server is supported for use by a Windows Server–based installation of vCenter Server, but it is not supported by the vCenter Server virtual appliance.

For smaller environments, users have the option of using Microsoft SQL Server 2008 Express Edition or, if using the virtual appliance, an embedded database. As of this writing, VMware had not yet published any sizing recommendations regarding the use of the embedded database. As I stated in the sidebar "My View on the vCenter Virtual Appliance," the use of the vCenter virtual appliance with the embedded database is probably best suited for smaller environments.

Users should use SQL Server 2008 Express Edition only when their vSphere deployment will be limited in size; otherwise, users should plan on using a separate database server. If you are starting out with a small environment that will work with SQL Server 2008 Express Edition, note that it is possible to upgrade to a more full-featured version of SQL Server at a later date. More information on upgrading SQL Server 2008 Express is available on the Microsoft website (www.microsoft.com).

USING SQL SERVER 2008 EXPRESS EDITION

SQL Server 2008 Express Edition is the minimum database available as a backend to the Windows Server–based version of vCenter Server.

Microsoft SQL Server 2008 Express Edition has physical limitations that include the following:

◆ One CPU maximum

◆ 1 GB maximum of addressable RAM

◆ 4 GB database maximum

Large virtual enterprises will quickly outgrow these SQL Server 2008 Express Edition limitations. Therefore, you might assume that any virtual infrastructures using SQL Server 2008 Express Edition are smaller deployments with little projections, if any, for growth. VMware suggests using SQL Server 2008 Express Edition only for deployments with five or fewer hosts and 50 or fewer VMs.

Because the separate database server is independently installed and managed, some additional configuration is required. Later in this chapter, the section "Installing vCenter Server" provides detailed information about working with separate database servers and the specific configuration that is required for each.

So, how does an organization go about choosing which separate database server to use? The selection of which database server to use with vCenter Server is typically a reflection of what an organization already uses or is already licensed to use. Organizations that already have Oracle may decide to continue to use Oracle for vCenter Server; organizations that are predominantly based on Microsoft SQL Server will likely choose to use SQL Server to support vCenter Server. The choice of which version of vCenter Server—Windows Server–based or virtual appliance—will also affect this decision, since the supported databases are different for each version. You should choose the database engine with which you are most familiar and that will support both the current and projected size of the virtual infrastructure.

With regard to the hardware requirements for the database server, the underlying database server will largely determine those requirements. VMware provides some general guidelines around Microsoft SQL Server in the white paper "VirtualCenter Database Performance for Microsoft SQL Server 2005," available on VMware's website at `www.vmware.com/files/pdf/vc_database_performance.pdf`. Although written with VirtualCenter 2.5 in mind, this information applies to newer versions of vCenter Server as well. In a typical configuration with standard logging levels, an SQL Server instance with two CPU cores and 4 GB of RAM allocated to the database application should support all but the very largest or most demanding environments.

If you are planning on running the database server and vCenter Server on the same hardware, you should adjust the hardware requirements accordingly.

Appropriately sizing hardware for vCenter Server and the separate database server is good and necessary. Given the central role that vCenter Server plays in a vSphere environment, though, you must also account for availability.

Planning for vCenter Server Availability

Planning for a vCenter Server deployment is more than just accounting for CPU and memory resources. You must also create a plan for business continuity and disaster recovery. Remember, features such as vSphere vMotion, vSphere Storage vMotion, vSphere DRS, and—to a certain extent–vSphere HA stop functioning or are significantly impacted when vCenter Server is unavailable. While vCenter Server is down, you won't be able to clone VMs or deploy new VMs from templates. You also lose centralized authentication and role-based administration of the ESXi hosts. Clearly, there are reasons why you might want vCenter Server to be highly available.

Keep in mind, too, that the heart of the vCenter Server content is stored in a backend database. Any good disaster-recovery or business-continuity plan must also include instructions on how to handle data loss or corruption in the backend database, and the separate database server (if running on a separate physical computer or in a separate VM) should be designed and deployed in a resilient and highly available fashion. This is especially true in larger environments.

There are a few different ways to approach this concern. First, I'll discuss how to protect vCenter Server, and then I'll talk about protecting the separate database server.

First, vCenter Server Heartbeat—a product available from VMware since VirtualCenter/vCenter Server 2.5 to provide high availability with little or no downtime—will be available with support for vCenter Server 5 upon release or shortly after the release of vSphere 5 (vCenter Server 5 support is slated for vCenter Heartbeat 6.4). Using vCenter Server Heartbeat will automate both the process of keeping the active and passive vCenter Server instances synchronized and the process of failing over from one to another (and back again). The website at `www.vmware.com/products/vcenter-server-heartbeat` has more information on vCenter Server Heartbeat.

If the vCenter Server computer is a physical server, one way to provide availability is to create a standby vCenter Server system that you can turn on in the event of a failure of the online vCenter Server computer. After failure, you bring the standby server online and attach it to the existing SQL Server database, and then the hosts can be added to the new vCenter Server computer. In this approach, you'll need to find mechanisms to keep the primary and secondary/standby vCenter Server systems synchronized with regard to filesystem content, configuration settings, and the roles and permissions stored in an Active Directory Application Mode (ADAM) instance (see the sidebar "One Pitfall of Using a Standby vCenter Server Computer"). The use of the Linux-based virtual appliance might make this approach easier, since it does not use ADAM (it doesn't support linked mode operation) and, because it is a VM, can be cloned (a process you'll see in more detail in Chapter 10).

A variation on that approach is to keep the standby vCenter Server system as a VM. You can use physical-to-virtual (P2V) conversion tools to regularly "back up" the physical vCenter Server instance to a standby VM. This method reduces the amount of physical hardware required and leverages the P2V process as a way of keeping the two vCenter Servers synchronized. Obviously, this sort of approach is viable for a Windows Server–based installation on a physical system but not applicable to the virtual appliance version of vCenter Server.

As a last resort for recovering vCenter Server, it's possible to just reinstall the software, point to the existing database, and connect the host systems. Of course, this assumes that the database is housed on a separate system from vCenter Server itself. The installation of vCenter Server is not a time-consuming process. Ultimately, the most important part of the vCenter Server recovery plan is to ensure that the database server is redundant and protected.

ONE PITFALL OF USING A STANDBY VCENTER SERVER COMPUTER

Although vCenter Server stores most of its information in the database managed by the separate database server, the Windows Server–based version of vCenter Server also uses Microsoft ADAM to store roles and permissions. Any availability scheme that involves a standby vCenter Server computer—be it a physical or virtual instance—runs the risk of losing roles or permissions in vCenter Server if the appropriate steps aren't taken to ensure this data is kept current. In addition, processes used to create the standby vCenter Server computer that don't ensure a consistent copy of the ADAM database also run the risk of losing roles or permissions within vCenter Server. Be aware of this pitfall if you plan to use a standby vCenter Server in your environment.

For high availability of the database server supporting vCenter Server, you can configure the backend database on a cluster. Figure 3.4 illustrates using an SQL Server cluster for the backend database. This figure also shows a standby vCenter Server system. Methods used to provide high availability for the database server are in addition to whatever steps you might take to protect vCenter Server itself. Other options might include using SQL log shipping to create a database replica on a separate system. If using clustering or log shipping/database replication is not available or is not within fiscal reach, you should strengthen your database backup strategy to support easy recovery in the event of data loss or corruption. Using the native SQL Server tools, you can create a backup strategy that combines full, differential, and transaction log backups. This strategy allows you to restore data up to the minute when the loss or corruption occurred.

The suggestion of using a VM as a standby system for a physical computer running vCenter Server naturally brings me to the last topic: should you run vCenter Server in a VM? That's quite a question, and it's one that I'll answer next.

FIGURE 3.4
A good disaster recovery plan for vCenter Server should include a quick means of regaining the user interface as well as ensuring the data is highly available and protected against damage.

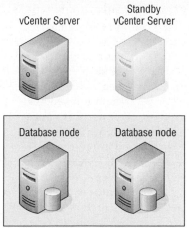

VIRTUALIZING VCENTER SERVER

Another option for vCenter Server is to install it into a VM. Although you might hesitate to do so, there are really some great advantages to doing this. vCenter Server installed as a VM offers increased portability, snapshot functionality, and cloning functionality. It can also be easier to increase resource allocation in the event the vCenter Server instance needs more memory, for example.

Although there are advantages to installing vCenter Server in a VM, you should also understand the limitations. Features such as cold migration, cloning, and editing hardware are not available for the VM running vCenter Server. In addition, there could be considerations for running vCenter Server as a VM in conjunction with a distributed virtual switch. You'll learn about distributed virtual switches in Chapter 5, "Creating and Configuring Virtual Networks."

Running vCenter Server in a VM is a supported option, as further evidenced by vSphere 5's inclusion of a Linux-based virtual appliance edition of vCenter Server.

Running vCenter Server in a VM

You certainly have the option of skipping a physical server entirely and running vCenter Server as a VM. This gives you several advantages, including snapshots, vMotion, vSphere HA, and vSphere DRS.

Snapshots are a feature I'll discuss in detail in Chapter 9. At a high level, snapshot functionality gives you the ability to return to a specific point in time for your VM, in this case, your vCenter Server VM. vMotion gives you the portability required to move the server from host to host without experiencing server downtime. But what happens when a snapshot is corrupted or the VM is damaged to the point it will not run? With vCenter Server as your VM, you can make regular copies of the virtual disk file and keep a "clone" of the server ready to go in the event of server failure. The clone will have the same system configuration used the last time the virtual disks were copied. Given that the bulk of the data processing by vCenter Server ends up in a backend database running on a different server, this should not be very different. However, remember that the Windows Server–based version of vCenter Server uses an ADAM database to store roles and permissions, so roles and permissions on the clone will "roll back" to the point in time at which the clone was created. Additionally, if you are using the vCenter Server virtual appliance with the embedded database, you could run into issues with snapshots and reverting to snapshots. This might or might not be an issue, but be sure to plan accordingly. Figure 3.5 illustrates the setup of a manual cloning of a vCenter Server VM.

FIGURE 3.5

If vCenter Server is a VM, its virtual disk file can be copied regularly and used as the hard drive for a new VM, effectively providing a point-in-time restore in the event of complete server failure or loss.

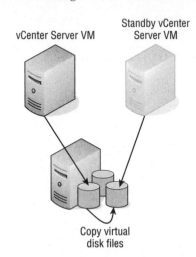

vCenter Server VM

Standby vCenter Server VM

Copy virtual disk files

By now, you have a good understanding of the importance of vCenter Server in a large enterprise environment and some of the considerations that go into planning for a vCenter Server deployment. You also have a good idea of the features, functions, and role of vCenter Server. With this information in mind, let's install vCenter Server. The next section mainly focuses on the installation of the Windows Server–based version of vCenter Server; for information on the vCenter Server virtual appliance, refer to the section "Deploying the vCenter Server Virtual Appliance."

Installing vCenter Server

Depending on the size of the environment to be managed, installing vCenter Server can be simple. In small environments, the vCenter Server installer can install and configure all the necessary components. For larger environments, installing vCenter Server in a scalable and resilient fashion is a bit more involved and requires a few different steps. For example, supporting more than 1,000 ESXi hosts or more than 10,000 VMs requires installing multiple vCenter Server instances in a linked mode group, a scenario that I'll discuss later in this chapter in the section "Installing vCenter Server in a Linked Mode Group." You also know that the majority of vCenter Server deployments need a separate database server installed and configured to support vCenter Server. The exception would be the very small deployments in which SQL Server 2008 Express Edition is sufficient.

The majority of this section is applicable only to installing vCenter Server on a Windows Server–based computer (physical or virtual). However, some tasks—such as the tasks required for preparing separate database servers—are applicable to the use of the vCenter Server virtual appliance as well.

VCENTER SERVER PREINSTALLATION TASKS

Before you install vCenter Server, ensure that the computer has been updated with the latest updates, such as Windows Installer 3.1 and all required .NET components, from the Microsoft Windows Update site at www.update.microsoft.com/microsoftupdate/v6/default.aspx.

Depending on the database engine you will use, different configuration steps are required to prepare the database server for vCenter Server, and these steps must be completed before you can actually install vCenter Server. If you are planning on using SQL Server 2008 Express Edition—and you're aware of the limitations of using this edition, as described earlier in the sidebar "Using SQL Server 2008 Express Edition"—you can skip ahead to the section "Running the vCenter Server Installer." Otherwise, let's take a closer look at working with a separate database server and what is required.

Configuring the vCenter Server Backend Database Server

As noted previously, vCenter Server stores the majority of its information in a backend database, usually using a separate database server. It's important to realize that the backend database is a key component to this infrastructure. The backend database server should be designed and deployed accordingly. Without the backend database, you will find yourself rebuilding an entire infrastructure.

VCENTER SERVER BUSINESS CONTINUITY

Losing the server that runs vCenter Server might result in a small period of downtime; however, losing the backend database to vCenter Server could result in days of downtime and extended periods of rebuilding.

On the backend database server, vCenter Server requires specific permissions on its database. After that database is created and configured appropriately, connecting vCenter Server to its backend database requires that an Open Database Connectivity (ODBC) data source name (DSN) be created on the vCenter Server system. The ODBC DSN should be created under the context of a database user who has full rights and permissions to the database that has been created specifically for storing vCenter Server data.

In the following sections, we'll take a closer look at working with the two most popular database servers used in conjunction with vCenter Server: Oracle and Microsoft SQL Server. Although other database servers are supported for use with vCenter Server, Oracle and SQL Server are officially supported and account for the vast majority of all installations.

> **DO I NEED A 32-BIT DATA SOURCE NAME OR A 64-BIT DATA SOURCE NAME?**
>
> vCenter Server 5 requires a supported 64-bit version of Windows and also requires the use of a 64-bit DSN.

WORKING WITH ORACLE DATABASES

Perhaps because Microsoft SQL Server was designed as a Windows-based application, like vCenter Server, working with Oracle as the backend database server involves a bit more effort than using Microsoft SQL Server.

To use Oracle 10*g* or 11*g*, you need to install Oracle and create a database for vCenter Server to use. Although it is supported to run Oracle on the same computer as vCenter Server, it is not a configuration I recommend. Still, in the event you have valid business reasons for doing so, I'll walk you through the steps for configuring Oracle to support vCenter Server both locally (on the same computer as vCenter Server) and remotely (on a different computer than vCenter Server). If you are deploying the vCenter Server virtual appliance, then only the remote Oracle configuration applies. Both of these sets of instructions assume that you have already created the database you are going to use.

> **SPECIAL PATCHES NEEDED FOR ORACLE 10*g* RELEASE 2**
>
> For Oracle 10g Release 2, you must apply patch 10.2.0.4 to both the client and the Oracle database server in order to support vCenter Server.

Perform the following steps to prepare Oracle for vCenter Server if your Oracle database resides on the same computer as vCenter Server:

1. Log in to an SQL*Plus session with the system account to create a database user. Run the following SQL command to create a user with the correct permissions:

```
CREATE USER "vpxadmin" PROFILE "DEFAULT" IDENTIFIED BY "vcdbpassword"
DEFAULT TABLESPACE
"VPX" ACCOUNT UNLOCK;
grant connect to VPXADMIN;
grant resource to VPXADMIN;
grant create view to VPXADMIN;
grant create sequence to VPXADMIN;
grant create table to VPXADMIN;
grant create materialized view to VPXADMIN;
grant execute on dbms_lock to VPXADMIN;
grant execute on dbms_job to VPXADMIN;
grant unlimited tablespace to VPXADMIN;
```

If the RESOURCE role doesn't have CREATE PROCEDURE, CREATE TABLE, and CREATE SEQUENCE privileges assigned, you'll need to grant them to the vCenter Server database user.

2. Run the following SQL command to create the vCenter Server database:

```
CREATE SMALLFILE TABLESPACE "VPX" DATAFILE 'C:\Oracle\ORADATA\VPX\VPX.DBF'
SIZE 1G AUTOEXTEND ON NEXT 10M MAXSIZE UNLIMITED LOGGING EXTENT MANAGEMENT
LOCAL SEGMENT SPACE MANAGEMENT AUTO;
```

Modify the path to the database as appropriate for your installation.

3. Now you need to assign a user permission to this newly created tablespace. While you are still connected to SQL*Plus, run the following SQL command:

```
CREATE USER vpxAdmin IDENTIFIED BY vpxadmin DEFAULT TABLESPACE vpx;
```

4. Install the Oracle client and the ODBC driver.

5. Modify the TNSNAMES.ORA file to reflect where your Oracle database is located:

```
VC=
(DESCRIPTION=
(ADDRESS_LIST=
(ADDRESS=(PROTOCOL=TCP)(HOST=localhost)(PORT=1521))
)
(CONNECT_DATA=
(SERVICE_NAME=VPX)
)
)
```

The HOST= value should be set to localhost if you are accessing the Oracle database locally or the name of the remote Oracle database server if you are accessing the database remotely. Specify the remote host as a fully-qualified domain name (FQDN), such as pod-1-blade-8.v12nlab.net.

6. Create the ODBC DSN. When you are creating the DSN, be sure to specify the service name as listed in TNSNAMES.ORA (in this example, VPX).

7. While logged in to SQL*Plus with the system account, run the following SQL command to enable database monitoring via the vCenter Server user:

```
grant select on v_$system_event to VPXADMIN;
grant select on v_$sysmetric_history to VPXADMIN;
grant select on v_$sysstat to VPXADMIN;
grant select on dba_data_files to VPXADMIN;
grant select on v_$loghist to VPXADMIN;
```

8. After you complete the vCenter Server installation, copy the Oracle JDBC driver (ojdbc13.jar) to the tomcat\lib folder under the VMware vCenter Server installation folder.

After the Oracle database is created and configured appropriately and the ODBC DSN is established, you're ready to install vCenter Server.

> **vCENTER SERVER AND ORACLE**
>
> You can find all the downloadable files required to make vCenter Server work with Oracle on Oracle's website at www.oracle.com/technology/software/index.html.

WORKING WITH MICROSOFT SQL SERVER DATABASES

In light of the existing widespread deployment of Microsoft SQL Server 2005 and Microsoft SQL Server 2008, it is common to find SQL Server as the backend database for vCenter Server. This is not to say that Oracle does not perform as well or that there is any downside to using Oracle. Microsoft SQL Server just happens to be implemented more commonly than Oracle and therefore is a more common database server for vCenter Server.

If you are considering the use of Microsoft SQL Server as the separate database server for the backend database, keep in mind that the vCenter Server virtual appliance does not support Microsoft SQL Server.

Connecting vCenter Server to a Microsoft SQL Server database, like the Oracle implementation, requires a few specific configuration tasks, as follows:

♦ vCenter Server supports both Windows and mixed mode authentication. Be aware of which authentication type the SQL Server is using because this setting will affect other portions of the vCenter Server installation.

♦ You must create a new database for vCenter Server. Each vCenter Server computer—remember that there may be multiple instances of vCenter Server running in a linked mode group—will require its own SQL database.

♦ You must create an SQL login that has full access to the database you created for vCenter Server. If the SQL Server is using Windows authentication, this login must be linked to a domain user account; for mixed mode authentication, the associated domain user account is not required.

♦ You must set the appropriate permissions for this SQL login by mapping the SQL login to the dbo user on the database created for vCenter Server. In SQL Server 2005/2008, you do this by right-clicking the SQL login, selecting Properties, and then choosing User Mapping.

♦ The SQL login must not only have dbo (db_owner) privileges on the database created for vCenter Server, but the SQL login must also be set as the owner of the database. Figure 3.6 shows a new SQL database being created with the owner set to the vCenter Server SQL login.

♦ Finally, the SQL login created for use by vCenter Server must also have dbo (db_owner) privileges on the MSDB database but only for the duration of the installation process. This permission can and should be removed after installation is complete.

If you have an existing SQL Server 2005/2008 database that needs to be used as the backend for vCenter Server, you can use the sp_changedbowner stored procedure command to change the database ownership accordingly. For example, EXEC sp_changedbowner @loginame='vcdbuser', @map='true' would change the database owner to a SQL login named vcdbuser.

You need to take these steps prior to creating the ODBC DSN to the SQL Server database.

FIGURE 3.6
SQL Server
2005/2008
databases that
vCenter Server uses
must be owned
by the account
vCenter Server uses
to connect to the
database.

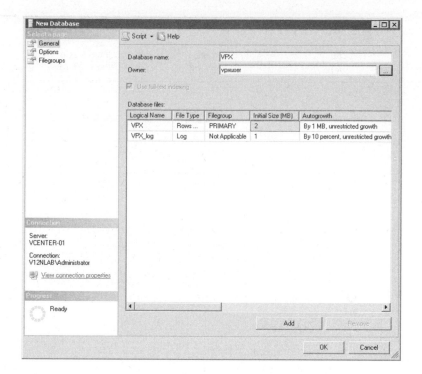

SQL SERVER PERMISSIONS

Not only will most database administrators cringe at the thought of overextending privileges to an SQL Server computer, but also it is not good practice to do so. As a strong security practice, it is best to minimize the permissions of each account that accesses the SQL Server computer. Therefore, in the case of the vCenter Server installation procedure, you will need to grant an SQL Server user account the db_owner membership on the MSDB database. However, after the installation is complete, this role membership can and should be removed. Normal day-to-day operation of and access to the vCenter Server database does not require this permission. It is a temporary requirement needed for the installation of vCenter Server.

After your database is set up, you can create the ODBC DSN to be used during the vCenter Server installation wizard. SQL Server 2005 and SQL Server 2008 require the use of the SQL Native Client. Because vCenter Server requires SQL Server 2005 or 2008, you're required to use the SQL Native Client. If you do not find the SQL Native Client option while creating the ODBC DSN, you can download it from Microsoft's website or install it from the SQL Server installation media.

After the SQL Native Client has been installed—if it wasn't installed already—then you are ready to create the ODBC DSN that vCenter Server uses to connect to the SQL Server instance hosting its database. This ODBC DSN must be created on the computer where vCenter Server will be installed.

Perform the following steps to create an ODBC DSN to a SQL Server 2005/2008 database:

1. Log onto the computer where vCenter Server will be installed later.

   You need to log on with an account that has administrative permissions on that computer.

2. Open the Data Sources (ODBC) applet from the Administrative Tools menu.

3. Select the System DSN tab.

4. Click the Add button.

5. Select the SQL Native Client from the list of available drivers, and click the Finish button.

   If the SQL Native Client is not in the list, you can download it from Microsoft's website or install it from the SQL Server installation media.

   Go back and install the SQL Native Client; then restart this process.

6. The Create New Data Source To SQL Server dialog box opens. In the Name text box, type the name you want to use to reference the ODBC DSN.

   Make note of this name—this is the name you will give to vCenter Server during installation to establish the database connection.

7. In the Server drop-down list, select the SQL Server 2005/2008 computer where the database was created, or type the name of the computer running SQL Server 2005/2008 that has already been prepared for vCenter Server.

   Be sure that whatever name you enter here can be properly resolved; I generally recommend using the fully qualified domain name.

8. Click the Next button.

9. Choose the correct authentication type, depending upon the configuration of the SQL Server instance.

   If you are using SQL Server authentication, you also need to supply the SQL login and password created earlier for use by vCenter Server.

   Click Next.

10. If the default database is listed as Master, select the Change The Default Database To check box, and then select the name of the vCenter Server database as the default. Click Next.

11. None of the options on the next screen—including the options for changing the language of the SQL Server system messages, regional settings, and logging options—need to be changed. Click Finish to continue.

12. On the summary screen, click the Test Data Source button to test the ODBC DSN.

    If the tests do not complete successfully, double-check the SQL Server and SQL database configuration outlined previously.

13. Click OK to return to the ODBC Data Source Administrator, which will now have the new System DSN you just created listed.

At this point, you are ready to actually install vCenter Server.

CONFIGURING IBM DB2 DATABASES FOR VCENTER SERVER

Configuring IBM DB2 for use with vCenter Server is similar to configuring Oracle or Microsoft SQL Server:

1. Configure an IBM DB2 database user or group.

2. Add the database instance Registry variables.

3. Add the client instance Registry variables.

4. Create a DB2 database.

5. Create the DB2 database schema.

6. Configure the connection to the DB2 database.

7. Configure the IBM DB2 database user to enable database monitoring.

Full details on how to accomplish these specific steps are found in the vSphere Installation and Setup Guide, available from VMware's website at www.vmware.com.

Running the vCenter Server Installer

With the database in place and configured, you can now install vCenter Server. After you've done that, you can add servers and continue configuring your virtual infrastructure, including adding vCenter Server instances in a linked mode group.

USE THE LATEST VERSION OF VCENTER SERVER

Remember that the latest version of vCenter Server is available for download from www.vmware.com/download. It is often best to install the latest version of the software to ensure the highest levels of compatibility, security, and simplicity.

The vCenter Server installation takes only a few minutes and is not administratively intensive, assuming you've completed all of the preinstallation tasks. You can start the vCenter Server installation by double-clicking autorun.exe inside the vCenter Server installation directory.

The VMware vCenter Installer, shown in Figure 3.7, is the central point for a number of installations:

- vCenter Server
- vSphere Client
- vSphere Web Client (Server)
- vSphere Update Manager

Chapter 4 provides more detail on vSphere Update Manager. You already installed the vSphere Client in Chapter 2. For now, I'll focus just on vCenter Server.

FIGURE 3.7
The VMware
vCenter Installer
offers options
for installing
several different
components.

If you will be using Windows authentication with a separate SQL Server database server, there's an important step here before you go any farther. For the vCenter Server services to be able to connect to the SQL database, these services need to run in the context of the domain user account that was granted permission to the database. Be sure that you know the username and password of the account that was granted permission to the backend database before proceeding. You'll also want to be sure that you've created an ODBC DSN with the correct information. You'll need the information for the ODBC DSN as well as the user account when you install vCenter Server. If you are using SQL authentication, you'll need to know the SQL login and password. I'll assume that you will use integrated Windows authentication.

After you've logged on as an administrative user to the computer that will run vCenter Server, then start the vCenter Server installation process by clicking the link for vCenter Server in the VMware vCenter Installer, shown previously in Figure 3.7. If you are running a version of Windows Server that uses User Account Control, you could be prompted to allow the installer to run; if so, select Yes. After you select a language for the installation, you arrive at the installation wizard for vCenter Server.

Perform the following steps to install vCenter Server:

1. Click Next to begin the installation wizard.

2. Click Next to proceed past the end-user patent agreement.

3. Click I Agree To The Terms In The License Agreement, and click Next.

4. Supply a username, organization name, and license key.

   Note that both user name and organization are required. If you don't have a license key yet, you can continue installing vCenter Server in evaluation mode.

5. At this point you must select whether to use SQL Server 2008 Express Edition or a separate database server.

If the environment will be small (a single vCenter Server with fewer than five hosts or fewer than 50 VMs), then using SQL Server 2008 Express is acceptable. For all other deployments, select Use An Existing Supported Database, and select your ODBC DSN from the drop-down list. If you forgot to create the ODBC DSN, you'll need to create it and restart the installation process in order to continue.

For the rest of this procedure, I'll assume that you are using an existing supported database. Select the correct ODBC DSN, and click Next.

ODBC TO DB

An ODBC DSN must be defined, and the name must match in order to move past the database configuration page of the installation wizard. Remember to set the appropriate authentication strategy and user permissions for an existing database server. If you receive an error at this point in the installation, revisit the database configuration steps. Remember to set the appropriate database ownership and database roles.

---

6. If you are using SQL authentication, then the next screen prompts for the SQL login and password that have permissions to the SQL database created for vCenter Server. Login information is not required if you are using Windows authentication, so you can just leave these fields blank.

   If the SQL Server Agent service is not running on the SQL Server computer, you'll receive an error at this step and won't be able to proceed. Make sure the SQL Server Agent service is running.

7. Unless you have specifically configured the database server differently than the default settings, a dialog box pops up warning you about the Full recovery model and the possibility that transaction logs may grow to consume all available disk space.

IMPLICATIONS OF THE SIMPLE RECOVERY MODEL

If your SQL Server database is configured for the Full recovery model, the installer suggests reconfiguring the vCenter Server database into the Simple recovery model. What the warning does not tell you is that doing this means that you will lose the ability to back up transaction logs for the vCenter Server database. If you leave the database set to Full recovery, be sure to work with the database administrator to routinely back up and truncate the transaction logs. By having transaction log backups from a database in Full recovery, you have the option to restore to an exact point in time should any type of data corruption occur. If you alter the recovery model as suggested, be sure you are making consistent full backups of the database, but understand that you will be able to recover only to the point of the last full backup because transaction logs will be unavailable.

---

8. The next screen prompts for account information for the vCenter Server services.

   If you are using Windows authentication with an SQL database, then you should populate the username and password fields with the correct user information. The "correct user" in this context is the domain user account granted permission on the SQL database. If you are using SQL authentication, then the account information is not as important, although you may want to run the vCenter Server services under an account other than the system account (this is a recommended practice for many Windows Server–based applications).

9. Select the directory where you want vCenter Server to be installed, and click Next.

10. If this is the first vCenter Server installation in your environment, then select Create A Standalone VMware vCenter Server Instance. Click Next.

I'll cover the other option in the section "Installing vCenter Server in a Linked Mode Group."

VCENTER SERVER AND IIS

Despite the fact that vCenter Server is accessible via a web browser, it is not necessary to install Internet Information Services on the vCenter Server computer. vCenter Server access via a browser relies on the Apache Tomcat web service that is installed as part of the vCenter Server installation. IIS should be uninstalled because it can cause conflicts with Apache Tomcat.

---

11. The next screen provides the option for changing the default TCP and UDP ports on which vCenter Server operates. Unless you have specific reason to change them, I recommend accepting the defaults. The ports listed on this screen include the following:

◆ TCP ports 80 and 443 (HTTP and HTTPS)

◆ UDP port 902

◆ TCP ports 8080 and 8443

◆ TCP port 60099

◆ TCP ports 389 and 636

12. To help optimize the performance of vCenter Server for your environment, select the inventory size that matches your deployment. Figure 3.8 shows these options. Click Next to continue.

13. Click Install to begin the installation.

14. Click Finish to complete the installation.

Upon completion of the vCenter Server installation, browsing to vCenter Server's URL (`http://<server name>` or `http://<server ip address>`) will turn up a page that allows for the installation of the vSphere Client.

The vSphere Client connected to vCenter Server should be the primary management tool for managing ESXi hosts and their respective VMs. As I've mentioned on several occasions already, the vSphere Client can connect directly to ESXi hosts under the context of a local user account defined on each ESXi host, or it can connect to a vCenter Server instance under the context of a Windows user account defined in Active Directory or the local SAM of the vCenter Server computer. Using vCenter Server along with Active Directory user accounts is the recommended deployment scenario.

FIGURE 3.8
The vCenter Server installation program will optimize the performance of vCenter Server and its components based on your selection on this screen.

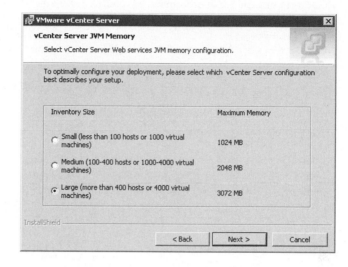

After the installation of vCenter Server, there will be a number of new services installed to facilitate the operation of vCenter Server. These services include the following:

◆ vCenter Inventory Service.

◆ VMware vCenter Orchestrator Configuration (supports the Orchestrator workflow engine, which I'll describe briefly in Chapter 14, "Automating VMware vSphere.")

◆ VMware VirtualCenter Management Web services.

◆ VMware VirtualCenter Server is the core of vCenter Server and provides centralized management of ESX/ESXi hosts and VMs.

◆ VMware vSphere Profile-Driven Storage Service.

◆ VMwareVCMSDS is the Microsoft ADAM instance that supports multiple vCenter Server instances in a linked mode group and is used for storing roles and permissions. Note that ADAM is used for storing roles and permissions both in stand-alone installations as well as installations with a linked mode group.

As a vSphere administrator, you should be familiar with the default states of these services. In times of troubleshooting, check the status of the services to see whether they have changed. Keep in mind the dependencies that exist between vCenter Server and other services on the network. For example, if the vCenter Server service is failing to start, be sure to check that the system has access to the SQL Server (or Oracle or DB2) database. If vCenter Server cannot access the database because of a lack of connectivity or the database service is not running, then it will not start.

As additional features and extensions are installed, additional services will also be installed to support those features. For example, installing vSphere Update Manager will install an additional service called VMware Update Manager Service. You'll learn more about vSphere Update Manager in Chapter 4.

Your environment may be one that requires only a single instance of vCenter Server running. If that's the case, you're ready to get started managing ESXi hosts and VMs. However, some of you might need more than one vCenter Server instance, so I'll show you how to install additional vCenter Server instances in a linked mode group.

Installing vCenter Server in a Linked Mode Group

What is a linked mode group, and why might you want to install multiple instances of vCenter Server into such a group? If you need more ESXi hosts or more VMs than a single vCenter Server instance can handle, or if for whatever other reason you need more than one instance of vCenter Server, you can install multiple instances of vCenter Server and have those instances share inventory and configuration information for a centralized view of all the virtualized resources across the enterprise. These multiple instances of vCenter Server that share information among them are referred to as a *linked mode group*.

In a linked mode environment, there are multiple vCenter Server instances, and each of the instances has its own set of hosts, clusters, and VMs. However, when a user logs into a vCenter Server instance using the vSphere Client, that user sees all the vCenter Server instances where he or she has permissions assigned. This allows a user to perform actions on any ESXi host managed by any vCenter Server within the linked mode group.

vCenter Server linked mode uses Microsoft ADAM to replicate information between the instances. The replicated information includes the following:

◆ Connection information (IP addresses and ports)

◆ Certificates and thumbprints

◆ Licensing information

◆ User roles and permissions

There are a few different reasons why you might need multiple vCenter Server instances running in a linked mode group. With vCenter Server 4.0, one common reason was the size of the environment. With the dramatic increases in capacity incorporated into vCenter Server 4.1 and vCenter Server 5, the need for multiple vCenter Server instances due to size will likely decrease. However, you might still use multiple vCenter Server instances. You might prefer to deploy multiple vCenter Server instances in a linked mode group to accommodate organizational or geographic constraints, for example.

Table 3.1 shows the maximums for a single instance of vCenter Server for versions 4.0, 4.1, and 5.0. Using a linked mode group is necessary if you need to manage more than the number of ESXi hosts or VMs listed.

TABLE 3.1: MAXIMUM NUMBER OF HOSTS OR VMS PER VCENTER SERVER INSTANCE

ITEM	VCENTER SERVER 4.0	VCENTER SERVER 4.1	VCENTER SERVER 5.0
ESXi hosts per vCenter Server instance	200	1,000	1,000
VMs per vCenter Server instance	3,000	10,000	10,000

Before you install additional vCenter Server instances, you must verify the following prerequisites:

◆ All computers that will run vCenter Server in a linked mode group must be members of a domain. The servers can exist in different domains only if a two-way trust relationship exists between the domains.

◆ DNS must be operational. Also, the DNS name of the servers must match the server name.

◆ The servers that will run vCenter Server cannot be domain controllers or terminal servers.

◆ You cannot combine vCenter Server 5 instances in a linked mode group with earlier versions of vCenter Server.

Each vCenter Server instance must have its own backend database, and each database must be configured as outlined earlier with the correct permissions. The databases can all reside on the same database server, or each database can reside on its own database server.

USING MULTIPLE VCENTER SERVER INSTANCES WITH ORACLE

If you are using Oracle, you'll need to make sure that each vCenter Server instance has a different schema owner or uses a dedicated Oracle server for each instance.

After you have met the prerequisites, installing vCenter Server in a linked mode group is straightforward. You follow the steps outlined previously in "Installing vCenter Server" until you get to step 10. In the previous instructions, you installed vCenter Server as a stand-alone instance in step 10. This sets up a master ADAM instance that vCenter Server uses to store its configuration information.

This time, however, at step 10 you simply select the option Join A VMware vCenter Server Group Using Linked Mode To Share Information.

When you select to install into a linked mode group, the next screen also prompts for the name and port number of a remote vCenter Server instance. The new vCenter Server instance uses this information to replicate data from the existing server's ADAM repository.

After you've provided the information to connect to a remote vCenter Server instance, the rest of the installation follows the same steps.

You can also change the linked mode configuration after the installation of vCenter Server. For example, if you install an instance of vCenter Server and then realize you need to create a linked mode group, you can use the vCenter Server Linked Mode Configuration icon on the Start menu to change the configuration.

Perform the following steps to join an existing vCenter Server installation to a linked mode group:

1. Log into the vCenter Server computer as an administrative user, and run vCenter Server Linked Mode Configuration from the Start Menu.

2. Click Next at the Welcome To The Installation wizard For VMware vCenter Server screen.

3. Select Modify Linked Mode Configuration, and click Next.

4. To join an existing linked mode group, select Join vCenter Server To An Existing Linked Mode Group Or Another Instance, and click Next. This is shown in Figure 3.9.

FIGURE 3.9
You can join an existing vCenter Server instance to a linked mode group.

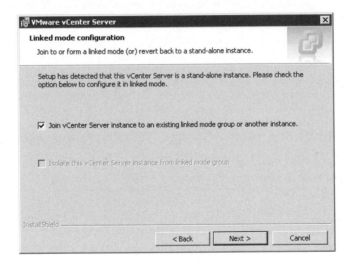

5. A warning appears reminding you that you cannot join vCenter Server 5 with older versions of vCenter Server. Click OK.

6. Supply the name of the server and the LDAP port. Specify the server name as a fully-qualified domain name.

   It's generally not necessary to modify the LDAP port unless you know that the other vCenter Server instance is running on a port other than the standard port.

   Click Next to continue.

7. Click Continue to proceed.

8. Click Finish.

Using this same process, you can also remove an existing vCenter Server installation from a linked mode group. Figure 3.10 shows how the installation wizard changes to allow you to remove an instance from the group.

FIGURE 3.10
If the vCenter Server instance is already in a linked mode group, you can also remove (or isolate) the instance.

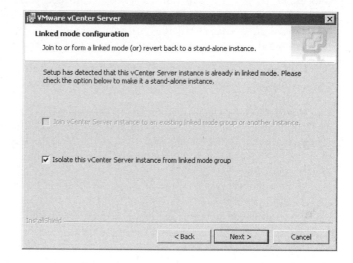

After the additional vCenter Server is up and running in the linked mode group, logging in via the vSphere Client displays all the linked vCenter Server instances in the inventory view, as you can see in Figure 3.11.

FIGURE 3.11
In a linked mode environment, the vSphere Client shows all the vCenter Server instances for which a user has permission.

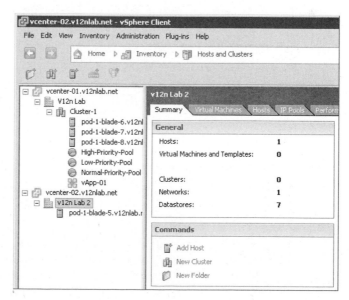

One quick note about linked mode: while the inventory and permissions are shared among all the linked mode group members, each vCenter Server instance is managed separately, and each vCenter Server instance represents a vMotion domain. This means that you can't perform a vMotion migration between vCenter Server instances in a linked mode group. I'll discuss vMotion in detail in Chapter 12, "Balancing Resource Utilization."

Installing vCenter Server onto a Windows Server–based computer, though, is only one of the options available for getting vCenter Server running in your environment. For those environments that don't need linked mode support or that want a full-featured virtual appliance with all the necessary network services, the vCenter Server virtual appliance is a good option. I'll discuss the vCenter Server virtual appliance in the next section.

Deploying the vCenter Server Virtual Appliance

The vCenter Server virtual appliance is a Linux-based VM that comes prepackaged and preinstalled with vCenter Server. Rather than creating a new VM, installing a guest operating system, and then installing vCenter Server, you only need to deploy the virtual appliance. I discussed the vCenter Server virtual appliance earlier in this chapter in the section "Choosing the Version of vCenter Server."

The vCenter Server virtual appliance comes as an OVF template. I'll discuss OVF templates in great detail in Chapter 10, but for now I'll simply explain them as an easy way to distribute "prepackaged VMs."

I'll assume that you've already downloaded the files for the vCenter Server virtual appliance from VMware's website at `www.vmware.com`. You'll need these files before you can proceed with deploying the vCenter Server virtual appliance.

Perform the following steps to deploy the vCenter Server virtual appliance:

1. Launch the vSphere Client and connect to an ESXi host.

   You could connect to a vCenter Server instance, but if you are deploying the vCenter Server virtual appliance, you most likely do not already have a vCenter Server instance up and running.

2. From the File menu, select Deploy OVF Template.

3. At the first screen of the Deploy OVF Template wizard, click the Browse button to find the OVF file you downloaded for the vCenter Server virtual appliance.

4. After you've selected the OVF file, click Next.

5. Review the details of the vCenter Server virtual appliance, as shown in Figure 3.12. Click Next when you're ready to proceed.

6. Supply a display name for the vCenter Server virtual appliance, and click Next.

7. Select a destination datastore, and click Next.

8. Select the disk provisioning type (Thick Provision Lazy Zeroed, Thick Provision Eager Zeroed, or Thin Provision).

FIGURE 3.12
The vCenter Server
virtual appliance
comes preinstalled
with SuSE Linux 11
and vCenter Server.

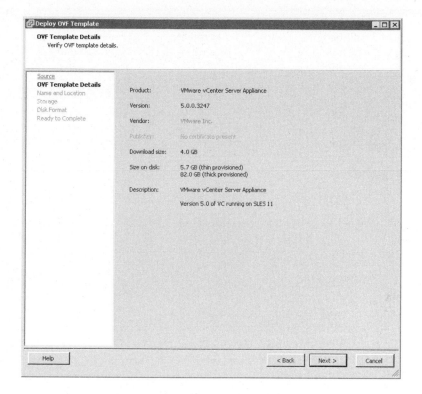

Chapter 6 and Chapter 9 provide more details on the different disk provisioning types. In all likelihood, you'll want to use Thin Provision to help you conserve disk space.

Click Next.

9. Click Finish to start deploying the virtual appliance.

A progress window like the one shown in Figure 3.13 will display while the vCenter Server virtual appliance is being deployed to the ESXi host.

FIGURE 3.13
This dialog box
provides informa-
tion on the status of
the vCenter Server
virtual appliance
deployment.

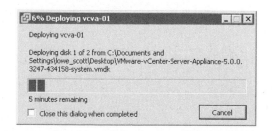

10. Once the vCenter Server virtual appliance is fully deployed, go ahead and power it on.

    You can use the VM console to watch the virtual appliance boot up. Eventually, it will display a virtual appliance management screen like the one shown in Figure 3.14.

FIGURE 3.14
This management screen lets you configure network access to the vCenter Server virtual appliance.

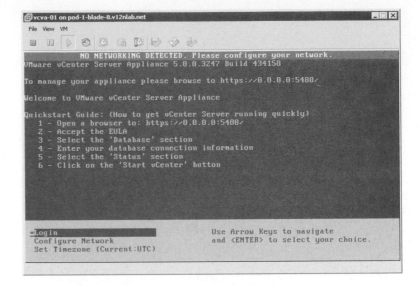

11. Use the arrow keys to select Configure Network, and press Enter. A prompt-driven network configuration script will start running.

12. If you want to assign an additional IPv6 address, press Y; otherwise, press N. Press Enter after pressing either Y or N.

13. If you want to use a DHCP v4 server instead of a statically assigned IP address, press Enter.

    In this instance, let's give the virtual appliance a static IP address, so press N and then press Enter.

14. Enter an IPv4 address and press Enter.

15. Enter the network mask and press Enter.

16. Enter the default gateway and press Enter.

17. Enter IP addresses for a primary and secondary DNS server, and press Enter after each address.

18. Supply the fully-qualified domain name for the virtual appliance.

19. Specify Y or N, depending on whether a proxy is required to access the Internet.

    Many organizations do not employ proxy servers for server-oriented systems.

20. Review the network configuration, and press Y if it is correct.

The vCenter Server virtual appliance will reconfigure its network settings and return you to the management console. From this point forward, all the configuration is handled via a web browser. As you can see in Figure 3.14, once networking has been established there are three major tasks to getting the virtual appliance up and running:

◆ Accept the End-User License Agreement (EULA).

◆ Configure the database.

◆ Start the vCenter Server services.

I'll take a look at each of these steps in the next few sections.

Accepting the End-User License Agreement

To accept the EULA, open a web browser and navigate to port 5480 on the IP address of the vCenter Server virtual appliance, using a URL such as `https://10.1.9.116:5480`, where `10.1.9.116` should be replaced with the IP address assigned to the virtual appliance. You might be prompted with a warning about an invalid certificate; accept the certificate and continue on to the site. You'll eventually reach the login screen for the virtual appliance, as shown in Figure 3.15.

FIGURE 3.15
You must first log in to the vCenter Server virtual appliance before you can change any configuration settings.

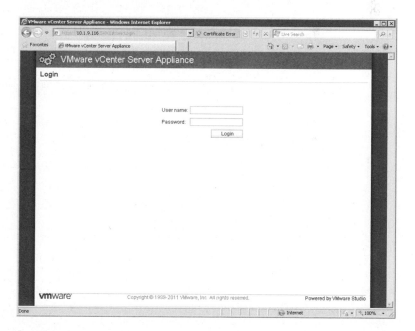

The default username and password for the vCenter Server virtual appliance distributed by VMware are `root` and `vmware`.

Immediately upon login, you will be presented with a copy of the VMware EULA for the vCenter Server virtual appliance. Review the EULA, and then click the Accept EULA button on the right side of the window (you might need to scroll over to see it).

Next, you'll need to configure the database connection.

Configuring the Database

Like the Windows Server–based version of vCenter Server, the vCenter Server virtual appliance requires a backend database in order to function properly. The virtual appliance supports Oracle, DB2, and a local embedded database.

To configure the database settings, click the vCenter Server tab on the VMware vCenter Server Appliance web administration screen, and then select Database. From there, you'll have an option to select Embedded, Oracle, and DB2. As I mentioned previously, Microsoft SQL Server is not supported for use with the virtual appliance.

The instructions provided previously for configuring Oracle or DB2 are still applicable; you need to perform those steps before you configure the database connection. Once the database has been properly configured, you can specify the database name, server, port, username, and password to use when connecting.

If you are using the embedded DB2 database, simply select Embedded from the Database Type drop-down list. No further configuration is required.

Once you enter your settings, use the Test Settings button to verify that they work correctly. If they are correct, use the Save Settings button to save the settings for use by vCenter Server.

When you've configured your database settings accordingly, you're ready to start the vCenter Server services.

Starting the vCenter Server Services

After you've accepted the EULA and configured the database, you can start the vCenter Server services on the virtual appliance. This is accomplished from the vCenter Server ➤ Status screen using the Start vCenter button on the right. After a few minutes, the services will start (use the Refresh button to refresh the screen to see that the services are currently shown as Running).

You'll now be able to launch the vSphere Client and connect to this instance of the vCenter Server virtual appliance. Remember the default username and password; you'll use those for the vSphere Client as well.

Installing or deploying vCenter Server is just the beginning. Before you're ready to start using vCenter Server in earnest, you must become a bit more familiar with the user interface and how to create and manage objects in vCenter Server.

Exploring vCenter Server

You access vCenter Server via the vSphere Client, which you installed previously. The vSphere Client is installed either through the home page of an ESXi host or through the home page of a vCenter Server instance. When you launch the vSphere Client, you are prompted to enter the IP address or name of the server to which you will connect, along with security credentials. vCenter Server supports pass-through authentication, enabled by the check box Use Windows Session Credentials. When this check box is selected, the username and password are grayed out, and authentication to the vCenter Server is handled using the currently logged-on account.

The first time that you connect to a vCenter Server instance, you receive a Security Warning dialog box. This security warning appears because the vSphere Client uses HTTP over Secure Sockets Layer (HTTPS) to connect to vCenter Server while the vCenter Server is using a Secure Sockets Layer (SSL) certificate from an "untrusted" source.

To correct this error, you have the following two options:

◆ You can select the box Install This Certificate And Do Not Display Any Security Warnings For *server.domain.com*. This option installs the SSL certificate locally so that the system running the vSphere Client will no longer consider it to be an untrusted certificate.

◆ You can install your own SSL certificate from a trusted certification authority on the vCenter Server.

After the vSphere Client connects to vCenter Server, you will notice a Getting Started tab that facilitates the construction of a new datacenter. The starting point for the vCenter Server inventory is the vCenter Server itself, while the building block of the vCenter Server inventory is called a *datacenter*. I'll discuss the concept of the datacenter and building out your vCenter Server inventory in the section "Creating and Managing a vCenter Server Inventory."

REMOVING THE GETTING STARTED TABS

If you prefer not to see the Getting Started tabs in the vSphere Client, you can turn them off. From the vSphere Client menu, select Edit ➢ Client Settings, and deselect the box Show Getting Started Tabs.

Clicking the Create A Datacenter link allows you to create a datacenter. The Getting Started wizard would then prompt you to add an ESXi host to vCenter Server, but before you do that, you should acquaint yourself with the vSphere Client interface when it's connected to vCenter Server.

What's in the vCenter Server Home Screen?

So far, you've seen only the Hosts And Clusters inventory view. This is where you manage ESXi hosts, clusters, and VMs. Hosts and VMs you already understand; clusters I'll discuss later in this chapter in the section "Creating and Managing a vCenter Server Inventory." To see the rest of what vCenter Server has to offer, click the Home button on the navigation bar; you'll see a screen similar to the screen shown in Figure 3.16 (there may or may not be additional icons here, depending on the plug-ins you have installed).

The home screen lists all the various features that vCenter Server has to offer in managing ESXi hosts and VMs:

◆ Under Inventory, vCenter Server offers several views, including Search, Hosts And Clusters, VMs And Templates, Datastores And Datastore Clusters, and Networking.

◆ Under Administration, vCenter Server has screens for managing roles, viewing and managing current sessions, licensing, viewing system logs, managing vCenter Server settings, and viewing the status of the vCenter Server services.

◆ Under Management, there are areas for scheduled tasks, events, maps, host profiles, VM storage profiles, and customization specifications.

Many of these features are explored in other areas of the book. For example, networking is discussed in Chapter 5, and datastores are discussed in Chapter 6, "Creating and Configuring Storage Devices." Chapter 10 discusses templates and customization specifications, and Chapter 8 discusses roles and permissions. A large portion of the rest of this chapter is spent just on vCenter Server's inventory view.

FIGURE 3.16
The vCenter Server
home screen shows
the full selection
of features within
vCenter Server.

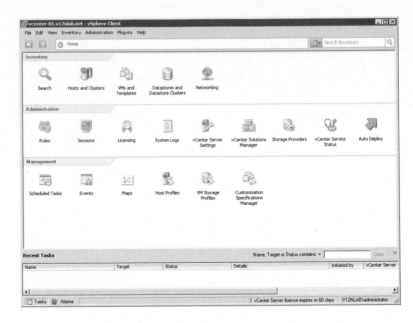

From the home screen, you can click any of the icons shown there to navigate to that area. But vCenter Server and the vSphere Client also have another way to navigate quickly and easily, and that's called the *navigation bar*.

Using the Navigation Bar

Across the top of the vSphere Client, just below the menu bar, is the navigation bar. The navigation bar shows you exactly where you are in the various screens that vCenter Server provides.

If you click any portion of the navigation bar, a drop-down menu appears. The options that appear illustrate a key point about the vSphere Client and vCenter Server: the menu options and tabs that appear within the application are context sensitive, meaning they change depending on what object is selected or active. You'll learn more about this topic throughout the chapter.

Of course, you can also use the menu bar, where the View menu will be the primary method whereby you would switch between the various screens that are available to you. The vSphere Client also provides numerous keyboard shortcuts, making it even easier to flip quickly from one area to another with very little effort.

Now you're ready to start creating and managing the vCenter Server inventory.

Creating and Managing a vCenter Server Inventory

As a vSphere administrator, you will spend a significant amount of time using the vSphere Client. Out of that time, you will spend a great deal of it working with the various inventory views available in vCenter Server, so I think it's quite useful that I first explain them.

Understanding Inventory Views and Objects

Every vCenter Server has a root object, the datacenter object, which serves as a container for all other objects. Prior to adding an object to the vCenter Server inventory, you must create at least one datacenter object (you can have multiple datacenter objects in a single vCenter Server instance). The objects found within the datacenter object depend on which inventory view is active. The navigation bar provides a quick and easy reminder of which inventory view is currently active. In the Hosts And Clusters inventory view, you will work with ESXi hosts, clusters, resource pools, and VMs. In the VMs And Templates view, you will work with folders, VMs, and templates. In the Datastores And Datastore Clusters view, you will work with datastores and datastore clusters; in the Networking view, you'll work with vSphere Standard Switches and vSphere Distributed Switches.

VCENTER SERVER INVENTORY DESIGN

If you are familiar with objects used in a Microsoft Windows Active Directory (AD), you may recognize a strong similarity in the best practices of AD design and the design of a vCenter Server inventory. A close parallel can even be drawn between a datacenter object and an organizational unit because both are the building blocks of their respective infrastructures.

You organize the vCenter Server inventory differently in different views. The Hosts And Clusters view is primarily used to determine or control where a VM is executing or how resources are allocated to a VM or group of VMs. You would not, typically, create your logical administrative structure in the Hosts And Clusters inventory view. This would be a good place, though, to provide structure around resource allocation or to group hosts into clusters according to business rules or other guidelines.

In VMs And Templates inventory view, though, the placement of VMs and templates within folders is handled irrespective of the specific host on which that VM is running. This allows you to create a logical structure for VM administration that remains, for the most part, independent of the physical infrastructure upon which those VMs are running. There is one very important tie between the VMs And Templates view and the Hosts And Clusters view: datacenter objects are shared between them. Datacenter objects span both the Hosts And Clusters view and the VMs And Templates view.

The naming strategy you provide for the objects in vCenter Server should mirror the way that network management is performed. For example, if you have qualified IT staff at each of your three datacenters across the country, then you would most likely create a hierarchical inventory that mirrors that management style. On the other hand, if your IT management was most profoundly set by the various departments in your company, then the datacenter objects might be named after each respective department. In most enterprise environments, the vCenter Server inventory will be a hybrid that involves management by geography, department, server type, and even project title.

The vCenter Server inventory can be structured as needed to support a company's IT management needs. Folders can be created above and below the datacenter object to provide higher or more granular levels of control that can propagate to lower-level child objects. In Chapter 8, "Securing VMware vSphere," I'll discuss the details around vCenter Server permissions and how you can use them in a vCenter Server hierarchy. Figure 3.17 shows a Hosts And Clusters view of a vCenter Server inventory that is based on a geographical management style.

FIGURE 3.17
Users can create folders above the datacenter object to grant permission at a level that can propagate to multiple datacenter objects or to create folders beneath a datacenter to manage the objects within the datacenter object.

Should a company use more of a departmental approach to IT resource management, then the vCenter Server inventory can be shifted to match the new management style. Figure 3.18 reflects a Hosts And Clusters inventory view based on a departmental management style.

FIGURE 3.18
A departmental vCenter Server inventory allows the IT administrator to implement controls within each organizational department.

In most enterprise environments, the vCenter Server inventory will be a hybrid of the different topologies. Perhaps one topology might be a geographical top level, followed by departmental management, followed by project-based resource configuration.

The Hosts And Clusters inventory view is just one view of the inventory, though. In addition to building your inventory structure in the Hosts And Clusters view, you also build your inventory structure in VMs And Templates. Figure 3.19 shows a sample VMs And Templates inventory view that organizes VMs by department.

FIGURE 3.19
The structure of the
VMs And Templates
inventory view is
separate from the
Hosts And Clusters
inventory view.

These inventory views are mostly separate and independent, although as I pointed out earlier they do share datacenter objects. For example, the Hosts And Clusters inventory view may reflect a physical or geographical focus, while the VMs And Templates inventory view may reflect a departmental or functional focus. Because permissions are granted based on these structures, organizations have the ability to build inventory structures that properly support their administrative structures. Chapter 8 will describe the security model of vCenter Server that will work hand in hand with the management-driven inventory design.

With that basic understanding of vCenter Server inventory views and the hierarchy of inventory objects behind you, it's time for you to actually build out your inventory structure and start creating and adding objects in vCenter Server.

Creating and Adding Inventory Objects

Before you can really build your inventory—in either Hosts And Clusters view or VMs And Templates view—you must get your ESXi hosts into vCenter Server. And before you can get your ESXi hosts into vCenter Server, you need to have a datacenter object.

CREATING A DATACENTER OBJECT

You might have created the datacenter object as part of the Getting Started wizard, but if you didn't, you must create one now. Don't forget that you can have multiple datacenter objects within a single vCenter Server instance.

Perform the following steps to create a datacenter object:

1. Launch the vSphere Client, if it is not already running, and connect to a vCenter Server instance.

2. From the View menu, select Inventory ➢ Hosts And Clusters, or press the Ctrl+Shift+H keyboard hotkey.

3. Right-click the vCenter Server object, and select Add Datacenter.

4. Type in a name for the new datacenter object. Press Enter, or click anywhere else in the window when you have finished.

If you already have a datacenter object, then you are ready to start adding ESXi hosts to vCenter Server.

MAKE SURE NAME RESOLUTION IS WORKING

Name resolution—the ability for one computer to match the hostname of another computer to its IP address—is a key component for a number of ESXi functions. I have witnessed a number of problems that were resolved by making sure that name resolution was working properly.

I strongly recommend you ensure that name resolution is working in a variety of directions. You will want to do the following:

◆ Ensure that the vCenter Server computer can resolve the hostnames of each and every ESXi host added to the inventory.

◆ Ensure that each and every ESXi host can resolve the hostname of the vCenter Server computer by which it is being managed.

◆ Ensure that each and every ESXi host can resolve the hostnames of the other ESXi hosts in the inventory, especially if those hosts might be combined into a vSphere HA cluster.

Although I've seen some recommendations about using the /etc/hosts file to hard-code the names and IP addresses of other servers in the environment, I don't recommend it. Managing the /etc/hosts file on every ESX host gets cumbersome very quickly and is error prone. In addition, ESXi doesn't support the /etc/hosts file. For the most scalable and reliable solution, ensure your Domain Naming System (DNS) infrastructure is robust and functional, and make sure that the vCenter Server computer and all ESXi hosts are configured to use DNS for name resolution. You'll save yourself a lot of trouble later by investing a little bit of effort in this area now.

Once you create at least one datacenter object, then you're ready to add your ESXi hosts to the vCenter Server inventory, as described in the next section.

ADDING ESXI HOSTS

In order for vCenter Server to manage an ESXi host, you must first add the ESXi host to vCenter Server. The process of adding an ESXi host into vCenter Server automatically installs a vCenter agent on the ESXi host through which vCenter Server communicates and manages the host.

Note that vCenter Server 5 does support adding and managing ESX/ESXi 4.*x* hosts to the inventory. I'll only describe adding ESXi 5 hosts to vCenter Server, but the process is nearly identical for other versions.

Perform the following steps to add an ESXi host to vCenter Server:

1. Launch the vSphere Client, if it is not already running, and connect to a vCenter Server instance.

2. From the View menu, select Inventory ➢ Hosts And Clusters, or press the Ctrl+Shift+H keyboard hotkey.

3. Right-click the datacenter object, and select Add Host.

4. In the Add Host Wizard, supply the IP address or fully qualified hostname and user account information for the host being added to vCenter Server. This will typically be the root account.

Although you supply the root password when adding the host to the vCenter Server inventory, vCenter Server uses the root credentials only long enough to establish a different set of credentials for its own use moving forward. This means that you can change the root password without worrying about breaking the communication and authentication between vCenter Server and your ESXi hosts. In fact, regular changes of the root password are considered a security best practice.

5. When prompted to decide whether to trust the host and an SHA1 fingerprint is displayed, click Yes.

   Strictly speaking, security best practices dictate that you should verify the SHA1 fingerprint before accepting it as valid. ESXi provides the SHA1 fingerprint in the View Support Information screen at the console.

6. The next screen displays a summary of the ESXi host being added, along with information on any VMs currently hosted on that server. Click Next.

7. Figure 3.20 shows the next screen, where you need to assign a license to the host being added.

   The option to add the host in evaluation mode is also available.

   Choose evaluation mode, or assign a license; then click Next.

FIGURE 3.20
Licenses can be assigned to an ESXi host as they are added to vCenter Server or at a later time.

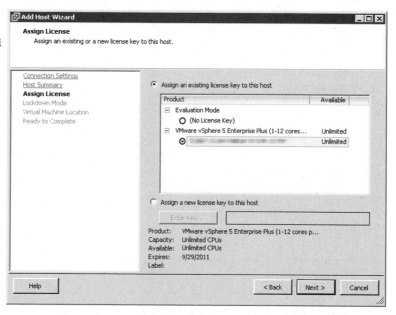

8. The next screen offers the option to enable lockdown mode. Lockdown mode ensures that the management of the host occurs via vCenter Server, not through the vSphere Client connected directly to the ESXi host. If you are adding an ESX 4.x host, this screen will not appear. Click Next.

9. Choose a location for this host's VMs, and click Next.

10. Click Finish at the summary screen.

11. Repeat this process for all the ESXi hosts you want to manage using this instance of vCenter Server.

Now compare the tabs in the pane on the right of the vSphere Client for the vCenter Server, data-center, and host objects. You can see that the tabs presented to you change depending on the object selected in the inventory tree. This is yet another example of how vCenter Server's user interface is context sensitive and changes the options available to the user depending on what is selected.

You can add hosts to vCenter Server and manage them as separate, individual entities, but you might prefer to group these hosts together into a cluster, another key object in the vCenter Server inventory. I'll describe clusters in the next section.

CREATING A CLUSTER

I've made a few references to clusters here and there, and now it's time to take a closer look at clusters. Clusters are administrative grouping of ESX/ESXi hosts. (Note I've referenced ESX here because ESX 4.x is supported by vCenter Server 5 and might be included in a cluster.) Once you have grouped hosts into a cluster, you have the ability to enable some of vSphere's most use-ful features. vSphere High Availability (HA), vSphere Distributed Resource Scheduler (DRS), and vSphere Fault Tolerance (FT) all work only with clusters. I'll describe these features in later chapters; Chapter 7, "Ensuring High Availability and Business Continuity," discusses vSphere HA and vSphere FT, while Chapter 12 discusses vSphere DRS.

Perform the following steps to create a cluster:

1. Launch the vSphere Client, if it is not already running, and connect to a vCenter Server instance.

2. Select a datacenter object in Hosts And Clusters inventory view.

3. From the Summary tab on the right, select New Cluster. This opens the New Cluster Wizard.

4. Supply a name for the cluster.

   Don't select Turn On vSphere HA or Turn On vSphere DRS; I'll explore these options later in the book (Chapter 7 and Chapter 12, respectively).

   Click Next.

5. Leave Disable EVC selected (the default), and click Next.

6. Leave the default option (Store The Swapfile In The Same Directory As The Virtual Machine) selected, and click Next.

7. Click Finish.

Once the cluster is created, adding hosts to a cluster is a matter of simply dragging the ESXi host object onto the cluster object, and vCenter Server will add the host to the cluster. You may be prompted about resource pools; refer to Chapter 11 for more information on what resource pools are and how they work.

Adding ESXi hosts to vCenter Server enables you to manage them with vCenter Server. You'll explore some of vCenter Server's management features in the next section.

Exploring vCenter Server's Management Features

After your ESXi hosts are managed by vCenter Server, you can take advantage of some of vCenter Server's management features:

◆ Basic host management tasks in Hosts And Clusters inventory view

◆ Basic host configuration

◆ Scheduled tasks

◆ Events

◆ Maps

◆ Host profiles

In the next few sections, you'll examine each of these areas in a bit more detail.

Understanding Basic Host Management

A great deal of the day-to-day management tasks for ESXi hosts in vCenter Server occur in the Hosts And Clusters inventory view. From this area, the context menu for an ESXi host shows some of the options available:

◆ Create a new VM.

◆ Create a new resource pool.

◆ Create a new vApp.

◆ Disconnect from the selected ESXi host.

◆ Enter maintenance mode.

◆ Add permission.

◆ Manage alarms for the selected ESXi host.

◆ Shut down, reboot, power on, or place the ESXi host into standby mode.

◆ Produce reports.

◆ Remove the ESXi host from vCenter Server.

The majority of these options are described in later chapters. Chapter 9 describes creating VMs, and Chapter 11 discusses resource pools. Chapter 8 covers permissions, and Chapter 13 discusses alarms and reports. The remaining actions—shutting down, rebooting, powering on, standing by, disconnecting, and removing from vCenter Server—are self-explanatory and do not need any additional explanation.

Additional commands may appear on this context menu as extensions are installed into vCenter Server or depending on the ESXi host's configuration. For example, after you install vSphere Update Manager, several new commands appear on the context menu for an ESXi host. In addition, ESXi hosts in a cluster enabled for vSphere HA would have additional options. You'll learn more about vSphere HA in Chapter 7.

In addition to the context menu, the tabs across the top of the right side of the vSphere Client window also provide some host-management features. Figure 3.21 shows some of the tabs; note the left/right arrows that allow you to scroll through the tabs when they don't all fit in the window.

FIGURE 3.21
When a host is selected in the inventory view, the tabs across the top right side of the window also provide host-management features.

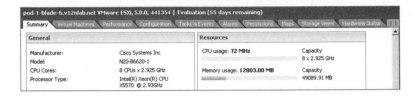

For the most part, these tabs correspond closely to the commands on the context menu. Here are the tabs that are displayed when a host is selected in the inventory view, along with a brief description of what each tab does:

Summary   The Summary tab gathers and displays information about the underlying physical hardware, the storage devices that are configured and accessible, the networks that are configured and accessible, and the status of certain features such as vMotion and vSphere FT. In addition, the Commands area of the Summary tab provides links to commonly performed host-management tasks.

Virtual Machines   The Virtual Machines tab lists the VMs currently running on that host. The list of VMs also provides summary information on the VM's status, provisioned versus used space, and how much CPU and RAM the VM is actually using.

Performance   The Performance tab displays performance information for the host, such as overall CPU utilization, memory utilization, disk I/O, and network throughput. I'll discuss this area in more detail in Chapter 13.

Configuration   The Configuration tab is where you will make configuration changes to the host. Tasks such as configuring storage, configuring network, changing security settings, configuring hardware, and so forth are all performed here.

Tasks & Events   All tasks and events related to the selected host are displayed here. The Tasks view shows all tasks, the target object, which account initiated the task, which vCenter Server was involved, and the result of the task. The Events view lists all events related to the selected host.

Alarms   The Alarms tab shows either triggered alarms or alarm definitions. If a host is using almost its entire RAM or if a host's CPU utilization is very high, you may see some triggered alarms. The Alarms Definition section allows you to define your own alarms.

Permissions   The Permissions tab shows permissions on the selected host. This includes permissions inherited from parent objects/containers as well as permissions granted directly to the selected host.

Maps   The Maps tab shows a graphical topology map of resources and VMs associated with that host. vCenter Server's Maps functionality is described in more detail later in this chapter.

Storage Views   The Storage Views tab brings together a number of important storage-related pieces of information. For each VM on the selected host, the Storage Views tab shows the current multipathing status, the amount of disk space used, the amount of snapshot space used, and the current number of disks.

Hardware Status   The Hardware Status tab displays sensor information on hardware components such as fans, CPU temperature, power supplies, network interface cards (NICs) and NIC firmware, and more.

Before I show you some of vCenter Server's other management features, I want to walk you through the Configuration tab, where you'll perform almost all of the ESXi host-configuration tasks and where you're likely to spend a fair amount of time, at least in the beginning.

Examining Basic Host Configuration

You've already seen the Configuration tab of an ESXi host, when in Chapter 2 I showed you how to configure NTP time synchronization. Now I want to spend a bit more time on it here. You'll be visiting this area quite often throughout this book. In Chapter 5, you'll use the Configuration tab for networking configuration, and in Chapter 6 you'll use the Configuration tab for storage configuration.

Figure 3.22 shows the commands available on the Configuration tab for an ESXi host that has just been added to vCenter Server.

FIGURE 3.22
The Configuration tab of an ESXi host offers a number of different commands to view or modify the host's configuration.

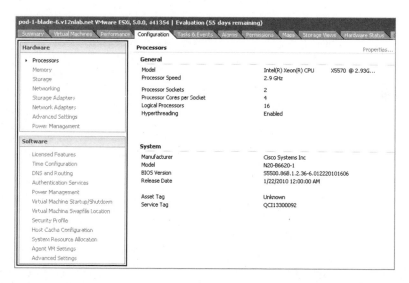

There are a lot of options here, so allow me to quickly run through these options and provide a brief explanation of each. First, here are the options available in the Hardware section of the Configuration tab:

Processors   In this section, vCenter Server provides details about the processors in the selected ESXi host as well as provides the ability to enable or disable hyperthreading on that ESXi host.

Memory   This area shows you the amount of memory installed in an ESXi host and how to modify the amount of memory assigned to the Service Console on an ESX host (applicable only for ESX 4.*x* hosts). For an ESXi host, this command only provides information about the memory in the host; there are no options to configure.

Storage   You'll explore this area extensively in Chapter 6; this is where you will add, remove, or configure datastores for use by ESXi hosts. Information about existing datastores is also available here.

Networking   In Chapter 5, I'll explore the functionality found in this section. You'll config- ure network connectivity for both hosts and VMs in this area.

Storage Adapters   This area provides information on the various storage adapters installed in the ESXi host as well as information on storage resources connected to those adapters. This is more of a physical view of storage, whereas the Storage area described earlier is more logi- cal in nature.

Network Adapters   The Network Adapters area in the Hardware section of the Configuration tab provides read-only information on the network adapters that are installed in the selected ESXi host.

Advanced Settings   This area is a bit misnamed; it allows you to configure VMDirectPath, a feature that allows for VMs to be attached directly to physical hardware in the ESXi host, bypassing the hypervisor.

Power Management   The Power Management area in the Hardware section of the Configuration tab allows you to set various power-management policies on the selected ESXi host.

In addition to the commands listed in the Hardware section, the Configuration tab offers these commands in the Software section:

Licensed Features   This command allows you to view the currently licensed features as well as to assign or change the license for the selected ESXi host.

Time Configuration   From here, you can configure time synchronization via NTP for the selected ESXi host. You saw this area in Chapter 2.

DNS And Routing   In this area, you can view and change the DNS and routing configura- tion for the selected ESXi host.

Authentication Services   I'll discuss this in more detail in Chapter 8, but this area allows you to configure how ESXi hosts authenticate users.

Power Management   If you want to use Distributed Power Management (DPM), you'll need to configure the ESXi hosts appropriately. This area is where that configuration occurs.

Virtual Machine Startup/Shutdown   If you want to have VMs start up or shut down automatically with the ESXi host, this area allows you to configure those settings. Here is also where you can define the startup order of VMs that are set to start up with the host.

Virtual Machine Swapfile Location   This area is where you will configure the location of the swapfiles for running VMs on the host. By default, the swapfile is stored in the same directory as the VM itself. When an ESXi host is in a cluster, the cluster setting overrides the per-host configuration.

Security Profile   This area allows you to configure which daemons (services) should run on the host. For older hosts running ESX 4.*x*, this area controls the Service Console firewall.

Host Cache Configuration   This area allows you to specify or view the amount of space on Solid State Drive (SSD)–backed datastores that can be used for swapping. Swapping to SSD as opposed to traditional disks is much faster, and this area allows you to control which SSD-backed datastores may be used for swapping.

System Resource Allocation   The System Resource Allocation area allows you to fine-tune the resource allocation for the selected ESXi host.

Agent VM Settings   Agent VMs are VMs that add specific supporting functionality to the virtual environment. Although they are VMs, they are considered part of the infrastructure. Examples include vShield Edge and vShield Endpoint, both of which use agent VMs to help supply their functionality.

Advanced Settings   The Advanced Settings area provides direct access to detailed configuration settings on the selected ESXi host. In the majority of instances, this is not an area you'll visit on a regular basis, but it is helpful to know where it is in the event you need to change a setting.

As you can see, vCenter Server provides all the tools that most administrators will need to manage ESXi hosts. Although these host-management tools are visible in the Hosts And Clusters inventory view, several of vCenter Server's other management features are found in the Management view, accessible from the View ➤ Management menu.

Using Scheduled Tasks

Selecting View ➤ Management ➤ Scheduled Tasks displays the Scheduled Tasks area of vCenter Server. You can also use the Ctrl+Shift+T keyboard shortcut.

From here, you can create jobs to run based on a defined logic. You can schedule the following list of tasks:

- Change the power state of a VM.
- Clone a VM.
- Deploy a VM from a template.
- Move a VM with vMotion.

◆ Move a VM's virtual disks with Storage vMotion.

◆ Create a VM.

◆ Make a snapshot of a VM.

◆ Add a host.

◆ Change the power settings for a cluster.

◆ Change resource settings for a resource pool or VM.

◆ Check compliance for a profile.

As you can see, vCenter Server supports quite a list of tasks you can schedule to run automatically. Because the information required for each scheduled task varies, the wizards are different for each of the tasks. Let's take a look at one task that you might find quite useful to schedule: adding a host.

Why might you want to schedule a task to add a host? Perhaps you know that you will be adding a host to vCenter Server, but you want to add the host after hours. You can schedule a task to add the host to vCenter Server later tonight, although keep in mind that the host must be reachable and responding when the task is created.

Perform the following steps to create a scheduled task to add a host to vCenter Server:

1. Launch the vSphere Client, if it is not already running, and connect to a vCenter Server instance.

2. After you connect to vCenter Server, navigate to the Scheduled Tasks area by selecting View ➢ Management ➢ Scheduled Tasks. You can also click the Scheduled Tasks icon on the vCenter Server home screen, or you can press Ctrl+Shift+T.

3. Right-click the blank area of the Scheduled Tasks list, and select New Scheduled Task.

4. From the list of tasks to schedule, select Add A Host.

5. The Add Host Wizard starts. Select the datacenter or cluster to which this new host will be added.

6. Supply the hostname, username, and password to connect to the host, just as if you were adding the host manually.

7. When prompted to accept the host's SHA1 fingerprint, click Yes.

8. The next three or four steps in the wizard—three steps for ESX, four steps for ESXi—are just like you are adding the host manually. Click Next after each step until you come to the point of scheduling the task.

9. Supply a task name, task description, frequency of the task, and schedule for the task. For adding a host, the frequency option doesn't really make sense.

10. Select if you want to receive email notification of the scheduled task when it completes and supply an email address. Note that vCenter Server must be configured with the name of an SMTP server it can use.

In my mind, scheduling the addition of an ESXi host is of fairly limited value. However, the ability to schedule tasks such as powering off a group of VMs, moving their virtual disks to a new datastore, and then powering them back on again is quite useful.

Using Events View in vCenter Server

The Events view in vCenter Server brings together all the events that have been logged by vCenter Server. Figure 3.23 shows the Events view with an event selected.

FIGURE 3.23
The Events view lets you view event details, search events, and export events.

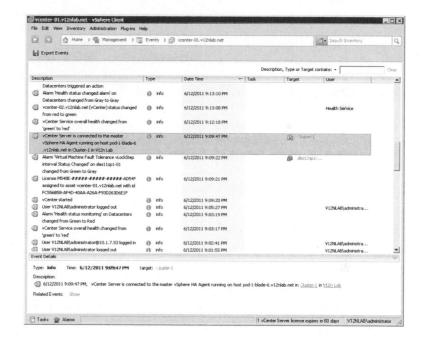

You can view the details of an event by simply clicking it in the list. Any text highlighted in blue is a hyperlink; clicking that text will take you to that object in vCenter Server. You can search through the events using the search box in the upper-right corner of the vSphere Client window, and just below the navigation bar is a button to export the events to a text file. Figure 3.24 shows the dialog box for exporting events.

FIGURE 3.24

Users have a number of options when exporting events out of vCenter Server to a text file.

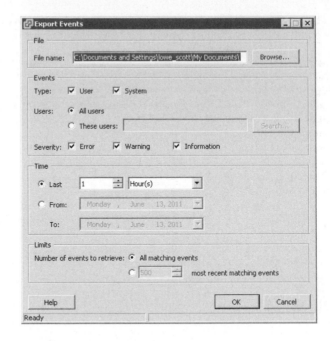

Using vCenter Server's Maps

The Maps feature of vCenter Server is a great tool for quickly reviewing your virtual infrastructure. Topology maps graphically represent the relationship that exists between different types of objects in the virtual infrastructure. The maps can display any of the following relationships:

◆ Host to VM

◆ Host to network

◆ Host to datastore

◆ VM to network

◆ VM to datastore

In addition to defining the relationships to display, you can include or exclude specific objects from the inventory. Perhaps you are interested only in the relationship that exists between the VMs and the networks on a single host. In this case, you can exclude all other hosts from the list of relationships by deselecting their icons in the vCenter Server inventory on the left side of the window. Figure 3.25 shows a series of topology maps defining the relationships for a set of objects in the vCenter Server inventory. For historical purposes or further analysis, you can save topology maps as JPG, BMP, PNG, GIF, TIFF, or EMF file format.

Topology maps are available from the menu by selecting View ➢ Management ➢ Maps, by using the navigation bar, or by using the Ctrl+Shift+M keyboard shortcut. You can also select an inventory object and then select the Maps tab. Figure 3.25 showed the Maps feature from the vCenter Server menu, and Figure 3.26 shows the Maps tab available for each inventory object (in this case, a cluster of ESXi hosts). In either case, the depth of the relationship can be identified by enabling or disabling options in the list of relationships on the right side of the maps display.

FIGURE 3.25
vCenter Server's Maps feature is a flexible, graphical utility that helps identify the relationships that exist among the various objects in the virtual infrastructure.

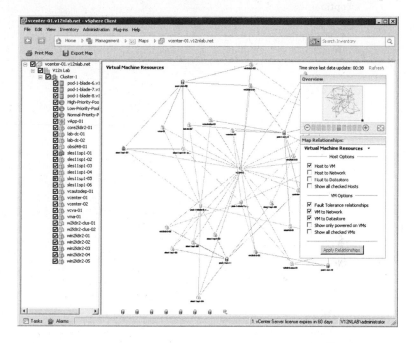

FIGURE 3.26
The Maps tab for inventory objects limits the scope of the map to the selected object.

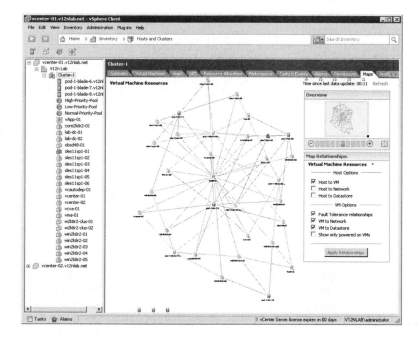

Selecting Maps from the View ⊳ Management menu shows you everything and then allows you to limit the scope of the relationship by enabling and disabling objects in the vCenter Server inventory. By selecting an inventory object and then viewing the topology map using the Maps tab, the focus is limited to just that object and you can't enable/disable certain objects. In both cases, the Overview mini-window lets you zoom in to view specific parts of the topology map or zoom out to view the whole topology map.

Working with Host Profiles

Host profiles are a powerful feature of vCenter Server. As you'll see in upcoming chapters, there can be a bit of configuration involved in setting up an ESXi host. Although vCenter Server and the vSphere Client make it easy to perform these configuration tasks, it's easy to overlook something. Additionally, making all these changes manually for multiple hosts can be time consuming and even more error prone. That's where host profiles can help.

A host profile is essentially a collection of all the various configuration settings for an ESXi host. This includes settings such as NIC assignments, virtual switches, storage configuration, date and time, and more. By attaching a host profile to an ESXi host, you can then compare the compliance of that host with the settings outlined in the host profile. If the host is compliant, then you know its settings are the same as the settings in the host profile. If the host is not compliant, then you can enforce the settings in the host profile to make it compliant. This provides administrators with a way not only to verify consistent settings across ESXi hosts but also to quickly and easily apply settings to new ESXi hosts.

To work with host profiles, select View ⊳ Management ⊳ Host Profiles, or use the Ctrl+Shift+P keyboard shortcut. Figure 3.27 shows the Host Profiles view in vCenter Server, where two different host profiles have been created but not yet attached to any hosts.

FIGURE 3.27
Host profiles provide a mechanism for checking and enforcing compliance with a specific configuration.

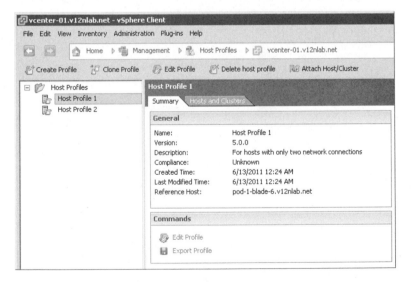

As you can see in Figure 3.27, there are five toolbar buttons across the top of the window, just below the navigation bar. These buttons allow you to create a new host profile, clone a host profile, edit an existing host profile, delete a host profile, and attach a host or cluster to a profile.

To create a new profile, you must either create one from an existing host or import a profile that was already created somewhere else. Creating a new profile from an existing host requires only that you select the reference host for the new profile. vCenter Server will then compile the host profile based on that host's configuration.

After you create a profile, you can edit the profile to fine-tune the settings contained in it. For example, you might need to change the IP addresses of the DNS servers found in the profile because they've changed since the profile was created.

Perform the following steps to edit the DNS server settings in a host profile:

1. If the vSphere Client isn't already running, launch it and connect to a vCenter Server instance.

2. From the menu, select View ➤ Management ➤ Host Profiles.

3. Right-click the host profile to be edited, and select Edit Profile.

4. From the tree menu on the left side of the Edit Profile window, navigate to Networking Configuration ➤ DNS Configuration.

   Figure 3.28 shows this area.

FIGURE 3.28
To make changes to a number of ESXi hosts at the same time, put the settings into a host profile, and attach the profile to the hosts.

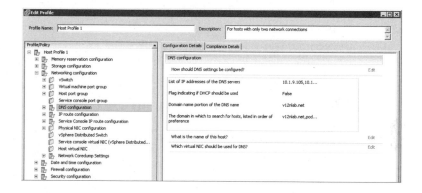

5. Click the blue Edit link to change the values shown in the host profile.

6. Click OK to save the changes to the host profile.

Although this procedure only describes how to change DNS settings, the steps for changing other settings within a host profile are much the same. This allows you to quickly create a host profile based on a reference host but then customize the host profile until it represents the correct "golden configuration" for your hosts.

Host profiles don't do anything until they are attached to ESXi hosts. Click the Attach Host/ Cluster toolbar button just below the navigation bar in the vSphere Client to open a dialog box that allows you to select one or more ESXi hosts to which the host profile should be attached.

After a host profile has been attached to an ESXi host, checking for compliance is as simple as right-clicking that host on the Hosts And Clusters tab and selecting Host Profile ➢ Check Compliance from the context menu.

If an ESXi host is found noncompliant with the settings in a host profile, you can then place the host in maintenance mode and apply the host profile. When you apply the host profile, the settings found in the host profile are enforced on that ESXi host to bring it into compliance. Note that some settings, such as changing the Service Console memory on an ESX 4.*x* host, require a reboot in order to take effect.

To truly understand the power of host profiles, consider a group of ESXi hosts in a cluster. I haven't discussed clusters yet, but as you'll see elsewhere in the book—especially in Chapter 5 and Chapter 6—ESXi hosts in a cluster need to have consistent settings. Without a host profile, you would have to manually review and configure these settings on each host in the cluster. With a host profile that captures those settings, adding a new host to the cluster is a simple two-step process:

1. Add the host to vCenter Server and to the cluster.

2. Attach the host profile and apply it.

That's it. The host profile will enforce all the settings on this new host that are required to bring it into compliance with the settings on the rest of the servers in the cluster. This is a huge advantage for larger organizations that need to quickly deploy new ESXi hosts.

Host profiles are also hugely important when using vSphere Auto Deploy to create a stateless environment. In stateless environments using Auto Deploy, configuration settings aren't persistent between reboots. In order to keep your stateless ESXi hosts properly configured, you'll want to use host profiles to apply the proper settings so that the host retains a consistent configuration over time, even when it's rebooted.

At this point, you have installed vCenter Server, added at least one ESXi host, and explored some of vCenter Server's features for managing settings on ESXi hosts. Now I'll cover how to manage some of the settings for vCenter Server itself.

Managing vCenter Server Settings

To make it easier for vSphere administrators to find and change the settings that affect the behavior or operation of vCenter Server, VMware centralized these settings into a single area within the vSphere Client user interface. This single area, found on the Administration menu in vCenter Server, allows for post-installation configuration of vCenter Server. In fact, it even contains configuration options that are not provided during installation. The Administration menu contains the following items:

◆ Custom Attributes

◆ vCenter Server Settings

◆ Role

◆ Session

◆ Edit Message Of The Day

◆ Export System Logs

Of these commands on the Administration menu, the Custom Attributes commands and the vCenter Server Settings are particularly important, so I'll review those two areas first, starting with Custom Attributes.

Custom Attributes

The Custom Attributes option lets you define custom identification or information options for VMs, hosts, or both (global). This is a pretty generic definition; perhaps a more concrete example will help. Say that you want to add metadata to each VM to identify whether it is an application server, an infrastructure server (that is, DHCP server, DNS server), or a domain controller.

To accomplish this task, you could add a custom VM attribute named Virtual Machine Role. To add this custom attribute, select Administration ➢ Custom Attributes. This opens the Custom Attributes dialog box, and from there you can click Add to create a new custom attribute. You can create a custom attribute that is global in nature or that applies only to ESXi hosts or VMs.

CUSTOM ATTRIBUTES AREN'T TRULY GLOBAL

Custom attributes are scoped per vCenter Server, meaning that you define these attributes separately on each vCenter Server instance, even when they are running in a linked mode group.

After you create this Virtual Machine Role custom attribute, you can edit the attribute data on the Summary tab of a VM (because this was a custom attribute for VMs). After the custom attribute is added, it appears in the Annotations section of the object. You can use the Edit button to open the Edit Annotations window and add the required metadata, as shown in Figure 3.29.

With the metadata clearly defined for various objects, you can then search based on that data. Figure 3.30 shows a custom search for all VMs whose Virtual Machine Role custom attribute contains the text "Infra."

FIGURE 3.29
You can add meta-data to objects by editing the values of the custom attributes.

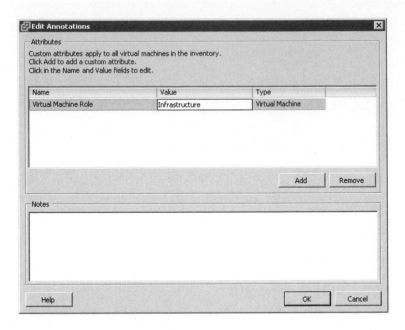

FIGURE 3.30
After you've defined the data for a custom attribute, you can use it as search criteria for quickly finding objects with similar metadata.

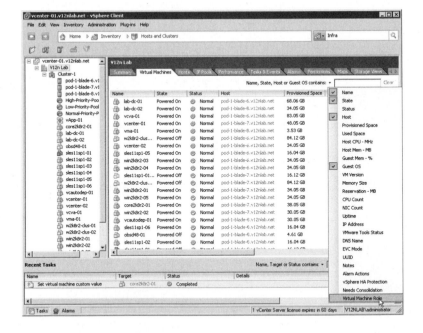

Using custom attributes to build metadata around your ESXi hosts and VMs is quite powerful, and the integration with the vSphere Client's search functionality makes very large inventories much more manageable.

But the Administration menu is about more than just custom attributes and metadata; it's also about configuring vCenter Server itself. The vCenter Server Settings command on the Administration menu gives you access to change the settings that control how vCenter Server operates, as you'll see in the next section.

vCenter Server Settings

The vCenter Server Settings dialog box contains 13 vCenter Server settings:

◆ Licensing

◆ Statistics

◆ Runtime Settings

◆ Active Directory

◆ Mail

◆ SNMP

◆ Ports

◆ Timeout Settings

◆ Logging Options

◆ Database

◆ Database Retention Policy

◆ SSL Settings

◆ Advanced Settings

When you have vCenter Server instances running in a linked mode group, the Current vCenter drop-down box lets you view the settings for each vCenter Server instance in the group.

Each of these settings controls a specific area of interaction or operation for vCenter Server that I briefly discuss next:

Licensing The Licensing configuration page of the vCenter Server Settings dialog box, shown in Figure 3.31, provides the parameters for how vCenter Server is licensed. The options include using an evaluation mode or applying a license key to this instance of vCenter Server. If this vCenter Server instance will also manage ESX 3.x hosts, then this dialog box provides an option for specifying the license server those hosts should use.

FIGURE 3.31
Licensing vCenter Server is managed through the vCenter Server Settings dialog box.

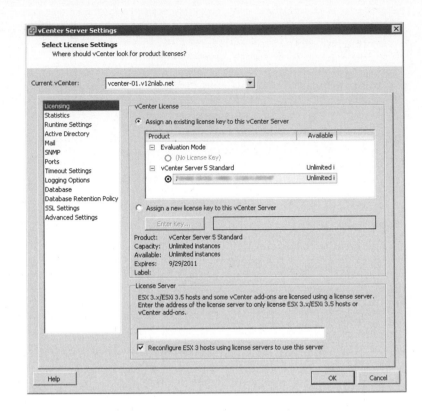

When an evaluation of vSphere and vCenter Server is no longer required and the appropriate licenses have been purchased, you must deselect the evaluation option and add a license key.

Statistics   The Statistics page, shown in Figure 3.32, offers the ability to configure the collection intervals and the system resources for accumulating statistical performance data in vCenter Server. In addition, it also provides a database-sizing calculator that can estimate the size of a vCenter Server database based on the configuration of statistics intervals. By default, the following four collection intervals are available:

◆ Past day: 5 minutes per sample at statistics level 1

◆ Past week: 30 minutes per sample at statistics level 1

◆ Past month: 2 hours per sample at statistics level 1

◆ Past year: 1 day per sample at statistics level 1

FIGURE 3.32
You can customize statistics collection intervals to support broad or detailed logging.

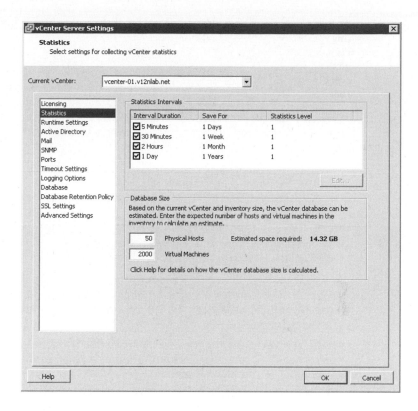

By selecting an interval from the list and clicking the Edit button, you can customize the interval configuration. You can set the interval, how long to keep the sample, and what statistics level (level 1 through level 4) vCenter Server will use.

The Statistics Collection level offers the following four collection levels defined in the user interface:

Level 1   Has the basic metrics for average usage of CPU, memory, disk, and network. It also includes data about system uptime, system heartbeat, and DRS metrics. Statistics for devices are not included.

Level 2   Includes all the average, summation, and rollup metrics for CPU, memory, disk, and network. It also includes system uptime, system heartbeat, and DRS metrics. Maximum and minimum rollup types as well as statistics for devices are not included.

Level 3   Includes all metrics for all counter groups, including devices, except for minimum and maximum rollups. Maximum and minimum rollup types are not included.

Level 4   Includes all metrics that vCenter Server supports.

DATABASE ESTIMATES

By editing the statistics collection configuration, you can see the estimated database size change accordingly. For example, by reducing the one-day collection interval to one minute as opposed to five minutes, the database size jumps from an estimated 14.32 GB to an estimated 26.55 GB. Similarly, if the collection samples taken once per day are kept for five years instead of one year, the database size jumps from an estimated 14.32 GB to an estimated 29.82 GB. The collection intervals and retention durations should be set to a level required by your company's audit policy.

Runtime Settings The Runtime Settings area lets you configure the vCenter Server Unique ID, the IP address used by vCenter Server, and the server name of the computer running vCenter Server. The unique ID will be populated by default, and changing it requires a restart of the vCenter Server service. These settings would normally require changing only when running multiple vCenter Server instances in the same environment. It is possible conflicts might exist if not altered.

Active Directory This page includes the ability to set the Active Directory timeout value, a limit for the number of users and groups returned in a query against the Active Directory database, and the validation period (in minutes) for synchronizing users and groups used by vCenter Server.

Mail The Mail page might be the most commonly customized page because its configuration is crucial to the sending of alarm results, as you'll see in Chapter 13. The mail SMTP server name or IP address and the sender account will determine the server and the account from which alarm results will be sent.

SNMP The SNMP configuration page is where you would configure vCenter Server for integration with a Systems Network Management Protocol (SNMP) management system. The receiver URL should be the name or IP address of the server with the appropriate SNMP trap receiver. The SNMP port, if not configured away from the default, should be set at 162, and the community string should be configured appropriately (Public is the default). vCenter Server supports up to four receiver URLs.

Ports The Ports page is used to configure the HTTP and HTTPS ports used by vCenter Server.

Timeout Settings This area, the Timeout Settings area, is where you configure client connection timeouts. The settings by default allow for a 30-second timeout for normal operations or 120 seconds for long operations.

Logging Options The Logging Options page, shown in Figure 3.33, customizes the level of detail accumulated in vCenter Server logs. The logging options include the following:

◆ None (Disable Logging)

◆ Errors (Errors Only)

◆ Warning (Errors And Warnings)

- ◆ Information (Normal Logging)

- ◆ Verbose (Verbose)

- ◆ Trivia (Trivia)

FIGURE 3.33
vCenter Server
offers several
options for config-
uring the amount of
data to be stored in
vCenter Server logs.

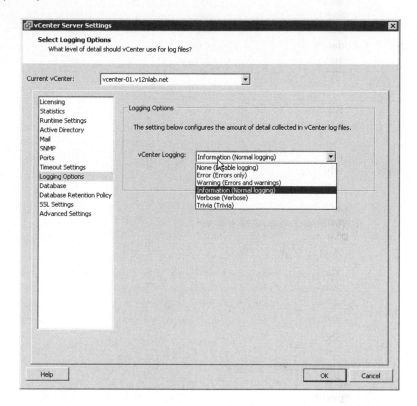

By default, vCenter Server stores its logs at `C:\Documents and Settings\All Users\Application Data\VMware\VMware VirtualCenter\Logs` (on Windows Server 2003) or `C:\ProgramData\VMware\VMware VirtualCenter\Logs` (on Windows Server 2008 and Windows Server 2008 R2).

Database   The Database page lets you configure the maximum number of connections to the backend database.

Database Retention Policy   To limit the growth of the vCenter Server database, you can configure a retention policy. vCenter Server offers options for limiting the length of time that both tasks and events are retained in the backend database.

SSL Settings   This page includes the ability to configure a certificate validity check between vCenter Server and the vSphere Client. If enabled, both systems will check the trust of the SSL certificate presented by the remote host when performing tasks such as adding a host to inventory or establishing a remote console to a VM.

Advanced Settings   The Advanced Settings page provides for an extensible configuration interface.

Roles

After the vCenter Server Settings command on the Administration menu is the Roles command.

The Roles option from the Administration menu is available only when the view is set to Administration and the Roles tab is selected. This menu works like a context menu that offers the ability to add, edit, rename, or remove roles based on what object is selected.

Chapter 8 describes vCenter Server's roles in detail.

Sessions

The Sessions menu option is available only when the view is set to Administration ➤ Sessions. The Sessions view allows for terminating all sessions and editing the text that makes up the message of the day (MOTD). The currently used session identified by the status "This Session" cannot be terminated.

Edit Message of the Day

As the name suggests, this menu item allows for editing the MOTD. The MOTD is displayed to users each time they log in to vCenter Server. This provides an excellent means of distributing information regarding maintenance schedules or other important information.

As extensions are added to vCenter Server—such as vSphere Update Manager or vSphere Auto Deploy—additional commands may appear on the Administration menu.

The next chapter, Chapter 4, discusses one such extension to vCenter Server, and that is vSphere Update Manager.

Export System Logs

This command allows you to export the logs from vCenter Server and/or one or more ESXi hosts. When you select this command from the Administration menu, the dialog box shown in Figure 3.34 appears. From this dialog box, you can choose which logs you want to export and the filesystem location where you would like the logs stored.

Perform the following tasks to export system logs out of vCenter Server:

1. With the vSphere Client running and connected to a vCenter Server instance, select Administration ➤ Export System Logs.

    The Export System Logs Wizard shown in Figure 3.34 appears.

2. Expand the tree and select the datacenter, cluster, or host objects whose logs you want to export.

3. If you want vCenter Server and vSphere Client logs included, leave Include Information From vCenter Server And vSphere Client selected. Click Next.

4. Select the log(s) you want to export. By default, all logs except Testing and PerformanceSnapshot are selected. Use the blue Select All and Deselect All hyperlinks to help with selecting the desired logs.

5. If you want to include performance data, select Include Performance Data and adjust the intervals, if necessary. Click Next.

6. Specify a local path to save the logs, and then click Next.

7. Review the settings and click Finish.

FIGURE 3.34
You can export logs from vCenter Server and one or more ESXi hosts easily from this dialog box.

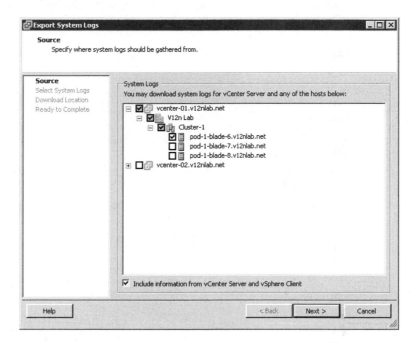

MORE OPTIONS FOR EXPORTING LOGS

On the File menu there is also an Export ➢ Export System Logs option. If you select the vCenter Server object and then choose this menu item, you'll get the same dialog box as if you'd selected Administration ➢ Export System Logs. If, however, you select an ESXi host or a VM, the dialog box changes to show you log export options that are specific to the currently selected inventory object.

After you click Finish, one or more tasks will appear in the Tasks pane of the vSphere Client to track the progress of exporting the system logs, and a Downloading System Logs Bundles dialog box appears, like the one shown in Figure 3.35.

FIGURE 3.35
The Downloading
System Logs
Bundles dialog box
shows the status
of the various log
export tasks.

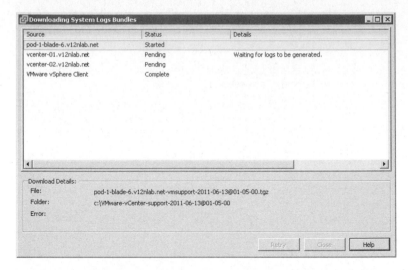

In the location you selected, vCenter Server will create a folder named `VMware-vCenter-support-year-mo-day@time;` in that folder you'll find the system logs for the vCenter Server computer, the selected ESXi hosts, and the computer running the vSphere Client. Figure 3.36 has a screenshot of some log files exported from vCenter Server.

FIGURE 3.36
These logs are for
vCenter Server, a
single ESXi host,
and the com-
puter running the
vSphere Client.

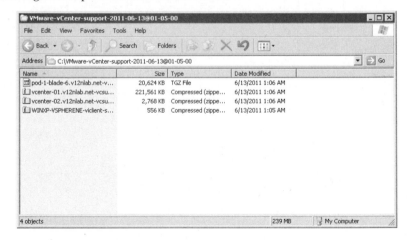

I'll continue to explore vCenter Server's functionality in the coming chapters. The next chapter, Chapter 4, explores the functionality added to vCenter Server by the vSphere Update Manager extension.

The Bottom Line

Understand the features and role of vCenter Server.   vCenter Server plays a central role in the management of ESXi hosts and VMs. Key features such as vMotion, Storage vMotion, vSphere DRS, vSphere HA, and vSphere FT are all enabled and made possible by vCenter Server. vCenter Server provides scalable authentication and role-based administration based on integration with Active Directory.

> **Master It** Specifically with regard to authentication, what are three key advantages of using vCenter Server?

Plan a vCenter Server deployment. Planning a vCenter Server deployment includes selecting a backend database engine, choosing an authentication method, sizing the hardware appropriately, and providing a sufficient level of high availability and business continuity. You must also decide whether you will run vCenter Server as a VM or on a physical system. Finally, you must decide whether you will use the Windows Server–based version of vCenter Server or deploy the vCenter Server virtual appliance.

> **Master It** What are some of the advantages and disadvantages of running vCenter Server as a VM?

> **Master It** What are some of the advantages and disadvantages of using the vCenter Server virtual appliance?

Install and configure a vCenter Server database. vCenter Server supports several enterprise-grade database engines, including Oracle and Microsoft SQL Server. IBM DB2 is also supported. Depending on the database in use, there are specific configuration steps and specific permissions that must be applied in order for vCenter Server to work properly.

> **Master It** Why is it important to protect the database engine used to support vCenter Server?

Install and configure vCenter Server. vCenter Server is installed using the VMware vCenter Installer. You can install vCenter Server as a stand-alone instance or join a linked mode group for greater scalability. vCenter Server will use a predefined ODBC DSN to communicate with the separate database server.

> **Master It** When preparing to install vCenter Server, are there any concerns about which Windows account should be used during the installation?

Use vCenter Server's management features. vCenter Server provides a wide range of management features for ESXi hosts and VMs. These features include scheduled tasks, topology maps, host profiles for consistent configurations, and event logging.

> **Master It** Your manager has asked you to prepare an overview of the virtualized environment. What tools in vCenter Server will help you in this task?

## Chapter 4

Installing and Configuring vSphere Update Manager

Software patches are an unfortunate fact of life in today's IT departments. Most organizations recognize that software updates are necessary to correct problems or flaws and to add new features. Fortunately, VMware offers a tool to help centralize, automate, and manage these patches for vSphere. This tool is called vSphere Update Manager (VUM).

In this chapter you will learn to

◆ Install VUM and integrate it with the vSphere Client

◆ Determine which hosts or VMs need to be patched or upgraded

◆ Use VUM to upgrade VM hardware or VMware Tools

◆ Apply patches to ESXi hosts and older ESX hosts

◆ Upgrade hosts and coordinate large-scale datacenter upgrades

◆ Utilize alternative approaches to VUM updates when required

Overview of vSphere Update Manager

VUM is a tool designed to help VMware administrators automate and streamline the process of applying updates, which could be patches or upgrades, to their vSphere environment. VUM is fully integrated within vCenter Server and offers the ability to scan and remediate ESXi hosts, host extensions (such as EMC's Powerpath/VE multipathing software), older ESX and ESXi hosts (circa 3.5, 4.0, and 4.1), and virtual appliances. VUM can also upgrade VMware Tools and upgrade VM hardware. VUM is also the vehicle used to install and update the Cisco Nexus 1000V third-party distributed virtual switch. The Cisco Nexus 1000V is covered in Chapter 5, "Creating and Configuring Virtual Networks."

MAJOR VUM 5 CHANGES

If you have used previous incarnations of VUM with vSphere 4, it is worth noting that there are some substantial changes that affect VUM.

As we have already covered in the previous chapters, vSphere 5 has only the ESXi variant of the hypervisor. With ESX being retired, VUM 5 has a new capability to migrate ESX 4.*x* hosts across to ESXi. Unfortunately, because of the size the /boot partition was allocated in ESX 3.*x*, these hosts cannot be migrated to ESXi 5. Any ESX 4.*x* hosts that had previously been upgraded from ESX 3.*x* will not have the required minimum 350 MB of space in the /boot partition. In these cases a fresh install is required, so you'll need to consider how you want to migrate their settings.

Despite "vanilla" ESX being replaced wholesale with ESXi in vSphere 5.0, VUM 5.0 still supports the great patching capabilities for legacy 3.5 and 4 ESX/ESXi servers and upgrades for 4.*x* hosts. So in this chapter there will often be callouts to ESX or ESX/ESXi, when most of the rest of this book is bereft of such references; but these are here purposefully. Companies will work in a mixed mode of hosts during their migration to vSphere 5, and many will keep older ESX hosts for some time, so this capability of VUM is worth remembering.

Finally, the big change in VUM itself with vSphere 5 is the removal of the guest OS patching feature. Previously, VUM could scan certain supported versions of Windows and Linux guest OSes and apply updates to the OS and even some of their applications. This is a substantial change in VUM's direction. Realistically, it was difficult for VMware to keep up with an ever-changing landscape of OSes and guest applications. Organizations on the whole already had trusted, more-native methods to manage this regular guest patching. Also, VUM could suffer from scaling issues, trying to cope with large deployments of VMs. vCenters are capable of holding a large number of hosts these days, and therefore the number of VMs can be appreciable. Trying to maintain patching on all the potential VMs as vCenter scaled up was something that VUM would struggle to support.

VUM integrates itself tightly with vSphere's inherent cluster features. It can use the Distributed Resource Scheduler (DRS) for nondisruptive updating of ESX/ESXi hosts, by moving its VMs between hosts in the cluster and avoiding downtime. It can coordinate itself with the cluster's Distributed Power Management (DPM), High Availability (HA), and Fault Tolerance (FT) settings to ensure that they don't prevent VUM from updating at any stage. With vSphere 5, the cluster can even calculate if it can remediate multiple hosts at once while still appeasing its cluster constraints, speeding up the overall patching process.

The whole VUM experience is fully *synthesized* with vCenter, allowing the configuration and remediation work to be carried out in the same vSphere Client. VUM uses two views: the administrative view, where you can configure VUM settings and manage baselines, and a compliance view, where you can scan and remediate vSphere objects. When applying updates to VMs, VUM can apply snapshots to them to enable rollback in the event of problems. It can identify when hardware upgrades and VMware Tools are needed and combine them into a single, actionable task.

To help keep your vSphere environment patched and up to date, VUM utilizes your company's Internet connection to download information about available updates, the products to which those updates apply, and the actual updates themselves. Based on rules and policies that are defined and applied by the VMware administrator using the vSphere Client, VUM will then apply updates to hosts and VMs. The installation of updates can be scheduled, and even VMs that are powered off or suspended can have updates applied to them in an automated fashion.

UPGRADING, PATCHING, AND UPDATING WITHOUT DISCOMBOBULATION

Several common terms sometimes lead to confusion. *Upgrading* refers to the process of bringing the object to a new version, which often includes new features and capabilities. For example, for hosts, this can mean moving from 4.1 to 5.0 or, when the next minor version is available, from 5.0 to 5.*x*. VM hardware, virtual appliances, and host extensions all tend to be associated with upgrades, because they are usually rip-and-replace–type software changes.

The term *patching* is usually reserved for applying remedial software changes to individual host components. This will normally change the host's build number but not its version number. Often these are rolled up into host *updates*, so expect ESXi 5 to receive 5.0 Update 1 before you see a 5.*x* version change. However, and certainly somewhat confusingly, the term *updates* is often used to explain the generic process of both patching and upgrading. So applying updates might include host patches (some of which might be rolled into a host update) and various upgrades.

Regardless of the terminology used, it is useful to think about updating in terms of how routine it is — in fact, this is the way this chapter splits it up. Routine updates would include host patches, host updates, and upgrading a VM's VMware Tools. These are the sort of remediation tasks you could expect to perform on, say, a monthly basis, as many guest OS patches are, and should be more trivial to test and apply. Nonroutine updates are the upgrades to hosts and VM hardware. These updates will often change the functionality of the object, so they need to be tested in your environment to make sure they are fully "sociable" and to understand how best to take advantage of the new capabilities that the upgrades are likely to bring.

The one gray area is upgrading host extensions and virtual appliances, because they need to be evaluated on a case-by-case basis. Some of their upgrades will be simple improvements; others can bring significant changes to the way they work. You need to evaluate each extension and appliance upgrade and decide for yourself how much testing is required before you deploy it.

Putting VUM to work in your vSphere deployment involves installing and configuring VUM, setting up baselines, scanning hosts and VMs, and applying patches.

Installing vSphere Update Manager

VUM installs from the vCenter Server DVD installation media and requires that a vCenter Server instance be already installed. You will find that installing VUM is much like installing vCenter Server, which you saw in the previous chapter.

You perform the following high-level steps to install VUM:

1. Configure VUM's database.

2. Create an Open Database Connectivity (ODBC) data source name (DSN) for VUM.

3. Install VUM.

4. (Optional) Install the Update Manager Download Service (UMDS) if desired.

5. Install the VUM plug-in for the vSphere Client.

VUM has a one-to-one relationship with vCenter. That is, for every vCenter instance you need a separate VUM install, and each VUM can provide update services to only one vCenter. The one exception to this is that you can share the job of downloading patches between multiple VUMs (and therefore multiple vCenters) with the use of an optional component known as Update Manager Download Services (UMDS), which is discussed in the section "Installing the Update Manager Download Service (Optional)."

If you have multiple vCenters that are connected via Linked Mode you can use VUM, but a separate instance is still required for each vCenter. All the installation, configuration, permissions, update scanning, and remediation are done on a per-VUM basis because they operate independently.

As discussed previously, with vSphere 5 there are now two deployment options for vCenter: the conventional Windows installation and the new Linux-based prebuilt vCenter Virtual Appliance (VCVA). VUM can happily connect to either installation; however, for obvious reasons, your choice helps to shape your deployment model. If you have a Windows-based vCenter, you can either install VUM on the same server instance or use a separate Windows install. However, because the VCVA is Linux based, if you are opting for this you will have to install VUM on its own Windows install, because there is no Linux version of VUM yet.

Defining the Requirements

VUM requires access to a dedicated vCenter instance, so your vSphere licensing must include vCenter. This therefore excludes the free stand-alone ESXi hypervisor version currently available.

The VUM server should have 2 GB of RAM at a minimum, and if installed on the same server as vCenter itself, there should be at least 4 GB. We discuss various database options in the next section, but you should avoid installing VUM on the same database as vCenter (it can be on the same server; it just should not be on the same database).

Even though VUM is a 32-bit application, it can only be installed on a 64-bit version of Windows. Windows Server 2003 SP2 and 2008 are supported. During the install, you will receive a warning if you attempt to put the download repository on a drive with less than 120 GB of free space.

AVOID INSTALLING VUM ON A VM THAT SITS ON A HOST THAT IT REMEDIATES

Be wary of installing VUM on a VM running on a host in a cluster that it is responsible for remediating. If DRS is disabled on the cluster at any stage, or the cluster has a problem migrating this VUM VM to another host, then to prevent VUM from shutting itself down, the remediation will fail.

Table 4.1 shows the default ports that need to be opened if any of your components are separated by a firewall.

Table 4.1: **Firewall requirements for VUM**

PORT	SOURCE	DESTINATION	PROTOCOL	DESCRIPTION
80	VUM	vCenter	TCP	Inter VUM–vCenter communications
80 & 443	VUM	Internet	TCP	Retrieving updates and metadata
902	VUM	Hosts	TCP	Pushing upgrade files
8084	Client plug-in	VUM	TCP	SOAP listening
9084	Hosts	VUM	TCP	HTTP service for patch downloads
9087	Client plug-in	VUM	TCP	Uploading upgrade files

Configuring VUM's Database

Like vCenter Server, VUM requires its own database. Where vCenter Server uses the database to store configuration and performance statistics, VUM uses a database to store patch metadata.

SUPPORTED DATABASE SERVERS

VUM's database support is similar to that of vCenter Server but not identical. For example, although DB2 is supported by vCenter Server, DB2 is not supported by VUM. In general, most versions of SQL Server 2005, 2008, and Oracle 10g/11g are supported by VUM. For the most up-to-date database compatibility matrix, refer to the latest *vSphere Compatibility Matrixes*, available from VMware's website.

For small installations (up to 5 hosts and 50 VMs), VUM can use an instance of SQL Server 2008 R2 Express Edition (SQL Express). SQL Express is included on the VMware vCenter media, and the VUM installation will automatically install and configure the SQL Express instance appropriately. No additional work is required outside of the installation routine. However, as you learned in Chapter 3, "Planning and Installing vCenter Server," SQL Express does have some limitations, so plan accordingly. If you do plan on using SQL Express, you can skip ahead to the section "Installing VUM."

If you decide against using SQL Express, you must now make another decision: where do you put the VUM database? Although it is possible for VUM to use the same database as vCenter Server, it is strongly recommended that you use a separate database, even if you keep both databases on the same physical computer. For environments with fewer than 30 hosts, it's generally safe to keep these databases on the same computer, but moving beyond 30 hosts or 300 VMs, it's recommended to separate the vCenter Server and VUM databases onto different physical computers. When you move beyond 100 hosts or 1,000 VMs, you should be sure to use separate database servers for both the vCenter Server database and the VUM database as well as separate servers for vCenter Server and the VUM server software. Other factors, such as high availability or capacity, may also affect this decision. Aside from knowing which database server you'll use, the decision to use a single computer versus multiple computers won't affect the procedures described in this section.

In either case, whether hosting the VUM database on the same computer as the vCenter Server database or not, there are specific configuration steps that you'll need to follow, just as you did when installing vCenter Server. You'll need to create and configure the database, assign ownership, and grant permissions to the MSDB database. Be sure to complete these steps before trying to install VUM, because this information is required during installation.

Perform the following steps to create and configure a Microsoft SQL Server 2005/2008 database for use with VUM:

1. Launch the SQL Server Management Studio application. When prompted to connect to a server, connect to a supported database server running SQL Server 2005 SP2 or later. Select Database Engine as the server type.

2. From the Object Explorer on the left side, expand the server node at the top level.

3. Right-click the Databases node and select New Database.

4. In the New Database window, specify a database name. Use a name that is easy to identify, such as VUM or vSphereUM.

5. Set the owner of the new database.

   Unless you are running the separate database on the same computer as VUM, you will need to set the owner of the database to a SQL login; integrated Windows authentication is not supported with a remote database.

   Figure 4.1 shows a new database being created with an SQL login set as the owner.

6. For ideal performance, set the location of the database and log files so they are on different physical disks than the operating system and the patch repository. Scroll along to the right of the large pane to set the locations.

   Figure 4.2 shows the database and log files stored on a separate drive from the operating system.

7. After the settings are configured, click OK to create the new database.

MSDB PERMISSIONS SHOULDN'T PERSIST BEYOND THE INSTALL

VUM requires dbo permissions on the MSDB database during the install to create the required tables. You can and should remove the dbo permissions on the MSDB database after the installation of VUM is complete. They are not needed after installation, as with the vCenter Server setup.

As with the vCenter Server database, the login that VUM will use to connect to the database server must have dbo permissions on the new database as well as on the MSDB database. You should remove the permissions on the MSDB database after installation is complete.

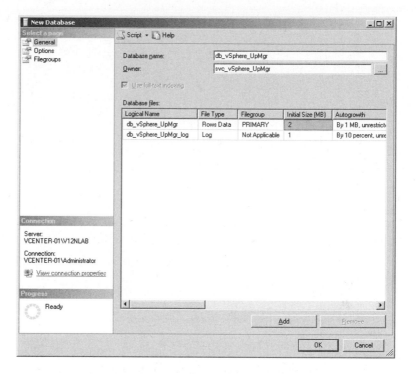

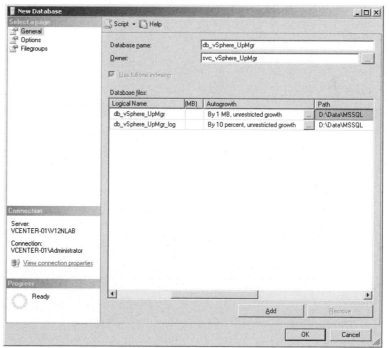

Creating the Open Database Connectivity Data Source Name

After you configure the separate database server, you must create an ODBC DSN to connect to the backend database. You'll need to have the ODBC DSN created before you start VUM installation, and because VUM is a 32-bit application, the ODBC DSN must be a 32-bit DSN. This is true even though VUM installs only on a 64-bit version of Windows.

Perform the following steps to create an ODBC DSN for the VUM database:

1. Run the 32-bit ODBC Administrator application found at `%systemroot%\SysWOW64\odbcad32.exe`.

   The 32-bit ODBC Administrator application looks identical to the 64-bit version, and there doesn't appear be any way to distinguish between the two. If you're unsure which one you launched, exit and restart to be sure that you have the correct version.

IS THERE ANY WAY TO TELL THE DIFFERENCE?

There is a way to tell the difference between the 64-bit and 32-bit versions of the ODBC Data Source Administrator application: the 64-bit and 32-bit system DSNs are not shared between the two applications. So, if you see your vCenter Server DSN listed on the System DSN tab, you're running the 64-bit version of the tool (because vCenter Server requires a 64-bit DSN).

---

2. Select the System DSN tab.

3. Click the Add button.

4. From the list of available drivers, select the correct driver for the database server you're using.

   As with vCenter Server, you will need to ensure the correct ODBC driver is installed for the database server hosting the VUM database. For SQL Server 2005/2008, select the SQL Server Native Client.

5. On the first screen of the Create A New Data Source Wizard, fill in the name of the DSN, a description, and the name of the server to which this DSN will connect.

   Be sure to make a note of the DSN name; you'll need this information later. Click Next when you're finished.

6. On the next screen you need to supply an authentication type and credentials to connect to the separate database server. Select With SQL Server Authentication Using A Login ID And Password Entered By The User, and specify a SQL login and password that are valid on the database server and that have the appropriate permissions assigned to the VUM and MSDB databases. Click Next.

   Windows Integrated Authentication is an option only if you have installed the database server component locally on the same server as VUM. It is advised that you use SQL Server Authentication in all cases, even if the database is local, because it makes moving the database easier in the future should your environment grow and require scaling beyond a local instance.

7. Change the default database to the one you created in Figure 4.1 and click Next.

8. Click Finish.

9. In the ODBC Microsoft SQL Server Setup dialog box, click the Test Data Source connection to verify the settings.

   If the results say the tests completed successfully, click OK twice to return to the ODBC Data Source Administrator window. If not, go back and double-check the settings and change them as needed.

   With the database created and the ODBC connection defined, you're now ready to proceed with the installation of VUM.

Installing VUM

Now that you have met all the prerequisites — at least one instance of vCenter Server running and accessible across the network, a separate database running and configured appropriately, and an ODBC DSN defined to connect to the preconfigured database — you can start the VUM installation. Before you begin, make sure that you have made a note of the ODBC DSN you defined previously and the SQL login and password configured for access to the database. You'll need these pieces of information during the installation.

Perform the following steps to install VUM:

1. Insert the vCenter Server DVD into the computer.

   The VMware vCenter Installer runs automatically; if it does not, simply double-click the DVD drive in My Computer to invoke AutoPlay.

2. Select vSphere Update Manager and click Install.

3. Choose the correct language for the installation, and click OK.

4. On the Welcome To The InstallShield Wizard For VMware vSphere Update Manager screen, click Next to start the installation.

5. Click Next to continue past the End-User Patent Agreement.

6. Accept the terms in the license agreement, and click Next.

7. The Support Information screen clarifies that VUM 5 does not support guest OS patching or upgrades from ESX/ESXi 3.x. Leave the check box Download Updates From Default Sources Immediately After Installation ticked, unless the VUM server does not have access to the Internet or you want to postpone a large Internet download until a more convenient time. Click Next.

8. Fill out the next screen with the correct IP address or hostname, HTTP port, username, and password for the vCenter Server instance to which this VUM server will be associated. If you have created a service account to use for VUM, enter it here. Click Next when the information is complete.

9. Select to either install an SQL 2008 Express instance or to use an existing database instance. If you are using a supported separate database server, select the correct DSN from the list, and click Next.

As described previously, using a supported database instance requires that you have already created the database and ODBC DSN. If you haven't created the ODBC DSN yet, you'll need to exit the installation, create the DSN, and restart the installation.

10. The next screen prompts you for user credentials to connect to the database specified in the DSN and configured for use by VUM. Supply the username and password for the SQL login you created before starting the installation, as shown in Figure 4.3.

FIGURE 4.3
Supply the correct username and password for the VUM database.

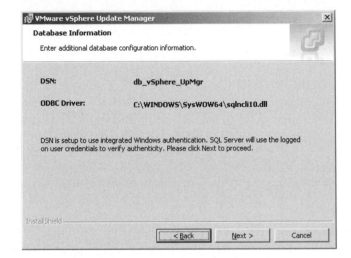

11. If the SQL Server database is set to the Full recovery model (the default), a dialog box pops up warning you about the need for regular backups.

Click OK to dismiss the dialog box and continue with the installation, but be sure to arrange for regular backups of the database. Otherwise, the database transaction logs could grow to consume all available space.

12. Unless there is a need to change the default port settings, leave the default settings, as shown in Figure 4.4. If there is a proxy server that controls access to the Internet, click the check box labeled Yes, I Have Internet Connection And I Want To Configure Proxy Settings Now. Otherwise, if there isn't a proxy or if you don't know the correct proxy configuration, leave the box deselected, and click Next.

CONFIGURING PROXY SETTINGS DURING INSTALLATION

If you forget to select the box to configure proxy settings during installation, fear not! All is not lost. After you install VUM, you can use the vSphere Client to set the proxy settings accordingly. Just be aware that VUM's first attempt to download patch information will fail because it can't access the Internet.

FIGURE 4.4
The VUM installation provides the option to configure proxy settings. If there is no proxy, leave the box deselected.

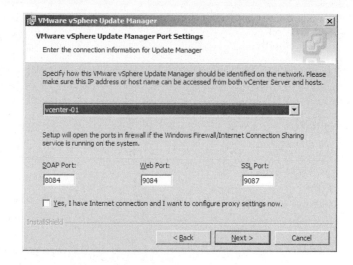

13. VUM downloads patches and patch metadata from the Internet and stores them locally for use in remediating hosts and guests.

The next screen allows you to specify where to install VUM as well as where to store the patches, as shown in Figure 4.5. Use the Change button to modify the location of the patches to a location with sufficient storage capacity.

In Figure 4.6, you can see where a drive different from the system drive has been selected to store the downloaded patches.

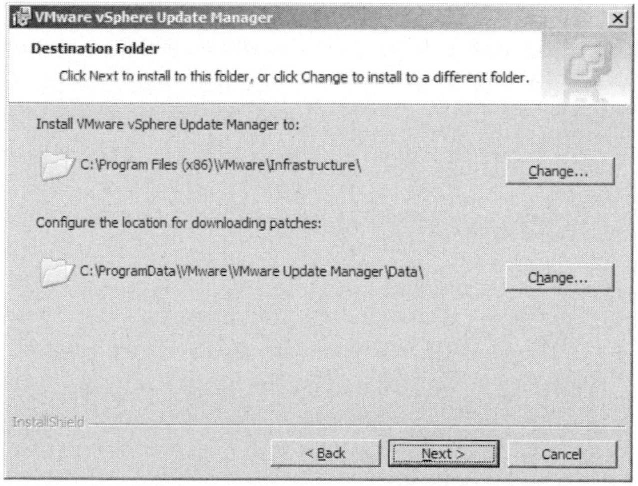

FIGURE 4.5
The default settings for VUM place the application files and the patch repository on the system drive.

FIGURE 4.6
During installation, you can tell VUM to store the downloaded patches on a drive other than the system drive.

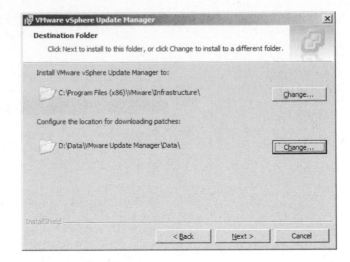

14. If you select a drive or partition with less than 120 GB, a dialog box will pop up warning you to be sure you have sufficient space to download the appropriate patches. Click OK to proceed.

15. Click Install to install VUM.

16. Click Finish when the installation is complete.

Installing the Update Manager Download Service (Optional)

An optional step in the deployment of VUM is the installation of the Update Manager Download Service (UMDS). UMDS provides a centralized download repository. Installing UMDS is especially useful in two situations. First, UMDS is beneficial when you have multiple VUM servers; using UMDS prevents consuming more bandwidth than necessary because the updates need to be downloaded only once. Instead of each VUM server downloading a full copy, multiple VUM servers can leverage the centralized UMDS repository. The second situation in which UMDS is beneficial is in environments where the VUM servers do not have direct Internet access. Internet access is required to download the updates and update metadata, so you can use UMDS to download and distribute the information to the individual VUM servers.

To install UMDS on a server, browse the vCenter DVD installation media. UMDS, like VUM, can be installed only on 64-bit servers. From the root of the DVD there is a umds folder. Within that folder run the executable VMware-UMDS.exe.

UMDS is a command-line tool. By default the UMDS tool is installed in c:\Program Files (x86)\VMware\Infrastructure\Update Manager.

You can configure many options in UMDS, but to start using it, you need to configure the following three settings:

1. Specify the updates to download using the –S switch.

2. Download the updates with the –D switch.

3. Export the updates and metadata with the –E switch.

Full details of all the command's switch options are available from the in-built help, by running `vmware-umds -H`. Figure 4.7 shows the UMDS utility being run from the command prompt. Along with the basic switches that can be seen in Figure 4.7, the full help file provides all the arguments and provides a series of examples of common usage tasks.

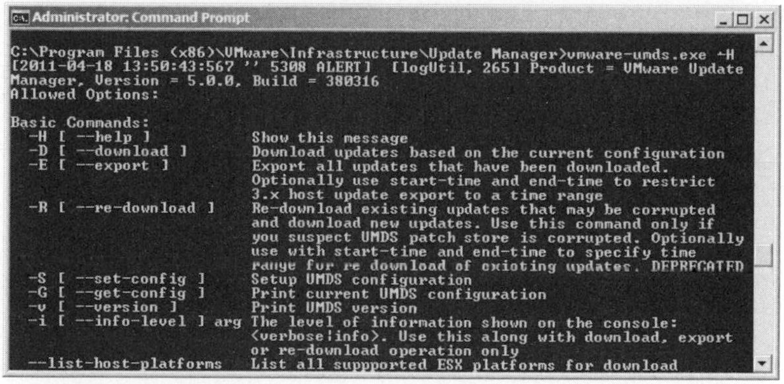

FIGURE 4.7
You must configure the UMDS utility at the command prompt.

```
Administrator: Command Prompt                                              _ □ X

C:\Program Files (x86)\VMware\Infrastructure\Update Manager>vmware-umds.exe -H
[2011-04-18 13:50:43:567 '' 5308 ALERT] [logUtil, 265] Product = VMware Update
Manager, Version = 5.0.0, Build = 380316
Allowed Options:

Basic Commands:
  -H [ --help ]              Show this message
  -D [ --download ]          Download updates based on the current configuration
  -E [ --export ]            Export all updates that have been downloaded.
                             Optionally use start-time and end-time to restrict
                             3.x host update export to a time range
  -R [ --re-download ]       Re-download existing updates that may be corrupted
                             and download new updates. Use this command only if
                             you suspect UMDS patch store is corrupted. Optionally
                             use with start-time and end-time to specify time
                             range for re download of existing updates. DEPRECATED
  -S [ --set-config ]        Setup UMDS configuration
  -G [ --get-config ]        Print current UMDS configuration
  -v [ --version ]           Print UMDS version
  -i [ --info-level ] arg    The level of information shown on the console:
                             <verbose|info>. Use this along with download, export
                             or re-download operation only
  --list-host-platforms      List all suppported ESX platforms for download
```

There are two different designs for using UMDS:

◆ The VUM server does not have network connectivity to the UMDS server. In this case you need to move the downloaded patches and metadata to a removable media drive and physically transfer the data via old-fashioned "sneakernet."

◆ The VUM server can connect to the UMDS server. Although the VUM server may not be allowed to connect directly to the Internet, if it can hit the UMDS, then it can effectively use it as a web proxy. You need to configure a web server on the UMDS server, such as IIS or Apache. Then the VUM server can connect to the UMDS server and download its patches. This is also typically the approach you would take if you wanted to use UMDS as a centralized download server for several VUM instances.

At this point VUM is installed, but you have no way to manage it. In order to manage VUM, you must install the VUM plug-in for vCenter Server and the vSphere Client, as we discuss in the next section.

Installing the vSphere Update Manager Plug-in

The tools to manage and configure VUM are implemented as a vCenter Server plug-in and are completely integrated into vCenter Server and the vSphere Client. However, to access these tools, you must first install and register the plug-in in the vSphere Client. This enables the vSphere Client to manage and configure VUM by adding an Update Manager tab and some extra context menu commands to objects in the vSphere Client. vSphere Client plug-ins are managed on a per-client basis; that is, each installation of the vSphere Client needs to have the plug-in installed in order to access the VUM administration tools.

Perform the following steps to install the VUM plug-in for each instance of the vSphere Client:

1. Launch the vSphere Client if it isn't already running and connect to the vCenter Server that has VUM associated with it.

2. From the vSphere Client's Plug-ins menu, select Manage Plug-ins.

3. Find the vSphere Update Manager extension, and click the blue Download And Install link, as shown in Figure 4.8.

FIGURE 4.8
Installing the vSphere Client plug-in is done from within the vSphere Client.

4. Run through the installation of the vSphere Update Manager extension, selecting the language, agreeing to the license terms, and completing the installation.

5. After the installation is complete, the status of the plug-in is listed as Enabled. Click Close to return to the vSphere Client.

The VUM plug-in is now installed into this instance of the vSphere Client. Remember that the VUM plug-in is per instance of the vSphere Client, so you need to repeat this process on each installation of the vSphere Client. If you have the vSphere Client installed on your desktop workstation and your laptop, you'll need to install the plug-in on both systems as well. After that is done, you are ready to configure VUM for your environment.

---

vSphere Web Client

At the time of writing, with the initial release of vSphere 5.0, the new Web Client did not have a VUM plug-in available. Unless you resort to the PowerCLI command line (discussed in "Using vSphere Update Manager PowerCLI"), all VUM-related tasks can only be performed through the Windows-based vSphere Client.

Reconfiguring the VUM or UMDS Installation with the Update Manager Utility

When you install VUM or UMDS on a server, a small reconfiguration utility is silently installed. This tool, the Update Manager Utility, allows you change some of the fundamental installation settings without the need to reinstall either VUM or UMDS.

The settings that the tool allows you to change are these:

◆ Proxy settings

◆ Database username and password

◆ vCenter Server IP address

◆ SSL certificate (provides a set of instructions to follow)

Perform the following steps to run the Update Manager Utility:

1. Stop the Update Manager service on the server.

2. Browse to the utility's directory. By default this is: `c:\Program Files (x86)\VMware\Infrastructure\Update Manager`.

3. Run the executable `VMwareUpdateManagerUtility.exe`.

The utility is a simple GUI tool that steps through these VUM/UMDS settings.

Upgrading VUM from a Previous Version

It is possible to upgrade VUM from any VUM installation that is version 4.0 or above. When the VUM 5.0 install starts, it will recognize the previous version and offer to upgrade it. You can choose to delete the previously downloaded patches and start afresh or keep the existing downloads and potentially save some bandwidth. Remember that like the install itself, the account that VUM uses to connect to the database will need dbo permissions on the MSDB database during the upgrade procedure. You will not be able to change the patch repository's location using an upgrade.

VUM 5.0 is installable only on 64-bit versions of Windows. If you have a 4.x VUM install on 32-bit Windows, you need to migrate the data to a new 64-bit server first. There is a special tool on the vCenter installation DVD in the `datamigration` folder to help you back up and restore a previous installation to a new machine.

Configuring vSphere Update Manager

After you have installed and registered the plug-in with the vSphere Client, a new Update Manager icon appears on the vSphere Client home page. Additionally, in the Hosts And Clusters or VMs And Templates inventory view, a new tab labeled Update Manager appears on objects in the vSphere Client. From this Update Manager tab, you can scan for patches, create and attach baselines, stage patches to hosts, and remediate hosts and guests.

Clicking the Update Manager icon at the vSphere Client home page takes you to the main VUM administration screen. Figure 4.9 shows that this area is divided into seven main sections: Baselines And Groups, Configuration, Events, Notifications, Patch Repository, ESXi Images, and VA Upgrades. Initially, like many other areas of the vSphere Client, you will also see a leading Getting Started tab.

FIGURE 4.9
The tabs in the Update Manager Administration area within the vSphere Client.

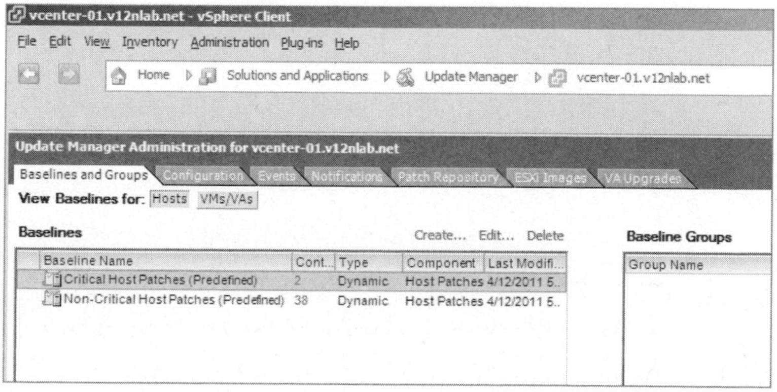

These seven tabs comprise the major areas of configuration for VUM, so let's take a closer look at each section:

Baselines And Groups   Baselines are a key part of how VUM works. In order to keep ESX/ESXi hosts and VMs updated, VUM uses *baselines*.

VUM uses several different types of baselines. First, baselines are divided into host baselines, designed to be used in updating ESX/ESXi hosts, and VM/VA baselines, which are designed to be used to update VMs and virtual appliances.

Baselines are further subdivided into patch baselines, upgrade baselines, and host extension baselines. Patch baselines define lists of patches to be applied to an ESX/ESXi host; upgrade baselines define how to upgrade an ESX/ESXi host, the VM's hardware, VMware Tools, or a virtual appliance. There's also another type of baseline for hosts, known as host extension baselines; these are used to manage the extensions installed onto your ESX/ESXi hosts.

Finally, patch baselines are divided again into dynamic baselines and fixed baselines. Dynamic baselines can change over time; for example, all security host patches since a certain date. But fixed baselines remain constant; for example, a specific host patch that you want to ensure is applied to your hosts.

WHEN SHOULD YOU USE FIXED BASELINES OR DYNAMIC BASELINES?

Fixed baselines are best used to apply a specific fix to a group of hosts. For example, let's say that VMware released a specific fix for ESX/ESXi that you wanted to be sure that all your hosts had installed. By creating a fixed baseline that included just that patch and attaching that baseline to your hosts, you could ensure that your hosts had that specific fix installed. Another use for fixed baselines is to establish the approved set of patches that you have tested and are now ready to deploy to the environment as a whole.

Dynamic baselines, on the other hand, are best used to keep systems current with the latest sets of patches. Because these baselines evolve over time, attaching them to your hosts can help you understand just how current your systems are (or aren't!).

VMware provides a few baselines with VUM when it's installed. The baselines that are present upon installation include the following:

◆ Two dynamic host patch baselines named Critical Host Patches and Non-Critical Host Patches

◆ A dynamic baseline for upgrading VMware Tools to match the host

◆ A dynamic baseline for upgrading VM hardware to match the host

◆ A dynamic VA upgrade baseline named VA Upgrade To Latest

Although these baselines provide a good starting point, many users will need to create additional baselines that better reflect their organizations' specific patching policy or procedures. For example, organizations may want to ensure that ESX/ESXi hosts are kept fully patched with regard to security patches but not necessarily critical non-security patches. This can be accomplished by creating a custom dynamic baseline.

Perform the following steps to create a new dynamic host patch baseline for security-related ESX/ESXi host patches:

1. Launch the vSphere Client, and connect to the vCenter Server instance with which VUM is registered.

2. In the vSphere Client, navigate to the Update Manager Administration area via the vCenter home page, and click the Baselines And Groups tab.

3. Just under the tab bar, you need to select the correct baseline type, Hosts or VMs/VAs. In this case, click the Hosts button.

4. Click the Create link in the area to the right of the list of baselines (not the Create link for the Baseline Groups on the far right). This launches the New Baseline Wizard.

5. Supply a name and description for the new baseline, and select Host Patch as the baseline type. Click Next.

6. Select Dynamic, and click Next.

7. On the next screen you define the criteria for the patches to be included in this baseline. Select the correct criteria for the baseline you are defining, and then click Next.

   Figure 4.10 shows a sample selection set — in this case, all security-related patches.

FIGURE 4.10
Dynamic baselines contain a set of criteria that determine which patches are included in the baseline and which are not.

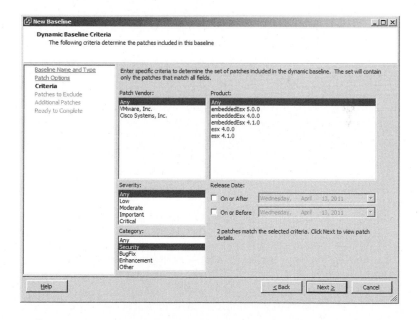

8. Select any patches that match the selection criteria but that you want to exclude from the baseline.

Use the up/down arrows to move patches out of or into the exclusion list in the lower pane, respectively. In this case, don't exclude any patches and just click Next.

9. Now you have the option to permanently include any patches that are available but that were not automatically included by the selection criteria.

Once again, use the up/down arrows to remove patches or add patches to be included, respectively. Don't add any additional patches; just click Next.

10. Click Finish to create the baseline.

You can now use this baseline to determine which ESX/ESXi hosts are not compliant with the latest security patches by attaching it to one or more hosts, a procedure you'll learn later in this chapter in the section "Routine Updates."

Groups, or baseline groups, are simply combinations of nonconflicting baselines. You might use a baseline group to combine multiple dynamic patch baselines, like the baseline group shown in Figure 4.11. In that example, a baseline group is defined that includes the built-in Critical Host Patches and Non-Critical Host Patches baselines. By attaching this baseline group to your ESX/ESXi hosts, you would be able to ensure that your hosts had all available patches installed.

FIGURE 4.11
Combining multiple dynamic baselines into a baseline group provides greater flexibility in managing patches.

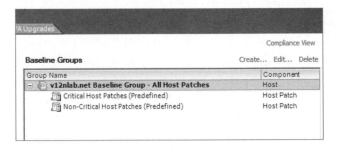

You can also use baseline groups to combine different types of baselines. Each baseline group can include one of each type of upgrade baseline. For a host baseline group, there is only one type of upgrade baseline — a host upgrade. For VM/VA upgrade baselines, there are multiple types: VA Upgrades, VM Hardware Upgrades, and VM Tools Upgrades. When you are working with a host baseline group, you also have the option of adding a host extension baseline into the baseline group. This ability to combine different types of baselines together into a baseline group simplifies the application of multiple baselines to objects in your vCenter Server hierarchy.

Another use for baseline groups would be to combine a dynamic patch policy and a fixed patch policy into a baseline group. For example, there might be a specific fix for your ESX/ESXi hosts, and you want to ensure that all your hosts have all the critical patches — easily handled by the built-in Critical Host Patches dynamic baseline — as well as the specific fix. To do this, create a fixed baseline for the specific patch you want included, and then combine it in a baseline group with the built-in Critical Host Patches dynamic baseline.

Figure 4.12 shows an example of a host baseline group that combines different types of host baselines. In this example, a baseline group is used to combine a host upgrade baseline and dynamic patch baselines. This would allow you to upgrade an ESX/ESXi host and then ensure that the host has all the applicable updates for the new version.

FIGURE 4.12
Use baseline groups to combine host upgrade and dynamic host patch baselines.

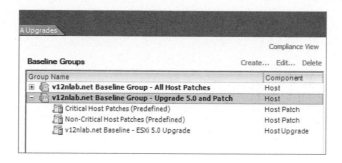

Perform the following steps to create a host baseline group combining multiple host baselines:

1. Launch the vSphere Client if it isn't already running, and connect to the vCenter Server instance with which VUM is registered.

2. Navigate to the Update Manager Administration area, and make sure the Baselines And Groups tab is selected.

3. In the upper-right corner of the Update Manager Administration area, click the Create link to create a new baseline group. This starts the New Baseline Group Wizard.

4. Type in a name for the new baseline group, and select Host Baseline Group as the baseline type. Click Next.

5. Because we haven't yet discussed how to create a host upgrade baseline, you probably don't have an upgrade baseline listed. Instead, for this procedure, you will combine a dynamic and a fixed-host patch baseline. Select None and click Next to skip attaching an upgrade baseline to this host baseline group.

6. Place a check mark next to each individual baseline to include in this baseline group, as shown in Figure 4.13, and click Next.

7. If you want to include a host extension baseline, select the desired host extension baseline and click Next. Otherwise, just click Next to proceed without adding a host extension baseline.

8. On the summary screen, review the settings, and click Finish to create the new baseline group.

The new baseline group you just created is now included in the list of baseline groups, and you can attach it to ESX/ESXi hosts or clusters to identify which of them are not compliant with the baseline.

You'll see more about host upgrade baselines in the section "Upgrading Hosts with vSphere Update Manager."

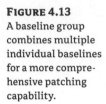

FIGURE 4.13
A baseline group combines multiple individual baselines for a more comprehensive patching capability.

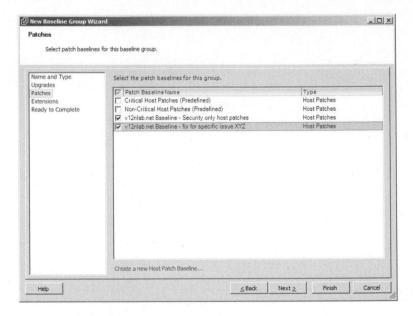

Configuration   The bulk of the configuration of VUM is performed on the Configuration tab. From here, users can configure the full range of VUM settings, including network connectivity, download settings, download schedule, notification check schedule, VM settings, ESX/ESXi host settings, and vApp settings. These are some of the various options that you can configure:

> **Network Connectivity**   Under Network Connectivity, you can change the ports on which VUM communicates. In general, there is no need to change these ports, and you should leave them at the defaults.
>
> **Download Settings**   The Patch Download Settings area allows you to configure what types of patches VUM will download and store. If your environment does not have any ESX 3.x hosts, you can configure VUM not to download these patches by deselecting the sources, as shown in Figure 4.14. You can add custom URLs to download third-party patches.
>
> This is also the area in the settings where you can point to a web server configured on a UMDS instance if you are centralizing your downloads. Setting VUM to use a download server is done with the Use A Shared Repository radio button. You can also import offline patch bundles, distributed as zip files, to add collections of VMware or third-party patches and updates.
>
> The Download Settings area is also where you would set the proxy configuration, if a proxy server is present on your network. VUM needs access to the Internet in order to download the patches and patch metadata, so if a proxy server controls Internet access, you must configure the proxy settings here in order for VUM to work.

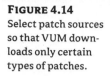

FIGURE 4.14
Select patch sources so that VUM downloads only certain types of patches.

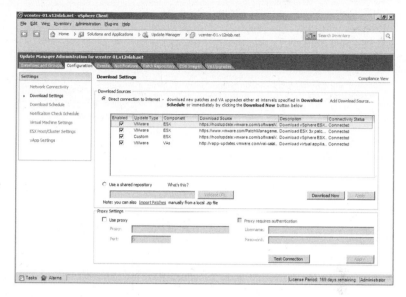

Download Schedule The Download Schedule area allows you to control the timing and frequency of patch downloads. Click the Edit Patch Downloads link in the upper-right corner of this area to open the Schedule Update Download Wizard, which allows you to specify the schedule for patch downloads as well as gives you the opportunity to configure email notifications.

EMAIL NOTIFICATIONS REQUIRE SMTP SERVER CONFIGURATION

To receive any email notifications that you might configure in the Schedule Update Download Wizard, you must also configure the SMTP server in the vCenter Server settings, accessible from the Administration menu of the vSphere Client.

Notification Check Schedule VUM regularly checks for notifications about patch recalls, patch fixes, and other alerts. The schedule for checking for these notifications is configured in this area. As with the Patch Download Schedule, you can click the Edit Notifications link in the upper-right corner of the window to edit the schedule VUM uses to check for notifications.

VM Settings Under VM Settings, vSphere administrators configure whether to use VM snapshots when applying upgrades to VMs. As you'll see in Chapter 7, "Ensuring High Availability and Business Continuity," snapshots provide the ability to capture a VM's state at a given point and then roll back to that captured state if so desired. Having the ability, via a snapshot, to undo the installation of a driver from a VMware Tools upgrade can be incredibly valuable. Be careful not to keep the snapshot for an unnecessary length of time, because it can affect the VM's performance and, more importantly, can cause storage issues because it can grow and fill your datastore unexpectedly.

Figure 4.15 shows the default settings that enable snapshots.

FIGURE 4.15
By default, VM snapshots are enabled for use with VUM.

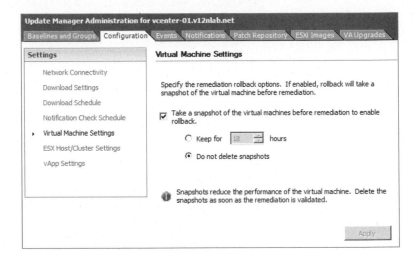

ESX Host/Cluster Settings   The ESX Host/Cluster Settings area provides controls for fine-tuning how VUM handles maintenance mode operations. Before an ESX/ESXi host is patched or upgraded, it is first placed into maintenance mode. When the ESX/ESXi host is part of a cluster that has VMware Distributed Resource Scheduler (DRS) enabled, this will also trigger automatic vMotions of VMs to other hosts in the cluster. These settings allow you to control what happens if a host fails to go into maintenance mode and how many times VUM retries the maintenance mode operation. The default settings specify that VUM will retry three times to place a host in maintenance mode.

You can configure whether VUM will disable certain cluster features in order to perform remediation. Otherwise, VUM may not perform updates on the hosts with these features enabled. The features that VUM can control are Distributed Power Management (DPM), High Availability Admission Control, and Fault Tolerance (FT). You can opt to let the cluster determine if more than one host can be updated at once, while safely maintaining compliance with the rest of the cluster settings. If so, then multiple hosts can be patched or upgraded at once.

Lastly, you can select whether to patch any PXE-booted ESXi 5.x hosts.

PATCHING STATELESS PXE-BOOTED SERVERS

When you patch a PXE-booted server, those changes won't survive the host's next reboot, because it will revert to the network image. You should apply these patches to the image itself for them to remain persistent.

So why apply them to the hosts?

VUM can apply live install patches, which do not require a host reboot. This means that you can quickly apply a patch to a fleet of PXE-booted ESXi hosts without needing to reboot them, or update and test the images, in order to pick up an important patch.

vApp Settings   The vApp Settings allow you to control whether VUM's smart reboot feature is enabled for vApps. vApps are teams, if you will, of VMs. Consider a multitier application that consists of a frontend web server, a middleware server, and a backend database server. These three different VMs and their respective guest OSes could be combined into a vApp. The smart reboot feature simply restarts the different VMs within the vApp in a way that accommodates inter-VM dependencies. For example, if the database server has to be patched and rebooted, then it is quite likely that the web server and the middleware server will also need to be rebooted, and they shouldn't be restarted until after the database server is back up and available again. The default setting is to leverage smart reboot.

Events   The Events tab lists the VUM-specific events logged. As shown in Figure 4.16, the Events tab lists actions taken by administrators as well as automatic actions taken by VUM. Administrators can sort the list of events by clicking the column headers, but there is no functionality to help users filter out only the events they want to see. There is also no way to export events from here.

FIGURE 4.16
The Events tab lists events logged by VUM during operation and can be a good source of information for troubleshooting.

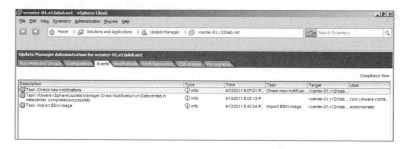

However, you can also find the events listed in the holistic Management ➤ Events area of vCenter Server home page (or via the Ctrl+Shift+E keyboard shortcut), and that area does include some filtering functionality as well as the ability to export the events. The Export Events button, shown in Figure 4.17 in the upper-left corner, allows you to export events to a file.

FIGURE 4.17
Events from VUM Manager are included in the Management area of vCenter Server, where information can be exported or filtered.

The functionality of the Management ➤ Events area of vCenter Server was discussed in detail in Chapter 3.

Notifications   This tab displays any notifications gathered by VUM regarding patch recalls, patch fixes, and other alerts issued by VMware.

For example, if VMware recalled a patch, VUM would mark the patch as recalled. This prevents you from installing the recalled patch. A notification that the patch was recalled would be displayed in the Notifications area. Similarly, if a patch is fixed, VUM would update the new patch and include a notification that the patch has been updated.

Patch Repository   The Patch Repository tab shows all the patches that are currently in VUM's patch repository. From here, you can also view the details of any specific patch by right-clicking the patch and selecting Show Patch Detail or by double-clicking a patch. Figure 4.18 shows the additional information displayed about a patch when you select Show Patch Detail from the context menu (right click).

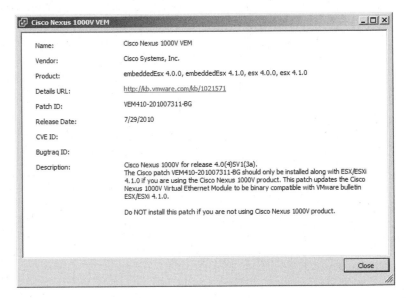

FIGURE 4.18
The Patch Repository tab also offers more detailed information about each of the items in the repository.

This particular item shown in Figure 4.18 is the Virtual Ethernet Module for the Cisco Nexus 1000V, a third-party distributed virtual switch that is discussed in detail in Chapter 5.

The Import Patches link in the upper-right corner of the Patch Repository tab allows you to upload patches directly into the repository. Importing patches here is the same as importing them on the Configuration ➢ Download Settings page.

ESXi Images   This is the area where you will upload ISO files for upgrading ESX/ESXi. These ISO files are the same images used to create the CD installation media for a base ESXi install. You can find more information on this task in the section "Upgrading Hosts With vSphere Update Manager."

VA Upgrades   The VA Upgrades tab lists any suitable virtual appliances upgrades. You can view different versions, see a log of all the changes that have been made since the previous version, and accept any required licensing agreements. For a virtual appliance to be upgradable via VUM, it must have been built with VMware's own free Studio package (at least version 2.0 must have been used).

Having examined the different areas present within VUM, let's now take a look at actually using VUM to patch hosts and VMs.

Routine Updates

VUM uses the term *remediation* to refer to the process of applying patches and upgrades to a vSphere object. As described in the previous section, VUM uses baselines to create lists of patches based on certain criteria. By attaching a baseline to a host or VM and performing a scan, VUM can determine whether that object is compliant or noncompliant with the baseline. Compliance with the baseline means that the host or VM has all the patches included in the baseline currently installed and is up to date; noncompliance means that one or more patches are missing and the target is not up to date.

After compliance with one or more baselines or baseline groups has been determined, the vSphere administrator can remediate — or *patch* — the hosts or VMs. Optionally, the administrator can also stage patches to ESX/ESXi hosts before remediation.

The first step in this process is actually creating the baselines that you will attach to your ESX/ESXi hosts or VMs. How to create a host patch baseline was covered in "Baselines And Groups," so you have already seen this process. The next step is attaching a baseline to — or detaching a baseline from — ESX/ESXi hosts or VMs. Let's take a closer look at how to attach and detach baselines.

Attaching and Detaching Baselines or Baseline Groups

Before you patch a host or guest, you must determine whether an ESX/ESXi host or VM is compliant or noncompliant with one or more baselines or baseline groups. Defining a baseline or baseline group alone is not enough. To determine compliance, the baseline or baseline group must first be attached to a host or VM. After it is attached, the baseline or baseline group becomes the "measuring stick" that VUM uses to determine compliance with the list of patches included in the attached baselines or baseline groups.

Attaching and detaching baselines is performed in one of vCenter Server's Inventory views. To attach or detach a baseline or baseline groups for ESX/ESXi hosts, you need to be in the Hosts And Clusters view; for VMs, you need to be in the VMs And Templates view. In both cases, you'll use the Update Manager tab to attach or detach baselines or baseline groups.

In both views, baselines and baseline groups can be attached to a variety of objects. In the Hosts And Clusters view, baselines and baseline groups can be attached to datacenters, clusters, or individual ESX/ESXi hosts. In the VMs And Templates view, baselines and baseline groups can be attached to datacenters, folders, or specific VMs. Because of the hierarchical nature of the vCenter Server inventory, a baseline attached at a higher level will automatically apply to eligible child objects as well. You may also find yourself applying different baselines or baseline groups at different levels of the hierarchy; for example, there may be a specific baseline that applies to all hosts in the environment but another baseline that applies only to a specific subset of hosts.

Let's look at attaching a baseline to a specific ESX/ESXi host. The process is much the same, if not identical, for attaching a baseline to a datacenter, cluster, folder, or VM.

Perform the following steps to attach a baseline or baseline group to an ESX/ESXi host:

1. Launch the vSphere Client if it is not already running, and connect to a vCenter Server instance.

   This instance of vCenter Server should have an instance of VUM associated with it.

Because VUM is integrated with and depends on vCenter Server, you cannot manage, attach, or detach VUM baselines when connected directly to an ESX/ESXi host.

2. From the menu, select View ➢ Inventory ➢ Hosts And Clusters, or press the Ctrl+Shift+H keyboard shortcut.

3. In the inventory tree on the left, select the ESX/ESXi host to which you want to attach a baseline or baseline group.

4. From the pane on the right, use the double-headed arrows to scroll through the list of tabs until you can see the Update Manager tab, and then select it.

The screen shown in Figure 4.19 shows the Update Manager tab for a specific ESX/ESXi that has no baselines or baseline groups attached.

FIGURE 4.19
The Update Manager tab of an ESX/ESXi host shows what baselines and baseline groups, if any, are currently attached.

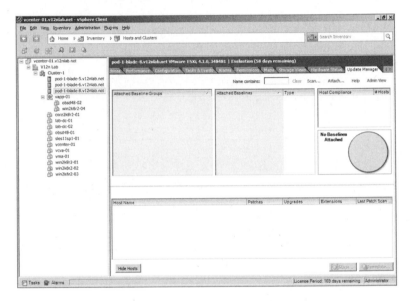

5. Click the Attach link in the upper-right corner; this link opens the Attach Baseline Or Group dialog box.

6. Select the baselines and/or baseline groups that you want to attach to this ESX/ESXi host, and then click Attach.

The steps for attaching a baseline or baseline group to a VM with a guest OS installed are similar, but let's walk through the process anyway. A very useful baseline to point out is named VMware Tools Upgrade To Match Host. This baseline is a default baseline that is defined upon installation of VUM, and its purpose is to help you identify which VMs have guest OSes running outdated versions of the VMware Tools. As you'll see in Chapter 7, the VMware Tools are an important piece of optimizing your guest OSes to run in a virtualized environment, and it's great that VUM can help identify which VMs have guest OSes with an outdated version of the VMware Tools installed.

Perform the following steps to attach a baseline to a datacenter so that it applies to all the objects under the datacenter:

1. Launch the vSphere Client if it is not already running, and connect to a vCenter Server instance. The vCenter Server instance to which you connect should have an instance of VUM associated with it.

2. Switch to the VMs And Templates inventory view by selecting View ➢ Inventory ➢ VMs And Templates, by using the navigation bar, or by using the Ctrl+Shift+V keyboard shortcut.

3. Select a datacenter object from the inventory on the left.

4. From the contents pane on the right, click the Update Manager tab.

5. Right-click a blank area of the list of baselines or baseline groups, and select Attach from the context menu. This opens the Attach Baseline Or Group dialog box.

6. Click to select the VMware Tools Upgrade To Match Host upgrade baseline, and then click Attach.

After you attach this baseline, you'll see the screen change to show that VUM is unsure about whether the systems to which this baseline has been applied are in compliance with the baseline. The screen will look something like Figure 4.20.

FIGURE 4.20
VUM is unsure if the objects to which the baseline has been attached are in compliance with the baseline.

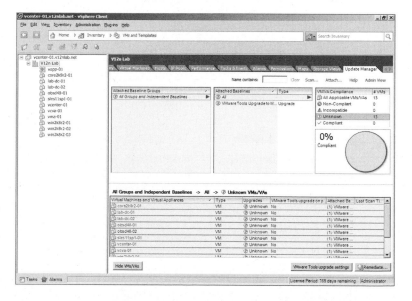

In the event that you need to detach a baseline from an object, you can simply right-click the attached baseline or baseline group while on the Update Manager tab for an object. The only command that is available is the Detach Baseline command, which then takes you to a screen that also allows you to detach the baseline from other objects to which it is attached. Figure 4.21 shows how VUM allows you to detach the selected baseline or baseline group from other objects at the same time (it does not allow you to detach baselines from objects that have inherited the baseline, only those that have been explicitly attached to each child object).

FIGURE 4.21
When detaching a baseline or baseline group, VUM offers the option to detach it from other objects at the same time.

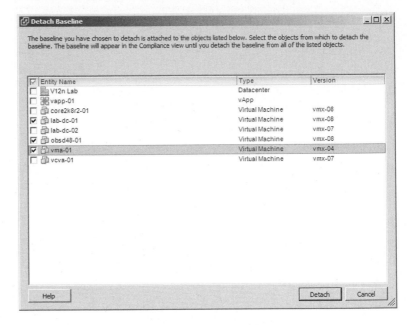

In much the same way as simply defining a baseline or baseline group wasn't enough, simply attaching a baseline or baseline group to an ESX/ESXi host or VM isn't enough to determine compliance or noncompliance. To determine compliance or noncompliance with a baseline or baseline group, you need to perform a scan.

Performing a Scan

The next step after attaching a baseline is to perform a scan. The purpose of a scan is to determine the compliance, or noncompliance, of an object with the baseline. If the object being scanned matches what's defined in the baseline, then the object — be it an ESX/ESXi host, VM, or virtual appliance instance — is compliant. If something is missing from the object, then it's noncompliant.

While the process of scanning these objects within vCenter Server is essentially the same, there are enough differences in the processes and requirements to make it worthwhile examining each one.

SCANNING VMs

You might perform any of three different types of scans against a VM and virtual appliances using VUM:

1. Scan the installed version of VMware Tools to see if it's the latest version.

2. Scan the VM hardware to see if it's the latest version.

3. Scan a virtual appliance to see if a new version is available and if it can be upgraded. The process for actually conducting a scan is identical in all three instances except for the check box that indicates what type of scan you'd like to perform, as shown in Figure 4.22.

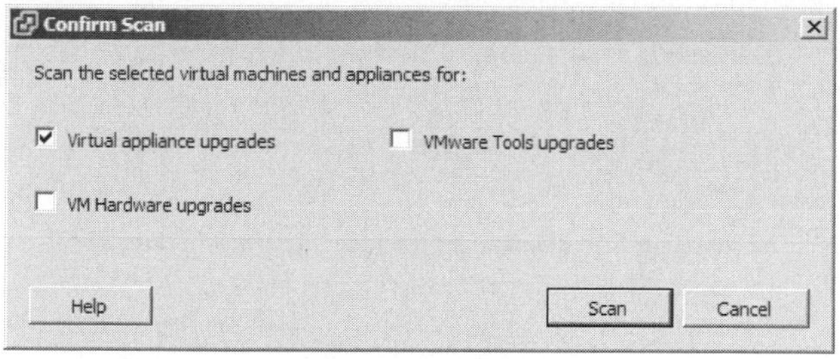

FIGURE 4.22
Different types
of scans are initi-
ated depending on
the check boxes
selected at the start
of the scan.

What differs among these three types of scans are the requirements needed in order to perform a scan:

Scanning for VMware Tools Upgrades   If you scan a VM for VMware Tools upgrades and that VM does not have the VMware Tools installed, the scan will succeed but VUM will report the VM as Incompatible. In order to get a Compliant or Non-compliant report, some version of the VMware Tools needs to already be running within the guest OS installed in the VM. Other than that requirement, VUM has no other restrictions. VUM can scan both online and offline VMs and templates.

Scanning for VM Hardware Upgrades   Scanning for VM hardware upgrades requires that the latest version of the VMware Tools be installed in the VM. This, of course, means that a guest OS is installed in the VM. You can perform VM hardware upgrade scans on both online as well as offline VMs and templates.

Scanning Virtual Appliances   Scanning virtual appliances for virtual appliance upgrades can only be performed on virtual appliances created with VMware Studio 2.0 or later. In addition, because of the nature of virtual appliances as prepackaged installations of a guest OS and applications, it's generally not recommended to scan virtual appliances for VMware Tools upgrades or VM hardware upgrades. Virtual appliances are generally distributed in such a way that if the developer of the virtual appliance wants to update VMware Tools or the VM hardware, he or she will create a new version of the appliance and distribute the entire appliance.

UNMANAGED VMWARE TOOLS

Creators of virtual appliances have the option of installing Operating System Specific Packages (OSP) for VMware Tools. Because installing VMware Tools through the vSphere Client is mutually exclusive to using the OSP VMware Tools, the OSP VMware Tools will report Unmanaged as the status in the vSphere Client. In addition, performing scans of virtual appliances for VMware Tools upgrades will report the virtual appliance as Incompatible. It's not something to be concerned about, because it allows the virtual appliance creators to use the native operating system packaging tools to more effectively manage the driver updates.

SCANNING ESX/ESXi HOSTS

As with VMs, the requirements for being able to scan an ESX/ESXi host vary depending on the type of scan VUM is performing. In all cases, the ESX/ESXi hosts need to be online and reachable via the network from the VUM server.

Scanning for Patches   You can perform a patch scan on hosts running ESX 3.5 or later or ESX 3i version 3.5 or later.

Scanning for Extensions   You can scan for extensions only on hosts running ESX/ESXi 4.0 or later.

Scanning for Host Upgrades   You can scan hosts running ESX 3.5 or later or ESX 3i version 3.5 or later for upgrades. However, 3.5 hosts can only be upgraded to version 4 with VUM, because of a limitation in the default partitioning. Version 4 hosts can be upgraded to ESXi 5.

Now that you have a better idea of the requirements for performing a scan, let's look at the steps involved. Keep in mind that performing a scan on a VM and performing a scan on a virtual appliance are extremely similar processes.

Perform the following steps to initiate a scan of an ESX/ESXi host for patches, extensions, or upgrades after a baseline is attached:

1. Launch the vSphere Client if it is not already running, and connect to a vCenter Server instance that has a VUM instance associated with it.

2. Go to the Hosts And Clusters inventory view by selecting View ➢ Inventory ➢ Hosts And Clusters, by using the navigation bar, or by pressing the Ctrl+Shift+H keyboard shortcut.

3. Select an ESX/ESXi host from the inventory tree on the left.

4. From the content pane on the right, scroll through the list of tabs, and select the Update Manager tab.

5. Click the Scan link in the upper-right corner.

6. Select whether you want to scan for patches and extensions, upgrades, or both, and then click Scan.

When the scan is complete, the Update Manager tab will update to show whether the object is compliant or noncompliant. Compliance is measured on a per-baseline basis. In Figure 4.23, you can see that the selected ESXi host is compliant with both the Critical Host Patches baseline as well as the Non-Critical Host Patches baseline. This means the host is compliant overall. If a host is noncompliant with at least one attached baseline, the host is considered noncompliant.

When you are viewing the Update Manager tab for an object that contains other objects, such as a datacenter, cluster, or folder, then compliance might be mixed. That is, some objects might be compliant, while other objects might be noncompliant. Figure 4.24 shows a cluster with mixed compliance reports. In this particular case, you're looking at a compliance report for VMware Tools upgrades to match the host. The compliance report shows objects that are compliant (VMware Tools are up to date), noncompliant (VMware Tools are outdated), and incompatible (VMware Tools cannot be installed for some reason).

FIGURE 4.23
When multiple baselines are attached to an object, compliance is reflected on a per-baseline basis.

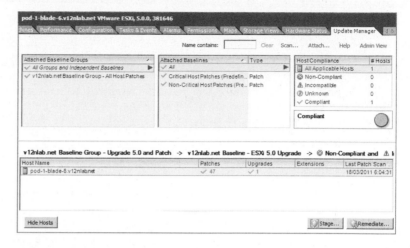

FIGURE 4.24
VUM can show partial compliance when viewing objects that contain other objects.

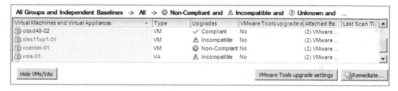

VUM can report an object as Incompatible for a number of reasons. In this particular case, VUM is reporting two objects as Incompatible when scanning for VMware Tools. Taking a closer look at Figure 4.24, you can see that these two objects are a VM named sles11sp1-01 and a virtual appliance named vma-01. The VM is reported as incompatible because this is a fresh VM with no guest OS installed yet, and the vMA is reporting Incompatible because it is a virtual appliance running the OSP VMware Tools, which are not intended to be managed by the vSphere Client.

Depending on the type of scan you are performing, scans can be fairly quick. Scanning a large group of VMs for VMware Tools upgrades or VM hardware upgrades may also be fairly quick. Scanning a large group of hosts for patches, on the other hand might be more time consuming and more resource intensive. Combining several tasks at the same time can also slow down scans, while they run concurrently.

After the scanning is complete and compliance is established, you are ready to fix the noncompliant systems. Before we discuss remediation, let's first look at staging patches to ESX/ESXi hosts.

Staging Patches

If the target of remediation — that is, the object within vCenter Server that you are trying to remediate and make compliant with a baseline — is an ESX/ESXi host, an additional option exists. VUM offers the option of staging patches to ESX/ESXi hosts. Staging a patch to an ESX/ESXi host copies the files across to the host to speed up the actual time of remediation. Staging is not a required step; you can update hosts without staging the updates first, if you prefer. VUM won't stage patches to a PXE-booted ESXi host.

Staging host patches is particularly useful for companies whose VUM-connected hosts are spread across slow WAN links. This can substantially reduce the outage required on such sites, especially if the WAN link is particularly slow or the patches themselves are very large. Hosts do not need to be in maintenance mode while patches are being staged, but do during the remediation phase. Staging patches reduces the maintenance mode period associated with remediation. Staging patches also allows the uploads to be scheduled for a time when heavy WAN utilization is more appropriate, allowing the administrator to remediate the host at a more agreeable time.

Perform the following steps to stage patches to an ESX/ESXi host using VUM:

1. Launch the vSphere Client if it is not already running, and connect to a vCenter Server instance.

2. Navigate to the Hosts And Clusters view by selecting View ➤ Inventory ➤ Hosts And Clusters, by using the Ctrl+Shift+H keyboard shortcut, or using the navigation bar.

3. From the inventory list on the left, select an ESX/ESXi host.

4. From the content pane on the right, scroll through the tabs, and select the Update Manager tab.

5. Click the Stage button in the bottom-right corner of the content pane, or right-click the host and select Stage Patches. Either method activates the Stage Wizard.

6. Select the baselines for the patches you want to be staged, and click Next to proceed.

7. The next screen allows you to deselect any specific patches you do not want to be staged. If you want all the patches to be staged, leave them all selected, and click Next.

8. Click Finish at the summary screen to start the staging process.

After the staging process is complete, the Tasks pane at the bottom of the vSphere Client reflects this, as shown in Figure 4.25.

FIGURE 4.25
The vSphere Client reflects when the process of staging patches is complete.

After you stage patches to the ESX/ESXi hosts, you can begin the task of remediating.

Remediating Hosts

After you have attached a baseline to a host, scanned the host for compliance, and optionally staged the updates to the host, you're ready to remediate, or update, the ESX/ESXi host.

REMEDIATION

The term *remediation* is simply VMware parlance to mean the process of applying patches or upgrades to an object to bring it up to a compliant level.

Perform the following steps to patch an ESX/ESXi host:

1. Launch the vSphere Client if it is not already running, and connect to a vCenter Server instance.

2. Switch to the Hosts And Clusters view by using the navigation bar, by using the Ctrl+Shift+H keyboard shortcut, or by selecting View ➢ Inventory ➢ Hosts And Clusters.

3. Select an ESX/ESXi host from the inventory tree on the left.

4. From the content pane on the right, select the Update Manager tab. You might need to scroll through the available tabs in order to see the Update Manager tab.

5. In the lower-right corner of the window, click the Remediate button. You can also right-click the ESX/ESXi host and select Remediate from the context menu.

6. The Remediate dialog box displays, as shown in Figure 4.26. From here, select the baselines or baseline groups that you want to apply. Click Next.

FIGURE 4.26
The Remediate dialog box allows you to select the baselines or baseline groups against which you would like to remediate an ESX/ESXi host.

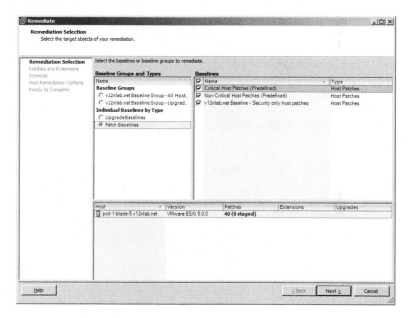

7. Deselect any patches or extensions that you don't want applied to the ESX/ESXi host.

   This allows you to customize the exact list of patches. Click Next after you've deselected any patches to exclude.

8. Specify a name and description for the remediation task. Also, choose whether you want the remediation to occur immediately or whether it should run at a specific time.

   Figure 4.27 shows these options.

FIGURE 4.27
When remediating a host, you need to specify a name for the remediation task and a schedule for the task.

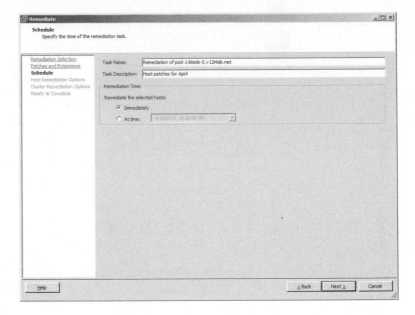

9. The Host Remediation Options page gives you the option to modify the default settings for how VUM should handle a host's VMs if it has to enter maintenance mode. It also lets you patch PXE-booted ESXi hosts but warns you that those changes will be lost on the next power cycle. Figure 4.28 shows the options available during this stage. Make any changes required and click Next.

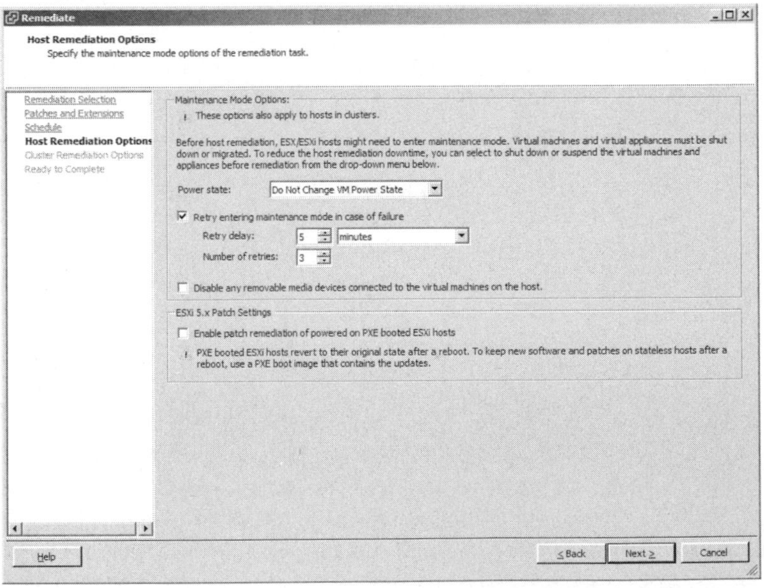

FIGURE 4.28
Host remediation options available if the host has to enter maintenance mode

10. If the host is a member of a cluster, you can choose whether to disable any of the cluster settings for DPM, HA, and FT, if you think they may interfere with the remediation process. VUM version 5 now has the option to remediate several hosts at once if the cluster has sufficient compute resources to meet the other cluster controls. In Figure 4.29 you can see the full gamut of cluster options.

FIGURE 4.29
Cluster options during host remediation

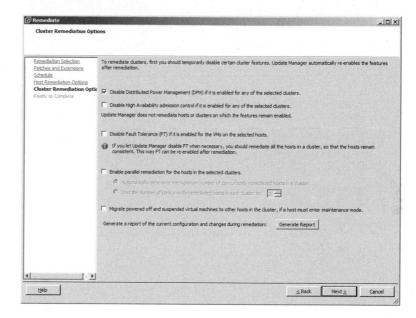

11. Review the summary screen, and click Finish if everything is correct. If there are any errors, use the Back button to double-check and change the settings.

If you selected to have the remediation occur immediately, which is the default setting, VUM initiates a task request with vCenter Server. You'll see this task, as well as some related tasks, in the Tasks pane at the bottom of the vSphere Client.

If necessary, VUM automatically puts the ESX/ESXi host into maintenance mode. If the host is a member of a DRS-enabled cluster, putting the host into maintenance mode will, in turn, initiate a series of vMotion operations to migrate all VMs to other hosts in the cluster. After the patching is complete, VUM automatically reboots the host, if it is required, and then takes the host out of maintenance mode.

KEEPING HOSTS PATCHED IS IMPORTANT

Keeping your ESX/ESXi hosts patched is important. We all know this, but too often VMware administrators forget to incorporate this key task into their operations.

VUM makes keeping your hosts patched much easier, but you still need to actually do it! Be sure to take the time to establish a regular schedule for applying host updates and take advantage of VUM's integration with vMotion, vCenter Server, and VMware Distributed Resource Scheduler (DRS) to avoid downtime for your end users during the patching process.

Upgrading the VMware Tools

VUM can scan and remediate not only ESX/ESXi hosts but also the VMware Tools running inside your VMs. The VMware Tools are an important part of your virtualized infrastructure. The basic idea behind the VMware Tools is to provide a set of virtualization-optimized drivers for all the guest OSes that VMware supports with VMware vSphere. These virtualization-optimized drivers help provide the highest levels of performance for guest OSes running on VMware vSphere, and it's considered a best practice to keep the VMware Tools up to date whenever possible. You can find a more complete and thorough discussion of the VMware Tools in Chapter 7.

To help with that task, VUM comes with a prebuilt upgrade baseline named VMware Tools Upgrade To Match Host. This baseline can't be modified or deleted from within the vSphere Client, and its sole purpose is to help vSphere administrators identify VMs that are not running a version of VMware Tools that is appropriate for the host on which they are currently running.

In general, follow the same order of operations for remediating VMware Tools as you did for ESX/ESXi hosts:

1. Attach the baselines to the VMs you want to scan and remediate.

2. Scan the VMs for compliance with the attached baseline.

3. Remediate the VMware Tools inside the VMs, if they are noncompliant.

The procedure for attaching a baseline was described in the section "Attaching and Detaching Baselines or Baseline Groups" and the process of performing a scan for compliance with a baseline was also described in the section "Performing a Scan."

If you have attached a baseline to a VM and scanned the VMware Tools on that VM for compliance with the baseline, the next step is actually remediating the VMware Tools inside the VM.

Perform the following steps to remediate the VMware Tools:

1. Launch the vSphere Client if it is not already running, and connect to an instance of vCenter Server.

2. Using the menu, navigate to the VMs And Templates area by selecting View ➢ Inventory ➢ VMs And Templates. You can also use the navigation bar or the Ctrl+Shift+V keyboard shortcut.

3. Right-click the VM that you want to remediate, and select Remediate from the context menu. To remediate several VMs, select an object farther up the hierarchy. This displays the Remediate dialog box.

4. In the Remediate dialog box, select the VMware Tools Upgrade To Match Host baseline, and then click Next.

5. Provide a name for the remediation task, and select a schedule for the task. Different schedules are possible for powered-on VMs, powered-off VMs, and suspended VMs, as shown in Figure 4.30.

6. Select an appropriate schedule for each of the different classes of VMs, and then click Next.

7. If you want to take a snapshot of the VM, supply a name for the snapshot and a description.

FIGURE 4.30
VUM supports different schedules for remediating powered-on VMs, powered-off VMs, and suspended VMs.

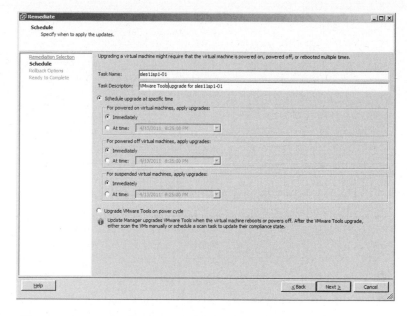

You may also specify a maximum age for the snapshot and whether to snapshot the VM's memory. The default settings, as shown in Figure 4.31, are Do Not Delete Snapshots and Take A Snapshot Of The VMs Before Remediation To Enable Rollback.

FIGURE 4.31
VUM integrates with vCenter Server's snapshot functionality to allow remediation operations to be rolled back in the event of a problem.

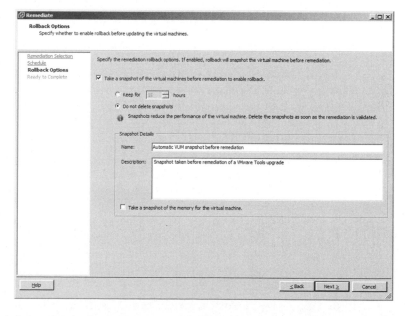

8. Review the information in the summary screen. If anything is incorrect, use the Back button to double-check and change the settings. Otherwise, click Finish to start the remediation.

In general, a reboot of the guest OS is required after the VMware Tools upgrade is complete, although this varies from guest OS to guest OS. Most Windows versions require a reboot, so plan accordingly. Where multiple VMs are joined together in a vApp, VUM and vCenter Server will coordinate restarting the VMs within the vApp to satisfy inter-VM dependencies unless you turned off Smart Reboot in the VUM configuration.

When you are dealing with VMs brought into a VMware vSphere environment from previous versions of VMware Infrastructure, you must be sure to first upgrade VMware Tools to the latest version and then deal with upgrading VM hardware, which is explained after the "Upgrading Hosts with vSphere Update Manager" section. By upgrading the VMware Tools first, you ensure that the appropriate drivers are already loaded into the guest OS when you upgrade the VM hardware.

Upgrading Virtual Appliances and Host Extensions

Once again, you follow the same overall procedure to upgrade virtual appliances and host extensions in VUM as you do with VMware Tools from the previous section:

1. Attach the baseline.

2. Scan for compliance.

3. Remediate.

However, it is worth noting that both virtual appliances and host extensions are less likely to be upgraded quite so routinely. When upgraded they are replaced wholesale, and their settings are migrated across to the new version.

Virtual appliances and host extensions are often provided by third-party hardware or software providers. Each vendor will make their own decisions regarding what changes to functionality are included in these upgrades. For some, you may find that the upgrade includes merely minor bug fixes and no change in the way the appliance or extension works. On the other hand, another upgrade might bring significant changes to how it operates.

For this reason, it is prudent to treat each upgrade to a virtual appliance or host extension as something that needs to be tested thoroughly before running through a wide-scale upgrade.

Now let's look at the last major piece of VUM's functionality: upgrading vSphere hosts.

Upgrading Hosts with vSphere Update Manager

Upgrading vSphere ESXi 5.0 to the newest versions when they become available, and upgrading legacy vSphere 4.x ESX and ESXi hosts to ESXi 5.0, is principally a three-stage process. Although ESX and ESXi are fundamentally very different hypervisors, VUM can seamlessly upgrade either variant to ESXi 5. In fact, while running the Upgrade Wizard, which we'll step through later in this section, if you blink, you won't even spot the difference.

Perform the following steps to upgrade a host server with VUM 5.0:

1. Import an ESXi image and create a host upgrade baseline.

2. Upgrade the host by remediating with the upgrade baseline.

3. Upgrade the VMs' VMware Tools and hardware.

Strictly speaking, the last point is not part of the host upgrade procedure. However, most of the time when you upgrade VMs' hardware, it is immediately following a host upgrade (at least you should be upgrading them at that time!).

Importing an ESXi Image and Creating the Host Upgrade Baseline

Previous versions of vSphere used Update Bundles to upgrade hosts. These offline bundle zip files are still used by vSphere to patch hosts and third-party software but not for host upgrades. In VUM 5.0, all host upgrades use the same image file that is used to install ESXi.

Perform the following steps to import the ISO file into VUM and create the baseline:

1. Launch the vSphere Client if it is not already running, and connect to a vCenter Server instance.

2. Navigate to the Update Manager Administration area by using the navigation bar or by selecting View ➢ Solutions And Applications ➢ Update Manager.

3. Click the ESXi Images tab.

4. Click the blue Import ESXi Image link in the top-right corner of this tab.

5. Use the Browse button, shown in Figure 4.32, to select the new ESXi ISO file. Click Next.

FIGURE 4.32
Select the ESXi image to use for the host upgrade.

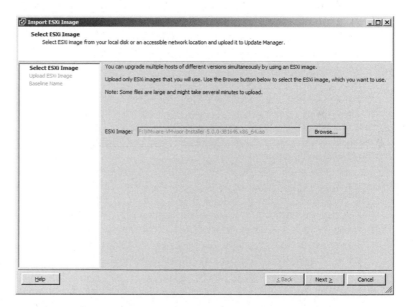

6. Monitor the progress of the file upload, as shown in Figure 4.33; this might take a few minutes to complete. Once the file import is complete, verify the summary information and click Next.

FIGURE 4.33
ESXi image import

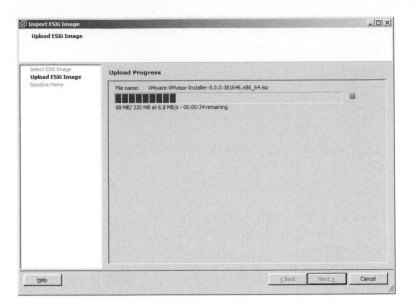

7. Take this opportunity to let the Wizard create a Host Upgrade Baseline for you by leaving the checkbox selected. Give the baseline a name and appropriate description and click Finish. Figure 4.34 shows an image uploaded into the list of imported images. When an image is selected, the lower pane lists all the software packages included in the image and their version number.

FIGURE 4.34
All the packages contained in the imported ESXi image are shown.

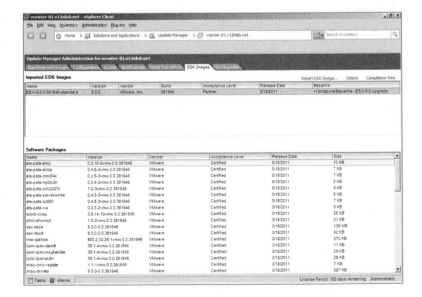

Upgrading a Host

After you've created a host upgrade baseline, you can use this baseline to upgrade an ESX/ESXi host following the same basic sequence of steps outlined previously to remediate other vSphere objects:

1. Attach the baseline to the ESX/ESXi hosts that you want to upgrade. Refer to the previous section "Attaching and Detaching Baselines or Baseline Groups" for a review of how to attach a baseline to an ESX/ESXi host or several hosts.

2. Scan the ESX/ESXi hosts for compliance with the baseline. Don't forget to select to scan for upgrades when presented with the scan options.

3. Remediate the host.

BACK UP YOUR HOST CONFIGURATION AS REQUIRED

Unlike previous host upgrades methods, VUM no longer supports rollbacks after a problematic upgrade. Before you start the upgrade, make sure you have sufficient information about the state of the host to restore or rebuild the host if required.

The Remediate Wizard is similar to the process discussed in the section "Remediating Hosts" (Figure 4.25 through Figure 4.31), but there are enough differences to warrant reviewing the process.

Perform the following steps to upgrade an ESX/ESXi host with a VUM host upgrade baseline:

1. Launch the vSphere Client if it is not already running, and connect to a vCenter Server instance.

2. Switch to the Hosts And Clusters view by using the navigation bar, by using the Ctrl+Shift+H keyboard shortcut, or by selecting View ➢ Inventory ➢ Hosts And Clusters.

3. Select the ESX/ESXi host from the inventory tree on the left.

4. From the content pane on the right, select the Update Manager tab. You might need to scroll through the available tabs in order to see the Update Manager tab.

5. In the lower-right corner of the window, click the Remediate button. You can also right-click the ESX/ESXi host and select Remediate from the context menu.

6. The Remediate dialog box displays, as shown in Figure 4.35. From here, ensure that the Upgrade Baselines is selected in the Groups and Types frame, then choose the baseline that you want to apply. Click Next.

7. Select the check box to accept the license terms, and then click Next.

8. If you are upgrading the hosts from vSphere 4, the next screen gives you the option to explicitly ignore any third-party software on the host that might prevent a host upgrade, as shown in Figure 4.36.

FIGURE 4.35
Select the correct upgrade baseline in the right pane if multiple versions are listed.

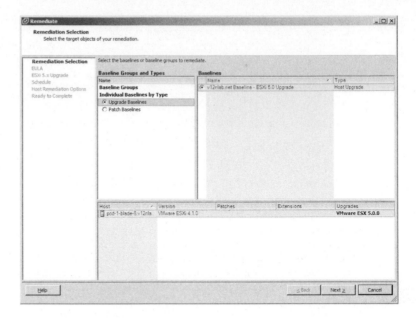

FIGURE 4.36
Upgrades can ignore third-party software on legacy hosts.

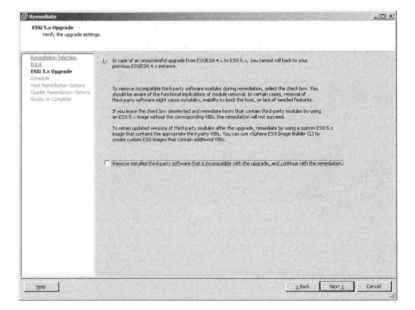

9. Specify a name, description, and a schedule for the remediation task, and then click Next.

10. Choose how the host's VMs should react to the host entering maintenance mode, and click Next.

11. The next page gives you the same cluster options shown in Figure 4.29. You can control how the host's cluster should conform to its own DPM, HA, and FT settings and whether to allow multiple hosts to be upgraded at the same time if the cluster has sufficient resources. Select the options required and click Next.

12. Review the summary, and use the Back button if any settings need to be changed. Click Finish when the settings are correct.

VUM then proceeds with the host upgrade at the scheduled time (Immediately is the default setting in the Wizard). The upgrade will be an unattended upgrade, and at the end of the upgrade the host automatically reboots.

Surprisingly enough, considering the inherent differences between ESX and ESXi, VMware has done a great job of hiding the complex differences during this upgrade procedure. In fact, unless you knew which type of host you had selected to upgrade beforehand, the only way you can tell during the Remediate Wizard is the version of host discreetly listed in the lower pane shown in Figure 4.35.

After upgrading all the hosts in a cluster, you should consider upgrading the VMs' VMware Tools and then their virtual hardware version. Upgrading a VMs´ hardware can prevent that VM from running on older hosts, which is why you should ensure all the hosts in the same cluster are upgraded first. Otherwise, you can restrict the efficiency of fundamental cluster operations such as DRS and HA.

Keeping in mind that you should upgrade the VMs' VMware Tools first, discussed in the section "Upgrading the VMware Tools," let's look at how to upgrade the virtual hardware.

Upgrading VM Hardware

So far, the idea of VM hardware hasn't been discussed but the topic is covered in Chapter 9, "Creating and Managing VMs." For now, suffice it to say that VMs brought into a VMware vSphere environment from previous versions of ESX/ESXi will have outdated VM hardware. By far the most common occurrence of this will be after upgrading a host. In order to use all the latest functionality of VMware vSphere with these VMs, you will have to upgrade the VM hardware. To help with this process, VUM includes the ability to scan for and remediate VMs with out-of-date VM hardware.

VUM already comes with a VM upgrade baseline that addresses this: the VM Hardware Upgrade To Match Host baseline. This baseline is predefined and can't be changed or deleted from within the vSphere Client. The purpose of this baseline is to determine whether a VM's hardware is current. vSphere 5.0 VMs use hardware version 8 by default. Hardware version 7 is the version used by vSphere 4.0 and 4.1, and ESX/ESXi 3 used VM hardware version 4.

To upgrade the virtual VM version, you again follow the same general sequence:

1. Attach the baseline.

2. Perform a scan.

3. Remediate.

To attach the baseline, follow the same procedures outlined in the section "Attaching and Detaching Baselines or Baseline Groups." Performing a scan is much the same as well; be sure you select the VM Hardware upgrades option when initiating a scan in order for VUM to detect outdated VM hardware. Even if the correct baseline is attached, outdated VM hardware won't be detected during a scan unless you select this box.

PLANNING FOR DOWNTIME

Remediation of VMs found to be noncompliant — for example, found to have outdated VM hardware — is again much like the other forms of remediation that have already been discussed. The important thing to note is that VM hardware upgrades are done while the VM is powered off. This means you must plan for downtime in the environment in order to remediate this issue.

VUM performs VM hardware upgrades only when the VM is powered off. It's also important to note that VUM might not be able to conduct an orderly shutdown of the guest OS in order to do the VM hardware upgrade. To avoid an unexpected shutdown of the guest OS when VUM powers off the VM, specify a schedule in the dialog box shown previously in Figure 4.30 that provides you with enough time to perform an orderly shutdown of the guest OS first.

Depending on which guest OS and which version are running inside the VM, the user may see prompts for "new hardware" after the VM hardware upgrade is complete. If you've followed the recommendations and the latest version of the VMware Tools is installed, then all the necessary drivers should already be present, and the "new hardware" should work without any real issues.

 Real World Scenario

KEEP A RECORD OF YOUR VM'S IP ADDRESSES

The most common problem faced with upgrading VM Hardware is losing the VM's IP address. This occurs if VMware Tools has not been upgraded properly before starting the Hardware upgrade process. Normally the new VMware Tools can record the VM's IP settings, and if a new VM Hardware upgrade changes the network card's driver, the Tools can migrate the IP settings across automatically. However, the VMware Tools can drop the settings for several reasons, such as not realizing there was an issue with the Tools before proceeding further, not allowing for enough reboots after the Tools upgrade, OS issues caused by the new drivers, and so forth.

While this shouldn't happen, it is seen often enough that a quick plan B is in order. One simple approach, prior to initiating the remediation step, is to list all the VMs to be upgraded in the VMs And Templates view. Right-click one of the columns, and add the IP address to the view. Then from the File menu, select Export List To A Spreadsheet. This way, should one or more VMs lose their IP settings in the upgrade, you have a quick reference you can pull up. It's not foolproof, but this 30-second action might just save you some time trawling through DNS records if things go awry.

Although you might find virtual appliances with old versions of virtual hardware, it's advisable to treat these as special cases and wait for the software vendors to include the hardware upgrade in the next version. Virtual appliances are custom built and tuned by the vendors for their purpose. They are often released with older hardware so they are compatible with as many versions of vSphere as possible. If a new version of VM hardware is available that the vendor thinks would benefit their appliance, it's likely that they will provide a new version of their appliance to take advantage of it.

You can find more information on VM hardware and VM hardware versions in Chapter 7.

By combining some of the different features of VUM, you can greatly simplify the process of upgrading your virtualized infrastructure to the latest version of VMware vSphere through an orchestrated upgrade.

Performing an Orchestrated Upgrade

A specific use case for baseline groups is the *orchestrated upgrade*. An orchestrated upgrade involves the use of a host baseline group and a VM/VA baseline group that, when run sequentially, will help automate the process of moving an organization's environment fully into VMware vSphere 5. Quite simply, it upgrades your hosts and then your VMs in one job.

Consider this sequence of events:

1. You create a host baseline group that combines a host upgrade baseline with a dynamic host patch baseline to apply the latest updates.

2. You create a VM baseline group that combines two different VM upgrade baselines — the VMware Tools upgrade baseline and the VM hardware upgrade baseline.

3. You schedule the host baseline group to execute, followed at some point by the VM baseline group.

4. The host baseline group upgrades the hosts from ESX/ESXi 4.*x* to ESXi 5.0 and installs all applicable patches and updates.

5. The VM baseline group upgrades the VMware Tools and then upgrades the VM hardware to version 8.

When these two baseline groups have completed, all the hosts and VMs affected by the baselines will be upgraded and patched. Most, if not all, of the tedious tasks surrounding upgrading the VMware Tools and the VM hardware have been automated. Congratulations! You've just simplified and automated the upgrade path for your virtual environment.

Investigating Alternative Update Options

In most circumstances, using the VUM tools in the vSphere Client is the easiest and most efficient method of keeping your hosts, VMs, and virtual appliances patched and at the latest, greatest level. However, there are sometimes circumstances where you want to look beyond the standard tools and investigate the alternatives. As you'll learn, vSphere can be updated in several other ways.

Using vSphere Update Manager PowerCLI

vSphere takes advantage of Microsoft's PowerShell scripting environment with the PowerCLI extensions that are discussed in Chapter 14, "Automating VMware vSphere."

Without getting ahead of ourselves, it's worth noting the PowerCLI tools that are available to script many of VUM's functions. The VUM PowerCLI cmdlets cover the most common tasks like working with baselines, scanning, staging, and remediating vSphere objects. Figure 4.37 shows the list of cmdlets currently available.

To use the VUM PowerCLI, you need to first install the vSphere PowerCLI and then download and install the Update Manager PowerCLI package. More information on the use of this package can be garnered from VMware's own "VMware vSphere Update Manager PowerCLI Installation and Administration Guide" for VUM 5.0.

FIGURE 4.37
VUM PowerCLI
cmdlets available

Upgrading and Patching without vSphere Update Manager

You can maintain your vSphere environment, keeping the elements patched and upgraded, without resorting to the use of VUM. Also, you may want to use VUM for certain updating tasks but take an alternative approach for others. For example, you might not want to use VUM in the following situations:

◆ You are using the free stand-alone vSphere ESXi hypervisor, which does not come with vCenter. Without a licensed vCenter, you can't use VUM.

◆ You have only a small environment with one or two small host servers. To maximize the use of your server hardware for VMs, you don't want the infrastructure overhead of another application and another database running.

◆ You rely heavily on scripting to manage your environment, and you would like to take advantage of tools that don't need PowerShell, such as the PowerCLI toolset that VMware offers.

◆ You don't want to use VUM for host upgrades, because you choose to always run fresh host rebuilds when required.

◆ You already have kick-start scripts, PowerShell post-install scripts, Host Profiles, EDA/ UDA tools, or you want to set up an AutoDeploy server to control the installation and upgrading of your hosts.

So, what alternatives are available?

Upgrading and Patching Hosts   To upgrade your legacy 4.0 ESX or ESXi hosts to vSphere 5.0, you have two non-VUM options. You can run through an interactive install from the ESXi 5.0 CD media, choosing an in-place upgrade. Or you can run a kick-start scripted upgrade along with the same ESXi 5.0 media, to perform an unattended upgrade. No command-line utility can upgrade an older ESX or ESXi host to 5.0.

For upgrades from ESXi 5.0 to newer versions, you can likewise use an interactive or unattended upgrade. If you have used VMware's AutoDeploy technology to rollout vSphere 5.0, then you will be able to leverage this tool to upgrade or patch it to the latest updates. ESXi 5.0 hosts can also be patched and upgraded with the vCLI command-line `esxcli` tool.

The `esxupdate` and `vihostupdate` tools are no longer supported for ESXi 5.0 updates.

Upgrading VMs   Without VUM, upgrading VM hardware can only be done via the vSphere Client. If the hosts are connected to a vCenter, then your connected client can manually upgrade the hardware. You must shut down the VMs yourself and initialize each upgrade. Even without vCenter you can still upgrade each VM by connecting your client straight at the host. Similarly, the VMware Tools can be upgraded in each guest OS manually from within the VM's console. You must mount the VMware Tools from your vSphere Client.

The `vmware-vmupgrade.exe` tool should not be used to upgrade VMs anymore.

Now you're ready to start taking advantage of the new networking functionality available in VMware vSphere in Chapter 5.

The Bottom Line

Install VUM and integrate it with the vSphere Client.   vSphere Update Manager (VUM) is installed from the VMware vCenter installation media and requires that vCenter Server has already been installed. Like vCenter Server, VUM requires the use of a backend database server. Finally, you must install a plug-in into the vSphere Client in order to access, manage, or configure VUM.

Master It   You have VUM installed, and you've configured it from the vSphere Client on your laptop. One of the other administrators on your team is saying that she can't access or configure VUM and that there must be something wrong with the installation. What is the most likely cause of the problem?

Determine which ESX/ESXi hosts or VMs need to be patched or upgraded.   Baselines are the "measuring sticks" whereby VUM knows whether an ESX/ESXi host or VM instance is up to date. VUM compares the ESX/ESXi hosts or guest OSes to the baselines to determine whether they need to be patched and, if so, what patches need to be applied. VUM also uses baselines to determine which ESX/ESXi hosts need to be upgraded to the latest version or which VMs need to have their VM hardware upgraded. VUM comes with some predefined baselines and allows administrators to create additional baselines specific to their environments. Baselines can be fixed — the contents remain constant — or they can be dynamic, where the contents of the baseline change over time. Baseline groups allow administrators to combine baselines and apply them together.

Master It In addition to ensuring that all your ESX/ESXi hosts have the latest critical and security patches installed, you also need to ensure that all your ESX/ESXi hosts have another specific patch installed. This additional patch is noncritical and therefore doesn't get included in the critical patch dynamic baseline. How do you work around this problem?

Use VUM to upgrade VM hardware or VMware Tools. VUM can detect VMs with outdated VM hardware versions and guest OSes that have outdated versions of the VMware Tools installed. VUM comes with predefined baselines that enable this functionality. In addition, VUM has the ability to upgrade VM hardware versions and upgrade the VMware Tools inside guest OSes to ensure that everything is kept up to date. This functionality is especially helpful after upgrading your ESX/ESXi hosts to version 5.0 from a previous version.

Master It You've just finished upgrading your virtual infrastructure to VMware vSphere. What two additional tasks should you complete?

Apply patches to ESX/ESXi hosts. Like other complex software products, VMware ESX and VMware ESXi need software patches applied from time to time. These patches might be bug fixes or security fixes. To keep your ESX/ESXi hosts up to date with the latest patches, VUM can apply patches to your hosts on a schedule of your choosing. In addition, to reduce downtime during the patching process or perhaps to simplify the deployment of patches to remote offices, VUM can also stage patches to ESX/ESXi hosts before the patches are applied.

Master It How can you avoid VM downtime when applying patches (for example, remediating) to your ESX/ESXi hosts?

Apply patches to Windows guests. VUM can check the compliance status of your ESXi hosts and your legacy ESX/ESXi hosts, your VM hardware, VMware Tools, and certified virtual appliances. To ensure your software stack has all the available software patches and security fixes applied, you also need to consider the state of the guest OSes and applications running within the VMs.

Master It You are having a discussion with another VMware vSphere administrator about keeping hosts and guests updated. The other administrator insists that you can use VUM to keep guest OSes updated as well. Is this accurate?

Chapter 5

Creating and Configuring Virtual Networks

Eventually, it all comes back to the network. Having servers running VMware ESXi with VMs stored on a highly redundant Fibre Channel SAN is great, but they are ultimately useless if the VMs cannot communicate across the network. What good is the ability to run 10 production systems on a single host at less cost if those production systems aren't available? Clearly, virtual networking within ESXi is a key area for every vSphere administrator to understand fully.

In this chapter, you will learn to

◆ Identify the components of virtual networking

◆ Create virtual switches (vSwitches) and distributed virtual switches (dvSwitches)

◆ Install and perform the basic configuration of the Cisco Nexus 1000V

◆ Create and manage NIC teaming, VLANs, and private VLANs

◆ Configure virtual switch security policies

Putting Together a Virtual Network

Designing and building virtual networks with ESXi and vCenter Server bears some similarities to designing and building physical networks, but there are enough significant differences that an overview of components and terminology is warranted. So, I'll take a moment here to define the various components involved in a virtual network, and then I'll discuss some of the factors that affect the design of a virtual network:

vSphere Standard Switch   A software-based switch that resides in the VMkernel and provides traffic management for VMs. Users must manage vSwitches independently on each ESXi host.

vSphere Distributed Switch   A software-based switch that resides in the VMkernel and provides traffic management for VMs and the VMkernel. Distributed vSwitches are shared by and managed across entire clusters of ESXi hosts. You might see vSphere Distributed Switch abbreviated as vDS; I'll use the term *dvSwitch* throughout this book.

Port/port Group   A logical object on a vSwitch that provides specialized services for the VMkernel or VMs. A virtual switch can contain a VMkernel port or a VM port group. On a vSphere Distributed Switch, these are called *dvPort groups*.

VMkernel Port   A specialized virtual switch port type that is configured with an IP address to allow vMotion, iSCSI storage access, network attached storage (NAS) or Network File System (NFS) access, or vSphere Fault Tolerance (FT) logging. Now that vSphere 5 includes only VMware ESXi hosts, a VMkernel port also provides management connectivity for managing the host. A VMkernel port is also referred to as a *vmknic*.

NO MORE SERVICE CONSOLE PORTS

Because vSphere 5 does not include VMware ESX with a traditional Linux-based Service Console, pure vSphere 5 environments will not use a Service Console port (or *vswif*). In ESXi, a VMkernel port that is enabled for management traffic replaces the Service Console port. Note that vSphere 5 does support ESX 4.*x*, though, and ESX 4.*x* would use a Service Console port. Because this book primarily focuses on vSphere 5, I don't provide any information on Service Console ports or how to create them.

VM Port Group   A group of virtual switch ports that share a common configuration and allow VMs to access other VMs or the physical network.

Virtual LAN   A logical LAN configured on a virtual or physical switch that provides efficient traffic segmentation, broadcast control, security, and efficient bandwidth utilization by providing traffic only to the ports configured for that particular virtual LAN (VLAN).

Trunk Port (Trunking)   A port on a physical switch that listens for and knows how to pass traffic for multiple VLANs. It does this by maintaining the VLAN tags for traffic moving through the trunk port to the connected device(s). Trunk ports are typically used for switch-to-switch connections to allow VLANs to pass freely between switches. Virtual switches support VLANs, and using VLAN trunks allows the VLANs to pass freely into the virtual switches.

Access Port   A port on a physical switch that passes traffic for only a single VLAN. Unlike a trunk port, which maintains the VLAN identification for traffic moving through the port, an access port strips away the VLAN information for traffic moving through the port.

Network Interface Card Team   The aggregation of physical network interface cards (NICs) to form a single logical communication channel. Different types of NIC teams provide varying levels of traffic load balancing and fault tolerance.

vmxnet Adapter   A virtualized network adapter operating inside a guest operating system (guest OS). The vmxnet adapter is a high-performance, 1 Gbps virtual network adapter that operates only if the VMware Tools have been installed. The vmxnet adapter is sometimes referred to as a *paravirtualized* driver. The vmxnet adapter is identified as Flexible in the VM properties.

vlance Adapter   A virtualized network adapter operating inside a guest OS. The vlance adapter is a 10/100 Mbps network adapter that is widely compatible with a range of operating systems and is the default adapter used until the VMware Tools installation is completed.

e1000 Adapter   A virtualized network adapter that emulates the Intel e1000 network adapter. The Intel e1000 is a 1 Gbps network adapter. The e1000 network adapter is the most common in 64-bit VMs.

Now that you have a better understanding of the components involved and the terminology that you'll see in this chapter, I'll discuss how these components work together to form a virtual network in support of VMs and ESXi hosts.

Your answers to the following questions will, in large part, determine the design of your virtual networking:

- Do you have or need a dedicated network for management traffic, such as for the management of physical switches?

- Do you have or need a dedicated network for vMotion traffic?

- Do you have an IP storage network? Is this IP storage network a dedicated network? Are you running iSCSI or NAS/NFS?

- How many NICs are standard in your ESXi host design?

- Do the NICs in your hosts run 1 Gb Ethernet or 10 Gb Ethernet?

- Is there a need for extremely high levels of fault tolerance for VMs?

- Is the existing physical network composed of VLANs?

- Do you want to extend the use of VLANs into the virtual switches?

As a precursor to setting up a virtual networking architecture, you need to identify and document the physical network components and the security needs of the network. It's also important to understand the architecture of the existing physical network, because that also greatly influences the design of the virtual network. If the physical network can't support the use of VLANs, for example, then the virtual network's design has to account for that limitation.

Throughout this chapter, as I discuss the various components of a virtual network in more detail, I'll also provide guidance on how the various components fit into an overall virtual network design. A successful virtual network combines the physical network, NICs, and vSwitches, as shown in Figure 5.1.

Because the virtual network implementation makes VMs accessible, it is essential that the virtual network be configured in a manner that supports reliable and efficient communication around the different network infrastructure components.

FIGURE 5.1
Successful virtual
networking is a
blend of virtual and
physical
network adapters
and switches.

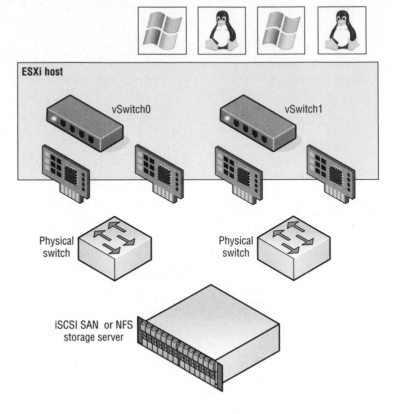

Working with vSphere Standard Switches

The networking architecture of ESXi revolves around the creation and configuration of virtual switches (vSwitches). These virtual switches are either vSphere Standard Switches or vSphere Distributed Switches. In this section, I'll discuss vSphere Standard Switches, hereafter called vSwitches; I'll discuss vSphere Distributed Switches in the next section.

You create and manage vSwitches through the vSphere Client or through the vSphere CLI using the `vicfg-vswitch` command, but they operate within the VMkernel. Virtual switches provide the connectivity to provide communication

- ◆ Between VMs within an ESXi host
- ◆ Between VMs on different ESXi hosts
- ◆ Between VMs and physical machines on the network
- ◆ For VMkernel access to networks for vMotion, iSCSI, NFS, or fault tolerance logging (and management on ESXi)

Take a look at Figure 5.2, which shows the vSphere Client depicting a virtual switch on a host running ESXi 5.

FIGURE 5.2
Virtual switches alone can't provide connectivity; they need ports or port groups and uplinks.

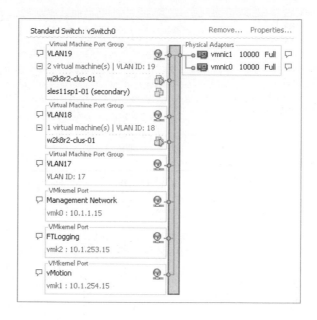

In this figure, the vSwitch isn't depicted alone; it also requires ports or port groups and uplinks. Without uplinks, a virtual switch can't communicate with the rest of the network; without ports or port groups, a vSwitch can't provide connectivity for the VMkernel or the VMs. It is for this reason that most of our discussion about virtual switches centers on ports, port groups, and uplinks.

First, though, let's take a closer look at vSwitches and how they are both similar to, yet different from, physical switches in the network.

Comparing Virtual Switches and Physical Switches

Virtual switches in ESXi are constructed by and operate in the VMkernel. Virtual switches, or vSwitches, are not managed switches and do not provide all the advanced features that many new physical switches provide. You cannot, for example, telnet into a vSwitch to modify settings. There is no command-line interface (CLI) for a vSwitch, apart from the vSphere CLI commands such as `vicfg-vswitch`. Even so, a vSwitch operates like a physical switch in some ways. Like its physical counterpart, a vSwitch functions at Layer 2, maintains MAC address tables, forwards frames to other switch ports based on the MAC address, supports VLAN configurations, is capable of trunking by using IEEE 802.1q VLAN tags, and is capable of establishing port channels. Similar to physical switches, vSwitches are configured with a specific number of ports.

Despite these similarities, vSwitches do have some differences from physical switches. A vSwitch does not support the use of dynamic negotiation protocols for establishing 802.1q trunks or port channels, such as Dynamic Trunking Protocol (DTP) or Port Aggregation Protocol (PAgP). A vSwitch cannot be connected to another vSwitch, thereby eliminating a potential loop configuration. Because there is no possibility of looping, the vSwitches do not run Spanning Tree Protocol (STP). Looping can be a common network problem, so this is a real benefit of vSwitches.

CREATING AND CONFIGURING VIRTUAL SWITCHES

By default, every virtual switch is created with 128 ports. However, only 120 of the ports are available, and only 120 are displayed when looking at a vSwitch configuration through the vSphere Client. Reviewing a vSwitch configuration via the vicfg-vswitch command shows the entire 128 ports. The 8-port difference is attributed to the fact that the VMkernel reserves 8 ports for its own use.

After a virtual switch is created, you can adjust the number of ports to 8, 24, 56, 120, 248, 504, 1016, 2040, or 4088. These are the values that are reflected in the vSphere Client. But, as noted, there are 8 ports reserved, and therefore the command line will show 16, 32, 64, 128, 256, 512, 1024, 2048, and 4096 ports for virtual switches.

Changing the number of ports in a virtual switch requires a reboot of the ESXi host on which the vSwitch was altered.

SPANNING TREE PROTOCOL

In physical switches, Spanning Tree Protocol (STP) offers redundancy for paths and prevents loops in the network topology by locking redundant paths in a standby state. Only when a path is no longer available will STP activate the standby path.

It is possible to link vSwitches together using a VM with Layer 2 bridging software and multiple virtual NICs, but this is not an accidental configuration and would require some effort to establish.

Some other differences of vSwitches from physical switches include the following:

◆ A vSwitch authoritatively knows the MAC addresses of the VMs connected to that vSwitch, so there is no need to learn MAC addresses from the network.

◆ Traffic received by a vSwitch on one uplink is never forwarded out another uplink. This is yet another reason why vSwitches do not run STP.

◆ A vSwitch does not need to perform Internet Group Management Protocol (IGMP) snooping because it knows the multicast interests of the VMs attached to that vSwitch.

As you can see from this list of differences, you simply can't use virtual switches in the same way you can use physical switches. You can't use a virtual switch as a transit path between two physical switches, for example, because traffic received on one uplink won't be forwarded out another uplink.

With this basic understanding of how vSwitches work, let's now take a closer look at ports and port groups.

Understanding Ports and Port Groups

As described previously in this chapter, a vSwitch allows several different types of communication, including communication to and from the VMkernel and between VMs. To help distinguish between these different types of communication, ESXi uses ports and port groups. A vSwitch without any ports or port groups is like a physical switch that has no physical ports; there is no way to connect anything to the switch, and it is, therefore, useless.

Port groups differentiate between the types of traffic passing through a vSwitch, and they also operate as a boundary for communication and/or security policy configuration. Figure 5.3 and Figure 5.4 show the two different types of ports and port groups that you can configure on a vSwitch:

◆ VMkernel port

◆ VM port group

FIGURE 5.3
Virtual switches can contain two connection types: VMkernel port and VM port group.

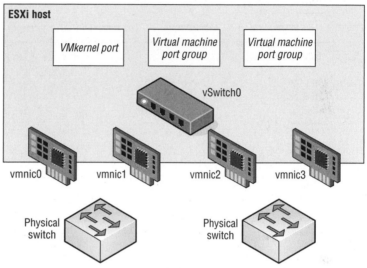

FIGURE 5.4
You can create virtual switches with both connection types on the same switch.

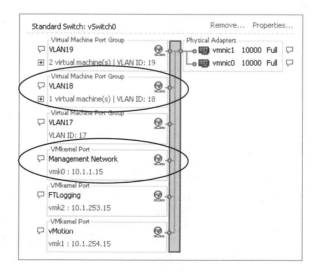

Because a vSwitch cannot be used in any way without at least one port or port group, you'll see that the vSphere Client combines the creation of new vSwitches with the creation of new ports or port groups.

As shown in Figure 5.2, though, ports and port groups are only part of the overall solution. The uplinks are the other part of the solution that you need to consider because they provide external network connectivity to the vSwitches.

Understanding Uplinks

Although a vSwitch provides for communication between VMs connected to the vSwitch, it cannot communicate with the physical network without uplinks. Just as a physical switch must be connected to other switches in order to provide communication across the network, vSwitches must be connected to the ESXi host's physical NICs as uplinks in order to communicate with the rest of the network.

Unlike ports and port groups, uplinks aren't necessarily required in order for a vSwitch to function. Physical systems connected to an isolated physical switch that has no uplinks to other physical switches in the network can still communicate with each other — just not with any other systems that are not connected to the same isolated switch. Similarly, VMs connected to a vSwitch without any uplinks can communicate with each other but cannot communicate with VMs on other vSwitches or physical systems.

This sort of configuration is known as an *internal-only* vSwitch. It can be useful to allow VMs to communicate with each other but not with any other systems. VMs that communicate through an internal-only vSwitch do not pass any traffic through a physical adapter on the ESXi host. As shown in Figure 5.5, communication between VMs connected to an internal-only vSwitch takes place entirely in the software and happens at whatever speed the VMkernel can perform the task.

FIGURE 5.5
VMs communicating through an internal-only vSwitch do not pass any traffic through a physical adapter.

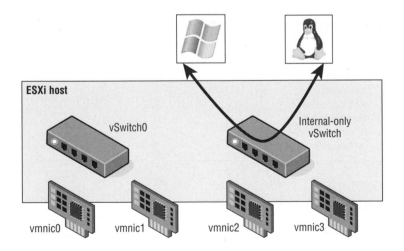

> **NO UPLINK, NO VMOTION**
>
> VMs connected to an internal-only vSwitch are not vMotion capable. However, if the VM is discon-nected from the internal-only vSwitch, a warning will be provided, but vMotion will succeed if all other requirements have been met. The requirements for vMotion are covered in Chapter 12, "Balancing Resource Utilization."

For VMs to communicate with resources beyond the VMs hosted on the local ESXi host, a vSwitch must be configured to use at least one physical network adapter, or uplink. A vSwitch can be bound to a single network adapter or bound to two or more network adapters.

A vSwitch bound to at least one physical network adapter allows VMs to establish communi-cation with physical servers on the network or with VMs on other ESXi hosts. That's assuming, of course, that the VMs on the other ESXi hosts are connected to a vSwitch that is bound to at least one physical network adapter. Just like a physical network, a virtual network requires con-nectivity from end to end. Figure 5.6 shows the communication path for VMs connected to a vSwitch bound to a physical network adapter. In the diagram, when vm1 on pod-1-blade-5 needs to communicate with vm2 on pod-1-blade-8, the traffic from the VM passes through vSwitch0 (via a VM port group) to the physical network adapter to which the vSwitch is bound. From the physical network adapter, the traffic will reach the physical switch (PhySw1). The physical switch (PhySw1) passes the traffic to the second physical switch (PhySw2), which will pass the traffic through the physical network adapter associated with the vSwitch on pod-1-blade-8. In the last stage of the communication, the vSwitch will pass the traffic to the destination virtual machine vm2.

FIGURE 5.6
A vSwitch with a single network adapter allows VMs to communicate with physical servers and other VMs on the network.

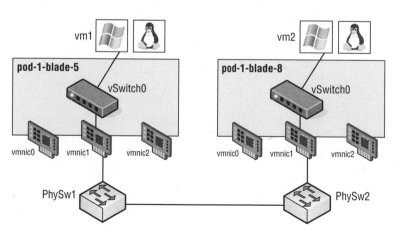

The vSwitch associated with a physical network adapter provides VMs with the amount of bandwidth the physical adapter is configured to support. All the VMs will share this band-width when communicating with physical machines or VMs on other ESXi hosts. In this way, a vSwitch is once again similar to a physical switch. For example, a vSwitch bound to a network adapter with a 1 Gbps maximum speed will provide up to 1 Gbps of bandwidth for the VMs connected to it; similarly, a physical switch with a 1 Gbps uplink to another physical switch provides up to 1 Gbps of bandwidth between the two switches for systems attached to the physical switches.

A vSwitch can also be bound to multiple physical network adapters. In this configuration, the vSwitch is sometimes referred to as a *NIC team*, but in this book I'll use the term *NIC team* or *NIC teaming* to refer specifically to the grouping of network connections together, not to refer to a vSwitch with multiple uplinks.

UPLINK LIMITS

Although a single vSwitch can be associated with multiple physical adapters as in a NIC team, a single physical adapter cannot be associated with multiple vSwitches. ESXi hosts can have up to 32 e1000 network adapters, 32 Broadcom TG3 Gigabit Ethernet network ports, or 16 Broadcom BNX2 Gigabit Ethernet network ports. ESXi hosts support up to eight 10 Gigabit Ethernet adapters.

Figure 5.7 and Figure 5.8 show a vSwitch bound to multiple physical network adapters. A vSwitch can have a maximum of 32 uplinks. In other words, a single vSwitch can use up to 32 physical network adapters to send and receive traffic from the physical switches. Binding multiple physical NICs to a vSwitch offers the advantage of redundancy and load distribution. In the section "Configuring NIC Teaming," you'll dig deeper into the configuration and workings of this sort of vSwitch configuration.

FIGURE 5.7
A vSwitch using NIC teaming has multiple available adapters for data transfer. NIC teaming offers redundancy and load distribution.

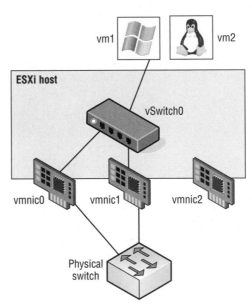

FIGURE 5.8
Virtual switches using NIC teaming are identified by the multiple physical network adapters assigned to the vSwitch.

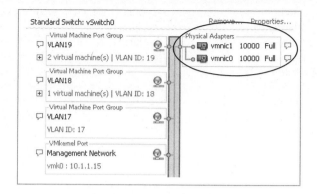

So, we've examined vSwitches, ports and port groups, and uplinks, and you should have a basic understanding of how these pieces begin to fit together to build a virtual network. The next step is to delve deeper into the configuration of the various types of ports and port groups, because they are so essential to virtual networking. I'll start with a discussion on management networking.

Configuring Management Networking

Management traffic is a special type of network traffic that runs across a *VMkernel port*. VMkernel ports provide network access for the VMkernel's TCP/IP stack, which is separate and independent from the network traffic generated by VMs. The ESXi management network, however, is treated a bit differently than "regular" VMkernel traffic in two ways:

◆ First, the ESXi management network is automatically created when you install ESXi. In order for the ESXi host to be reachable across the network, it must have a management network configured and working. So, the ESXi installer automatically sets up an ESXi management network.

◆ Second, the Direct Console User Interface (DCUI) — the user interface that exists when working at the physical console of a server running ESXi — provides a mechanism for configuring or reconfiguring the management network but not any other forms of networking on that host.

Although the vSphere Client offers an option to enable management traffic when configuring networking, as you can see in Figure 5.9, it's unlikely that you'll use this option very often. After all, in order to use this option to configure management networking from within the vSphere Client, the ESXi host must already have functional management networking in place (vCenter Server communicates with ESXi over the management network). You might use this option if you were creating additional management interfaces. To create additional management network interfaces, you would use the procedure described later (in the section "Configuring VMkernel Networking") for creating VMkernel ports using the vSphere Client, simply enabling the Use This Port Group For Management Traffic option while creating the VMkernel port.

FIGURE 5.9
The vSphere Client offers a way to enable management networking when configuring networking.

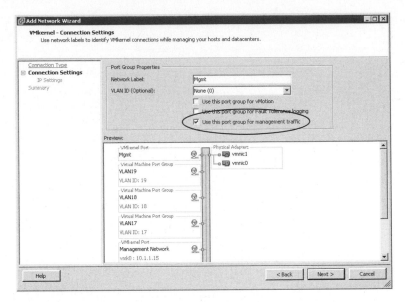

In the event that the ESXi host is unreachable — and therefore cannot be configured using the vSphere Client — you'll need to use the DCUI to configure the management network. Perform the following steps to configure the ESXi management network using the DCUI:

1. At the server's physical console or using a remote console utility such as the HP iLO, press F2 to enter the System Customization menu.

   If prompted to log in, enter the appropriate credentials.

2. Use the arrow keys to highlight the Configure Management Network option, as shown in Figure 5.10, and press Enter.

FIGURE 5.10
To configure ESXi's equivalent of the Service Console port, use the Configure Management Network option in the System Customization menu.

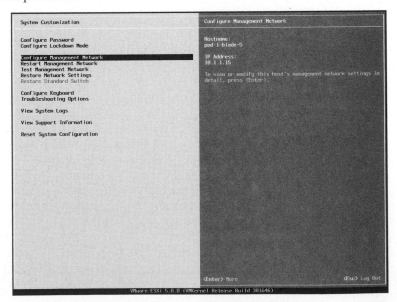

3. From the Configure Management Network menu, select the appropriate option for configuring ESXi management networking, as shown in Figure 5.11.

You cannot create additional management network interfaces from here; you can only modify the existing management network interface.

FIGURE 5.11
From the Configure Management Network menu, users can modify assigned network adapters, change the VLAN ID, or alter the IP configuration.

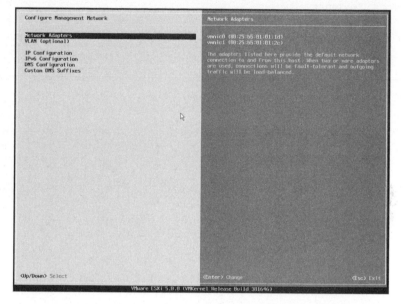

4. When finished, follow the screen prompts to exit the management networking configuration.

If prompted to restart the management networking, select Yes; otherwise, restart the management networking from the System Customization menu, as shown in Figure 5.12.

FIGURE 5.12
The Restart Management Network option restarts ESXi's management networking and applies any changes that were made.

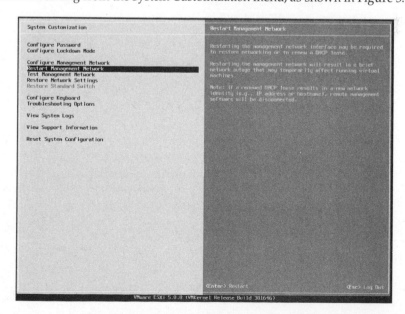

In looking at Figure 5.10 and Figure 5.12, you'll also see options for testing the management network, which lets you be sure that the management network is configured correctly. This is invaluable if you are unsure of the VLAN ID or network adapters that you should use.

I also want to point out the Restore Network Settings option, shown in Figure 5.13. This restores the network configuration to a management-enabled VMkernel port with a single uplink on a single vSwitch — a handy option if you're working with vSphere Distributed Switches (a topic I tackle later in this chapter).

FIGURE 5.13
Use the Restore Network Settings option to revert to an "out of the box" network configuration.

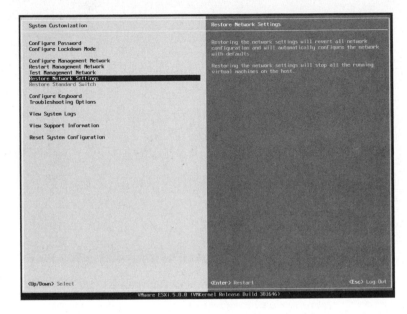

Let's expand our discussion of VMkernel networking away from just management traffic and take a closer look at the other types of VMkernel traffic, as well as how to create and configure VMkernel ports.

Configuring VMkernel Networking

VMkernel networking carries management traffic, but it also carries all other forms of traffic that originate with the ESXi host itself (i.e., any traffic that isn't generated by VMs running on that ESXi host). As shown in Figure 5.14 and Figure 5.15, VMkernel ports are used for vMotion, iSCSI, NAS/NFS access, and vSphere FT. With ESXi, VMkernel ports are also used for management. In Chapter 6 I detail the iSCSI and NAS/NFS configurations; in Chapter 12 I provide details of the vMotion process and how vSphere FT works. These discussions provide insight into the traffic flow between VMkernel and storage devices (iSCSI/NFS) or other ESXi hosts (for vMotion or vSphere FT). At this point, you should be concerned only with configuring VMkernel networking.

FIGURE 5.14

A VMkernel port is associated with an interface and assigned an IP address for accessing iSCSI or NFS storage devices or for performing vMotion with other ESXi hosts.

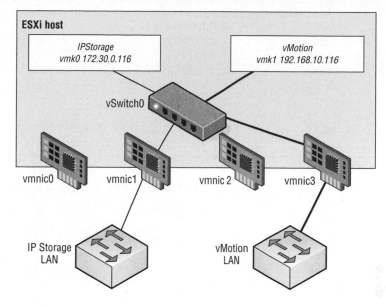

FIGURE 5.15

The port labels for VMkernel ports should be as descriptive as possible.

A VMkernel port actually comprises two different components: a port on a vSwitch and a VMkernel network interface, also known as a *vmknic*. Creating a VMkernel port using the vSphere Client combines the task of creating the port group and the VMkernel NIC.

Perform the following steps to add a VMkernel port to an existing vSwitch using the vSphere Client:

1. Use the vSphere Client to establish a connection to a vCenter Server or an ESXi host.

2. Click the hostname in the inventory pane on the left, select the Configuration tab in the details pane on the right, and then choose Networking from the Hardware menu.

3. Click Properties for the virtual switch to host the new VMkernel port.

4. Click the Add button, select the VMkernel radio button option, and click Next.

5. Type the name of the port in the Network Label text box.

6. If necessary, specify the VLAN ID for the VMkernel port.

7. Select the various functions that will be enabled on this VMkernel port, and then click Next. For a VMkernel port that will be used only for iSCSI or NAS/NFS traffic, all check boxes should be deselected, as shown in Figure 5.16.

Select Use This Port Group For vMotion if this VMkernel port will host vMotion traffic; otherwise, leave the check box deselected.

Similarly, select the Use This Port Group For Fault Tolerance Logging check box if this VMkernel port will be used for vSphere FT traffic. Select Use This Port Group For Management Traffic if you want to create an additional management interface.

FIGURE 5.16
VMkernel ports can carry IP-based storage traffic, Fault Tolerance logging traffic, or management traffic.

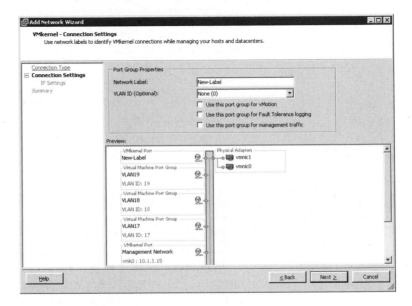

8. Enter an IP address for the VMkernel port. Ensure the IP address is a valid IP address for the network to which the physical NIC is connected. You do not need to provide a default gateway if the VMkernel does not need to reach remote subnets.

9. Click Next to review the configuration summary, and then click Finish.

After you complete these steps, you can use the `vicfg-vswitch` command — either from an instance of the vSphere Management Assistant or from a system with the vSphere CLI installed — which shows the new VMkernel port, and the `vicfg-vmknic` command, which shows the new VMkernel NIC that was created:

```
esxcfg-vmknic --list
```

To help illustrate the different parts — the VMkernel port and the VMkernel NIC, or vmknic — that are created during this process, let's again walk through the steps for creating a VMkernel port using the vSphere Management Assistant.

Perform the following steps to create a VMkernel port on an existing vSwitch using the command line:

1. Using `PuTTY.exe` (Windows) or a terminal window (Linux or Mac OS X), establish an SSH session to the vSphere Management Assistant.

2. Enter the following command to add a port group named VMkernel to vSwitch0:

   `vicfg-vswitch --server <vCenter host name> --vihost <ESXi host name> --username <vCenter administrative user> -A VMkernel vSwitch0`

3. Use the `vicfg-vswitch` command to list the vSwitch and the port groups. Note that the port group exists, but nothing has been connected to it (the Used Ports column shows 0).

   `vicfg-vswitch --server <vCenter host name> --vihost <ESXi host name> --username <vCenter administrative user> --list`

4. Enter the following command to assign an IP address and subnet mask to the VMkernel port created in the previous step:

   `vicfg-vmknic --server <vCenter host name> --vihost <ESXi host name> --username <vCenter administrative user> -a -i 172.30.0.114 -n 255.255.255.0 VMkernel`

5. Repeat the command from step 3 again, noting now how the Used Ports column has incremented to 1.

This indicates that a vmknic has been connected to a virtual port on the port group. Figure 5.17 shows the output of the `vicfg-vswitch` command after completing step 4.

FIGURE 5.17
Using the CLI helps drive home the fact that the port group and the VMkernel port are separate objects.

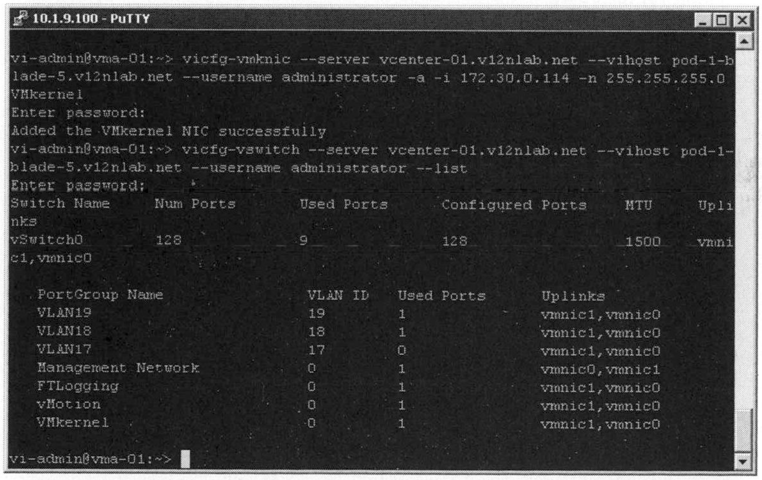

Aside from the default ports required for the management network, no VMkernel ports are created during the installation of ESXi, so all the non-management VMkernel ports that may be required in your environment will need to be created, either using the vSphere Client or via CLI using the vSphere CLI or the vSphere Management Assistant.

Only one type of port or port group remains, and that is a VM port group.

Configuring VM Networking

The second type (or port group) to discuss is the VM port group. The VM port group is quite different from a VMkernel port. Both of the other ports have a one-to-one relationship with an interface: each VMkernel NIC, or vmknic, requires a matching VMkernel port on a vSwitch. In addition, these interfaces require IP addresses that are used for management or VMkernel network access.

A VM port group, on the other hand, does not have a one-to-one relationship, and it does not require an IP address. For a moment, forget about vSwitches and consider standard physical switches. When you install or add an unmanaged physical switch into your network environment, that physical switch does not require an IP address: you simply install the switches and plug in the appropriate uplinks that will connect them to the rest of the network.

A vSwitch created with a VM port group is really no different. A vSwitch with a VM port group acts just like an additional unmanaged physical switch. You need only plug in the appropriate uplinks — physical network adapters, in this case — that will connect that vSwitch to the rest of the network. As with an unmanaged physical switch, an IP address does not need to be configured for a VM port group to combine the ports of a vSwitch with those of a physical switch. Figure 5.18 shows the switch-to-switch connection between a vSwitch and a physical switch.

FIGURE 5.18
A vSwitch with a VM port group uses an associated physical network adapter to establish a switch-to-switch connection with a physical switch.

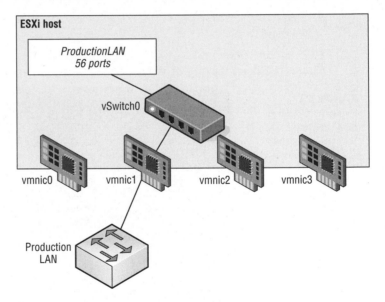

Perform the following steps to create a vSwitch with a VM port group using the vSphere Client:

1. Use the vSphere Client to establish a connection to a vCenter Server or an ESXi host.

2. Click the hostname in the inventory pane on the left, select the Configuration tab in the details pane on the right, and then select Networking from the Hardware menu.

3. Click Add Networking to start the Add Network Wizard.

4. Select the Virtual Machine radio button, and click Next.

5. Because you are creating a new vSwitch, select the check box that corresponds to the network adapter to be assigned to the new vSwitch.

   Be sure to select the NIC connected to the switch that can carry the appropriate traffic for your VMs.

6. Type the name of the VM port group in the Network Label text box.

7. Specify a VLAN ID, if necessary, and click Next.

8. Click Next to review the virtual switch configuration, and then click Finish.

If you are a command-line junkie, you can create a VM port group from the vSphere CLI as well. You can probably guess the commands that are involved from the previous examples, but I'll walk you through the process anyway.

Perform the following steps to create a vSwitch with a VM port group using the command line:

1. Using PuTTY.exe (Windows) or a terminal window (Linux or Mac OS X), establish an SSH session to a running instance of the vSphere Management Assistant.

2. Enter the following command to add a virtual switch named vSwitch1:

   ```
   vicfg-vswitch --server <vCenter host name> --vihost <ESXi host name>
   --username <vCenter administrative user> -a vSwitch1
   ```

3. Enter the following command to bind the physical NIC vmnic1 to vSwitch1:

   ```
   vicfg-vswitch --server <vCenter host name> --vihost <ESXi host name>
   --username <vCenter administrative user> -L vmnic1 vSwitch1
   ```

   By binding a physical NIC to the vSwitch, you provide network connectivity to the rest of the network for VMs connected to this vSwitch. Again, remember that you can assign a physical NIC to only one vSwitch at a time.

4. Enter the following command to create a VM port group named ProductionLAN on vSwitch1:

   ```
   vicfg-vswitch --server <vCenter host name> --vihost <ESXi host name>
   --username <vCenter administrative user> -A ProductionLAN vSwitch1
   ```

Of the different connection types — VMkernel ports and VM port groups — vSphere administrators will spend most of their time creating, modifying, managing, and removing VM port groups.

PORTS AND PORT GROUPS ON A VIRTUAL SWITCH

A vSwitch can consist of multiple connection types, or each connection type can be created in its own vSwitch.

Configuring VLANs

Several times so far we've referenced the use of the VLAN ID when configuring a VMkernel port and a VM port group. As defined previously in this chapter, a virtual LAN (VLAN) is a logical LAN that provides efficient segmentation, security, and broadcast control while allowing traffic to share the same physical LAN segments or same physical switches. Figure 5.19 shows a typical VLAN configuration across physical switches.

FIGURE 5.19
Virtual LANs provide secure traffic segmentation without the cost of additional hardware.

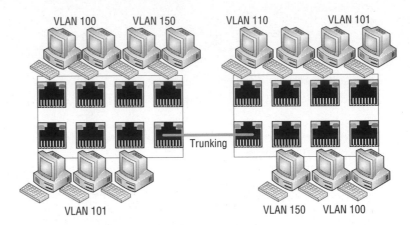

VLANs utilize the IEEE 802.1Q standard for *tagging*, or marking, traffic as belonging to a particular VLAN. The VLAN tag, also known as the VLAN ID, is a numeric value between 1 and 4094, and it uniquely identifies that VLAN across the network. Physical switches such as the ones depicted in Figure 5.19 must be configured with ports to trunk the VLANs across the switches. These ports are known as *trunk* (or *trunking*) ports. Ports not configured to trunk VLANs are known as *access* ports and can carry traffic only for a single VLAN at a time.

USING VLAN ID 4095

Normally the VLAN ID will range from 1 to 4094. In the ESXi environment, however, a VLAN ID of 4095 is also valid. Using this VLAN ID with ESXi causes the VLAN tagging information to be passed through the vSwitch all the way up to the guest OS. This is called *virtual guest tagging* (VGT) and is useful only for guest OSes that support and understand VLAN tags.

VLANs are an important part of ESXi networking because of the impact they have on the number of vSwitches and uplinks that are required. Consider this:

◆ The management network needs access to the network segment carrying management traffic.

◆ Other VMkernel ports, depending upon their purpose, may need access to an isolated vMotion segment or the network segment carrying iSCSI and NAS/NFS traffic.

◆ VM port groups need access to whatever network segments are applicable for the VMs running on the ESXi hosts.

Without VLANs, this configuration would require three or more separate vSwitches, each bound to a different physical adapter, and each physical adapter would need to be physically connected to the correct network segment, as illustrated in Figure 5.20.

FIGURE 5.20
Supporting multiple networks without VLANs can increase the number of vSwitches and uplinks that are required.

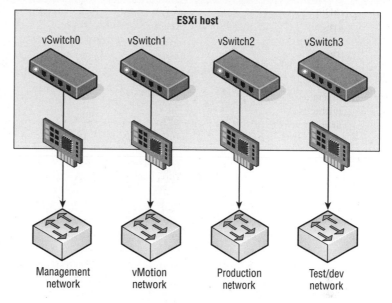

Add in an IP-based storage network and a few more VM networks that need to be supported, and the number of required vSwitches and uplinks quickly grows. And this doesn't even take uplink redundancy, for example NIC teaming, into account!

VLANs are the answer to this dilemma. Figure 5.21 shows the same network as in Figure 5.20, but with VLANs this time.

FIGURE 5.21
VLANs can reduce the number of vSwitches and uplinks required.

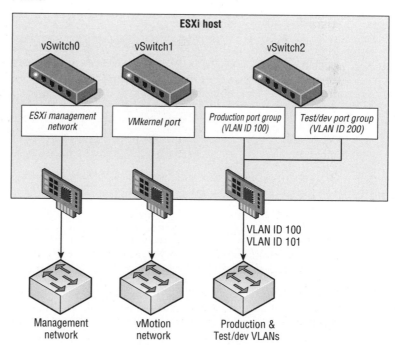

While the reduction from Figure 5.20 to Figure 5.21 is only a single vSwitch and a single uplink, you can easily add more VM networks to the configuration in Figure 5.21 by simply adding another port group with another VLAN ID. Blade servers provide an excellent example of when VLANs offer tremendous benefit. Because of the small form factor of the blade casing, blade servers have historically offered limited expansion slots for physical network adapters. VLANs allow these blade servers to support more networks than they would be able to otherwise.

NO VLAN NEEDED

Virtual switches in the VMkernel do not need VLANs if an ESXi host has enough physical network adapters to connect to each of the different network segments. However, VLANs provide added flexibility in adapting to future network changes, so the use of VLANs where possible is recommended.

As shown in Figure 5.21, VLANs are handled by configuring different port groups within a vSwitch. The relationship between VLANs and port groups is not a one-to-one relationship; a port group can be associated with only one VLAN at a time, but multiple port groups can be associated with a single VLAN. Later in this chapter when I discuss security settings (in the section "Configuring Virtual Switch Security"), you'll see some examples of when you might have multiple port groups associated with a single VLAN.

To make VLANs work properly with a port group, the uplinks for that vSwitch must be connected to a physical switch port configured as a trunk port. A trunk port understands how to pass traffic from multiple VLANs simultaneously while also preserving the VLAN IDs on the traffic. Figure 5.22 shows a snippet of configuration from a Cisco Catalyst 3560G switch for a couple of ports configured as trunk ports.

FIGURE 5.22
The physical switch ports must be configured as trunk ports in order to pass the VLAN information to the ESXi hosts for the port groups to use.

```
!
interface GigabitEthernet0/6
 switchport trunk encapsulation dot1q
 switchport trunk native vlan 999
 switchport mode trunk
 spanning-tree portfast trunk
!
interface GigabitEthernet0/7
 switchport trunk encapsulation dot1q
 switchport trunk native vlan 999
 switchport mode trunk
 spanning-tree portfast trunk
!
```

THE NATIVE VLAN

In Figure 5.22, you might notice the `switchport trunk native vlan 999` command. The default native VLAN is VLAN ID 1. If you need to pass traffic on VLAN 1 to the ESXi hosts, you should designate another VLAN as the native VLAN using this command. I recommend creating a dummy VLAN, like 999, and setting that as the native VLAN. This ensures that all VLANs will be tagged with the VLAN ID as they pass into the ESXi hosts.

When the physical switch ports are correctly configured as trunk ports, the physical switch passes the VLAN tags up to the ESXi server, where the vSwitch tries to direct the traffic to a port group with that VLAN ID configured. If there is no port group configured with that VLAN ID, the traffic is discarded.

Perform the following steps to configure a VM port group using VLAN ID 31:

1. Use the vSphere Client to establish a connection to a vCenter Server or an ESXi host.

2. Click the hostname in the inventory pane on the left, select the Configuration tab in the details pane on the right, and then select Networking from the Hardware menu.

3. Click the Properties link for the vSwitch where the new port group should be created.

4. Click the Add button, select the Virtual Machine radio button, and then click Next.

5. Type the name of the VM port group in the Network Label text box.

   Embedding the VLAN ID and a brief description into the name of the port group is strongly recommended, so typing something like **VLANXXX-NetworkDescription** would be appropriate, where XXX represents the VLAN ID.

6. Type **31** in the VLAN ID (Optional) text box, as shown in Figure 5.23.

   You will want to substitute a value that is correct for your network here.

FIGURE 5.23
You must specify the correct VLAN ID in order for a port group to receive traffic intended for a particular VLAN.

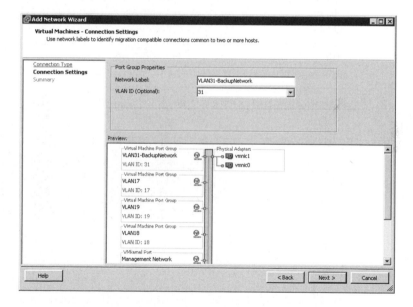

7. Click Next to review the vSwitch configuration, and then click Finish.

As you've probably gathered by now, you can also use the `vicfg-vswitch` command from the vSphere CLI to create or modify the VLAN settings for ports or port groups. I won't go through the steps here, because the commands are extremely similar to what I've shown you already.

Although VLANs reduce the costs of constructing multiple logical subnets, keep in mind that VLANs do not address traffic constraints. Although VLANs logically separate network segments, all the traffic still runs on the same physical network underneath. For bandwidth-intensive network operations, the disadvantage of the shared physical network might outweigh the scalability and cost savings of a VLAN.

CONTROLLING THE VLANS PASSED ACROSS A VLAN TRUNK

You might see the `switchport trunk allowed vlan` command in some Cisco switch configurations as well. This command allows you to control what VLANs are passed across the VLAN trunk to the device at the other end of the link — in this case, an ESXi host. You will need to ensure that all the VLANs that are defined on the vSwitches are also included in the `switchport trunk allowed vlan` command, or else those VLANs not included in the command won't work.

Configuring NIC Teaming

We know that in order for a vSwitch and its associated ports or port groups to communicate with other ESXi hosts or with physical systems, the vSwitch must have at least one uplink. An *uplink* is a physical network adapter that is bound to the vSwitch and connected to a physical network switch. With the uplink connected to the physical network, there is connectivity for the VMkernel and the VMs connected to that vSwitch. But what happens when that physical network adapter fails, when the cable connecting that uplink to the physical network fails, or the upstream physical switch to which that uplink is connected fails? With a single uplink, network connectivity to the entire vSwitch and all of its ports or port groups is lost. This is where NIC teaming comes in.

NIC teaming involves connecting multiple physical network adapters to single vSwitch. NIC teaming provides redundancy and load balancing of network communications to the VMkernel and VMs.

Figure 5.24 illustrates NIC teaming conceptually. Both of the vSwitches have two uplinks, and each of the uplinks connects to a different physical switch. Note that NIC teaming supports all the different connection types, so it can be used with ESXi management networking, VMkernel networking, and networking for VMs.

Figure 5.25 shows what NIC teaming looks like from within the vSphere Client. In this example, the vSwitch is configured with an association to multiple physical network adapters (uplinks). As mentioned in the previous section, the ESXi host can have a maximum of 32 uplinks; these uplinks can be spread across multiple vSwitches or all tossed into a NIC team on one vSwitch. Remember that you can connect a physical NIC to only one vSwitch at a time.

Building a functional NIC team requires that all uplinks be connected to physical switches in the same broadcast domain. If VLANs are used, then all the switches should be configured for VLAN trunking, and the appropriate subset of VLANs must be allowed across the VLAN trunk. In a Cisco switch, this is typically controlled with the `switchport trunk allowed vlan` statement.

In Figure 5.26, the NIC team for vSwitch0 will work, because both of the physical switches share VLAN100 and are therefore in the same broadcast domain. The NIC team for vSwitch1, however, will not work because the physical network adapters do not share a common broadcast domain.

FIGURE 5.24
Virtual switches with multiple uplinks offer redundancy and load balancing.

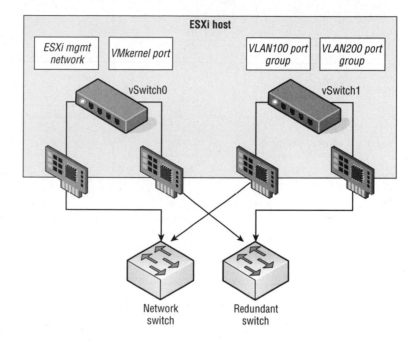

FIGURE 5.25
The vSphere Client shows when multiple physical network adapters are associated to a vSwitch using NIC teaming.

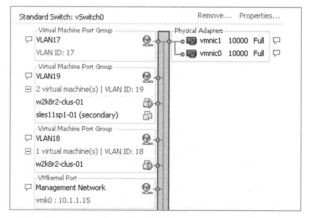

FIGURE 5.26
All the physical
network adapters
in a NIC team must
belong to the same
Layer 2 broadcast
domain.

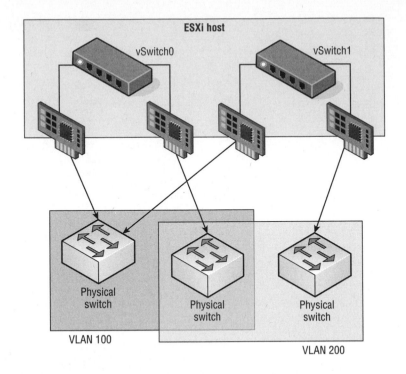

CONSTRUCTING NIC TEAMS

NIC teams should be built on physical network adapters located on separate bus architectures. For example, if an ESXi host contains two onboard network adapters and a PCI Express–based quad-port network adapter, a NIC team should be constructed using one onboard network adapter and one network adapter on the PCI bus. This design eliminates a single point of failure.

Perform the following steps to create a NIC team with an existing vSwitch using the vSphere Client:

1. Use the vSphere Client to establish a connection to a vCenter Server or an ESXi host.

2. Click the hostname in the inventory pane on the left, select the Configuration tab in the details pane on the right, and then select Networking from the Hardware menu.

3. Click Properties for the virtual switch that will be assigned a NIC team, and select the Network Adapters tab.

4. Click Add and select the appropriate adapter from the Unclaimed Adapters list, as shown in Figure 5.27. Click Next.

5. Adjust the Policy Failover Order as needed to support an active/standby configuration.

6. Review the summary of the virtual switch configuration, click Next, and then click Finish.

FIGURE 5.27
Create a NIC team
using unclaimed
network adapters
that belong to the
same Layer 2
broadcast domain
as the original
adapter.

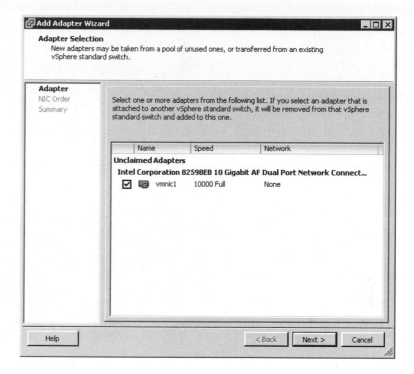

After a NIC team is established for a vSwitch, ESXi can then perform load balancing for that vSwitch. The load-balancing feature of NIC teaming does not function like the load-balancing feature of advanced routing protocols. Load balancing across a NIC team is not a product of identifying the amount of traffic transmitted through a network adapter and shifting traffic to equalize data flow through all available adapters. The load-balancing algorithm for NIC teams in a vSwitch is a balance of the number of connections — not the amount of traffic. NIC teams on a vSwitch can be configured with one of the following four load-balancing policies:

- vSwitch port-based load balancing (default)
- Source MAC-based load balancing
- IP hash-based load balancing
- Explicit failover order

The last option, explicit failover order, isn't really a "load-balancing" policy; instead, it uses the user-specific failover order. More information on the failover order is provided in the section "Configuring Failover Detection and Failover Policy."

OUTBOUND LOAD BALANCING

The load-balancing feature of NIC teams on a vSwitch applies only to the outbound traffic.

REVIEWING VIRTUAL SWITCH PORT-BASED LOAD BALANCING

The vSwitch port-based load-balancing policy that is used by default uses an algorithm that ties (or pins) each virtual switch port to a specific uplink associated with the vSwitch. The algorithm attempts to maintain an equal number of port-to-uplink assignments across all uplinks to achieve load balancing. As shown in Figure 5.28, this policy setting ensures that traffic from a specific virtual network adapter connected to a virtual switch port will consistently use the same physical network adapter. In the event that one of the uplinks fails, the traffic from the failed uplink will failover to another physical network adapter.

FIGURE 5.28
The vSwitch port-based load-balancing policy assigns each virtual switch port to a specific uplink. Failover to another uplink occurs when one of the physical network adapters experiences failure.

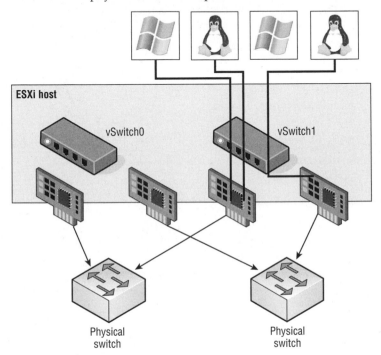

You can see how this policy does not provide dynamic load balancing but does provide redundancy. Because the port to which a VM is connected does not change, each VM is tied to a physical network adapter until failover occurs regardless of the amount of network traffic that is generated. Looking at Figure 5.28, imagine that the Linux VM and the Windows VM on the far left are the two most network-intensive VMs. In this case, the vSwitch port-based policy has assigned both of the ports used by these VMs to the same physical network adapter. This could create a situation in which one physical network adapter is much more heavily utilized than some of the other network adapters in the NIC team.

The physical switch passing the traffic learns the port association and therefore sends replies back through the same physical network adapter from which the request initiated. The vSwitch port-based policy is best used when the number of virtual network adapters is greater than the number of physical network adapters. In the case where there are fewer virtual network adapters than physical adapters, some physical adapters will not be used. For example, if five VMs are connected to a vSwitch with six uplinks, only five vSwitch ports will be assigned to exactly five uplinks, leaving one uplink with no traffic to process.

REVIEWING SOURCE MAC-BASED LOAD BALANCING

The second load-balancing policy available for a NIC team is the source MAC-based policy, shown in Figure 5.29. This policy is susceptible to the same pitfalls as the vSwitch port-based policy simply because the static nature of the source MAC address is the same as the static nature of a vSwitch port assignment. Like the vSwitch port-based policy, the source MAC-based policy is best used when the number of virtual network adapters exceeds the number of physical network adapters. In addition, VMs are still not capable of using multiple physical adapters unless configured with multiple virtual network adapters. Multiple virtual network adapters inside the guest OS of a VM will provide multiple source MAC addresses and therefore offer an opportunity to use multiple physical network adapters.

FIGURE 5.29

The source MAC based load-balancing policy, as the name suggests, ties a virtual network adapter to a physical network adapter based on the MAC address.

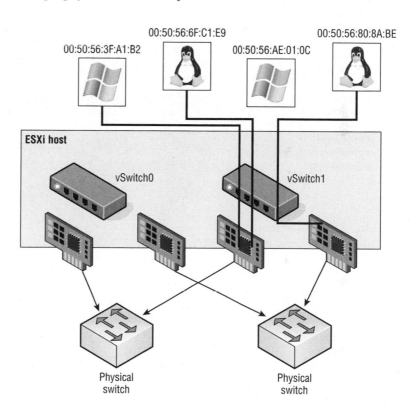

VIRTUAL SWITCH TO PHYSICAL SWITCH

To eliminate a single point of failure, you can connect the physical network adapters in NIC teams set to use the vSwitch port-based or source MAC-based load-balancing policies to different physical switches; however, the physical switches must belong to the same Layer 2 broadcast domain. Link aggregation using 802.3ad teaming is not supported with either of these load-balancing policies.

REVIEWING IP HASH-BASED LOAD BALANCING

The third load-balancing policy available for NIC teams is the IP hash-based policy, also called the *out-IP* policy. This policy, shown in Figure 5.30, addresses the limitation of the other two policies that prevents a VM from accessing two physical network adapters without having two virtual network adapters. The IP hash-based policy uses the source and destination IP addresses to calculate a hash. The hash determines the physical network adapter to use for communication. Different combinations of source and destination IP addresses will, quite naturally, produce different hashes. Based on the hash, then, this algorithm could allow a single VM to communicate over different physical network adapters when communicating with different destinations, assuming that the calculated hashes lead to the selection of a different physical NIC.

FIGURE 5.30
The IP hash-based policy is a more scalable load-balancing policy that allows VMs to use more than one physical network adapter when communicating with multiple destination hosts.

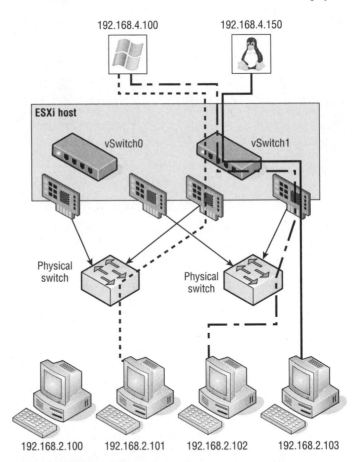

BALANCING FOR LARGE DATA TRANSFERS

Although the IP hash-based load-balancing policy can more evenly spread the transfer traffic for a single VM, it does not provide a benefit for large data transfers occurring between the same source and destination systems. Because the source-destination hash will be the same for the duration of the data load, it will flow through only a single physical network adapter.

Unless the physical hardware supports it, a vSwitch with the NIC teaming load-balancing policy set to use the IP-based hash must have all physical network adapters connected to the same physical switch. Some newer switches support link aggregation across physical switches, but otherwise all the physical network adapters will need to connect to the same switch. In addition, the switch must be configured for link aggregation. ESXi supports standard 802.3ad teaming in static (manual) mode — sometimes referred to as EtherChannel in Cisco networking environments — but does not support the Link Aggregation Control Protocol (LACP) or Port Aggregation Protocol (PAgP) commonly found on switch devices. Link aggregation will increase throughput by combining the bandwidth of multiple physical network adapters for use by a single virtual network adapter of a VM.

Another consideration to point out when using IP hash-based load balancing policy is that all physical NICs must be set to active instead of configuring some as active and some as passive. This is due to the nature of how IP hash-based load balancing works between the virtual switch and the physical switch.

Figure 5.31 shows a snippet of the configuration of a Cisco switch configured for link aggregation.

FIGURE 5.31

The physical switches must be configured to support the IP hash-based load-balancing policy.

```
interface Port-channel2
 description Link aggregate for ESX server
 switchport trunk encapsulation dot1q
 switchport trunk native vlan 999
 switchport mode trunk
!
interface GigabitEthernet0/1
 switchport trunk encapsulation dot1q
 switchport trunk native vlan 999
 switchport mode trunk
 channel-group 2 mode on
 spanning-tree portfast trunk
!
```

Perform the following steps to alter the NIC teaming load-balancing policy of a vSwitch:

1. Use the vSphere Client to establish a connection to a vCenter Server or an ESXi host.

2. Click the hostname in the inventory pane on the left, select the Configuration tab in the details pane on the right, and then select Networking from the Hardware menu.

3. Click the Properties for the virtual switch, select the name of virtual switch from the Configuration list, and then click the Edit button.

4. Select the NIC Teaming tab, and then select the desired load-balancing strategy from the Load Balancing drop-down list, as shown in Figure 5.32.

FIGURE 5.32

Select the load-balancing policy for a vSwitch on the NIC Teaming tab.

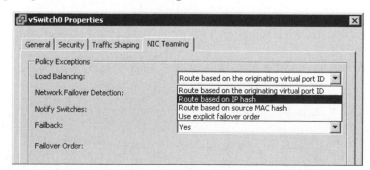

5. Click OK and then click Close.

Now that I've explained the load-balancing policies — with the exception of explicit failover order, which I'll discuss in the next section — let's take a deeper look at the failover and failback of uplinks in a NIC team. There are two parts to consider: failover detection and failover policy.

CONFIGURING FAILOVER DETECTION AND FAILOVER POLICY

Failover detection with NIC teaming can be configured to use either a link status method or a beacon-probing method.

The link status failover-detection method works just as the name suggests. Failure of an uplink is identified by the link status provided by the physical network adapter. In this case, failure is identified for events like removed cables or power failures on a physical switch. The downside to the link status failover-detection setting is its inability to identify misconfigurations or pulled cables that connect the switch to other networking devices (for example, a cable connecting one switch to an upstream switch.)

OTHER WAYS OF DETECTING UPSTREAM FAILURES

Some network switch manufacturers have also added features into their network switches that assist in the task of detecting upstream network failures. In the Cisco product line, for example, there is a feature known as *link state tracking* that enables the switch to detect when an upstream port has gone down and react accordingly. This feature can reduce or even eliminate the need for beacon probing.

The beacon-probing failover-detection setting, which includes link status as well, sends Ethernet broadcast frames across all physical network adapters in the NIC team. These broadcast frames allow the vSwitch to detect upstream network connection failures and will force failover when Spanning Tree Protocol blocks ports, when ports are configured with the wrong VLAN, or when a switch-to-switch connection has failed. When a beacon is not returned on a physical network adapter, the vSwitch triggers the failover notice and reroutes the traffic from the failed network adapter through another available network adapter based on the failover policy.

Consider a vSwitch with a NIC team consisting of three physical network adapters, where each adapter is connected to a different physical switch and each physical switch is connected to a single physical switch, which is then connected to an upstream switch, as shown in Figure 5.33. When the NIC team is set to the beacon-probing failover-detection method, a beacon will be sent out over all three uplinks.

After a failure is detected, either via link status or beacon probing, a failover will occur. Traffic from any VMs or VMkernel ports is rerouted to another member of the NIC team. Exactly which member that might be, though, depends primarily on the configured failover order.

Figure 5.34 shows the failover order configuration for a vSwitch with two adapters in a NIC team. In this configuration, both adapters are configured as active adapters, and either or both adapters may be used at any given time to handle traffic for this vSwitch and all its associated ports or port groups.

Now look at Figure 5.35. This figure shows a vSwitch with three physical network adapters in a NIC team. In this configuration, one of the adapters is configured as a standby adapter. Any adapters listed as standby adapters will not be used until a failure occurs on one of the active adapters, at which time the standby adapters activate in the order listed.

FIGURE 5.33
The beacon-probing failover-detection policy sends beacons out across the physical network adapters of a NIC team to identify upstream network failures or switch misconfigurations.

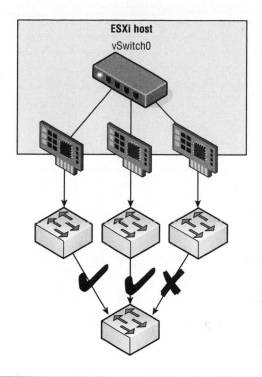

FIGURE 5.34
The failover order helps determine how adapters in a NIC team are used when a failover occurs.

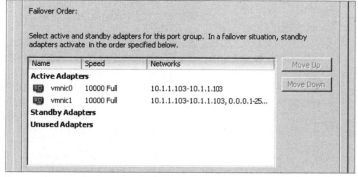

FIGURE 5.35
Standby adapters automatically activate when an active adapter fails.

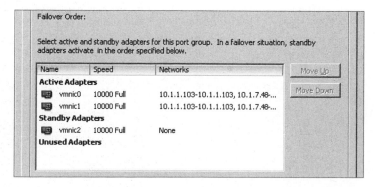

Now take a quick look back at Figure 5.32. You'll see an option there labeled Use Explicit Failover Order. This is the explicit failover order policy that I mentioned toward the beginning of the "Configuring NIC Teaming" section. If you select that option instead of one of the other load-balancing options, then traffic will move to the next available uplink in the list of active adapters. If no active adapters are available, then traffic will move down the list to the standby adapters. Just as the name of the option implies, ESXi will use the order of the adapters in the failover order to determine how traffic will be placed on the physical network adapters. Because this option does not perform any sort of load balancing whatsoever, it's generally not recommended, and one of the other options is used instead.

The Failback option controls how ESXi will handle a failed network adapter when it recovers from failure. The default setting, Yes, as shown in Figure 5.36, indicates the adapter will be returned to active duty immediately upon recovery, and it will replace any standby adapter that may have taken its place during the failure. Setting Failback to No means that the recovered adapter remains inactive until another adapter fails, triggering the replacement of the newly failed adapter.

FIGURE 5.36
By default, a
vSwitch using
NIC teaming has
Failback enabled
(set to Yes).

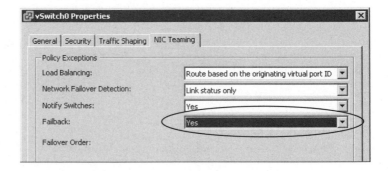

USING FAILBACK WITH VMKERNEL PORTS AND IP-BASED STORAGE

I recommend setting Failback to No for VMkernel ports you've configured for IP-based storage. Otherwise, in the event of a "port-flapping" issue — a situation in which a link may repeatedly go up and down quickly — performance is negatively impacted. Setting Failback to No in this case protects performance in the event of port flapping.

Perform the following steps to configure the Failover Order policy for a NIC team:

1. Use the vSphere Client to establish a connection to a vCenter Server or an ESXi host.

2. Click the hostname in the inventory pane on the left, select the Configuration tab in the details pane on the right, and then select Networking from the Hardware menu.

3. Click Properties for the virtual switch, select the name of virtual switch from the Configuration list, and then click the Edit button.

4. Select the NIC Teaming tab.

5. Use the Move Up and Move Down buttons to adjust the order of the network adapters and their location within the Active Adapters, Standby Adapters, and Unused Adapters lists, as shown in Figure 5.37.

FIGURE 5.37

Failover order for a NIC team is determined by the order of network adapters as listed in the Active Adapters, Standby Adapters, and Unused Adapters lists.

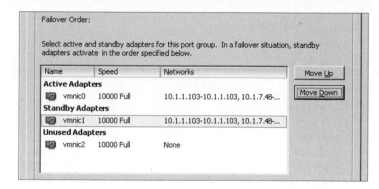

6. Click OK, and then click Close.

When a failover event occurs on a vSwitch with a NIC team, the vSwitch is obviously aware of the event. The physical switch that the vSwitch is connected to, however, will not know immediately. As shown in Figure 5.38, a vSwitch includes a Notify Switches configuration setting, which, when set to Yes, will allow the physical switch to immediately learn of any of the following changes:

◆ A VM is powered on (or any other time a client registers itself with the vSwitch)

◆ A vMotion occurs

◆ A MAC address is changed

◆ A NIC team failover or failback has occurred

FIGURE 5.38

The Notify Switches option allows physical switches to be notified of changes in NIC teaming configurations.

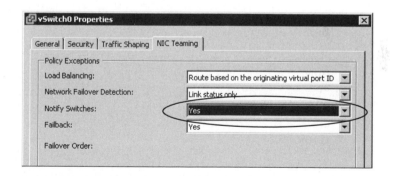

TURNING OFF NOTIFY SWITCHES

The Notify Switches option should be set to No when the port group has VMs using Microsoft Network Load Balancing (NLB) in Unicast mode.

In any of these events, the physical switch is notified of the change using the Reverse Address Resolution Protocol (RARP). RARP updates the lookup tables on the physical switches and offers the shortest latency when a failover event occurs.

Although the VMkernel works proactively to keep traffic flowing from the virtual networking components to the physical networking components, VMware recommends taking the following actions to minimize networking delays:

◆ Disable Port Aggregation Protocol (PAgP) and Link Aggregation Control Protocol (LACP) on the physical switches.

◆ Disable Dynamic Trunking Protocol (DTP) or trunk negotiation.

◆ Disable Spanning Tree Protocol (STP).

VIRTUAL SWITCHES WITH CISCO SWITCHES

VMware recommends configuring Cisco devices to use PortFast mode for access ports or PortFast trunk mode for trunk ports.

Using and Configuring Traffic Shaping

By default, all virtual network adapters connected to a vSwitch have access to the full amount of bandwidth on the physical network adapter with which the vSwitch is associated. In other words, if a vSwitch is assigned a 1 Gbps network adapter, then each VM configured to use the vSwitch has access to 1 Gbps of bandwidth. Naturally, if contention becomes a bottleneck hindering VM performance, NIC teaming will help. However, as a complement to NIC teaming, it is also possible to enable and to configure traffic shaping. Traffic shaping involves the establishment of hard-coded limits for peak bandwidth, average bandwidth, and burst size to reduce a VM's outbound bandwidth capability.

As shown in Figure 5.39, the Peak Bandwidth value and the Average Bandwidth value are specified in kilobits per second, and the Burst Size value is configured in units of kilobytes. The value entered for the Average Bandwidth dictates the data transfer per second across the virtual vSwitch. The Peak Bandwidth value identifies the maximum amount of bandwidth a vSwitch can pass without dropping packets. Finally, the Burst Size value defines the maximum amount of data included in a burst. The burst size is a calculation of bandwidth multiplied by time. During periods of high utilization, if a burst exceeds the configured value, packets are dropped in favor of other traffic; however, if the queue for network traffic processing is not full, the packets are retained for transmission at a later time.

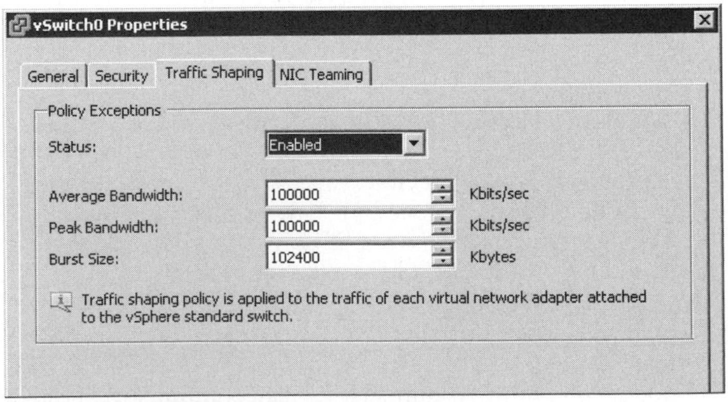

FIGURE 5.39
Traffic shaping reduces the outbound bandwidth available to a port group.

> **TRAFFIC SHAPING AS A LAST RESORT**
>
> Use the traffic-shaping feature sparingly. Traffic shaping should be reserved for situations where VMs are competing for bandwidth and the opportunity to add network adapters is removed by limitations in the expansion slots on the physical chassis. With the low cost of network adapters, it is more worthwhile to spend time building vSwitch devices with NIC teams as opposed to cutting the bandwidth available to a set of VMs.

Perform the following steps to configure traffic shaping:

1. Use the vSphere Client to establish a connection to a vCenter Server or an ESXi host.

2. Click the hostname in the inventory pane on the left, select the Configuration tab in the details pane on the right, and then select Networking from the Hardware menu.

3. Click the Properties for the virtual switch, select the name of the virtual switch or port group from the Configuration list, and then click the Edit button.

4. Select the Traffic Shaping tab.

5. Select the Enabled option from the Status drop-down list.

6. Adjust the Average Bandwidth value to the desired number of kilobits per second.

7. Adjust the Peak Bandwidth value to the desired number of kilobits per second.

8. Adjust the Burst Size value to the desired number of kilobytes.

Bringing It All Together

By now you've seen how all the various components of ESXi virtual networking interact with each other — vSwitches, ports and port groups, uplinks and NIC teams, and VLANs. But how do you assemble all these pieces into a usable whole?

The number and the configuration of the vSwitches and port groups are dependent on several factors, including the number of network adapters in the ESXi host, the number of IP subnets, the existence of VLANs, and the number of physical networks. With respect to the configuration of the vSwitches and VM port groups, there is no single correct configuration that will satisfy every scenario. It is true, however, to say that the greater the number of physical network adapters in an ESXi host, the more flexibility you will have in your virtual networking architecture.

Later in the chapter I'll discuss some advanced design factors, but for now let's stick with some basic design considerations. If the vSwitches created in the VMkernel are not going to be configured with multiple port groups or VLANs, you will be required to create a separate vSwitch for every IP subnet or physical network to which you need to connect. This was illustrated previously in Figure 5.20 in our discussion about VLANs. To really understand this concept, let's look at two more examples.

Figure 5.40 shows a scenario in which there are five IP subnets that your virtual infrastructure components need to reach. The VMs in the production environment must reach the production LAN, the VMs in the test environment must reach the test LAN, the VMkernel needs to access the IP storage and vMotion LANs, and finally the ESXi host must have access to the management LAN. In this scenario, without the use of VLANs and port groups, the ESXi host must have five different vSwitches and five different physical network adapters. (Of course, this doesn't account for redundancy or NIC teaming for the vSwitches.)

Real World Scenario

WHY DESIGN IT THAT WAY?

During the virtual network design process I am often asked a number of different questions, such as why virtual switches should not be created with the largest number of ports to leave room to grow, or why multiple vSwitches should be used instead of a single vSwitch (or vice versa). Some of these questions are easy to answer; others are a matter of experience and, to be honest, personal preference.

Consider the question about why vSwitches should not be created with the largest number of ports. As you'll see in Table 5.1, the maximum number of ports in a virtual switch is 4,088, and the maximum number of ports across all switches on a host is 4,096. This means that if virtual switches are created with the 1,016 ports, only 4 virtual switches can be created. If you're doing a quick calculation of 1,016 × 4 and realizing it is not 4,096, don't forget that virtual switches actually have 8 reserved ports, as I pointed out earlier. Therefore, the 1,016-port switch actually has 1,024 ports. Calculate 1,024 × 4, and you will arrive at the 4,096-port maximum for an ESXi host.

Other questions aren't necessarily so clear cut. I have found that using multiple vSwitches can make it easier to shift certain networks to dedicated physical networks; for example, if a customer wants to move their management network to a dedicated physical network for greater security, this is more easily accomplished when using multiple vSwitches instead of a single vSwitch. The same can be said for using VLANs.

In the end, though, many areas of virtual networking design are simply areas of personal preference and not technical necessity. Learning to determine which areas are which will go a long way to helping you understand your virtualized networking environment.

FIGURE 5.40
Without the use of port groups and VLANs in the vSwitches, each IP subnet will require a separate vSwitch with the appropriate connection type.

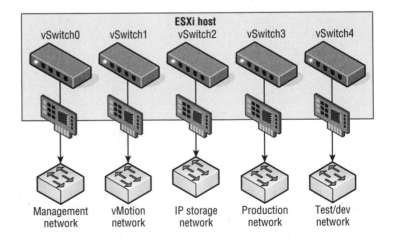

Figure 5.41 shows the same configuration, but this time using VLANs for the Management, vMotion, Production, and Test/Dev networks. The IP storage network is still a physically separate network.

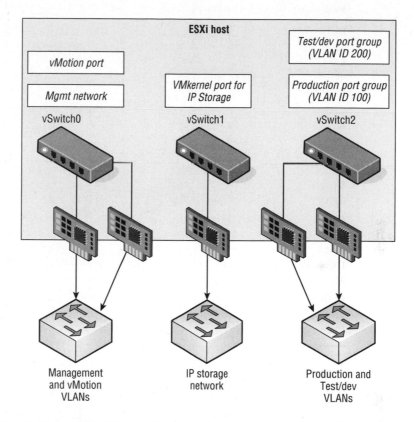

FIGURE 5.41
The use of the physically separate IP storage network limits the reduction in the number of vSwitches and uplinks.

The configuration in Figure 5.41 still uses five network adapters, but this time you're able to provide NIC teaming for all the networks except for the IP storage network.

If the IP storage network had been configured as a VLAN, the number of vSwitches and uplinks could have been even further reduced. Figure 5.42 shows a possible configuration that would support this sort of scenario.

This time, you're able to provide NIC teaming to all the traffic types involved — Management, vMotion, IP storage, and VM traffic — using only a single vSwitch with multiple uplinks.

Clearly, there is a tremendous amount of flexibility in how vSwitches, uplinks, and port groups are assembled to create a virtual network capable of supporting your infrastructure. Even given all this flexibility, though, there are limits. Table 5.1 lists some of the limits of ESXi networking.

FIGURE 5.42
With the use of port groups and VLANs in the vSwitches, even fewer vSwitches and uplinks are required.

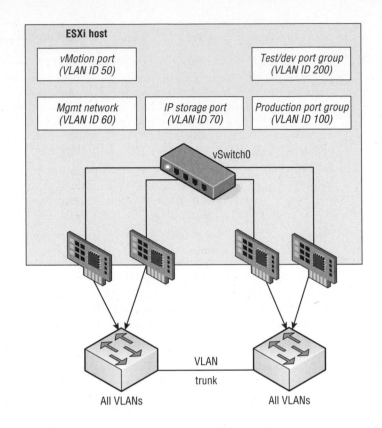

TABLE 5.1:   Configuration maximums for ESXi networking components (vSphere Standard Switches)

CONFIGURATION ITEM	MAXIMUM
Number of vSwitches	248
Ports per vSwitch	4,088
Maximum ports per host (vSS/vDS)	4,096
Port groups per vSwitch	256
Uplinks per vSwitch	32
Number of VMkernel NICs	16
Maximum active ports per host (vSS/vDS)	1,016

VIRTUAL SWITCH CONFIGURATIONS: DON'T GO TOO BIG OR TOO SMALL

Although you can create a vSwitch with a maximum of 4,088 ports (really 4,096), it is not recommended if you anticipate growth. Because ESXi hosts cannot have more than 4,096 ports, if you create a vSwitch with 4,088 ports, then you are limited to a single vSwitch on that host. With only a single vSwitch, you may not be able to connect to all the networks that you need. In the event you do run out of ports on an ESXi host and need to create a new vSwitch, you can reduce the number of ports on an existing vSwitch. That change requires a reboot to take effect, but vMotion allows you to move the VMs to a different host to prevent VM downtime.

You also want to be sure that you account for scenarios such as a host failure, when VMs will be restarted on other hosts using vSphere HA (described in more detail in Chapter 7, "Ensuring High Availability and Business Continuity"). In this case, if you make your vSwitch too small (for example, not enough ports), then you could run into an issue there also.

My key takeaway: virtual switch sizing is the factor of multiple variables that you need to consider, so plan carefully! I recommend creating virtual switches with enough ports to cover existing needs, projected growth, and failover capacity.

With all the flexibility provided by the different virtual networking components, you can be assured that whatever the physical network configuration might hold in store, there are several ways to integrate the virtual networking. What you configure today may change as the infrastructure changes or as the hardware changes. ESXi provides enough tools and options to ensure a successful communication scheme between the virtual and physical networks.

Working with vSphere Distributed Switches

So far our discussion has focused solely on vSphere Standard Switches (just vSwitches). Starting with vSphere 4 and continuing with vSphere 5, there is another option: vSphere Distributed Switches.

Whereas vSwitches are managed per host, a vSphere Distributed Switch functions as a single virtual switch across all the associated ESXi hosts. There are a number of similarities between a vSphere Distributed Switch and a Standard vSwitch:

◆ Like a vSwitch, a vSphere Distributed Switch provides connectivity for VMs and VMkernel interfaces.

◆ Like a vSwitch, a vSphere Distributed Switch leverages physical network adapters as uplinks to provide connectivity to the external physical network.

◆ Like a vSwitch, a vSphere Distributed Switch can leverage VLANs for logical network segmentation.

Of course, there are differences as well, but the biggest of these is that a vSphere Distributed Switch spans multiple servers in a cluster instead of each server having its own set of vSwitches. This greatly reduces complexity in clustered ESXi environments and simplifies the addition of new servers to an ESXi cluster.

VMware's official abbreviation for a vSphere Distributed Switch is vDS. For ease of reference and consistency with other elements in the vSphere user interface, we'll refer to vSphere Distributed Switches from here on as *dvSwitches*.

Creating a vSphere Distributed Switch

The process of creating a dvSwitch is twofold. First, you create the dvSwitch and then you add ESXi hosts to the dvSwitch. To help simplify the process, vSphere automatically includes the option to add an ESXi host to the dvSwitch during the process of creating it.

Perform the following steps to create a new dvSwitch:

1. Launch the vSphere Client, and connect to a vCenter Server instance. You must connect to vCenter Server; dvSwitches require vCenter Server.

2. On the vSphere Client home screen, select the Networking option under Inventory.

3. Right-click the Datacenter object in the inventory pane on the left, and select New vSphere Distributed Switch from the context menu.

   This launches the Create vSphere Distributed Switch wizard.

4. First, select the version of the dvSwitch you'd like to create. Figure 5.43 shows the options for dvSwitch versions.

   Three options are available:

   ◆ vSphere Distributed Switch Version: 4.0: This type of dvSwitch is compatible back to vSphere 4.0 and limits the dvSwitch to features supported only by vSphere 4.0.

   ◆ vSphere Distributed Switch Version: 4.1.0: This type of dvSwitch adds support for Load-Based Teaming and Network I/O Control. This version is supported by vSphere 4.1 and later.

   ◆ vSphere Distributed Switch Version: 5.0.0: This version is compatible only with vSphere 5.0 and later and adds support for all the new features such as user-defined network resource pools, Network I/O Control, NetFlow, and port mirroring.

   In this case, select vSphere Distributed Switch Version 5.0.0 and click Next.

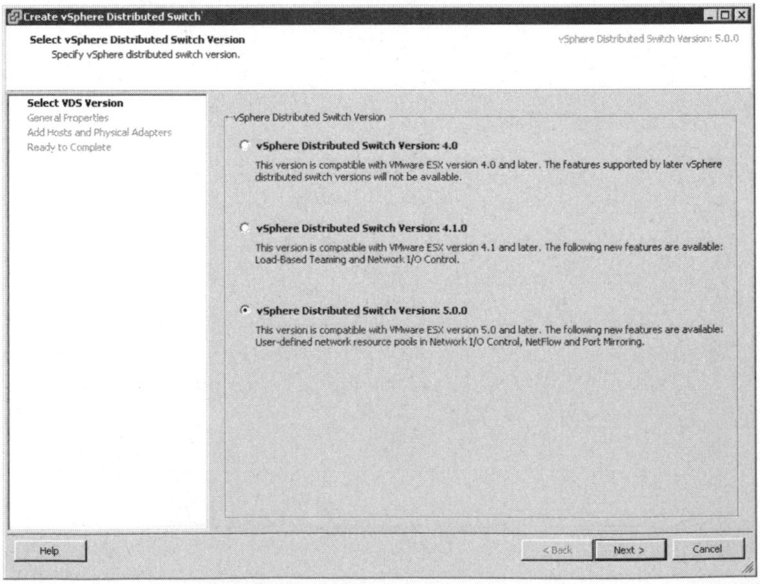

FIGURE 5.43
If you want to support all the features included in vSphere 5, you must use a Version 5.0.0 dvSwitch.

5. Specify a name for the dvSwitch, and specify the number of dvUplink ports, as illustrated in Figure 5.44. Click Next.

FIGURE 5.44

The number of dvUplink ports controls how many physical adapters from each host can serve as uplinks for the distributed switch.

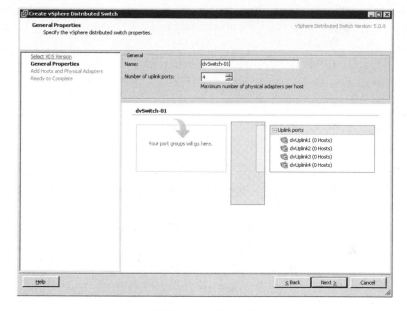

6. On the next screen, you can choose to add hosts to the dvSwitch now or add them later. To add hosts now, select Add Now and select unused physical adapters from each applicable host.

These physical adapters will be configured as uplinks connected to a dvUplink port. Figure 5.45 shows a single host being added to a dvSwitch during creation.

FIGURE 5.45

Users can add ESXi hosts to a vSphere Distributed Switch during or after creation.

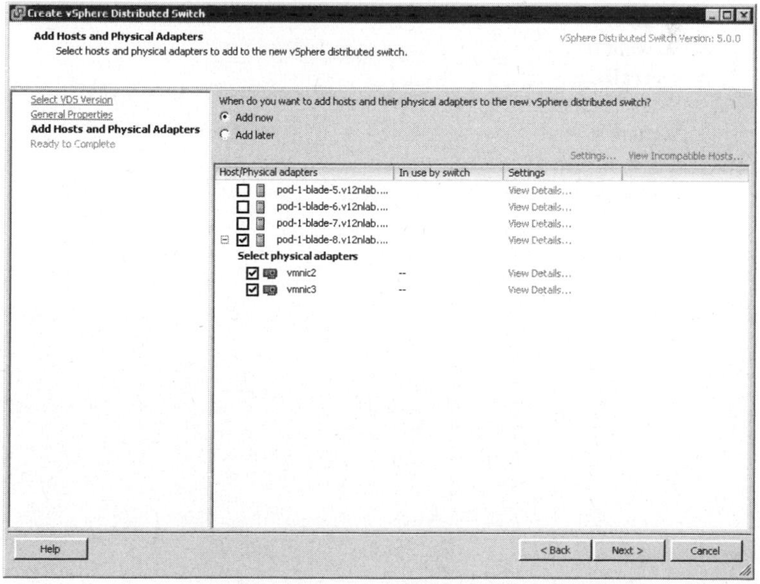

7. If you need to change the number of virtual ports assigned per host, click the blue Settings hyperlink in the upper-right area of the Create vSphere Distributed Switch dialog box.

   This will display the vSphere Distributed Switch – Host Properties dialog box, where you can change the maximum number of ports per host.

8. To view any ESXi hosts that are incompatible with the dvSwitch you've selected to create, click the View Incompatible Hosts hyperlink in the upper-right area of the Create vSphere Distributed Switch dialog box.

   This will display any ESXi hosts that are incompatible with this dvSwitch.

9. Click Next once you have finished adding hosts to the dvSwitch.

10. To create a default dvPort group, leave the box selected labeled Automatically Create A Default Port Group (the default), as shown in Figure 5.46. Click Finish.

FIGURE 5.46
By default, a dvPort group is created during the creation of the distributed switch.

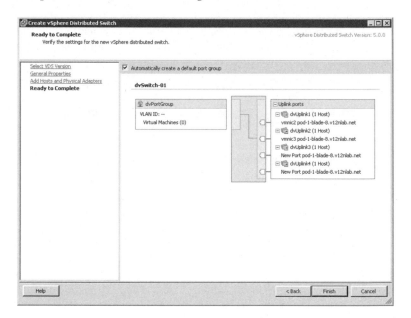

Upon completion of the Create vSphere Distributed Switch wizard, a new dvSwitch, a dvPort group for the uplinks, and the default dvPort group will appear in the inventory list. Using the vSphere CLI or the vSphere Management Assistant will show you the new vSphere Distributed Switch and dvPort groups, but because of the shared nature of the dvSwitch, configuration of the distributed switch occurs in the vSphere Client connected to vCenter Server.

VSPHERE DISTRIBUTED SWITCHES REQUIRE VCENTER SERVER

This may seem obvious, but it's important to point out that because of the shared nature of a vSphere Distributed Switch, vCenter Server is required. That is, you cannot have a vSphere Distributed Switch in an environment that is not being managed by vCenter Server.

After creating a vSphere Distributed Switch, it is relatively easy to add another ESXi host. When the additional ESXi host is created, all of the dvPort groups will automatically be propagated to the new host with the correct configuration. This is the distributed nature of the dvSwitch — as configuration changes are made via the vSphere Client, vCenter Server pushes those changes out to all participating hosts in the dvSwitch. VMware administrators used to managing large ESXi clusters and having to repeatedly create vSwitches and port groups across all the servers individually will be very pleased with the reduction in administrative overhead that dvSwitches offer.

Perform the following steps to add another host to an existing dvSwitch:

1. Launch the vSphere Client, and connect to a vCenter Server instance.

2. On the vSphere Client home screen, select the Networking option under Inventory.

   You can also use the Ctrl+Shift+N keyboard shortcut to navigate to the Networking inventory view.

3. Select an existing vSphere Distributed Switch in the inventory pane on the left, click the Summary tab in the details pane on the right, and select Add Host from the Commands section.

   This launches the Add Host To vSphere Distributed Switch wizard, as shown in Figure 5.47.

FIGURE 5.47
Adding a host to an existing vSphere Distributed Switch uses the same format as adding hosts during creation of the dvSwitch.

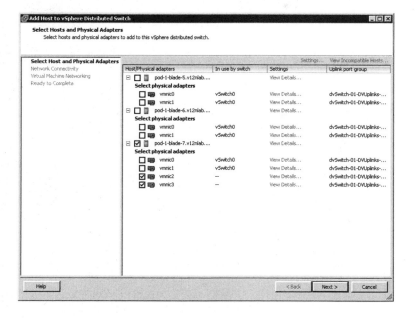

4. Select the physical adapters on the host being added that should be connected to the dvSwitch's dvUplinks port group as uplinks for the distributed switch, and then click Next.

5. If you would like to migrate any VMkernel interfaces, the next screen offers the opportunity to migrate them to the dvSwitch. Leave all VMkernel interfaces (referred to here as virtual adapters) unselected and click Next.

I'll show you how to migrate these later in this chapter.

6. Similarly, if you'd like to migrate any VM networking, select Migrate Virtual Machine Networking and choose the VMs you'd like to migrate to the dvSwitch.

   For now, leave Migrate Virtual Machine Networking unselected and click Next.

7. At the summary screen, review the changes being made to the dvSwitch — which are help-fully highlighted in the graphical display of the dvSwitch, as shown in Figure 5.48 — and click Finish if everything is correct.

FIGURE 5.48
Changes made to a dvSwitch when adding a new ESXi host are highlighted on the summary screen.

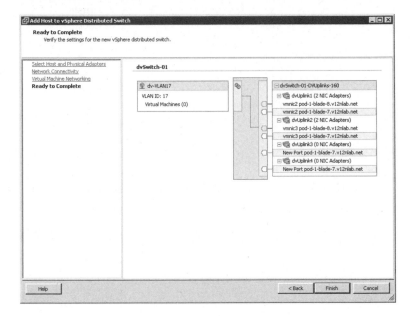

DvSwitch Total Ports and Available Ports

With vSphere Standard Switches, the VMkernel reserved eight ports for its own use, creating a discrepancy between the total number of ports listed in different places. When looking at a dvSwitch, you may think the same thing is true — a dvSwitch with two hosts will have a total port count of 136, with only 128 ports remaining. Where are the other eight ports? Those are the ports in the dvUplink port group, reserved for uplinks. For every host added to a dvSwitch, another four ports (by default) are added to the dvUplinks port group. So, a dvSwitch with three hosts would have 140 total ports with 128 available, a dvSwitch with four hosts would have 144 total ports with 128 available, and so forth. If a value other than four was selected as the maximum number of uplinks, then the difference between total ports and available ports would be that value times the number of hosts in the dvSwitch.

Removing an ESXi Host from a Distributed vSwitch

Naturally, you can also remove ESXi hosts from a dvSwitch. A host can't be removed from a dvSwitch if it still has VMs connected to a dvPort group on that dvSwitch. This is analogous to trying to delete a standard vSwitch or a port group while a VM is still connected; this, too, is prevented. To allow the host to be removed from the dvSwitch, all VMs will need to be moved to a standard vSwitch or a different dvSwitch.

Perform the following steps to remove an individual host from a dvSwitch:

1. Launch the vSphere Client, and connect to a vCenter Server instance.

2. On the vSphere Client home screen, select the Networking option under Inventory. You can also select the View menu and then choose Inventory ➤ Networking, or you can press the keyboard hotkey (Ctrl+Shift+N).

3. Select an existing vSphere Distributed Switch in the inventory pane on the left, and click the Hosts tab in the details pane on the right.

   A list of hosts currently connected to the selected dvSwitch displays.

4. Right click the ESXi host to be removed, and select Remove From vSphere Distributed Switch from the context menu, as shown in Figure 5.49.

FIGURE 5.49
Use the context menu on the host while in the Networking Inventory view to remove an ESXi host from a dvSwitch.

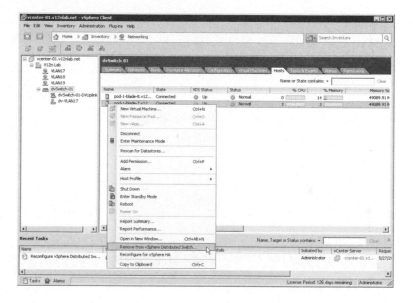

5. If any VMs are still connected to the dvSwitch, the vSphere Client throws an error similar to the one shown in Figure 5.50.

   To correct this error, reconfigure the VM(s) to use a different dvSwitch or vSwitch, or migrate the VMs to a different host using vMotion. Then proceed with removing the host from the dvSwitch.

RECONFIGURING VM NETWORKING WITH A DRAG-AND-DROP OPERATION

While in the Networking view (View ➤ Inventory ➤ Networking), you can use drag and drop to reconfigure a VM's network connection. Simply drag the VM onto the desired network and drop it. vCenter Server reconfigures the VM to use the selected virtual network.

6. If there were no VMs attached to the dvSwitch, or after all VMs are reconfigured to use a different vSwitch or dvSwitch, the host is removed from the dvSwitch.

In addition to removing individual ESXi hosts from a dvSwitch, you can also remove the entire dvSwitch.

FIGURE 5.50
The vSphere Client won't allow a host to be removed from a dvSwitch if a VM is still attached.

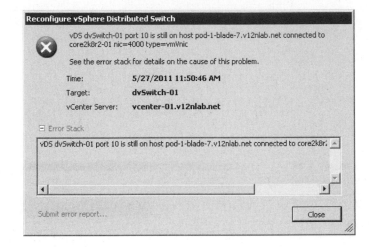

Removing a Distributed vSwitch

Removing the last ESXi host from a dvSwitch does not remove the dvSwitch itself. If you want to get rid of the dvSwitch entirely, you must remove the dvSwitch and not just remove the hosts from the dvSwitch. When you remove a dvSwitch, it is removed from all hosts and removed from the vCenter Server inventory as well.

Removing a dvSwitch is possible only if no VMs have been assigned to a dvPort group on the dvSwitch. Otherwise, the removal of the dvSwitch is blocked with an error message similar to the one displayed previously in Figure 5.50. Again, you'll need to reconfigure the VM(s) to use a different vSwitch or dvSwitch before the operation can proceed. Refer to Chapter 9, "Creating and Managing Virtual Machines," for more information on modifying a VM's network settings.

Perform the following steps to remove the dvSwitch if no VMs are using the dvSwitch or any of the dvPort groups on that dvSwitch:

1. Launch the vSphere Client, and connect to a vCenter Server instance.

2. On the vSphere Client home screen, select the Networking option under Inventory.

   You can also select the View menu and then choose Inventory ➢ Networking, or you can press the keyboard hotkey (Ctrl+Shift+N).

3. Select an existing vSphere Distributed Switch in the inventory pane on the left.

4. Right-click the dvSwitch and select Remove, or choose Remove from the Edit menu. Select Yes in the confirmation dialog box that appears.

5. The dvSwitch and all associated dvPort groups are removed from the inventory and from any connected hosts.

The bulk of the configuration for a dvSwitch isn't performed for the dvSwitch itself but rather for the dvPort groups on that dvSwitch.

Creating and Configuring dvPort Groups

With vSphere Standard Switches, port groups are the key to connectivity for the VMkernel and for VMs. Without ports and port groups on a vSwitch, nothing can be connected to that vSwitch. The same is true for vSphere Distributed Switches. Without a dvPort group, nothing can be connected to a dvSwitch, and the dvSwitch is, therefore, unusable. In this section, you'll take a closer look at creating and configuring dvPort groups.

Perform the following steps to create a new dvPort group:

1. Launch the vSphere Client, and connect to a vCenter Server instance.

2. On the vSphere Client home screen, select the Networking option under Inventory. Alternately, from the View menu, select Inventory ➢ Networking.

3. Select an existing vSphere Distributed Switch in the inventory pane on the left, click the Summary tab in the details pane on the right, and select New Port Group in the Commands section.

This launches the Create Distributed Port Group Wizard, as illustrated in Figure 5.51.

FIGURE 5.51
The Create Distributed Virtual Port Group Wizard allows the user to specify the name of the dvPort group, the number of ports, and the VLAN type.

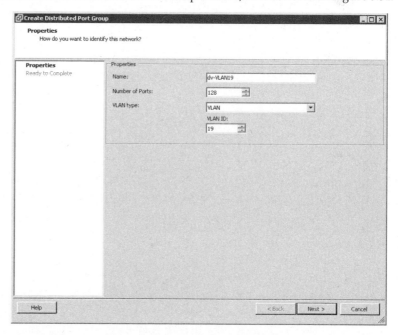

The name of the dvPort group and the number of ports are self-explanatory, but the options under VLAN Type need a bit more explanation:

◆ With VLAN Type set to None, the dvPort group will receive only untagged traffic. In this case, the uplinks must connect to physical switch ports configured as access ports, or they will receive only untagged/native VLAN traffic.

◆ With VLAN Type set to VLAN, you'll then need to specify a VLAN ID. The dvPort group will receive traffic tagged with that VLAN ID. The uplinks must connect to physical switch ports configured as VLAN trunks.

◆ With VLAN Type set to VLAN Trunking, you'll then need to specify the range of allowed VLANs. The dvPort group will pass the VLAN tags up to the guest OSes on any connected VMs.

◆ With VLAN Type set to Private VLAN, you'll then need to specify a Private VLAN entry. Private VLANs are described in detail later in this section.

Specify a descriptive name for the dvPort group, select the appropriate number of ports, select the correct VLAN type, and then click Next.

4. On the summary screen, review the settings, and click Finish if everything is correct.

After a dvPort group has been created, you can select that dvPort group in the VM configuration as a possible network connection, as shown in Figure 5.52.

FIGURE 5.52
A dvPort group is selected as a network connection for VMs, just like port groups on a Standard vSwitch.

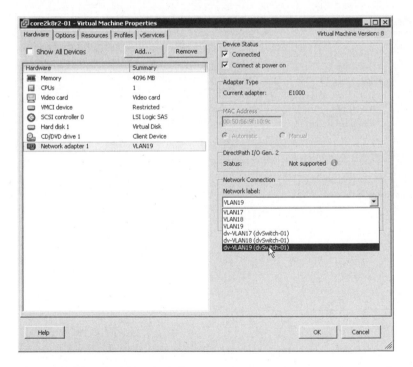

After creating a dvPort group, selecting the dvPort group in the inventory on the left side of the vSphere Client provides you with the option to get more information about the dvPort group and its current state:

◆ The Summary tab provides exactly that — summary information such as the total number of ports in the dvPort group, the number of available ports, any configured IP pools, and the option to edit the settings for the dvPort group.

◆ The Ports tab lists the dvPorts in the dvPort group, their current status, attached VMs, and port statistics, as illustrated in Figure 5.53.

FIGURE 5.53
The Ports tab shows all the dvPorts in the dvPort group along with port status and port statistics.

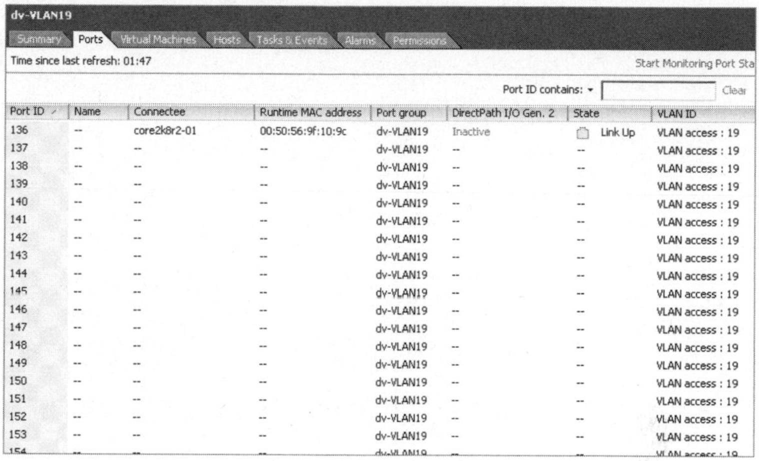

To update the port status or statistics, click the link in the upper-right corner labeled Start Monitoring Port State. That link then changes to Stop Monitoring Port State, which you can use to disable port monitoring.

◆ The Virtual Machines tab lists any VMs currently attached to that dvPort group. The full range of VM operations — such as editing VM settings, shutting down the VM, and migrating the VM — is available from the context menu of a VM listed in this area.

◆ The Hosts tab lists all ESXi hosts currently participating in the dvSwitch that hosts this dvPort group. As with VMs, right-clicking a host here provides a context menu with the full range of options, such as creating a new VM, entering maintenance mode, checking host profile compliance, or rebooting the host.

◆ The Tasks & Events tab lists all tasks or events associated with this dvPort group.

◆ The Alarms tab shows any alarms that have been defined or triggered for this dvPort group.

◆ The Permissions tab shows permissions that have been applied to (or inherited by) this dvPort group.

To delete a dvPort group, right-click the dvPort group and select Delete. If any VMs are still attached to that dvPort group, the vSphere Client prevents the deletion of the dvPort group and logs an error message into the Tasks pane of the vSphere Client. This error is also visible on the Tasks And Events tab of the dvPort group.

To delete the dvPort group, you first have to reconfigure the VM to use a different dvPort group or a different vSwitch or dvSwitch. You can either edit the settings of the VM, or just use drag and drop in the Networking inventory view to reconfigure the VM's network settings.

To edit the configuration of a dvPort group, use the Edit Settings link in the Commands section on the dvPort group's Summary tab. This produces the dialog box shown in Figure 5.54.

The various options along the left side of the dvPort group Settings dialog box allow you to modify different aspects of the dvPort group.

FIGURE 5.54
The Edit Settings command for a dvPort group allows you to modify the configuration of the dvPort group.

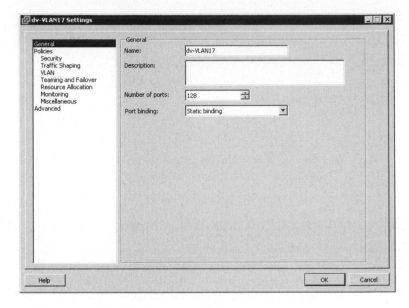

DIFFERENT OPTIONS ARE AVAILABLE DEPENDING ON THE DVSWITCH VERSION

Recall that you can create different versions of dvSwitches in the vSphere Client. Certain configuration options — like Resource Allocation and Monitoring — are only available with a version 5.0.0 vSphere Distributed Switch.

Let's focus now on modifying VLAN settings, traffic shaping, and NIC teaming for the dvPort group. Policy settings for security and monitoring follow later in this chapter.

Perform the following steps to modify the VLAN settings for a dvPort group:

1. Launch the vSphere Client, and connect to a vCenter Server instance.

2. On the vSphere Client home screen, select the Networking option under Inventory. Alternately, from the View menu, select Inventory ➢ Networking.

3. Select an existing dvPort group in the inventory pane on the left, select the Summary tab in the details pane on the right, and click the Edit Settings option in the Commands section.

4. In the dvPort Group Settings dialog box, select the VLAN option under Policies from the list of options on the left.

5. Modify the VLAN settings by changing the VLAN ID or by changing the VLAN Type setting to VLAN Trunking or Private VLAN.

Refer to Figure 5.51 for the different VLAN configuration options.

6. Click OK when you have finished making changes.

Perform the following steps to modify the traffic-shaping policy for a dvPort group:

1. Launch the vSphere Client, and connect to a vCenter Server instance.

2. On the vSphere Client home screen, select the Networking option under Inventory. Alternately, from the View menu, select Inventory ≻ Networking.

3. Select an existing dvPort group in the inventory pane on the left, select the Summary tab in the details pane on the right, and click the Edit Settings option in the Commands section.

4. Select the Traffic Shaping option from the list of options on the left of the dvPort group settings dialog box, as illustrated in Figure 5.55.

FIGURE 5.55
You can apply both ingress and egress traffic-shaping policies to a dvPort group on a dvSwitch.

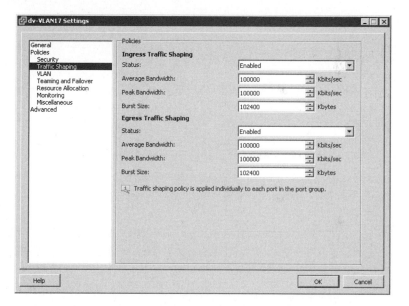

Traffic shaping was described in detail in the section "Using and Configuring Traffic Shaping." The big difference here is that with a dvSwitch, you can apply traffic-shaping policies to both ingress and egress traffic. With vSphere Standard Switches, you could apply traffic-shaping policies only to egress (outbound) traffic. Otherwise, the settings here for a dvPort group function as described earlier.

5. Click OK when you have finished making changes.

Perform the following steps to modify the NIC teaming and failover policies for a dvPort group:

1. Launch the vSphere Client, and connect to a vCenter Server instance.

2. On the vSphere Client home screen, select the Networking option under Inventory. Alternately, from the View menu, select Inventory ➢ Networking.

3. Select an existing dvPort group in the inventory pane on the left, select the Summary tab in the details pane on the right, and click the Edit Settings option in the Commands section.

4. Select the Teaming And Failover option from the list of options on the left of the dvPort group Settings dialog box, as illustrated in Figure 5.56.

FIGURE 5.56
The Teaming And Failover item in the dvPort group Settings dialog box provides options for modifying how a dvPort group uses dvUplinks.

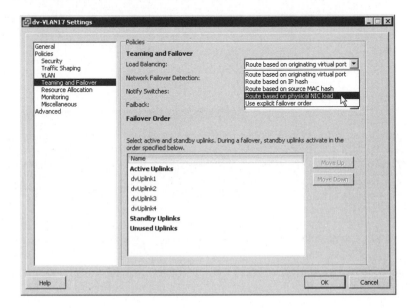

These settings were described in detail in the section "Configuring NIC Teaming," with one notable exception — version 4.1 and version 5.0 dvSwitches support a new load-balancing type, Route Based On Physical NIC Load. When this load-balancing policy is selected, ESXi checks the utilization of the uplinks every 30 seconds for congestion. In this case, congestion is defined as either transmit or receive traffic greater than 75 percent mean utilization over a 30-second period. If congestion is detected on an uplink, ESXi will dynamically reassign the VM to a different uplink.

REQUIREMENTS FOR LOAD-BASED TEAMING

Load-Based Teaming (LBT) requires that all upstream physical switches be part of the same Layer 2 (broadcast) domain. In addition, VMware recommends that you enable the PortFast or PortFast Trunk option on all physical switch ports connected to a dvSwitch that is using Load-Based Teaming.

---

5. Click OK when you have finished making changes.

If you browse through the available settings, you might notice a Blocked policy option. This is the equivalent of disabling a group of ports in the dvPort group. Figure 5.57 shows that the Block All Ports setting is set to either Yes or No. If you set the Block policy to Yes, then all traffic to and from that dvPort group is dropped. Don't set the Block policy to Yes unless you are prepared for network downtime for all VMs attached to that dvPort group!

FIGURE 5.57
The Block policy is set to either Yes or No. Setting the Block policy to Yes disables all the ports in that dvPort group.

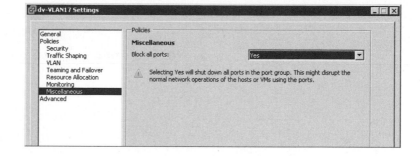

Managing Adapters

With a dvSwitch, managing adapters — both virtual and physical — is handled quite differently than with a standard vSwitch. Virtual adapters are VMkernel interfaces, so by managing virtual adapters, I'm really talking about managing VMkernel traffic — management, vMotion, IP-based storage, and Fault Tolerance logging — on a dvSwitch. Physical adapters are, of course, the physical network adapters that serve as uplinks for the dvSwitch. Managing physical adapters means adding or removing physical adapters connected to ports in the dvUplinks dvPort group on the dvSwitch.

Perform the following steps to add a virtual adapter to a dvSwitch:

1. Launch the vSphere Client, and connect to a vCenter Server instance.

2. On the vSphere Client home screen, select the Hosts And Clusters option under Inventory. Alternately, from the View menu, select Inventory ➤ Hosts And Clusters. The Ctrl+Shift+H hotkey also takes you to the correct view.

3. Select an ESXi host in the inventory pane on the left, click the Configuration tab in the details pane on the right, and select Networking from the Hardware list.

4. Click to change the view from vSphere Standard Switch to vSphere Distributed Switch, as illustrated in Figure 5.58.

FIGURE 5.58
To manage virtual adapters, switch the Networking view to vSphere Distributed Switch in the vSphere Client.

5. Click the Manage Virtual Adapters link. This opens the Manage Virtual Adapters dialog box, as shown in Figure 5.59.

FIGURE 5.59
The Manage Virtual
Adapters dialog
box allows users to
create VMkernel
interfaces, referred
to here as virtual
adapters.

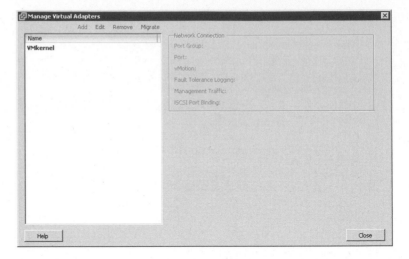

6. Click the Add hyperlink. The Add Virtual Adapter Wizard appears, offering you the option to either create a new virtual adapter or migrate existing virtual adapters.

   Creating a new virtual adapter involves providing new information about the VMkernel port and then attaching the new virtual adapter to an existing dvPort group. The wizard also prompts for IP address information because that is required when creating a VMkernel interface. Refer to the earlier sections about configuring ESXi management and VMkernel networking for more information.

   In the section "Creating a vSphere Distributed Switch," I mentioned that I would show you how to migrate virtual adapters. This is where you would migrate a virtual adapter. In the Add Virtual Adapter dialog box, select Migrate Existing Virtual Adapters and click Next.

7. For each current virtual adapter, select the new destination port group on the dvSwitch. Deselect the box next to the current virtual adapters that you don't want to migrate right now.

   This is illustrated in Figure 5.60. Click Next to continue.

8. Review the changes to the dvSwitch — which are helpfully highlighted for easy identification — and click Finish to commit the changes.

   After creating or migrating a virtual adapter, the same dialog box allows for changes to the virtual port, such as modifying the IP address, changing the dvPort group to which the adapter is assigned, or enabling features such as vMotion or Fault Tolerance logging. You would remove virtual adapters using this dialog box as well.

   The Manage Physical Adapters link allows you to add or remove physical adapters connected to ports in the dvUplinks port group on the dvSwitch. Although you can specify physical adapters during the process of adding a host to a dvSwitch, as shown earlier, it might be necessary at times to connect a physical NIC to a port in the dvUplinks port group on the dvSwitch after the host is already participating in the dvSwitch.

   Perform the following steps to add a physical network adapter in an ESXi host to the dvUplinks port group on the dvSwitch:

1. Launch the vSphere Client, and connect to a vCenter Server instance.

2. On the vSphere Client home screen, select the Hosts And Clusters option under Inventory. Alternately, from the View menu, select Inventory ➤ Hosts And Clusters. The Ctrl+Shift+H hotkey will also take you to the correct view.

3. Select an ESXi host in the inventory list on the left, click the Configuration tab in the details pane on the right, and select Networking from the Hardware list.

4. Click to change the view from vSphere Standard Switch to vSphere Distributed Switch.

5. Click the Manage Physical Adapters link. This opens the Manage Physical Adapters dialog box, as shown in Figure 5.61.

FIGURE 5.60
For each virtual adapter migrating to the dvSwitch, you must assign the virtual adapter to an existing dvPort group.

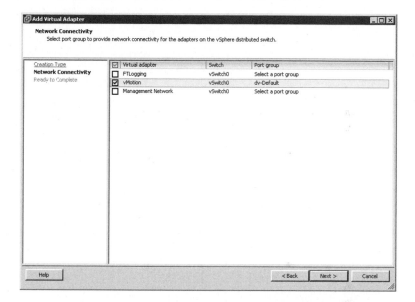

FIGURE 5.61
The Manage Physical Adapters dialog box provides information on physical NICs connected to the dvUplinks port group and allows you to add or remove uplinks.

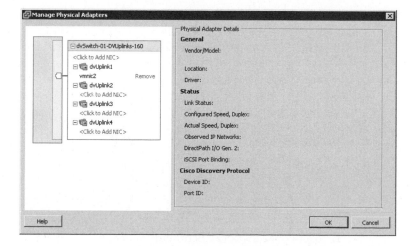

6. To add a physical network adapter to the dvUplinks port group, click the Click To Add NIC link.

7. In the Add Physical Adapter dialog box, select the physical adapter to be added to the dvUplinks port group, and click OK.

8. Click OK again to return to the vSphere Client.

In addition to being able to migrate virtual adapters, you can use vCenter Server to assist in migrating VM networking between vSphere Standard Switches and vSphere Distributed Switches, as shown in Figure 5.62.

FIGURE 5.62

The Migrate Virtual Machine Networking tool automates the process of migrating VMs from vSwitches to dvSwitches and back again.

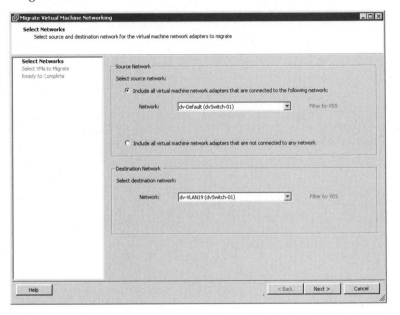

This tool, accessed using the Migrate Virtual Machine Networking link on the Summary tab of a dvSwitch, will reconfigure all selected VMs to use the selected destination network. This is a lot easier than individually reconfiguring a bunch of VMs! In addition, this tool allows you to easily migrate VMs both *to* a dvSwitch as well as *from* a dvSwitch. Let's walk through the process so that you can see how it works.

Perform the following steps to migrate VMs from a vSphere Standard Switch to a vSphere Distributed Switch:

1. Launch the vSphere Client, and connect to a vCenter Server instance.

2. Navigate to the Networking inventory view.

3. Select a dvSwitch from the inventory tree on the left, select the Summary tab, and click the Migrate Virtual Machine Networking link from the Commands section.

   This launches the Migrate Virtual Machine Networking wizard.

4. Select the source network that contains the VMs you'd like to migrate.

If you prefer to work by dvSwitch and dvPort group, click the Filter By VDS link.

5. Select the destination network to which you'd like the VMs to be migrated.

Again, use the Filter By VDS link if you'd rather select the destination by dvSwitch and dvPort group.

6. Click Next when you've finished selecting the source and destination networks.

7. A list of matching VMs is generated, and each VM is analyzed to determine if the destination network is Accessible or Inaccessible to the VM.

Figure 5.63 shows a list with both Accessible and Inaccessible destination networks. A destination network might show up as Inaccessible if the ESXi host on which that VM is running isn't part of the dvSwitch (as is the case in this instance). Select the VMs you want to migrate; then click Next.

FIGURE 5.63
You cannot migrate VMs matching your source network selection if the destination network is listed as Inaccessible.

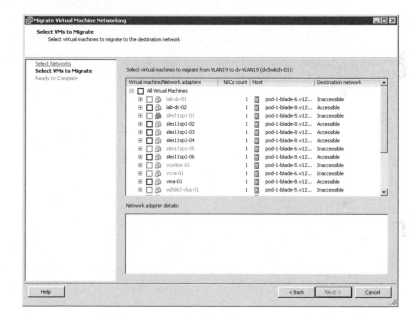

8. Click Finish to start the migration of the selected VMs from the specified source network to the selected destination network.

You'll see a Reconfigure Virtual Machine task spawn in the Tasks pane for each VM that needs to be migrated.

Keep in mind that this tool can migrate VMs from a vSwitch to a dvSwitch or from a dvSwitch to a vSwitch — you only need to specify the source and destination networks accordingly.

Now that I've covered the basics of dvSwitches, I'd like to delve into a few advanced topics. First up is network monitoring using NetFlow.

Using NetFlow on vSphere Distributed Switches

NetFlow is a mechanism for efficiently reporting IP-based traffic information as a series of *traffic flows*. Traffic flows are defined as the combination of source and destination IP address, source and destination TCP or UDP ports, IP, and IP Type of Service (ToS). Network devices that support NetFlow will track and report information on the traffic flows, typically sending this information to a NetFlow collector. Using the data collected, network administrators gain detailed insight into the types and amount of traffic flows across the network.

In vSphere 5.0, VMware introduced support for NetFlow with vSphere Distributed Switches (only on version 5.0.0 dvSwitches). This allows ESXi hosts to gather detailed per-flow information and report that information to a NetFlow collector.

Configuring NetFlow is a two-step process:

1. Configure the NetFlow properties on the dvSwitch.

2. Enable or disable NetFlow (the default is disabled) on a per–dvPort group basis.

Let's take a closer look at these steps.

To configure the NetFlow properties for a dvSwitch, perform these steps:

1. Launch the vSphere Client, and connect to a vCenter Server instance.

2. Select View ➤ Inventory ➤ Networking to navigate to the Networking inventory view, where you'll see your configured dvSwitches and dvPort groups listed.

3. Select the dvSwitch for which you'd like to configure the NetFlow properties, and click the Edit Settings link in the Commands section of the Summary tab.

   This opens the dvSwitch Settings dialog box.

4. Click the NetFlow tab.

5. As shown in Figure 5.64, specify the IP address of the NetFlow collector, the port on the NetFlow collector, and an IP address to identify the dvSwitch.

6. You can modify the Advanced Settings if advised to do so by your networking team.

7. If you want the dvSwitch to only process internal traffic flows — that is, traffic flows from VM to VM on that host — select Process Internal Flows Only.

8. Click OK to commit the changes and return to the vSphere Client.

After you configure the NetFlow properties for the dvSwitch, you then enable NetFlow on a per-dvPort group basis. The default setting is Disabled.

Perform these steps to enable NetFlow on a specific dvPort group:

1. In the vSphere Client, switch to the Networking inventory view.

2. Select the dvPort group for which NetFlow should be enabled.

3. Click the Summary tab and then click Edit Settings in the Commands area.

   You can also right-click the dvPort group and select Edit Settings from the context menu.

4. The dvPort group Settings dialog box appears. Click Monitoring from the list of options on the left.

This displays the NetFlow setting, as shown in Figure 5.65.

FIGURE 5.64

You'll need the IP address and port number for the NetFlow collector in order to send flow information from a dvSwitch.

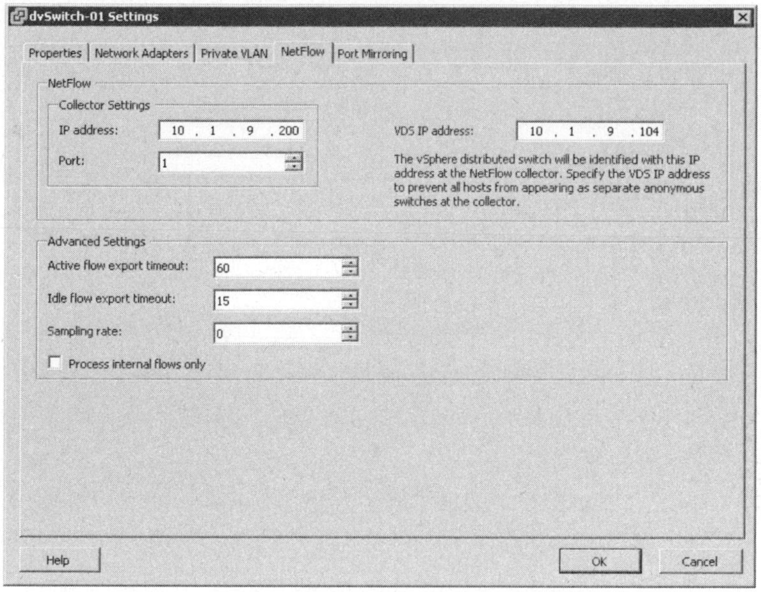

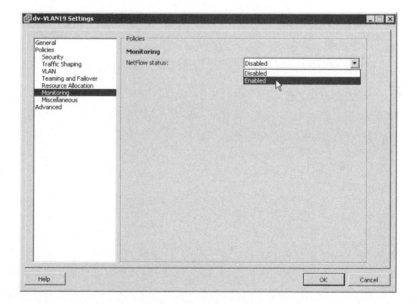

FIGURE 5.65

NetFlow is disabled by default. You enable NetFlow on a per–dvPort group basis.

5. From the NetFlow Status drop-down list, select Enabled.

6. Click OK to save the changes to the dvPort group.

This dvPort group will start capturing NetFlow statistics and reporting that information to the specified NetFlow collector.

Another feature that was present in previous versions of vSphere but has been expanded in vSphere 5.0 is support for switch discovery protocols, as discussed in the next section.

Enabling Switch Discovery Protocols

Previous versions of vSphere supported Cisco Discovery Protocol (CDP), a protocol for exchanging information between network devices. However, it required using the command line to enable and configure CDP.

In vSphere 5.0, VMware added support for Link Layer Discovery Protocol (LLDP), an industry-standardized form of CDP, and provided a location within the vSphere Client where CDP/LLDP support can be configured.

Perform the following steps to configure switch discovery support:

1. In the vSphere Client, switch to the Networking inventory view.

2. Select the dvSwitch for which you'd like to configure CDP or LLDP support and click Edit Settings.

   You can also right-click the dvSwitch and select Edit Settings from the context menu.

3. Click Advanced.

4. Configure the dvSwitch for CDP or LLDP support, as shown in Figure 5.66.

   This figure shows the dvSwitch configured for LLDP support, both listening (receiving LLDP information from other connected devices) and advertising (sending LLDP information to other connected devices).

FIGURE 5.66
LLDP support enables dvSwitches to exchange discovery information with other LLDP-enabled devices over the network.

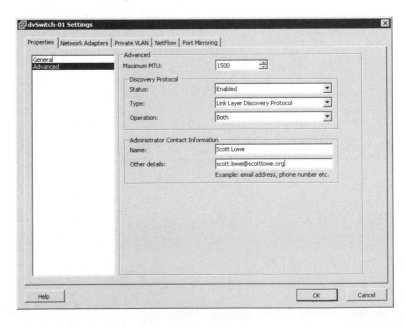

5. Click OK to save your changes.

Once the ESXi hosts participating in this dvSwitch start exchanging discovery information, you can view that information from the physical switch(es). For example, on most Cisco switches the `show cdp neighbor` command will display information about CDP-enabled network devices, including ESXi hosts. Entries for ESXi hosts will include information on the physical NIC use and the vSwitch involved.

The final advanced networking topic I'll review is private VLANs. Private VLANs were first added in vSphere 4.0, and support for private VLANs continues in vSphere 5.

Setting Up Private VLANs

Private VLANs (PVLANs) are an advanced networking feature of vSphere that build on the functionality of vSphere Distributed Switches. Private VLANs are possible only when using dvSwitches and are not available to use with vSphere Standard Switches.

I'll provide a quick overview of private VLANs. PVLANs are a way to further isolate ports within a VLAN. For example, consider the scenario of hosts within a demilitarized zone (DMZ). Hosts within a DMZ rarely need to communicate with each other, but using a VLAN for each host quickly becomes unwieldy for a number of reasons. By using PVLANs, you can isolate hosts from each other while keeping them on the same IP subnet. Figure 5.67 provides a graphical overview of how PVLANs work.

FIGURE 5.67
Private VLANs can help isolate ports on the same IP subnet.

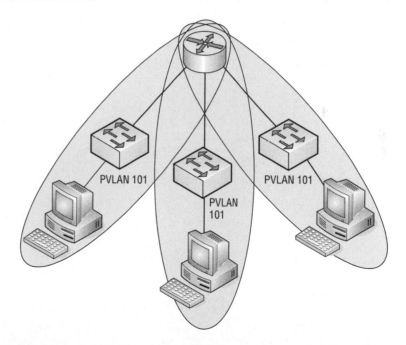

PVLANs are configured in pairs: the primary VLAN and any secondary VLANs. The primary VLAN is considered the *downstream* VLAN; that is, traffic to the host travels along the primary VLAN. The secondary VLAN is considered the *upstream* VLAN; that is, traffic from the host travels along the secondary VLAN.

To use PVLANs, first configure the PVLANs on the physical switches connecting to the ESXi hosts, and then add the PVLAN entries to the dvSwitch in vCenter Server.

Perform the following steps to define PVLAN entries on a dvSwitch:

1. Launch the vSphere Client, and connect to a vCenter Server instance.

2. On the vSphere Client home screen, select the Networking option under Inventory. Alternately, from the View menu, select Inventory ➢ Networking or press the Ctrl+Shift+N hotkey.

3. Select an existing dvSwitch in the inventory pane on the left, select the Summary tab in the details pane on the right, and click the Edit Settings option in the Commands section.

4. Select the Private VLAN tab.

5. Add a primary VLAN ID to the list on the left.

6. For each primary VLAN ID in the list on the left, add one or more secondary VLANs to the list on the right, as shown in Figure 5.68.

FIGURE 5.68
Private VLAN entries consist of a primary VLAN and one or more secondary VLAN entries.

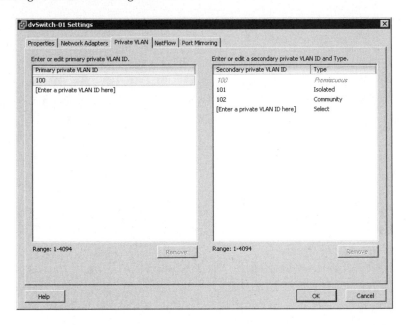

Secondary VLANs are classified as one of the two following types:

◆ Isolated: Ports placed in secondary PVLANs configured as isolated are allowed to communicate only with promiscuous ports in the same secondary VLAN. I'll explain promiscuous ports shortly.

♦ Community: Ports in a secondary PVLAN are allowed to communicate with other ports in the same secondary PVLAN as well as with promiscuous ports.

Only one isolated secondary VLAN is permitted for each primary VLAN. Multiple secondary VLANs configured as community VLANs are allowed.

7. When you finish adding all the PVLAN pairs, click OK to save the changes and return to the vSphere Client.

After the PVLAN IDs have been entered for a dvSwitch, you must create a dvPort group that takes advantage of the PVLAN configuration. The process for creating a dvPort group was described previously. Figure 5.69 shows the Create Distributed Port Group wizard for a dvPort group that uses PVLANs.

FIGURE 5.69
When creating a dvPort group with PVLANs, the dvPort group is associated with both the primary VLAN ID and a secondary VLAN ID.

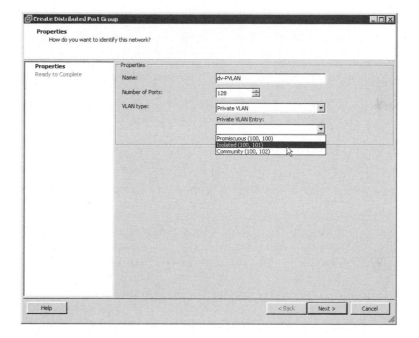

In Figure 5.69 you can see the term *promiscuous* again. In PVLAN parlance, a promiscuous port is allowed to send and receive Layer 2 frames to any other port in the VLAN. This type of port is typically reserved for the default gateway for an IP subnet — for example, a Layer 3 router.

PVLANs are a powerful configuration tool but also a complex configuration topic and one that can be difficult to understand. For additional information on PVLANs, I recommend visiting Cisco's website at www.cisco.com and searching for *private VLANs*.

As with vSphere Standard Switches, vSphere Distributed Switches provide a tremendous amount of flexibility in designing and configuring a virtual network. But, as with all things, there are limits to the flexibility. Table 5.2 lists some of the configuration maximums for vSphere Distributed Switches.

TABLE 5.2: Configuration maximums for ESXi networking components (vSphere Distributed Switches)

CONFIGURATION ITEM	MAXIMUM
Switches per vCenter Server	32
Maximum ports per host (vSS/vDS)	4,096
vDS ports per vCenter instance	30,000
ESXi hosts per vDS	350
Static port groups per vCenter instance	5,000
Ephemeral port groups per vCenter instance	256

As if adding vSphere Distributed Switches to vSphere and ESXi 4.0 wasn't a big enough change from earlier versions of VMware Infrastructure, there's something even bigger in store for you: the very first third-party vSphere Distributed Switch: the Cisco Nexus 1000V.

Installing and Configuring the Cisco Nexus 1000V

The Cisco Nexus 1000V is a third-party vSphere Distributed Switch, the first of its kind. Built as part of a joint engineering effort between Cisco and VMware and released with vSphere 4.0, the Nexus 1000V completely changes the dynamics in how the networking and server teams interact in environments using vSphere 4 and later.

Prior to the arrival of the Cisco Nexus 1000V, the reach of the networking team ended at the uplinks from the ESXi host to the physical switches. The networking team had no visibility into and no control over the networking inside the ESXi hosts. The server team, which used the vSphere Client to create and manage vSwitches and port groups, handled that functionality. The Cisco Nexus 1000V changes all that. Now the networking group will create the port groups that will be applied to VMs, and the server group will simply attach VMs to the appropriate port group — modeling the same behavior in the virtual environment as exists in the physical environment. In addition, organizations gain per-VM network statistics and much greater insight into the type of traffic that's found on the ESXi hosts.

The Cisco Nexus 1000V has the following two major components:

◆ The Virtual Ethernet Module (VEM), which executes inside the ESXi hypervisor and replaces the standard vSwitch functionality. The VEM leverages the vSphere Distributed Switch APIs to bring features like quality of service (QoS), private VLANs, access control lists, NetFlow, and SPAN to VM networking.

◆ The Virtual Supervisor Module (VSM), which is a Cisco NX-OS instance running as a VM (note that Cisco also sells a hardware appliance, called the Nexus 1010, that can provide a Nexus 1000V VSM). The VSM controls multiple VEMs as one logical modular switch. All configuration is performed through the VSM and propagated to the VEMs automatically.

The Nexus 1000V supports redundant VSMs, a configuration in which there is both a primary VSM and a secondary VSM.

The Cisco Nexus 1000V marks a new era in virtual networking. Let's take a closer look at installing and configuring the Nexus 1000V, starting with the installation process.

Installing the Cisco Nexus 1000V

Installing the Nexus 1000V is a two-step process:

◆ You must first install at least one VSM. If you are going to set up redundant VSMs, you'll need to wait to create the secondary VSM until after you've gotten the primary VSM up, running, and attached to vCenter Server.

◆ After a VSM is up and running, you use the VSM to push out the VEMs to the various ESXi hosts that use the Nexus 1000V as their dvSwitch.

Fortunately, users familiar with setting up a VM have an advantage in setting up the VSM because it operates as a VM. However, before attempting to set up the VSM as a VM, there are some dependencies that must be addressed. Specifically, you should be sure that you — or the appropriate networking individuals — have performed the following tasks before starting installation of the Nexus 1000V:

◆ You must identify three VLANs to be used by the Nexus 1000V VSM and VEMs: one VLAN for management traffic, one VLAN for control traffic, and one VLAN for packet traffic. These VLANs are not the same as the VLANs that you will configure on the Nexus 1000V to carry VM traffic or ESXi host traffic; these VLANs are used by the Nexus 1000V for VSM-VEM connectivity. The management VLAN can be the same VLAN that you use for management of the ESXi hosts themselves, if desired.

◆ You must configure the physical upstream switches to carry traffic from the relevant VLANs to the ESXi host(s) that will support the VSMs and VEMs. This generally means configuring the upstream switch ports as 802.1Q VLAN trunks and allowing all relevant VLANs across the VLAN trunk. The commands to do this vary from manufacturer to manufacturer; on most Cisco switches, you would use the `switchport mode trunk` and `switchport trunk allowed vlan` commands.

◆ On upstream physical switches, you should ensure you are filtering Bridge Protocol Data Units (BPDUs). Either globally enable BPDU filter and BPDU Guard, or use the `spanning-tree bpdu filter` and `spanning-tree bpdu guard` commands on the specific interfaces where the Nexus 1000V dvSwitch uplinks will connect.

◆ Ports on upstream physical switches also require the use of the `portfast trunk`, `portfast edge trunk`, or `spanning-tree port type edge trunk` commands (the command varies based on the switch model). These are Cisco-specific commands, so for other vendors other commands would be necessary.

◆ The ESXi host that will support the VSM must already have the appropriate VLANs configured and supported, including the control and packet VLANs.

For more complete and detailed information on these dependencies, I encourage you to refer to the official Cisco Nexus 1000V documentation. Once you've satisfied these requirements, then you're ready to start installing the Nexus 1000V VSM.

OVF TEMPLATE FOR THE NEXUS 1000V VSM

Earlier versions of the Nexus 1000V that supported vSphere 4.x provided an Open Virtualization Format (OVF) template that simplified the deployment of the VSM (OVF templates are something that I discuss in greater detail in Chapter 10). At the time of this writing, an OVF template was not available for the vSphere 5.0-compatible version of the Nexus 1000V, and so I've modified the instructions accordingly.

SETTING UP THE NEXUS 1000V VSM

After you've fulfilled all the necessary dependencies and requirements, the first step is to set up the first Nexus 1000V VSM.

Perform the following steps to install a Nexus 1000V VSM:

1. Use the vSphere Client to establish a connection to a vCenter Server or an ESXi host. Although the Nexus 1000V requires vCenter Server, the initial creation of the VSM could be done directly on an ESXi host if necessary.

2. Create a new VM with the following specifications:

   ◆ Guest OS: Other Linux (64-bit)

   ◆ Memory: 2 GB

   ◆ CPUs: One vCPU

   ◆ Network adapters: Three e1000 network adapters

   ◆ Virtual disk: 3 GB with LSI Logic Parallel adapter (Thin Provisioned virtual disks are not supported)

   For more information on creating VMs and specifying these values, refer to Chapter 7.

3. After the VM has been created, edit the VM to reserve 1500 MHz of CPU capacity and 2 GB of RAM. More information on reservations is found in Chapter 11.

4. Configure the network adapters so that the first e1000 adapter connects to a VLAN created for control traffic, the second e1000 adapter connects to the management VLAN, and the third e1000 network adapter connects to a VLAN created for packet traffic. These are the three VLANs that you identified earlier in this chapter.

   It is very important that the adapters are configured *in exactly* this order.

4. Attach the Nexus 1000V VSM ISO image to the VM's CD-ROM drive, and configure the CD-ROM to be connected at startup, as shown in Figure 5.70.

5. Power on the VM.

FIGURE 5.70

The ISO image for the Nexus 1000V VSM should be attached to the VM's CD-ROM drive for installation.

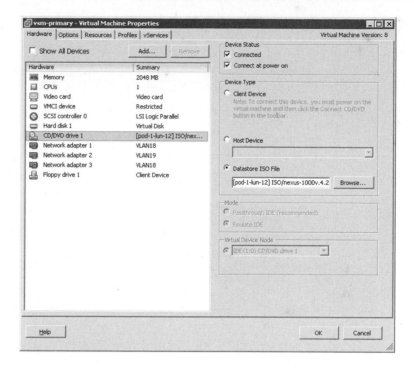

6. From the boot menu, select Install Nexus 1000V And Bring Up The New Image.

7. After the installation is complete, walk through the initial setup dialog.

   During the initial setup dialog, a series of questions prompt you for information such as the password for the admin user account; the VLAN IDs for the management, packet, and data VLANs; the IP address to be assigned to the VSM; and the default gateway for the VSM. When prompted for HA role, enter "standalone"; if you are going to set up redundant VSMs, you'll perform that task later.

Once the VSM is up and running, the next step will be to connect it to vCenter Server. To help ensure a smooth process, I'd recommend using the ping command to double-check connectivity to both the VSM and the vCenter Server. This might help identify network connectivity issues, such as connecting the virtual NICs in the VSM in the wrong order, that would prevent successful completion of the next step.

If network connectivity to the VSM and to vCenter Server is working, then you're ready to proceed with connecting the Nexus 1000V VSM to vCenter Server.

CONNECTING THE NEXUS 1000V VSM TO VCENTER SERVER

In early versions of the Nexus 1000V, multiple separate steps were needed to connect the VSM to vCenter Server for proper communications. Not too long after the initial release of the Nexus 1000V, Cisco released a web-based tool to help with the installation. These instructions will assume the use of the web-based tool to connect the VSM with vCenter Server.

To connect the Nexus 1000V VSM to vCenter Server using the web-based configuration tool, perform these steps:

1. Open a web browser and navigate to the IP address you assigned to the VSM during the initial setup dialog. For example, if you provided the IP address 10.1.9.110 during the initial setup dialog, you would navigate to `http://10.1.9.110` in the web browser.

2. Click the Launch Installer Application hyperlink.

3. If prompted to run the application, click Run.

4. After a few moments, the Nexus 1000V Installation Management Center will launch. At the first screen, enter the admin password for the VSM (you provided this password during the initial setup dialog). Click Next to proceed to the next step.

5. Supply the information needed to connect to your vCenter Server instance. This includes the vCenter Server IP address, port number (default is 443), username, and password. This is illustrated in Figure 5.71. Make sure that Use A Configuration File is set to No, then click Next to continue.

FIGURE 5.71
You must supply the necessary information to connect the VSM to vCenter Server.

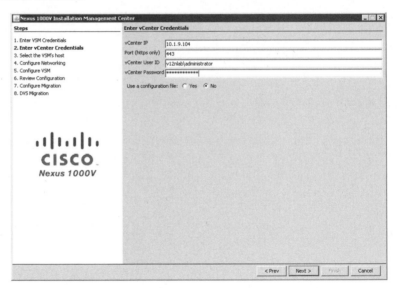

6. Select the cluster or ESXi host where the VSM VM is currently running. Click Next.

7. At the Configure Networking screen, select the VSM VM from the drop-down list of VMs.

8. Under Please Choose A Configuration Option, you have three options:

- If you select Default L2: Choose The Management VLAN For All Port Groups, then the management, control, and packet interfaces on the Nexus 1000V VSM will use the management VLAN. Select the option only if you are sharing a single VLAN for all three VSM-VEM traffic types.

◆ If you select Advanced L2: Configure Each Port Group Individually, then you'll have the option of selecting the appropriate port group or creating a new port group for each of the three interfaces on the VSM. Select this option if the management, control, or packet VLANs are on a separate VLAN from the others.

◆ If you select Advanced L3: Configure Port Groups for L3, you'll have the ability to specify Layer 3 (routed) connectivity for the VSM interfaces. Select this option only if the VSM and the VEM will be separated by a router.

In most instances, I recommend either the Default L2 or the Advanced L2 option, depending on how your VLANs are configured. Once you've selected the right option, click Next to continue.

9. At the Configure VSM screen, you must supply the information requested by the installation application. This includes information like the VSM switch name, admin password, IP address, default gateway, HA role, domain ID, SVS datacenter name (the name of the datacenter object in vCenter Server), and the native (or untagged) VLAN. Click Next once you're finished filling in the fields.

10. If you want to save the configuration out to a file for future reference or use, click Save Configuration To File and then select a destination file. Otherwise, click Next to proceed.

11. The Nexus 1000V Installation Management Center will proceed though a series of steps. As each step is completed, a green check mark will appear next to it. At certain points during this process, you might also notice tasks appearing in the Tasks pane of the vSphere Client as the application performs the necessary steps to integrate the VSM with vCenter Server.

12. When the checklist is complete, the application will automatically proceed to the next step. When prompted if you want to migrate this host and its networks, select No. Click Next.

13. At the Summary screen, review the configuration and then click Close. Integration of the VSM with vCenter Server is now complete.

Integration of the VSM with vCenter Server results in the creation of a vSphere Distributed Switch. If you navigate to the Networking inventory view, you can see the new dvSwitch that was created by the Nexus 1000V Installation Management Center.

At this point, you have the VSM connected to and communicating with vCenter Server. The next step is to configure a system uplink port profile; this is the equivalent of the dvUplinks dvPort group used by native dvSwitches and will contain the physical network adapters that will connect the Nexus 1000V to the rest of the network. While this port profile isn't required for the VSM, it is required by the VEM, and it's necessary to have this port profile in place before adding ESXi hosts to the Nexus 1000V and deploying the VEM onto those hosts.

1. Using PuTTY.exe (Windows) or a terminal window (Linux or Mac OS X), establish an SSH session to the VSM, and log in as the admin user.

2. Enter the following command to activate configuration mode:

```
config t
```

3. Enter the following commands to create the system uplink port profile:

```
port-profile type ethernet system-uplink
switchport mode trunk
switchport trunk allowed vlan 18, 19
no shut
system vlan 18, 19
vmware port-group
state enabled
```

The order of the commands is important; some commands, like the `system vlan` command, won't be accepted by the VSM until the allowed VLANs are defined and the port is in an active state (accomplished with the `no shut` command). Additionally, any VLANs that you want to define as system VLANs must already be created on the Nexus 1000V using the `vlan` command.

Replace the VLAN IDs on the `system vlan` statement with the VLAN IDs of the control and packet VLANs. Likewise, specify the control and packet VLANs — along with any other VLANs that should be permitted across these uplinks — on the `switchport trunk allowed vlan` command.

If you would like to specify a different name for the dvPort group in vCenter Server than the name given in the `port-profile` statement, append that name to the `vmware-port group` command, like this:

```
vmware port-group dv-SystemUplinks
```

4. Use the `exit` command to exit out of configuration mode to privileged EXEC mode. Depending on where you are in the configuration, you might need to use this command more than once. You can also use Ctrl+Z to exit directly to privileged EXEC mode.

5. Copy the running configuration to the startup configuration so that it is persistent across reboots:

```
copy run start
```

The purpose of this port profile is to provide the configuration for the physical NICs in the servers that will participate in the Nexus 1000V distributed virtual switch. Without this port profile in place before adding your first ESXi host, the Nexus 1000V wouldn't know how to configure the uplinks, and the host would become unreachable across the network. You'd then be forced to use the Direct Console User Interface (DCUI) to restore the default virtual network configuration on this host.

With the port profile for the uplinks in place, the one step remaining in the installation of the Nexus 1000V is adding ESXi hosts. The next section covers this procedure.

ADDING ESXi HOSTS TO THE NEXUS 1000V

Like installing the Nexus 1000V VSM, the process of adding ESXi hosts to the Nexus 1000V is a two step process:

◆ First, you must ensure the VEM is deployed to all ESXi hosts that you plan to add to the dvSwitch.

◆ Once the VEM is deployed to the ESXi hosts, you can add them to the Nexus 1000v distributed virtual switch.

I'll discuss each of these steps in the sections below.

Deploying the VEM to an ESXi Host

The process for deploying the VEM to an ESXi host will depend on whether you have vSphere Update Manager (VUM) present in your environment. If VUM is present and configured with the Nexus 1000V software, then VUM will automatically push the VEM onto an ESXi host when you add the ESXi host to the distributed virtual switch. No additional effort is required once VUM has been configured; the process is automatic. You only need to configure VUM to point to a software repository that contains the Nexus 1000V software. This process is described in Chapter 4, "Installing and Configuring vSphere Update Manager."

If, on the other hand, you are not using VUM or you have not configured VUM with the Nexus 1000V software, then you'll have to install the VEM manually before adding an ESXi host to the distributed virtual switch.

Perform these steps to manually install the VEM onto an ESXi host:

1. Using the Datastore Browser in the vSphere Client, upload the VIB file for the Nexus 1000V VEM into a datastore accessible from the ESXi host on which you want to install the VEM. This process is described in Chapter 9 in the section "Working With Installation Media."

2. Run this command, either from a system with the vSphere CLI (vCLI) installed or from the vSphere Management Assistant:

   ```
   esxcli --server ESXi host IP address software vib install
   /vmfs/volumes/VMFS datastore name/path to VIB file
   ```

3. If prompted for username and/or password, supply the appropriate credentials to authenticate to the ESXi host.

4. After a couple of minutes, the command will complete and, if successful, will return a message that the operation completed successfully. Repeat these steps for each ESXi host you are going to add to the Nexus 1000V distributed virtual switch.

With the VSM configured and connected to vCenter Server and the VEM installed on the ESXi hosts, you're ready to add hosts to the Nexus 1000V distributed virtual switch.

Adding an ESXi Host to the Nexus 1000V

Adding an ESXi host to the Nexus 1000V is, for the most part, very much like adding an ESXi host to a VMware dvSwitch.

Perform these steps to add an ESXi host to the Nexus 1000V distributed virtual switch:

1. If it's not already running, launch the vSphere Client and connect to the vCenter Server instance with which the VSM is connected.

   Although you could connect directly to an ESXi host to create the VSM VM and install the VEM, you must connect to vCenter Server to add a host to the Nexus 1000V dvSwitch. In addition, since there can be multiple instances of vCenter Server, it must be the instance of vCenter Server with which the VSM has been connected.

2. Navigate to the Networking inventory view.

3. Right-click on the dvSwitch object that represents the Nexus 1000V and select Add Host. This launches the Add Host To vSphere Distributed Switch wizard.

4. Place a check mark next to each ESXi host you want to add to the Nexus 1000V dvSwitch.

5. For each ESXi host, place a check mark next to the physical NICs you want to use as uplinks for the Nexus 1000V.

   I generally recommend migrating only a single physical NIC over to the Nexus 1000V until you've verified that the dvSwitch is working as expected. Once you've confirmed that the Nexus 1000V configuration is correct and works, then you can migrate the remaining physical NICs.

6. For each selected physical NIC on each ESXi host, select the desired uplink port group on the Nexus 1000V. Unless you've created additional uplink port groups, there will be only the single uplink port group you created earlier in the section "Connecting the Nexus 1000V VSM to vCenter Server."

MULTIPLE UPLINK GROUPS

One key change between a native dvSwitch and the Cisco Nexus 1000V is that the Nexus 1000V supports multiple uplink groups. When adding a host to the Nexus dvSwitch, be sure to place the physical network adapters for that host into the appropriate uplink group(s).

---

7. When you're finished selecting ESXi hosts, physical NICs, and uplink port groups, click Next.

8. If you are prompted to migrate one or more VMkernel ports, choose not to migrate them. You can migrate them manually after you've verified the operation of the Nexus 1000V. I described the process for migrating both physical and virtual adapters in the "Managing Adapters" section of this chapter. Click Next.

9. If you are prompted to migrate VM networking, choose not to migrate them. You can migrate VM networking configurations manually after you've verified the operation of the Nexus 1000V. Instructions for migrating VM networking configurations are also provided in the "Managing Adapters" section in this chapter. Click Next to continue.

10. Click Finish to complete adding the ESXi host to the Nexus 1000V.

If you didn't install the VEM manually but are using VUM instead, VUM will automatically push the VEM to the ESXi host as part of adding the host to the Nexus 1000V distributed virtual switch. If you installed the VEM manually, then the host is added to the dvSwitch.

You can verify that the host was added to the Nexus 1000V and that the VEM is working properly by logging into to the VSM and using the show module command. For each ESXi host added and working properly, there will be a Virtual Ethernet Module listed in the output of the command.

Removing a host from a Nexus 1000V distributed virtual switch is the same as for a native dvSwitch, so refer to those procedures in the section "Removing an ESXi Host from a Distributed vSwitch" for more information.

So you've installed the Nexus 1000V, but what's next? In the next section, I'll take a closer look at some common configuration tasks for the Nexus 1000V.

Configuring the Cisco Nexus 1000V

All configuration of the Nexus 1000V is handled by the VSM, typically at the CLI via SSH or Telnet. Like other members of the Cisco Nexus family, the Nexus 1000V VSM runs NX-OS, which is similar to Cisco's Internetwork Operating System (IOS). Thanks to the increasing popularity of Cisco's Nexus switches and the similarity between NX-OS and IOS, I expect that many IT professionals will be able to transition into NX-OS without too much difficulty.

The bulk of the configuration of the Nexus 1000V VSM is performed during installation. After installing the VSM and the VEMs and adding ESXi hosts to the dvSwitch, most configuration tasks after that involve creating, removing, or modifying *port profiles*. Port profiles are the Nexus 1000V counterpart to VMware distributed virtual port groups (dvPort groups). Every dvPort group on a Nexus 1000V corresponds to a port profile.

Earlier in this section I described how the Nexus 1000V brings the same creation-consumption model to the virtualized environment that currently exists in the physical environment. I'd like to expand a bit more on that concept to help further clarify the relationship between port profiles and vSphere port groups. In the physical data center environment, the networking team *creates* the appropriate configuration on the physical switches, and the server team *consumes* that configuration by connecting to the necessary ports. With the Nexus 1000V, the networking team *creates* the appropriate configuration on the VSM with port profiles. Those port profiles are automatically pushed into vCenter Server as dvPort groups. The server team then *consumes* that configuration by connecting VMs to the necessary dvPort group. Port profiles are the creation side of the model; port groups are the consumption side.

Now that you have a better understanding of the importance and necessity of port profiles in a Nexus 1000V environment, let's walk through the process for creating a port profile.

Perform the following steps to create a new port profile:

1. Using PuTTY.exe (Windows) or a terminal window (Linux or Mac OS X), establish an SSH session to the VSM, and log in as the admin user.

2. If you are not already in privileged EXEC mode, indicated by a hash sign after the prompt, enter privileged EXEC mode with the enable command, and supply the password.

3. Enter the following command to enter configuration mode:

   config t

4. Enter the following commands to create a new port profile:

   ```
   port-profile type vethernet port-profile-name
   switchport mode access
   switchport access vlan 17
   vmware port-group VMware-dvPort-Group-Name
   no shut
   state enabled
   ```

These commands create a port profile and matching dvPort group in vCenter Server. In this example, ports in this dvPort group will be assigned to VLAN 17. Obviously, you can change the VLAN ID on the `switchport access vlan` statement, and you can change the name of the dvPort group using the `vmware port-group` statement.

Note that the `no shut` command is important; without it, virtual Ethernet ports created from this port profile will be administratively down and will not send or receive traffic.

5. Use the `end` command to exit configuration mode and return to privileged EXEC mode.

6. Copy the running configuration to the startup configuration so that it is persistent across reboots:

```
copy run start
```

Upon completion of these steps, a dvPort group, either with the name specified on the `vmware port-group` statement or with the name of the port profile, will be listed in the vSphere Client under Inventory ➢ Networking.

Perform the following steps to delete an existing port profile and the corresponding dvPort group:

1. Using `PuTTY.exe` (Windows) or a terminal window (Linux or Mac OS X), establish an SSH session to the VSM, and log in as the admin user.

2. If you are not already in privileged EXEC mode, indicated by a hash sign after the prompt, enter privileged EXEC mode with the `enable` command, and supply the password.

3. Enter the following command to enter configuration mode:

```
config t
```

4. Enter the following commands to create a new port profile:

```
no port-profile type vethernet port-profile-name
```

If there are any VMs assigned to the dvPort group, the VSM CLI will respond with an error message indicating that the port profile is currently in use. You must reconfigure the VM(s) in question to use a different dvPort group before this port profile can be removed.

5. The port profile and the matching dvPort group are removed. You will be able to see the dvPort group being removed in the Tasks list at the bottom of the vSphere Client.

6. Use the `end` command to exit configuration mode and return to privileged EXEC mode.

7. Copy the running configuration to the startup configuration so that it is persistent across reboots:

```
copy run start
```

Perform the following steps to modify an existing port profile and the corresponding dvPort group:

1. Using PuTTY.exe (Windows) or a terminal window (Linux or Mac OS X), establish an SSH session to the VSM, and log in as the admin user.

2. If you are not already in privileged EXEC mode, indicated by a hash sign after the prompt, enter privileged EXEC mode with the enable command, and supply the password.

3. Enter the following command to enter configuration mode:

   config t

4. Enter the following commands to configure a specific port profile:

   port-profile type vethernet *port-profile-name*

5. Change the name of the associated dvPort group with this command:

   vmware port-group *New-VMware-dvPort-Group-Name*

   If there are any VMs assigned to the dvPort group, the VSM CLI will respond with an error message indicating that the port profile was updated locally but not updated in vCenter Server. You must reconfigure the VM(s) in question to use a different dvPort group and re-peat this command in order for the change to take effect.

6. Change the access VLAN of the associated dvPort group with this command (replace 19 with an appropriate VLAN ID from your environment):

   switchport access vlan *19*

7. Remove the associated dvPort group, but leave the port profile intact with this command:

   no state enabled

8. Shut down the ports in the dvPort group with this command:

   shutdown

Because the VSM runs NX-OS, a wealth of options is available for configuring ports and port profiles. For more complete and detailed information on the Cisco Nexus 1000V, refer to the official Nexus 1000V documentation and the Cisco website at www.cisco.com.

Configuring Virtual Switch Security

Even though vSwitches and dvSwitches are considered to be "dumb switches" — with the exception of the Nexus 1000V — you can configure them with security policies to enhance or ensure Layer 2 security. For vSphere Standard Switches, you can apply security policies at the vSwitch or at the port group level. For vSphere Distributed Switches, you apply security policies only at the dvPort group level. The security settings include the following three options:

◆ Promiscuous Mode

◆ MAC Address Changes

◆ Forged Transmits

Applying a security policy to a vSwitch is effective, by default, for all connection types within the switch. However, if a port group on that vSwitch is configured with a competing security policy, it will override the policy set at the vSwitch. For example, if a vSwitch is configured with a security policy that rejects the use of MAC address changes but a port group on the switch is configured to accept MAC address changes, then any VMs connected to that port group will be allowed to communicate even though it is using a MAC address that differs from what is configured in its VMX file.

The default security profile for a vSwitch, shown in Figure 5.72, is set to reject Promiscuous mode and to accept MAC address changes and forged transmits. Similarly, Figure 5.73 shows the default security profile for a dvPort group on a dvSwitch.

FIGURE 5.72
The default security profile for a vSwitch prevents Promiscuous mode but allows MAC address changes and forged transmits.

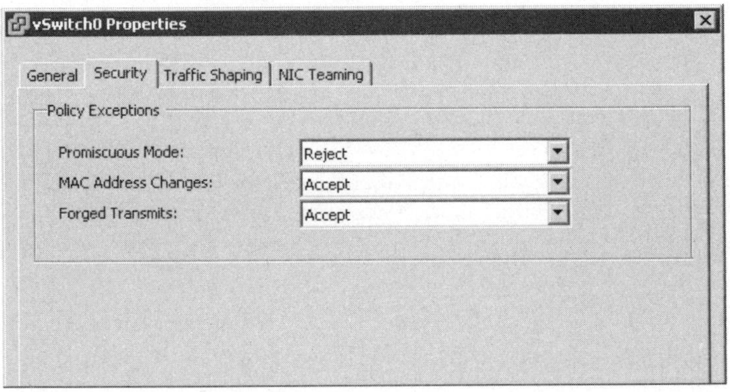

FIGURE 5.73
The default security profile for a dvPort group on a dvSwitch matches that for a standard vSwitch.

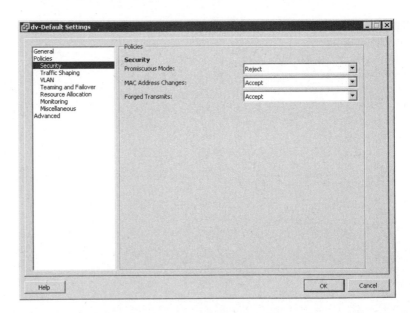

Each of these security options is explored in more detail in the following sections.

Understanding and Using Promiscuous Mode

The Promiscuous Mode option is set to Reject by default to prevent virtual network adapters from observing any of the traffic submitted through the vSwitch. For enhanced security, allowing Promiscuous mode is not recommended because it is an insecure mode of operation that allows a virtual adapter to access traffic other than its own. Despite the security concerns, there are valid reasons for permitting a switch to operate in Promiscuous mode. An intrusion-detection system (IDS) requires the ability to identify all traffic to scan for anomalies and malicious patterns of traffic.

Previously in this chapter, I talked about how port groups and VLANs did not have a one-to-one relationship and that there might be occasions when you have multiple port groups on a vSwitch configured with the same VLAN ID. This is exactly one of those situations — you have a need for a system, the IDS, to see traffic intended for other virtual network adapters. Rather than granting that ability to all the systems on a port group, you can create a dedicated port group for just the IDS system. It will have the same VLAN ID and other settings but will allow Promiscuous Mode instead of rejecting Promiscuous mode. This allows you, the administrator, to carefully control which systems are allowed to use this powerful and potentially security-threatening feature.

As shown in Figure 5.74, the virtual switch security policy will remain at the default setting of Reject for the Promiscuous Mode option, while the VM port group for the IDS will be set to Accept. This setting will override the virtual switch, allowing the IDS to monitor all traffic for that VLAN.

FIGURE 5.74
Promiscuous mode, though a reduction in security, is required when using an intrusion-detection system.

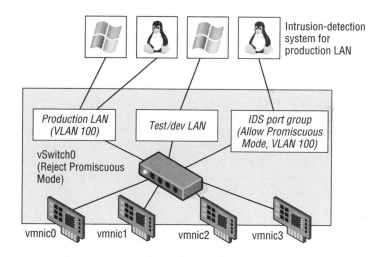

Allowing MAC Address Changes and Forged Transmits

When a VM is created with one or more virtual network adapters, a MAC address is generated for each virtual adapter. Just as Intel, Broadcom, and others manufacture network adapters that include unique MAC address strings, VMware is a network adapter manufacturer that has its own MAC prefix to ensure uniqueness. Of course, VMware doesn't actually manufacture anything because the product exists as a virtual NIC in a VM. You can see the 6-byte, randomly generated MAC addresses for a VM in the configuration file (.vmx) of the VM, as shown in

Figure 5.75. A VMware-assigned MAC address begins with the prefix 00:50:56 or 00:0C:29. In previous versions of ESXi, the value of the fourth set (XX) would not exceed 3F to prevent conflicts with other VMware products, but this appears to have changed in vSphere 5. The fifth and sixth sets (YY:ZZ) are generated randomly based on the Universally Unique Identifier (UUID) of the VM that is tied to the location of the VM. For this reason, when a VM location is changed, a prompt appears prior to successful boot. The prompt inquires about keeping the UUID or generating a new UUID, which helps prevent MAC address conflicts.

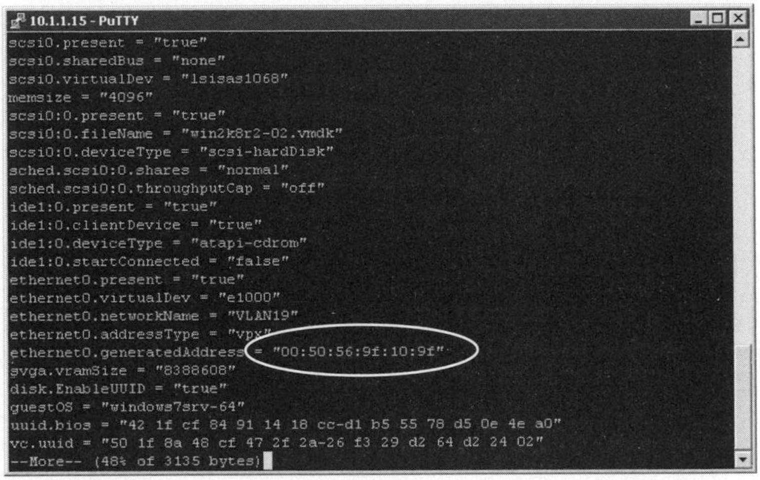

FIGURE 5.75
A VM's initial MAC address is automatically generated and listed in the configuration file for the VM.

```
10.1.1.15 - PuTTY
scsi0.present = "true"
scsi0.sharedBus = "none"
scsi0.virtualDev = "lsisas1068"
memsize = "4096"
scsi0:0.present = "true"
scsi0:0.fileName = "win2k8r2-02.vmdk"
scsi0:0.deviceType = "scsi-hardDisk"
sched.scsi0:0.shares = "normal"
sched.scsi0:0.throughputCap = "off"
ide1:0.present = "true"
ide1:0.clientDevice = "true"
ide1:0.deviceType = "atapi-cdrom"
ide1:0.startConnected = "false"
ethernet0.present = "true"
ethernet0.virtualDev = "e1000"
ethernet0.networkName = "VLAN19"
ethernet0.addressType = "vpx"
ethernet0.generatedAddress = "00:50:56:9f:10:9f"
svga.vramSize = "8388608"
disk.EnableUUID = "true"
guestOS = "windows7srv-64"
uuid.bios = "42 1f cf 84 91 14 18 cc-d1 b5 55 78 d5 0e 4e a0"
vc.uuid = "50 1f 8a 48 cf 47 2f 2a-26 f3 29 d2 64 d2 24 02"
--More-- (48% of 3135 bytes)
```

MANUALLY SETTING THE MAC ADDRESS

Manually configuring a MAC address in the configuration file of a VM does not work unless the first three bytes are VMware-provided prefixes and the last three bytes are unique. If a non-VMware MAC prefix is entered in the configuration file, the VM will not power on.

All VMs have two MAC addresses: the initial MAC and the effective MAC. The initial MAC address is the MAC address discussed in the previous paragraph that is generated automatically and that resides in the configuration file. The guest OS has no control over the initial MAC address. The effective MAC address is the MAC address configured by the guest OS that is used during communication with other systems. The effective MAC address is included in network communication as the source MAC of the VM. By default, these two addresses are identical. To force a non-VMware-assigned MAC address to a guest operating system, change the effective MAC address from within the guest OS, as shown in Figure 5.76.

The ability to alter the effective MAC address cannot be removed from the guest OS. However, the ability to let the system function with this altered MAC address is easily addressable through the security policy of a vSwitch. The remaining two settings of a virtual switch security policy are MAC Address Changes and Forged Transmits. Both of these security policies are concerned with allowing or denying differences between the initial MAC address in the configuration file and the effective MAC address in the guest OS. As noted earlier, the default security policy is to accept the differences and process traffic as needed.

FIGURE 5.76

A VM's source MAC address is the effective MAC address, which by default matches the initial MAC address configured in the VMX file. The guest OS, however, may change the effective MAC address.

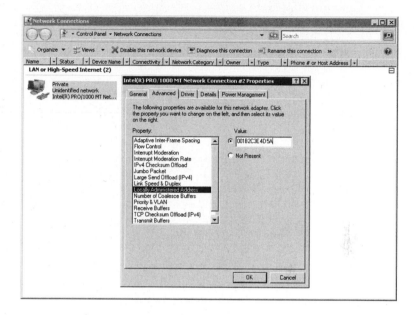

The difference between the MAC Address Changes and Forged Transmits security settings involves the direction of the traffic. MAC Address Changes is concerned with the integrity of incoming traffic, while Forged Transmits oversees the integrity of outgoing traffic. If the MAC Address Changes option is set to Reject, traffic will not be passed through the vSwitch to the VM (incoming) if the initial and the effective MAC addresses do not match. If the Forged Transmits option is set to Reject, traffic will not be passed from the VM to the vSwitch (outgoing) if the initial and the effective MAC addresses do not match. Figure 5.77 highlights the security restrictions implemented when MAC Address Changes and Forged Transmits are set to Reject.

FIGURE 5.77

The MAC Address Changes and Forged Transmits security options deal with incoming and outgoing traffic, respectively.

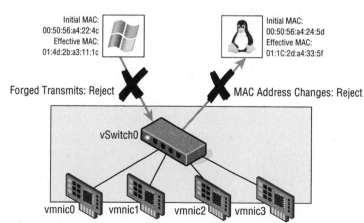

For the highest level of security, VMware recommends setting MAC Address Changes, Forged Transmits, and Promiscuous Mode on each vSwitch to Reject. When warranted or necessary, use port groups to loosen the security for a subset of VMs to connect to the port group.

VIRTUAL SWITCH POLICIES FOR MICROSOFT NETWORK LOAD BALANCING

As with anything, there are, of course, exceptions. For VMs that will be configured as part of a Microsoft Network Load Balancing (NLB) cluster set in Unicast mode, the VM port group must allow MAC address changes and forged transmits. Systems that are part of an NLB cluster will share a common IP address and virtual MAC address.

The shared virtual MAC address is generated by using an algorithm that includes a static component based on the NLB cluster's configuration of Unicast or Multicast mode plus a hexadecimal representation of the four octets that make up the IP address. This shared MAC address will certainly differ from the MAC address defined in the VMX file of the VM. If the VM port group does not allow for differences between the MAC addresses in the VMX and guest OS, NLB will not function as expected. VMware recommends running NLB clusters in Multicast mode because of these issues with NLB clusters in Unicast mode.

Perform the following steps to edit the security profile of a vSwitch:

1. Use the vSphere Client to establish a connection to a vCenter Server or an ESXi host.

2. Click the hostname in the inventory pane on the left, select the Configuration tab in the details pane on the right, and then select Networking from the Hardware menu.

3. Click the Properties link for the virtual switch.

4. Click the name of the virtual switch under the Configuration list, and then click the Edit button.

5. Click the Security tab, and make the necessary adjustments.

6. Click OK, and then click Close.

Perform the following steps to edit the security profile of a port group on a vSwitch:

1. Use the vSphere Client to establish a connection to a vCenter Server or an ESXi host.

2. Click the hostname in the inventory pane on the left, select the Configuration tab in the details pane on the right, and then select Networking from the Hardware menu.

3. Click the Properties link for the virtual switch.

4. Click the name of the port group under the Configuration list, and then click the Edit button.

5. Click the Security tab, and make the necessary adjustments.

6. Click OK, and then click Close.

Perform the following steps to edit the security profile of a dvPort group on a dvSwitch:

1. Use the vSphere Client to establish a connection to a vCenter Server instance.

2. On the vSphere Client home screen, select the Networking option under Inventory. Alternatively, from the View menu, select Inventory ➤ Networking.

3. Select an existing dvPort group in the inventory pane on the left, select the Summary tab in the details pane on the right, and click the Edit Settings option in the Commands section.

4. Select Security from the list of policy options on the left side of the dialog box.

5. Make the necessary adjustments to the security policy.

6. Click OK to save the changes and return to the vSphere Client.

Managing the security of a virtual network architecture is much the same as managing the security for any other portion of your information systems. Security policy should dictate that settings be configured as secure as possible to err on the side of caution. Only with proper authorization, documentation, and change-management processes should security be reduced. In addition, the reduction in security should be as controlled as possible to affect the least number of systems if not just the systems requiring the adjustments.

The Bottom Line

Identify the components of virtual networking.   Virtual networking is a blend of virtual switches, physical switches, VLANs, physical network adapters, virtual adapters, uplinks, NIC teaming, VMs, and port groups.

    Master It   What factors contribute to the design of a virtual network and the components involved?

Create virtual switches (vSwitches) and distributed virtual switches (dvSwitches).   vSphere introduces a new type of virtual switch, the vSphere Distributed Virtual Switch, as well as continuing to support the host-based vSwitch (now referred to as the vSphere Standard Switch) from previous versions. vSphere Distributed Switches bring new functionality to the vSphere networking environment, including private VLANs and a centralized point of management for ESXi clusters.

    Master It   You've asked a fellow vSphere administrator to create a vSphere Distributed Virtual Switch for you, but the administrator is having problems completing the task because they can't find the right command-line switches for `vicfg-vswitch`. What should you tell this administrator?

Install and perform basic configuration of the Cisco Nexus 1000V.   The Cisco Nexus 1000V is the first third-party Distributed Virtual Switch for vSphere. Running Cisco's NX-OS, the Nexus 1000V uses a distributed architecture that supports redundant supervisor modules and provides a single point of management. Advanced networking functionality like quality of service (QoS), access control lists (ACLs), and SPAN ports is made possible via the Nexus 1000V.

> **Master It** A vSphere administrator is trying to use the vSphere Client to make some changes to the VLAN configuration of a dvPort group configured on a Nexus 1000V, but the option to edit the settings for the dvPort group isn't showing up. Why?

Create and manage NIC teaming, VLANs, and private VLANs. NIC teaming allows for virtual switches to have redundant network connections to the rest of the network. Virtual switches also provide support for VLANs, which provide logical segmentation of the network, and private VLANs, which provide added security to existing VLANs while allowing systems to share the same IP subnet.

> **Master It** You'd like to use NIC teaming to bond multiple physical uplinks together for greater redundancy and improved throughput. When selecting the NIC teaming policy, you select Route Based On IP Hash, but then the vSwitch seems to lose connectivity. What could be wrong?

Configure virtual switch security policies. Virtual switches support security policies for allowing or rejecting Promiscuous Mode, allowing or rejecting MAC address changes, and allowing or rejecting forged transmits. All of the security options can help increase Layer 2 security.

> **Master It** You have a networking application that needs to see traffic on the virtual network that is intended for other production systems on the same VLAN. The networking application accomplishes this by using Promiscuous mode. How can you accommodate the needs of this networking application without sacrificing the security of the entire virtual switch?

Chapter 6

Creating and Configuring Storage Devices

The storage infrastructure supporting VMware vSphere has always been a critical element of any virtual infrastructure. This chapter will help you with all the elements required for a proper storage subsystem design, starting with vSphere storage fundamentals at the datastore and VM level and extending to best practices for configuring the storage array. Good storage design is critical for anyone building a virtual datacenter.

In this chapter, you will learn to

◆ Differentiate and understand the fundamentals of shared storage, including SANs and NAS

◆ Understand vSphere storage options

◆ Configure storage at the vSphere layer

◆ Configure storage at the VM layer

◆ Leverage best practices for SAN and NAS storage with vSphere

Reviewing the Importance of Storage Design

Storage design has always been important, but it becomes more so as vSphere is used for larger workloads, for mission-critical applications, for larger clusters, and as the basis for Infrastructure as a Service (IaaS)–based offerings in a nearly 100 percent virtualized datacenter. You can probably imagine why this is the case:

Advanced Capabilities   Many of vSphere's advanced features depend on shared storage; vSphere High Availability (HA), vMotion, vSphere Distributed Resource Scheduler (DRS), vSphere Fault Tolerance (FT), and VMware vCenter Site Recovery Manager all have a critical dependency on shared storage.

Performance   People understand the benefits that virtualization brings—consolidation, higher utilization, more flexibility, and higher efficiency. But often, people have initial questions about how vSphere can deliver performance for individual applications when it is inherently consolidated and oversubscribed. Likewise, the overall performance of the VMs and the entire vSphere cluster are both dependent on shared storage, which is also highly consolidated and oversubscribed.

Availability   The overall availability of your virtualized infrastructure—and by extension, the VMs running on that infrastructure—is dependent on the shared storage infrastructure. Designing high availability into this infrastructure element is paramount. If the storage is not available, vSphere HA will not be able to recover, and the aggregate community of VMs can be affected. (I discuss vSphere HA in detail in Chapter 7, "Ensuring High Availability and Business Continuity.")

While design choices at the server layer can make the vSphere environment relatively more or less optimal, design choices for shared resources such as networking and storage can sometimes make the difference between virtualization success and failure. This is especially true for storage because of its critical role. The importance of storage design and storage design choices remains true regardless of whether you are using storage area networks (SANs), which present shared storage as disks or logical units (LUNs); network attached storage (NAS), which presents shared storage as remotely accessed filesystems; or a mix of both. Done correctly, you can create a shared storage design that lowers the cost and increases the efficiency, performance, availability, and flexibility of your vSphere environment.

This chapter breaks down these topics into the following main sections:

◆   "Examining Shared Storage Fundamentals" covers broad topics of shared storage that are critical with vSphere, including hardware architectures, protocol choices, and key terminology. Although these topics will be applicable to any environment that uses shared storage, understanding these core technologies is a prerequisite to understanding how to apply storage technology in a vSphere implementation.

◆   "Implementing vSphere Storage Fundamentals" covers how storage technologies covered in the previous section are applied and used in vSphere environments. This section is broken down into a section on VMFS datastores ("Working with VMFS Datastores"), raw device mappings ("Working with Raw Device Mappings"), NFS datastores ("Working with NFS Datastores"), and VM-level storage configurations ("Working with VM-Level Storage Configuration").

◆   "Leveraging SAN and NAS Best Practices" covers how to pull together all the topics discussed to move forward with a design that will support a broad set of vSphere environments.

Examining Shared Storage Fundamentals

vSphere 5 offers numerous storage choices and configuration options relative to previous versions of vSphere or to non-virtualized environments. These choices and configuration options apply at two fundamental levels: the virtualization layer and the VM layer. The storage requirements for a vSphere environment and the VMs it supports are unique, making broad generalizations impossible. The requirements for any given vSphere environment span use cases ranging from virtual servers to desktops to templates and virtual CD/DVD (ISO) images. The virtual server use cases vary from light utility VMs with few storage performance considerations to the largest database workloads possible, with incredibly important storage layout considerations.

Let's start by examining this at a fundamental level. Figure 6.1 shows a simple three-host vSphere environment attached to shared storage.

FIGURE 6.1
When ESXi hosts are connected to same shared storage, they share its capabilities.

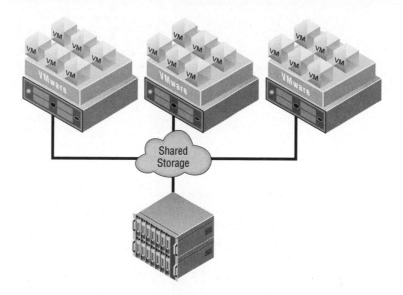

It's immediately apparent that the ESXi hosts and the VMs will be contending for the shared storage asset. In a way similar to how ESXi can consolidate many VMs onto a single ESXi host, the shared storage consolidates the storage needs of all the VMs.

What are the implications of this? The VMs will depend on and share the performance characteristics of the underlying storage configuration that supports them, just as they depend on and share the performance characteristics of the compute platform. When sizing or designing the compute platform, you hone in on key attributes like CPU speed (measured in megahertz), memory (measured in megabytes), and virtual CPU (vCPU) configuration. Similarly, when sizing or designing the storage solution, you focus on attributes like capacity (gigabytes or terabytes) and performance, which is measured in bandwidth (megabytes per second, or MBps), throughput (I/O operations per second or IOps), and latency (in milliseconds).

DETERMINING PERFORMANCE REQUIREMENTS

How do you determine the storage performance requirements of an application that will be virtualized, a single ESXi host, or even a complete vSphere environment? There are many rules of thumb for key applications, and the best practices for every application could fill a book. Here are some quick considerations:

◆ Online transaction processing (OLTP) databases need low latency (as low as you can get, but a few milliseconds is a good target). They are also sensitive to input/output operations per second (IOps), because their I/O size is small (4 KB to 8 KB). TPC-C and TPC-E benchmarks generate this kind of I/O pattern.

◆ Decision support system/business intelligence databases and SQL Servers that support Microsoft Office SharePoint Server need high bandwidth, which can be hundreds of megabytes per second because their I/O size is large (64 KB to 1 MB). They are not particularly sensitive to latency; TPC-H benchmarks generate the kind of I/O pattern used by these use cases.

Continues

DETERMINING PERFORMANCE REQUIREMENTS *(CONTINUED)*

◆ Copying files, deploying from templates, using Storage vMotion, and backing up VMs (within the guest or from a proxy server via vSphere Storage APIs) without using array-based approaches generally all need high bandwidth. In fact, the more, the better.

So, what does vSphere need? The answer is basic—the needs of the vSphere environment are the aggregate sum of all the use cases across all the VMs, which can cover a broad set of requirements. If the VMs are *all* small-block workloads and you don't do backups inside guests (which generate large-block workloads), then it's all about IOps. If the VMs are *all* large-block workloads, then it's all about MBps. More often than not, a virtual datacenter has a mix, so the storage design should be flexible enough to deliver a broad range of capabilities—but without overbuilding.

How can you best determine what you will need? With small workloads, too much planning can result in overbuilding. You can use simple tools, including VMware Capacity Planner, Windows Perfmon, and top in Linux, to determine the I/O pattern of the applications and OSes that will be virtualized.

Also, if you have many VMs, consider the aggregate performance requirements, and don't just look at capacity requirements. After all, 1,000 VMs with 10 IOps each need an aggregate of 10,000 IOps, which is 50 to 80 fast spindle's worth, regardless of the capacity (in gigabytes or terabytes) needed.

Use large pool designs for generic, light workload VMs.

Conversely, focused, larger VM I/O workloads (such as virtualized SQL Servers, SharePoint, Exchange, and other use cases) should be where you spend some time planning and thinking about layout. There are numerous VMware published best practices and a great deal of VMware partner reference architecture documentation that can help with virtualizing Exchange, SQL Server, Oracle, and SAP workloads. I have listed a few resources for you:

◆ Exchange

www.vmware.com/solutions/business-critical-apps/exchange/resources.html

◆ SQL Server

www.vmware.com/solutions/business-critical-apps/sql/resources.html

◆ Oracle

www.vmware.com/solutions/business-critical-apps/oracle/

◆ SAP

www.vmware.com/partners/alliances/technology/sap-resources.html

---

As with performance, the overall availability of the vSphere environment and the VMs is dependent on the same shared storage infrastructure, so a robust design is paramount. If the storage is not available, vSphere HA will not be able to recover, and the consolidated community of VMs will be affected.

Note that I said the "consolidated community of VMs." That statement underscores the need to typically put more care and focus on the availability of the configuration than on the performance or capacity requirements. In virtual configurations, the availability impact of storage issues is more pronounced, so greater care needs to be used in an availability design than in the physical world. It's not just one workload being affected—it's multiple workloads.

At the same time, advanced vSphere options such as Storage vMotion and advanced array techniques allow you to add, move, or change storage configurations nondisruptively, making it unlikely that you'll create a design where you can't nondisruptively fix performance issues.

Before going too much further, it's important to cover several basics of storage:

◆ Local storage versus shared storage

◆ Common storage array architectures

◆ RAID technologies

◆ Midrange and enterprise storage array design

◆ Protocol choices

I'll start with a brief discussion of local storage versus shared storage.

Comparing Local Storage with Shared Storage

An ESXi host can have one or more storage options actively configured, including the following:

◆ Local SAS/SATA/SCSI storage

◆ Fibre Channel

◆ Fibre Channel over Ethernet (FCoE)

◆ iSCSI using software and hardware initiators

◆ NAS (specifically, NFS)

◆ InfiniBand

Local storage is used in a limited fashion with vSphere in general because so many of vSphere's advanced features—such as vMotion, vSphere HA, vSphere DRS, and vSphere FT—require shared storage. With vSphere Auto Deploy and the ability to deploy ESXi images directly to RAM at boot time coupled with host profiles to automate the configuration, in some environments local storage in vSphere 5 serves even less of a function than it did in previous versions.

So, how carefully do you need to design your local storage? The answer is simple—generally speaking, careful planning is not necessary for storage local to the ESXi host. ESXi stores very little locally, and by using host profiles and distributed virtual switches, it can be easy and fast to replace a failed ESXi host. During this time, vSphere HA will make sure the VMs are running on the other ESXi hosts in the cluster. Don't sweat HA design in local storage for ESXi. Spend the effort making your shared storage design robust.

 **Real World Scenario**

NO LOCAL STORAGE? NO PROBLEM!

What if you don't *have* local storage? (Perhaps you have a diskless blade system, for example.) There are many options for diskless systems, including booting from Fibre Channel/iSCSI SAN and network-based boot methods like vSphere Auto Deploy (discussed in Chapter 2, "Planning and Installing VMware ESXi"). There is also the option of using USB boot, a technique that I've employed on numerous occasions in lab environments. Both Auto Deploy and USB boot give you some flexibility in quickly reprovisioning hardware or deploying updated versions of vSphere, but there are some quirks, so plan accordingly. Refer to Chapter 2 for more details on selecting the configuration of your ESXi hosts.

Shared storage is the basis for most vSphere environments because it supports the VMs themselves and because it is a requirement for many of vSphere's features. Shared storage in both SAN configurations (which encompasses Fibre Channel, FCoE, and iSCSI) and NAS is always highly consolidated. This makes it efficient. As I mentioned previously, in the same way that vSphere can take many servers with 10 percent utilized CPU and memory and consolidate them to make them 80 percent utilized, SAN/NAS can take the direct attached storage in physical servers that are 10 percent utilized and consolidate them to 80 percent utilization.

As you can see, shared storage is a key design point. It's therefore important to understand some of the array architectures that vendors use to provide shared storage to vSphere environments. The high-level overview in the following section is neutral on specific storage array vendors, because the internal architectures vary tremendously.

Defining Common Storage Array Architectures

This section is remedial for anyone with basic storage experience, but is needed for vSphere administrators with no storage knowledge. For people unfamiliar with storage, the topic can be a bit disorienting at first. Servers across vendors tend to be relatively similar, but the same logic can't be applied to the storage layer because core architectural differences between storage vendor architectures are vast. In spite of that, storage arrays have several core architectural elements that are consistent across vendors, across implementations, and even across protocols.

The elements that make up a shared storage array consist of external connectivity, storage processors, array software, cache memory, disks, and bandwidth:

External Connectivity The external (physical) connectivity between the storage array and the hosts (in this case, the ESXi hosts) is generally Fibre Channel or Ethernet, though InfiniBand and other rare protocols exist. The characteristics of this connectivity define the maximum bandwidth (given no other constraints, and there usually are other constraints) of the communication between the ESXi host and the shared storage array.

Storage Processors Different vendors have different names for storage processors, which are considered the brains of the array. They handle the I/O and run the array software. In most modern arrays, the storage processors are not purpose-built application-specific integrated circuits (ASICs), but instead are general-purpose CPUs. Some arrays use PowerPC, some use specific ASICs, and some use custom ASICs for specific purposes. But in general, if you cracked open an array, you would most likely find an Intel or AMD CPU.

Array Software Although hardware specifications are important and can define the scaling limits of the array, just as important are the functional capabilities the array software provides. The array software is at least as important as the array hardware. The capabilities of modern storage arrays are vast—similar in scope to vSphere itself—and vary wildly among vendors. At a high level, the following list includes some examples of these array capabilities; this is not an exhaustive list but does include the key functions:

- Remote storage replication for disaster recovery. These technologies come in many flavors with features that deliver varying capabilities. These include varying recovery point objectives (RPOs)—which are a reflection of how current the remote replica is at any time, ranging from synchronous to asynchronous and continuous. Asynchronous RPOs can range from minutes to hours, and continuous is a constant remote journal that can recover to varying RPOs. Other examples of remote replication technologies are technologies that drive synchronicity across storage objects or "consistency technology," compression, and many other attributes, such as integration with VMware vCenter Site Recovery Manager

◆ Snapshot and clone capabilities for instant point-in-time local copies for test and development and local recovery. These also share some of the ideas of the remote replication technologies like "consistency technology," and some variations of point-in-time protection and replicas also have TiVo-like continuous journaling locally and remotely, where you can recover/copy any point in time

◆ Capacity-reduction techniques such as archiving and deduplication

◆ Automated data movement between performance/cost storage tiers at varying levels of granularity

◆ LUN/filesystem expansion and mobility, which means reconfiguring storage properties dynamically and nondisruptively to add capacity or performance as needed

◆ Thin provisioning, which typically involves allocation of storage on demand as applications and workloads require it

◆ Storage quality of service (QoS), which means prioritizing I/O to deliver a given MBps, IOps, or latency

The array software defines the "persona" of the array, which in turn impacts core concepts and behavior in a variety of ways. Arrays generally have a "file server" persona (sometimes with the ability to do some block storage by presenting a file as a LUN) or a "block" persona (generally with no ability to act as a file server). In some cases, arrays are combinations of file servers and block devices.

Cache Memory   Every array differs as to how cache memory is implemented, but all have some degree of nonvolatile memory used for various caching functions—delivering lower latency and higher IOps throughput by buffering I/O using write caches and storing commonly read data to deliver a faster response time using read caches. Nonvolatility (meaning ability to survive a power loss) is critical for write caches because the data is not yet committed to disk, but it's not critical for read caches. Cached performance is often used when describing shared storage array performance maximums (in IOps, MBps, or latency) in specification sheets. These results are generally not reflective of real-world scenarios. In most real-world scenarios, performance tends to be dominated by the disk performance (the type and number of disks) and is helped by write caches in most cases, but only marginally by read caches (with the exception of large relational database management systems, which depend heavily on read-ahead cache algorithms). One vSphere use case that is helped by read caches is a situation where many boot images are stored only once (through the use of vSphere or storage array technology), but this is also a small subset of the overall VM I/O pattern.

Disks   Arrays differ as to which type of disks (often called *spindles*) they support and how many they can scale to support. Drives are described according to two different attributes. First, drives are often separated by the drive interface they use: Fibre Channel, serial-attached SCSI (SAS), and serial ATA (SATA). In addition, drives—with the exception of enterprise flash drives (EFDs)—are also described by their rotational speed, noted in revolutions per minute

(RPM). Fibre Channel drives typically come in 15K RPM and 10K RPM variants, SATA drives are usually found in 5,400 RPM and 7,200 RPM variants, and SAS drives are usually 15K RPM or 10K RPM variants. Second, EFDs, which are becoming mainstream, are solid state and have no moving parts; therefore rotational speed does not apply. The type of disks and the number of disks are very important. Coupled with how they are configured, this is usually the main determinant of how a storage object (either a LUN for a block device or a filesystem for a NAS device) performs. Shared storage vendors generally use disks from the same disk vendors, so this is an area where there is commonality across shared storage vendors. The following list is a quick reference on what to expect under a random read/write workload from a given disk drive:

- 7,200 RPM SATA: 80 IOps

- 10K RPM SATA/SAS/Fibre Channel: 120 IOps

- 15K RPM SAS/Fibre Channel: 180 IOps

- A commercial solid-state drive (SSD) based on Multi-Level Cell (MLC) technology: 1,000–2,000 IOps

- An Enterprise Flash Drive (EFD) based on Single-Level cell (SLC) technology and much deeper, very high-speed memory buffers: 6,000–30,000 IOps

Bandwidth (Megabytes per second)   Performance tends to be more consistent across drive types when large-block, sequential workloads are used (such as single-purpose workloads like archiving or backup to disk), so in these cases, large SATA drives deliver strong performance at a low cost.

Explaining RAID

Redundant Array of Inexpensive (sometimes "Independent") Disks (RAID) is a fundamental and critical method of storing the same data several times. RAID is used not only to increase the data availability (by protecting against the failure of a drive) but also to scale performance beyond that of a single drive. Every array implements various RAID schemes (even if it is largely invisible in file server persona arrays where RAID is done below the filesystem, which is the primary management element).

Think of it this way: disks are mechanical, spinning, rust-colored surfaces. The read/write heads are flying microns above the surface. While they are doing this, they read minute magnetic field variations, and using similar magnetic fields, they write data by affecting surface areas also only microns in size.

THE "MAGIC" OF DISK DRIVE TECHNOLOGY

It really is a technological miracle that magnetic disks work at all. What a disk does all day long is analogous to a 747 flying 600 miles per hour 6 inches off the ground and reading pages in a book while doing it!

In spite of the technological wonder of hard disks, they have unbelievable reliability statistics. But they do fail—and fail predictably, unlike other elements of a system. RAID schemes address this by leveraging multiple disks together and using copies of data to support I/O until the drive can be replaced and the RAID protection can be rebuilt. Each RAID configuration tends to have different performance characteristics and different capacity overhead impact.

I recommend that you view RAID choices as one factor among several in your design, not as the most important but not as the least important either. Most arrays layer additional constructs on top of the basic RAID protection. (These constructs have many different names, but ones that are common are *metas*, *virtual pools*, *aggregates*, and *volumes*.)

Remember, all the RAID protection in the world won't protect you from an outage if the connectivity to your host is lost, if you don't monitor and replace failed drives and allocate drives as hot spares to automatically replace failed drives, or if the entire array is lost. It's for these reasons that it's important to design the storage network properly, to configure hot spares as advised by the storage vendor, and to monitor for and replace failed elements. Always consider a disaster-recovery plan and remote replication to protect from complete array failure.

Let's examine the RAID choices:

RAID 0   This RAID level offers no redundancy and no protection against drive failure (see Figure 6.2). In fact, it has a *higher* aggregate risk than a single disk because any single disk failing affects the whole RAID group. Data is spread across all the disks in the RAID group, which is often called a *stripe*. Although it delivers fast performance, this is the only RAID type that is not appropriate for any production vSphere use because of the availability profile.

FIGURE 6.2
In a RAID 0 configuration, the data is striped across all the disks in the RAID set, providing very good performance but very poor availability.

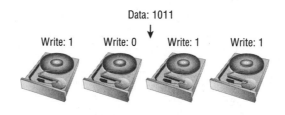

RAID 1, 1+0, 0+1   These mirrored RAID levels offer high degrees of protection but at the cost of 50 percent loss of usable capacity (see Figure 6.3). This is versus the raw aggregate capacity of the sum of the capacity of the drives. RAID 1 simply writes every I/O to two drives and can balance reads across both drives (because there are two copies). This can be coupled with RAID 0 to form RAID 1+0 (or RAID 10), which mirrors a stripe set, or to form RAID 0+1, which stripes data across pairs of mirrors. This has the benefit of being able to withstand multiple drives failing, but only if the drives fail on different elements of a stripe on different mirrors. The other benefit of mirrored RAID configuration is that, in the case of a failed drive, rebuild times can be very rapid, which shortens periods of exposure.

Parity RAID (RAID 5, RAID 6)   These RAID levels use a mathematical calculation (an XOR parity calculation) to represent the data across several drives. This tends to be a good compromise between the availability of RAID 1 and the capacity efficiency of RAID 0. RAID 5 calculates the parity across the drives in the set and writes the parity to another drive. This parity block calculation with RAID 5 is rotated among the arrays in the RAID 5 set. (RAID 4 is a variant that uses a dedicated parity disk rather than rotating the parity across drives.)

FIGURE 6.3
This RAID 10 2+2 configuration provides good performance and good availability, but at the cost of 50 percent of the usable capacity.

Parity RAID schemes can deliver very good performance, but there is always some degree of write penalty. For a full-stripe write, the only penalty is the parity calculation and the parity write, but in a partial-stripe write, the old block contents need to be read, a new parity calculation needs to be made, and all the blocks need to be updated. However, generally modern arrays have various methods to minimize this effect.

Read performance, on the other hand, is generally excellent, because a larger number of drives can be read from than with mirrored RAID schemes. RAID 5 nomenclature refers to the number of drives in the RAID group, so Figure 6.4 would be referred to as a RAID 5 4+1 set. In the figure, the storage efficiency (in terms of usable to raw capacity) is 80 percent, which is much better than RAID 1 or 10.

FIGURE 6.4
A RAID 5 4+1 configuration offers a balance between performance and efficiency.

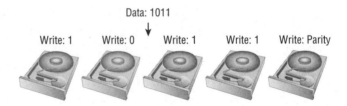

RAID 5 can be coupled with stripes, so RAID 50 is a pair of RAID 5 sets with data striped across them.

When a drive fails in a RAID 5 set, I/O can be fulfilled using the remaining drives and the parity drive, and when the failed drive is replaced, the data can be reconstructed using the remaining data and parity.

A KEY RAID 5 CONSIDERATION

One downside to RAID 5 is that only one drive can fail in the RAID set. If another drive fails before the failed drive is replaced and rebuilt using the parity data, data loss occurs. The period of exposure to data loss because of the second drive failing should be mitigated.

The period of time that a RAID 5 set is rebuilding should be as short as possible to minimize the risk. The following designs aggravate this situation by creating longer rebuild periods:

◆ Very large RAID groups (think 8+1 and larger), which require more reads to reconstruct the failed drive.

◆ Very large drives (think 1 TB SATA and 500 GB Fibre Channel drives), which cause more data to be rebuilt.

♦ Slower drives that struggle heavily during the period when they are providing the data to rebuild the replaced drive and simultaneously support production I/O (think SATA drives, which tend to be slower during the random I/O that characterizes a RAID rebuild). The period of a RAID rebuild is actually one of the most stressful parts of a disk's life. Not only must it service the production I/O workload, but it must also provide data to support the rebuild, and it is known that drives are statistically more likely to fail during a rebuild than during normal duty cycles.

The following technologies all mitigate the risk of a dual drive failure (and most arrays do various degrees of each of these items):

♦ Using proactive hot sparing, which shortens the period of the rebuild substantially by automatically starting the hot spare *before* the drive fails. The failure of a disk is generally preceded with read errors (which are recoverable; they are detected and corrected using on-disk parity information) or write errors, both of which are noncatastrophic. When a threshold of these errors occurs *before* the disk itself fails, the failing drive is replaced by a hot spare by the array. This is much faster than the rebuild after the failure, because the bulk of the failing drive can be used for the copy and because only the portions of the drive that are failing need to use parity information from other disks.

♦ Using smaller RAID 5 sets (for faster rebuild) and striping the data across them using a higher-level construct.

♦ Using a second parity calculation and storing this on another disk.

As described in the sidebar "A Key RAID 5 Consideration," one way to protect against data loss in the event of a single drive failure in a RAID 5 set is to use another parity calculation. This type of RAID is called RAID 6 (RAID-DP is a RAID 6 variant that uses two dedicated parity drives, analogous to RAID 4). This is a good choice when large RAID groups and SATA are used.

Figure 6.5 shows an example of a RAID 6 4+2 configuration. The data is striped across four disks, and a parity calculation is stored on the fifth disk. A second parity calculation is stored on another disk. RAID 6 rotates the parity location with I/O, and RAID-DP uses a pair of dedicated parity disks. This provides good performance and good availability but a loss in capacity efficiency. The purpose of the second parity bit is to withstand a second drive failure during RAID rebuild periods. It is important to use RAID 6 in place of RAID 5 if you meet the conditions noted in the previous sidebar and are unable to otherwise use the mitigation methods noted.

FIGURE 6.5
A RAID 6 4+2 configuration offers protection against double drive failures.

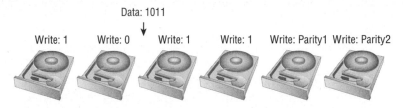

While this is a reasonably detailed discussion of RAID levels, what you should take from this discussion is that you shouldn't worry about it too much. There are generally more important considerations. Just don't use RAID 0. Use hot spare drives and follow the vendor best practices on hot spare density. EMC, for example, generally recommends one hot spare for every 30 drives in its arrays. Just be sure to check with your storage vendor for their specific recommendations. Compellent, for example, recommends one hot spare per drive type and per drive shelf.

For most vSphere implementations, RAID 5 is a good balance of capacity efficiency, performance, and availability. Use RAID 6 if you have to use large SATA RAID groups or don't have proactive hot spares. RAID 10 schemes still make sense in conditions that need significant write performance. Remember that for your vSphere environment it doesn't all have to be one RAID type; in fact, mixing different RAID types can be very useful to deliver different tiers of performance/availability.

For example, you can use most datastores with RAID 5 as the default LUN configuration, sparingly use RAID 10 schemes where needed, and use Storage vMotion to nondisruptively make the change for the particular VM that needs it.

You should definitely make sure that you have enough spindles in the RAID group to meet the aggregate workload of the LUNs you create in that RAID group. The RAID type will affect the ability of the RAID group to support the workload, so keep RAID overhead (like the RAID 5 write penalty) in mind. Fortunately, some storage arrays have the ability to nondisruptively add spindles to a RAID group to add performance as needed, so if you find that you need more performance, you can correct it. Storage vMotion can also help you manually balance workloads.

Now let's take a closer look at some specific storage array design architectures that will impact your vSphere storage environment.

Understanding Midrange and Enterprise Storage Array Design

There are some major differences in physical array design that can be pertinent in a vSphere design.

Traditional midrange storage arrays are generally arrays with dual-storage processor cache designs where the cache is localized to one storage processor or another, but commonly mirrored between them. (Remember that all vendors call storage processors something slightly different; sometimes they are called *controllers*, *heads*, *engines*, or *nodes*.) In cases where one of the storage processors fails, the array remains available, but in general, performance is degraded (unless you drive the storage processors to only 50 percent storage processor utilization during normal operation).

Enterprise storage arrays are generally considered to be those that scale to many more controllers and a much larger global cache (memory can be accessed through some common shared model). In these cases, multiple elements can fail while the array is being used at a very high degree of utilization—without any significant performance degradation. Other characteristics of enterprise arrays are support for mainframes and other characteristics that are beyond the scope of this book.

Hybrid designs exist as well, such as scale-out designs where they can scale out to more than two storage processors but without the features otherwise associated with enterprise storage arrays. Often these are iSCSI-only arrays and leverage iSCSI redirection techniques (which are not options of the Fibre Channel or NAS protocol stacks) as a core part of their scale-out design.

Where it can be confusing is that VMware and storage vendors use the same words to express different things. To most storage vendors, an *active-active* storage array is an array that can service I/O on all storage processor units at once, and an *active-passive* design is a system where one storage process is idle until it takes over for the failed unit. VMware has specific nomenclature for these terms that is focused on the model for a *specific LUN*. VMware defines active-active and active-passive arrays in the following way (this information is taken from the *vSphere Storage Guide*):

Active-Active Storage System   An active-active storage system provides access to LUNs simultaneously through all available storage ports without significant performance degradation. Barring a path failure, all paths are active at all times.

Active-Passive Storage System   In an active-passive storage system, one storage processor is actively providing access to a given LUN. Other processors act as backup for the LUN and can be actively servicing I/O to other LUNs. In the event of the failure of an active storage port, one of the passive storage processors can be activated to handle I/O.

Asymmetrical Storage System   An asymmetrical storage system supports Asymmetric Logical Unit Access (ALUA), which allows storage systems to provide different levels of access per port. This permits the hosts to determine the states of target ports and establish priority for paths. (See the sidebar "The Fine Line between Active-Active and Active-Passive" for more details on ALUA.)

Virtual Port Storage System   Access to all LUNs is provided through a single virtual port. These are active-active devices where the multiple connections are disguised behind the single virtual port. Virtual port storage systems handle failover and connection balancing transparently, which is often referred to as "transparent failover."

This distinction between array types is important because VMware's definition is based on the multipathing mechanics, not whether you can use both storage processors at once. The active-active and active-passive definitions apply equally to Fibre Channel (and FCoE) and iSCSI arrays, and the virtual port definition applies to only iSCSI (because it uses an iSCSI redirection mechanism that is not possible on Fibre Channel/FCoE).

THE FINE LINE BETWEEN ACTIVE-ACTIVE AND ACTIVE-PASSIVE

Wondering why VMware specifies "without significant performance degradation" in the active-active definition? The reason is found within ALUA, a standard supported by many midrange arrays. vSphere supports ALUA with arrays that implement ALUA compliant with the SPC-3 standard.

Midrange arrays usually have an internal interconnect between the two storage processors used for write cache mirroring and other management purposes. ALUA was an addition to the SCSI standard that enables a LUN to be presented on its primary path and on an asymmetrical (significantly slower) path via the secondary storage processor, transferring the data over this internal interconnect.

The key is that the "non-optimized path" generally comes with a significant performance degradation. The midrange arrays don't have the internal interconnection bandwidth to deliver the same response on both storage processors, because there is usually a relatively small, or higher latency, internal interconnect used for cache mirroring that is used for ALUA versus enterprise arrays that have a very-high-bandwidth internal model.

Without ALUA, on an array with an active-passive LUN ownership model, paths to a LUN are shown as active, standby (designates that the port is reachable but is on a processor that does not have the LUN), and dead. When the failover mode is set to ALUA, a new state is possible: active non-optimized. This is not shown distinctly in the vSphere Client GUI, but looks instead like a normal active path. The difference is that it is not used for any I/O.

So, should you configure your midrange array to use ALUA? Follow your storage vendor's best practice. For some arrays this is more important than others. Remember, however, that the non-optimized paths will not be used even if you select the Round Robin policy. An active-passive array using ALUA is not functionally equivalent to an active-passive array where all paths are used. This behavior can be different if using a third-party multipathing module—see the "Reviewing Multipathing" section.

By definition, all enterprise arrays are active-active arrays (by VMware's definition), but not all midrange arrays are active-passive. To make things even more confusing, not all active-active arrays (again, by VMware's definition) are enterprise arrays!

So, what do you do? What kind of array architecture is the right one for VMware? The answer is simple: as long as you select one on VMware's Hardware Compatibility List (HCL), they all work; you just need to understand how the one *you* have works.

Most customers' needs are well met by midrange arrays, regardless of whether they have an active-active, active-passive, or virtual port (iSCSI only) design or whether they are NAS devices. Generally, only the most mission-critical virtual workloads at the highest scale require the characteristics of enterprise-class storage arrays. In these cases, *scale* refers to VMs that number in the thousands, datastores that number in the hundreds, local and remote replicas that number in the hundreds, and the highest possible workloads—all that perform consistently even after component failures.

The most important considerations are as follows:

◆ If you have a midrange array, recognize that it is possible to oversubscribe the storage processors significantly. In such a situation, if a storage processor fails, performance will be degraded. For some customers, that is acceptable because storage processor failure is rare. For others, it is not, in which case you should limit the workload on either storage processor to less than 50 percent or consider an enterprise array.

◆ Understand the failover behavior of your array. Active-active arrays use the fixed-path selection policy by default, and active-passive arrays use the most recently used (MRU) policy by default. (See the "Reviewing Multipathing" section for more information.)

◆ Do you need specific advanced features? For example, if you want to do disaster recovery, make sure your array has integrated support on the VMware vCenter Site Recovery Manager HCL. Or, do you need array-integrated VMware snapshots? Do they have integrated management tools? Do they have a vSphere Storage API road map? Ask your array vendor to illustrate its VMware integration and the use cases it supports.

I'm now left with the last major area of storage fundamentals before I move on to discussing storage in a vSphere-specific context. The last remaining area deals with choosing a storage protocol.

Choosing a Storage Protocol

vSphere offers several shared storage protocol choices, including Fibre Channel, FCoE, iSCSI, and Network File System (NFS), which is a form of NAS. A little understanding of each goes a long way in designing the storage for your vSphere environment.

REVIEWING FIBRE CHANNEL

SANs are most commonly associated with Fibre Channel storage, because Fibre Channel was the first protocol type used with SANs. However, *SAN* refers to a network topology, not a connection protocol. Although people often use the acronym *SAN* to refer to a Fibre Channel SAN, it is completely possible to create a SAN topology using different types of protocols, including iSCSI, FCoE, and InfiniBand.

SANs were initially deployed to mimic the characteristics of local or direct attached SCSI devices. A SAN is a network where storage devices (logical units—or LUNs—just like on a SCSI or SAS controller) are presented from a storage target (one or more ports on an array) to one or more initiators. An initiator is usually a host bus adapter (HBA) or converged network adapter (CNA), though software-based initiators are available for iSCSI and FCoE. See Figure 6.6.

FIGURE 6.6
A Fibre Channel SAN presents LUNs from a target array (in this case an EMC Symmetrix VMAX) to a series of initiators (in this case a Cisco Virtual Interface Controller).

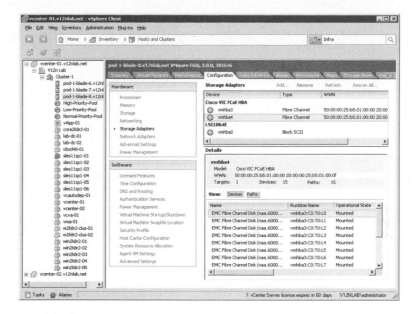

Today, Fibre Channel HBAs have roughly the same cost as high-end multiported Ethernet interfaces or local SAS controllers, and the per-port cost of a Fibre Channel switch is about twice that of a high-end managed Ethernet switch.

Fibre Channel uses an optical interconnect (though there are copper variants), which is used since the Fibre Channel protocol assumes a very high-bandwidth, low-latency, and loss-less physical layer. Standard Fibre Channel HBAs today support very-high-throughput, 4 Gbps and 8 Gbps connectivity in single-, dual-, and even quad-ported options. Older, obsolete HBAs supported only 2 Gbps. Some HBAs supported by ESXi are the QLogic QLE2462 and Emulex LP10000. You can find the authoritative list of supported HBAs on the VMware HCL at `www.vmware.com/resources/compatibility/search.php`. For end-to-end compatibility (in other words, from host to HBA to switch to array), every storage vendor maintains a similar compatibility matrix. For example, EMC e-Lab is generally viewed as the most expansive storage interoperability matrix.

Although in the early days of Fibre Channel there were many different types of cables and there was the interoperability of various Fibre Channel initiators, firmware revisions, switches, and targets (arrays), today interoperability is broad. Still, it is always a best practice to check and maintain your environment to be current with the vendor interoperability matrix. From a connectivity standpoint, almost all cases use a common OM2 (orange-colored cables) multi-mode duplex LC/LC cable, as shown in Figure 6.7. There is a newer OM3 (aqua-colored cables) standard that is used for longer distances and is generally used for 10 Gbps Ethernet and 8 Gbps Fibre Channel (which otherwise have shorter distances using OM2). They all plug into standard optical interfaces.

FIGURE 6.7
A standard Fibre Channel multi-mode duplex LC/LC fiber-optic cable. Historically viewed as more expensive than Ethernet, they cost roughly the same as Cat5e. This 3-meter cable, for example, cost $5 U.S.

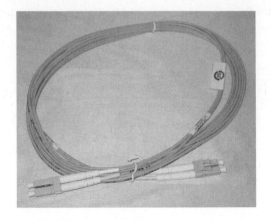

The Fibre Channel protocol can operate in three modes: point-to-point (FC-P2P), arbitrated loop (FC-AL), and switched (FC-SW). Point-to-point and arbitrated loop are rarely used today for host connectivity, and they generally predate the existence of Fibre Channel switches. FC-AL is commonly used by some array architectures to connect their backend spindle enclosures (vendors give different hardware names to them, but they're the hardware elements that contain and support the physical disks) to the storage processors, but even in these cases, most modern array designs are moving to switched designs, which have higher bandwidth per disk enclosure.

Fibre Channel can be configured in several topologies. On the left in Figure 6.8, point-to-point configurations were used in the early days of Fibre Channel storage prior to broad adoption of SANs. (However, with modern, extremely high-array port densities, point-to-point is making a bit of a comeback.) On the right is an arbitrated loop configuration. This is almost never used in host configuration, but is sometimes used in array backend connectivity. Both types have become rare for host connectivity with the prevalence of switched Fibre Channel SAN (FC-SW).

FIGURE 6.8
Fibre Channel supports both point-to-point and arbitrated loop topologies.

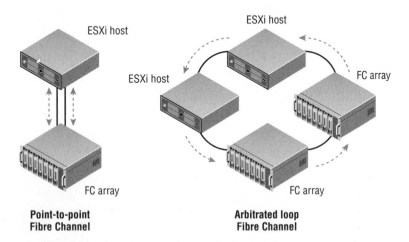

As Figure 6.9 shows, each ESXi host has a minimum of two HBA ports, and each is physically connected to two Fibre Channel switches. Each switch has a minimum of two connections to two redundant front-end array ports (across storage processors).

FIGURE 6.9
The most common Fibre Channel configuration: a switched Fibre Channel (FC-SW) SAN. This enables the Fibre Channel LUN to be easily presented to all the hosts while creating a redundant network design.

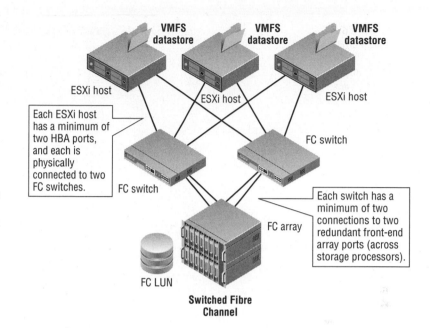

Each ESXi host has a minimum of two HBA ports, and each is physically connected to two FC switches.

Each switch has a minimum of two connections to two redundant front-end array ports (across storage processors).

VMFS datastore

ESXi host

FC switch

FC array

FC LUN

Switched Fibre Channel

HOW DIFFERENT IS FCOE?

Aside from discussions of the physical media and topologies, the concepts for FCoE are almost identical to those of Fibre Channel. This is because FCoE was designed to be seamlessly interoperable with existing Fibre Channel–based SANs.

All the objects (initiators, targets, and LUNs) on a Fibre Channel SAN are identified by a unique 64-bit identifier called a *worldwide name* (WWN). WWNs can be worldwide port names (a port on a switch) or node names (a port on an endpoint). For anyone unfamiliar with Fibre Channel, this concept is simple. It's the same technique as Media Access Control (MAC) addresses on Ethernet. Figure 6.10 shows an ESXi host with FCoE CNAs, where the highlighted CNA has the following worldwide node name: worldwide port name (WWnN: WWpN):

50:00:00:25:b5:01:00:00 20:00:00:25:b5:01:00:0f

Like Ethernet MAC addresses, WWNs have a structure. The most significant two bytes are used by the vendor (the four hexadecimal characters starting on the left) and are unique to the vendor, so there is a pattern for QLogic or Emulex HBAs or array vendors. In the previous example, these are Cisco CNAs connected to an EMC Symmetrix VMAX storage array.

Fibre Channel and FCoE SANs also have a critical concept of zoning. Fibre Channel switches implement zoning to restrict which initiators and targets can see each other as if they were on a common bus. If you have Ethernet networking experience, the idea is somewhat analogous to VLANs with Ethernet.

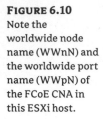

FIGURE 6.10
Note the worldwide node name (WWnN) and the worldwide port name (WWpN) of the FCoE CNA in this ESXi host.

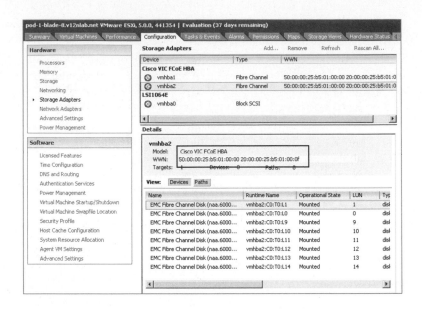

IS THERE A FIBRE CHANNEL EQUIVALENT TO VLANS?

Actually, yes, there is. Virtual Storage Area Networks (VSANs) were adopted as a standard in 2004. Like VLANs, VSANs provide isolation between multiple logical SANs that exist on a common physical platform. This enables SAN administrators greater flexibility and another layer of separation in addition to zoning.

Zoning is used for the following two purposes:

◆ To ensure that a LUN that is required to be visible to multiple hosts in a cluster (for example in a vSphere cluster, a Microsoft cluster, or an Oracle RAC cluster) has common visibility to the underlying LUN, while ensuring that hosts that should *not* have visibility to that LUN do not. For example, it's used to ensure that VMFS volumes aren't visible to Windows servers (with the exception of backup proxy servers using software that leverages the vSphere Storage APIs for Data Protection).

◆ To create fault and error domains on the SAN fabric, where noise, chatter, and errors are not transmitted to all the initiators/targets attached to the switch. Again, it's somewhat analogous to one of the uses of VLANs to partition very dense Ethernet switches into broadcast domains.

Zoning is configured on the Fibre Channel switches via simple GUIs or CLI tools and can be configured by port or by WWN:

◆ Using port-based zoning, you would zone by configuring your Fibre Channel switch to "put port 5 and port 10 into a zone that we'll call zone_5_10." Any device (and therefore any WWN) you physically plug into port 5 could communicate only to a device (or WWN) physically plugged into port 10.

♦ Using WWN-based zoning, you would zone by configuring your Fibre Channel switch to "put WWN from this HBA and these array ports into a zone we'll call ESXi_4_host1_CX_SPA_0." In this case, if you moved the cables, the zones would move to the ports with the matching WWNs.

You can see in the ESXi configuration shown in Figure 6.11 that the LUN itself is given an unbelievably long name that combines the initiator WWN (the one starting with 50/20), the Fibre Channel switch ports (the one starting with 50), and the Network Address Authority (NAA) identifier. This provides an explicit name that uniquely identifies not only the storage device but also the full end-to-end path.

FIGURE 6.11
The Manage Paths dialog box shows both the new explicit storage object name and the runtime (shorthand) name.

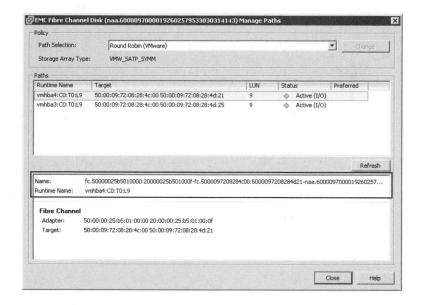

This is also shown in a shorthand runtime name, but the full name is explicit and always globally unique (I'll give you more details on storage object naming later in this chapter, in the sidebar titled "What Is All the Stuff in the Storage Devices List?").

Zoning should not be confused with LUN masking. *Masking* is the ability of a host or an array to intentionally ignore WWNs that it *can* actively see (in other words, that are zoned to it). Masking is used to further limit what LUNs are presented to a host (commonly used with test and development replicas of LUNs).

You can put many initiators and targets into a zone and group zones together, as illustrated in Figure 6.12. For features like vSphere HA, vSphere DRS, and vMotion, ESXi hosts must have shared storage to which all applicable hosts have access. Generally, this means that every ESXi host in a vSphere environment must be zoned such that it can see each LUN. Also, every initiator (HBA or CNA) needs to be zoned to all the front-end array ports that *could* present the LUN. So, what's the best configuration practice? The answer is single initiator/single target zoning.

This creates smaller zones, creates less cross talk, and makes it more difficult to administratively make an error that removes a LUN from all paths to a host or many hosts at once with a switch configuration error.

FIGURE 6.12

There are many ways to configure zoning. From left to right: multi-initiator/multi-target zoning, single-initiator/multi-target zoning, and single-initiator/single-target zoning.

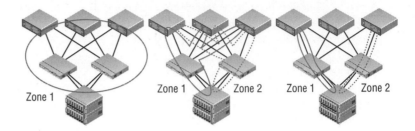

Remember that the goal is to ensure that every LUN is visible to all the nodes in the vSphere cluster. The left side of the figure is how most people who are not familiar with Fibre Channel start—multi-initiator zoning, with all array ports and all the ESXi Fibre Channel initiators in one massive zone. The middle is better—with two zones, one for each side of the dual-fabric Fibre Channel SAN design, and each zone includes all possible storage processors' front-end ports (critically, at least one from each storage processor!). The right one is the best and recommended zoning configuration—single-initiator/single-target zoning.

When using single-initiator/single-target zoning as shown in the figure, each zone consists of a single initiator and a single target array port. This means you'll end up with multiple zones for each ESXi host, so that each ESXi host can see all applicable target array ports (again, at least one from each storage processor/controller!). This reduces the risk of administrative error and eliminates HBA issues affecting adjacent zones, but it takes a little more time to configure and results in a larger number of zones overall. It is always critical to ensure that each HBA is zoned to at least one front-end port on each storage processor.

REVIEWING FIBRE CHANNEL OVER ETHERNET

As I mentioned in the sidebar titled "How Different Is FCoE?", FCoE was designed to be interoperable and compatible with Fibre Channel. In fact, the FCoE standard is maintained by the same T11 body as Fibre Channel (the current standard is FC-BB-5). At the upper layers of the protocol stacks, Fibre Channel and FCoE look identical.

It's at the lower levels of the stack that the protocols diverge. Fibre Channel as a protocol doesn't specify the physical transport it runs over. However, unlike TCP, which has retransmission mechanics to deal with a lossy transport, Fibre Channel has far fewer mechanisms for dealing with loss and retransmission, which is why it requires a lossless, low-jitter, high-bandwidth physical layer connection. It's for this reason that Fibre Channel traditionally is run over relatively short optical cables rather than the unshielded twisted-pair (UTP) cables that Ethernet uses.

To address the need for lossless Ethernet, the IEEE created a series of standards—all of which had been approved and finalized at the time of this writing—that make 10 Gb Ethernet lossless for FCoE traffic. Three key standards, all part of the Data Center Bridging (DCB) effort, make this possible:

- Priority Flow Control (PFC, also called Per-Priority Pause)
- Enhanced Transmission Selection (ETS)
- Datacenter Bridging Exchange (DCBX)

Used together, these three protocols allow Fibre Channel frames to be encapsulated into Ethernet frames, as illustrated in Figure 6.13, and transmitted in a lossless manner. Thus, FCoE uses whatever physical cable plant that 10 Gb Ethernet uses. Today, 10 GbE connectivity is generally optical (same cables as Fibre Channel) and Twinax (which is a pair of coaxial copper cables), InfiniBand-like CX cables, and some emerging 10 Gb unshielded twisted pair (UTP) use cases via the new 10GBase-T standard. Each has its specific distance-based use cases and varying interface cost, size, and power consumption.

FIGURE 6.13
FCoE simply encapsulates Fibre Channel frames into Ethernet frames for transmission over a lossless Ethernet transport.

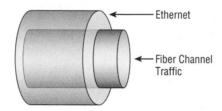

Ethernet

Fiber Channel Traffic

WHAT ABOUT DATACENTER ETHERNET OR CONVERGED ENHANCED ETHERNET?

Datacenter Ethernet (DCE) and Converged Enhanced Ethernet (CEE) are prestandard terms used to describe a lossless Ethernet network. DCE describes Cisco's prestandard implementation of the DCB standards; CEE was a multivendor effort of the same nature.

Because FCoE uses Ethernet, why use FCoE instead of NFS or iSCSI over 10 Gb Ethernet? The answer is usually driven by the following two factors:

- There are existing infrastructure, processes, and tools in large enterprises that are designed for Fibre Channel, and they expect WWN addressing, not IP addresses. This provides an option for a converged network and greater efficiency, without a "rip and replace" model. In fact, early prestandard FCoE implementations did not include elements required to cross multiple Ethernet switches. These elements, part of something called FCoE Initialization Protocol (FIP), are part of the official FC-BB-5 standard and are required in order to comply with the final standard. This means that most FCoE switches in use today function as FCoE/LAN/Fibre Channel bridges. This makes them excellent choices to integrate and extend existing 10 GbE/1 GbE LANs and Fibre Channel SAN networks. The largest cost savings, power savings, cable and port reduction, and impact on management simplification are on this layer from the ESXi host to the first switch.

- Certain applications require a lossless, extremely low-latency transport network model— something that cannot be achieved using a transport where dropped frames are normal and long-window TCP retransmit mechanisms are the protection mechanism. Now, this is a very high-end set of applications, and those historically were not virtualized. However, in the era of vSphere 5, the goal is to virtualize every workload, so I/O models that can deliver those performance envelopes while still supporting a converged network become more important.

In practice, the debate of iSCSI versus FCoE versus NFS on 10 Gb Ethernet infrastructure is not material. All FCoE adapters are converged adapters, referred to as converged network adapters (CNAs). They support native 10 GbE (and therefore also NFS and iSCSI) as well as FCoE simultaneously, and they appear in the ESXi host as multiple 10 GbE network adapters and multiple Fibre Channel adapters. If you have FCoE support, in effect you have it all. All protocol options are yours.

A list of FCoE CNAs supported by vSphere can be found in the I/O section of the VMware compatibility guide.

UNDERSTANDING iSCSI

iSCSI brings the idea of a block storage SAN to customers with no Fibre Channel infrastructure. iSCSI is an IETF standard for encapsulating SCSI control and data in TCP/IP packets, which in turn are encapsulated in Ethernet frames. Figure 6.14 shows how iSCSI is encapsulated in TCP/IP and Ethernet frames. TCP retransmission is used to handle dropped Ethernet frames or significant transmission errors. Storage traffic can be intense relative to most LAN traffic. This makes it important that you minimize retransmits, minimize dropped frames, and ensure that you have "bet-the-business" Ethernet infrastructure when using iSCSI.

FIGURE 6.14
Using iSCSI, SCSI control and data are encapsulated in both TCP/IP and Ethernet frames.

Although Fibre Channel is often viewed as having higher performance than iSCSI, in many cases iSCSI can more than meet the requirements for many customers, and a carefully planned and scaled-up iSCSI infrastructure can, for the most part, match the performance of a moderate Fibre Channel SAN.

Also, iSCSI and Fibre Channel SANs are roughly comparable in complexity and share many of the same core concepts. Arguably, getting the first iSCSI LUN visible to an ESXi host is simpler than getting the first Fibre Channel LUN visible for people with expertise with Ethernet but not Fibre Channel, since understanding worldwide names and zoning is not needed. However, as you saw previously, these are not complex topics. In practice, designing a scalable, robust iSCSI network requires the same degree of diligence that is applied to Fibre Channel. You should use VLAN (or physical) isolation techniques similarly to Fibre Channel zoning, and you need to scale up connections to achieve comparable bandwidth. Look at Figure 6.15, and compare it to the switched Fibre Channel network diagram in Figure 6.9.

Each ESXi host has a minimum of two VMkernel ports, and each is physically connected to two Ethernet switches. (Recall from Chapter 5, "Creating and Configuring Virtual Networks," that VMkernel ports are used by the hypervisor for network traffic such as IP-based storage traffic, like iSCSI or NFS.) Storage and LAN are isolated—physically or via VLANs. Each switch has a minimum of two connections to two redundant front-end array network interfaces (across storage processors).

FIGURE 6.15

Notice how the topology of an iSCSI SAN is the same as a switched Fibre Channel SAN.

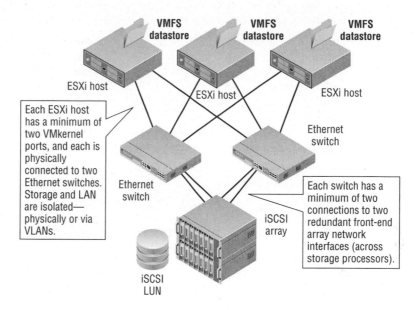

The one additional concept to focus on with iSCSI is the concept of *fan-in ratio*. This applies to all shared storage networks, including Fibre Channel, but the effect is often most pronounced with Gigabit Ethernet (GbE) networks. Across all shared networks, there is almost always a higher amount of bandwidth available across all the host nodes than there is on the egress of the switches and front-end connectivity of the array. It's important to remember that the host bandwidth is gated by congestion wherever it occurs. Don't minimize the array port-to-switch configuration. If you connect only four GbE interfaces on your array and you have 100 hosts with two GbE interfaces each, then expect contention, because your fan-in ratio is too large.

Also, when examining iSCSI and iSCSI SANs, many core ideas are similar to Fibre Channel and Fibre Channel SANs, but in some cases there are material differences. Let's look at the terminology:

iSCSI Initiator   An iSCSI initiator is a logical host-side device that serves the same function as a physical host bus adapter in Fibre Channel/FCoE or SCSI/SAS. iSCSI initiators can be software initiators (which use host CPU cycles to load/unload SCSI payloads into standard TCP/IP packets and perform error checking) or hardware initiators (the iSCSI equivalent of a Fibre Channel HBA or FCoE CNA). Examples of software initiators that are pertinent to vSphere administrators are the native ESXi software initiator and the guest software initiators available in Windows XP and later and in most current Linux distributions. Examples of iSCSI hardware initiators are add-in cards like the QLogic QLA 405x and QLE 406x host bus adapters. These cards perform all the iSCSI functions in hardware. An iSCSI initiator is identified by an iSCSI qualified name (referred to as an IQN). An iSCSI initiator uses an iSCSI network portal that consists of one or more IP addresses. An iSCSI initiator "logs in" to an iSCSI target.

iSCSI Target   An iSCSI target is a logical target-side device that serves the same function as a target in Fibre Channel SANs. It is the device that hosts iSCSI LUNs and masks to specific iSCSI initiators. Different arrays use iSCSI targets differently—some use hardware, some use software implementations—but largely this is unimportant. More important is that an iSCSI target doesn't necessarily map to a physical port as is the case with Fibre Channel; each array does this differently. Some have one iSCSI target per physical Ethernet port; some have one iSCSI target per iSCSI LUN, which is visible across multiple physical ports; and some have logical iSCSI targets that map to physical ports and LUNs in any relationship the administrator configures within the array. An iSCSI target is identified by an iSCSI Qualified Name (an IQN). An iSCSI target uses an iSCSI network portal that consists of one or more IP addresses.

iSCSI Logical Unit   An iSCSI LUN is a LUN hosted by an iSCSI target. There can be one or more LUNs behind a single iSCSI target.

iSCSI Network Portal   An iSCSI network portal is one or more IP addresses that are used by an iSCSI initiator or iSCSI target.

iSCSI Qualified Name   An iSCSI qualified name (IQN) serves the purpose of the WWN in Fibre Channel SANs; it is the unique identifier for an iSCSI initiator, target, or LUN. The format of the IQN is based on the iSCSI IETF standard.

Challenge Authentication Protocol   CHAP is a widely used basic authentication protocol, where a password exchange is used to authenticate the source or target of communication. Unidirectional CHAP is one way; the source authenticates to the destination, or, in the case of iSCSI, the iSCSI initiator authenticates to the iSCSI target. Bidirectional CHAP is two-way; the iSCSI initiator authenticates to the iSCSI target, and vice versa, before communication is established. Although Fibre Channel SANs are viewed as intrinsically secure because they are physically isolated from the Ethernet network, and although initiators not zoned to targets cannot communicate, this is not by definition true of iSCSI. With iSCSI, it is possible (but not recommended) to use the same Ethernet segment as general LAN traffic, and there is no intrinsic zoning model. Because the storage and general networking traffic could share networking infrastructure, CHAP is an optional mechanism to authenticate the source and destination of iSCSI traffic for some additional security. In practice, Fibre Channel and iSCSI SANs have the same security and same degree of isolation (logical or physical).

IP Security   IPsec is an IETF standard that uses public-key encryption techniques to secure the iSCSI payloads so that they are not susceptible to man-in-the-middle security attacks. Like CHAP for authentication, this higher level of optional security is part of the iSCSI standards because it is possible (but not recommended) to use a general-purpose IP network for iSCSI transport—and in these cases, not encrypting data exposes a security risk (for example, a man-in-the-middle attack could determine data on a host it can't authenticate to by simply reconstructing the data from the iSCSI packets). IPsec is relatively rarely used, because it has a heavy CPU impact on the initiator and the target.

Static/Dynamic Discovery   iSCSI uses a method of discovery where the iSCSI initiator can query an iSCSI target for the available LUNs. Static discovery involves a manual configuration, whereas dynamic discovery issues an iSCSI-standard `SendTargets` command to one of the iSCSI targets on the array. This target then reports all the available targets and LUNs to that particular initiator.

iSCSI Naming Service   The iSCSI Naming Service (iSNS) is analogous to the Domain Name System (DNS); it's where an iSNS server stores all the available iSCSI targets for a very large iSCSI deployment. iSNS is rarely used.

Figure 6.16 shows the key iSCSI elements in a logical diagram. This diagram shows iSCSI in the broadest sense.

FIGURE 6.16
The iSCSI IETF standard has several different elements.

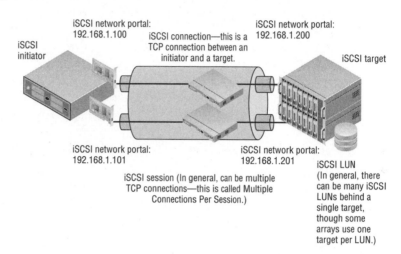

In general, the iSCSI session can be multiple TCP connections, called *Multiple Connections Per Session*. Note that this cannot be done in VMware. An iSCSI initiator and iSCSI target can communicate on an iSCSI network portal that can consist of one or more IP addresses. The concept of network portals is done differently on each array; some arrays always have one IP address per target port, while some arrays use network portals extensively. The iSCSI initiator logs into the iSCSI target, creating an iSCSI session. It is possible to have many iSCSI sessions for a single target, and each session can have multiple TCP connections (Multiple Connections Per Session, which isn't currently supported by vSphere). There can be varied numbers of iSCSI LUNs behind an iSCSI target—many or just one. Every array does this differently. I'll discuss the particulars of the vSphere software iSCSI initiator implementation in detail in the "Adding a LUN via iSCSI" section.

What about the debate regarding hardware iSCSI initiators (iSCSI HBAs) versus software iSCSI initiators? Figure 6.17 shows the differences among software iSCSI on generic network interfaces, network interfaces that do TCP/IP offload, and full iSCSI HBAs. Clearly there are more things the ESXi host needs to process with software iSCSI initiators, but the additional CPU is relatively light. Fully saturating several GbE links will use only roughly one core of a modern CPU, and the cost of iSCSI HBAs is usually less than the cost of slightly more CPU. Keep the CPU overhead in mind as you craft your storage design, but don't let it be your sole criterion.

FIGURE 6.17
Some parts of the stack are handled by the adapter card versus the ESXi host CPU in various implementations.

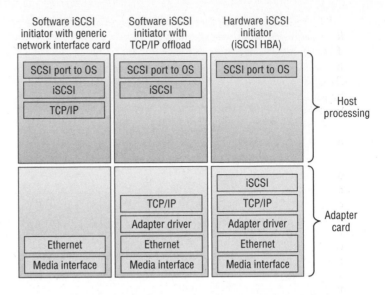

Prior to vSphere 5, one thing that remained the exclusive domain of the iSCSI HBAs was booting from an iSCSI SAN. vSphere 5 includes support for iSCSI Boot Firmware Table (iBFT), a mechanism that enables booting from iSCSI SAN with a software iSCSI initiator. You must have appropriate support for iBFT in the hardware. One might argue that using Auto Deploy would provide much of the same benefit as booting from an iSCSI SAN, but each approach has its advantages and disadvantages.

iSCSI is the last of the block-based shared storage options available in vSphere; now I move on to the Network File System (NFS), the only NAS protocol that vSphere supports.

JUMBO FRAMES ARE SUPPORTED

VMware ESXi does support jumbo frames for all VMkernel traffic, including both iSCSI and NFS, and should be used where possible. However, it is then critical to configure a consistent, larger maximum transfer unit (MTU) size on *all* devices in all the possible networking paths; otherwise, Ethernet frame fragmentation will cause communication problems.

UNDERSTANDING THE NETWORK FILE SYSTEM

NFS protocol is a standard originally developed by Sun Microsystems to enable remote systems to access a filesystem on another host as if it were locally attached. vSphere implements a client compliant with NFSv3 using TCP.

When NFS datastores are used by vSphere, no local filesystem (such as VMFS) is used. The filesystem is on the remote NFS server. This means that NFS datastores need to handle the same access control and file-locking requirements that vSphere delivers on block storage using the vSphere Virtual Machine File System, or VMFS (I'll describe VMFS in more detail in the section "Examining the vSphere Virtual Machine File System"). NFS servers accomplish this through traditional NFS file locks.

The movement of the filesystem from the ESXi host to the NFS server also means that you don't need to handle zoning/masking tasks. This makes configuring an NFS datastore one of the easiest storage options to simply get up and running. On the other hand, it also means that all of the high availability and multipathing functionality that is normally part of a Fibre Channel, FCoE, or iSCSI storage stack is gone; instead, this functionality has to be provided by the networking stack. I'll discuss the implications of this in the section titled "Crafting a Highly Available NFS Design."

Figure 6.18 shows the configuration and topology of an NFS configuration. Note the similarities to the topologies in Figures 6.9 and 6.15.

FIGURE 6.18

The configuration and topology of an NFS configuration is similar to iSCSI from a connectivity standpoint but very different from a configuration standpoint.

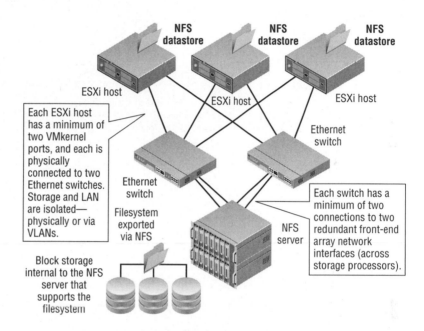

Technically, any NFS server that complies with NFSv3 over TCP will work with vSphere (vSphere does not support NFS over UDP), but similar to the considerations for Fibre Channel and iSCSI, the infrastructure needs to support your entire vSphere environment. Therefore, I recommend you use only NFS servers that are explicitly on the VMware HCL.

Using NFS datastores moves the elements of storage design associated with LUNs from the ESXi hosts to the NFS server. Instead of exposing block storage—which uses the RAID techniques that I described earlier for data protection—and allowing the ESXi hosts to create a filesystem (VMFS) on those block devices, the NFS server uses its block storage—protected using RAID—and creates its own filesystems on that block storage. These filesystems are then exported via NFS and mounted on your ESXi hosts.

In the early days of using NFS with VMware, NFS was categorized as being a lower-performance option for use with ISOs and templates but not production VMs. If production VMs were used on NFS datastores, the historical recommendation would have been to relocate the VM swap to block storage. Although it is true that NAS and block architectures are different and, likewise, their scaling models and bottlenecks are generally different, this perception is mostly rooted in how people have used NAS historically.

The reality is that it's absolutely possible to build an enterprise-class NAS infrastructure. NFS datastores can support a broad range of virtualized workloads and do not require you to relocate the VM swap. However, in cases where NFS will be supporting a broad set of production VM workloads, you will need to pay attention to the NFS server backend design and network infrastructure. You need to apply the same degree of care to bet-the-business NAS as you would if you were using block storage via Fibre Channel, FCoE, or iSCSI. With vSphere, your NFS server isn't being used as a traditional file server, where performance and availability requirements are relatively low. Rather, it's being used as an NFS server supporting a mission-critical application—in this case the vSphere environment and all the VMs on those NFS datastores.

I mentioned previously that vSphere implements an NFSv3 client using TCP. This is important to note because it directly impacts your connectivity options. Each NFS datastore uses two TCP sessions to the NFS server: one for NFS control traffic and the other for NFS data traffic. In effect, this means that the vast majority of the NFS traffic for a single datastore will use a single TCP session. Consequently, this means that link aggregation (which works on a per-flow basis from one source to one target) will use only one Ethernet link per datastore, regardless of how many links are included in the link aggregation group. To be able to use the aggregate throughput of multiple Ethernet interfaces, multiple datastores are needed, and no single datastore will be able to use more than one link's worth of bandwidth. The approach available to iSCSI (multiple iSCSI sessions per iSCSI target) is not available in the NFS use case. I'll discuss techniques for designing high-performance NFS datastores in the section titled "Crafting a Highly Available NFS Design."

As in the previous sections that covered the common storage array architectures, the protocol choices available to the vSphere administrator are broad. You can make most vSphere deployments work well on all protocols, and each has advantages and disadvantages. The key is to understand and determine what will work best for you. In the following section, I'll summarize how to make these basic storage choices.

Making Basic Storage Choices

Most vSphere workloads can be met by midrange array architectures (regardless of active-active, active-passive, asymmetrical, or virtual port design). Use enterprise array designs when mission-critical and very large-scale virtual datacenter workloads demand uncompromising availability and performance linearity.

As shown in Table 6.1, each storage protocol choice can support most use cases. It's not about one versus the other but rather about understanding and leveraging their differences and applying them to deliver maximum flexibility.

TABLE 6.1: Storage Choices

FEATURE	FIBRE CHANNEL SAN	iSCSI SAN	NFS
ESXi boot (boot from SAN)	Yes	Hardware initiator or software initiator with iBFT support	No
VM boot	Yes	Yes	Yes

TABLE 6.1:   Storage Choices   *(CONTINUED)*

FEATURE	FIBRE CHANNEL SAN	ISCSI SAN	NFS
Raw device mapping	Yes	Yes	No
Dynamic extension	Yes	Yes	Yes
Availability and scaling model	Storage stack (PSA), ESXi LUN queues, array configuration	Storage stack (PSA), ESXi LUN queues, array configuration	Network Stage (NIC teaming and routing), network and NFS server configuration
VMware feature support (vSphere HA, vMotion, Storage vMotion, vSphere FT)	Yes	Yes	Yes

Picking a protocol type has historically been focused on the following criteria:

vSphere Feature Support   Although major VMware features such as vSphere HA and vMotion initially required VMFS, they are now supported on all storage types, including raw device mappings (RDMs) and NFS datastores. vSphere feature support is generally not a protocol-selection criterion, and there are only a few features that lag on RDMs and NFS, such as native vSphere snapshots on physical compatibility mode RDMs or the ability to create RDMs on NFS.

Storage Capacity Efficiency   Thin provisioning behavior at the vSphere layer, universally and properly applied, drives a very high efficiency, regardless of protocol choice. Applying thin provisioning at the storage array (on both block and NFS objects) delivers a higher overall efficiency than applying it only at the virtualization layer. Emerging additional array capacity efficiency techniques (such as detecting and reducing storage consumed when there is information in common using compression and data deduplication) are currently most efficiently used on NFS datastores, but are expanding to include block use cases. One common error is to look at storage capacity (GB) as the sole vector of efficiency—in many cases, the performance envelope requires a fixed number of spindles even with advanced caching techniques. Often in these cases, efficiency is measured in spindle density, not in GB. For most vSphere customers, efficiency tends to be a function of operational process, rather than protocol or platform choice.

Performance   Many vSphere customers see similar performance regardless of a given protocol choice. Properly designed iSCSI and NFS over Gigabit Ethernet can support very large VMware deployments, particularly with small-block (4 KB–64 KB) I/O patterns that characterize most general Windows workloads and don't need more than roughly 80 MBps of 100 percent read or write I/O bandwidth or 160 MBps of mixed I/O bandwidth. This difference in the throughput limit is due to the 1 Gbps/2 Gbps bidirectional nature of 1GbE—pure read or pure write workloads are unidirectional, but mixed workloads are bidirectional.

Fibre Channel (and by extension, FCoE) generally delivers a better performance envelope with very large-block I/O (VMs supporting DSS database workloads or SharePoint), which tends to demand a high degree of throughput. Less important generally but still important for some workloads, Fibre Channel delivers a lower-latency model and also tends to have a faster failover behavior because iSCSI and NFS always depend on some degree of TCP retransmission for loss and, in some iSCSI cases, ARP—all of which drive failover handling into tens of seconds versus seconds with Fibre Channel or FCoE. Load balancing and scale-out with IP storage using multiple Gigabit Ethernet links with IP storage can work for iSCSI to drive up throughput. Link aggregation techniques can help, but they work only when you have many TCP sessions. Because the NFS client in vSphere uses a single TCP session for data transmission, link aggregation won't improve the throughput of individual NFS datastores. Broad availability of 10 Gb Ethernet brings higher-throughput options to NFS datastores.

You can make every protocol configuration work in almost all use cases; the key is in the details (covered in this chapter). In practice, the most important thing is what you know and feel comfortable with.

The most flexible vSphere configurations tend to use a combination of both VMFS (which requires block storage) and NFS datastores (which require NAS), as well as RDMs on a selective basis (block storage).

The choice of which block protocol should be used to support the VMFS and RDM use cases depends on the enterprise more than the technologies and tends to follow this pattern:

◆ iSCSI for customers who have never used and have no existing Fibre Channel SAN infrastructure

◆ Fibre Channel for those with existing Fibre Channel SAN infrastructure that meets their needs

◆ FCoE for those upgrading existing Fibre Channel SAN infrastructure

vSphere can be applied to a very broad set of use cases—from the desktop/laptop to the server and on the server workloads—ranging from test and development to heavy workloads and mission-critical applications. A simple one-size-fits-all model can work, but only for the simplest deployments. The advantage of vSphere is that all protocols and all models are supported. Becoming fixated on one model means that not everything is virtualized that can be and the enterprise isn't as flexible and efficient as it can be.

Now that you've learned about the basic principles of shared storage and determined how to make the basic storage choices for your environment, it's time to see how these are applied in vSphere.

Implementing vSphere Storage Fundamentals

This section of the chapter examines how the shared storage technologies covered previously are applied in vSphere. I will cover these elements in a logical sequence, starting with core vSphere storage concepts. Next, I'll cover the storage options in vSphere for datastores to contain groups of VMs (VMFS datastores and NFS datastores). I'll follow that discussion with options for presenting disk devices directly into VMs (raw device mappings). Finally, I'll examine VM-level storage configuration details.

Reviewing Core vSphere Storage Concepts

One of the core concepts of virtualization is encapsulation. What used to be a physical system is encapsulated by vSphere, resulting in VMs that are represented by a set of files. Chapter 9, "Creating and Managing Virtual Machines," provides more detail on the specific files that compose a VM and their purpose. For reasons I've described already, these VM files reside on the shared storage infrastructure (with the exception of a raw device mapping, or RDM, which I'll discuss shortly).

In general, vSphere uses a shared-everything storage model. All ESXi hosts in a vSphere environment use commonly accessed storage objects using block storage protocols (Fibre Channel, FCoE, or iSCSI, in which case the storage objects are LUNs) or network attached storage protocols (NFS, in which case the storage objects are NFS exports). Depending on the environment, these storage objects will be exposed to the majority of your ESXi hosts, although not necessarily to all ESXi hosts in the environment. In Chapter 7, I'll again review the concept of a cluster, which is a key part of features like vSphere HA and vSphere DRS. Within a cluster, you'll want to ensure that all ESXi hosts have visibility and access to the same set of storage objects.

Before I get into the details of how to configure the various storage objects in vSphere, I need to first review some core vSphere storage technologies, concepts, and terminology. This information will provide a foundation upon which I will build later in the chapter. I'll start with a look at the vSphere Virtual Machine File System, a key technology found in practically every vSphere deployment.

EXAMINING THE VSPHERE VIRTUAL MACHINE FILE SYSTEM

The vSphere Virtual Machine File System (VMFS) is a common configuration option for many vSphere deployments. It's similar to NTFS for Windows Server and ext3 for Linux. Like these filesystems, it is native; it's included with vSphere and operates on top of block storage objects. If you're leveraging any form of block storage, you're using VMFS.

The purpose of VMFS is to simplify the storage environment. It would clearly be difficult to scale a virtual environment if each VM directly accessed its own storage rather than storing the set of files on a shared volume. VMFS creates a shared storage pool that is used for one or more VMs.

While similar to NTFS and ext3, VMFS differs from these common filesystems in several important ways:

◆ It was designed to be a clustered filesystem from its inception; neither NTFS nor ext3 is a clustered filesystem. Unlike many clustered filesystems, it is simple and easy to use.

◆ VMFS's simplicity is derived from its simple and transparent distributed locking mechanism. This is generally much simpler than traditional clustered filesystems with network cluster lock managers.

◆ VMFS enables simple direct-to-disk, steady-state I/O that results in high throughput at a low CPU overhead for the ESXi hosts.

◆ Locking is handled using metadata in a hidden section of the filesystem, as illustrated in Figure 6.19. The metadata portion of the filesystem contains critical information in the form of on-disk lock structures (files), such as which ESXi host is the current owner of a given VM, ensuring that there is no contention or corruption of the VM.

FIGURE 6.19
VMFS stores
metadata in a
hidden area of the
first extent.

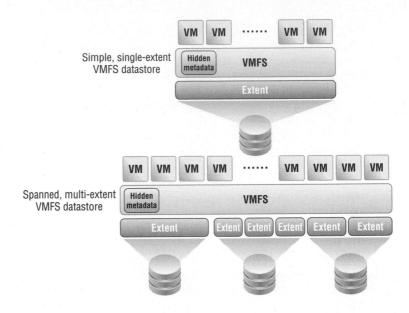

- Depending on the storage array's support for vSphere, when these on-disk lock structures are updated, the ESXi host doing the update momentarily locks the LUN using a nonpersistent SCSI lock (SCSI Reserve/Reset commands). This operation is completely transparent to the vSphere administrator.

- These metadata updates do *not* occur during normal I/O operations and do not represent a fundamental scaling limit.

- During the metadata updates, there is minimal impact to the production I/O (covered in a VMware white paper at www.vmware.com/resources/techresources/1059. This impact is negligible to the other hosts accessing the same VMFS datastore and more pronounced on the ESXi host holding the SCSI lock.

- These metadata updates occur during the following:

  - The creation of a file in the VMFS datastore (powering on a VM, creating/deleting a VM, or taking a snapshot, for example)

  - Actions that change the ESXi host that owns a VM (vMotion and vSphere HA)

  - Changes to the VMFS filesystem itself (extending the filesystem or adding a filesystem extent)

---

vSphere 5 and SCSI-3 Dependency

In vSphere 5, like vSphere 4, only SCSI-3–compliant block storage objects are supported. Most major storage arrays have, or can be upgraded via their array software to, full SCSI-3 support, but check with your storage vendor before doing so. If your storage array doesn't support SCSI-3, the storage details shown on the Configuration tab for the vSphere host will not display correctly.

> In spite of this requirement, vSphere still uses SCSI-2 reservations for general ESXi-level SCSI reservations (not to be confused with guest-level reservations). This is important for Asymmetrical Logical Unit Access (ALUA) support, covered in the "Reviewing Multipathing" section.

vSphere 4 used VMFS version 3 (VMFS-3), and vSphere 5 continues to provide support for VMFS-3. VMFS-3 supports datastores up to just shy of 2 TB (2 TB minus 512 bytes, to be precise). While many have claimed this to be a "32-bit vs. 64-bit" limitation, it actually stems from the use of MBR (Master Boot Record) partition management instead of GPT (GUID partition tables). While this amount seems quite large, in enterprise environments the 2 TB ceiling could be constrictive.

Fortunately, VMFS-3 supports the ability to reside on one or more partitions (referred to as *extents*). In fact, VMFS-3 supports up to 32 extents in a single VMFS-3 datastore, for a maximum size of up to 64 TB. You can add these extents nondisruptively, as I'll show you later in the section "Expanding a VMFS Datastore."

It is a widely held misconception that having a VMFS-3 datastore that spans multiple extents is *always* a bad idea and acts as a simple concatenation of the filesystem. In practice, although adding an extent adds more space to the datastore as a concatenated space, as new objects (VMs) are placed in the datastore, VMFS-3 will randomly distribute those new file objects across the various extents without waiting for the original extent to be full. VMFS-3 allocates the initial blocks for a new file randomly in the filesystem, and subsequent allocations for that file are sequential (this has been VMFS-3's behavior since the early days of ESX 3.0). This means that files are distributed across the filesystem and, in the case of spanned VMFS volumes, across multiple LUNs. This will naturally distribute VMs across multiple extents.

LOCKING IN A MULTI-EXTENT VMFS CONFIGURATION

Note that the metadata that VMFS uses is always stored in the first extent of a VMFS datastore. This means that in VMFS volumes that span extents, the effects of SCSI locking during the short moments of metadata updates apply only to the LUN backing the first extent. The vSphere Storage APIs could modify this behavior; see the section "Uncovering the vSphere Storage APIs" for more information.

In addition, having a VMFS datastore that comprises multiple extents across multiple LUNs increases the parallelism of the underlying LUN queues. This is a topic I'll revisit later in the section "Reviewing the Importance of LUN Queues."

Also widely unknown is that VMFS-3 datastores that span extents are more resilient than generally believed. Removing the LUN supporting a VMFS-3 extent will *not* make the spanned VMFS datastore unavailable. The exception is the first extent in the VMFS-3 datastore, which contains the metadata for VMFS (see Figure 6.19); removing this will result in the datastore being unavailable. However, this is no better or worse than a single-extent VMFS volume. Removing an extent affects only the portion of the datastore supported by that extent; reconnecting the LUN restores full use of that portion of the VMFS-3 datastore. VMFS-3 and VMs are relatively resilient to this *crash-consistent* behavior (a common term for filesystem behavior after a hard shutdown or crash). While they are *crash-resilient*, note that just like any action that removes a datastore or portion of a datastore while VMs are active, the removal of a VMFS extent *can* result in corrupted VMs and should not be done intentionally.

VMFS-3 also supported multiple block sizes (ranging from 1 MB to 8 MB). The VMFS-3 block size determined the maximum file size; to create files of up to approximately 2 TB on a VMFS-3 volume, you had to use 8 MB block sizes. Here are the VMFS-3 block sizes and corresponding maximum file sizes:

◆ 1 MB block size meant a maximum file size of 256 GB.

◆ 2 MB block size meant a maximum file size of 512 GB.

◆ 4 MB block size meant a maximum file size of 1 TB.

◆ 8 MB block size meant a maximum file size of approximately 2 TB.

Once set, the VMFS-3 block size could not be changed, so if you selected a 1 MB block size when creating the VMFS-3 datastore, then you were limited to creating virtual disks of up to 256 GB of that datastore. VMs that needed a virtual disk larger than 256 GB could not be stored on that datastore.

In addition to supporting VMFS-3, vSphere 5 introduces VMFS version 5 (VMFS-5). Only hosts running ESXi 5.0 or later support VMFS-5; hosts running ESX/ESXi 4.x will not be able to see or access VMFS-5 datastores. VMFS-5 offers a number of advantages over VMFS-3:

◆ VMFS-5 datastores can now grow up to 64 TB in size using only a single extent. Datastores built on multiple extents are still limited to 64 TB as well.

◆ VMFS-5 datastores use a single block size of 1 MB, but you are allowed to create files of up to approximately 2 TB on VMFS-5 datastores.

◆ VMFS-5 uses a more efficient sub-block allocation size of only 8 KB, compared to 64 KB for VMFS-3.

◆ VMFS-5 allows for the creation of physical-mode RDMs for devices in excess of 2 TB in size. (VMFS-3 limited RDMs to 2 TB in size. I'll cover RDMs later in the section "Working with Raw Device Mappings.")

Even better than the improvements in VMFS-5 is the fact that you can upgrade VMFS-3 datastores to VMFS-5 in place and online—without any disruption to the VMs running on that datastore. You're also not required to upgrade VMFS-3 datastores to VMFS-5, which further simplifies the migration from vSphere 4 to vSphere 5.

Later in this chapter in the section "Working with VMFS Datastores," I'll provide more details on how to create, expand, delete, and upgrade VMFS datastores.

Closely related to VMFS is the idea of multipathing, a topic that I will discuss in the next section.

REVIEWING MULTIPATHING

Multipathing is the term used to describe how a host, such as an ESXi host, manages storage devices that have multiple ways (or paths) to access them. Multipathing is extremely common in Fibre Channel and FCoE environments and is also found in iSCSI environments. I won't go so far as to say that multipathing is strictly for block-based storage environments, but I will say that multipathing for NFS is generally handled much differently than for block storage.

In vSphere 4, VMware and VMware technology partners spent considerable effort over-hauling how the elements of the vSphere storage stack that deal with multipathing work. This architecture, known as the Pluggable Storage Architecture (PSA), is present in vSphere 5 as well. Figure 6.20 shows an overview of the PSA.

FIGURE 6.20
vSphere's Pluggable Storage Architecture is highly modular and extensible.

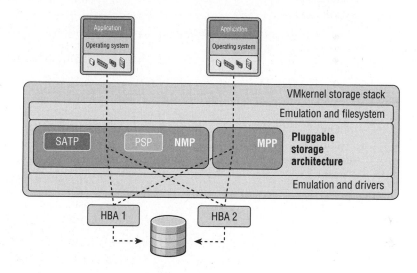

One of the key goals in the development of the PSA was to make vSphere multipathing much more flexible. Pre–vSphere 4 versions of VMware ESX/ESXi had a rigid set of lists that determined failover policy and multipathing policy, and this architecture was updated only with major VMware releases. With the PSA's modular architecture, vSphere administrators have a much more flexible approach.

Four different modules compose the PSA:

- Native multipathing plug-in (NMP)
- Storage array type plug-in (SATP)
- Path selection plug-in (PSP)
- Multipathing plug-in (MPP)

Any given ESXi host can have multiple modules in use at any point and can be connected to multiple arrays, and you can configure the combination of modules used (an NMP/SATP/PSP combination or an MPP) on a LUN-by-LUN basis.

Let's see how they work together.

Understanding the NMP Module

The NMP module handles overall MPIO behavior and array identification. The NMP leverages the SATP and PSP modules and isn't generally configured in any way.

Understanding SATP Modules

SATP modules handle path failover for a given storage array and determine the failover type for a LUN.

vSphere ships with SATPs for a broad set of arrays, with generic SATPs for non-specified arrays and a local SATP for local storage. The SATP modules contain the rules on how to handle array-specific actions or behavior, as well as any specific operations needed to manage array paths. This is part of what makes the NMP modular (unlike the NMP in prior versions); it doesn't need to contain the array-specific logic, and additional modules for new arrays can be added without changing the NMP. Using the SCSI Array ID reported by the array via a SCSI query, the NMP selects the appropriate SATP to use. After that, the SATP monitors, deactivates, and activates paths (and when a manual rescan occurs, detects new paths)—providing information up to the NMP. The SATP also performs array-specific tasks such as activating passive paths on active/passive arrays.

To see what array SATP modules exist, enter the following command from the vCLI (I ran this from the vSphere Management Assistant):

esxcli –s *vcenter-01* –h *pod-1-blade-7* storage nmp satp list

Figure 6.21 shows the results this command returns (note that the default PSP for a given SATP is also shown):

FIGURE 6.21
Only the SATPs for the arrays to which an ESXi host is connected are loaded.

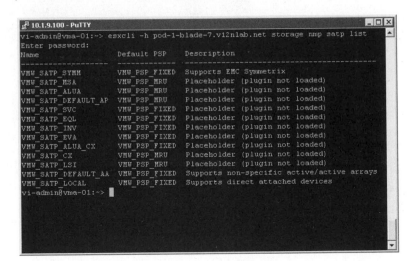

Understanding PSP Modules

The PSP module handles the actual path used for every given I/O.

The NMP assigns a default PSP, which can be overridden manually for every LUN based on the SATP associated with that device. This command (and the output captured in Figure 6.22) shows you the three PSPs vSphere includes by default:

esxcli –s *vcenter-01* –h *pod-1-blade-7* storage nmp psp list

Each of these PSPs performs path selection slightly differently:

◆ Most Recently Used (noted as VMW_PSP_MRU) selects the path it used most recently. If this path becomes unavailable, the ESXi host switches to an alternative path and continues to use the new path while it is available. This is the default for active/passive array types.

◆ Fixed (noted as VMW_PSP_FIXED) uses the designated preferred path, if it has been configured. Otherwise, it uses the first working path discovered at system boot time. If the ESXi
host cannot use the preferred path, it selects a random alternative available path. The ESXi
host automatically reverts to the preferred path as soon as the path becomes available. This
is the default for active/active array types (or active/passive arrays that use ALUA with
SCSI-2 reservation mechanisms—in these cases, they appear as active/active).

◆ Round Robin (noted as VMW_PSP_RR) rotates the path selection among all available paths
and enables basic load balancing across the paths. This is neither a weighted algorithm nor
responsive to queue depth, but is a significant improvement. In prior ESXi versions, there
was no way to load balance a LUN, and customers needed to statically distribute LUNs
across paths, which was a poor proxy for true load balancing.

FIGURE 6.22
vSphere ships with
three default PSPs.

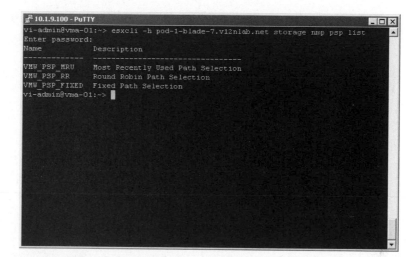

WHICH PSP IS RIGHT IF YOU'RE USING ALUA?

What do you do if your array can be configured to use ALUA—and therefore could use the Fixed,
MRU, or Round Robin policy? See the "Understanding Midrange and Enterprise Storage Array
Design" section for information on ALUA.

The Fixed and MRU path failover policies deliver failover only and work fine with active-active and
active-passive designs, regardless of whether ALUA is used. Of course, they both drive workloads
down a single path. Ensure that you manually select active I/O paths that are the "good" ports,
which are the ones where the port is on the storage processor owning the LUN. You don't want to
select the "bad" ports, which are the higher-latency, lower-throughput ones that transit the internal
interconnect to get to the LUN.

The out-of-the-box load-balancing policy in vSphere (Round Robin) doesn't use the non-optimized
paths (though they are noted as active in the vSphere Client). Third-party multipathing plug-ins
that are aware of the difference between the asymmetrical path choices can optimize an ALUA
configuration.

Perform the following steps to see what SATP (and PSP) is being used for a given LUN in the vSphere Client:

1. In the vSphere Client, navigate to the Datastore And Datastore Clusters inventory view.

2. Select a datastore from the list on the left; then select the Configuration tab on the right.

3. Click the Properties hyperlink.

This opens the Datastore Properties dialog box.

4. Click the Manage Paths button.

This opens the Datastore Manage Paths dialog box. The SATP will be listed near the top of this dialog box, as shown in Figure 6.23.

FIGURE 6.23
The SATP for this datastore is VMW_SATP_SYMM, which is the default SATP for EMC Symmetrix arrays.

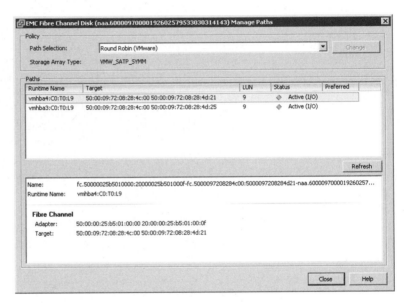

In this example, the array is an EMC Symmetrix VMAX, so the default SATP reports this as an active/active array, and the generic VMW_SATP_SYMM is selected.

The default PSP is Fixed (VMware), but this has been manually changed to Round Robin (VMware). A change in the PSP takes place *immediately* when you change it. There is no confirmation. Note that the PSP is configurable on a LUN-by-LUN basis.

WHAT IS ALL THE STUFF IN THE STORAGE DEVICES LIST?

In the runtime name, the *C* is the channel identifier, the *T* is the target identifier, and the *L* is the LUN number.

And that long text string starting with *naa*? This is the Network Address Authority ID, which is a unique identifier for the target and a LUN. This ID is guaranteed to be persistent through reboots and is used throughout vSphere. You can copy the NAA ID to the clipboard of the system running the vSphere Client by right-clicking the name in the configuration screen and selecting "Copy Identifier to Clipboard."

Understanding MPP Modules

The MPP module can add significantly enhanced multipathing to vSphere, and for the given LUNs it supports, it replaces the NMP, SATP, and PSP. The MPP claim policy (the LUNs that it manages) is defined on a LUN-by-LUN and array-by-array basis, and MPPs can coexist with NMP.

Because it replaces the NMP, SATP, and PSP, the MPP can change the path selection normally handled by the PSP. This allows the MPP to provide more sophisticated path selection than the VMware-supplied PSPs are capable of offering—including selecting by host queue depth and, in some cases, the array target port state. As a result of this more sophisticated path selection, an MPP could offer notable performance increases or other new functionality not present in vSphere by default.

The PSA was written not only to be modular but also to support third-party extensibility; third-party SATPs, PSPs, and MPPs are technically possible. At the time of this writing, only a couple MPPs were generally available, though other vendors are likely to create third-party SATPs, PSPs, and potentially full MPPs. Once the MPP is loaded on an ESXi host via the vSphere Client's host update tools, all multipathing for LUNs managed by that MPP become fully automated.

AN EXAMPLE OF A THIRD-PARTY MPP

EMC PowerPath/VE is a third-party multipathing plug-in that supports a broad set of EMC and non-EMC array types. PowerPath/VE dramatically enhances load balancing, performance, and availability using the following techniques:

◆ Better availability through active management of intermittent path behavior

◆ Better availability through more rapid path state detection

◆ Better availability through automated path discovery behavior without manual rescan

◆ Better performance through better path selection using weighted algorithms, which is critical in cases where the paths are unequal (ALUA)

◆ Better performance by monitoring and adjusting the ESXi host queue depth to select the path for a given I/O, shifting the workload from heavily used paths to lightly used paths

◆ Better performance with some arrays by predictive optimization based on the array port queues (which are generally the first point of contention and tend to affect all the ESXi hosts simultaneously; without predictive advance handling, they tend to cause simultaneous path choice across the ESXi cluster)

Previously in this chapter, in the section on VMFS, I mentioned that one potential advantage to having a VMFS datastore spanned across multiple extents on multiple LUNs would be to increase the parallelism of the LUN queues. In addition, in this section you've heard me mention how a third-party MPP might make multipathing decisions based on host or target queues. Why is queuing so important? I'll review queuing in the next section.

REVIEWING THE IMPORTANCE OF LUN QUEUES

Queues are an important construct in block storage environments (across all protocols, including Fibre Channel, FCoE, and iSCSI). Think of a queue as a line at the supermarket checkout.

Queues exist on the server (in this case the ESXi host), generally at both the HBA and LUN levels. They also exist on the storage array. Every array does this differently, but they all have the same concept. Block-centric storage arrays generally have these queues at the target ports, array-wide, and array LUN levels, and finally at the spindles themselves. File-centric storage arrays generally have queues at the target ports and array-wide, but abstract the array LUN queues because the LUNs actually exist as files in the filesystem. However, file-centric designs have internal LUN queues underneath the filesystems themselves and then ultimately at the spindle level—in other words, it's internal to how the file server accesses its own storage.

The queue depth is a function of how fast things are being loaded into the queue and how fast the queue is being drained. How fast the queue is being drained is a function of the amount of time needed for the array to service the I/O requests. This is called the *service time*, and in the supermarket checkout it is the speed of the person behind the checkout counter (ergo, the array service time).

CAN I VIEW THE QUEUE?

To determine how many outstanding items are in the queue, use `resxtop`, hit U to get to the storage screen, and look at the QUED column.

The array service time itself is a function of many things, predominantly the workload, then the spindle configuration, then the write cache (for writes only), then the storage processors, and finally, with certain rare workloads, the read caches.

So why is all this important? Well, for most customers it will never come up, and all queuing will be happening behind the scenes. However, for some customers, LUN queues are one of the predominant things with block storage architectures that determines whether your VMs are happy or not from a storage performance perspective.

When a queue overflows (either because the storage configuration is insufficient for the steady-state workload or because the storage configuration is unable to absorb a burst), it causes many upstream effects to slow down the I/O. For IP-focused people, this effect is analogous to TCP windowing, which should be avoided for storage just as queue overflow should be avoided.

You can change the default queue depths for your HBAs and for each LUN. (See www.vmware.com for HBA-specific steps.) After changing the queue depths on the HBAs, a second step is needed at the VMkernel layer. You must increase the amount of outstanding disk requests from the VMs to VMFS to match the HBA setting. You can do this in the ESXi advanced settings, specifically Disk.SchedNumReqOutstanding, as shown in Figure 6.24. In general, the default settings for LUN queues and Disk.SchedNumReqOutstanding are the best. I don't recommend changing these values unless instructed to do so by VMware or your storage vendor.

If the queue overflow is not a case of dealing with short bursts but rather that you are under-configured for the steady state workload, making the queues deeper can have a downside: higher latency. Then it overflows anyway. This is the predominant case, so before increasing your LUN queues, check the array service time. If it's taking more than 10 milliseconds to service I/O requests, you need to improve the service time, usually by adding more spindles to the LUN or by moving the LUN to a faster-performing tier.

The last topic I'll cover before moving on to more hands-on topics is a relatively new feature to vSphere, first introduced in vSphere 4.1 and expanded in vSphere 5.0: the vSphere Storage APIs.

FIGURE 6.24
It is possible to adjust the advanced properties for advanced use cases, increasing the maximum number of outstanding requests allowed to match adjusted queues.

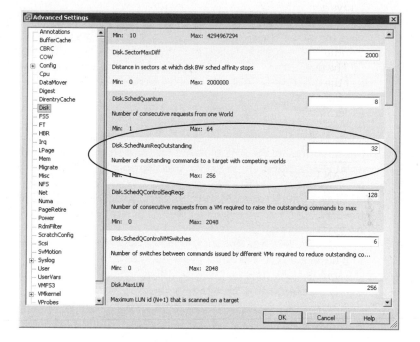

UNCOVERING THE VSPHERE STORAGE APIs

Formerly known as the vStorage APIs, the vSphere Storage APIs aren't necessarily application programming interfaces (APIs) in the truest sense of the word. In some cases, yes, but in other cases, they are simply storage commands that vSphere leverages.

There are several broad families of storage APIs that vSphere offers:

- vSphere Storage APIs for Array Integration
- vSphere Storage APIs for Storage Awareness
- vSphere Storage APIs for Site Recovery
- vSphere Storage APIs for Multipathing
- vSphere Storage APIs for Data Protection

Because of the previous naming convention (vStorage APIs), some of these technologies are more popularly known by their acronyms. Table 6.2 maps the well-known acronyms to their new official names.

TABLE 6.2: vSphere Storage API acronyms

WELL-KNOWN ACRONYM	OFFICIAL NAME
VAAI	vSphere Storage APIs for Array Integration
VASA	vSphere Storage APIs for Storage Awareness
VADP	vSphere Storage APIs for Data Protection

In this book, for consistency with what is found in the community and the marketplace, I'll use the well-known acronyms when I refer to these technologies.

As I mentioned previously, some of these technologies are truly APIs. The Storage APIs for Multipathing are the APIs that VMware partners can use to create third-party MPPs, SATPs, and PSPs for use in the PSA. Similarly, the Storage APIs for Site Recovery encompass the actual programming interfaces that enable array vendors to make their storage arrays work with VMware's Site Recovery Manager product, and the Storage APIs for Data Protection are the APIs that third-party companies can use to build virtualization-aware and virtualization-friendly backup solutions.

There are two sets remaining that I haven't yet mentioned, and that's because I'd like to delve into those a bit more deeply. I'll start with the Storage APIs for Array Integration.

Exploring the vSphere Storage APIs for Array Integration

The vSphere Storage APIs for Array Integration (more popularly known as VAAI) were first introduced in vSphere 4.1 as a means of offloading storage-related operations from the ESXi hosts to the storage array. Although VAAI is largely based on SCSI commands ratified by the T10 committee in charge of the SCSI standards, it does require appropriate support from storage vendors, so you'll want to check with your storage vendor to see what is required in order to support VAAI. In addition to the VAAI features introduced in vSphere 4.1, vSphere 5 introduces even more storage offloads (popularly referred to as VAAIv2). Here's a quick rundown of the storage offloads available in vSphere 5:

Hardware-Assisted Locking   Also called atomic test and set (ATS), this feature supports discrete VM locking without the use of SCSI reservations. In the section titled "Examining the vSphere Virtual Machine File System," I briefly described how vSphere uses SCSI reservations when VMFS metadata needs to be updated. Hardware-assisted locking allows for disk locking per sector instead of locking the entire LUN. This offers a dramatic increase in performance when lots of metadata updates are necessary (such as powering on many VMs at the same time).

Hardware-Accelerated Full Copy   Support for hardware-accelerated full copy allows storage arrays to make full copies of data completely internal to the array instead of requiring the ESXi host to read and write the data. This causes a significant reduction in the storage traffic between the host and the array, and can reduce the time required to perform operations like cloning VMs or deploying new VMs from templates.

Hardware-Accelerated Block Zeroing   Sometimes called write same, this functionality allows storage arrays to zero out large numbers of blocks to provide newly allocated storage without any previously written data. This can speed up operations like creating VMs and formatting virtual disks.

Thin Provisioning   vSphere 5 adds an additional set of hardware offloads around thin provisioning. First, vSphere 5 is thin provisioning aware, meaning that it will recognize when a LUN presented by an array is thin provisioned. In addition, vSphere 5 adds the ability to reclaim dead space (space no longer used) via the T10 UNMAP command; this will help keep space utilization in thin-provisioned environments in check. Finally, vSphere 5 adds support for providing advance warning of thin-provisioned out-of-space conditions and provides better handling for true out-of-space conditions.

STANDARDS-BASED OR PROPRIETARY?

So is the functionality of VAAI standards-based or proprietary? Well, the answer is a little of both. In vSphere 4.1, the hardware-accelerated block zeroing was fully T10 compliant, but the hardware-assisted locking and hardware-accelerated full copy were not fully T10 compliant and required specific support from the array vendors. In vSphere 5, all three of these features are fully T10 compliant, as is the thin-provisioning support, and will work with any array that is also T10 compliant.

The NAS offloads, however, are not standards-based and will require specific plug-ins from the NAS vendors in order to take advantage of these offloads.

---

vSphere 5 also introduces hardware offloads for NAS:

Reserve Space   This functionality allows for the creation of thick-provisioned VMDKs on NFS datastores, much like what is possible on VMFS datastores.

Full File Clone   The Full File Clone functionality allows offline VMDKs to be cloned (copied) by the NAS device.

Lazy File Clone   This feature allows NAS devices to create native snapshots for the purpose of space-conservative VMDKs for virtual desktop infrastructure (VDI) environments. It's specifically targeted at emulating the Linked Clone functionality vSphere offers on VMFS datastores.

Extended Statistics   When leveraging the Lazy File Clone feature, this feature allows more accurate space reporting.

In all cases, support for VAAI requires that the storage vendor's array be fully T10 compliant (for block-level VAAI commands) or support VMware's file-level NAS offloads via a vendor-supplied plug-in. Check with your storage vendor to determine what firmware revisions, software levels, or other requirements are necessary to support VAAI/VAAIv2 with vSphere 5.

The vSphere Client reports VAAI support, so it's easy to determine if your array has been recognized as VAAI capable by vSphere. Figure 6.25 shows a series of datastores; note the status of the Hardware Acceleration column.

Figure 6.26 shows another list of datastores; in this list, you can see that some datastores clearly report Supported in the Hardware Acceleration column.

vSphere determines the hardware acceleration status for VMFS datastores and NFS data stores differently. For VMFS datastores, if at least one of the various SCSI commands is unsupported but others are supported, then the status will be listed as Unknown. If all the commands are unsupported, it will list Not Supported; if all the commands are supported, it will list Supported. You can gather a bit more detail about which commands are supported or not supported using the `esxcli` command-line utility from the vSphere Management Assistant. Run this command:

```
esxcli -s vcenter-01 -h pod-1-blade-5 storage core device vaai status get
```

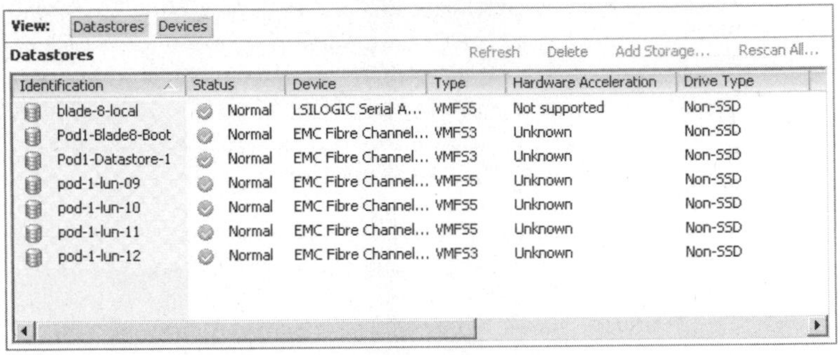

FIGURE 6.25
A datastore is reported as Unknown if not all the hardware offload features are supported.

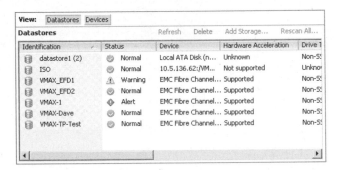

FIGURE 6.26
If all hardware offload features are supported, the Hardware Acceleration status is listed as Supported.

You'll get output that looks something like Figure 6.27; note that some of the commands are listed as unsupported, but block zero is supported. Because there is at least one supported and one unsupported, vSphere reports the status as Unknown.

FIGURE 6.27
The VAAI support is partial—some are listed as supported while others are listed as unsupported—so the vSphere Client reports hardware acceleration as Unknown.

If you run this command against an array where all the commands are supported, you'll get output like what is shown in Figure 6.28.

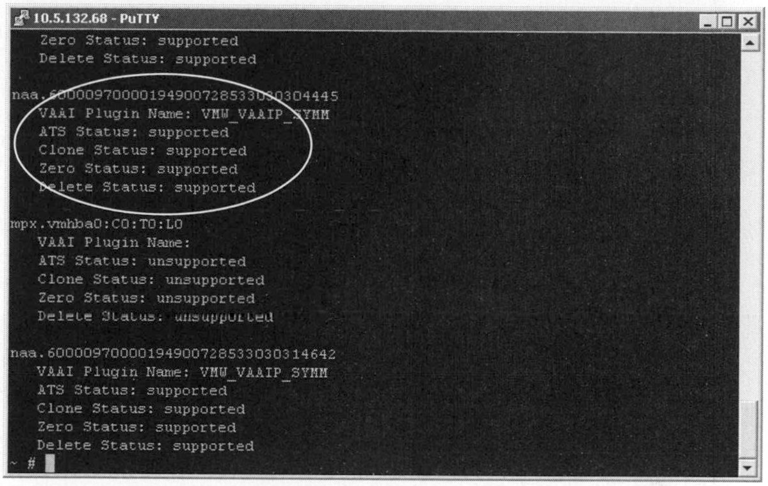

FIGURE 6.28

When all the VAAI commands are supported, the vSphere Client will report hardware acceleration as Supported.

For the inquisitive types who are interested in just a bit more detail on how VAAI works and fits into the vSphere PSA, try running this command from the vSphere Management Assistant:

```
esxcli -s vcenter-01 -h pod-1-blade-8 storage core claimrules list -c all
```

The output will look something like Figure 6.29.

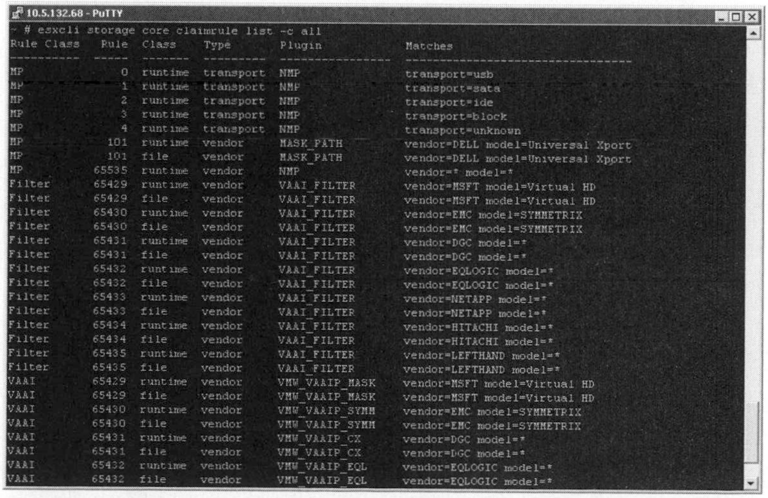

FIGURE 6.29

VAAI works hand-in-hand with claimrules that are used by the PSA for assigning an SATP and PSP for detected storage devices.

This output shows you that VAAI works in conjunction with the claimrules that the PSA uses when determining the SATP and PSP for a given storage device.

YOU CAN DISABLE VAAI IF NECESSARY

There might be situations where disabling VAAI is required. Some advanced SAN fabric features, for example, aren't currently compatible with VAAI. To disable VAAI, set the value of the following advanced settings to zero:

◆ /VMFS3/HardwareAcceleratedLocking

◆ /DataMoverHardwareAcceleratedMove

◆ /DataMover/HardwareAcceleratedInit

No reboot is necessary for this change to take effect. To re-enable VAAI, change the value for these advanced settings back to 1.

VAAI is not the only mechanism for advanced storage integration with vSphere; with vSphere 5, VMware also introduced the Storage APIs for Storage Awareness. I'll describe those in the next section.

Exploring the vSphere Storage APIs for Storage Awareness

The vSphere Storage APIs for Storage Awareness, more commonly known as VASA (from its previous name, the vStorage APIs for Storage Awareness), enables more advanced out-of-band communication between storage arrays and the virtualization layer. At a high level, VASA operates in the following manner:

◆ The storage array communicates its capabilities to the VASA provider. These capabilities could be just about anything: replication status, snapshot capabilities, storage tier, drive type, or IOps capacity. Exactly what capabilities are communicated to the VASA provider are strictly determined by the storage vendor.

◆ The VASA provider communicates these capabilities to vCenter Server. This allows vSphere administrators to, for the very first time, see storage capabilities within vCenter Server.

To enable this communication, you must have a VASA provider supplied by your storage vendor. This VASA provider might be a separate VM supplied by the storage vendor, or it might be an additional service provided by the software on the array. The one restriction that VMware does place on the VASA provider is that it can't run on the same computer as vCenter Server. Once you have this VASA provider, you'll then add it to vCenter Server using the Storage Providers icon on the vSphere Client home screen, shown in Figure 6.30.

Once the storage provider has been added to vCenter Server, it will communicate storage capabilities up to vCenter Server.

However, the presence of these storage capabilities is only half the picture. The other half of the picture is what the vSphere administrator does with these capabilities: build profile-driven VM storage policies, as I describe in the next section.

EXAMINING PROFILE-DRIVEN STORAGE

Working in conjunction with VASA, the principle behind profile-driven storage is simple: allow vSphere administrators to build VM storage profiles that describe the specific storage attributes that a VM requires. Then, based on that VM storage profile, allow vSphere administrators to place VMs on datastores that are compliant with that storage profile, thus ensuring that the needs of the VM are properly serviced by the underlying storage.

FIGURE 6.30

The Storage Providers area is where you go to enable communication between the VASA provider and vCenter Server.

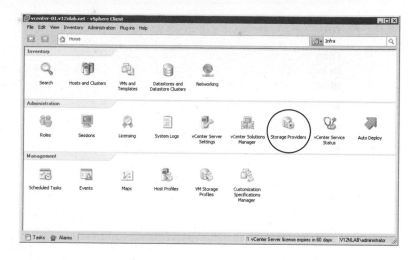

Working with profile-driven storage involves the following three steps:

1. Use VASA to populate system storage capabilities and/or create user-defined storage capabilities. System capabilities are automatically propagated to datastores; user-defined capabilities must be manually assigned.

2. Create VM storage profiles that define the specific features a VM requires from the underlying storage.

3. Assign a VM storage profile to a VM and then check its compliance (or noncompliance) with the assigned VM storage profile.

I'll provide the details on how to accomplish step 2 and step 3 later in this chapter in the section "Creating and Assigning VM Storage Profiles." In the section "Assigning a Storage Capability to a Datastore," I'll show you how to assign a user-defined storage capability to a datastore.

In the "Creating and Assigning VM Storage Profiles" section, I'll show you how to create a VM storage profile and then determine the compliance or noncompliance of a VM with that storage profile.

For now, I'd like to show you how to create a user-defined storage capability. Keep in mind that the bulk of the power of profile-driven storage comes from the interaction with VASA to automatically gather storage capabilities from the underlying array. However, you might find it necessary or useful to define one or more additional storage capabilities that you can use in building your VM storage profiles.

Perform the following steps to create a user-defined storage capability:

1. In the vSphere Client, navigate to the Home screen and click the VM Storage Profiles icon, as shown in Figure 6.31.

2. In the VM Storage Profiles screen, click Manage Storage Capabilities.

   This will bring up the Manage Storage Capabilities dialog box.

3. Click Add to create a new user-defined storage capability.

4. In the Add Storage Capability dialog box, provide a name and description for the new user-defined capability.

FIGURE 6.31
The VM Storage Profiles area in the vSphere Client is one place to create user-defined storage capabilities. You can also create them from the Datastores and Datastore Clusters inventory view.

Figure 6.32 shows an example of a user-defined storage capability. Click OK when you've finished supplying a name and description.

FIGURE 6.32
You'll need to supply a name and description for each new user-defined storage capability.

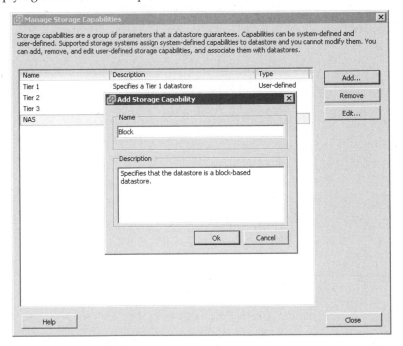

5. Click Close in the Manage Storage Capabilities dialog box when you've finished adding user-defined storage capabilities.

Any system-provided storage capabilities supplied by VASA will also show up in the Manage Storage Capabilities dialog box.

You'll come back to the VM Storage Profiles area of the vSphere Client later in this chapter when I show you how to create a VM storage profile and assign it to a VM.

Now that I've covered some vSphere-specific storage basics, let's move on to working with VMFS datastores.

Working with VMFS Datastores

It's time to shift the focus away from concepts and into practice. In this section, I'll take a look at working with VMFS datastores. As you learned in the previous section, VMFS is the filesystem that vSphere uses for all block-based storage, so it's common. Working with VMFS datastores will be a daily task that you, as a vSphere administrator, will be responsible for accomplishing.

Let's start with adding a VMFS datastore. Every VMFS datastore is backed by a LUN, so first I'll need to review the process for adding a LUN to your ESXi hosts. The process for adding a LUN will vary based on the block storage protocol, so the next two sections will describe adding a LUN via Fibre Channel or FCoE (these are essentially the same) and via iSCSI.

ADDING A LUN VIA FIBRE CHANNEL

Adding a LUN to vSphere via Fibre Channel is really more of a task for the storage administrator (who might also be the vSphere administrator in some environments!). As I mentioned previously in the "Reviewing Fibre Channel" section, making a LUN visible over a Fibre Channel SAN involves a few steps, only one of which is done in the vSphere environment:

1. Zone the Fibre Channel SAN so that the ESXi host(s) can see the target port(s) on the storage array.

2. On the storage array, present the LUN to the ESXi host(s). This procedure varies from vendor to vendor. In a NetApp environment, this involves adding the host's WWNs to an initiator group (or *igroup*); in an EMC environment, it involves creating a storage group. Refer to your specific storage vendor's instructions.

3. Rescan for new storage devices on the ESXi host.

That last step is the only step that involves the vSphere environment. There are two ways to rescan for new storage devices: you can rescan a specific storage adapter, or you can rescan all storage adapters.

Perform the following steps to rescan only a specific storage adapter:

1. In the vSphere Client, navigate to the Configuration tab for a specific ESXi host in the Hosts And Clusters inventory view.

2. In the Hardware section, select Storage Adapters.

   This will display the storage adapters recognized in the selected ESXi host.

3. Right-click a storage adapter and select Rescan.

   You'll note that two tasks appear in the Tasks pane of the vSphere Client: a task for rescanning the selected HBA and a task for rescanning VMFS.

   The task for rescanning the HBA is pretty straightforward; this is a query to the device to see if new storage devices are available. If new storage devices are available to the adapter, they will appear in the Details pane of the Storage Adapters area in the vSphere Client (see Figure 6.33).

   The second task is a bit different. The VMFS rescan is triggered automatically, and it scans available storage devices for an existing VMFS datastore. If it finds an existing VMFS datastore, it will attempt to mount the VMFS datastore and make it available to the

ESXi host. Automatically triggering the VMFS rescan simplifies the process of making new VMFS datastores available to ESXi hosts.

In addition to rescanning just a single HBA or CNA, you can also rescan all storage adapters. This method might give you just a bit more control; it allows you to specify whether you'd like to scan the HBA, scan for VMFS datastores, or both.

FIGURE 6.33
The Storage
Adapters area
of a host's
Configuration tab
shows the details
for storage devices.

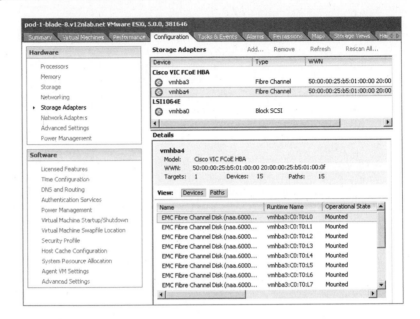

Perform the following steps to rescan all storage adapters:

1. In the vSphere Client, navigate to the Configuration tab for a specific ESXi host in the Hosts And Clusters inventory view.

2. From the Hardware section, select Storage Adapters.

3. Click the Rescan All hyperlink in the upper-right corner of the content pane.

4. If you want to only scan for new LUNs that have been zoned or presented to the ESXi host, select Scan For New Storage Devices and deselect Scan For New VMFS Volumes.

   If you want to scan only for new VMFS datastores, deselect Scan For New Storage Devices and select Scan For New VMFS Volumes.

   If you want to do both, simply click OK (both are selected by default). You'll see the appropriate tasks appear in the Tasks pane of the vSphere Client.

YOU CAN ALSO RESCAN AN ENTIRE CLUSTER

If you right-click a cluster object in the Hosts And Clusters inventory view, you can also rescan an entire cluster for new storage objects.

Assuming that the zoning of your Fibre Channel SAN is correct and that the storage has been presented to the ESXi host properly, your new LUN should appear in the Details pane shown previously in Figure 6.33.

Once the LUN is visible, you're ready to create a new VMFS datastore on the LUN, but before I get to that, I need to cover the process for adding a LUN via FCoE.

ADDING A LUN VIA FCoE

The process for adding a LUN via FCoE really depends on one key question: are you using a CNA where the FCoE is handled in hardware, or are you using vSphere 5's new software-based FCoE initiator?

In previous versions of vSphere, FCoE was supported strictly in hardware, meaning that you could use FCoE only if you had an FCoE CNA installed in your ESXi host. In this configuration, the CNA drivers presented the CNAs to the ESXi host as if they were Fibre Channel HBAs. Therefore, the process of adding a LUN to an ESXi host using hardware-based FCoE was virtually identical to the process I described previously in the section "Adding a LUN via Fibre Channel." Because it's so similar, I won't repeat those steps here.

However, vSphere 5 adds the ability to perform FCoE in software via an FCoE software initiator. There is still an element of hardware support required, though; only certain network interface cards that support partial FCoE offload are supported. Refer to the *vSphere Compatibility Guide* or the vSphere HCL.

Assuming you have a supported NIC, the process for configuring the software FCoE initiator is twofold: configure the FCoE networking and then activate the software FCoE adapter.

Perform the following steps to configure the networking for software FCoE:

1. Log in to the vSphere Client, and connect to an ESXi host or to a vCenter Server instance.

2. Navigate to the Hosts And Clusters inventory view.

3. Select a host from the inventory panel and then click the Configuration tab.

4. From the Hardware section, select Networking. Make sure you are in the vSphere Standard Switch view.

5. Use the Add Networking link to create a new vSphere Standard Switch with a VMkernel port.

   When selecting uplinks for the new vSwitch, be sure to select the NIC that supports partial FCoE offload. You can add multiple NICs to a single vSwitch, or you can add each FCoE offload-capable NIC to a separate vSwitch. However, once you add the NICs to a vSwitch, don't remove them or you'll disrupt the FCoE traffic.

   For more information on creating a vSphere Standard Switch, creating a VMkernel port, or selecting uplinks for a vSwitch, refer to Chapter 5.

6. Once you've configured the network, click Storage Adapters in the Hardware section of the Configuration tab.

   (You should still be on this tab after completing the network configuration.)

7. Click Add, select Software FCoE Adapter, and click OK.

8. On the Add Software FCoE Adapter dialog box, select the appropriate NIC (one that supports partial FCoE offload and that was used as an uplink for the vSwitch you created previously) from the drop-down list of physical adapters.

9. Click OK.

OTHER NETWORKING LIMITATIONS FOR SOFTWARE FCoE

Don't move a network adapter port from one vSwitch to another when FCoE traffic is active, or you'll run into problems. If you made this change, moving the network adapter port back to the original vSwitch will correct the problem. Reboot your ESXi host if you need to move the network adapter port permanently.

Also, be sure to use a VLAN for FCoE that is not used for any other form of networking on your ESXi host.

Double-check that you've disabled Spanning Tree Protocol (STP) on the ports that will support software FCoE from your ESXi host. Otherwise, the FCoE Initialization Protocol (FIP) exchange might be delayed and cause the software adapter not to function properly.

---

vSphere will create a new adapter in the list of Storage Adapters. Once the adapter is created, you can right-click the adapter to view its properties, such as getting the WWN assigned to the software adapter. You'll use that WWN in the zoning and LUN presentation as described in the section on adding a LUN via Fibre Channel. After you've completed the zoning and LUN presentation, you can rescan the adapter to see the new LUN appear.

The next procedure I'll review is adding a LUN with iSCSI.

ADDING A LUN VIA iSCSI

As with FCoE, the procedure for adding a LUN via iSCSI depends on whether you are doing hardware-based iSCSI (using an iSCSI HBA) or leveraging vSphere's software iSCSI initiator.

If you are using a hardware iSCSI solution, the configuration takes place in the iSCSI HBA itself. The instructions for configuring your iSCSI HBA will vary from vendor to vendor, so once again I'll refer you to your specific vendor's documentation on how to configure your iSCSI HBA to properly connect to your iSCSI SAN. Once the iSCSI HBA is configured, then the process for adding a LUN via hardware-based iSCSI is much like the process I described for Fibre Channel in the section "Adding a LUN via Fibre Channel," so I won't repeat the steps here.

If you instead choose to use vSphere's software iSCSI initiator, then you can take advantage of iSCSI connectivity without the need for iSCSI hardware installed in your server.

As with the software FCoE adapter, there are a couple of different steps involved in setting up the software iSCSI initiator:

1. Configure networking for the software iSCSI initiator.

2. Activate and configure the software iSCSI initiator.

The following sections describe these steps in more detail.

Configuring Networking for the Software iSCSI Initiator

With iSCSI, although the Ethernet stack can technically be used to perform some multipathing and load balancing, this is not how iSCSI is generally designed. iSCSI uses the same multipath I/O (MPIO) storage framework as Fibre Channel and FCoE SANs. As a result, a specific networking configuration is required to support this framework. In particular, you'll need to configure the networking so that each path through the network uses only a single physical NIC. The MPIO framework can then use each NIC as a path and perform the appropriate multipathing functions. This configuration also allows iSCSI connections to scale across multiple NICs; using Ethernet-based techniques like link aggregation will increase overall throughput but will not increase throughput for any single iSCSI target.

Perform the following steps to configure the virtual networking properly for the software iSCSI initiator:

1. In the vSphere Client, navigate to the Hosts And Clusters inventory view and select an ESXi host from the inventory panel.

2. Select the Configuration tab and then click Networking. Make sure you are in the vSphere Standard Switch view.

   (You can also use a vSphere Distributed Switch, but for simplicity I'll use a vSwitch in this procedure.)

3. Create a new vSwitch with at least two uplinks. Make sure all uplinks are listed as active NICs in the vSwitch's failover order.

USING SHARED UPLINKS VS. DEDICATED UPLINKS

Generally, a bet-the-business iSCSI configuration will use a dedicated vSwitch with dedicated uplinks. However, if you are using 10 Gigabit Ethernet, you may only have two uplinks. In this case, you will have to use a shared vSwitch and shared uplinks. If at all possible, I recommend configuring Quality of Service on the vSwitch, either by using a vSphere Distributed Switch with Network I/O Control or by using the Cisco Nexus 1000V and QoS. This will help ensure that iSCSI traffic is granted the appropriate network bandwidth so that your storage performance doesn't suffer.

---

4. Create a VMkernel port for use by iSCSI. Configure the VMkernel port to use only one of the available uplinks on the vSwitch.

5. Repeat step 4 for each uplink on the vSwitch. Ensure that each VMkernel port is assigned only one active uplink and that no uplinks are shared between VMkernel ports.

   Figure 6.34 shows the NIC Teaming tab for an iSCSI VMkernel port; note that only one uplink is listed as an active NIC.

WHAT'S THE MAXIMUM NUMBER OF LINKS THAT YOU CAN USE FOR ISCSI?

You can use the method shown previously to drive I/O down eight separate vmnics. Testing has shown that vSphere is able to drive 9 Gbps of iSCSI throughput through a single ESXi host.

For more information on how to create a vSwitch, assign uplinks, create VMkernel ports, or modify the NIC failover order for a vSwitch or VMkernel port, refer to Chapter 5.

When you finish with the networking configuration, you're ready for the next step.

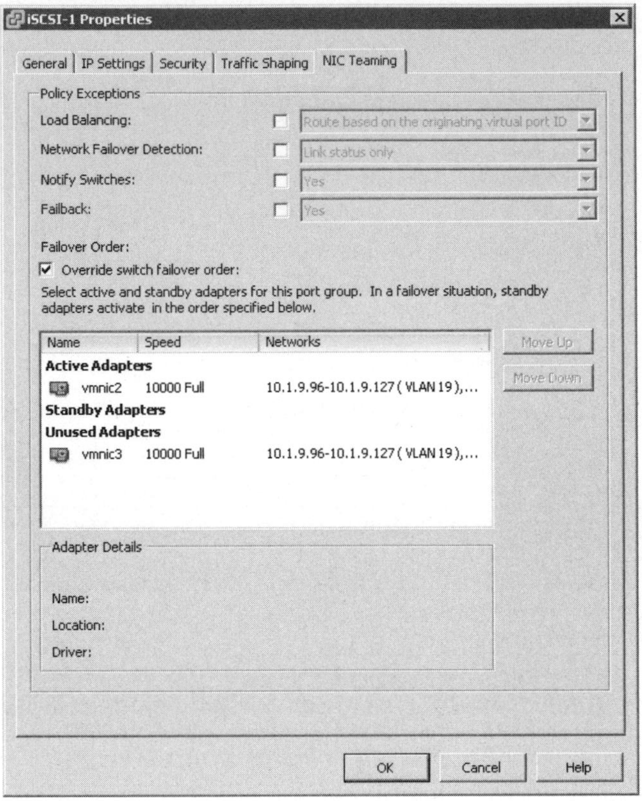

FIGURE 6.34
For proper iSCSI
multipathing and
scalability, only
one uplink can be
active for each iSCSI
VMkernel port.

Activating and Configuring the Software iSCSI Initiator

After configuring the network appropriately for iSCSI, perform these steps to activate and configure the software iSCSI initiator:

1. In the vSphere Client, navigate to the Hosts And Clusters inventory view and select an ESXi host from the inventory panel.

2. Click the Configuration tab and select Storage Adapters.

3. Click the Add hyperlink. From the Add Storage Adapter dialog box, select Add Software iSCSI Adapter and click OK.

4. A dialog box will appear, informing you that a software iSCSI will be added to the list of storage adapters. Click OK.

   After a few moments, a new storage adapter under the iSCSI Software Adapter will appear, as shown in Figure 6.35.

5. Right-click the new adapter and select Properties. This opens the iSCSI Initiator Properties dialog box.

6. Click the Network Configuration tab.

7. Click the Add button to add a VMkernel port binding.

This will create the link between a VMkernel port used for iSCSI traffic and a physical NIC.

FIGURE 6.35
This storage
adapter is where
you will perform all
the configuration
for the software
iSCSI initiator.

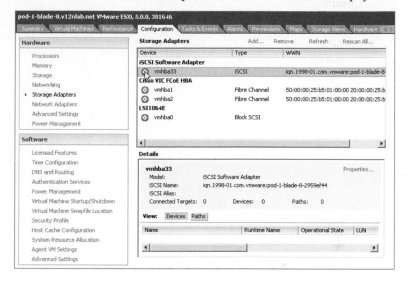

THE VMKERNEL PORT BINDINGS GUI IS NEW

In previous versions of vSphere, binding VMkernel interfaces to physical NICs for iSCSI multipathing had to be done at the command-line interface.

8. From the Bind With VMkernel Network Adapter dialog box, select a compliant port group.

A compliant port group is a port group with a VMkernel port configured with only a single physical uplink. Figure 6.36 shows an example of two compliant port groups you could select to bind to the VMkernel network adapter.

Click OK after selecting a compliant port group.

9. Repeat step 8 for each VMkernel port and uplink you created previously when configuring the network for iSCSI.

When you've finished, the iSCSI Initiator Properties dialog box will look something like Figure 6.37.

10. Select the Dynamic Discovery tab and click Add.

11. In the Add Send Target Server dialog box, enter the IP address of the iSCSI target. Click OK when you've finished.

Configuring discovery tells the iSCSI initiator what iSCSI target it should communicate with to get details about storage that is available to it and actually has the iSCSI initiator log in to the target—which makes it known to the iSCSI target. This also populates all the other known iSCSI targets and populates the Static Discovery entries.

FIGURE 6.36
Only compliant port groups will be listed as available to bind with the VMkernel adapter.

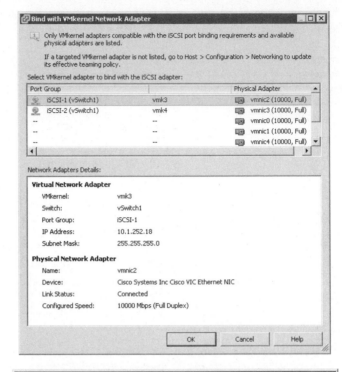

FIGURE 6.37
This configuration allows for robust multipathing and greater bandwidth for iSCSI storage configurations.

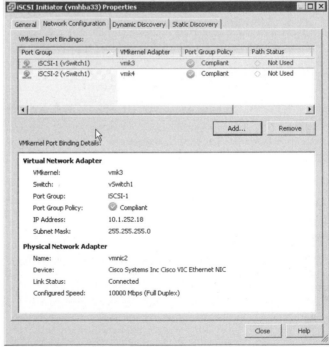

If you've already performed the necessary masking/presentation tasks on the iSCSI array to make LUNs available, then the LUN should now show up in the list of devices on the software iSCSI adapter, and you can use that LUN to create a VMFS datastore. If you haven't already presented the LUN to the ESXi host, you'll need to do so according to your vendor's instructions (every array vendor is different). After presenting the storage to the host, a rescan of the iSCSI adapter—using the procedure I outlined in the "Adding a LUN via Fibre Channel" section—should cause the device to show up.

TROUBLESHOOTING iSCSI LUNs

If you're having a problem getting the iSCSI LUN to show up on your ESXi host, check the following troubleshooting list:

◆ Are you able to ping the iSCSI target from the initiator? (Use the Direct Console User Interface (DCUI) test connectivity from the ESXi host, or enable the ESXi shell and use the vmkping command.)

◆ Is the physical cabling correct? Are the link lights showing a connected state on the physical interfaces on the ESXi host, the Ethernet switches, and the iSCSI arrays?

◆ Are your VLANs configured correctly? If you've configured VLANs, have you properly configured the same VLAN on the host, the switch, and the interface(s) that will be used on the array for the iSCSI target?

◆ Is your IP routing correct and functional? Have you properly configured the IP addresses of the VMkernel port and the interface(s) that will be used on the array for the iSCSI target? Are they on the same subnet? If not, they should be. Although iSCSI can be routed, it's not a good idea because routing adds significant latency and isn't involved in a bet-the-business storage Ethernet network. In addition, it's generally not recommended in vSphere environments.

◆ Is iSCSI traffic being allowed through any firewalls? If the ping succeeds but subsequently the iSCSI initiator can't log into the iSCSI target, check whether TCP port 3620 is being blocked by a firewall somewhere in the path. Again, the general recommendation is to avoid firewalls in the midst of the iSCSI data path wherever possible to avoid introducing additional latency.

◆ Is your CHAP configuration correct? Have you correctly configured authentication on both the iSCSI initiator and the iSCSI target?

Now that you have a LUN presented and visible to the ESXi hosts, you can add (or create) a VMFS datastore on that LUN. I'll cover this process in the next section.

CREATING A VMFS DATASTORE

Once you have a LUN available to the ESXi hosts, you can create a VMFS datastore.

Before starting this process, you'll want to double-check to verify that the LUN you will be using for the new VMFS datastore is shown under the configuration's Storage Adapters list. (LUNs appear in the bottom of the vSphere Client properties pane associated with a storage adapter.) If you've provisioned a LUN that doesn't appear, rescan for new devices.

Perform the following steps to configure a VMFS datastore on an available LUN:

1. Launch the vSphere Client if it isn't already running, and connect to a vCenter Server instance.

2. Navigate to the Hosts And Clusters inventory view, and select an ESXi host from the inventory tree.

3. Click the Configuration tab on the right, and then select Storage from the list of commands in the Hardware section.

4. Click the Add Storage hyperlink to launch the Add Storage wizard.

ANOTHER WAY TO OPEN THE ADD STORAGE WIZARD

You can also access the Add Storage wizard in the Datastores And Datastore Clusters inventory view by right-clicking the datacenter object and selecting Add Datastore from the context menu.

5. The first screen of the Add Storage wizard prompts you for the storage type. Because you will be creating a VMFS datastore, select Disk/LUN, and click Next.

   (I'll show you how to use the Add Storage wizard to create an NFS datastore in the "Working with NFS Datastores" section later in this chapter.)

6. Select the LUN on which you want to create the new VMFS datastore.

   For each visible LUN, you will see the LUN name and identifier information, along with the LUN number and its size (and the VMFS label if it has been previously used). Figure 6.38 shows a single LUN available on which to create a VMFS datastore.

   After you've selected the LUN you want to use, click Next.

7. Select whether you'd like to create a VMFS-5 datastore or a VMFS-3 datastore.

   I described the differences between VMFS-5 and VMFS-3 in the section titled "Examining the vSphere Virtual Machine File System."

   Click Next after selecting a version.

8. The next screen, displayed for you in Figure 6.39, shows a summary of the details of the LUN selected and the action that will be taken; if it's a new LUN (no preexisting VMFS partition), the wizard will note that a VMFS partition will be created.

   Click Next to continue.

   If the selected LUN has an existing VMFS partition, you will be presented with some different options; see the "Expanding a VMFS Datastore" section for more information.

9. Name the datastore.

   I recommend that you use as descriptive a name as possible. You might also consider using a naming scheme that includes an array identifier, a LUN identifier, a protection detail (RAID type and whether it is replicated remotely for disaster recovery purposes), or other key configuration data. Clear datastore naming can help the vSphere administrator later in determining VM placement and can help streamline troubleshooting if a problem arises.

Click Next after you've entered a name for the datastore.

FIGURE 6.38
You'll choose from a list of available LUNs when creating a new VMFS datastore.

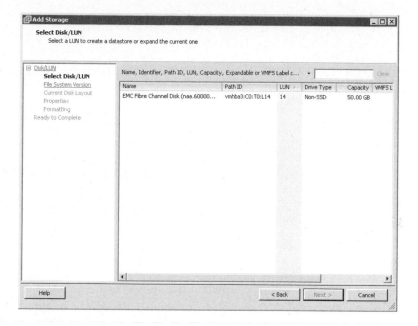

FIGURE 6.39
The Current Disk Layout screen provides information on the partitioning action that will be taken to create a VMFS datastore on the selected LUN.

10. If you selected VMFS-3 in step 7, you'll need to select the VMFS allocation size, as shown in Figure 6.40.

For VMFS-5 datastores, you won't need to select a VMFS allocation size (VMFS-5 always uses a 1 MB block size).

Refer back to "Examining the vSphere Virtual Machine File System" for more information on block sizes and their impact.

FIGURE 6.40
Select the VMFS-3 allocation size; this defines the minimum size of any filesystem allocation but also the maximum size for any individual file.

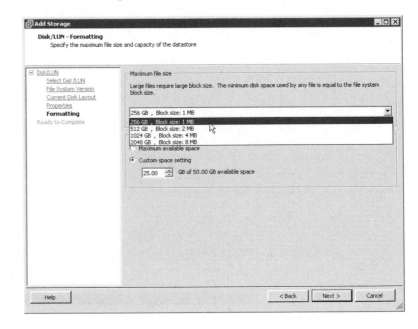

11. For both VMFS-5 and VMFS-3, in the Capacity section you'll specify how you want to utilize the space on the selected LUN.

Generally speaking, you will select Maximize Available Space to use all the space available on the LUN. If, for whatever reason, you can't or don't want to use all of the space available on the LUN, select Custom Space Setting and specify the size of the VMFS datastore you are creating. Click Next when you are ready to proceed.

12. At the final summary screen, double-check all the information. If everything is correct, click Finish; otherwise, use the Back button to go back and make any changes.

When you click Finish and complete the creation of the datastore, vSphere will trigger the remaining hosts in the same cluster to rescan for new devices. This ensures that the other hosts in the cluster will also see the LUN and the VMFS datastore on that LUN. You will still need to rescan for devices (using the process I provided previously in the sections on adding a LUN) for ESXi hosts that are not in the same cluster.

Once you've created a VMFS datastore, there are some additional tasks that you might need to complete. Although these tasks are storage-related, I've included them in other areas of the book. Here's a quick reference to some of the other tasks you might need to perform on a VMFS datastore:

- You might want to enable Storage I/O Control, a mechanism for enforcing prioritized access to storage I/O resources. For more information on Storage I/O Control, refer to the "Controlling Storage I/O Utilization" section of Chapter 11, "Managing Resource Allocation."

- You might want to create a datastore cluster for the purposes of enabling Storage DRS. To learn more about Storage DRS and datastore clusters, refer to "Introducing and Working with Storage DRS" in Chapter 12, "Balancing Resource Utilization."

- You might want or need to create some alarms on this new VMFS datastore. For more information on alarms, refer to the "Using Alarms" section in Chapter 13, "Monitoring VMware vSphere Performance."

Creating new VMFS datastores is not the only way to make additional space available to vSphere for use by VMs. Depending on your configuration, you might be able to expand an existing VMFS datastore, as I'll describe in the next section.

EXPANDING A VMFS DATASTORE

Recall from my previous discussion of VMFS (in the "Examining the vSphere Virtual Machine File System" section) that I mentioned that VMFS supports multiple extents. In previous versions of vSphere, administrators could use multiple extents as a way of getting past the 2 TB limit for VMFS-3 datastores. By combining multiple extents, vSphere administrators could take VMFS-3 datastores up to 64 TB (32 extents of 2 TB each). VMFS-5 eliminates this need because it now supports single-extent VMFS volumes of up to 64 TB in size. However, adding extents is not the only way to expand a VMFS datastore.

If you have a VMFS datastore (either VMFS-3 or VMFS-5), there are two ways of expanding the datastore to make more space available:

- You can dynamically expand the VMFS datastore.

  VMFS can be easily and dynamically expanded in vSphere without adding extents, as long as the underlying LUN has more capacity than was configured in the VMFS data store. Many modern storage arrays have the ability to nondisruptively add capacity to a LUN; when combined with the ability to nondisruptively expand a VMFS volume, this gives you a great deal of flexibility as a vSphere administrator. This is true for both VMFS-3 and VMFS-5.

- You can add an extent.

  You can also expand a VMFS datastore by adding an extent. You need to add an extent if the datastore is a VMFS-3 datastore that has already hit its size limit (2 TB minus 512 bytes) or if the underlying LUN on which the datastore resides does not have any additional free space available. This latter condition would apply for VMFS-3 as well as VMFS-5 datastores.

These procedures are extremely similar; many of the steps in both procedures are exactly the same.

Perform these steps to expand a VMFS datastore (either by nondisruptively expanding the datastore on the same LUN or by adding an extent):

1. In the vSphere Client, navigate to the Datastores And Datastore Clusters inventory view.

2. Select a datastore from the inventory tree on the left, and then click the Configuration tab on the right.

3. From the Configuration tab, click the Properties hyperlink to open the Volume Properties dialog box, shown in Figure 6.41.

FIGURE 6.41
From the Volume Properties dialog box, you can increase the size of the datastore.

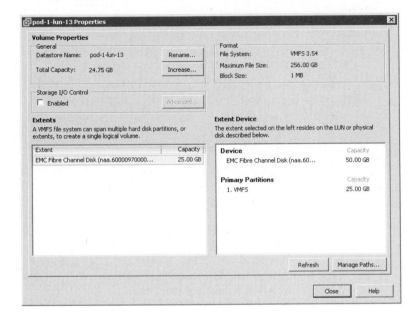

4. Click the Increase button. This will open the Increase Datastore Capacity wizard.

   You'll note that this looks similar to the Add Storage wizard you saw previously when creating a new VMFS datastore.

5. If the underlying LUN has free space available, then the Expandable column will report Yes, as shown in Figure 6.42. Select this LUN to nondisruptively expand the VMFS data store using the free space on the same LUN.

   If the underlying LUN has no additional free space available, the Expandable column will report No, and you must expand the VMFS datastore by adding an extent. Select an available LUN.

   Click Next when you are ready to proceed.

6. If you are expanding the VMFS datastore using free space on the LUN, the Current Disk Layout screen will report that the free space will be used to expand the volume.

If you are adding an extent to the VMFS datastore, the Current Disk Layout screen will indicate that a new partition will be created.

FIGURE 6.42
If the Expandable column reports Yes, the VMFS volume can be expanded into the available free space.

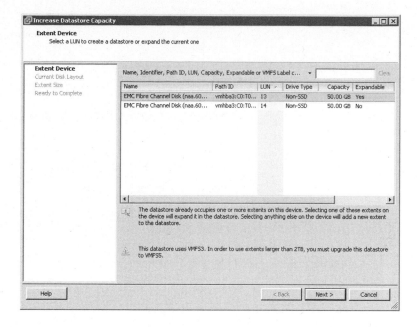

Click Next to proceed.

7. Regardless of the method you're using—expanding into free space on the LUN or adding an extent—if you are expanding a VMFS-3 datastore, you'll note that the block size drop-down list is grayed out. You don't have an option to change the VMFS block size when expanding a VMFS-3 datastore.

8. If you didn't want to use or couldn't use all of the free space on the underlying LUN, you could change the capacity from Maximize Available Space to Custom Space Setting and specify the amount. Generally, you will leave the default of Maximize Available Space selected. Click Next.

9. Review the summary information and, if everything is correct, click Finish.

If you added an extent to the datastore, the datastore properties pane in Datastores And Datastore Clusters inventory view will reflect the fact that the datastore now has at least two extents. This is also shown in the Datastore Properties dialog box, as you can see in Figure 6.43.

Regardless of the procedure used to expand the datastore, it is nondisruptive—there is no need to evacuate VMs or incur downtime.

Another nondisruptive task is upgrading a datastore from VMFS-3 to VMFS-5, a procedure that I describe in the following section.

FIGURE 6.43
This 100 GB
datastore actually
comprises two 50
GB extents.

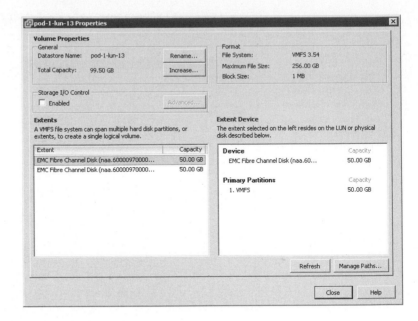

UPGRADING A DATASTORE FROM VMFS-3 TO VMFS-5

As I mentioned in the "Examining the vSphere Virtual Machine File System" section, vSphere 5 introduces a new version of VMFS called VMFS-5. VMFS-5 offers a number of new features, all of which I described previously. To take advantage of these new features, you'll need to upgrade your VMFS datastores from VMFS-3 to VMFS-5. Keep in mind that upgrading your datastores to VMFS-5 is required only if you need to take advantage of the features available in VMFS-5.

To help vSphere administrators keep clear about which datastores are VMFS-3 and which datastores are VMFS-5, VMware added that information in multiple places through the vSphere Client. Figure 6.44 shows the Configuration tab for an ESXi host; note the datastore listing in the Storage section includes a column for VMFS version.

Figure 6.45 shows the Details pane for a datastore, found on the Configuration tab for a data store in Datastores And Datastore Clusters view. Again, note that the VMFS version is included in the information provided about that datastore. This view, by the way, is also a great view to see information about storage capabilities (used by profile-driven storage), the path policy in use, and whether or not Storage I/O Control is enabled for this datastore. The datastore in Figure 6.45 does have a user-defined storage capability assigned and has Storage I/O Control enabled.

Perform the following steps to upgrade a datastore from VMFS-3 to VMFS-5:

1. Log into the vSphere Client, if it isn't already running.

2. Navigate to the Datastores And Datastore Clusters inventory view and select a datastore from the inventory panel.

3. Select the Configuration tab.

4. Click the Upgrade To VMFS-5 hyperlink.

FIGURE 6.44
The columns in the Datastores list can be rearranged and reordered, and they include a column for VMFS version.

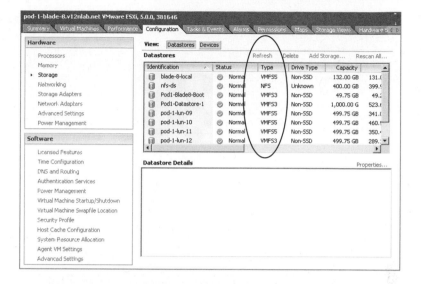

FIGURE 6.45
Among the other details listed for a datastore, the VMFS version is also included.

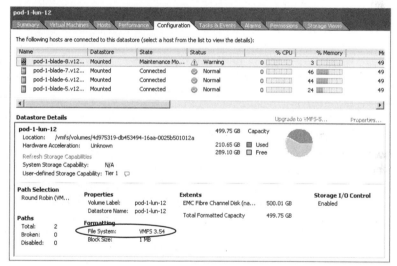

5. If you are clear to proceed—meaning that all hosts attached are running at least ESXi 5.0 and support VMFS-5—a dialog box will appear to that effect. Click OK to start the upgrade of the datastore.

6. The VMFS-5 upgrade will start. A task will appear in the Tasks pane for the upgrade; when the upgrade is complete, the vSphere Client will trigger a VMFS rescan on the attached hosts so that they also recognize that the datastore has been upgraded to VMFS-5.

Once a datastore has been upgraded to VMFS-5, you cannot downgrade it back to VMFS-3.

ONE POTENTIAL REASON NOT TO UPGRADE VMFS-3 DATASTORES

Although you can upgrade a VMFS-3 datastore to VMFS-5, the underlying block size of the datastore does not change. This means that you could run into situations where Storage vMotion operations between an upgraded VMFS-3 datastore and a newly created VMFS-5 datastore could be slower than expected. This is because vSphere won't take advantage of hardware offloads when the block sizes are different between the source and destination datastores. For this reason, you might prefer to migrate your VMs off the VMFS-3 datastore and recreate it as a native VMFS-5 datastore instead of upgrading it.

I'd like to make one final note about VMFS versions. You'll note in the screenshot in Figure 6.45 that the selected datastore is running VMFS 3.54. vSphere 5 uses VMFS version 3.54 and VMFS version 5.54. For datastores running previous versions of VMFS-3 (say, VMFS 3.46), there is no need or any way to upgrade to VMFS 3.54. VMware only provides an upgrade path for moving from VMFS-3 to VMFS-5.

Figure 6.45 shows a datastore that has a user-defined storage capability assigned. As you know already, this is part of the functionality of profile-driven storage. Let's take a look at how to assign a capability to a datastore.

ASSIGNING A STORAGE CAPABILITY TO A DATASTORE

As I explained previously in the "Examining Profile-Driven Storage" section, you have the ability to define your own set of storage capabilities. These user-defined storage capabilities will be used in conjunction with system-provided storage capabilities (supplied by VASA) in determining the compliance or noncompliance of a VM with its assigned VM storage profile. I'll discuss the creation of VM storage profiles and compliance later in this chapter in the section "Creating and Assigning VM Storage Profiles." In this section, I'm just going to show you how to assign a user-defined storage capability to a datastore.

Perform these steps to assign a user-defined storage capability to a datastore:

1. Launch the vSphere Client if it's not already running, and connect to a vCenter Server instance.

   Profile-driven storage requires vCenter Server.

2. Navigate to either the Hosts And Clusters inventory view or the Datastores And Datastore Clusters inventory view.

3. Right-click a datastore and select Assign User-Defined Storage Capability.

   This brings up the Assign User-Defined Storage Capability dialog box captured in Figure 6.46.

4. From the Name drop-down list, select the user-defined storage capability you'd like to assign to the selected datastore.

Note that you can only assign a single user-defined storage capability to each datastore. If you need to create a new user-defined storage capability, use the New button.

5. Click OK after you've selected the capability to assign to the datastore.

FIGURE 6.46
From this dia-
log box, you can
assign a single
user-defined stor-
age capability to a
datastore.

vCenter Server will assign the selected capability to the datastore, and it will show up in the datastore details view you saw previously in Figure 6.45.

Keep in mind that you can assign only one user-defined storage capability per datastore. The VASA provider can also only assign a single system-provided storage capability to each datastore. This means that datastores may have up to 2 capabilities assigned: one system-provided capability and one user-defined capability.

There are other properties about a datastore that you might also need to edit or change, such as renaming a datastore. I'll describe that process in the next section.

RENAMING A VMFS DATASTORE

You can rename a VMFS datastore in two ways:

◆ Right-click a datastore object and select Rename. The Rename command is available for data store objects in the Resources list only when a host is selected in the Hosts And Clusters inventory view or for datastore objects in the Datastores And Datastore Clusters inventory view.

◆ Click the Rename button in the Volume Properties dialog box, accessed by right-clicking a datastore object and selecting Properties. Figure 6.47 shows the Volume Properties dialog box with the Rename button highlighted.

Both methods will produce the same result; the datastore will be renamed to the new name. You can use whichever method best suits you.

In Figure 6.47, you'll also note the Manage Paths button in the lower-right corner. Modifying the multipathing policy for a VMFS datastore is another important function with which any vSphere administrator should be familiar.

FIGURE 6.47
You can use the Rename button to change the name of the datastore.

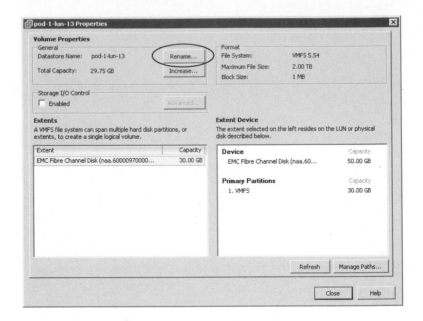

MODIFYING THE MULTIPATHING POLICY FOR A VMFS DATASTORE

Previously in this chapter, in the section "Reviewing Multipathing," I described vSphere's Pluggable Storage Architecture (PSA) and how it manages multipathing for block-based storage devices. VMFS datastores are built on block-based storage devices, and so viewing or changing the multipathing configuration for a VMFS datastore is an integral part of working with VMFS datastores.

Changing the multipathing policy for a VMFS datastore is done using the Manage Paths button in the Datastore Properties dialog box. I've highlighted the Manage Paths button in Figure 6.48.

FIGURE 6.48
You'll use the Manage Paths button in the Datastore Properties dialog box to modify the multipathing policy.

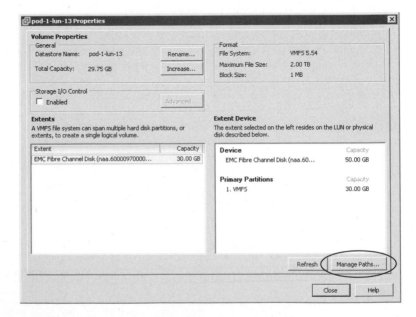

Once you select Manage Paths, the Manage Paths dialog box comes up. Figure 6.49 shows the Manage Paths dialog box. From this screenshot and from the information I've provided in this chapter, you should be able to deduce a couple of key facts:

◆ This VMFS datastore is hosted on an active-active storage array; the currently assigned policy is Fixed (VMware), which is the default for an active-active array.

◆ This VMFS datastore resides on a LUN hosted by an EMC Symmetrix array. This is noted by the SATP, listed here at VMW_SATP_SYMM.

FIGURE 6.49

This datastore resides on an active-active array; specifically, an EMC Symmetrix. You can tell this by the currently assigned path selection policy and the storage array type information.

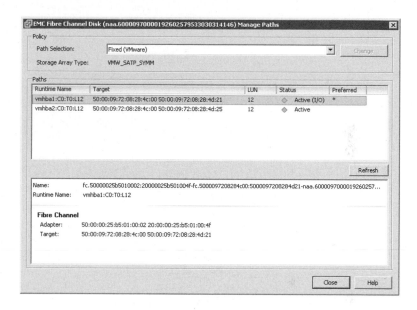

To change the multipathing policy, simply select a new policy from the Path Selection drop-down list and click Change. One word of caution: choosing the wrong path selection policy for your specific storage array can cause problems, so be sure to choose a path selection policy recommended by your storage vendor. In this particular case, the Round Robin policy is also supported by active-active arrays such as the EMC Symmetrix VMAX hosting this LUN, so I'll change the path selection to Round Robin (VMware).

Changes to the path selection are immediate and do not require a reboot.

I'm nearing the end of the section on VMFS datastores, but I do need to cover two more topics. First, I'll discuss managing copies of VMFS datastores, and then I'll wrap up this section with a quick review of removing VMFS datastores.

MANAGING VMFS DATASTORE COPIES

Every VMFS datastore has a Universally Unique Identifier (UUID) embedded in the filesystem. When you clone or replicate a VMFS datastore, the copy of the datastore is a byte-for-byte copy, right down to the UUID. If you attempt to mount the LUN that has the copy of the VMFS datastore, vSphere will see this as a duplicate copy and will require that you do one of two things:

◆ Unmount the original and mount the copy with the same UUID.

◆ Keep the original mounted and write a new signature to the copy.

Other storage operations might also cause this behavior. If you change the LUN ID after creating a VMFS datastore, vSphere will recognize that the UUID is now associated with a new device (vSphere uses the NAA ID to track the devices) and will follow this behavior.

In either case, vSphere provides a GUI in the Add Storage wizard that allows you to clearly choose which option you'd like to use in these situations:

◆ Choose Keep Existing Signature if you want to mount the datastore copy without writing a new signature. vSphere won't allow UUID collisions, so you can only mount without resignaturing if the original datastore has been unmounted or no longer exists (this is the case if you change the LUN ID, for example). If you mount a datastore copy without resignaturing and then later want to mount the original, you'll need to unmount the copy first.

◆ Choose Assign A New Signature if you want to write a new signature onto the VMFS datastore. This will allow you to have both the copy and the original mount as separate and distinct datastores. Keep in mind this process is irreversible—you can't undo the resignaturing operation. If the resignatured datastore contains any VMs, you will likely need to reregister those VMs in vCenter Server, because the paths to the VM's configuration files will have changed. "Adding or Registering Existing VMs," in Chapter 9, describes how to reregister a VM.

Let's take a look at removing a VMFS datastore.

Removing a VMFS Datastore

Removing a VMFS datastore is, fortunately, as straightforward as it seems. To remove a VMFS datastore, simply right-click the datastore object and select Delete. The vSphere Client will prompt for confirmation—reminding you that you will lose all the files associated with all VMs on this datastore—before actually deleting the datastore.

As with many of the other datastore-related tasks I've shown you, the vSphere Client will trigger a VMFS rescan for other ESXi hosts so that all hosts are aware that the VMFS datastore has been deleted.

Like resignaturing a datastore, deleting a datastore is irreversible. Once you delete a datastore, you can't recover the datastore or any of the files that were stored in that datastore. Be sure to double-check that you're deleting the right datastore before you proceed!

Let's now shift from working with VMFS datastores to working with another form of block-based storage, albeit one that is far less frequently used: raw device mappings, or RDMs.

Working with Raw Device Mappings

Although the concept of shared pool mechanisms (like VMFS or NFS datastores) for VMs works well for many use cases, there are certain use cases where a storage device must be presented directly to the guest operating system (guest OS) inside a VM.

vSphere provides this functionality via a raw device mapping. RDMs are presented to your ESXi hosts and then via vCenter Server directly to a VM. Subsequent data I/O bypasses the VMFS and volume manager completely, though management is handled via a mapping file that is stored on a VMFS volume.

IN-GUEST iSCSI AS AN ALTERNATIVE TO RDMs

In addition to using RDMs to present storage devices directly to the guest OS inside a VM, you can also use in-guest iSCSI software initiators. I'll provide more information on that scenario in the "Using In-Guest iSCSI Initiators" section later in this chapter.

RDMs should be viewed as a tactical tool in the vSphere administrators' toolkit rather than a common use case. A common misconception is that RDMs perform better than VMFS. In reality, the performance delta between the storage types is within the margin of error of tests. Although it is possible to oversubscribe a VMFS or NFS datastore (because they are shared resources) and not an RDM (because it is presented to specific VMs only), this is better handled through design and monitoring rather than through the extensive use of RDMs. In other words, if your concerns about oversubscription of a storage resource are driving the choice of an RDM over a shared datastore model, simply choose to not put multiple VMs in the pooled datastore.

You can configure RDMs in two different modes:

Physical Compatibility Mode (pRDM)   In this mode, all I/O passes directly through to the underlying LUN device, and the mapping file is used solely for locking and vSphere management tasks. Generally, when a storage vendor says "RDM" without specifying further, it means physical compatibility mode RDM. You might also see this referred to as a pass-through disk.

Virtual Mode (vRDM)   In this mode, all I/O travels through the VMFS layer. Generally, when VMware says "RDM" without specifying further, it means a virtual mode RDM.

Contrary to common misconception, both modes support almost all vSphere advanced functions such as vSphere HA and vMotion, but there is one important difference: virtual mode RDMs can be included in a vSphere snapshot, while physical mode RDMs cannot. This inability to take a native vSphere snapshot of a pRDM also means that features that depend on snapshots don't work with pRDMs. In addition, a virtual mode RDM can go from virtual mode RDM to a virtual disk via Storage vMotion, but a physical mode RDM cannot.

PHYSICAL OR VIRTUAL? BE SURE TO ASK!

When a feature specifies RDM as an option, make sure to check the type: physical compatibility mode or virtual mode.

The most common use case for RDMs are VMs configured as Microsoft Windows clusters. In Windows Server 2008, this is called Windows Failover Clusters (WFC), and in Windows Server 2003, this is called Microsoft Cluster Services (MSCS). In Chapter 7, the "Introducing Windows Failover Clustering" section provides full details on how to use RDMs with Windows Server–based clusters.

Another important use case of pRDMs is that they can be presented from a VM to a physical host interchangeably. This gives pRDMs a flexibility that isn't found with virtual mode RDMs or virtual disks. This flexibility is especially useful in cases where an independent software vendor

(ISV) hasn't yet embraced virtualization and indicates that virtual configurations are not supported. In this sort of instance, the RDMs can easily be moved to a physical host to reproduce the issue on a physical machine. As an example, this is useful in Oracle on vSphere use cases.

In a small set of use cases, storage vendor features and functions depend on the guest directly accessing the LUN and therefore need pRDMs. For example, certain arrays, such as EMC Symmetrix, use in-band communication for management to isolate management from the IP network. This means the management traffic is communicated via the block protocol (most commonly Fibre Channel). In these cases, EMC gatekeeper LUNs are used for host-array communication and, if they are used in a VM (commonly where EMC Solutions Enabler is used), require pRDMs.

Finally, another example of storage features that are associated with RDMs are those related to storage array features such as application-integrated snapshot tools. These are applications that integrate with Microsoft Exchange, SQL Server, SharePoint, Oracle, and other applications to handle recovery modes and actions. Examples include EMC's Replication Manager, NetApp's SnapManager family, and Dell/EqualLogic's Auto Volume Replicator tools. Previous generations of these tools required the use of RDMs, but most of the vendors now can manage these without the use of RDMs and integrate with vCenter Server APIs. Check with your array vendor for the latest details.

In Chapter 7, I show you how to create an RDM, and I briefly discuss RDMs in Chapter 9.

I'm now ready to shift away from block-based storage in a vSphere environment and move into a discussion of working with NAS/NFS datastores.

Working with NFS Datastores

NFS datastores are used in much the same way as VMFS datastores: as shared pools of storage for VMs. Although VMFS and NFS are both shared pools of storage for VMs, they are different in other ways. The two most important differences between VMFS and NFS datastores are as follows:

◆ The filesystem itself is not managed or controlled by the ESXi host; rather, ESXi is using the NFS protocol via an NFS client to access a remote filesystem managed by the NFS server.

◆ All the vSphere elements of high availability and performance scaling design are not part of the storage stack, but are part of the networking stack of the ESXi host.

These differences create some unique challenges in properly architecting an NFS-based solution. This is not to say that NFS is in any way inferior to block-based storage protocols; rather, the challenges that NFS presents are simply different challenges that many storage-savvy vSphere administrators have probably not encountered before. Networking-savvy vSphere administrators are going to be quite familiar with some of these behaviors, which center on the use of link aggregation and its behavior with TCP sessions.

Before going into detail on how to create or remove an NFS datastore, I'd like to first address some of the networking-related considerations.

CRAFTING A HIGHLY AVAILABLE NFS DESIGN

High-availability design for NFS datastores is substantially different from block storage devices. Block storage devices use MPIO, which is an end-to-end path model. For Ethernet networking and NFS, the domain of link selection is from one Ethernet MAC to another Ethernet MAC, or one link hop. This is configured from the host to switch, from switch to host, and from NFS server to switch, and switch to NFS server; Figure 6.50 shows the comparison. In the figure, "link aggregation" refers to NIC teaming where multiple connections are bonded together for greater aggregate throughput (with some caveats, as I'll explain in a moment).

FIGURE 6.50
NFS uses the networking stack, not the storage stack, for high availability and load balancing.

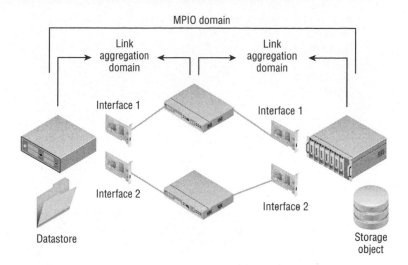

The mechanisms used to select one link or another are fundamentally the following:

◆ A NIC teaming/link aggregation choice, which is set up per TCP connection and is either static (set up once and permanent for the duration of the TCP session) or dynamic (can be renegotiated while maintaining the TCP connection, but still always on only one link or the other).

◆ A TCP/IP routing choice, where an IP address (and the associated link) is selected based on layer 3 routing—note that this doesn't imply that traffic crosses subnets via a gateway, only that the ESXi host selects the NIC or a given datastore based on the IP subnet.

Figure 6.51 shows the basic decision tree.

The path on the left has a topology that looks like Figure 6.52. Note that the little arrows mean that link aggregation/static teaming is configured from the ESXi host to the switch and on the switch to the ESXi host; in addition, note that there is the same setup on both sides for the switch-to-NFS server relationship.

The path on the right has a topology that looks like Figure 6.53. You can use link aggregation/teaming on the links in addition to the routing mechanism, but this has limited value—remember that it won't help with a single datastore. Routing is the selection mechanism for the outbound NIC for a datastore, and each NFS datastore should be reachable via an alias on both subnets.

The key to understanding why NIC teaming and link aggregation techniques cannot be used to scale up the bandwidth of a single NFS datastore is how TCP is used in the NFS case. Remember that the MPIO-based multipathing options used for block storage and iSCSI in particular are not options here, because NFS datastores use the networking stack, not the storage stack. The VMware NFS client uses two TCP sessions per datastore (as shown in Figure 6.54): one for control traffic and one for data flow. The TCP connection for the data flow is the vast majority of the bandwidth. With all NIC teaming/link aggregation technologies, Ethernet link choice is based on TCP connections. This happens either as a one-time operation when the connection is established with NIC teaming or dynamically, with 802.3ad. Regardless, there's always only one active link per TCP connection and therefore only one active link for all the data flow for a single NFS datastore.

FIGURE 6.51
The choices to configure highly available NFS datastores depend on your network infrastructure and configuration.

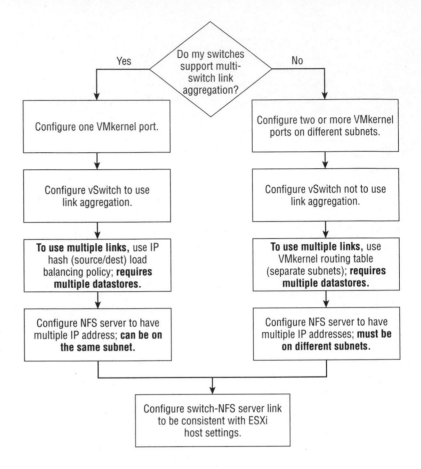

FIGURE 6.52
If you have a network switch that supports multi-switch link aggregation, you can easily create a network team that spans switches.

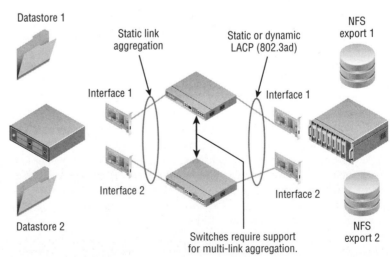

FIGURE 6.53
If you have a basic network switch without multi-switch link aggregation or don't have the experience or control of your network infrastructure, you can use VMkernel routing by placing multiple VMkernel network interfaces on separate vSwitches and different subnets.

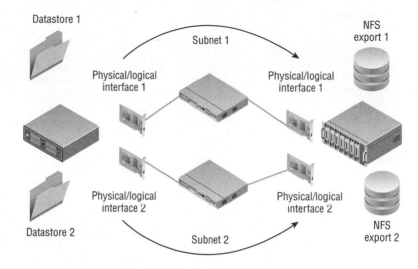

FIGURE 6.54
Every NFS datastore has two TCP connections to the NFS server but only one for data.

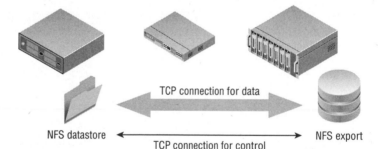

This highlights that, as with VMFS, the "one big datastore" model is not a good design principle. In the case of VMFS, it's not a good model because of the extremely large number of VMs and the implications on LUN queues (and to a far lesser extent, SCSI locking impact). In the case of NFS, it is not a good model because the bulk of the bandwidth would be on a single TCP session and therefore would use a single Ethernet link (regardless of network interface teaming, link aggregation, or routing). This has implications for supporting high-bandwidth workloads on NFS, as I'll explore later in this section.

Another consideration of highly available design with NFS datastores is that NAS device failover is generally longer than for a native block device. Block storage devices generally can fail over after a storage processor failure in seconds (or milliseconds). NAS devices, on the other hand, tend to fail over in tens of seconds and can take longer depending on the NAS device and the configuration specifics. There are NFS servers that fail over faster, but these tend to be relatively rare in vSphere use cases. This long failover period should not be considered intrinsically negative but rather a configuration question that determines the fit for NFS datastores, based on the VM service level agreement (SLA) expectation.

The key questions are these:

◆ How much time elapses before ESXi does something about a datastore being unreachable?

◆ How much time elapses before the guest OS does something about its virtual disk not responding?

FAILOVER IS NOT UNIQUE TO NFS

The concept of failover exists with Fibre Channel and iSCSI, though, as noted in the text, it is generally in shorter time intervals. This time period depends on specifics of the HBA configuration, but typically it is less than 30 seconds for Fibre Channel/FCoE and 60 seconds for iSCSI. Depending on your multipathing configuration within vSphere, path failure detection and switching to a different path might be much faster (near instantaneous).

The answer to both questions is a single word: timeouts. Timeouts exist at the vSphere layer to determine how much time should pass before a datastore is marked as unreachable, and timeouts exist within the guest OS to control the behavior of the guest OS. Let's look at each of these.

At the time of this writing, both EMC and NetApp recommend the same ESXi failover settings. Because these recommendations change, please be sure to refer to the latest recommendations from your storage vendor to be sure you have the right settings for your environment. Based on your storage vendor's recommendations, you can change the timeout value for NFS datastores by changing the values in the Advanced Settings dialog box, shown in Figure 6.55.

FIGURE 6.55

When configuring NFS datastores, it's important to extend the ESXi host timeouts to match the vendor best practices. This host is not configured with the recommended settings.

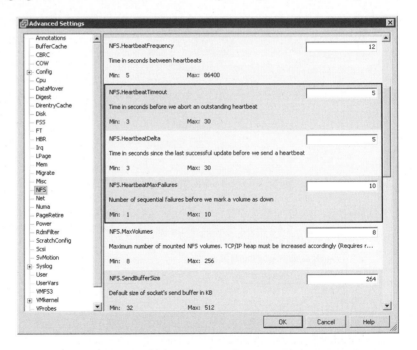

The current settings (at the time of this writing) that both EMC and NetApp recommend are as follows:

◆ NFS.HeartbeatDelta (NFS.HeartbeatFrequency in ESX 3.x): 12

◆ NFS.HeartbeatTimeout: 5

◆ NFS.HeartbeatMaxFailures: 10

You should configure these settings across all ESXi hosts that will be connected to NFS datastores.

Here's how these settings work:

◆ Every NFS.HeartbeatDelta (or 12 seconds), the ESXi host checks to see that the NFS datastore is reachable.

◆ Those heartbeats expire after NFS.HeartbeatTimeout (or 5 seconds), after which another heartbeat is sent.

◆ If NFS.HeartbeatMaxFailures (or 10) heartbeats fail in a row, the datastore is marked as unavailable, and the VMs crash.

This means that the NFS datastore can be unavailable for a maximum of 125 seconds before being marked unavailable, which covers the large majority of failover events (including those for both NetApp and EMC NAS devices serving NFS to a vSphere environment).

What does a guest OS see during this period? It sees a nonresponsive SCSI disk on the vSCSI adapter (similar to the failover behavior of a Fibre Channel or iSCSI device, though the interval is generally shorter). The disk timeout is how long the guest OS will wait while the disk is nonresponsive before throwing an I/O error. This error is a delayed write error, and for a boot volume it will result in the guest OS crashing. Windows Server, for example, has a disk timeout default of 60 seconds. A recommendation is to increase the guest OS disk timeout value to match the NFS datastore timeout value. Otherwise, the VMs can time out their boot storage (which will cause a crash) while ESXi is still waiting for the NFS datastore within the longer timeout value. Without extending the guest timeout, if vSphere HA is configured for VM monitoring, the VMs will reboot (when the NFS datastore returns), but obviously extending the timeout is preferable to avoid this extra step and the additional delay and extra I/O workload it generates.

Perform the following steps to set operating system timeout for Windows Server to match the 125-second maximum set for the datastore. You'll need to be logged into the Windows Server system as a user who has administrative credentials.

1. Back up your Windows Registry.

2. Select Start ➤ Run, type **regedit.exe**, and click OK.

3. In the left panel hierarchy view, double-click HKEY_LOCAL_MACHINE, then System, then CurrentControlSet, then Services, and then Disk.

4. Select the TimeOutValue value, and set the data value to 125 (decimal).

There are two sub-cases of NFS that I want to examine briefly before I start showing you how to create and manage NFS datastores: large bandwidth workloads and large throughput workloads. Each of these cases deserves a bit of extra attention when planning your highly available design for NFS.

Supporting Large Bandwidth (MBps) Workloads on NFS

Bandwidth for large I/O sizes is generally gated by the transport link (in this case the TCP session used by the NFS datastore being 1 Gbps or 10 Gbps) and overall network design. At larger scales, the same care and design should be applied that would be applied for iSCSI or Fibre Channel networks. In this case, it means carefully planning the physical network/VLAN, implementing end-to-end jumbo frames, and leveraging enterprise-class Ethernet switches with sufficient buffers to handle significant workload. At 10 GbE speeds, features such as TCP Segment Offload (TSO) and other offload mechanisms, as well as the processing power and I/O architecture of the NFS server, become important for NFS datastore and ESXi performance.

So, what is a reasonable performance expectation for bandwidth on an NFS datastore? From a bandwidth standpoint, where 1 Gbps Ethernet is used (which has 2 Gbps of bandwidth bidirectionally), the reasonable bandwidth limits are 80 MBps (unidirectional 100 percent read or 100 percent write) to 160 MBps (bidirectional mixed read/write workloads) for a single NFS datastore. The limits scale accordingly with 10 Gigabit Ethernet. Because of how TCP connections are handled by the ESXi NFS client, and because of how networking handles link selection in link aggregation or layer 3 routing decisions, almost all the bandwidth for a single NFS datastore will always use only one link. If you therefore need more bandwidth from an NFS datastore than a single Gigabit Ethernet link can provide, you have no other choice than to migrate to 10 Gigabit Ethernet, because link aggregation won't help (as I explained previously in this section).

Supporting Large Throughput (IOps) Workloads on NFS

High-throughput (IOps) workloads are usually gated by the backend configuration (as true of NAS devices as it is with block devices) and not the protocol or transport, since they are also generally low bandwidth (MBps). By *backend*, I mean the array target. If the workload is cached, then it's determined by the cache response, which is almost always astronomical. However, in the real world, most often the performance is not determined by cache response; the performance is determined by the spindle configuration that supports the storage object. In the case of NFS datastores, the storage object is the filesystem, so the considerations that apply at the ESXi host for VMFS (disk configuration and interface queues) apply within the NFS server. Because the internal architecture of an NFS server varies so greatly from vendor to vendor, it's almost impossible to provide recommendations, but here are a couple of examples. On a NetApp FAS array, the IOps achieved is primarily determined by the FlexVol/aggregate/RAID group configuration. On an EMC VNX array, it is likewise primarily determined by the Automated Volume Manager/dVol/RAID group configuration. Although there are other considerations (at a certain point, the scale of the interfaces on the array and the host's ability to generate I/Os become limited, but up to the limits that users commonly encounter), performance is far more often constrained by the backend disk configuration that supports the filesystem. Make sure your filesystem has sufficient backend spindles in the container to deliver performance for all the VMs that will be contained in the filesystem exported via NFS.

With these NFS storage design considerations in mind, let's move forward with creating and mounting an NFS datastore.

THERE'S ALWAYS AN EXCEPTION TO THE RULE

Thus far, in the "Working with NFS Datastores" section, I've been talking about how NFS *always* uses only a single link, and how you *always* need to use multiple VMkernel ports and multiple NFS exports in order to utilize multiple links. In vSphere 5, it turns out there's an exception to that rule.

Normally, vSphere requires that you mount an NFS datastore using the same IP address or hostname and path on all hosts (you'll see this in the section "Creating and Mounting an NFS Datastore"). However, in vSphere 5, you do have the ability to use a DNS hostname that resolves to multiple IP addresses. In this case, the vSphere NFS client will actually use all the different IP addresses behind the hostname. This is the exception to the rule—in this sort of configuration, the NFS client could end up using multiple links in a link aggregate for increased overall throughput between the ESXi host and the NFS datastore.

CREATING AND MOUNTING AN NFS DATASTORE

In this procedure, I will show you how to create and mount an NFS datastore in vSphere. Although I use the term *create* here, it's a bit of a misnomer; the filesystem is actually created on the NFS server and just exported. That process I can't really show you, because the procedures vary so greatly from vendor to vendor. What works for one vendor to create an NFS datastore is likely to be different for another vendor.

Before you start, ensure that you completed the following steps:

1. You created at least one VMkernel port for NFS traffic. If you intend to use multiple VMkernel ports for NFS traffic, ensure that you configure your vSwitches and physical switches appropriately, as described previously in "Crafting a Highly Available NFS Design."

2. You configured your ESXi host for NFS storage according to the vendor's best practices, including timeout values and any other settings. At the time of this writing, many storage vendors recommend an important series of advanced ESXi parameter settings to maximize performance (including increasing memory assigned to the networking stack and changing other characteristics). Be sure to refer to your storage vendor's recommendations for using their product with vSphere.

3. You created a filesystem on your NAS device and exported it via NFS. A key part of this configuration is the specifics of the NFS export itself; the ESXi NFS client must have full root access to the NFS export. If the NFS export was exported with `root squash`, the filesystem will not be able to mount on the ESXi host. (Root users are downgraded to unprivileged filesystem access. On a traditional Linux system, when `root squash` is configured on the export, the remote systems are mapped to the "nobody" account.) You have one of two options for NFS exports that are going to be used with ESXi hosts:

    ◆ Use the `no_root_squash` option, and give the ESXi hosts explicit read/write access.

    ◆ Add the ESXi host's IP addresses as root-privileged hosts on the NFS server.

For more information on setting up the VMkernel networking for NFS traffic, refer to Chapter 5; for more information on setting up your NFS export, refer to your storage vendor's documentation.

After you complete these steps, you're ready to mount an NFS datastore.

Perform the following steps to mount an NFS datastore on an ESXi host:

1. Make a note of the IP address on which the NFS export is hosted as well as the name (and full path) of the NFS export; you'll need this information later in this process.

2. Launch the vSphere Client and connect to an ESXi host or to a vCenter Server instance.

3. In the vSphere Client, navigate to the Datastores And Datastore Clusters inventory view.

4. Right-click the datacenter object and select Add Datastore. This launches the Add Storage wizard.

5. Select the specific ESXi host to which you'd like to add the NFS datastore, and click Next.

6. At the Select Storage Type screen, select Network File System. Click Next.

7. At the Locate Network File System screen, you'll need to supply three pieces of information:

   ◆ You'll need to supply the IP address on which the NFS export is hosted. If you don't know this information, you'll need to go back to your storage array and determine what IP address it is using to host the NFS export.

   In general, identifying the NFS server by IP addresses is recommended, but it is not recommended to use a hostname because it places an unnecessary dependency on DNS and because generally it is being specified on a relatively small number of hosts. There are, of course, some cases where a hostname may be applicable—for example, where NAS virtualization techniques are used to provide transparent file mobility between NFS servers—but this is relatively rare.

   Also, refer to the sidebar titled "There's Always an Exception to the Rule"; that sidebar describes another configuration in which you might want to use a hostname that resolves to multiple IP addresses.

   ◆ You'll need to supply the folder or path to the NFS export. Again, this is determined by the NFS server and the settings on the NFS export.

   ◆ Finally, you'll need to supply a datastore name. As with VMFS datastores, I recommend a naming scheme that identifies the NFS server and other pertinent information in the datastore name for easier troubleshooting.

   Figure 6.56 shows an example of the Locate Network File System screen of the Add Storage wizard, where I've supplied the necessary information.

FIGURE 6.56
Mounting an NFS datastore requires that you know the IP address and the export name from the NFS server.

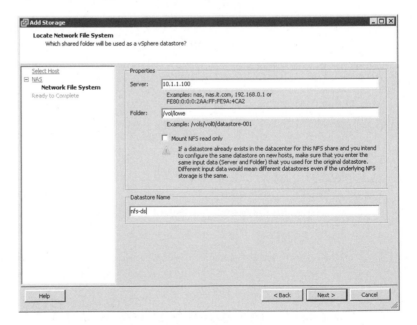

8. If the NFS datastore should be read-only, then select Mount NFS Read Only.

You might need to mount a read-only NFS datastore if the datastore contains only ISO images, for example.

Click Next to continue.

9. Review the information at the summary screen. If everything is correct, click Finish to continue; otherwise, go back and make the necessary changes.

When you click Finish, the vSphere Client will mount the NFS datastore on the selected ESXi host and the new NFS datastore will appear in the list of datastores, as you can see in Figure 6.57.

TROUBLESHOOTING NFS CONNECTIVITY

If you're having problems getting an NFS datastore to mount, the following list can help you troubleshoot the problem:

◆ Are you able to ping the IP address of the NFS export from the ESXi host? (Use the Direct Console User Interface (DCUI) to test connectivity from the ESXi host, or enable the ESXi shell and use the vmkping command.)

◆ Is the physical cabling correct? Are the link lights showing a connected state on the physical interfaces on the ESXi host, the Ethernet switches, and the NFS server?

◆ Are your VLANs configured correctly? If you've configured VLANs, have you properly configured the same VLAN on the host, the switch, and the interface(s) that will be used on your NFS server?

◆ Is your IP routing correct and functional? Have you properly configured the IP addresses of the VMkernel port and the interface(s) that will be used on the NFS server? Are they on the same subnet? If not, they should be. Although you can route NFS traffic, it's not a good idea because routing adds significant latency and isn't involved in a bet-the-business storage Ethernet network. In addition, it's generally not recommended in vSphere environments.

◆ Is the NFS traffic being allowed through any firewalls? If the ping succeeds but you can't mount the NFS export, check to see if NFS is being blocked by a firewall somewhere in the path. Again, the general recommendation is to avoid firewalls in the midst of the data path wherever possible to avoid introducing additional latency.

◆ Are jumbo frames configured correctly? If you're using jumbo frames, have you configured jumbo frames on the VMkernel port, the vSwitch or distributed vSwitch, all physical switches along the data path, and the NFS server?

◆ Are you allowing the ESXi host root access to the NFS export?

Unlike VMFS datastores in vSphere, you need to add the NFS datastore on each host in the vSphere environment. Also, it's important to use consistent NFS properties (for example, a consistent IP/domain name), as well as common datastore names; this is not enforced. VMware provides a helpful reminder on the Locate Network File System screen, which you can see in Figure 6.56.

Once the NFS datastore is mounted, you can use it as you would any other datastore—you can select it as a Storage vMotion source or destination, you can create virtual disks on the NFS datastore, or you can map ISO images stored on an NFS datastore into a VM as a virtual CD/DVD drive.

FIGURE 6.57
NFS datastores are listed in among VMFS datastores, but the information provided for each is different.

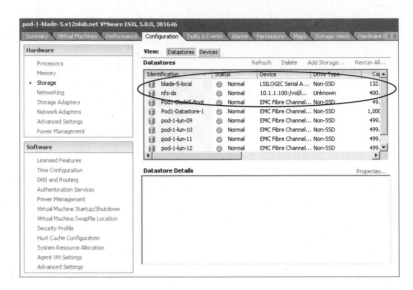

As you can see, using NFS requires a simple series of steps, several fewer than using VMFS. And yet, with the same level of care, planning, and attention to detail, you can create robust NFS infrastructures that provide the same level of support as traditional block-based storage infrastructures.

So far I've examined both block-based storage and NFS-based storage at the hypervisor level. But what if you need a storage device presented directly to a VM, not a shared container, as is the case with VMFS and NFS datastores? The next section discusses some common VM-level storage configuration options.

Working with VM-Level Storage Configuration

Let's move from ESXi- and vSphere-level storage configuration to the storage configuration details for individual VMs.

In this section, I'll review virtual disks and the types of virtual disks supported in vSphere. Next I'll review the virtual SCSI controllers. Then I'll move into a discussion of VM storage profiles and how to assign them to a VM, and I'll wrap up this section with a brief exploration of using an in-guest iSCSI initiator to access storage resources.

INVESTIGATING VIRTUAL DISKS

Virtual disks (referred to as VMDKs because of the file extension used by vSphere) are how VMs encapsulate their disk devices (if not using RDMs), and warrant further discussion. Figure 6.58 shows the properties of a VM. Hard disk 1 is a 30 GB thick-provisioned virtual disk on a VMFS datastore. Hard disk 2, conversely, is an RDM.

FIGURE 6.58
This VM has both
a virtual disk on a
VMFS datastore
and an RDM.

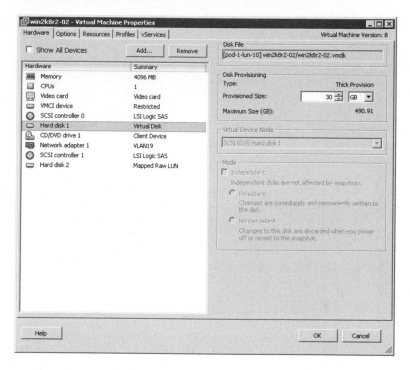

I discussed RDMs previously in the section "Working with Raw Device Mappings," and I'll discuss RDMs in a bit more detail in Chapter 7 as well. As you know already, RDMs are used to present a storage device directly to a VM instead of encapsulating the disk into a file on a VMFS datastore.

Virtual disks come in three formats:

Thin-Provisioned Disk   In this format, the size of the VDMK file on the datastore is only as much as is used (or was at some point used) within the VM itself. Figure 6.59 illustrates this concept. For example, if you create a 500 GB virtual disk and place 100 GB of data in it, the VMDK file will be 100 GB in size. As I/O occurs in the guest, the VMkernel zeroes out the space needed right before the guest I/O is committed and grows the VMDK file similarly. Sometimes, this is referred to as a *sparse file*. Note that space deleted from the guest OS's filesystem won't necessarily be released from the VMDK; if you added 50 GB of data but then turned around and deleted 50 GB of data, the space wouldn't necessarily be released to the hypervisor so that the VMDK can shrink in size. (Some guest OSes support the necessary T10 SCSI commands to address this situation.)

FIGURE 6.59
A thin-provisioned
virtual disk uses
only as much as the
guest OS in the VM
uses.

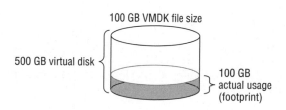

Thick Provision Lazy Zeroed   In this format (sometimes referred to as a flat disk), the size of the VDMK file on the datastore is the size of the virtual disk that you create, but within the file, it is not pre-zeroed. For example, if you create a 500 GB virtual disk and place 100 GB of data in it, the VMDK will appear to be 500 GB at the datastore filesystem, but it contains only 100 GB of data on disk. This is shown in Figure 6.60. As I/O occurs in the guest, the VMkernel zeroes out the space needed right before the guest I/O is committed, but the VDMK file size does not grow (since it was already 500 GB).

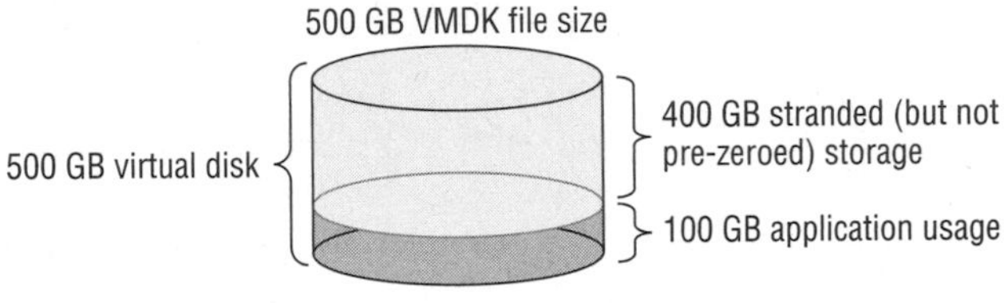

FIGURE 6.60
A flat disk doesn't pre-zero unused space, so if you are using array-level thin provisioning, only 100 GB is used.

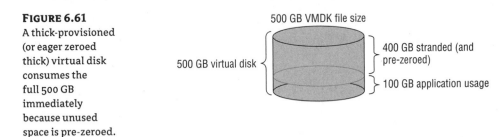

Thick Provisioned Eager Zeroed   Thick provisioned eager zeroed virtual disks, also referred to as eagerly zeroed disks or eagerzeroedthick disks, are truly thick. In this format, the size of the VDMK file on the datastore is the size of the virtual disk that you create, and within the file, it is pre-zeroed, as illustrated in Figure 6.61. For example, if you create a 500 GB virtual disk and place 100 GB of data in it, the VMDK will appear to be 500 GB at the datastore filesystem, and it contains 100 GB of data and 400 GB of zeros on disk. As I/O occurs in the guest, the VMkernel does not need to zero the blocks prior to the I/O occurring. This results in slightly improved I/O latency and fewer backend storage I/O operations during initial I/O operations to new allocations in the guest OS, but it results in significantly more backend storage I/O operation up front during the creation of the VM. If the array supports VAAI, vSphere can offload the up-front task of zeroing all the blocks and reduce the initial I/O and time requirements.

FIGURE 6.61
A thick-provisioned (or eager zeroed thick) virtual disk consumes the full 500 GB immediately because unused space is pre-zeroed.

This third type of virtual disk occupies more space than the first two, but it is required if you are going to use vSphere FT. (If they are thin-provisioned or flat virtual disks, conversion occurs automatically when the vSphere FT feature is enabled.)

As you'll see in Chapter 12 when I discuss Storage vMotion, you can convert between these virtual disk types using Storage vMotion.

ALIGNING VIRTUAL DISKS

Do you need to align the virtual disks? The answer is yes. Although not absolutely mandatory, it's recommended that you follow VMware's recommended best practices for aligning the volumes of guest OSes—and do so across all vendor platforms and all storage types. These are the same as the very mature standard techniques for aligning the partitions in standard physical configurations from most storage vendors.

Why do this? Aligning a partition aligns the I/O along the underlying RAID stripes of the array, which is particularly important in Windows environments (Windows Server 2008 automatically aligns partitions). This alignment step minimizes the extra I/Os by aligning the I/Os with the array RAID stripe boundaries. Extra I/O work is generated when the I/Os cross the stripe boundary with all RAID schemes, as opposed to a full stripe write. Aligning the partition provides a more efficient use of what is usually the most constrained storage array resource—IOps. If you align a template and then deploy from a template, you maintain the correct alignment.

Why is it important to do this across vendors and across protocols? Changing the alignment of the guest OS partition is a difficult operation once data has been put in the partition—so it is best done up front when creating a VM or when creating a template.

Some of these types of virtual disks are supported in certain environments and others are not. VMFS datastores support all three types of virtual disks (thin, flat, and thick), but NFS datastores support only thin unless the NFS server supports the VAAIv2 NAS extensions and vSphere has been configured with the vendor-supplied plug-in. Figure 6.62 shows the screen for creating a new virtual disk for a VM (a procedure I'll describe in full detail in Chapter 9) on a VMFS datastore; Figure 6.63 shows the same screen for an NFS datastore that does not have the VAAIv2 extension support.

FIGURE 6.62
VMFS datastores support all three virtual disk types.

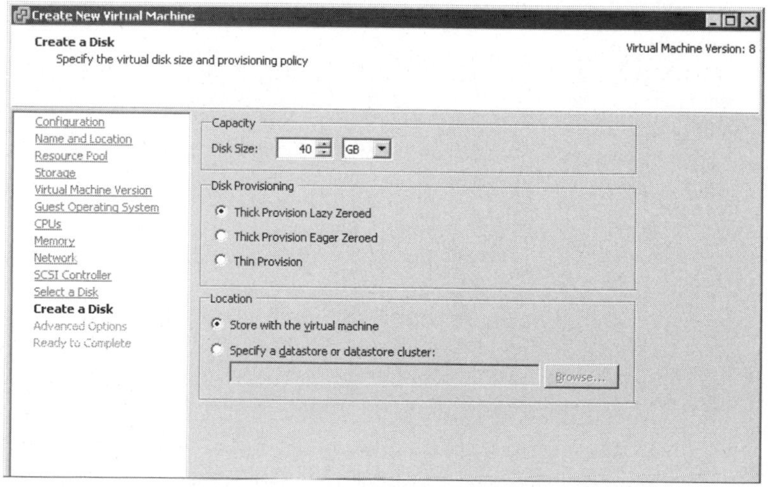

FIGURE 6.63
Without VAAIv2
NAS support, NFS
datastores support
only thin-
provisioned disks.

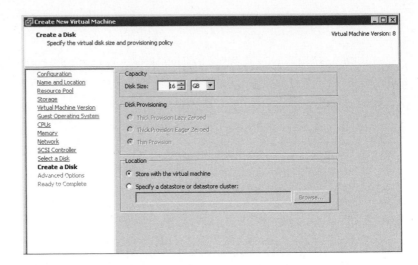

Is there a way to tell which type of virtual disk a VM is using? Certainly. In all three cases, the free space indication within the guest OS is always going to indicate the maximum size of the virtual disk, so you won't be able to use that. Fortunately, VMware provides several other ways to determine the disk type:

◆ In the Datastore Browser, VMware includes both a Size column and a Provisioned Size column, as you can see in Figure 6.64. This allows you to clearly see the maximum size of a thin-provisioned virtual disk as well as the current space usage. Virtual disks that are not thin provisioned won't have both columns or will report both sizes the same.

FIGURE 6.64
The Size and
Provisioned Size
columns tell you
the current and
maximum space
allocations for a
thin-provisioned
disk.

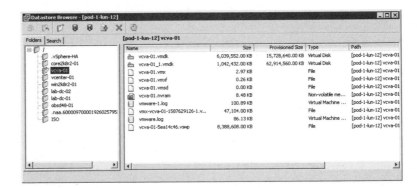

◆ On the Summary tab of a VM, the vSphere Client provides statistics on currently provisioned space, not-shared space, and used space. Figure 6.65 shows the statistics for a deployed instance of the vCenter Server virtual appliance.

◆ Finally, the VM Properties dialog box will also display the virtual disk type for a selected virtual disk in a VM. Using the same deployed instance of the vCenter virtual appliance as an example, Figure 6.66 shows the information supplied in this dialog box. You can't determine current space usage, but you can at least determine what type of disk is configured.

FIGURE 6.65

The Summary tab of a VM will report the total provisioned space as well as the used space.

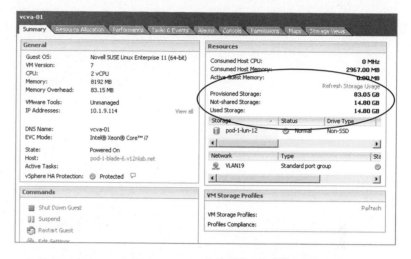

FIGURE 6.66

The VM Properties dialog box tells you what kind of disk is configured, but doesn't provide current space usage statistics.

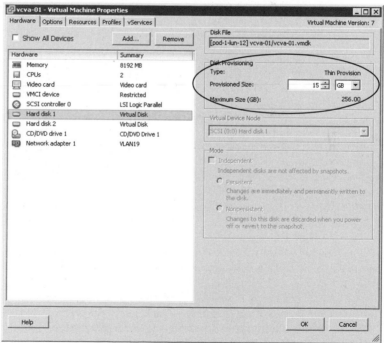

Closely related to virtual disks are the virtual SCSI adapters that are present within every VM.

EXPLORING VIRTUAL SCSI ADAPTERS

Virtual SCSI adapters are what you configure in your VMs and to what you will attach virtual disks and RDMs. In the guest OS, each virtual SCSI adapter has its own HBA queue, so for intense storage workloads, there are advantages to configuring multiple virtual SCSI adapters within a single guest.

There are four types of virtual SCSI adapters in ESXi, as shown in Figure 6.67.

FIGURE 6.67

There are various virtual SCSI adapters that a VM can use. You can configure up to four virtual SCSI adapters for each VM.

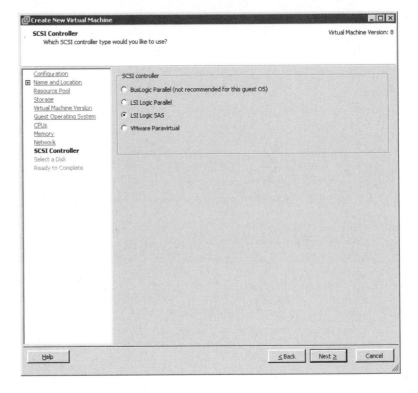

Table 6.3 summarizes the information about the four types of virtual SCSI adapters available for you to use.

As you can see from Table 6.3, two of these adapters—the LSI Logic SAS and VMware Paravirtual—are available only for VM hardware version 7 or higher. The LSI Logic SAS controller is the default SCSI adapter suggested for VMs running Windows Server 2008 and 2008 R2, while the LSI Logic parallel SCSI controller is the default for Windows Server 2003. Many of the various Linux flavors default to the BusLogic parallel SCSI adapters.

The BusLogic and LSI Logic controllers are pretty straightforward; they emulate a known SCSI controller. The VMware Paravirtual SCSI adapter, though, is a different kind of controller.

In short, paravirtualized devices (and their corresponding drivers) are specifically optimized to communicate more directly with the underlying VM Monitor (VMM); they deliver higher throughput and lower latency, and they usually significantly lower the CPU impact of the I/O operations. This is the case with the VMware Paravirtual SCSI adapter in vSphere. I'll discuss paravirtualized drivers in greater detail in Chapter 9.

TABLE 6.3: Virtual SCSI Adapters in vSphere 5

VIRTUAL SCSI ADAPTER	VM HARDWARE VERSIONS SUPPORTED	DESCRIPTION
BusLogic Parallel	4, 7, 8	This virtual SCSI adapter emulates the BusLogic parallel SCSI adapter. The BusLogic adapter is well supported for older guest OSes but doesn't perform as well as some other virtual SCSI adapters.
LSI Logic Parallel	4, 7, 8	The LSI Logic parallel SCSI virtual adapter is well suited for and well supported by newer guest OSes. Both LSI Logic controllers provide equivalent performance.
LSI Logic SAS	7, 8	The LSI Logic SAS controller is a better choice than LSI Logic parallel when the guest OS is phasing out support for parallel SCSI in favor of SAS. Performance between the two controllers is equivalent.
VMware Paravirtual	7, 8	The VMware Paravirtual SCSI adapter is a virtualization-optimized controller that provides higher throughput with lower CPU overhead but at the cost of guest OS compatibility.

Compared to other virtual SCSI adapters, the paravirtualized SCSI adapter shows improvements in performance for virtual disks as well as improvements in the number of IOps delivered at any given CPU utilization. The paravirtualized SCSI adapter also shows improvements (decreases) in storage latency as observed from the guest OS.

If the paravirtualized SCSI adapter works so well, why not use it for everything? Well, for one, this is an adapter type that exists only in vSphere environments, so you won't find the drivers for the paravirtualized SCSI adapter on the install disk for most guest OSes. In general, I recommend using the virtual SCSI adapter suggested by vSphere for the boot disk and the paravirtualized SCSI adapter for any other virtual disks, especially other virtual disks with active workloads.

As you can see, there are lots of options for configuring VM-level storage. When you factor in different datastores and different protocol options, how can you ensure that VMs are placed on the right storage? This is where VM storage profiles come into play.

CREATING AND ASSIGNING VM STORAGE PROFILES

VM storage profiles are a key component of profile-driven storage, a topic I touched on in the section "Examining Profile-Driven Storage." By leveraging system-provided storage capabilities supplied by a VASA provider (which is provided by the storage vendor), as well as user-defined storage capabilities, you can build VM storage profiles that help shape and control how VMs are allocated to storage.

Let's start with creating a VM storage profile.

Perform the following steps to create a VM storage profile:

1. In the vSphere Client, navigate to the VM Storage Profiles area. You can use the navigation bar, select View ➢ Management ➢ VM Storage Profiles from the menu bar, or use the Ctrl+Shift+Y keyboard shortcut.

2. Click Create VM Storage Profile to launch the Create New VM Storage Profile wizard.

3. At the first screen, supply a name and a description for the new VM storage profile. Click Next when you're ready to proceed.

4. At the Select Storage Capabilities screen, select all the storage capabilities that should be present for this VM storage profile. Keep in mind that a datastore may have, at most, two capabilities assigned: one system-provided capability and one user-defined capability. Creating a VM storage profile with more than two capabilities selected will result in all datastores being listed as Incompatible, because no datastore can have more than two capabilities assigned.

   This is an "and" selection—storage must have all of the selected capabilities in order to be considered compliant with the VM storage profile. Figure 6.68 shows a sample VM storage profile being created that requires the user-defined capability named NAS.

FIGURE 6.68
This VM storage profile requires a specific user-defined storage capability.

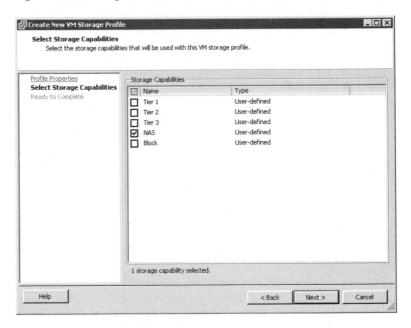

5. Click Next after you've finished selecting storage capabilities.

6. At the Summary screen, review the settings. If everything is correct, click Finish; otherwise, use the Back button to go back and make changes.

The new VM storage profile will appear in the list of defined profiles. If you need to edit the profile—change the name, add capabilities, or remove capabilities—you can simply right-click the VM storage profile and select Edit VM Storage Profile.

Similarly, if you need to delete a VM storage profile, simply right-click the existing VM storage profile and select Delete VM Storage Profile.

The second part of working with VM storage profiles is to enable VM storage profiles in the environment. To enable VM storage profiles, click the Enable VM Storage Profiles button. Figure 6.69 is the dialog box that appears.

FIGURE 6.69

The Enable VM Storage Profiles dialog box shows the current status of VM profiles and licensing compliance for the feature.

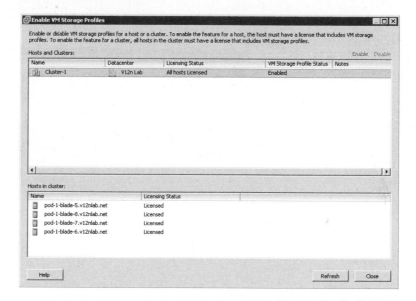

To enable VM storage profiles, click the Enable hyperlink. The Enable hyperlink will appear disabled, as it does in Figure 6.69, if the feature has already been enabled (you can't enable VM storage profiles if they are already enabled). In that case, you can use the Disable hyperlink to turn the feature off.

Once the feature is enabled, a new area appears on the Summary tab for a VM that shows compliance or noncompliance with the assigned VM storage profile. For a VM that does not have a storage profile assigned—and I'll show you how to assign one shortly—then the box is empty, like the one shown in Figure 6.70.

FIGURE 6.70

This VM does not have a VM storage profile assigned yet.

Perform these steps to assign a VM storage profile to a VM:

1. In the vSphere Client, navigate to either the Hosts And Clusters inventory view or the VMs And Templates inventory view.

2. Right-click a VM from the inventory panel and select Edit Settings.

3. In the VM Properties dialog box, select the Profiles tab.

4. From the drop-down list under Home VM Storage Profile, select the VM storage profile you want to assign to the VM's configuration and configuration-related files.

5. To have the VM's virtual disks use the same VM storage profile, click the Propagate To Disks button.

6. Otherwise, for each virtual disk listed, select the VM storage profile you want associated with that virtual disk.

Figure 6.71 shows a VM with one VM storage profile assigned to the VM configuration files and another VM storage profile assigned to the virtual disk.

FIGURE 6.71

Each virtual disk can have its own VM storage profile, so that you tailor VM storage capabilities on a per-virtual disk basis.

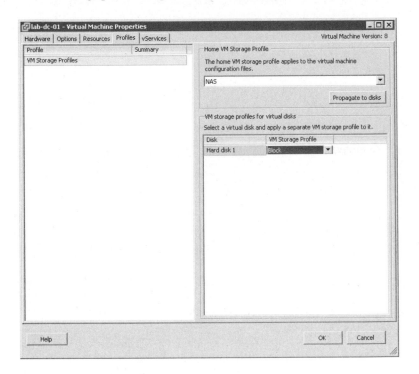

7. Click OK to save the changes to the VM and apply the storage profile.

After a VM storage profile is assigned, this area will show the compliance (or noncompliance) of the VM's current storage with the assigned storage profile, as in Figure 6.72 and Figure 6.73.

FIGURE 6.72

This VM's current storage is compliant with its assigned VM storage profile.

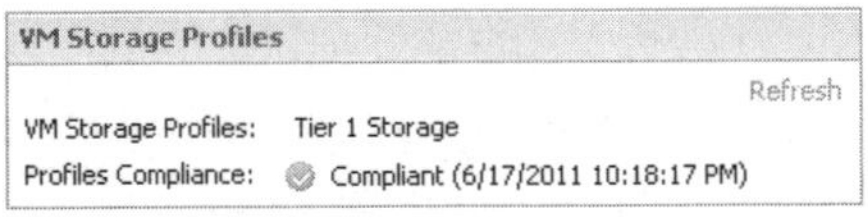

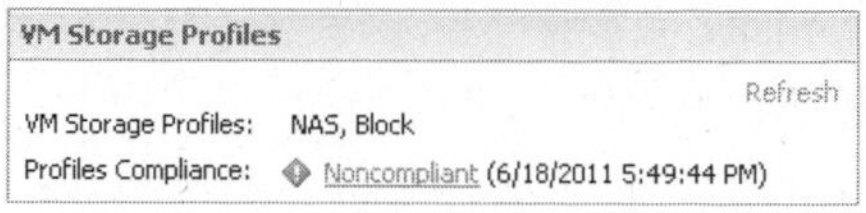

FIGURE 6.73

The storage capabilities specified in this VM storage profile don't match the capabilities of the VM's current storage location.

Figure 6.72 and Figure 6.73 also show the date and time of the last compliance check. Note that you can force a compliance check by clicking the Refresh hyperlink.

When I discuss creating VMs and adding virtual disks to a VM in Chapter 9, I'll revisit the concept of profile-driven storage and VM storage profiles.

In addition to the various methods I've shown you so far for accessing storage from a VM, there's still one method left: using an in-guest iSCSI initiator.

USING IN-GUEST ISCSI INITIATORS

I mentioned in the section "Working with Raw Device Mappings" that RDMs were not the only way to present storage devices directly to a VM. You also have the option of using an in-guest iSCSI initiator to bypass the hypervisor and access storage directly.

The decision whether to use in-guest iSCSI initiators will depend on numerous factors, including, but not limited to, your storage configuration (does your array support iSCSI?), your networking configuration (do you have enough network bandwidth to support the additional iSCSI traffic on the VM-facing networks?), your application needs (do you have applications that need or are specifically designed to work with in-guest iSCSI initiators, or applications that need RDMs that could work with in-guest iSCSI initiators instead?), consolidation target (can you afford the extra CPU and memory overhead in the VMs as a result of using an in-guest iSCSI initiator?), and your guest OS (is there a software iSCSI initiator for your particular guest OS?).

Should you decide to use an in-guest iSCSI initiator, keep in mind the following tips:

◆ The storage that you access via the in-guest initiator will be separate from the NFS and VMFS datastores you'll use for virtual disks. Keep this in mind so that you can plan your storage configuration accordingly.

◆ You will be placing more load and more visibility on the VM networks because all iSCSI traffic will bypass the hypervisor. You'll also be responsible for configuring and supplying redundant connections and multipathing separately from the configuration you might have supplied for iSCSI at the hypervisor level. This could result in a need for more physical NICs in your server than you had planned.

◆ If you are using 10 Gigabit Ethernet, you might need to create a more complex QoS/Network I/O Control configuration to ensure that the in-guest iSCSI traffic is appropriately prioritized.

◆ You'll lose Storage vMotion functionality for storage accessed via the in-guest iSCSI initiator because the hypervisor is not involved.

◆ For the same reason, vSphere snapshots would not be supported for in-guest iSCSI initiator-access storage.

As with so many different areas in vSphere, there is no absolute wrong or right choice, only the correct choice for your environment. Review the impact of using iSCSI initiators in the guest OSes and, if it makes sense for your environment, proceed as needed.

THIN PROVISIONING: SHOULD YOU DO IT IN THE ARRAY OR IN VMWARE?

The general answer is that *both* are right.

If your array supports thin provisioning, it's generally more efficient to use array-level thin provisioning in most operational models. If you thick provision at the LUN or filesystem level, there will always be large amounts of unused space until you start to get it highly utilized, unless you start small and keep extending the datastore, which operationally is heavyweight.

Also, when you use thin-provisioning techniques at the array level using NFS or block storage, you always benefit. In vSphere, the common default virtual disk types—both thin and flat (with the exception of thick provisioned, which in vSphere is used far more rarely)—are friendly to storage array-level thin provisioning since they don't pre-zero the files.

Thin provisioning also tends to be more efficient the larger the scale of the thin pool. On an array, this construct (often called a *pool*) tends to be larger than a single datastore and therefore more efficient, because thin provisioning is more efficient at larger scales of thinly provisioned objects in the oversubscribed pool.

Is there a downside to thin on thin? Not really, if you are able and willing to carefully monitor usage at both the vSphere layer and the storage layer. Use vSphere or third-party usage reports in conjunction with array-level reports, and set thresholds with notification and automated action on both the vSphere layer and the array level, if your array supports that. (See Chapter 13 for more information on creating alarms to monitor datastores.) Why? Even though vSphere 5 adds thin-provisioning awareness and support, thin provisioning still needs to be carefully managed for out-of-space conditions, because you are oversubscribing an asset that has no backdoor. Unlike the way VMware oversubscribes guest memory that can use VM swap if needed, if you run out of actual capacity for a datastore, the VMs on that datastore will be affected. When you use thin on thin, it can be marginally more efficient but can accelerate the transition to oversubscription and an outage.

An example here is instructive. If the total amount of provisioned space at the virtual disk layer in a datastore is 500 GB with thick virtual disks, then the datastore needs to be at least 500 GB in size, and therefore the LUN or NFS exported filesystem would need to look as if it were at least 500 GB in size. Now, those thick virtual disks are not actually using 500 GB; imagine that they have 100 GB of used space, and the remainder is empty. If you use thin provisioning at the storage array level, you provision a LUN or filesystem that is 500 GB, but only 100 GB in the pool is used. The space used cannot exceed 500 GB, so monitoring is needed only at the storage layer.

Conversely, if you use thin virtual disks, technically the datastore needs to be only 100 GB in size. The exact same amount of storage is being used (100 GB), but clearly there is a possibility of quickly needing more than 100 GB, since the virtual disks could grow up to 500 GB without any administrative action—with only the VMs writing more data in their guest OSes. Therefore, the datastore *and* the underlying storage LUN/filesystem must be monitored closely, and the administrator must be ready to respond with more storage on the array and grow the datastore if needed.

There are only two exceptions to the "always thin provision at the array level if you can" guideline. The first is in the most extreme performance use cases, because the thin-provisioning architectures generally have a performance impact (usually marginal—and this varies from array to array) compared to a traditional thick-storage configuration. The second is large, high-performance RDBMS storage objects when the amount of array cache is significantly smaller than the database; ergo, the actual backend spindles are tightly coupled to the host I/O. These database structures have internal logic that generally expect I/O locality, which is a fancy way of saying that they structure data expecting the on-disk structure to reflect their internal structure. With very large array caches, the host and the backend spindles with RDBMS-type workloads can be decoupled, and this consideration is irrelevant. These two cases are important but rare. "Always thin provision at the array level if you can" is a good general guiding principle.

In the last section of this chapter, I'll pull together everything you've learned in the previous sections and summarize with some recommended practices.

Leveraging SAN and NAS Best Practices

After all the discussion of configuring and managing storage in vSphere environments, these are the core principles:

- Pick a storage architecture for your immediate and midterm scaling goals. Don't design for extreme growth scenarios. You can always use Storage vMotion to migrate up to larger arrays.

- Consider using VMFS and NFS together; the combination provides a great deal of flexibility.

- When sizing your initial array design for your entire vSphere environment, think about availability, performance (IOps, MBps, latency), and then capacity—always together and generally in that order.

The last point in the previous list cannot be overstated. People who are new to storage tend to think primarily in the dimension of storage capacity (TB) and neglect availability and performance. Capacity is generally not the limit for a proper storage configuration. With modern large-capacity disks (300 GB+ per disk is common) and capacity reduction techniques such as thin provisioning, deduplication, and compression, you can fit a *lot* on a very small number of disks. Therefore, capacity is not always the driver of efficiency.

To make this clear, an example scenario will help. First, let's work through the capacity-centered planning dynamic:

◆ You determine you will have 150 VMs that are 50 GB in size each.

◆ This means that at a minimum, if you don't apply any special techniques, you will need 7.5 TB (150 × 50 GB). Because of extra space for vSphere snapshots and VM swap, you assume 25 percent overhead, so you plan 10 TB of storage for your vSphere environment.

◆ With 10 TB, you could fit that on approximately 13 large 1 TB SATA drives (assuming a 10+2 RAID 6 and one hot spare.

◆ Thinking about this further and trying to be more efficient, you determine that while the virtual disks will be configured to be 50 GB, on average they will need only 20 TB, and the rest will be empty, so you can use thin provisioning at the vSphere or storage array layer. Using this would reduce the requirement to 3 TB, and you decide that with good use of vSphere managed datastore objects and alerts, you can cut the extra space down from 25 percent to 20 percent. This reduces the requirement down to 3.6 TB.

◆ Also, depending on your array, you may be able to deduplicate the storage itself, which has a high degree of commonality. Assuming a conservative 2:1 deduplication ratio, you would then need only 1.5 TB of capacity—and with an additional 20 percent for various things, that's 1.8 TB.

◆ With only 1.8 TB needed, you could fit that on a very small 3+1 RAID 5 using 750 GB drives, which would net 2.25 TB.

This would be much cheaper, right? Much more efficient, right? After all, we've gone from 13 1 TB spindles to four 750 GB spindles.

It's not that simple. This will be clear going through this a second time, but this time working through the same design with a performance-centered planning dynamic:

◆ You determine you will have 150 VMs (the same as before).

◆ You look at their workloads, and although they spike at 200 IOps, they average at 50 IOps, and the duty cycle across all the VMs doesn't seem to spike at the same time, so you decide to use the average.

◆ You look at the throughput requirements and see that although they spike at 200 MBps during a backup, for the most part, they drive only 3 MBps. (For perspective, copying a file to a USB 2 memory stick can drive 12 MBps—so this is a small amount of bandwidth for a server.) The I/O size is generally small—in the 4 KB size.

◆ Among the 150 virtual purpose machines, while most are general-purpose servers, there are 10 that are "big hosts" (for example, Exchange servers and some SharePoint backend SQL Servers) that require specific planning, so you put them aside to design separately using the reference architecture approach. The remaining 140 VMs can be characterized as needing an average of 7,000 IOps (140 × 50 IOps) and 420 MBps of average throughput (140 × 3 MBps).

◆ Assuming no RAID losses or cache gains, 7,000 IOps translates to the following:

   ◆ 39 15K RPM Fibre Channel/SAS drives (7,000 IOps/180 IOps per drive)

   ◆ 59 10K RPM Fibre Channel/SAS drives (7,000 IOps/120 IOps per drive)

- ◆ 87 5,400 RPM SATA drives (7,000 IOps/80 IOps per drive)

- ◆ 7 enterprise flash drives (7,000 IOps/1000 IOps per drive)

◆ Assuming no RAID losses or cache gains, 420 MBps translates into 3,360 Mbps. At the array and the ESXi hosts layers, this will require the following:

- ◆ Two 4 Gbps Fibre Channel array ports (although it could fit on one, you need two for high availability).

- ◆ Two 10 GbE ports (though it could fit on one, you need two for high availability).

- ◆ Four 1 GbE ports for iSCSI or NFS. NFS will require careful multi-datastore planning to hit the throughput goal because of how NFS works in link aggregation configurations. iSCSI will require careful multipathing configuration to hit the throughput goal.

◆ If using block devices, you'll need to distribute VMs across datastores to design the data stores and backing LUNs themselves to ensure that they can support the IOps of the VMs they contain to ensure that the queues don't overflow.

◆ It's immediately apparent that the SATA drives are not ideal in this case (they would require 87 spindles!). At the time of writing this book, the sweet spot in the disk market from a combined price/capacity/performance standpoint is the 300 GB 15K RPM drives, and that's reflected in this configuration. Using these 300 GB 15K RPM drives (without using Enterprise Flash Drives), at a minimum you will have 11.7 TB of raw capacity, assuming 10 percent RAID 6 capacity loss (10.6 TB usable). This is more than enough to store the thickly provisioned VMs, not to mention their thinly provisioned and then deduplicated variations.

◆ Will thin provisioning and deduplication techniques save capacity? Yes. Could you use that saved capacity? Maybe, but probably not. Remember, we've sized the configuration to meet the IOps workload—unless the workload is lighter than we measured or the additional workloads you would like to load on those spindles generate no I/O during the periods the VMs need it. The spindles will all be busy servicing the existing VMs, and additional workloads will increase the I/O service time.

What's the moral of the story? That thin provisioning and data deduplication have no usefulness? That performance is all that matters?

No. The moral of the story is that to be efficient you need to think about efficiency in multiple dimensions: performance, capacity, power, operational simplicity, and flexibility. Here is a simple five-step sequence you can use to guide the process:

1. Look at your workload, and examine the IOps, MBps, and latency requirements.

2. Put the outliers to one side, and plan for the average.

3. Use reference architectures and a focused plan to design a virtualized configuration for the outlier heavy workloads.

4. Plan first on the most efficient way to meet the aggregate performance workloads.

5. Then, by using the performance configuration developed in step 4, back into the most efficient capacity configuration to hit that mark. Some workloads are performance bound (ergo, step 4 is the constraint), and some are capacity bound (ergo, step 5 is the constraint).

Let's quantify all this learning into applicable best practices:

When thinking about performance

◆ Do a little engineering by simple planning or estimation. Measure sample hosts, or use VMware Capacity Planner to profile the IOps and bandwidth workload of each host that will be virtualized onto the infrastructure. If you can't measure, at least estimate. For virtual desktops, estimate between 5 and 20 IOps. For light servers, estimate 50 to 100 IOps. Usually, most configurations are IOps bound, not throughput bound, but if you can, measure the average I/O size of the hosts (or again, use Capacity Planner). Although estimation can work for light server use cases, for heavy servers, don't ever estimate—measure them—it's so easy to measure, it's absolutely a "measure twice, cut once" case, particularly for VMs you know will have a heavy workload.

◆ For large applications (Exchange, SQL Server, SharePoint, Oracle, MySQL, and so on), the sizing, layout, and best practices for storage for large database workloads are not dissimilar to physical deployments and can be a good choice for RDMs or VMFS volumes with no other virtual disks. Also, leverage joint-reference architectures available from VMware and the storage vendors.

◆ Remember that the datastore will need to have enough IOps and capacity for the total of all the VMs. Just remember 80 to 180 IOps per spindle, depending on spindle type (refer to the "Disks" section in "Defining Common Storage Array Architectures" earlier in this chapter), to support the aggregate of all the VMs in it. If you just add up all the aggregate IOps needed by the sum of the VMs that will be in a datastore, you have a good approximation of the total. Additional I/Os are generated by the zeroing activity that occurs for thin and flat (but not thick, which is pre-zeroed up front), but this tends to be negligible. You lose some IOps because of the RAID protection, but you know you're in the ballpark if the number of spindles supporting the datastore (via a filesystem and NFS or a LUN and VMFS) times the number of IOps per spindle is more than the total number of IOps needed for the aggregate workload. Keep your storage vendor honest, and you'll have a much more successful virtualization project!

◆ Cache benefits are difficult to predict; they vary a great deal. If you can't do a test, assume they will have a large effect in terms of improving VM boot times with RDBMS environments on VMware, but almost no effect otherwise, so plan your spindle count cautiously.

When thinking about capacity

◆ Consider not only the VM disks in the datastores but also their snapshots, their swap, and their suspended state and memory. A good rule of thumb is to assume 25 percent more than from the virtual disks alone. If you use thin provisioning at the array level, oversizing the datastore has no downside, because only what is necessary is actually used.

◆ There is no exact best practice datastore-sizing model. Historically, people have recommended one fixed size or another. A simple model is to select a standard guideline for the number of VMs you feel comfortable with in a datastore, multiply that number by the average size of the virtual disks of each VM, add the overall 25 percent extra space, and use that as a standardized building block. Remember, VMFS and NFS datastores don't have an effective limit on the number of VMs—with VMFS you need to consider disk queuing and, to a much lesser extent, SCSI reservations; with NFS you need to consider the bandwidth to a single datastore.

◆ Be flexible and efficient. Use thin provisioning at the array level if possible, and if your array doesn't support it, use it at the VMware layer. It never hurts (so long as you monitor), but don't count on it resulting in needing fewer spindles (because of performance requirements).

◆ If your array doesn't support thin provisioning but does support extending LUNs, use thin provisioning at the vSphere layer, but start with smaller VMFS volumes to avoid oversizing and being inefficient.

◆ In general, don't oversize. Every modern array can add capacity dynamically, and you can use Storage vMotion to redistribute workloads. Use the new managed datastore function to set thresholds and actions, and then extend LUNs and the VMFS datastores using the new vSphere VMFS extension capability, or grow NFS datastores.

When thinking about availability

◆ Spend the bulk of your storage planning and configuration time to ensure your design has high availability. Check that array configuration, storage fabric (whether Fibre Channel or Ethernet), and NMP/MPP multipathing configuration (or NIC teaming/link aggregation and routing for NFS) are properly configured. Spend the effort to stay up to date with the interoperability matrices of your vendors and the firmware update processes.

◆ Remember, you can deal with performance and capacity issues as they come up nondisruptively (VMFS expansion/extends, array tools to add performance, and Storage vMotion). Something that affects the overall storage availability will be an emergency.

When deciding on a VM datastore placement philosophy, there are two common models: the predictive scheme and the adaptive scheme.

Predictive scheme

◆ Create several datastores (VMFS or NFS) with different storage characteristics, and label each datastore according to its characteristics.

◆ Locate each application in the appropriate RAID for its requirements by measuring the requirements in advance.

◆ Run the applications, and see whether VM performance is acceptable (or monitor the HBA queues as they approach the queue-full threshold).

◆ Use RDMs sparingly as needed.

Adaptive scheme

◆ Create a standardized datastore building-block model (VMFS or NFS).

◆ Place virtual disks on the datastore. Remember, regardless of what you hear, there's no practical datastore maximum number. The question is the performance scaling of the datastore.

◆ Run the applications and see whether disk performance is acceptable (on a VMFS data store, monitor the HBA queues as they approach the queue-full threshold).

- If performance is acceptable, you can place additional virtual disks on the datastore. If it is not, create a new datastore and use Storage vMotion to distribute the workload.

- Use RDMs sparingly.

My preference is a hybrid. Specifically, you can use the adaptive scheme coupled with starting with two wildly divergent datastore performance profiles (the idea from the predictive scheme), one for utility VMs and one for priority VMs.

Always read, follow, and leverage the key documentation:

- VMware's Fibre Channel and iSCSI SAN configuration guides

- VMware's HCL

- Your storage vendor's best practices/solutions guides

Sometimes the documents go out of date. Don't just ignore the guidance if you think it's incorrect; use the online community or reach out to VMware or your storage vendor to get the latest information.

Most important, have no fear!

Physical host and storage configurations have historically been extremely static, and the penalty of error in storage configuration from a performance or capacity standpoint was steep. The errors of misconfiguration would inevitably lead not only to application issues but to complex work and downtime to resolve. This pain of error has ingrained in administrators a tendency to overplan when it comes to performance and capacity.

Between the capabilities of modern arrays to modify many storage attributes dynamically and Storage vMotion (the ultimate "get out of jail free card"—including complete array replacement!), the penalty and risk are less about misconfiguration, and now the risk is more about oversizing or overbuying. You cannot be trapped with an underperforming configuration you can't change nondisruptively.

More important than any storage configuration or feature per se is to design a highly available configuration that meets your immediate needs and is as flexible to change as VMware makes the rest of the IT stack.

The Bottom Line

Differentiate and understand the fundamentals of shared storage, including SANs and NAS. vSphere depends on shared storage for advanced functions, cluster-wide availability, and the aggregate performance of all the VMs in a cluster. Designing high-performance and highly available shared storage infrastructure is possible on Fibre Channel, FCoE, and iSCSI SANs, and is possible using NAS; in addition, it's available for midrange to enterprise storage architectures. Always design the storage architecture to meet the performance requirements first, and then ensure that capacity requirements are met as a corollary.

Master It Identify examples where each of the protocol choices would be ideal for different vSphere deployments.

Master It Identify the three storage performance parameters and the primary determinant of storage performance and how to quickly estimate it for a given storage configuration.

Understand vSphere storage options. vSphere has three fundamental storage presentation models: VMFS on block, RDM, and NFS. The most flexible configurations use all three, predominantly via a shared-container model and selective use of RDMs.

Master It Characterize use cases for VMFS datastores, NFS datastores, and RDMs.

Master It If you're using VMFS and there's one performance metric to track, what would it be? Configure a monitor for that metric.

Configure storage at the vSphere layer. After a shared storage platform is selected, vSphere needs a storage network configured. The network (whether Fibre Channel or Ethernet based) must be designed to meet availability and throughput requirements, which is influenced by protocol choice and vSphere fundamental storage stack (and in the case of NFS, the network stack) architecture. Proper network design involves physical redundancy and physical or logical isolation mechanisms (SAN zoning and network VLANs). With connectivity in place, configure LUNs and VMFS datastores and/or NFS exports/NFS datastores using the predictive or adaptive model (or a hybrid model). Use Storage vMotion to resolve hot spots and other non-optimal VM placement.

Master It What would best identify an oversubscribed VMFS datastore from a performance standpoint? How would you identify the issue? What is it most likely to be? What would be two possible corrective actions you could take?

Master It A VMFS volume is filling up. What are three possible nondisruptive corrective actions you could take?

Master It What would best identify an oversubscribed NFS volume from a performance standpoint? How would you identify the issue? What is it most likely to be? What are two possible corrective actions you could take?

Configure storage at the VM layer. With datastores in place, create VMs. During the creation of the VMs, place VMs in the appropriate datastores and employ selective use of RDMs, but only where required. Leverage in-guest iSCSI where it makes sense, but understand the impact to your vSphere environment.

Master It Without turning the machine off, convert the virtual disks on a VMFS volume from thin to thick (eagerzeroedthick) and back to thin.

Master It Identify where you would use a physical compatibility mode RDM, and configure that use case.

Leverage best practices for SAN and NAS storage with vSphere. Read, follow, and leverage key VMware and storage vendors' best practices/solutions guide documentation. Don't oversize up front, but instead learn to leverage VMware and storage array features to monitor performance, queues, and backend load—and then nondisruptively adapt. Plan for performance first and capacity second. (Usually capacity is a given for performance requirements to be met.) Spend design time on availability design and on the large, heavy I/O VMs, and use flexible pool design for the general-purpose VMFS and NFS datastores.

Master It Quickly estimate the minimum usable capacity needed for 200 VMs with an average size of 40 GB. Make some assumptions about vSphere snapshots. What would be the raw capacity needed in the array if you used RAID 10? RAID 5 (4+1)? RAID 6 (10+2)? What would you do to nondisruptively cope if you ran out of capacity?

Master It Using the configurations in the previous question, what would the minimum amount of raw capacity need to be if there were actually only 20 GB of data in each VM, even though they are provisioning 40 GB and you used thick on an array that didn't support thin provisioning? What if the array *did* support thin provisioning? What if you used Storage vMotion to convert from thick to thin (both in the case where the array supports thin provisioning and in the case where it doesn't)?

Master It Estimate the number of spindles needed for 100 VMs that drive 200 IOps each and are 40 GB in size. Assume no RAID loss or cache gain. How many if you use 500 GB SATA 7,200 RPM? 300 GB 10K Fibre Channel/SAS? 300 GB 15K Fibre Channel/SAS? 160 GB consumer-grade SSD? 200 GB Enterprise Flash?

Chapter 7

Ensuring High Availability and Business Continuity

Ensuring high availability and business continuity is a key part of virtualization that is often overlooked or considered after the fact. It is equally as important as configuring storage devices and setting up virtual networking. Virtualization and VMware vSphere in particular enable new ways to provide high availability and business continuity. There are multiple layers where vSphere administrators can help provide high availability in a variety of ways depending on the needs of the business and the unique requirements of the organization. This chapter discusses some of the tools and techniques available for ensuring high availability and business continuity.

In this chapter, you will learn to

◆ Understand Windows clustering and the different types of clusters

◆ Use vSphere's built-in high-availability functionality

◆ Recognize differences between different high-availability solutions

◆ Understand additional components of business continuity

Understanding the Layers of High Availability

Even in non-virtualized environments, there are multiple ways to achieve high availability for OS instances and applications. When you introduce virtualization into the mix with vSphere, you gain additional methods of providing high availability. Figure 7.1 shows these different layers.

At each layer, there are tools and techniques for providing high availability and business continuity:

◆ Examples of high availability at the Application layer include Oracle Real Application Clusters (RAC).

◆ At the OS layer, solutions include OS clustering functionality, such as Windows Failover Clustering (WFC) for Windows Server.

◆ The Virtualization layer offers a number of features for high availability, including vSphere High Availability (HA) and vSphere Fault Tolerance (FT).

◆ High availability at the Physical layer is achieved through redundant hardware — multiple network interface cards (NICs) or host bus adapters (HBAs), multiple storage area network (SAN) switches and fabrics, multiple paths to storage, multiple controllers in storage arrays, redundant power supplies, and so forth.

FIGURE 7.1
Each layer has its own forms of high availability.

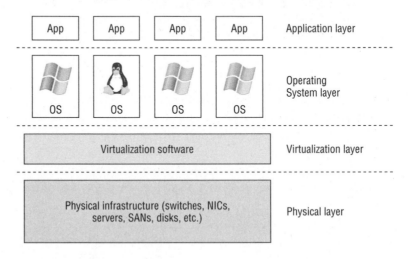

Each of these various technologies or techniques has its own strengths and weaknesses. For example, providing redundancy at the Physical layer is great, but it doesn't help with failures at the Application layer. Conversely, protecting against application failures is great but won't help much if the underlying hardware isn't redundant. As you set forth on a journey to establish high availability for your virtualized workloads, keep in mind that there is no "one size fits all" solution. Use the right tool for the job based on your specific requirements.

Given that this is a book on vSphere, I can cover only some of the various possibilities for ensuring high availability, so I'll focus my efforts on three key technologies or techniques that help provide high availability:

◆ OS clustering in Microsoft Windows

◆ ESXi host clustering using vSphere HA

◆ VM mirroring using vSphere FT

After a discussion of these three broad areas, I discuss some areas relating to business continuity.

First, though, let's start with a well-known technique for achieving high availability at the OS level: OS clustering, specifically clustering Microsoft Windows Server instances.

Clustering VMs

Because Windows Server 2008 and its predecessors are widely used in corporate and enterprise datacenters today, it's quite likely that at one point or another you've been asked to create or support a Windows-based cluster. There are two primary ways to use clustering to provide high availability for Windows Server 2008:

- Network Load Balancing (NLB) clustering

- Windows Failover Clustering (WFC)

While both of these methods are described as clustering, they are primarily targeted for very different purposes. NLB clustering is typically provided as a way to provide scalable performance, while WFC is usually focused on providing redundancy and high availability in the form of active/passive workload clustering.

Some experts say that vSphere HA eliminates the need for WFC because — as you'll see later in this chapter in the section "Implementing vSphere High Availability" — vSphere HA can provide failover in the event of a physical host failure. That's true, but it's important to understand that these high-availability mechanisms operate at different layers (refer back to Figure 7.1). WFC operates at the OS layer, providing redundancy in the event that one of the OS instances in the cluster fails. That OS failure could be the result of hardware failure. vSphere HA (and vSphere FT) operate at a layer beneath the OS and don't operate in exactly the same way. As I'll reiterate throughout this chapter, each of the high-availability mechanisms described in this chapter has advantages and disadvantages. You'll want to be sure you understand these so that you can choose the right approach for your specific environment.

Table 7.1 provides a quick overview of the clustering support provided by Windows Server 2003 and Windows Server 2008.

TABLE 7.1:   Windows Server 2003/2008 clustering support

OPERATING SYSTEM	NETWORK LOAD BALANCING	WINDOWS FAILOVER CLUSTERING
Windows Server 2003/2008 Web Edition	Yes (up to 32 nodes)	No
Windows Server 2003/2008 Standard Edition	Yes (up to 32 nodes)	No
Windows Server 2003/2008 Enterprise Edition	Yes (up to 32 nodes)	Yes (up to 8 nodes in 2003 and 16 nodes in 2008)
Windows Server 2003/2008 Datacenter Edition	Yes (up to 32 nodes)	Yes (up to 8 nodes in 2003 and 16 nodes in 2008)

I'll start this section with a quick review of NLB clustering and how you can use it in your vSphere environment.

Introducing Network Load Balancing Clustering

The Network Load Balancing configuration involves an aggregation of servers that balances the requests for applications or services. In a typical NLB cluster, all nodes are active participants in the cluster and are consistently responding to requests for services. If one of the nodes in the NLB cluster goes down, client connections are simply redirected to another available node in the NLB cluster. NLB clusters are most commonly deployed as a means of providing enhanced performance and availability. Because client connections could be directed to any available node within the cluster, NLB clusters are best suited for scenarios involving stateless connections and protocols, such as environments using Microsoft Internet Information Services (IIS), virtual private networking (VPN), or Microsoft Internet Security and Acceleration (ISA) Server, to name a few. Figure 7.2 summarizes the architecture of an NLB cluster made up of Windows-based VMs (the architecture is the same for physical systems).

FIGURE 7.2
An NLB cluster can contain up to 32 active nodes (only 5 are shown here) that distribute traffic equally across each node. The NLB software allows the nodes to share a common name and IP address that is referenced by clients.

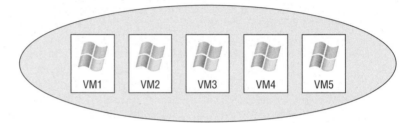

Load-balanced identity: www.v12nlab.net (10.1.1.10)

NETWORK LOAD-BALANCING SUPPORT FROM VMWARE

As of this writing, VMware supports NLB, but you will need to run NLB in Multicast mode to support vMotion and VMs on different physical hosts. You will also need to configure static Address Resolution Protocol (ARP) entries on the physical switch to achieve this, which greatly limits the scalability of the solution. If NLB is running in Unicast mode, then the VMs will all need to be running on the same host. Another option to consider would be the use of third-party load balancers to achieve the same results.

NLB clusters aren't the right fit for every application or workload. For applications and workloads that aren't a good fit for NLB, Microsoft offers Windows Failover Clustering. I describe this in the next section.

Introducing Windows Failover Clustering

Unlike NLB clusters, Windows Failover Clusters (which I'll refer to as server clusters or failover clusters from here on) are used solely for the sake of availability. Server clusters do not provide performance enhancements outside of high availability. In a typical server cluster, multiple nodes are configured to be able to own a service or application resource, but only one node owns the resource at a given time. Server clusters are most often used for applications like Microsoft Exchange, Microsoft SQL Server, and DHCP services, which each share a need for a common datastore. The common datastore houses the information accessible by the node that is online and currently owns the resource, as well as the other possible owners that could assume ownership in the event of failure. Each node requires at least two network connections: one for the production network and one for the cluster service heartbeat between nodes. Figure 7.3 details the structure of a server cluster built using physical systems (I'll illustrate several ways how server clusters are built with VMs later in this section).

FIGURE 7.3
Server clusters are best suited for applications and services like SQL Server, Exchange Server, DHCP, and so on, which use a common data set.

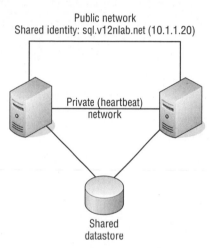

Public network
Shared identity: sql.v12nlab.net (10.1.1.20)

Private (heartbeat) network

Shared datastore

WINDOWS CLUSTERING STORAGE ARCHITECTURES

As you saw in Table 7.1, server clusters built on Windows Server 2003 can support only up to 8 nodes, and Windows Server 2008 can support up to 16 nodes when using a Fibre Channel–switched fabric. Storage architectures that use SCSI disks as direct attached storage or that use a Fibre Channel–arbitrated loop result in a maximum of only 2 nodes in a server cluster. Clustering VMs on an ESXi host utilizes a simulated SCSI shared storage connection and is therefore limited to only 2-node clustering.

Server clusters, when constructed properly, provide automatic failover of services and applications hosted across multiple cluster nodes. When multiple nodes are configured as a cluster for a service or application resource, as I said previously, only one node owns the resource at any given time. When the current resource owner experiences failure, causing a loss in the heartbeat between the cluster nodes, another node assumes ownership of the resource to allow continued access with minimal data loss. To configure multiple Windows Server 2008 nodes into a Microsoft cluster, the following requirements must be met:

◆ Nodes must be running either Enterprise Edition or Datacenter Edition of Windows Server 2008.

◆ All nodes should have access to the same storage device(s). The specific details of the storage device(s) and how they are shared will depend on how the cluster is built.

◆ All nodes should have two similarly connected and configured network adapters: one for the production (or public) network and one for the heartbeat (or private) network.

◆ All nodes should have Microsoft Cluster Services for the version of Windows that you are using.

Before I can provide you with the details on how to build a server cluster running Microsoft Windows Server 2008 on vSphere, I first need to discuss the different scenarios of how server clusters can be built.

REVIEWING VM CLUSTERING CONFIGURATIONS

Building a server cluster with Windows Server 2008 VMs requires one of three different configurations, as follows:

Cluster in a Box The clustering of two VMs on the same ESXi host is also known as a *cluster in a box*. This is the easiest of the three configurations to set up. No special configuration needs to be applied to make this configuration work.

Cluster across Boxes The clustering of two VMs that are running on different ESXi hosts is known as a *cluster across boxes*. VMware had restrictions in place for this configuration in earlier versions: the cluster node's C: drive must be stored on the host's local storage or local VMFS datastore, the cluster shared storage must be stored on Fibre Channel external disks, and you must use raw device mappings on the storage. In vSphere 4 and vSphere 5, this was changed and updated to allow .vmdk files on the SAN and to allow the cluster VM boot drive or C: drive on the SAN, but vMotion and vSphere Distributed Resource Scheduler (DRS) are not supported using Microsoft-clustered VMs.

Physical to Virtual Clustering The clustering of a physical server and a VM together is often referred as a *physical to virtual cluster*. This configuration of using physical and virtual servers together gives you the best of both worlds, and the only other added restriction is that you cannot use Virtual Compatibility mode with the RDMs.

I'll examine the cluster-in-a-box and the physical-to-virtual clustering configurations in more detail in the sections "Examining Cluster-in-a-Box Scenarios" and "Examining Physical-to-Virtual Clustering," respectively. I'll examine and show you how to build a cluster across boxes in the section "Examining Cluster-across-Boxes Configurations."

Building Windows-based server clusters has long been considered an advanced technology implemented only by those with high technical skills in implementing and managing high-availability environments. Although this might be more rumor than truth, it is certainly a more complex solution to set up and maintain.

Although you might achieve results setting up clustered VMs, you may not receive support for your clustered solution if you violate any of the clustering restrictions put forth by VMware. The following list summarizes and reviews the dos and don'ts of clustering VMs as published by VMware:

◆ 32-bit and 64-bit VMs can be configured as nodes in a server cluster.

◆ Majority node set clusters with application-level replication (for example, Microsoft Exchange 2007 Cluster Continuous Replication) are now supported.

◆ Only two-node clustering is allowed.

◆ Clustering is not supported on FCoE, iSCSI, or NFS datastores.

◆ Clustering does not support NIC teaming in the VMs.

◆ VMs configured as cluster nodes must use the LSI Logic SCSI adapter (for Windows Server 2003) or the LSI Logic SAS adapter (for Windows Server 2008) and the vmxnet network adapter.

◆ VMs in a clustered configuration are not valid candidates for vMotion, and they can't participate in vSphere HA, vSphere FT, or vSphere DRS. They can be part of a cluster that has these features enabled, but the features must be disabled for the VMs participating in the server cluster.

◆ VMs in a server cluster cannot use N_Port ID Virtualization.

◆ All the ESXi systems hosting VMs that are part of a server cluster must be running the same version of ESXi.

There is something else that you need to do. You must set the I/O timeout to 60 seconds or more by modifying `HKLM\System\CurrentControlSet\Services\Disk\TimeOutValue`, and if you re-create a cluster, you'll need to reset the value again.

So, let's get into some more details on clustering and look at the specific clustering options available in the virtual environment. I will start with the most basic design configuration, the cluster in a box.

EXAMINING CLUSTER-IN-A-BOX SCENARIOS

The cluster-in-a-box scenario involves configuring two VMs hosted by the same ESXi host as nodes in a server cluster. The shared disks of the server cluster can exist as `.vmdk` files stored on local Virtual Machine File System (VMFS) volumes or on a shared VMFS volume. Figure 7.4 details the configuration of a cluster in a box.

After reviewing the diagram of a cluster-in-a-box configuration, you might wonder why you would want to deploy such a thing. The truth is, you wouldn't want to deploy a cluster-in-a-box configuration because it still maintains a single point of failure. With both VMs running on the same host, if that host fails, both VMs fail. This architecture contradicts the very reason for creating failover clusters. A cluster-in-a-box configuration still contains a single point of failure that can result in downtime of the clustered application. If the ESXi host hosting the two-node cluster-in-a-box configuration fails, then both nodes are lost, and a failover does not occur. This setup might, and I use *might* loosely, be used only to "play" with clustering services or to test clustering services and configurations. But ultimately, even for testing, it is best to use the cluster-across-box configurations to get a better understanding of how this might be deployed in a production scenario.

FIGURE 7.4

A cluster-in-a-box configuration does not provide protection against a single point of failure. Therefore, it is not a common or suggested form of deploying Microsoft server clusters in VMs.

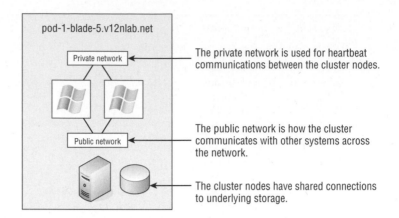

pod-1-blade-5.v12nlab.net

Private network — The private network is used for heartbeat communications between the cluster nodes.

Public network — The public network is how the cluster communicates with other systems across the network.

The cluster nodes have shared connections to underlying storage.

CONFIGURATION OPTIONS FOR VIRTUAL CLUSTERING

As suggested in the first part of this chapter, server clusters are deployed for high availability. High availability is not achieved by using a cluster-in-a-box configuration, and therefore you should avoid this configuration for any type of critical production applications and services.

EXAMINING CLUSTER-ACROSS-BOXES CONFIGURATIONS

Although the cluster-in-a-box scenario is more of an experimental or education tool for clustering, the cluster-across-boxes configuration provides a solid solution for critical VMs with stringent uptime requirements — for example, the enterprise-level servers and services like SQL Server and Exchange Server that are heavily relied on by the bulk of end users. The cluster-across-boxes scenario, as the name applies, draws its high availability from the fact that the two nodes in the cluster are managed on different ESXi hosts. In the event that one of the hosts fails, the second node of the cluster will assume ownership of the cluster group and its resources, and the service or application will continue responding to client requests.

The cluster-across-boxes configuration requires that VMs have access to the same shared storage, which must reside on a Fibre Channel storage device external to the ESXi hosts where the VMs run. The virtual hard drives that make up the operating system volume of the cluster nodes can be a standard VMDK implementation; however, the drives used as the shared storage must be set up as a special kind of drive called a *Raw Device Mapping* (RDM). An RDM is a feature that allows a VM to establish direct access to a LUN on a SAN device. I also discussed RDMs briefly in Chapter 6, "Creating and Configuring Storage Devices."

A cluster-across-boxes configuration requires a more complex setup than a cluster-in-a-box configuration. When clustering across boxes, all proper communication between VMs and all proper communication from VMs and storage devices must be configured properly. Figure 7.5 provides details on the setup of a two-node VM cluster-across-box configuration using Windows Server 2008 as the guest operating system (guest OS).

USING RAW DEVICE MAPPINGS IN YOUR VIRTUAL CLUSTERS

An RDM is not a direct access to a LUN, and it is not a normal virtual hard disk file. An RDM is a blend of the two. When adding a new disk to a VM, as you will soon see, the Add Hardware Wizard presents the RDMs as an option on the Select A Disk page. This page defines the RDM as having the ability to give a VM direct access to the SAN, thereby allowing SAN management. I know this seems like a contradiction to the opening statement of this sidebar; however, I'm getting to the part that, oddly enough, makes both statements true.

By selecting an RDM for a new disk, you're forced to select a compatibility mode for the RDM. An RDM can be configured in either Physical Compatibility mode or Virtual Compatibility mode. The Physical Compatibility mode option allows the VM to have direct raw LUN access. The Virtual Compatibility mode, however, is the hybrid configuration that allows raw LUN access but only through a VMDK file acting as a proxy. The following image details the architecture of using an RDM in Virtual Compatibility mode.

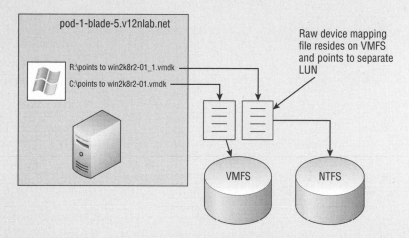

So, why choose one over the other if both are ultimately providing raw LUN access? Because the RDM in Virtual Compatibility mode uses a VMDK proxy file, it offers the advantage of allowing snapshots to be taken. By using the Virtual Compatibility mode, you will gain the ability to use snapshots on top of the raw LUN access in addition to any SAN-level snapshot or mirroring software. Or, of course, in the absence of SAN-level software, the VMware snapshot feature can certainly be a valuable tool. The decision to use Physical Compatibility or Virtual Compatibility is predicated solely on the opportunity and/or need to use VMware snapshot technology or when using physical-to-virtual clustering.

Make sure you document things well when you start using RDMs. Any storage that is presented to ESXi and is not formatted with VMFS will show up as available storage. If all the administrators are not on the same page, it is easy to take a LUN that was used for an RDM and reprovision that LUN as a VMFS datastore, effectively blowing away the RDM data in the process. I have seen this mistake happen firsthand, and let me tell you, the process is very quick to erase any data that is there. I have gone so far as to create a separate column in vCenter Server to list any RDM LUNs that are configured, to make sure everyone has a reference point.

FIGURE 7.5
A Microsoft cluster built on VMs residing on separate ESXi hosts requires shared storage access from each VM using an RDM.

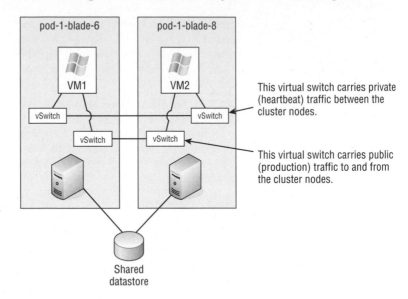

This virtual switch carries private (heartbeat) traffic between the cluster nodes.

This virtual switch carries public (production) traffic to and from the cluster nodes.

Let's keep moving and perform the following steps to configure Microsoft Cluster Services on Windows Server 2008 across VMs on separate ESXi hosts.

Creating the First Cluster Node in Windows Server 2008

Perform the following steps to create the first cluster node:

1. Using the vSphere Client, create a new VM, and install Windows Server 2008 (or clone an existing VM or template with Windows Server 2008 already installed).

   Refer to Chapter 9, "Creating and Managing Virtual Machines," for more details on creating VMs; refer to Chapter 10, "Using Templates and vApps," for more information on cloning VMs.

2. Configure the VM so that it has two NICs, as shown in Figure 7.6 — one for the public (production) network and one for the private (heartbeat) network. Assign IP addresses within Windows Server 2008 as needed. Shut down the VM after you have completed the networking configuration.

3. Right-click the new VM and select Edit Settings.

4. Click the Add button, select Hard Disk, and click Next.

5. Select the Raw Device Mappings radio button, and then click Next.

6. Select the appropriate target LUN from the list of available targets, and then click Next.

FIGURE 7.6
A node in a
Microsoft Windows
server cluster
requires at least
two NICs. One
adapter must be
able to commu-
nicate on the pro-
duction network,
and the second
adapter is config-
ured for internal
cluster heartbeat
communication.

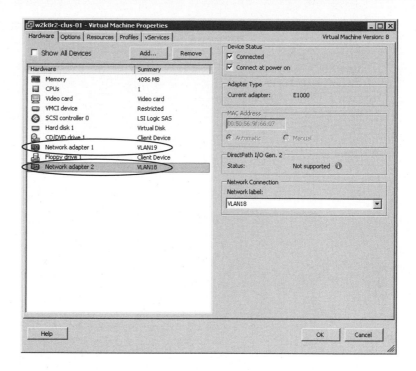

I'll remind you again: make sure you have the correct LUN, or you could overwrite important data!

7. Select Store With The Virtual Machine to keep the VMDK proxy file on the same datastore as the VM, and then click Next.

8. Select either Physical or Virtual for the RDM Compatibility mode.

Different versions have different requirements. In this case, select Physical and then click Next.

RDM REQUIREMENTS FOR WINDOWS SERVER 2003 AND WINDOWS SERVER 2008

When building a cluster across multiple ESXi hosts using Windows Server 2003, you can use Virtual mode RDMs. If you are using Windows Server 2008 to build the cluster across ESXi hosts, you must use Physical Compatibility mode.

---

9. Select the virtual device node to which the RDM should be connected, as shown in Figure 7.7, and then click Next.

Note that you must select a different SCSI node; you can't put the RDM on SCSI 0.

FIGURE 7.7

The virtual device node for the additional RDMs in a cluster node must be a different SCSI node.

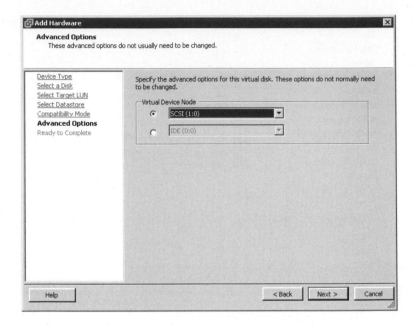

10. Click the Finish button.

11. Select the new SCSI controller that was added as a result of adding the RDMs on a separate SCSI controller.

12. Select the Physical radio button in the SCSI Bus Sharing options, as shown in Figure 7.8.

13. Repeat steps 2 through 9 to configure additional RDMs for shared storage locations needed by nodes of a Microsoft server cluster.

    In this case, I'm going to present a single RDM.

14. Power on the first node of the cluster. Verify that you've assigned valid IP addresses to the network adapters configured for the production and heartbeat networks. Then format the new drive representing the RDM and assign drive letters, as shown in Figure 7.9.

FIGURE 7.8
The SCSI bus sharing for the new SCSI adapter must be set to Physical to support running a Microsoft cluster across multiple ESXi hosts.

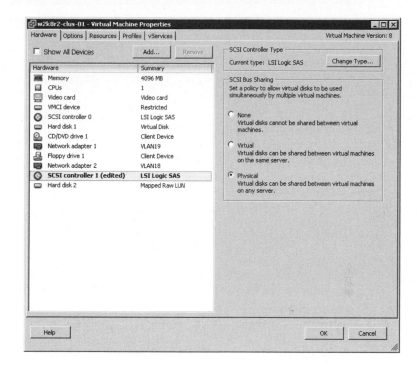

FIGURE 7.9
The RDM presented to the first cluster node is formatted and assigned a drive letter.

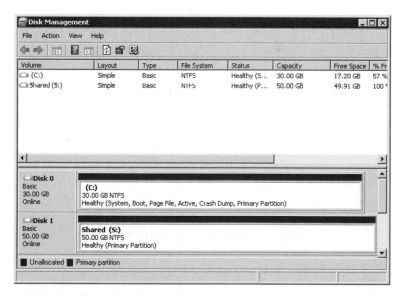

15. Proceed to the next section to configure the second cluster node and the respective ESXi host.

Creating the Second Cluster Node in Windows Server 2008

Perform the following steps to create the second cluster node:

1. Using the vSphere Client, create a second VM running Windows Server 2008 that is a member of the same Active Directory domain as the first cluster node. Ensure that the VM has two NICs and that the NICs have appropriate IP addresses assigned for the production (public) and heartbeat (private) networks.

2. Shut down the second VM.

3. Add the same RDMs to the second cluster node.

   This time around, you can't select Raw Device Mappings, because the LUN you selected when setting up the first node won't be listed (it's already been used). Instead, select Use An Existing Virtual Disk and then navigate to the location of the VMDK proxy file (if you selected Store With The Virtual Machine in step 7 of setting up the first node, you'll find a VMDK file there with the same size as the backing LUN).

   Be sure to use the same SCSI node values on the second VM. For example, if the first node used SCSI 1:0 for the first RDM, then configure the second node to use the same configuration. Don't forget to edit the SCSI bus sharing configuration for the new SCSI adapter (Physical SCSI bus sharing).

4. Power on the second VM.

5. Verify that the hard drives corresponding to the RDMs can be seen in Disk Manager. At this point, the drives will show a status of Healthy, but drive letters will not be assigned.

Creating the Failover Cluster in Windows Server 2008

Perform the following steps to create the management cluster:

1. Log into the first node as an administrative user.

2. Launch Server Manager from the Start menu, if it doesn't launch automatically.

3. Click Add Features.

4. From the list of features in the Add Features Wizard, select Failover Clustering and click Next.

5. Click Install. When the install is completed, click Close.

6. Repeat this process on the second node.

With Failover Clustering installed on both nodes, you can validate the cluster configuration to ensure that everything is configured properly:

1. Log into the first node as an administrative user.

2. From the Start menu, select Administrative Tools ➢ Failover Cluster Management.

3. Click Validate A Configuration. This launches the Validate A Configuration Wizard. Click Next to start the wizard.

4. Enter the names of both the first and second cluster nodes, clicking Add after each server name to add it to the list. Click Next.

5. Leave the default selection (Run All Tests) and click Next.

6. Click Next at the Confirmation step.

7. Review the report. If any errors are reported, follow the guidance to address the errors. Click Finish when you are done.

Now you're ready to create the cluster:

1. While still logged into the first node as an administrative user and still running Failover Cluster Management, click Create A Cluster.

2. At the first screen of the Create Cluster Wizard, click Next.

3. Enter the names of both nodes, and click Add after each server to add it to the list. Click Next to continue.

4. Select the option to not run the validation tests (you've already run them). Click Next.

5. Specify a cluster name and an IP address on the production (public) network. Click Next to continue.

6. Click Next at the Confirmation screen.

7. The Create Cluster Wizard will perform the necessary steps to create the cluster and bring the resources online. When it has completed, review the report and click Finish.

After the cluster is up and running, you can use the Failover Cluster Management application to add resources, applications, and services. Some applications, such as Microsoft SQL Server and Microsoft Exchange Server, not only are cluster-aware applications but also allow for the creation of a server cluster as part of the standard installation wizard. Other cluster-aware applications and services can be configured into a cluster using the cluster administrator. Refer to the documentation for Microsoft Windows Server 2008 and/or the specific application you want to cluster for more details.

EXAMINING PHYSICAL-TO-VIRTUAL CLUSTERING

The last type of clustering scenario to discuss is physical-to-virtual clustering. As you might have guessed, this involves building a cluster with two nodes where one node is a physical machine and the other node is a VM. Figure 7.10 details the setup of a two-node physical-to-virtual cluster.

The constraints surrounding the construction of a physical-to-virtual cluster are identical to those noted in the previous configuration. Likewise, the steps to configure the VM acting as a node in the physical-to-virtual cluster are identical to the steps outlined in the previous section, with one addition: you must set up the RDMs in Physical Compatibility mode, regardless of the version of Windows Server you're using. The VM must have access to all the same storage locations as the physical machine. The VM must also have access to the same pair of networks used by the physical machine for production and heartbeat communication, respectively.

FIGURE 7.10
Clustering physical machines with VM counterparts can be a cost-effective way of providing high availability.

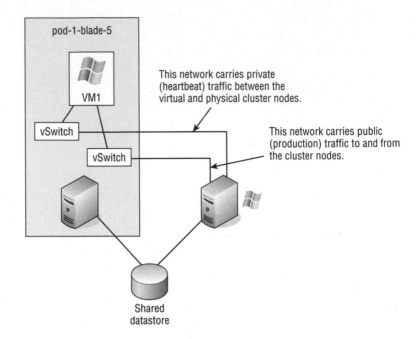

The advantage to implementing a physical-to-virtual cluster is the resulting high availability with reduced financial outlay. Physical-to-virtual clustering, because of the two-node limitation of VM clustering, ends up as an N+1 clustered solution, where N is the number of physical servers in the environment plus one additional physical server to host the VMs. In each case, each physical VM cluster creates a failover pair. With the scope of the cluster design limited to a failover pair, the most important design aspect in a physical-to-virtual cluster is the scale of the host running the ESXi host. As you may have figured, the more powerful the ESXi host, the more failover incidents it can handle. A more powerful ESXi host will handle multiple physical host failures better, whereas a less powerful ESXi host might handle only a single physical host failure before performance levels experience a noticeable decline. Figure 7.11 shows an example of many-to-one physical-to-virtual clustering.

OS CLUSTERING IS NOT LIMITED TO WINDOWS

Although I've only discussed Windows Server–based OS clustering methods in this section, you are not limited to Windows to use OS clustering. Other supported OSes also offer ways to provide high availability within the OS itself.

Now that I've covered OS clustering in Windows Server, let's take a look at VMware's version of high availability. VMware has a built-in option called vSphere High Availability (HA). As you'll see, vSphere HA uses a very different method than OS clustering to provide high availability.

FIGURE 7.11
Using a single powerful ESXi system to host multiple failover clusters is one use case for physical-to-virtual clustering.

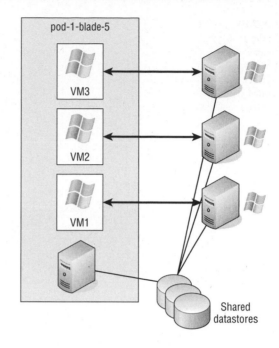

pod-1-blade-5

VM3

VM2

VM1

Shared datastores

Implementing vSphere High Availability

You've already seen how you can use OS clustering to provide high availability for OSes and applications. In addition to OS clustering, vSphere provides a feature intended to provide high availability at the virtualization layer as well. vSphere High Availability (HA) is a component of the vSphere product that provides for the automatic failover of VMs. Because the term "high availability" can mean different things to different people, it's important to understand the behavior of vSphere HA to ensure that you are using the right high-availability mechanism to meet the requirements of your organization. Depending on your requirements, one of the other high-availability mechanisms described in this chapter might be more appropriate.

A COMPLETE REWRITE FROM PREVIOUS VERSIONS

The underpinnings of vSphere HA underwent a complete rewrite for vSphere 5. If you are familiar with previous versions of vSphere, keep this in mind as you look at how vSphere HA behaves in this version.

Understanding vSphere High Availability

The vSphere HA feature is designed to provide an automatic restart of the VMs that were running on an ESXi host at the time it became unavailable, as shown in Figure 7.12.

FIGURE 7.12
vSphere HA provides an automatic restart of VMs that were running on an ESXi host when it failed.

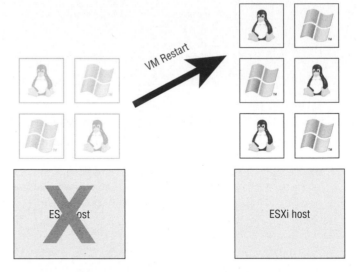

vSphere HA primarily targets ESXi host failures, but it can also be used to protect against VM- and application-level failures. In all cases, vSphere HA uses a restart of the VM as the mechanism for addressing the detected failure. This means there is a period of downtime when a failure occurs. Unfortunately, you can't calculate the exact duration of the downtime because it is unknown ahead of time how long it will take to boot a VM or a series of VMs. From this you can gather that at this point vSphere HA might not provide the same level of high availability as found in other high-availability solutions. Further, when a failover occurs between ESXi hosts as a result of the vSphere HA feature, there is a slight potential for data loss and/or filesystem corruption because the VM was immediately powered off when the server failed and then brought back up minutes later on another server. However, given the journaling filesystems in use by Windows and many distributions of Linux, this possibility is relatively slim.

 **Real World Scenario**

vSphere HA Experience in the Field

I want to mention my own personal experience with vSphere HA and the results I encountered. Your mileage might vary, but this should give you a reasonable expectation of what to expect. I had a VMware ESXi host that was a member of a five-node cluster. This node crashed sometime during the night, and when the host went down, it took anywhere from 15 to 20 VMs with it. vSphere HA kicked in and restarted all the VMs as expected.

What made this an interesting experience is that the crash must have happened right after the polling of the monitoring and alerting server. All the VMs that were on the general alerting schedule were restarted without triggering any alerts. We did have some of those VMs with a more aggressive monitoring that did trip off alerts that were recovered before anyone was able to log on to the system and investigate. I tried to argue the point that if an alert never fired, did the downtime really happen? I did not get too far with that argument but was pleased with the results.

> In another case, during testing I had a VM running on a two-node cluster. I pulled the power cords on the host that the VM was running to create the failure. My time to recovery from pull to ping was between five and six minutes. That's not too bad for general use but not good enough for all cases. vSphere Fault Tolerance (FT) can now fill that gap for even the most important and critical servers in your environment. I'll talk more about vSphere FT in a bit.

Understanding vSphere HA's Underpinnings

On the surface, the functionality of vSphere HA is similar to the functionality provided in previous versions of vSphere. Under the covers, though, vSphere HA uses a new VMware-developed tool known as Fault Domain Manager (FDM). FDM was developed from the ground up to replace Automated Availability Manager (AAM), which powered vSphere HA in earlier versions of vSphere. AAM had a number of notable limitations, including a strong dependence on name resolution and scalability limits. FDM was developed to address these limitations while still providing all the same functionality from earlier versions of vSphere. FDM also offers a couple of significant improvements over AAM:

- ◆ FDM uses a master/slave architecture that does not rely on primary/secondary host designations.

- ◆ FDM uses both the management network and storage devices for communication.

- ◆ FDM introduces support for IPv6.

- ◆ FDM addresses the issues of both network partition and network isolation.

FDM uses the concept of an agent that runs on each ESXi host. This agent is separate and decoupled from the vCenter management agents that vCenter uses to communicate with ESXi hosts (this management agent is known as vpxa). This agent gets installed into the ESXi hosts at `/opt/vmware/fdm` and stores its configuration files at `/etc/opt/vmware/fdm` (note that you must enable SSH and the ESXi shell in order to view these directories).

Although FDM is markedly different from AAM, as an end user you will notice very little difference in how vSphere HA operates. Therefore, I generally won't refer to FDM directly, but instead I'll refer to vSphere HA. I did want to bring it to your attention, though, so that you are aware of the underlying differences.

When vSphere HA is enabled, the vSphere HA agents participate in an election to pick a vSphere HA master. The vSphere HA master is responsible for a number of key tasks within a vSphere HA–enabled cluster:

- ◆ The vSphere HA master monitors slave hosts and will restart VMs in the event of a slave host failure.

- ◆ The vSphere HA master monitors the power state of all protected VMs. If a protected VM fails, it will restart the VM.

- ◆ The vSphere HA master manages the list of hosts that are members of the cluster and manages the process of adding and removing hosts from the cluster.

- ◆ The vSphere HA master manages the list of protected VMs. It updates this list after each user-initiated power-on or power-off operation. These updates are at the request of vCenter Server, which requests the master to protect or unprotect VMs.

♦ The vSphere HA master caches the cluster configuration. The master notifies and informs slave hosts of changes in the cluster configuration.

♦ The vSphere HA master host sends heartbeat messages to the slave hosts so that the slave hosts know the master is alive.

♦ The vSphere HA master reports state information to vCenter Server. vCenter Server typically communicates only with the master.

As you can see, the role of the vSphere HA master is quite important. For this reason, if the existing master fails, a new vSphere HA master is automatically elected. The new master will then take over the responsibilities listed here, including communication with vCenter Server.

DOES VCENTER SERVER TALK TO VSPHERE HA SLAVE HOSTS?

There are a few instances in which vCenter Server will talk to vSphere HA agents on slave hosts. Some of these instances include: when it is scanning for a vSphere HA master, when a host is reported as isolated or partitioned, or if the existing master informs vCenter that it cannot reach a slave agent.

Once an ESXi host in a vSphere HA–enabled cluster elects a vSphere HA master, all other hosts become slaves connected to that master. The responsibilities of the slave hosts include the following:

♦ A slave host watches the runtime state of the VMs running locally on that host. Significant changes in the runtime state of these VMs are forwarded to the vSphere HA master.

♦ vSphere HA slaves monitor the health of the master. If the master fails, slaves will participate in a new master election.

♦ vSphere HA slave hosts implement vSphere HA features that don't require central coordination by the master. This includes VM Health Monitoring.

The role of any given ESXi host within a vSphere HA–enabled cluster is noted on the Summary tab of the ESXi host within the vSphere Client. The composite screenshot in Figure 7.13 shows how the vSphere Client presents this information.

I mentioned that vSphere HA uses both the management network as well as storage devices to communicate. In the event that the master cannot communicate with a slave across the management network, the master can check its *heartbeat datastores* — selected datastores used by vSphere HA for communication — to see if the slave host is still alive. This functionality is what helps vSphere HA deal with network partition as well as network isolation.

Network partition is the term used to describe the situation in which one or more slave hosts cannot communicate with the master even though they still have network connectivity. In this case, vSphere HA is able to use the heartbeat datastores to detect whether the partitioned hosts are still live and whether action needs to be taken to protect VMs on those hosts.

Network isolation is the situation in which one or more slave hosts have lost all management network connectivity. Isolated hosts can neither communicate with the vSphere HA master nor communicate with other ESXi hosts. In this case, the slave host uses heartbeat datastores to notify the master that it is isolated. The slave host uses a special binary file, the `host-X-poweron` file, to notify the master. The vSphere HA master can then take the appropriate action to ensure that the VMs are protected. I'll discuss network isolation and how an ESXi host reacts to network isolation later in this chapter in the section "vSphere High Availability Isolation Response."

FIGURE 7.13

The status of an ESXi host as either master or slave is provided on the host's Summary tab. Here you can see both a master host and a slave host.

Figure 7.14 shows the files on a VMFS datastore that vSphere HA uses for storage heartbeating between the vSphere HA master and slave hosts.

In the section "Setting vSphere High Availability Datastore Heartbeating," I'll show you how to see which datastores are used as heartbeat datastores, as well as how to tell vSphere HA which datastores should or should not be used for heartbeating.

With this overview of the vSphere HA architecture and behavior under your belt, let's move on to enabling vSphere HA to protect your VMs.

Enabling vSphere High Availability

Let's review the requirements of vSphere HA. To implement vSphere HA, all of the following requirements should be met:

- All hosts in a vSphere HA-enabled cluster must have access to the same shared storage locations used by all VMs on the cluster. This includes any Fibre Channel, FCoE, iSCSI, and NFS datastores used by VMs.

- All hosts in a vSphere HA cluster should have an identical virtual networking configuration. If a new switch is added to one host, the same new switch should be added to all hosts in the cluster. If you are using a vSphere Distributed Switch (vDS), all hosts should be participating in the same vDS.

FIGURE 7.14
vSphere HA uses the host-X-poweron files for a slave host to notify the master that it has become isolated from the network.

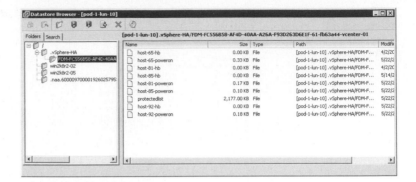

A TEST FOR VSPHERE HA

An easy and simple test for identifying vSphere HA capability for a VM is to perform a vMotion. The requirements of vMotion are actually more stringent than those for performing a vSphere HA failover, though some of the requirements are identical. In short, if a VM can successfully perform a vMotion across the hosts in a cluster, then it is safe to assume that vSphere HA will be able to power on that VM from any of the hosts. To perform a full test of a VM on a cluster with four nodes, perform a vMotion from node 1 to node 2, node 2 to node 3, node 3 to node 4, and finally node 4 back to node 1. If it works, then the VM has passed the test!

As with earlier versions, vSphere HA is a cluster-level configuration. In order to use vSphere HA to protect VMs, you must first place your ESXi hosts into a cluster. Remember, a VMware cluster represents a logical aggregation of CPU and memory resources. With vSphere HA, a cluster also represents a logical protection boundary. VMs can be protected by vSphere HA only if they are running on an ESXi host in a vSphere HA–enabled cluster. By editing the cluster settings, you can enable the vSphere HA feature for a cluster, as you can see in Figure 7.15.

When vSphere HA is enabled for a cluster, it will elect a master as described in the previous section. The other hosts in the cluster will become slave hosts connected to that master host. You can observe this process by watching the Tasks pane of the vSphere Client when you enable vSphere HA. Figure 7.16 shows an example of the tasks that are generated when you enable vSphere HA for a cluster.

After vSphere HA is enabled, there may be times when you need to temporarily halt it, such as during network maintenance windows. Previously I discussed the behavior of vSphere HA when a network partition or network isolation occurs. If you are going to be performing network maintenance that might trigger one of these events, uncheck Enable Host Monitoring to prevent vSphere HA from triggering isolation response or network partition behaviors. Note the Enable Host Monitoring check box shown in Figure 7.17; this is how you can temporarily disable the host-monitoring function of vSphere HA during times of network maintenance so as not to trigger network partition or network isolation behaviors.

FIGURE 7.15
vSphere HA is
enabled or disabled
for an entire cluster.

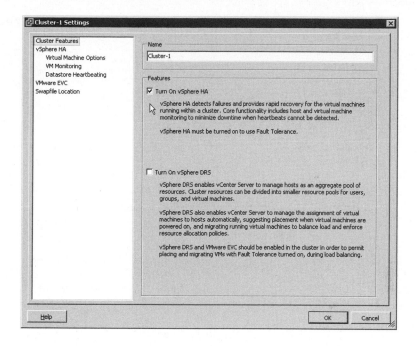

FIGURE 7.16
As you can see in
the Tasks pane,
vSphere HA elects a
master host when it
is enabled on a clus-
ter of ESXi hosts.

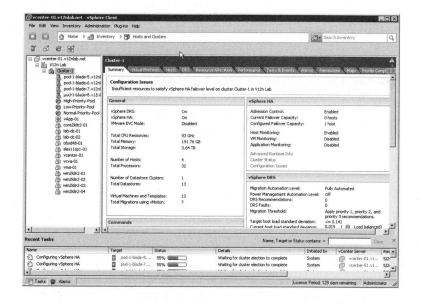

FIGURE 7.17
Deselecting Enable
Host Monitoring
when performing
network mainte-
nance will prevent
vSphere HA from
unnecessarily trig-
gering network
isolation or network
partition responses.

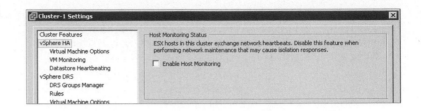

Configuring vSphere High Availability

After vSphere HA is enabled, configuring vSphere HA revolves around several key areas:

◆ Admission control and admission control policy

◆ VM options

◆ VM monitoring

◆ Datastore heartbeating

Each of these configuration areas is described in detail in the following sections.

SETTING THE VSPHERE HIGH AVAILABILITY ADMISSION CONTROL AND ADMISSION CONTROL POLICY

The vSphere HA Admission Control and Admission Control Policy settings control the behavior of the vSphere HA–enabled cluster with regard to cluster capacity. Specifically, should vSphere HA allow the user to power on more VMs than it has capacity to support in the event of a failure? Or should the cluster prevent more VMs from being powered on than it can actually protect? That is the basis for the admission control — and by extension, the admission control policy — settings.

Admission Control has two settings:

◆ Enable: Disallow VM power-on operations that violate availability constraints.

◆ Disable: Allow VM power-on operations that violate availability constraints.

These options go hand-in-hand with the Admission Control Policy settings, which I'll explain in a moment. First, though, let's take a closer look at the Admission Control settings. Consider for a moment that you have a cluster of four identical ESXi hosts. Running on these four ESXi hosts are a bunch of identically configured VMs. These VMs consume a total of 75 percent of the resources in the cluster. This cluster is configured for a single ESXi host failure (I'll go into more detail on these settings in a bit). Further, let's say now you want to power on one more VM, and the resource consumption by that VM will push you past the 75 percent resource usage mark. It is at this point that the Admission Control settings will come into play.

If Admission Control is set to Enabled, then vSphere HA would block the power-on operation of this additional VM. Why? Because the cluster is already at the limit of the capacity it could support if one of the ESXi hosts in the cluster failed (one host out of our four identical hosts is equal to 25 percent of the cluster's capacity). Because you've told vSphere HA to prevent power-on operations that violate availability constraints, vSphere HA will prevent you from starting more VMs than it has resources to protect. In effect, vSphere HA is guaranteeing you that you'll always have enough resources to restart all the protected VMs in the event of a failure.

If, on the other hand, Admission Control is set to Disabled, then vSphere HA will let you power on VMs until all of the cluster's resources are allocated. If there is an ESXi host failure at that point, it's possible that some of the VMs would not be able to be restarted because there are not sufficient resources to power on all the VMs. vSphere HA allowed you to exceed the availability constraints of the cluster.

OVERCOMMITMENT IN A vSPHERE HA–ENABLED CLUSTER

When the Admission Control setting is set to allow VMs to be powered on even if they violate availability constraints, you could find yourself in a position where there is more physical memory allocated to VMs than actually exists.

This situation, called *overcommitment*, can lead to poor performance on VMs that become forced to page information from fast RAM out to the slower disk-based swap file. Yes, your VMs will start, but after the host gets maxed out, the whole system and all VMs will slow down dramatically. This will increase the amount of time that HA will need to recover the VMs. What should have been a 20- to 30-minute recovery could end up being an hour or even more. Refer to Chapter 11, "Managing Resource Allocation," for more details on resource allocation and how vSphere handles memory overcommitment.

You should be able to see now how integral the Admission Control Policy settings are to the behavior of Admission Control. When Admission Control is enabled, the Admission Control Policy settings control its behavior by determining how many resources need to be reserved and the limit that the cluster can handle and still be able to tolerate failure.

The Admission Control Policy settings are illustrated in Figure 7.18.

There are three options for the Admission Control Policy:

◆ The first option, Host Failures The Cluster Tolerates, allows you to specify how many host failures the cluster should be configured to withstand. Because the ESXi hosts may have different amounts of RAM and/or CPU capacity and because the VMs in the cluster may have different levels of resource allocation, vSphere HA uses the idea of a slot to calculate the capacity of the cluster. I'll discuss slots in more detail in just a moment.

◆ The second option, Percentage Of Cluster Resources Reserved As Failover Spare Capacity, allows you to specify a percentage of the cluster's total resources that should be used for spare capacity in the event of a failure. You can specify different percentages for CPU and memory. The availability constraints are established by simply calculating the specified percentage of the cluster's total available resources.

◆ The third option, Specify Failover Hosts, allows you to specify one or more ESXi hosts as failover hosts. These hosts are used as spare capacity, and in the event of a failure, vSphere HA will use these hosts to restart VMs.

FIGURE 7.18
The Admission Control Policy settings will determine how a vSphere HA–enabled cluster determines availability constraints.

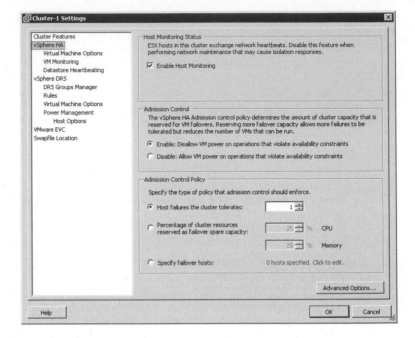

> **BE CAREFUL ABOUT USING FAILOVER HOSTS**
>
> When you select an ESXi host as a vSphere HA failover host, it's almost like putting that host into Maintenance mode. vSphere DRS, which I'll describe in more detail in Chapter 12, "Balancing Resource Utilization," won't place VMs here at startup and won't consider these hosts in its load-balancing calculations. You can't manually power on VMs on the failover host(s), either. These hosts are truly set aside as spare capacity.

For the most part, the Admission Control Policy settings are pretty easy to understand. The one part that can be confusing at times is the idea of a slot and a slot size, which is used by vSphere HA when the Admission Control Policy is set to Host Failures The Cluster Tolerates.

Why slots and slot sizes? vSphere HA uses slots and slot sizes because the ESXi hosts in the cluster might have different configurations: one host might have 8 CPU cores and 24 GB of RAM, while another host might have 12 CPU cores and 48 GB of RAM. Similarly, the VMs in the cluster are likely to have different resource configurations. One VM might need 4 GB of RAM, but another VM might require 8 GB of RAM. Some VMs will have 1 vCPU and other VMs will have 2 or even 4 vCPUs. Because vSphere doesn't know in advance which host will fail and which VMs will be affected by that failure (naturally), vSphere HA needed a way to establish a "least common denominator" to express the overall capacity of the cluster. Once that overall capacity of the cluster can be expressed, vSphere HA can set aside the appropriate amount of resources to protect against the configured number of host failures.

Here's how slots and slot sizes work. First, vSphere HA examines all the VMs in the cluster to determine the largest values for reserved memory and reserved CPU. For example, if one of the VMs in the cluster has a 2 GB memory reservation but all others do not have a memory reservation, vSphere HA will use 2 GB as the value to use for calculating slots based on memory. In the same fashion, if one VM has a reservation for 2 GHz of CPU capacity but all the other VMs don't have any reservation value, it will use 2 GHz as the value. Basically, vSphere HA constructs the least common denominator as a VM with the largest memory reservation and the largest CPU reservation.

WHAT IF THERE ARE NO RESERVATIONS?

vSphere HA uses reservations, described in Chapter 11, to calculate the slot size. If no VMs have reservations for CPU or memory, vSphere will use the default value of 32 MHz for CPU to calculate slot size. For memory, vSphere HA will use the largest memory overhead value when calculating the slot size.

Once it has constructed the least common denominator, vSphere HA then calculates the total number of slots that each ESXi host in the cluster could support. Then it determines how many slots the cluster could support if the host with the largest number of slots were to fail (a worst-case scenario). vSphere HA performs these calculations and comparisons for both CPU and memory and then uses the most restrictive result. If vSphere HA calculated 50 slots for memory and 100 slots for CPU, then 50 is the number vSphere HA uses. VMs are then assigned to the slots to determine how many slots are used and how many slots are free, and Admission Control uses this to determine whether additional VMs can be powered on (enough slots remain) or cannot be powered on (not enough slots are available).

The slot-size calculation algorithm just described can result in unexpected settings when you have an unbalanced cluster. An *unbalanced cluster* is a cluster with dramatically different ESXi hosts included in the cluster, such as a host with 12 GB of RAM along with an ESXi host with 96 GB of RAM in the same cluster. You might also have an unbalanced cluster if you have dramatically different resource reservations assigned to VMs in the cluster (for example, one VM with an 8 GB memory reservation while all the other VMs use much less than that). While you can fine-tune the behavior of the vSphere HA slot-calculation mechanism using advanced settings, it's generally not recommended. For these situations, you have a couple of options:

♦ You could place similarly sized VMs (or similarly sized hosts) in their own cluster.

♦ You could use percentage-based availability constraints (via the Percentage Of Cluster Resources Reserved As Failover Spare Capacity setting) instead of host failures or failover hosts.

Using reservations on resource pools might be another way to help alleviate the impact to slot size calculations, if the reservations are necessary. Refer to Chapter 11 for more details on both reservations and resource pools.

The next major area of configuration for vSphere HA is VM options.

CONFIGURING vSPHERE HIGH AVAILABILITY VM OPTIONS

Figure 7.19 shows the VM options that are available to control the behavior of VMs for vSphere HA. Two VM options are available for administrators to configure: VM Restart Priority and Host Isolation Response. Both options are configurable as a cluster default setting as well as a per-VM setting.

FIGURE 7.19

You can define cluster default VM options as well as per-VM options to customize the behavior of vSphere HA.

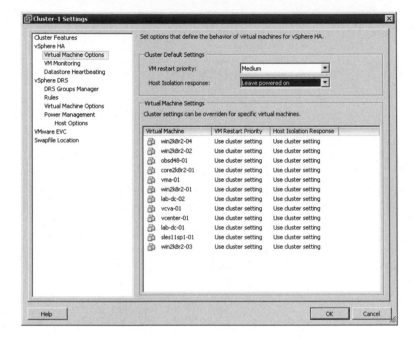

vSphere High Availability VM Restart Priority

Not all VMs are equal. Some VMs are more important or more critical and require higher priority when ensuring availability. When an ESXi host experiences failure and the remaining cluster nodes are tasked by vSphere HA with bringing VMs back online, they have a finite amount of resources to fill before there are no more resources to allocate to VMs that need to be powered on. This is especially true when Admission Control is set to Disabled, allowing more VMs to be powered on than the cluster could support given a failure. Rather than leave important VMs to chance, a vSphere HA–enabled cluster allows for the prioritization of VMs through VM Restart Priority.

The VM Restart Priority options for VMs in a vSphere HA–enabled cluster include Low, Medium, High, and Disabled. For those VMs that should be brought up first, the Restart Priority should be set to High. For those VMs that should be brought up if resources are available, the Restart Priority can be set to Medium or Low. For those VMs that will not be missed for a period of time and should not be brought online during the period of reduced resource availability, the Restart Priority should be set to Disabled. You can define a default restart priority for the entire cluster as well as define a per-VM restart priority. Figure 7.20 shows the VM Restart Priority set to Medium for the cluster and set to other levels for a few other VMs based on their importance to the organization.

FIGURE 7.20
Use the per-VM VM Restart Priority setting to specify which VMs should be restarted first or ignored entirely.

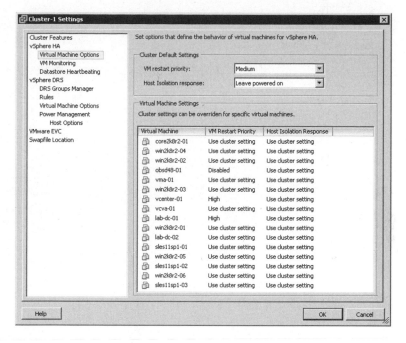

The restart priority is put into place only for the VMs running on the ESXi hosts that experience an unexpected failure. VMs running on hosts that have not failed are not affected by the restart priority. It is possible then that VMs configured with a restart priority of High might not be powered on by vSphere HA because of limited resources, which are in part because of lower-priority VMs that continue to run (again, only if Admission Control was set to Disabled). For example, as shown in Figure 7.21, the ESXi host pod-1-blade-5 hosts four VMs with a priority of High and four other VMs with priority values of Medium or Low. Meanwhile, pod-1-blade-6 and pod-1-blade-7 together hold 13 VMs, but of those VMs only two are considered of High priority. When pod-1-blade-5 fails, the FDM master host in the cluster will begin powering the VMs with a High priority. If vSphere DRS is enabled, the VMs will be automatically placed on one of the surviving hosts. However, assume there were only enough resources to power on three of the four VMs with High priority. That leaves a High-priority VM powered off while all other VMs of Medium and Low priorities continue to run on the remaining hosts.

At this point in the vSphere product suite, you can still manually remedy this imbalance. Any business continuity plan in a virtual environment built on vSphere should include a contingency plan that identifies VMs to be powered off to make resources available for those VMs with higher priority because of the network services they provide. If the budget allows, construct the vSphere HA cluster to ensure that there are ample resources to cover the needs of the critical VMs, even in times of reduced computing capacity. You can enforce guaranteed resource availability for restarting VMs by setting Admission Control to Enabled, as described previously in the section "Setting the vSphere High Availability Admission Control and Admission Control Policy."

FIGURE 7.21
High-priority VMs from a failed ESXi host might not be powered on because of a lack of resources — resources consumed by VMs with a lower priority that are running on the other hosts in a vSphere HA–enabled cluster.

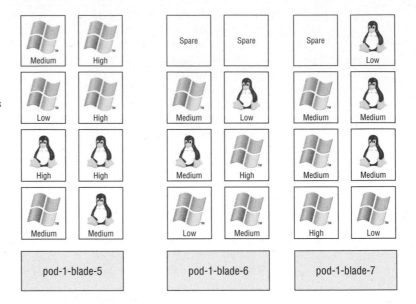

vSphere High Availability Isolation Response

Previously, I introduced FDM as the underpinning for vSphere HA and how it uses the ESXi management network to communicate between the master host and all connected slave hosts. When the vSphere HA master is no longer receiving status updates from a slave host, then the master assumes that host has failed and instructs the other connected slave hosts to spring into action to power on all the VMs that the missing node was running.

But what if the node with the missing heartbeat was not really missing? What if the heartbeat was missing, but the node was still running? This is the scenario I described in the section "Understanding vSphere HA's Underpinnings" when I discussed the idea of *network isolation*. When an ESXi host in a vSphere HA–enabled cluster is isolated — that is, it cannot communicate with the master host nor can it communicate with any other ESXi hosts or any other network devices — then the ESXi host triggers the isolation response configured in the dialog box shown in Figure 7.19. The default isolation response is Leave Powered On. You can change this setting (generally not recommended) either for the entire cluster (by changing the Cluster Default Settings for Host Isolation Response) or for one or more specific VMs.

Because vSphere HA uses both the ESXi management network as well as connected datastores (via datastore heartbeating) to communicate, network isolation is handled a bit differently in vSphere 5 than in previous versions of vSphere. In previous versions of vSphere, when a host was isolated it would automatically trigger the configured isolation response. A host considered itself isolated when it was not receiving heartbeats from any other hosts and when it could not reach the *isolation address* (by default, the default gateway on the management network).

With vSphere 5, the process for determining if a host is isolated is only slightly different. A host that is the master is looking for communication from its slave hosts; a host that is running as a slave is looking for updates from the master host. In either case, if the master or slave is not receiving any vSphere HA network heartbeat information, it will then attempt to contact the isolation address (by default, the default gateway on the management network). If it can reach the default gateway, then the ESXi host considers itself to be in a network partition state and reacts as described in the section titled "Understanding vSphere HA's Underpinnings." If the host can't reach the isolation address, then it considers itself isolated. Here is where vSphere 5's behavior diverges from the behavior of previous versions.

At this point, an ESXi host that has determined it is network-isolated will modify a special bit in the binary `host-X-poweron` file on all datastores that are configured for datastore heartbeating (more on that in the section titled "Setting vSphere High Availability Datastore Heartbeating"). The master sees that this bit, used to denote isolation, has been set and is therefore notified that this slave host has been isolated. When a master sees that a slave has been isolated, the master locks another file used by vSphere HA on the heartbeat datastore. When the isolated node sees that this file has been locked by a master, it knows that the master is assuming responsibility for restarting the VMs — remember that only a master can restart VMs — and the isolated host is then free to execute the configured isolation response. Therefore, even if the isolation response is set to Shut Down or Power Off, that action won't take place until the isolated slave has confirmed, via the datastore heartbeating structures, that a master has assumed responsibility for restarting the VMs.

The question still remains, though: should I change the Host Isolation Response setting?

The answer to this question is highly dependent on the virtual and physical network infrastructures in place. Let's look at a couple of examples.

Let's say we have a host in which both the ESXi management network and the VM networks are connected to the same virtual switch bound to a single network adapter (clearly not a generally recommended configuration). In this case, when the cable for the uplink on this vSwitch is unplugged, communication to the ESXi management network and every VM on that computer is lost. The solution, then, should be to shut down the VMs. When an ESXi host determines it is isolated and has confirmed that a master host has assumed responsibility for restarting the VMs, it can execute the isolation response so that the VMs can be restarted on another host with full network connectivity.

A more realistic example might be a situation in which a single vSwitch has two uplinks, but both uplinks go to the same physical switch. If this vSwitch hosts both the ESXi management and VM networks, then the loss of that physical switch means that both management traffic and VM traffic have been interrupted. Setting the Host Isolation Response to Shut Down would allow vSphere HA to restart those VMs on another ESXi host and restore connectivity to the VMs.

However, a network configuration that employs multiple uplinks, multiple vSwitches, and multiple physical switches, as shown in Figure 7.22, should probably leave the Host Isolation Response set to Leave Powered On, because it's unlikely that a network isolation event would also leave the VMs on that host inaccessible.

FIGURE 7.22
The option to leave VMs running when a host is isolated should be set only when the virtual and the physical networking infra-structures support high availability.

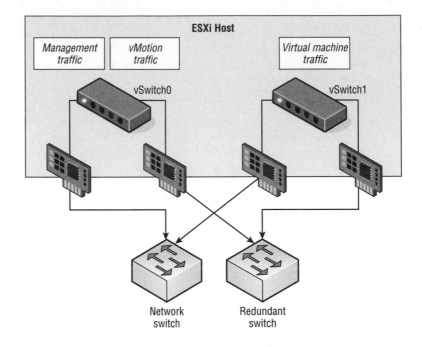

CONFIGURING THE ISOLATION RESPONSE ADDRESS

In some highly secure virtual environments, management access is limited to a single, non-routed management network. In these cases, the security plan calls for the elimination of the default gateway on the ESXi management network. The idea is to lock the ESXi management network onto the local subnet, thus preventing any type of remote network access to the management interfaces. The disadvantage, as you might have guessed, is that without a default gateway IP address configured for the management network, there is no isolation address to ping as a determination of network isolation status.

It is possible, however, to customize the isolation response address for scenarios just like this. The IP address can be any IP address but should be an IP address that is not going to be unavailable or taken from the network at any time.

Perform the following steps to define a custom isolation response address:

1. Use the vSphere Client to connect to a vCenter Server instance.

2. Open the Hosts And Clusters View, right-click an existing cluster, and select the Edit Settings option.

3. Click the vSphere HA node.

4. Click the Advanced Options button.

5. Enter **das.isolationaddress** in the Option column in the Advanced Options (HA) dialog box.

6. Enter the IP address to be used as the isolation response address for ESXi hosts that cannot communicate with the FDM master host.

7. Click the OK button twice.

This interface can also be configured with the following options:

◆ das.isolationaddress1: To specify the first address to try

◆ das.isolationaddress2: To specify the second address to try

◆ das.AllowNetwork: To specify a different port group to use for HA heartbeat

So far, you've only seen how vSphere HA handles ESXi host failures. In the next section, I'll show you how you can use vSphere HA to help protect against guest OS and application failures as well.

CONFIGURING vSPHERE HIGH AVAILABILITY VM MONITORING

In addition to monitoring for ESXi host failures and reacting accordingly, vSphere HA has the ability to look for guest OS and application failures. When a failure is detected, vSphere HA can restart the VM. Figure 7.23 shows the area of the Edit Cluster dialog box where you configure this behavior.

FIGURE 7.23
You can configure vSphere HA to monitor for guest OS and application heartbeats and restart a VM when a failure occurs.

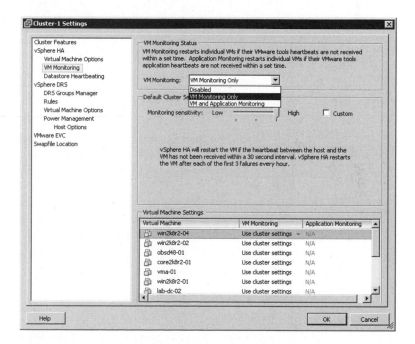

The foundation for this functionality is built into the VMware Tools, which I'll describe in greater detail in Chapter 9. The VMware Tools provide a series of heartbeats from the guest OS up to the ESXi host on which that VM is running. By monitoring these heartbeats in conjunction with disk and network I/O activity, vSphere HA can attempt to determine if the guest OS has failed. If there are no VMware Tools heartbeats, no disk I/O, and no network I/O for a period of time, then vSphere HA — if VM Monitoring is enabled — will restart the VM under the assumption that the guest OS has failed. To help with troubleshooting, vSphere also takes a screenshot of the VM's console right before vSphere HA restarts the VM. This might help capture any sort of diagnostic information, such as a kernel dump or blue-screen STOP error for Windows-based systems.

vSphere HA also has application monitoring. This functionality requires third-party software to take advantage of APIs built into VMware Tools to provide application-specific heartbeats to vSphere HA. By leveraging these APIs, third-party software developers can further extend the functionality of vSphere HA to protect against the failure of specific applications.

SYMANTEC APPHA

At the time of writing, the only product known to take advantage of the vSphere HA application-monitoring APIs is Symantec AppHA. AppHA enables application-specific functionality, such as restarting individual applications within the guest OS.

To enable VM or application monitoring, simply select the desired level of protection from the VM Monitoring drop-down list shown in Figure 7.23.

If you have enabled VM or application monitoring, you can then adjust the monitoring sensitivity. This slider bar controls how often vSphere HA will restart a VM based on a loss of VMware Tools heartbeats and a lack of disk and network I/O traffic. The slider bar also controls the failure window before which vSphere HA will restart a VM again after a maximum number of failures. Table 7.2 shows the values set by each position on the slider.

TABLE 7.2:   VM monitoring sensitivity settings

MONITORING SENSITIVITY SETTING	FAILURE INTERVAL	MAXIMUM FAILURES	FAILURE WINDOW
Low	2 minutes	3	7 days
Medium	1 minute	3	24 hours
High	30 seconds	3	1 hour

Here's how to read this information:

◆ Failure Interval: If vSphere HA doesn't detect any VMware Tools heartbeats, disk I/O, or network I/O within this time frame, it will consider the VM failed and will restart the VM.

◆ Maximum Failures: This is the maximum number of times vSphere HA will restart a VM within the specified failure window. If Maximum Failures is set at 3 and a VM is marked as failed a fourth time within the specified failure window, it will not be automatically restarted. This prevents vSphere HA from endlessly restarting problematic VMs.

◆ Failure Window: vSphere will only restart the VM a maximum number of times (Maximum Failures) within this time frame. If more failures occur within this period of time, the VM is not restarted.

If these predefined options aren't sufficient, you can select Custom and specify your own values for Failure Interval, Minimum Uptime (a value not exposed with the predefined settings), Maximum Per-VM Resets (Maximum Failures), and Maximum Resets Time Window (Failure Window). Figure 7.24 shows a custom VM Monitoring sensitivity configuration.

FIGURE 7.24

The Custom option provides specific control over how vSphere HA monitors VMs for guest OS failure.

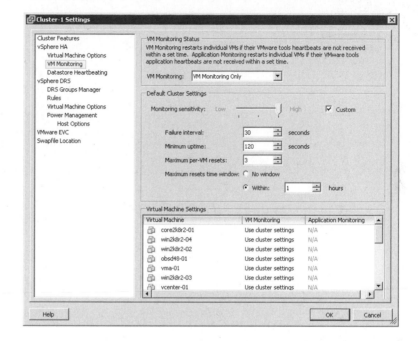

As with other areas of vSphere HA, you also have the option of configuring per-VM monitoring settings. This allows you, on a per-VM basis, to enable or disable VM monitoring and application monitoring sensitivity levels. Thus, if you need VM monitoring for only a few VMs, you can define a default cluster setting and then configure the exceptions accordingly.

The last configuration area for vSphere HA is datastore heartbeating, a new feature in vSphere 5.

SETTING VSPHERE HIGH AVAILABILITY DATASTORE HEARTBEATING

Datastore heartbeating is part of the new functionality found in vSphere HA in vSphere 5. By communicating through shared datastores when the ESXi management network is not available, vSphere HA provides greater protection against outages due to network partition or network isolation.

This part of the vSphere HA configuration allows you to specify which datastores should be used by vSphere HA for heartbeating. Figure 7.25 shows the Datastore Heartbeating section of the Edit Cluster dialog box.

FIGURE 7.25
Select the shared datastores that vSphere HA should use for datastore heartbeating.

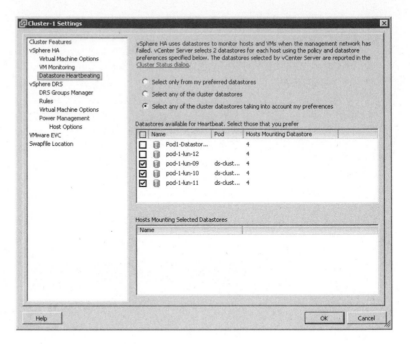

vSphere HA provides three different settings for how the administrator can influence the selection of datastores for heartbeating:

◆ The first option, Select Only From My Preferred Datastores, constrains vSphere HA to using only those datastores selected from the list of datastores. If one of those datastores becomes unavailable for whatever reason, vSphere HA will not perform heartbeating through a different datastore.

◆ The second option, Select Any Of The Cluster Datastores, disables the selection of datastores from the list. With this option, any cluster datastore could be used by vSphere HA for heartbeating.

◆ The last option is Select Any Of The Cluster Datastores Taking Into Account My Preferences. This is a bit of a blend of the previous two options. With this option, the administrator selects the preferred datastores that vSphere HA should use. vSphere HA chooses from among the datastores in that list. If one of the datastores becomes unavailable, vSphere HA will choose a different datastore, until none of the preferred datastores are available. At that point it will choose any available cluster datastore.

The last option is probably the most flexible, but how would you know which datastores were being used by vSphere HA? In the next section, "Managing vSphere High Availability," I'll show you how to tell which datastores vSphere HA is actually using for datastore heartbeating, as well as how to determine the slot size, see any cluster configuration issues, and gather information on the total number of protected and unprotected VMs.

Managing vSphere High Availability

Much of what vSphere HA does is calculated automatically: things like slot size, total number of slots, selection of hosts for datastore heartbeating, and the selection of master/slave role by FDM are just a few examples. Without proper exposure of these values, it would be difficult for administrators to properly manage vSphere HA and its operation. Fortunately, VMware included information about vSphere HA in the vSphere Client to help make it easier to manage vSphere HA.

Some of the information is pretty easy to find. For example, the Summary tab of an ESXi host in a vSphere HA–enabled cluster will show the master/slave status, as shown in Figure 7.13.

Similarly, the protected/unprotected status of a VM — indicating that the vSphere HA master has recognized that the VM has been powered on and has taken responsibility for restarting it in the event of a failure — is also noted on the Summary tab of a VM. You can see this in Figure 7.26.

FIGURE 7.26
This VM is currently listed as Unprotected by vSphere HA. This may be because the master has not yet been notified by vCenter Server that the VM has been powered on and needs to be protected.

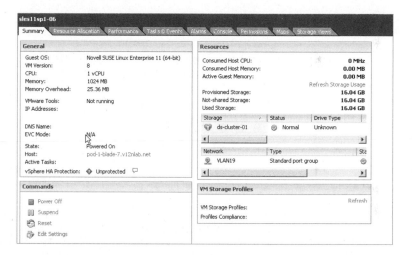

However, other pieces of information about vSphere HA are not quite so readily apparent. For example, on the Summary tab of a vSphere HA–enabled cluster in the section labeled vSphere HA, there are three unassuming hyperlinks. Let's take a look at each of these links and see what information they reveal about vSphere HA.

Clicking the first link, Advanced Runtime Info, displays the dialog box shown in Figure 7.27. As you can see in the figure, this dialog box exposes the vSphere HA calculations for slot size, total slots in cluster, used slots, available slots, and failover slots. This is very useful information to have. If you have Admission Control set to Enabled and aren't able to power on VMs that you think you should be able to power on, checking this dialog box for the slot size might reveal that the slot size is something very different that what you were expecting.

FIGURE 7.27
The vSphere HA Advanced Runtime Info dialog box holds a wealth of information about vSphere HA and its operation.

The second hyperlink, Cluster Status, reveals the dialog box shown in Figure 7.28. The vSphere HA Cluster Status dialog box has three tabs of information about vSphere HA:

◆ The Hosts tab lists the current vSphere HA master and the number of slave hosts connected to the master host. Although the vSphere HA master status is also displayed on the Summary tab for an ESXi host, using this dialog box might be easier and faster for clusters with a large number of hosts.

◆ The VMs tab shows the current number of protected and unprotected VMs. This gives you a quick "at a glance" protection summary and is a fast way to determine how many, if any, VMs are unprotected by vSphere HA.

◆ The Heartbeat Datastores tab shows which datastores are currently being used by vSphere HA for heartbeating. If you haven't explicitly defined which datastore can or should be used, this is where you can tell which datastores were selected by vSphere HA for heartbeating.

FIGURE 7.28
The current vSphere HA master, the number of protected and unprotected VMs, and the datastores used for heartbeating are some of the pieces of information exposed in the vSphere HA Cluster Status dialog box.

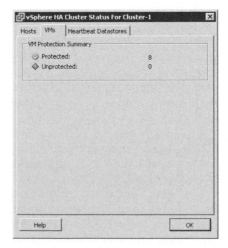

The third and final link, Configuration Issues, displays the Cluster Configuration Issues dialog box. Figure 7.29 shows an example Cluster Configuration Issues dialog box.

FIGURE 7.29

The Cluster Configuration Issues dialog box shows that this particular cluster has exceeded its configured failover capacity.

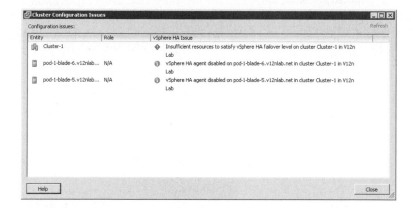

In the Cluster Configuration Issues dialog box, vSphere HA will display any configuration issues. For example, if the cluster has exceeded the configured failover capacity, like Cluster-1 shown in Figure 7.29, that will be displayed in the Cluster Configuration Issues dialog box. You might also see warnings about management network redundancy (if the ESXi management network isn't redundant and protected against single points of failure). Based on the issues displayed here, you can take the appropriate action to correct the problem or potential problem.

vSphere HA is a powerful feature, and I highly recommend its use in every vSphere implementation. However, vSphere HA does rely on restarting VMs in order to provide that level of high availability. What if there are applications for which you need a higher level of availability? vSphere offers that functionality with vSphere Fault Tolerance (FT). Based on VMware's vLockstep technology, vSphere FT provides zero downtime, zero data loss, and continuous availability for your applications.

That sounds pretty impressive, doesn't it? But how does it work? That's the focus of the next section.

Implementing vSphere Fault Tolerance

vSphere Fault Tolerance (FT) is the evolution of "continuous availability" that works by utilizing VMware vLockstep technology to keep a primary machine and a secondary machine in a virtual lockstep. This virtual lockstep is based on the record/playback technology that VMware introduced in VMware Workstation in 2006. vSphere FT will stream data that will be recorded (only nondeterministic events are recorded), and the replay will occur deterministically. By doing it this way, VMware has created a process that matches instruction for instruction and memory for memory to get identical results.

Deterministic means that the computer processor will execute the same instruction stream on the secondary VM so as to end up in the same state as the primary VM. On the other hand, nondeterministic events are functions, such as network/disk/keyboard I/O, as well as hardware interrupts. So, the record process will take the data stream, and the playback will perform all the keyboard actions and mouse clicks. It is pretty slick to move the mouse on the primary VM and see it also move on the secondary VM.

Before I show you how to enable vSphere FT for a VM, I need to cover some requirements in order to use vSphere FT. Because vSphere FT is matching instruction for instruction and memory for memory to create two identical VMs running on two different ESXi hosts, there are some fairly stringent requirements for vSphere FT. These requirements exist at three levels: at a cluster level, at a host level, and finally at a VM level.

vSphere FT has the following requirements at a cluster level:

◆ Host certificate checking must be enabled. This is the default for vCenter Server 4.1 and later, but if you upgraded from an earlier version of vCenter Server, you might need to enable this functionality.

◆ The cluster must have at least two ESXi hosts running the same FT version or build number. The FT version is displayed in the Fault Tolerance section of the ESXi host's Summary tab.

◆ vSphere HA must be enabled on the cluster. vSphere HA must be enabled before you can power on vSphere FT–enabled VMs.

◆ VMware EVC must be enabled if you want to use vSphere FT in conjunction with vSphere DRS. Otherwise, vSphere DRS will be disabled on any vSphere FT–enabled VMs.

In addition, vSphere FT has the following requirements on each ESXi host:

◆ The ESXi hosts must have access to the same datastores and networks.

◆ The ESXi hosts must have a Fault Tolerance logging network connection configured. This vSphere FT logging network requires at least Gigabit Ethernet connectivity, and 10 Gigabit Ethernet is recommended. Although VMware calls for dedicated vSphere FT logging NICs, NICs can be shared with other functions if necessary.

◆ The hosts must have CPUs that are vSphere FT compatible.

◆ Hosts must be licensed for vSphere FT.

◆ Hardware Virtualization (HV) must be enabled in the ESXi host's BIOS in order to enable CPU support for vSphere FT.

Finally, vSphere FT has the following requirements on any VM that is to be protected using vSphere FT:

◆ Only VMs with a single vCPU are supported with vSphere FT. VMs with more than one vCPU are not compatible with vSphere FT.

◆ VMs must be running a supported guest OS.

◆ VM files must be stored on shared storage that is accessible to all applicable ESXi hosts. vSphere FT supports Fibre Channel, FCoE, iSCSI, and NFS for shared storage.

◆ A VM's virtual disks must be in thick provisioned (eagerzeroedthick) format or a Virtual mode RDM. Physical mode RDMs are not supported.

◆ The VM must not have any snapshots. You must remove or commit snapshots before you can enable vSphere FT for a VM.

◆ The VM must not be a linked clone.

◆ The VM cannot have any USB devices, sound devices, serial ports, or parallel ports in its configuration. Remove these items from the VM configuration before attempting to enable vSphere FT.

◆ The VM cannot use N_Port ID Virtualization (NPIV).

◆ Nested page tables/extended page tables (NPT/EPT) are not supported. vSphere FT will disable NPT/EPT on VMs for which vSphere FT is enabled.

◆ The VM cannot use NIC passthrough or the older vlance network drivers. Turn off NIC passthrough and update the networking drivers to vmxnet2, vmxnet3, or E1000.

◆ The VM cannot have CD-ROM or floppy devices backed by a physical or remote device. You'll need to disconnect these devices or configure them to point to an ISO or FLP image on a shared datastore.

◆ The VM cannot use a paravirtualized kernel. Turn off paravirtualization in order to use vSphere FT.

As you can see, vSphere FT has some fairly stringent requirements in order to be properly supported.

vSphere FT also introduces some operational changes that must be taken into account as well:

◆ It is recommended that power management (also known as *power capping*) be turned off in the BIOS of any ESXi host that will participate in vSphere FT. This helps ensure uniformity in the CPU speeds of the ESXi hosts in the cluster.

◆ While you can use vMotion with a vSphere FT–protected VM, you cannot use Storage vMotion. By extension, this means that vSphere FT–protected VMs cannot take advantage of Storage DRS. To use Storage vMotion, you must first turn off vSphere FT.

◆ Hot-plugging devices is not supported, so you cannot make any virtual hardware changes when a vSphere FT–protected VM is powered on.

NO HARDWARE CHANGES INCLUDES NO NETWORK CHANGES

Changing the settings of a virtual network card while a VM is running requires that the network card be unplugged and then plugged back in. As a result, you can't make changes to virtual network cards while vSphere FT is running.

◆ Because snapshots aren't supported with vSphere FT, you can't back up VMs using any backup methodology that relies on snapshots. This includes any backup solution that leverages the vSphere Storage API for Data Protection as well as VMware Data Recovery. To back up a vSphere FT–enabled VM with one of these tools, you must first disable vSphere FT.

Be sure to keep these operational constraints in mind when deciding where and how to use vSphere FT in your environment.

Now you're ready to actually enable vSphere FT on a VM. Perform the following steps to enable vSphere FT:

1. If the vSphere Client is not already running, launch it and connect to a vCenter Server instance. vSphere FT is available only when using vCenter Server.

2. Navigate to the Hosts And Clusters or VMs And Templates inventory view. Right-click a running VM and then select Fault Tolerance ➢ Turn On Fault Tolerance, as shown in Figure 7.30.

FIGURE 7.30

You can turn on vSphere FT from the context menu for a VM.

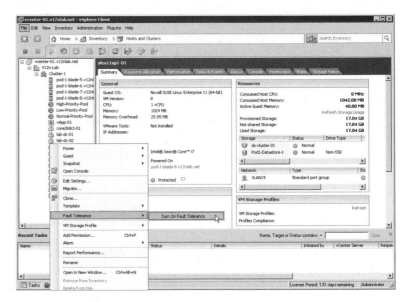

ERROR MESSAGE ABOUT "INCORRECT MONITOR MODE" WHEN ENABLING VSPHERE FAULT TOLERANCE

If you receive an error message when attempting to enable vSphere FT for a running VM and the error message mentions an "incorrect monitor mode," this is probably because your specific CPU family can enable vSphere FT for VMs only when they are powered down. Certain CPU families — most notably, the Intel "Nehalem" or Xeon 55xx series of CPUs — aren't able to enable vSphere FT when the VM is powered on. The workaround is to power the VM off and then enable vSphere FT.

3. A pop-up message appears to warn you that enabling vSphere FT will result in several changes. First, all virtual disks will be converted to Thick Provision Eager Zeroed disks, also called eagerzeroedthick disks (virtual disks with all blocks zeroed out ahead of time). Second, vSphere DRS will be disabled for this VM if VMware EVC is not enabled on the cluster. Third, the memory reservation for this VM will be set equal to the configured memory of the VM, as shown in Figure 7.31. Click Yes to turn on vSphere FT for the selected VM.

FIGURE 7.31
Several other config-
uration changes are
enforced when you
activate vSphere FT
on a VM.

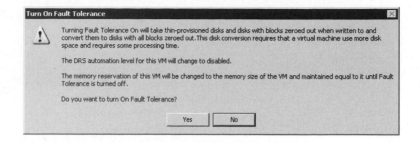

WILL vSPHERE FAULT TOLERANCE DISABLE vSPHERE DISTRIBUTED RESOURCE SCHEDULER FOR A VM?

If VMware EVC is not enabled on the cluster, then vSphere FT will disable DRS for the selected VM when vSphere FT is enabled. If VMware EVC is enabled, then vSphere 5 supports the use of vSphere DRS in conjunction with vSphere FT.

---

4. After you have selected to enable vSphere FT, the creation task begins, as shown in Figure 7.32.

If the VM's virtual disks were not already in the Thick Provision Eager Zeroed format, those disks will be converted. Depending on the size of the virtual disks, this might take quite some time.

FIGURE 7.32
vSphere FT must
convert existing
virtual disks to
Thick Provision
(eagerzeroedthick)
format.

5. Once the process is complete, the VM's icon in the inventory tree will change. Figure 7.33 shows a VM that has been enabled for vSphere FT.

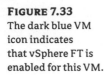

FIGURE 7.33
The dark blue VM
icon indicates
that vSphere FT is
enabled for this VM.

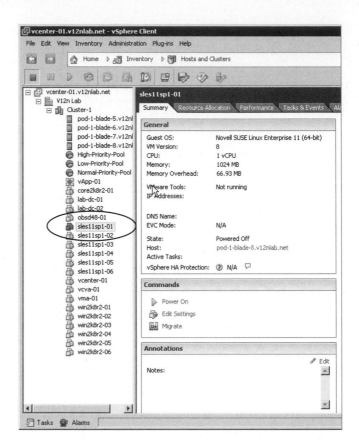

And that's it. It is literally that simple — at least on the surface.

Behind the scenes, after vSphere FT is turned on, vCenter Server will initiate the creation of the secondary VM by using a special type of vMotion. Both the primary and secondary VMs will share a common disk between them, and using VMware vLockstep, vSphere FT will then be able to keep the VMs in sync. vSphere FT uses a network connection between the ESXi hosts to keep the primary and secondary VMs in sync (recall from my earlier discussion of requirements that the ESXi hosts must have a Fault Tolerance logging connection established; Chapter 5 provides more detail on how to configure this network connection). Only the primary VM will respond to other systems across the network, which leaves the secondary VM a silent partner. You can almost compare this to active/passive cluster configuration in that only one node owns the shared network at a time. When the ESXi host supporting the primary VM fails, the secondary VM takes over immediately with no break in network connection. A reverse ARP is sent to the physical switch to notify the network of the new location of the VM. Does that sound familiar? It is exactly what vMotion does when the VM switches to a new host. Once the secondary VM becomes the primary, the creation of the new secondary VM is repeated until the sync is locked. After the sync is locked, as shown in Figure 7.34, you'll see green icons.

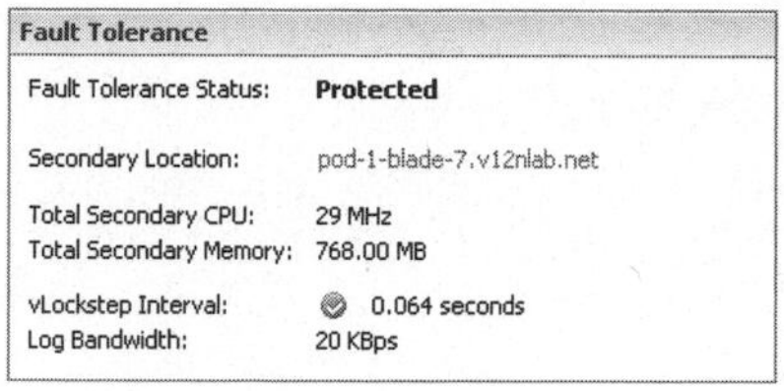

FIGURE 7.34

The vSphere Client shows vSphere FT status information in the Fault Tolerance area on the Summary tab of a VM.

Fault Tolerance	
Fault Tolerance Status:	**Protected**
Secondary Location:	pod-1-blade-7.v12nlab.net
Total Secondary CPU:	29 MHz
Total Secondary Memory:	768.00 MB
vLockstep Interval:	⊘ 0.064 seconds
Log Bandwidth:	20 KBps

Once you've met the requirements, there isn't any configuration to vSphere FT after you've enabled it.

Before wrapping up this discussion of vSphere FT, I want to discuss using vSphere FT in conjunction with vSphere HA and vSphere DRS. I'll start with vSphere FT and vSphere HA together.

Using vSphere Fault Tolerance with vSphere High Availability

vSphere FT works in conjunction with vSphere HA. Recall that vSphere HA must be enabled on both the cluster and the VM in order to enable vSphere FT. As I mentioned previously, if the ESXi host where the primary VM is running fails, the secondary VM takes over and a new secondary VM is created automatically to ensure protection. But what happens if there are multiple host failures?

In the event of multiple host failure, vSphere HA will restart the primary VM. vSphere FT will then re-create the secondary VM again on another host to ensure protection.

In the case of a guest OS failure, vSphere FT will take no action because, as far as FT is concerned, the VMs are in sync. Both VMs will fail at the same time and place. vSphere HA VM monitoring — if enabled — can detect the failure in the primary and restart it, and the secondary creation process will start again. Have you noticed a pattern about the secondary VMs? After the sync has failed, the secondary machine is always re-created. This helps avoid any potential split-brain issues with vSphere FT.

ONE OS IMAGE VERSUS TWO OS IMAGES

vSphere FT's behavior when it comes to guest OS failure is misunderstood by many people. If the guest OS in the primary VM crashes, the guest OS in the secondary VM is also going to crash. While these appear to be two separate guest OS instances, they are really one synchronized guest OS instance running in lockstep on two different ESXi hosts. A failure in one will mean a failure in both.

This is markedly different from traditional guest OS clustering solutions, which rely on two separate and distinct guest OS instances. If one of the guest OS instances fails, the other instance is still up and running and can take over for the failed instance. Microsoft Windows Failover Clustering is one example of this sort of configuration.

Understanding these differences between guest OS clustering and vSphere FT will help you choose the right high-availability mechanism for your particular application and needs.

Using vSphere Fault Tolerance with vSphere Distributed Resource Scheduler

vSphere FT can also interoperate and integrate with vSphere DRS. However, it requires the use of VMware EVC in order for this interoperability and integration to function properly.

When VMware EVC is enabled at the cluster level, vSphere FT can also take advantage of vSphere DRS. When VMware EVC is enabled and vSphere DRS is enabled and set to fully automated, vSphere DRS will make the initial placement recommendations for the fault-tolerant VMs, will include the fault-tolerant VMs during cluster rebalancing calculations and operations, and will allow you to assign a vSphere DRS automation level to the primary VM (the secondary VM assumes the same setting as the primary VM).

Without EVC, vSphere DRS is set to Disabled for the fault-tolerant VMs, initial placement is provided only for the secondary VM, and neither of the fault-tolerant VMs is included in cluster rebalancing calculations or operations.

Examining vSphere Fault Tolerance Use Cases

vSphere FT is not designed or meant to be run on all your VMs. You should use this service sparingly and take this form of fault tolerance only for your most important VMs. Suggested general guidelines recommend that there be no more than four to eight vSphere FT–protected VMs — primary or secondary — on any single ESXi host. Your mileage will vary, so be cautious in your own environment. Remember, once you have primary and secondary VMs locked and in sync, you will be using double the resources for a protected VM.

Now that we have looked at a couple of high-availability options, let's move on to planning and designing for disaster recovery.

Planning for Business Continuity

High availability is only part of the solution, one component in the bigger picture of business continuity. Business continuity is about ensuring that the business can continue operating in the face of some significant event. High availability deals with business continuity from a fairly narrow perspective: ensuring that the business can continue operating in the event of a physical server failure, an OS or application failure, or a network component failure. There are many more types of failures that you must account for and protect against, but I'll mention two primary ones here:

◆ First, you'll need to protect against the loss of data due to equipment failure, software malfunction, or simple user error (ever deleted something by mistake?).

◆ Second, you'll want to ensure you've done the necessary work around planning for disaster recovery, in the event your entire datacenter is rendered unusable or unavailable.

Most organizations have a policy or a set of policies that define the processes, procedures, tools, and technologies that help address these failure scenarios. As you review the information provided in this section, you'll want to be sure that any solution you are considering complies with your company's policy for business continuity. If your company doesn't yet have a policy for business continuity, now is a great time to create one!

In the next two sections, I'll look at both of these failure scenarios, along with some of the products and technologies that are applicable. First, let's start with data protection.

Providing Data Protection

Backups are an essential part of every IT department's responsibilities, yet they're often the source of the greatest conflict and frustration. Many organizations hoped that virtualizing would make backups easier, and in some ways it has. In other ways, it has made backups more difficult as well. In this section, I'll examine the basic methods for backing up VMs and then provide an overview of VMware Data Recovery, a backup solution provided by VMware to help with smaller implementations of vSphere.

EXAMINING VM BACKUP METHODS

There are two basic methods of backing up VMs in a VMware vSphere environment:

♦ Running a backup agent of some sort in the guest OS

♦ Leveraging vSphere snapshots and the vSphere Storage APIs for Data Protection (more popularly known as VADP)

While various backup applications might have slight variations, the basic methods remain the same. Each of these methods has its own advantages and disadvantages, and no one solution will be the right fit for all customers.

Figure 7.35 illustrates the flow of information when using backup agents inside the guest OS.

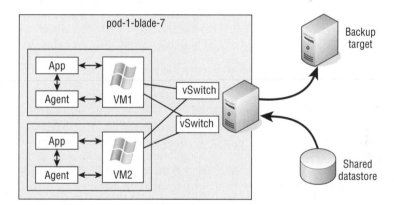

FIGURE 7.35
Running backup agents inside the guest OS can provide application- and OS-level integration, but not without some drawbacks.

As you can see from Figure 7.35, running a backup agent within the guest OS affords you OS-level and application-level awareness and integration. The backup agent can leverage the APIs of the guest OS to integrate with the OS and applications running in the OS (for example, by leveraging the Volume Shadow Copy Service in Microsoft Windows). This allows the backup agent to perform very granular backups, such as specific tables within a SQL database, particular mailboxes in Microsoft Exchange, or a subset of files within a Linux filesystem.

However, running backup agents within the guest OS has its drawbacks, too:

♦ The network traffic typically runs across the network, which can create network bottlenecks. This is especially true if the backup traffic runs across the same network as end user–facing traffic.

♦ To avoid bottlenecks with end user–facing traffic, organizations introduced dedicated backup networks. This means more NICs in the ESXi hosts, separate vSwitches, separate physical switches, additional vNICs in the VMs, and additional complexity in the guest OS and the solution as a whole. Separate backup networks can also complicate troubleshooting and operations.

◆ The backup agents are individually running in each guest OS instance, so as more and more VMs (and guest OS instances) are consolidated onto physical servers, this creates additional overhead. Given that the overall utilization of the physical hosts was higher anyway because of consolidation, this leaves little headroom for the backup process, which in turn often translates to longer backup windows.

◆ Some backup vendors charged a separate license for every installation of the backup agent, which had a negative impact on the financial benefits of virtualization and consolidation.

Despite these drawbacks, the tight OS- and application-level integration they offer make backup agents the preferred choice in areas where granularity and application integration are paramount.

The second primary way that backups are accomplished in the vSphere environment is to operate outside the guest OS. Instead, leverage the snapshot functionality of VMware vSphere to unlock the VM's virtual disks and then back up the virtual disks directly. When the backup of the virtual disk is complete, commit the snapshot and you're finished. The framework for driving this process in an automated fashion — so that backup vendors can make it easier to use — is the vSphere Storage APIs for Data Protection.

The overall process looks something like this:

1. The backup software requests a snapshot of the virtual disks for the VM to be backed up.

2. VMware vSphere creates a snapshot, and all writes to the virtual disks for that VM now start flowing into the delta disks. The base VMDK files are unlocked.

3. The backup application backs up the base VMDK files.

4. When the backup of the base VMDK files is complete, the backup software requests vSphere to commit the snapshot.

5. The writes in the delta disk are committed to the base VMDK, and the snapshot is removed.

6. The process repeats itself for the next VM.

VADP not only helps provide a standard interface for backup vendors to use to interact with vSphere for the purpose of backing up VMs, but it also introduces a couple of other useful features. Changed Block Tracking (CBT), for example, allows vSphere and backup applications to track which blocks in a VMDK have changed and back up only those changed blocks. You can consider CBT the VMDK block equivalent of the archive flag in DOS and NTFS.

Like in-guest backups, VADP-based backups also have advantages and disadvantages:

◆ There is generally less processor and memory overhead because there's no need to run a backup agent inside every guest OS instance. Depending on the environment, this might afford you the ability to achieve a higher consolidation ratio or provide better performance for your workloads.

◆ Because there is generally little to no coordination with applications running in the guest OS instances, VADP-based backups typically cannot provide the same level of backup/restore granularity as in-guest backups. There may also be issues ensuring application consistency.

◆ Depending on the implementation of the VADP-based backup solution, file-level restores may be difficult. Some of these solutions require that you restore the entire VM and then manually pull out the individual file or files that need to be restored. This is an operational consideration you'll want to be sure to incorporate in your evaluation.

Numerous backup vendors leverage VADP to perform VM backups. In fact, VMware itself provides an entry-level backup solution that leverages VADP. That solution is called VMware Data Recovery.

IMPLEMENTING VMWARE DATA RECOVERY

VMware Data Recovery (VDR) is a disk-based backup and recovery solution. This solution fully integrates with vCenter Server to enable centralized and efficient management backup jobs, and it also includes data deduplication. VDR leverages VADP to streamline the process of backing up VMs.

So, how does VDR work? VDR is composed of three main components. The first component is the VDR virtual backup appliance that will manage the backup and recovery process. The second component is the user interface plug-in for vCenter Server. The third and last component is the deduplicated destination storage.

Using the vCenter Server interface, you pick the VMs that you want to protect. You can then schedule the backup job, configure the data-retention policy, and select the destination disk that the backup will go to. vCenter Server will then send the job information to the VDR virtual backup appliance to start the backup process by initiating the point-in-time snapshots of the protected VM. Like its predecessor, VDR frees up network traffic on the LAN by mounting the snapshot directly to the VDR virtual backup appliance. After the snapshot is mounted, the virtual appliance begins streaming the block-level data directly to the destination storage. It is during this streaming process, before the data gets to the destination disks, that the VDR appliance will deduplicate the data to ensure the redundant data is eliminated. After all the data has been written to the destination disk, the VDR appliance will then dismount the snapshot and apply the snapshot to the VM.

Backups are no good if you can't recover the data, naturally. With VDR, the recovery process is a point-in-time file-level or complete system restoration. The VDR virtual backup appliance will retrieve and stream the specific blocks of data that are needed for the restore. The virtual appliance will efficiently transfer only that data that has changed. This speeds up and streamlines the process. When restoring a single file, or file-level restore, the process is initiated from inside the VM console.

In the end, the method you use to provide data protection isn't what's important. What's important is that you do provide data protection for your virtualized datacenter.

USING YOUR STORAGE ARRAY TO PROTECT DATA

Many of the storage vendors have started adding the ability to do point-in-time snapshots of the data on the array. The specifics of how the snapshots work will vary from vendor to vendor, and — as with so many other aspects of Information Technology — there are advantages and disadvantages to each approach. The result of this functionality is the ability to hold point-in-time views of your company's information for a predetermined amount of time. This time frame could be hours, days, weeks, or months depending on the amount of disk you have provided for this. These snapshots can serve as a "first line of defense" in data protection. Here's an example. Let's say a VM was deleted by accident. With point-in-time restore, you can dial back in time to right before the VM was deleted. Mount the LUN from that specific moment in time, and restore your VM. Keep in mind, though, that array-based snapshots should not be considered a replacement for more traditional data-protection solutions but rather as a complementary tool designed to work hand in hand with these solutions.

Recovering from Disasters

High availability is only half of the ability to keep your application/systems up in day-to-day operation. The other half is disaster recovery, which is the ability to recover from a catastrophic failure. Hurricane Andrew and Hurricane Katrina demonstrated the importance of having a well-thought-out and well-designed plan in place. They also showed the importance of being able to execute that plan. Datacenters disappeared from the power of these storms, and the data-centers that remained standing and functioning did not stay functioning long when the generators ran out of gas. I believe when Hurricane Katrina came to visit New Orleans, the aftermath drove the point home that businesses need to be prepared.

I can remember what life was like before virtualization. The disaster recovery (DR) team would show up, and the remote recovery site was slated with the task of recovering the enterprise in a timely manner. A timely manner back then was at least a few days to build and install the recovery servers and then restore the enterprise from the backup media.

Sounds simple, right? Well, in theory, it was supposed to be, but there are always problems that occur during the process. First, during the recovery process, you almost never get to restore your environment at the remote datacenter location to the same make and model that you have running in your current environment. After you restore your data from your backup media, one of the joys is the pretty blue screen that you get because the drivers are different. For the most part, after the restore is finished, you can rerun the installation of the drivers for the recovery servers, but Murphy tends to show up and lay down his law.

Second, the restore process itself is another form of literal contention. If your backup strategy is not designed to consider which servers you want to recover first, then during a disaster, when you try to restore and bring up systems based on importance, you will have a lot a time wasted waiting for tape machines to become available. This contention becomes even worse if your backups span more than one tape. Speaking of tapes, it was not uncommon for tapes to become corrupt and unreadable. It was common for backups to be done and the tapes to be sent off site, but the tapes were hardly tested until they were needed. If all goes well, in a few days you might be done, but to be honest, success was sometimes a hard thing to find.

That old-school methodology has advanced and has changed the future with it. Now, a majority of data is kept on the SAN, and the data is replicated to another SAN at your remote disaster recovery co-location site. So, your data is waiting for you when it becomes time to recover, which really speeds up the recovery process in general. At first this was an expensive undertaking because only the high-dollar enterprise SANs had this capability. Over the years, though, this is becoming more the standard and is now a must-have in just about any SAN environment.

To set up SAN replication, a company would purchase two SANs that would be set up at different locations, and the data would be replicated between the two sites. Many different vendors have replication solutions, and the particulars of these replication solutions vary from vendor to vendor. Some replication solutions use Fibre Channel (or Fibre Channel over IP, FCIP); others use standard TCP/IP connections. Some replication solutions support only that vendor's storage arrays (like EMC SRDF or NetApp SnapMirror), while other replication solutions support heterogeneous storage environments. Some replication solutions allow for replicated data to be "split off" for other purposes (might be good for backups); others don't have that functionality.

In spite of these differences, all replication solutions fall into one of two very broad buckets:

◆ Synchronous replication solutions

◆ Asynchronous replication solutions

In synchronous replication solutions, the primary array waits until the secondary array has acknowledged each write before sending a write acknowledgement back to the host, ensuring that the replicated copy of the data is always as current as the primary. This is where the resultant latency comes into play and increases significantly with the distance. This also means that synchronous replication solutions are generally limited in distance in order to keep the latency to a minimum.

Asynchronous replication solutions transfer data to the secondary array in chunks and do not wait for a write acknowledgement from the remote array before acknowledging the write to the host. Using this method, the remote copy of the data will never be as current as the primary copy, but this method can replicate data over very long distances (long distances translate into high latencies, generally) and with reduced bandwidth requirements.

In a vSphere environment, you can combine SAN replication — synchronous or asynchronous — with VMware Site Recovery Manager (SRM), a workflow automation tool that helps administrators with the task of orchestrating the startup of all the VMs in a datacenter. SRM is a great product but well outside the scope of this book. However, you can refer to the VMware SRM website at `www.vmware.com/products/site-recovery-manager/` for more information.

---

vSphere High Availability Failover with Synchronous Replication?

Earlier in this chapter I told you that you could not perform HA failover to another site. As a general rule, this is true — even with synchronous SAN replication. Although synchronous SAN replication ensures the data in the remote site is always up to date, every traditional replication product on the market today marks the replication target as read only. This means that you can't failover via vSphere HA, because the target datastore is read only. As new solutions are brought to market that enable read/write access to storage in multiple locations at the same time, this ability becomes a reality.

In this chapter, I explained that high availability is for increasing uptime, and business continuity is about ensuring the business can continue in the event of a significant adverse event. The bottom line, to be blunt, is that you'd better have both in place in your environment. High availability is an important part of any IT shop, and proper thought should be used when creating or designing a solution. However, you cannot stop there and absolutely must test, test, and test again any solution to make sure that it is working as designed and, most important, that it will work when you need it.

The Bottom Line

Understand Windows clustering and the types of clusters.   Windows clustering plays a central role in the design of any high-availability solution for both virtual and physical servers. Microsoft Windows clustering gives us the ability to have application failover to the secondary server when the primary server fails.

> **Master It**   Specifically with regard to Windows clustering in a virtual environment, what are three different types of cluster configurations that you can have?

> **Master It**   What is the key difference between NLB clusters and Windows Failover clusters?

Use VMware vSphere's built-in high-availability functionality.   VMware Virtual Infrastructure has high-availability options built in and available to you out of the box: vSphere High Availability (HA) and vSphere Fault Tolerance (FT). These options help you provide better uptime for your critical applications.

> **Master It**   What are the two types of high-availability options that VMware provides in vSphere, and how are they different?

Recognize differences between different high-availability solutions.   A high-availability solution that operates at the Application layer, like Oracle Real Application Cluster (RAC), is different in architecture and operation from an OS-level clustering solution like Windows Failover clustering. Similarly, OS-level clustering solutions are very different from hypervisor-based solutions such as vSphere HA or vSphere FT. Each approach has advantages and disadvantages, and today's administrators will likely need to use multiple approaches in their datacenter.

> **Master It**   Name one advantage of a hypervisor-based high-availability solution over an OS-level solution.

Understand additional components of business continuity.   There are other components of ensuring business continuity for your organization. Data protection (backups) and replication of your data to a secondary location are two areas that can help ensure business continuity needs are satisfied, even in the event of a disaster.

> **Master It**   What are three methods to replicate your data to a secondary location and what is the golden rule for any continuity plan?

Chapter 8

Securing VMware vSphere

On a scale of 1 to 10 in importance, security always rates close to a 10 in setting up and managing a vSphere environment. Well, maybe not — but it should. Even though VMware has increased the capabilities and features that come with its products, these same products and features must fit within the security policies applied to other servers. Most of the time, ESXi and vCenter Server fit easily and nicely within those security policies, but sometimes the process is a bit of a challenge. This chapter examines the tools and techniques that will help you ensure your vSphere environment appropriately follows the security policies of your organization.

In this chapter, you will learn to

◆ Configure and control authentication to vSphere

◆ Manage roles and access controls

◆ Control network access to services on ESXi hosts

◆ Integrate with Active Directory

Overview of vSphere Security

Like most other areas of security within information technology, securing a vSphere environment means securing all the different components of vSphere. Specifically, securing vSphere means securing the following components:

◆ The ESXi hosts

◆ vCenter Server

◆ The VMs, specifically the guest operating systems (guest OSes) running inside the VMs

◆ The applications running in the VMs

In this chapter I'll discuss the security considerations for the vSphere components: the ESXi hosts, vCenter Server, and the guest OSes running in your VMs. Each of these components has its own unique set of security challenges, and each of these components has different ways of addressing those security challenges. For example, ESXi has a different set of security challenges than the Windows-based vCenter Server or the Linux-based vCenter Server virtual appliance. I won't address how to secure the applications within your VMs because that task falls well outside the scope of this book. I do encourage you, however, to be sure to keep application-level security in mind as you work toward securing your vSphere environment. When considering how to secure the various components involved in a vSphere environment, the three different aspects to security that you must consider are these:

◆ Authentication

◆ Authorization

◆ Accounting

This model — often referred to as the AAA model — describes the way in which a user must be authenticated (properly identified as who he or she claims to be), authorized (enabled or permitted to perform a task, which also includes network access controls), and accounted (all actions are tracked and logged for future reference). In using this AAA model, you can ensure that you've covered the key aspects of securing the different components of a vSphere environment. I'll use the AAA model as a rough guideline to structure the discussion of securing vSphere in this chapter.

As you work your way through this chapter, keep in mind that some of the recommendations I make here have absolutely nothing to do with virtualization. Because virtualizing with vSphere affects many different areas of the datacenter, you also have to consider all those areas when you look at security. Further, some of the recommendations I make are ones that I've also made elsewhere in the book, so you might see some duplicate information. Security should be woven into every aspect of your vSphere design and implementation, so it's completely natural that you'll see some of the same tips during this focused discussion on security.

The first components I discuss securing are the ESXi hosts.

Securing ESXi Hosts

VMware ESXi sits at the heart of vSphere, so it's fully expected that any discussion of how to secure vSphere includes a discussion on how to secure ESXi. In this section, I'll discuss securing your ESXi hosts using the AAA model as a guiding framework, starting with the concept of authentication.

Working with ESXi Authentication

The majority of what you need to do as a vSphere administrator involves working with vCenter Server. Even so, it's still necessary to discuss how ESXi handles user authentication, because the mechanism vCenter Server uses to manage ESXi hosts also relies on ESXi authentication. Additionally, there are occasions where it might be necessary to connect directly to an ESXi host. Although using vCenter Server eliminates the largest part of the need to connect directly to an ESXi host, the need does not go away entirely. There are instances when a task cannot be accomplished through vCenter Server. Some examples include the following:

◆ vCenter Server is not available or is down.

◆ You are troubleshooting ESXi boot and configuration problems.

Because the need to authenticate to ESXi still exists (even if you are authenticating indirectly through vCenter Server), you need to understand what options exist for managing users and groups on ESXi hosts. There are two basic options: managing users and groups locally on each host or integrating with Active Directory. I'll cover each of these options in the following sections.

MANAGING USERS AND GROUPS LOCALLY

In most cases, the number and the frequency of use of local user accounts on an ESXi host have both diminished considerably. Usually, two or three accounts are all that are needed for access to an ESXi host. Why two or three and not just one? The best reason to have at least two accounts is in case one of the user accounts is unavailable during situations such as user vacations, sickness, or accidents. As you already know, users and groups on ESXi hosts are, by default, managed independently per ESXi host. Because the need for local accounts is so greatly diminished, many organizations find that the administrative overhead of managing only a couple of accounts across multiple ESXi hosts is an acceptable burden.

If this is the case in your environment, you have two ways of managing users and groups locally. You can use command-line tools, or you can use the vSphere Client. The method that is right for you will largely depend on your experience and preferences. For example, I feel very comfortable using the command line, so using the command-line interface (CLI) would be my first choice. However, if you are more comfortable with a Windows-based application, then the vSphere Client is the best option for you. I'll describe both methods in this section so you can choose the method that works best for you.

Perform the following steps to view local users and groups with the vSphere Client:

1. Launch the vSphere Client if it is not already running, and connect to an ESXi host.

   You cannot manage local users and groups in the vSphere Client while connected to a vCenter Server instance.

2. Select the ESXi host from the inventory list on the left.

3. Click the Local Users & Groups tab in the content pane on the right.

On the Local Users & Groups tab, you can create new users or groups, edit existing users or groups including changing the password, and delete users and groups. I'll walk through each of these tasks shortly.

You can also use the CLI to manage local users and groups. Although ESXi offers a local shell (I'll discuss the ESXi local shell in a bit more detail in the section "Controlling Local CLI Access"), the preferred way of using the CLI to work with ESXi is via the vSphere CLI (also referred to as the vCLI). Personally, I find using the vSphere Management Assistant (vMA) the best way of working with the vSphere CLI. As I show you the process for creating, editing, and deleting local users or groups in the next few sections, the CLI environment I'll use and describe is the vMA.

Let's take a look at creating a user or group, editing a user or group, and deleting a user or group.

Creating a Local User or Group

Perform the following steps (these steps assume you're already viewing the Local Users & Groups tab in the vSphere Client) to create a local user or group using the vSphere Client:

1. Right-click a blank area of the Local Users & Groups tab and select Add.

This opens the Add New User dialog box.

2. Supply a login and (optionally) a UID and username.

   If you do not supply a UID, the system will assign the next-available UID, starting at 500. If the ESXi host is being managed by vCenter Server, UID 500 might already be taken by the vpxuser account, which I'll explain later in this chapter in the section "Understanding the vpxuser Account."

3. Enter and confirm the password for the new user account.

4. If you want this user to be able to use the ESXi Shell, check Grant Shell Access To This User.

5. Under Group Membership, select Users from the drop-down list of groups and click Add.

   This adds the new user to the Users group.

6. Click OK to create the user with the specified values.

   The new user appears in the list of users.

In the section "Managing ESXi Host Permissions," I'll show you how to assign a role to this user to control what actions the user is allowed to perform.

Perform these steps to create a local group using the vSphere Client:

1. Click the Groups button near the top of the Local Users & Groups tab.

2. Right-click a blank area of the tab and select Add.

   This opens the Create New Group dialog box.

3. Specify a group name and, optionally, a group ID.

   If you do not specify a group ID, the system will assign one automatically, starting with 500.

4. From the drop-down list, select the user you'd like to add to this group and click Add. Repeat the process for each user you want to add.

5. Click OK to create the group and return to the vSphere Client.

   The new group will appear in the list of groups on the Local Users & Groups tab.

You can also use the CLI to create users and groups. From the vMA, you can use the `vicfg-user` command to create users and groups on a specific ESXi host.

Perform these steps to create a user or group using the CLI:

1. Establish an SSH session to the vMA.

2. From the vMA command prompt, enter this command to create a new user account on a specific ESXi host:

   ```
   vicfg-user --server server.domain.com --username root --entity user --login
   LoginName --operation add
   ```

   To create a new group, replace the `--entity` and `--login` parameters, like this:

```
vicfg-user --server server.domain.com --username root --entity group --group
GroupName --operation add
```

3. Depending on your vMA configuration, you might be prompted for a password to execute the command. Enter the password for the user specified in the previous command (root, in my example).

4. If you are creating a new user account, you will be prompted for the password for the new user. Enter the password you want assigned to the new user account you are creating, and then confirm that password when prompted again.

Figure 8.1 shows the vMA prompting for a password to perform the command as well as the password for the new user account.

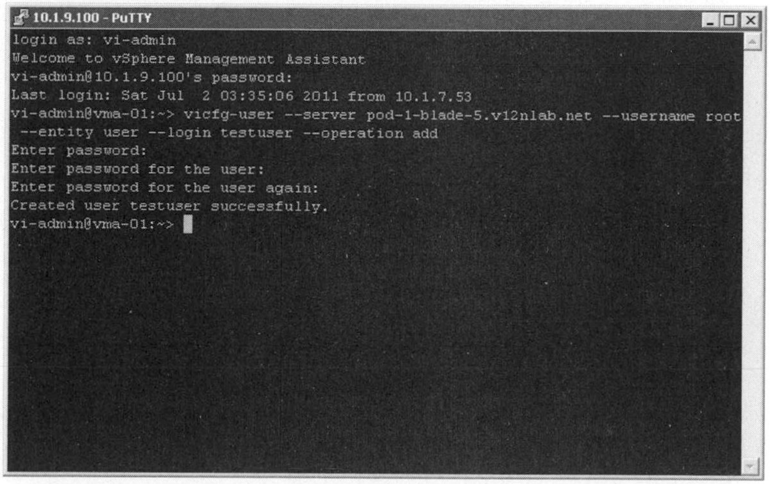

FIGURE 8.1
The vicfg-user command prompts for a password to execute the command and then prompts for a password for the new user you are creating.

```
login as: vi-admin
Welcome to vSphere Management Assistant
vi-admin@10.1.9.100's password:
Last login: Sat Jul  2 03:35:06 2011 from 10.1.7.53
vi-admin@vma-01:~> vicfg-user --server pod-1-blade-5.v12nlab.net --username root
--entity user --login testuser --operation add
Enter password:
Enter password for the user:
Enter password for the user again:
Created user testuser successfully.
vi-admin@vma-01:~>
```

As I mentioned previously, creating a new user or group is only part of the process; in order to use that account with the vSphere Client, you also need to assign a role. I'll cover roles and permissions in the section "Managing ESXi Host Permissions."

Now let's take a look at editing a user or group from both the vSphere Client and from the CLI.

Editing a Local User or Group

Perform the following steps to edit a local user or group using the vSphere Client:

1. Assuming you've already launched the vSphere Client and connected to an ESXi host, select the ESXi host from the inventory and click the Local Users & Groups tab.

2. Right-click the user you want to modify and select Edit.

   This opens the Edit User dialog box.

3. From the Edit User dialog box, make any necessary changes to the user account.

   As you can see from Figure 8.2, the login field cannot be changed.

FIGURE 8.2

For a user, you can change the UID, username, password, and group membership, but you can't change the login field.

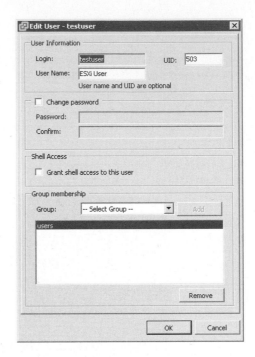

4. Click OK to make the changes to the selected user account.

To edit a group using the vSphere Client, the steps are almost identical to these. However, when editing a group, the context menu won't show an Edit command; you'll use Properties instead. Also, when editing a group, you can't change any properties of the group except its members.

Perform the following steps to edit a local user or group using the CLI:

1. Using PuTTY.exe (Windows) or a terminal window (Mac OS X or Linux), establish an SSH session to the vMA instance.

2. Use this command to modify a user account on a specific ESXi host:

   vicfg-user --server **pod-1-blade-5.v12nlab.net** --username **root** --entity user
   --login **LoginName** --newusername **"New Full Name"** --operation modify

   To modify a group, change the --entity and --login parameters, like this:

   Vicfg-user --server **pod-1-blade-5.v12nlab.net** --username **root** --entity group
   --operation modify --group **TestGroup** --adduser **testuser** --removeuser **bob**

As with the vSphere Client, editing a group via vicfg-user is limited to adding users to or removing users from the group.

3. If prompted for the password to execute the command (this will depend on your vMA configuration), enter the password for the user specified with the `--username` parameter.

Let's wrap up this discussion of managing local users and groups with a review of how to delete local users and groups from an ESXi host.

Deleting a Local User or Group

Perform the following steps to delete a local user or group from a specific ESXi host using the vSphere Client:

1. After you've connected to the desired ESXi host using the vSphere Client, select the ESXi host from the inventory and click the Local Users & Groups tab.

2. To delete a user, click the Users button. To delete a group, click the Groups button.

3. Right-click the user or group you want to remove, and select Remove from the context menu. When prompted for confirmation, select Yes.

Perform these steps to delete a local user or group using the vCLI:

1. Log into the vMA via SSH using PuTTY.exe (Windows) or a terminal window (Mac OS X or Linux).

2. Use the following command to remove a user:

```
vicfg-user --server pod-1-blade-5.v12nlab.net --username root --entity user
--operation delete --login UserName
```

To remove a group, change the `--entity` and `--login` parameters:

```
vicfg-user --server pod-1-blade-5.v12nlab.net --username root --entity group
--operation delete --group GroupName
```

Note that you cannot delete a group from the CLI without first removing all of its members. This limitation does not apply when deleting a group from the vSphere Client.

TO VC OR NOT TO VC

The best way to administer your vSphere environment is to connect the vSphere Client to a vCenter Server instance. Although you can connect the vSphere Client to an ESXi host directly, you lose a great deal of functionality. If you didn't purchase vCenter Server, you may have no other choice than to connect to the ESXi hosts. In such instances, you'd have to create user accounts locally on the ESXi hosts for VM administration as outlined in the section "Managing Users and Groups Locally."

Now that you have an idea of the specific steps used to manage users and groups locally on each ESXi host, what are the security challenges involved in doing so? And how can those security challenges be addressed? Here are just a couple of examples:

◆ You must manually manage users and groups separately on each and every ESXi host. If you forget to delete a user account for a departing employee on a specific ESXi host, you've just created a potential security problem.

◆ There is no way to centrally enforce password policies. Although you can set password policies on each ESXi host, you have to do this separately on every ESXi host in your environment. If you ever need to change the password policy, you must do so on each ESXi host individually.

You can address both of these particular security challenges by leveraging functionality provided by VMware with ESXi to integrate authentication into Active Directory, as you'll see in the next section.

ENABLING ACTIVE DIRECTORY INTEGRATION

You've already seen how, by default, ESXi uses local users and groups to assign permissions to directories and files. The presence of these local users and groups is the key to the ESXi security model, as you'll see in the section "Managing ESXi Host Permissions." Although these local users and groups form the foundation of the ESXi security model, managing these users and groups locally on every ESXi host in the enterprise can create a great deal of administrative overhead and has some security challenges, as I've already described.

What if you were able to continue to accommodate the need for local access to an ESXi host but in a way that avoided some of the security challenges of managing users and groups locally?

One answer to these security challenges is to use a centralized security authority. In vSphere 5, VMware includes the ability to use Microsoft Active Directory, a widely deployed directory service, as the centralized security authority for ESXi hosts. As you'll see in the section "Securing vCenter Server," the Windows-based version of vCenter Server already leverages Active Directory, so allowing your ESXi hosts to leverage the same security authority makes sense.

Before you can join your ESXi hosts into Active Directory, there are four prerequisites you need to satisfy:

◆ You must ensure that the time on your ESXi hosts is synchronized with the time on the Active Directory domain controllers. ESXi supports NTP, and in Chapter 2, "Planning and Installing VMware ESXi," I showed you how to configure NTP on your ESXi hosts.

◆ You must ensure that your ESXi hosts can resolve the Active Directory domain name and locate the domain controllers via DNS. Typically, this means configuring the ESXi hosts to use the same DNS servers as the Active Directory domain controllers.

◆ The fully qualified domain name (FQDN) of the ESXi host must use the same domain suffix as the Active Directory domain.

◆ You must create an ESX Admins group in Active Directory. Put the user accounts that should be permitted to connect to an ESXi host in this group. You can't use any other group name; it must be named ESX Admins.

Once you've satisfied these prerequisites, you can configure your ESXi host to authenticate to Active Directory.

Perform these steps to configure your ESXi host to use Active Directory as its centralized security authority:

1. Log into the ESXi host using the vSphere Client and authenticating with the root account (or an equivalent account).

2. Select the ESXi host from the inventory and click the Configuration tab.

3. From the Software section, select Authentication Services.

4. Click Properties in the upper-right corner.

5. From the Directory Services Configuration dialog box, select Active Directory from the Select Directory Service Type drop-down list.

6. Supply the DNS domain name of the Active Directory domain this ESXi host will use for authentication.

7. Click the Join Domain button.

8. Specify a username and password that has permission to allow the host to join the domain.

Once the ESXi host is joined to Active Directory, users will be able to authenticate to an ESXi host using their Active Directory credentials. Using the vSphere Client or the vCLI, users can use either the domain\username or username@domain syntax. From the vCLI, users must enclose the domain\username syntax in double quotes, as in this example:

```
vicfg-users --server pod-1-blade-5.v12nlab.net --username "v12nlab\administrator"
--entity group --operation list
```

To further simplify the use of the vMA, you can also configure the vMA to use Active Directory authentication.

Although managing how users authenticate is important, it's also important to control how users access ESXi hosts. In the next section, I'll examine how you can control access to your ESXi hosts.

Controlling Access to ESXi Hosts

The second part of the AAA model is authorization, which encompasses access control mechanisms that affect local access or network access. In this section, I'll describe the mechanisms available to you to control access to your ESXi hosts.

CONTROLLING LOCAL ACCESS

ESXi offers direct access via the server console through the Direct Console User Interface, or DCUI. I've shown you screenshots of the DCUI in various other parts of this book, such as Chapter 2.

Access to the DCUI is limited to users who have the Administrator role on that ESXi host. I haven't discussed the concept of roles yet (see "Managing ESXi Host Permissions" for more details), but this limitation on the DCUI allows you to control who is permitted to access the DCUI. Like other forms of security, it's important to secure access to the host via the physical server console, and limiting DCUI access to users with the Administrator role helps accomplish that goal.

Controlling Local CLI Access

ESXi has a CLI environment that is accessible from the server's physical console. However, by default, this CLI environment — known as the ESXi Shell — is disabled. If you need CLI access to ESXi, you must first enable the ESXi Shell. You can enable the ESXi Shell via the DCUI or via the vSphere Client.

Perform these steps to enable the ESXi Shell via the DCUI:

1. Access the console of the ESXi host using the physical server console or some KVM mechanism (many server vendors provide remote console functionality).

2. Press F2 to log into the DCUI. When prompted for username and password, supply a username and password with permission to access the DCUI (this user must have the Administrator role for this ESXi host).

3. Navigate down to Troubleshooting Options and press Enter.

4. Select Enable ESXi Shell.

   This enables the CLI environment on the ESXi host.

5. Press Escape until you return to the main DCUI screen.

6. Press Alt+F1 to access the CLI environment on that ESXi host.

   If your host is using local authentication, you can authenticate using a user account defined locally on that host. If your host is using Active Directory authentication as described in the previous section, you can log in using Active Directory credentials (using either the domain\username or username@domain syntax).

Perform the following steps to enable the ESXi Shell via the vSphere Client:

1. Connect to the ESXi host using the vSphere Client.

2. Select the ESXi host in the inventory, and click the Configuration tab.

3. From the Software section, select Security Profile.

4. Click the Properties hyperlink near Services.

   This opens the Services Properties dialog box.

5. Select ESXi Shell from the list of services and then click Options.

6. Click Start.

7. Click OK to return to the Services Properties dialog box.

    The status for the ESXi Shell should now be listed as Running.

8. Click OK to return to the vSphere Client.

    The ESXi Shell is now available.

You can now use the local CLI at the ESXi host's console. It's important to note, though, that VMware doesn't recommend regular, routine use of the ESXi Shell as your primary means of managing and maintaining ESXi. Instead, you should use the vSphere Client and/or the vMA and resort to the ESXi Shell only when absolutely necessary.

While following these steps gets you local CLI access, it doesn't get you remote CLI access. For remote CLI access, another step is required, as you'll see in the next section.

CONTROLLING REMOTE CLI ACCESS VIA SSH

Secure Shell, often referred to just as SSH, is a widely known and widely used encrypted remote console protocol. SSH was originally developed in 1995 to replace other protocols, such as `telnet`, `rsh`, and `rlogin`, that did not provide strong authentication and did not protect against password-sniffing attacks on the network. SSH gained rapid adoption, and the SSH-2 protocol is now a proposed Internet standard with the Internet Engineering Task Force (IETF).

ESXi includes SSH as a method of remote console access. This allows vSphere administrators to use an SSH client, such as `PuTTY.exe` on Windows or OpenSSH on Linux or Mac OS X, to remotely access the CLI of an ESXi host in order to perform management tasks. However, like the ESXi Shell, SSH access to an ESXi host is disabled by default. In order to gain remote CLI access to an ESXi host via SSH, you must first enable the ESXi Shell and enable SSH. You've already seen how to enable the ESXi Shell; now I'll show you how to enable SSH, both via the DCUI and via the vSphere Client.

Perform the following steps to enable SSH via the DCUI:

1. Access the console of the ESXi host using the physical server console or some KVM mechanism (many server vendors provide remote console functionality).

2. Press F2 to log into the DCUI. When prompted for username and password, supply a username and password with permission to access the DCUI (this user must have the Administrator role for this ESXi host).

3. Navigate down to Troubleshooting Options and press Enter.

4. Select Enable SSH. This enables the SSH server (or daemon) on the ESXi host.

5. Press Escape until you return to the main DCUI screen.

Perform these steps to enable SSH via the vSphere Client:

1. Connect to the ESXi host using the vSphere Client.

2. Select the ESXi host in the inventory and click the Configuration tab.

3. From the Software section, select Security Profile.

4. Click the Properties hyperlink near Services.

   This opens the Services Properties dialog box.

5. Select SSH from the list of services; then click Options.

6. Click Start.

7. Click OK to return to the Services Properties dialog box.

   The status for SSH should now be listed as Running.

8. Click OK to return to the vSphere Client. You can now use PuTTY.exe (Windows) or OpenSSH (Mac OS X, Linux, and other Unix variants) to establish an SSH session to the ESXi host.

As with local CLI access, VMware recommends against using SSH as a means of routinely managing your ESXi hosts. In fact, in previous versions of vSphere, SSH access to ESXi was unsupported. It is supported in this version of vSphere, but VMware still recommends against its regular use. If you want to use a CLI environment, I recommend getting familiar with the vMA as your primary CLI environment.

ROOT LOGIN VIA SSH IS ENABLED BY DEFAULT

Generally speaking, allowing the root user to log in to a host via SSH is considered a violation of security best practices. However, in vSphere 5, when SSH and the ESXi Shell are enabled, the root user is allowed to log in via SSH. This is yet one more reason to keep SSH and the ESXi Shell disabled during the normal course of operation.

Although VMware provides SSH as a means of accessing the CLI environment on an ESXi host, this version of SSH does not provide all the same flexibility as a "full" SSH installation. This further underscores the need to use SSH on an as-needed basis as well as the need for additional access controls for your ESXi hosts, such as a network firewall.

CONTROLLING NETWORK ACCESS VIA THE ESXI FIREWALL

ESXi ships with a firewall that controls network traffic into or out of the host. This firewall gives the vSphere administrator an additional level of control over what types of network traffic are allowed to enter or leave the ESXi hosts.

By default, the ESXi firewall allows only incoming and outgoing connections necessary for managing the VMs and the ESXi host. Some of the default ports open are as follows:

◆ TCP 443 and 902: vSphere Client, vCenter Agent

◆ UDP 53: Domain Name System (DNS) client

◆ TCP and UDP 427: Common Information Model (CIM) Service Location Protocol (SLP)

◆ TCP 8000: vMotion

◆ TCP 22: SSH

To see the full list of ports that are open on an ESXi host, use the vSphere Client connected directly to an ESXi host, as illustrated in Figure 8.3.

FIGURE 8.3
The Security Profile area of the Configuration tab in vCenter Server shows the current ESXi firewall configuration.

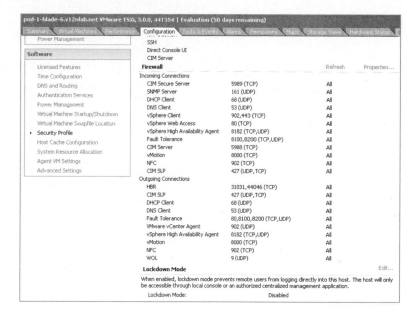

From this same area of the vSphere Client, you can also enable additional ports through the firewall or disable ports that are currently open. Unfortunately, there is no functionality provided to create your own custom definitions for traffic to be allowed through the firewall; you can only enable or disable services that are already defined.

Perform the following steps to enable or disable traffic through the ESXi firewall:

1. Launch the vSphere Client and connect to either an ESXi host or a vCenter Server instance.

2. Select an ESXi host from the inventory view and select the Configuration tab.

   If you connected to vCenter Server, you might need to navigate to the Hosts And Clusters inventory view first.

3. From the Software section, select Security Profile.

4. Click the Properties hyperlink to the right of the Firewall heading.

   This opens the Firewall Properties dialog box.

5. To enable a particular type of traffic through the ESXi firewall, select the check box next to that traffic type. To disable a type of traffic, deselect the check box for that traffic type.

6. Click OK to return to the vSphere Client.

The ESXi firewall also allows you to configure more fine-grained controls over network access by specifying specific source addresses from which traffic should be allowed. This gives you the ability to enable certain types of traffic through the ESXi firewall but restrict access to specific IP addresses or groups of IP addresses.

Perform these steps to limit access to a network service to a specific source:

1. Launch the vSphere Client and connect to either an ESXi host or a vCenter Server instance.

2. Select an ESXi host from the inventory view and select the Configuration tab.

   You might need to navigate to the Hosts And Clusters inventory view first if you are connected to a vCenter Server instance.

3. From the Software section, select Security Profile.

4. Click the Properties hyperlink to the right of the Firewall heading.

   This opens the Firewall Properties dialog box.

5. Select a particular port that is currently enabled through the firewall, and click the Firewall button.

   This opens the Firewall Settings dialog box.

6. To restrict access to a particular source, select Only Allow Connections From The Following Networks and specify a source address.

   You can specify the source address or addresses in three different formats:

   ◆ 192.168.1.24: A specific source IPv4 address

   ◆ 192.168.1.0/24: A specific subnet of source IPv4 addresses

   ◆ 2001::1/64: A subnet of source IPv6 addresses

   Figure 8.4 shows a source subnet of 10.0.0.0/8 configured for the selected network traffic.

FIGURE 8.4
Traffic to the selected network traffic on this ESXi host will be limited to addresses from the specified subnet.

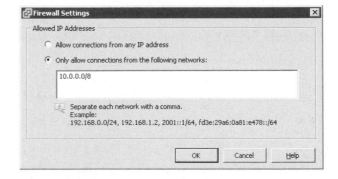

7. Click OK to close the Firewall Settings dialog box and return to the Firewall Properties dialog box.

8. Click OK to close the Firewall Properties dialog box and return to the vSphere Client.

This feature of the ESXi firewall gives you much more flexibility in not only defining what services are allowed into or out of your ESXi hosts but also in defining the source of the traffic into or out of the host. Maintaining the ESXi firewall configuration is an important part of ESXi host security.

Another recommended security practice is to isolate the ESXi management network so as to control network access to the management interfaces of your ESXi hosts. You can accomplish this using a network firewall, a technique I describe in the next section.

CONTROLLING NETWORK ACCESS TO THE ESXI MANAGEMENT INTERFACES

The ESXi firewall allows you to control access to specific TCP/IP ports on an ESXi host, but a further additional step to consider using is a network firewall to control access to the management interfaces of the ESXi host. Using a network firewall to enforce access control lists (ACLs) that govern which systems are allowed to make connections to the management interfaces of your ESXi hosts is a complementary step to using the ESXi firewall, and it follows the well-known recommended practice of using "defense in depth."

Should you choose to isolate the management interfaces of your ESXi hosts on a separate network segment, keep in mind the following two important considerations:

◆ Be sure to allow proper access from vCenter Server to the ESXi hosts. You can handle this by allowing the appropriate ports through the firewall or by adding an additional network interface on the isolated management segment to the vCenter Server system. Personally, I prefer the latter approach, but both approaches are perfectly valid.

◆ Don't forget to allow access from the vMA or from systems on which you will run PowerCLI scripts, if you'll be accessing the ESXi hosts directly. If the vMA or the PowerCLI scripts will be connecting to vCenter Server, then you just need to allow access to vCenter Server.

 Real World Scenario

USING A "JUMP BOX"

One technique that I've seen — and have used myself — in a fair number of installations is the use of a "jump box." This is a system — typically a Windows Server–based system — that has network interfaces to both the isolated management network as well as the rest of your network segments. You'll connect to the jump box and then connect from there to your vSphere environment using the vSphere Client, PowerCLI, vMA, or other tools. This neatly sidesteps the issue of having to create firewall rules to allow traffic into or out of the isolated management network but still provides access to manage the environment. If you are considering isolating the management interfaces of your ESXi hosts, this might be an approach to consider for your environment.

Controlling network access to your ESXi hosts is an important part of your overall security strategy, but it's also important to keep your ESXi hosts patched against security vulnerabilities.

Keeping ESXi Hosts Patched

Another key component in maintaining the security of your vSphere environment is keeping your ESXi hosts fully patched and up to date. On an as-needed basis, VMware releases security patches for ESXi. Failing to apply these security patches could expose your vSphere environment to potential security risks.

vSphere Update Manager (VUM) is the tool VMware supplies with vSphere to address this need. I discussed the VUM extensively in Chapter 4, "Installing and Configuring vSphere Update Manager." In order to keep your vSphere environment as secure as possible, you should strongly consider using VUM in your environment to keep your ESXi hosts patched.

In the next section, I'll move on to another aspect of authorization: the use of access controls to control what a user is allowed to do on an ESXi host after being authenticated.

Managing ESXi Host Permissions

I've shown you how to manage users and groups, both locally and through Active Directory integration, but there is another key aspect of ESXi host security to which I've referred but have not yet discussed. This is the concept of *roles*.

Both vCenter Server and ESXi hosts use the same structured security model to grant users the ability to manage portions of the virtual infrastructure. This model consists of users, groups, roles, privileges, and permissions, as shown in Figure 8.5.

FIGURE 8.5
vCenter Server and ESXi share a common security model for assigning access control.

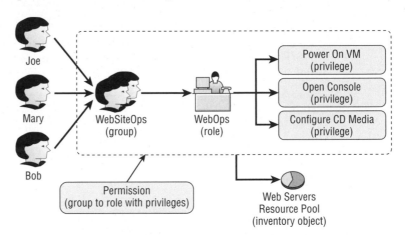

The items that differ between the non–vCenter Server environment and the vCenter Server environment are predominantly in the following two areas:

- The location of the user and group objects created

- The level of granularity of the roles and privileges available in each environment

You've already seen how ESXi can either use users and groups defined locally on each ESXi host or leverage Microsoft Active Directory as a centralized security authority. As you'll see later in the section "Securing vCenter Server," vCenter Server also leverages Active Directory as a centralized security authority, but it cannot and does not leverage local users and groups. This is the first key difference in managing permissions for environments that don't use vCenter Server versus environments that do use vCenter Server.

The second key difference is the level of granularity of the roles and privileges available in each environment. To explain this difference, I must first discuss and define roles and privileges.

For environments that don't have vCenter Server, or where the administrator chooses to have users authenticate directly to the ESXi hosts to perform management tasks, it is important to start with a discussion of the security model.

In the vCenter Server/ESXi security model's most basic format, users or groups are assigned to a role that has privileges. The user-role-privilege combination is then associated with an object in the inventory as a permission. This means there are four basic components to the vCenter Server/ESXi security model:

User or Group　A user is an authentication mechanism; a group is a way of collecting users. In earlier sections of this chapter, I showed you how to manage users and groups and how ESXi can leverage either local users and groups or users and groups from Active Directory. Users and groups form a basic building block of the security model.

Privilege　A privilege is an action that you can perform on an inventory object. This would include allocating space in a datastore, powering on a VM, configuring the network, or attaching a virtual CD/DVD to a VM.

Role　A role is a combination of a user or group with a collection of privileges. ESXi comes with some built-in roles, as I'll show you shortly, and you also have the ability to create your own custom roles.

Permission　A permission is the assignment of a role to an inventory object. For example, you might assign a role that has all privileges to a particular inventory object. Attaching the role to the inventory object creates a permission.

This flexible and modular security model provides a great deal of flexibility. vSphere administrators can either use the built-in roles provided with ESXi or create custom roles with custom sets of privileges and assign those custom roles to inventory objects in order to properly re-create the correct set of abilities in the virtual infrastructure. By associating roles with users or groups, vSphere administrators only need to define the role once; then, anytime someone needs those privileges, the administrator only needs to associate the appropriate user or group with the appropriate role. This can really help simplify the management of permissions.

An ESXi host has the following three default roles:

No Access　The No Access role works as the name suggests. This role prevents access to an object or objects in the inventory. The No Access role can be used if a user was granted access higher up in the inventory. The No Access role can also be used at lower-level objects to prevent object access. For example, if a user is granted permissions on the ESXi host but should be prevented access to a specific VM, you could use the No Access role on that specific VM.

Read-Only　Read-Only allows a user to see the objects within the vSphere Client inventory. It does not allow the user to interact with any of the visible objects in any way. For example, a user with the Read-Only permission would be able to see a list of VMs in the inventory but could not act on any of them.

Administrator　The Administrator role has the utmost authority, but it is only a role, and it needs to be assigned using a combination of a user or a group object and an inventory object such as a VM.

With only three built-in roles on ESXi hosts, the defaults don't leave room for much flexibility. In addition, the default roles just described can't be modified, so you can't customize the default roles. However, don't let that slow you down. Any limits created by the default roles are easily overcome by creating custom roles. You can create custom roles that will better suit your needs, or you can clone existing roles to make additional roles to modify for your own purposes.

Let's take a closer look at how to create a custom role.

CREATING CUSTOM ROLES

If you find that the default roles provided with ESXi don't suit your organization's needs with regard to permissions and management, then you should create custom roles to better map to your business needs. For example, assume that a set of users needs to interact with the console of a VM and also needs to change the CD and floppy media of those VMs. These needs aren't properly reflected in any of the default roles, so a custom role is necessary.

Perform the following steps to create a custom role named Operator:

1. Launch the vSphere Client if it is not already running, and connect to an ESXi host.

2. Navigate to the Administration area by using the navigation bar or by selecting View ➤ Administration ➤ Roles.

   You can also press the Ctrl+Shift+R keyboard shortcut.

3. Click the Add Role button.

4. Type the name of the new role in the Name text box (in this example, **Operator**), and then select the privileges that will be required by members of the role, as shown in Figure 8.6.

   The privileges shown in Figure 8.6 allow users or groups assigned to the Operator role to interact with the console of a VM, change the CD and floppy media and change the power state of a VM.

PERMISSIONS FOR CHANGING VIRTUAL MEDIA

To change floppy and CD media using floppy disk images (files with a `.flp` extension) and CD/DVD disk images (files with a `.iso` extension) that are stored on a SAN volume, you will also need to grant that group Browse Datastore privileges at the root of the hierarchy — in this case, at the ESXi host itself.

---

5. Click OK to complete the custom role creation.

The new Operator role is now defined, but it's not operational yet. You must still assign users or groups to the role and apply the role to the ESXi host and/or individual VM(s).

GRANTING PERMISSIONS

As simple and useful as roles are, they are not functional until a user or group is assigned to the role and then the role is assigned to an inventory object as a permission. Assume that a group of users exists that needs to interact with all VMs that are web servers. If access control is managed through the ESXi host, then you have to create a user account on that host (or leverage an Active Directory user account) together with a new group — for example, WebServerOps. Once these users and groups exist, you can execute the security model. (Refer to the sidebar "You Can't Mix

Active Directory Users and Local Groups" for more information on leveraging Active Directory when assigning roles.)

FIGURE 8.6

Custom roles strengthen management capabilities and add flexibility to permission delegations.

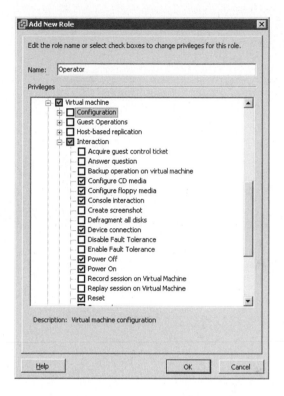

Perform the following steps to grant VM access control to a user or group:

1. Launch the vSphere Client if it is not already running, and connect to an ESXi host.

2. Right-click the object in the inventory tree on the left to which permission should be assigned, and click the Add Permission option. In this case, right-click the ESXi host.

3. Click the Add button in the Assign Permissions dialog box.

4. In the Select Users And Groups dialog box, select the appropriate user or group (for example, WebServerOps).

   Use the Domain drop-down box to show users and groups from Active Directory, if you've configured your ESXi host to integrate with Active Directory.

   Once you've found the user or group you want, click the Add button, and then click OK. This returns you to the Assign Permissions dialog box, where the user or group is listed on the left side of the dialog box.

5. From the Assigned Role drop-down list, choose the role to which the selected users or groups should be assigned. In this case, select Operator — the role you defined earlier — from the drop-down list to assign that role to the selected user or group.

You Can't Mix Active Directory Users and Local Groups

If you've integrated your ESXi hosts into Active Directory (as I described in the section "Enabling Active Directory Integration"), then you'll need to use Active Directory as your primary source for groups when assigning roles. While you can assign roles to a local group, that local group can't contain users from Active Directory. As a result, if you want to truly leverage Active Directory when assigning roles, you'll need to use Active Directory groups and not local groups.

What if you have an ESXi host that will host 30 VMs, and only 10 of those are the web server VMs? If you assign the permission at the ESXi host level, as I just demonstrated, then you'll assign that role to all 30 VMs, not just the 10 web server VMs. This is because when you assign a permission, an option named Propagate To Child Objects is enabled by default. Figure 8.7 shows the Assign Permissions dialog box; note the option to propagate permissions in the lower-right corner of the dialog box.

FIGURE 8.7
By default, assigning a permission to an object will propagate that permission to all child objects.

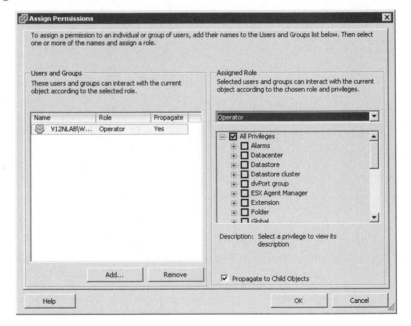

This option works like the inheritance settings in a Windows filesystem. It allows the privileges assigned in this role to be applied to objects beneath the selected object. For example, if the Operator role is applied as a permission on the ESXi host in the inventory panel and the Propagate To Child Objects option is enabled, all members of the Operator role will be able to interact with *all* the VMs hosted on the ESXi host. Although this certainly simplifies access control implementation, it adds another problem: the permissions of the Operator role have been overextended and now apply to all VMs and not just the web servers. With access control granted at the host level, members of the Operator role will be able to change floppy and CD media and use the console of the web server VMs, but they will also be able to do that on any other VM in the inventory.

To make this work as you would expect, you would have to assign permissions on each of the 10 web server VMs individually. Clearly, this is not an efficient process. Further growth resulting in more web server VMs would require additional administrative effort to ensure access control.

Alternatively, you could use the No Access role on the non-web-server–VMs to prevent access, but this method also does not scale well and requires administrative overhead.

This issue presents one of the drawbacks of managing access control on an individual ESXi host. Keep in mind as well that all of the steps we have discussed so far would have to be performed on each ESXi host in the virtual infrastructure. What if there were a way to organize the inventory of VMs? In other words, what if you could create a "container object" for the web server VMs, such as a folder, and put all the web server VMs into that folder? Then you could assign the group to the role at the parent object level and let inheritance take over. As shown in Figure 8.8, the problem is that folder objects are not possible on a single ESXi host. That means your only option is a resource pool.

FIGURE 8.8
Folder objects cannot be added to an individual ESXi host, leaving resource pools as the only viable option to group VMs.

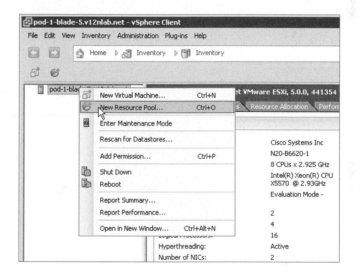

USING RESOURCE POOLS TO ASSIGN PERMISSIONS

A *resource pool* is actually a special object. Think of it as a folder of sorts. I'll discuss resource pools in much greater detail in Chapter 11, "Managing Resource Allocation"; I strongly urge you to read that chapter and understand the purpose behind resource pools and how they work before attempting to use them to organize your VMs. The focus here is on how resource pools can help you organize your VMs, but it's important to understand that using resource pools in this manner might have unintended side effects.

Perform the following steps to create a resource pool:

1. Launch the vSphere Client if it is not already running, and connect to an ESXi host.

2. Navigate to the inventory view by using the navigation bar, by using the Ctrl+Shift+H keyboard shortcut, or by selecting View ➢ Inventory ➢ Inventory from the menu.

3. Right-click the ESXi host, and select New Resource Pool, as shown previously in Figure 8.8.

4. Type a resource pool name in the Name text box, in this case **WebServers**.

5. Configure the resource allocations, if desired, to establish limits and reservations for the resource pool.

   The limit establishes a hard cap on the resource usage, while the reservations establish a resource guarantee.

6. Click OK.

So now that you've created the WebServers resource pool, you can place VMs into the resource pool, as shown in Figure 8.9. Putting VMs into a resource pool is simply a matter of creating new VMs in the resource pool (refer to Chapter 9, "Creating and Managing Virtual Machines," for creating new VMs) or dragging and dropping existing VMs into the resource pool.

FIGURE 8.9
As objects in the inventory, resource pools are potential levels of infrastructure management.

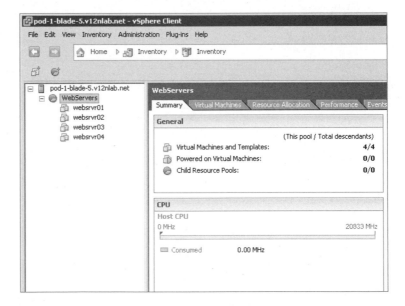

Additionally, resource pools become inventory objects to which permissions can be assigned. The same process you followed earlier, described in the section "Granting Permissions," applies here as well. Simply assign permission to the resource pool, and ensure that the Propagate To Child Objects check box is selected. Those permissions will also apply to all the VMs in the resource pool.

Using resource pools helps you accomplish a couple of key goals: better organization for your VMs and better control over permissions assigned to those VMs.

However, having said all of this, I must point out that I generally *do not recommend using resource pools in this way*. Although you can certainly use resource pools to organize VMs and assign permissions, resource pools are intended to help control resource allocation; they are not intended as a means of organizing VMs. In Chapter 11, I'll discuss resource allocation and why using resource pools solely for VM organization is generally not a good idea; I highly recommend reading that chapter and gaining a firm understanding of how resource pools affect resource allocation.

Now that I've shown you how to assign permissions, I need to show you how to remove permissions. Let's look at that next.

REMOVING PERMISSIONS

When your management needs change or if you've made some improper permissions assignments, you can remove permissions. In the section "Granting Permissions," you walked through the process of assigning the Operators role permission on the ESXi host. Now that you have a resource group in place to give you more granular control over permissions, you should remove the permissions you previously applied to the host.

Perform the following steps to remove permissions on an object in the inventory:

1. Launch the vSphere Client if it is not already running, and connect to an ESXi host.

2. Navigate to the inventory view using the navigation bar, the menu, or the keyboard shortcut.

3. Select the object in the inventory, and then select the Permissions tab.

   In this case, you need to remove the permissions from the ESXi host, so select the host from the inventory.

4. Right-click the permissions entry to be deleted from the list of existing permissions, and then click the Delete option.

You should see a warning indicating that users may retain their permissions because of assignments on parent objects higher in the hierarchy. In this case, you do want to remove the objects on the parent object (the ESXi host) because those permissions have been applied to the child object (the resource pool). In other cases, though, it might be necessary to keep permissions on the parent object.

After permissions are assigned throughout the inventory, it is easy to lose track of what has been previously done. Of course, if your company mandates documentation, there might already be a solid audit trail. However, it is easy to see existing role usage from within the vSphere Client.

IDENTIFYING PERMISSION USAGE

As the inventory of VMs and resource pools grows larger and more complex, it's very likely that the permissions granted to these various objects will also become complex. In addition, as company needs and management strategies change over time, these permissions need to change as well. Combined, these factors can create an environment where the permissions usage is quite complex and hard to decipher.

To help combat this issue, the vSphere Client's roles view helps administrators identify where roles have been assigned and what permissions have been granted in the inventory.

Perform the following steps to identify where a role has been assigned as a permission:

1. Launch the vSphere Client if it is not already running, and connect to an ESXi host.

2. Navigate to the roles view using the navigation bar, the Ctrl+Shift+R keyboard shortcut, or the View ➢ Administration ➢ Roles menu item.

3. Click the role whose usage you want to identify.

The details pane identifies where in the inventory hierarchy the role is used, as you can see illustrated in Figure 8.10.

FIGURE 8.10
The vSphere Client provides a break-down of where roles are currently in use.

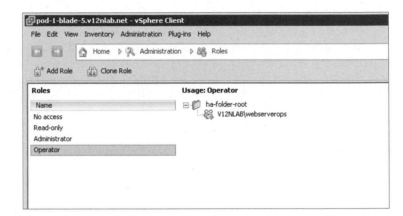

Using the vSphere Client's roles view allows you, the administrator, to track down where permissions have been assigned so that you can edit or remove permissions when necessary. But it's not only permissions that need to be removed — sometimes roles need to be removed, too.

EDITING AND REMOVING ROLES

Over time, it is almost inevitable that management needs will change. At times, you might have to create new roles, edit an existing role, or even delete a role. If the privileges assigned to a role are no longer applicable in your environment, you should edit the role to add or remove the necessary privileges.

Perform the following steps to edit a role:

1. Launch the vSphere Client if it is not already running, and connect to an ESXi host.

2. Navigate to the roles view using the navigation bar, the menu, or the keyboard shortcut.

3. Right-click the role you want to edit, and select Edit Role.

4. Make the desired changes by adding or removing privileges in the Edit Role dialog box. Click OK when you finish.

As I mentioned earlier in this chapter, ESXi won't allow you to edit the default roles.

If a role is no longer used, it should be removed to minimize the number of objects to be viewed and managed.

Perform the following steps to delete a role:

1. Launch the vSphere Client if it is not already running, and connect to an ESXi host.

2. Navigate to the roles view using the navigation bar, the Ctrl+Shift+R keyboard shortcut, or the View ➢ Administration ➢ Roles menu item.

3. Right-click the role to be deleted, and select Remove.

When a role is in use and is selected for removal, the ESXi host offers the opportunity to transfer the existing role members to a new role or to simply drop all members from the role. This eliminates the opportunity for accidentally deleting roles that are being used in the inventory.

Now that you understand how to work with local users, groups, roles, and permissions on an individual ESXi host, be aware that you are unlikely to do much of this. Managing local user accounts is administratively more cumbersome because of the lack of centralized management and authentication. Active Directory integration addresses a great deal of this, allowing you to collapse your user and group management into one centralized directory. However, you will still find that you perform most, if not all, of your access control work within vCenter Server. As you'll see in the section "Managing vCenter Server Permissions," vCenter Server offers greater flexibility than managing individual ESXi hosts.

The last area I'll discuss in this section on ESXi host security pertains to the third A in the AAA model: accounting. In other words, logging. Let's take a closer look at how to handle logs for your ESXi hosts.

Configuring ESXi Host Logging

Capturing information in the system logs is an important aspect of computer and network security. The system logs provide a record, or an accounting, of the actions performed, the events encountered, the errors experienced, and the state of the ESXi host and the VMs on that host.

Every ESXi host runs a syslog daemon (service) that captures events and logs them for future reference. Assuming that you've installed ESXi onto some local disks, the default location for the logs is on a 4 GB scratch partition that the ESXi installer creates. Although this provides long-term storage for the ESXi host logs, there is a centralized location for the logs, making analysis of the logs more difficult than it should be. An administrator would have to connect to each host individually in order to review the logs for that host.

Further, if you are booting from SAN or if you are using vSphere Auto Deploy, then there is no local scratch partition, and logs are stored in memory on the ESXi host — which means they disappear when the ESXi host is restarted. Clearly, this is not an ideal configuration. Not only does it lack centralized access to the logs, but it also lacks long-term storage for the logs.

The typical solution to both of these issues is the use of a third-party syslog server, a server that runs a syslog daemon and is prepared to accept the log entries from the various ESXi hosts. To make things easier, VMware supplies a syslog collector with vSphere 5 in three different forms:

- As an installable service you can install onto a Windows Server–based computer

- As a service preinstalled on the vCenter Server virtual appliance

- As part of the vMA's built-in syslog daemon

In this section, I'll show you how to install the VMware Syslog Collector on a Windows Server–based computer and how to configure your ESXi hosts to send their logs to this centralized syslog service.

Let's start with installing the VMware Syslog Collector.

INSTALLING THE VMWARE SYSLOG COLLECTOR

You can find the installer for the VMware Syslog Collector on the vCenter installation media. Figure 8.11 shows the link to the VMware Syslog Collector in the VMware vCenter Installer window.

FIGURE 8.11
You can install the VMware Syslog Collector from the vCenter Server installation media.

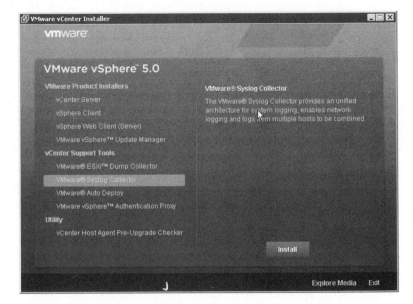

The Syslog Collector can operate as a stand-alone service, or you can install it as a vCenter Server–integrated instance. If you install it as a vCenter Server–integrated instance, you'll be able to view ESXi host logging settings from within the vSphere Client, as I'll show you later in this section. If you do plan to install it as a vCenter Server–integrated instance, you should install it either on the vCenter Server itself or on a Windows Server–based computer in the same domain as the vCenter Server system.

Perform these steps to install the Syslog Collector:

1. Log into a Windows Server–based system as a user with administrative credentials.

2. Insert the vCenter Server installation medium, either by physically inserting it into the computer or by attaching it as a virtual CD/DVD to the appropriate VM.

3. If the vCenter Server Installer does not auto-launch, double-click the CD/DVD drive in My Computer to start the installer.

4. From the vCenter Server Installer, select VMware Syslog Collector; then click Install.

5. Select the language for the installer; then click OK.

6. At the first screen of the VMware Syslog Collector installation wizard, click Next to get started.

7. Click Next to accept the End-User Patent Agreement.

8. Select I Accept The Terms Of The License Agreement, and click Next.

9. If you need to make changes to the installation directory or the log repository, click the appropriate Change button to select an alternate location.

10. If necessary, enter alternate values for the size of the log file before rotation and the number of log rotations to keep. In most instances, the default settings should be fine. Click Next to continue.

11. Select Standalone Installation to install VMware Syslog Collector without vCenter Server integration, or select VMware vCenter Server Installation to provide integration into vCenter Server (recommended). Click Next.

12. If you selected VMware vCenter Server Installation in the previous step, supply the IP address or hostname of the vCenter Server instance with which this installation should integrate. You'll also need to supply a username and password to authenticate to the vCenter Server computer. Click Next to continue when you're ready.

13. Click Next to accept the default port values and protocols, unless you know you have a specific reason to change them.

14. Click Next when prompted for how the Syslog Collector should identify itself on the network.

    The installation wizard will complete the installation of the VMware Syslog Collector.

15. Click Finish to complete the installation.

If you selected a vCenter-integrated installation, the next launch of the vSphere Client will show an additional icon on the home screen, as you can see in Figure 8.12.

Click the Network Syslog Collector icon for a list of the ESXi hosts that are currently logging to that collector. At first, the list will be empty because you haven't yet configured syslog on your ESXi hosts. That is the topic of the next section.

Configuring Syslog on ESXi Hosts

You have three different options for configuring syslog on your ESXi hosts:

◆ You can use the vSphere Client.

◆ You can use an installation of the vCLI, such as the vMA.

◆ You can use PowerShell.

In this section I'll focus only on using the vSphere Client and using the vCLI through the vMA.

FIGURE 8.12
The Syslog Collector
installation adds
the Network Syslog
Collector icon on
the home screen.

Configuring Syslog with the vSphere Client

The syslog configuration for an ESXi host is part of the advanced settings accessible through the vSphere Client.

Perform these steps to configure syslog on an ESXi host using the vSphere Client:

1. Launch the vSphere Client and log in to either an ESXi host or a vCenter Server instance.

   You can change the advanced setting for the syslog configuration logged directly into an ESXi host or into vCenter Server.

2. Select an ESXi host from the inventory screen (if you are using vCenter Server, you might need to navigate to the Hosts And Clusters inventory view first).

3. Select the Configuration tab; then click Advanced Settings under the Software section.

   This opens the Advanced Settings dialog box.

4. Navigate down through the list until you get to Syslog.

5. Expand Syslog and select Global.

6. Set the value of `Syslog.global.logHost` to the IP address or DNS name of the server where you installed the VMware Syslog Collector.

   Figure 8.13 shows a DNS name specified for the loghost.

7. Click OK to save the change to the advanced setting.

Because this is a per-ESXi host setting, you'll need to repeat this process with each ESXi host that should send its logs to this instance of the Syslog Collector.

FIGURE 8.13

The value of `Syslog.global. logHost` should be set to the IP address or DNS name of a syslog server, such as the VMware Syslog Collector.

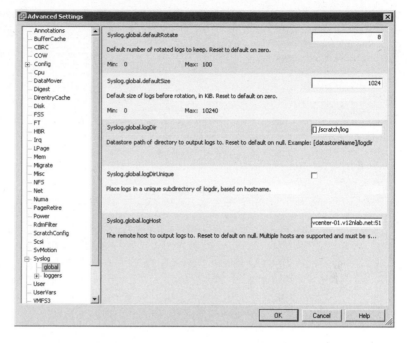

In addition to using the vSphere Client, you can also perform this configuration from the CLI, as I'll show you in the next section.

Configuring Syslog with the vMA

Perform these steps to configure an ESXi host's syslog settings with the vMA:

1. Using `PuTTY.exe` (Windows) or a terminal window (Linux or Mac OS X), establish an SSH session to the vMA.

2. From the vMA command prompt, use this command:

   `esxcli --server=`***vCenter Server*** `--vihost=`***ESXi host*** `--username=`***Administrative user account*** `system syslog config set --loghost=`***Syslog Collector server***

   If your vCenter Server is `vcenter-01.v12nlab.net`, your ESXi host is `pod-1-blade-5 .v12nlab.net`, your administrative username is `Administrator`, and your syslog server is `syslog.v12nlab.net`, the command would look like this:

   `esxcli --server=vcenter-01.v12nlab.net --vihost=pod-1-blade-5.v12nlab.net --username=administrator system syslog config set --loghost=syslog.v12nlab.net`

3. Repeat this process for each ESXi host, changing the value of the `--vihost` parameter as necessary.

Once you've configured all your ESXi hosts with the correct setting, selecting the Network Syslog Collector icon on the home screen of the vSphere Client will display a list of the hosts that are logging to this collector, as shown in Figure 8.14.

FIGURE 8.14
Each ESXi host will log to a separate subdirectory on the Syslog Collector host, as shown here in the vSphere Client.

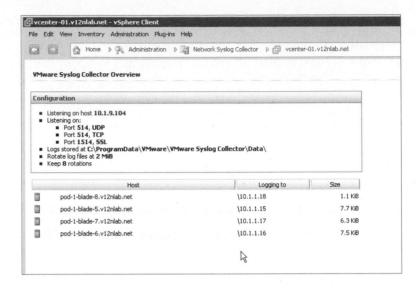

To view the actual logs, you'll need to navigate to the configured log directory on the syslog collector; there is no facility within the vSphere Client to examine the ESXi host logs.

I'll wrap up this section on ESXi host security with a quick look at some final security recommendations.

Reviewing Other ESXi Security Recommendations

In addition to all the security recommendations I've made so far with regard to ESXi hosts, there are some other recommended practices that you should also follow:

◆ Set a root password for the ESXi host. You can set the root password, if it has not already been set, via the server's console by pressing F2. More information on working with the ESXi console is available in Chapter 2.

◆ Use host profiles in vCenter Server. Host profiles can help ensure that the configuration of the ESXi hosts does not drift or change from the settings specified in the host profile. I discussed host profiles in Chapter 3, "Installing and Configuring vCenter Server."

◆ Enable Lockdown Mode for your ESXi hosts. Enabling Lockdown Mode disables console-based user access and direct access via the vSphere Client. Root access via the vSphere Management Assistant (vMA) is also restricted.

Now that you've looked at the various ways to secure your ESXi hosts, it's time to move on to securing vCenter Server, the second major component in your vSphere environment.

Securing vCenter Server

For the most part, discussing how to secure vCenter Server entails discussing how to secure the underlying OS. For environments that have deployed the Windows Server–based version of vCenter Server, this means securing Windows Server. For environments using the Linux-based vCenter Server virtual appliance, it means securing SuSE Linux. Because it's a virtual appliance, though, there isn't a lot that you can do to secure the preinstalled SuSE Linux instance.

Securing Windows Server — for those environments running the Windows Server–based version of vCenter Server — is a topic that has been discussed many, many times, so I won't go into great detail here. Some of the more common security recommendations include the following:

◆ Stay current on all Windows Server patches and updates. This helps protect you against potential security exploits.

◆ Harden the Windows Server installation using published best practices and guidelines from Microsoft.

In addition to these standard security recommendations, I can offer a few other security recommendations that are specific to vCenter Server:

◆ Be sure to stay current on vCenter Server patches and updates.

◆ Place the vCenter Server backend database on a separate system (physical or VM), if possible, and follow recommended practices to secure the separate system.

◆ If you are using Windows authentication with SQL Server, use a dedicated service account for vCenter Server — don't allow vCenter Server to share a Windows account with other services or applications.

◆ Be sure to secure the separate database server and backend database using published security practices from the appropriate vendor. This includes securing the database server itself (Microsoft SQL Server, IBM DB2, or Oracle) as well as the underlying OS for that database server (Windows Server, Linux, or other).

◆ Replace the default vCenter Server self-signed SSL certificate with a valid SSL certificate from a trusted root authority.

In addition to these recommendations, there are also some other steps you should take to ensure that vCenter Server — and the infrastructure being managed by vCenter Server — is appropriately secured and protected.

Once again using the AAA model as a rough structure for the security discussion, I'll start with a review of vCenter Server authentication.

Authenticating Users against vCenter Server

As with ESXi, users will need to authenticate against vCenter Server in order to perform any tasks. How you handle that authentication depends on which version of vCenter Server you've deployed in your environment. If you've deployed the Windows Server–based version of vCenter Server, then you must rely on Windows authentication; generally, this means Active Directory, although you could manage users and groups locally on the vCenter Server computer itself. If you've deployed the Linux-based vCenter Server virtual appliance, then you have the option of using either Network Information Service (NIS) or Active Directory. Because the Windows Server–based version and the Linux-based virtual appliance share Active Directory in common, I'll focus on the use of Active Directory in this discussion of authentication.

In this section, I'll cover these three topics:

- ◆ Configuring vCenter Server on Windows Server for authentication against Active Directory

- ◆ Configuring the vCenter Server virtual appliance for authentication against Active Directory

- ◆ Understanding how vCenter Server authenticates against ESXi

CONFIGURING vCENTER SERVER ON WINDOWS SERVER FOR ACTIVE DIRECTORY

When using vCenter Server on Windows Server, leveraging Active Directory is pretty simple: join the computer to an Active Directory domain before installing vCenter Server, and vCenter Server will — by virtue of how Windows integrates with Active Directory — automatically be able to take advantage of users and groups stored within Active Directory. If you choose not to join Active Directory, then the Windows-based version of vCenter Server will be able to use only user accounts and groups defined locally on that Windows Server–based system.

There is one configuration issue, however, with the default installation of vCenter Server onto a computer that is an Active Directory domain member. When vCenter Server is installed as a member server in an Active Directory domain, the default settings in vCenter Server extend permissions to users within Active Directory that aren't necessarily involved in the administration of the vSphere environment. Generally speaking, you only want to assign permission to those users who actually need it; this is part of the "principle of least privilege," a key concept in computer security.

The issue is this: by default, the local Administrators group — this is the Windows group defined locally on that specific Windows server — is given the Administrator role in vCenter Server (I'll discuss vCenter Server roles in more detail in the section "Managing vCenter Server Permissions"). This permission assignment happens at the vCenter Server object and propagates down to all child objects. Because the Domain Admins Domain Local group is a member of the local Administrators group, this means that the Domain Admins group is also given the Administrator role in vCenter Server. It has been my experience that in many organizations there are members of the Domain Admins group who don't have anything to do with the virtualization infrastructure. Granting those users privileges inside vCenter Server is a violation of security best practices; removing the default permissions for Domain Admins in vCenter Server is, therefore, a good idea.

Perform the following steps to remove the default permissions for Domain Admins in vCenter Server:

1. In Active Directory, create a Domain Local group named vSphere Administrators (or something similar).

   ESXi integration into Active Directory requires the presence of a group named ESX Admins; you could leverage this group here as well. Make the appropriate Active Directory domain user accounts members of this group. At the very least, be sure to place your own account in this group.

2. Log on to the vCenter Server computer as Administrator.

3. Create a local group, using the Local Users and Groups management console, named vSphere Admins, vCenter Admins, ESX Admins, or something similar.

This group is separate from the group created in Active Directory; this is a local group on the vCenter Server computer.

4. Add the Active Directory Domain Local group created in step 1 to this new local group. Also add the local Administrator account to this group.

5. Launch the vSphere Client, if it is not already running, and connect to the appropriate vCenter Server instance.

LATHER, RINSE, REPEAT

For multiple vCenter Server instances, you'll want to repeat this process on each vCenter Server. That is, you'll need to create a local group on each computer running vCenter Server, add the Domain Local group, and repeat the permissions assignment using the vSphere Client.

---

6. In the inventory tree on the left, select the vCenter Server object at the top of the tree.

7. Click the Permissions tab.

8. Right-click a blank area of the Permissions tab, and select Add Permission.

9. Add the local group you created in step 3, and assign that group the Administrator role. Be sure that the Propagate To Child Objects check box is selected.

10. Click OK to return to the Permissions tab. The new permission should be listed there.

11. Right-click the permission for Administrators, and select Remove. Click Yes in the dialog box prompting you for confirmation.

This removes the local Administrators group — and by extension the Domain Admins group — from the Administrator role on the vCenter Server object. Moving forward, only members of the Domain Local group you created will have permission within vCenter Server. You can add or remove users to that Domain Local group to control access to vCenter Server.

Of course, you will also want to create Active Directory groups to match up to other roles — custom or predefined — that you're using within vCenter Server to grant privileges to specific objects.

In the next section, I'll cover how to configure the vCenter Server virtual appliance for use with Active Directory.

CONFIGURING THE vCENTER SERVER VIRTUAL APPLIANCE FOR ACTIVE DIRECTORY

Two steps are required to leverage Active Directory with the Linux-based vCenter Server virtual appliance:

1. Enable Active Directory integration on the virtual appliance itself.

2. Add appropriate permissions to the vCenter Server hierarchy to allow Active Directory accounts to log in and manage the inventory objects.

Let's look at each of these steps.

Enabling Active Directory Integration on the Virtual Appliance

To enable the Active Directory integration of the virtual appliance, use the management interface of the virtual appliance. The vCenter Server virtual appliance offers a web-based management interface accessible on port 5480 of the IP address assigned to the virtual appliance. For example, if you assigned the IP address 10.1.1.100 to the virtual appliance, you could access the web-based management interface at `https://10.1.1.100:5480`. At this point, you'll be prompted to log into the virtual appliance. The default login credentials are username **root** and password **vmware**.

Perform these steps to enable Active Directory integration after you've logged into the management interface:

1. From the main web-based management screen, click the Authentication tab.

2. Select Active Directory.

3. Select Active Directory Enabled.

4. Supply the name of the Active Directory domain name and the username and password of an account that has permission to join the virtual appliance to the domain.

5. Click Save Settings.

   This screen notes that any change to the Active Directory configuration will require a restart of the virtual appliance, so the next step is to reboot the virtual appliance.

6. Select the System tab.

7. Click the Reboot button. When prompted for confirmation, select Reboot.

The virtual appliance will reboot.

You can monitor the progress of the reboot using the VM console within the vSphere Client. Once the virtual appliance has rebooted successfully, you can test the Active Directory integration by logging into the virtual appliance's web-based management interface using Active Directory credentials. You can use either the `domain\username` or the `username@domain` syntax to log in.

If the login is successful, you're ready to proceed to the next step. If not, you'll need to troubleshoot the Active Directory integration. The vCenter Server virtual appliance supports SSH logins, so you can log in via SSH and review the logs to see what errors were logged during the configuration.

If you're having problems with Active Directory integration, review the following list:

♦ Verify that the time on the virtual appliance is synchronized with the time on the Active Directory domain controllers.

♦ Ensure that the virtual appliance is able, via DNS, to resolve the domain name and locate the Active Directory domain controllers. This typically means using the same DNS servers that Active Directory uses.

♦ Verify that there is no firewall between the virtual appliance and the Active Directory domain controllers or that all necessary traffic is permitted through any firewalls that are present.

Once you've verified that the Active Directory integration is working, you're ready to proceed with the second step in configuring the vCenter Server virtual appliance for Active Directory.

Adding Permissions for Active Directory Users or Groups

Although you've successfully configured the Active Directory integration for the vCenter Server virtual appliance, you still can't use any Active Directory credentials to log in using the vSphere Client. In order to log in via the vSphere Client, you must first grant access to one or more Active Directory users or groups within the vCenter Server hierarchy.

Perform these steps to grant permissions to an Active Directory user or group in order to log into the vCenter Server virtual appliance via the vSphere Client:

1. Launch the vSphere Client, if it is not already running.

2. Specify the DNS name or IP address of the vCenter Server virtual appliance in the IP Address/Name field.

3. Specify the username **root** and the password **vmware**, and click Login to log in to the vCenter Server virtual appliance.

4. Select the vCenter Server object from the inventory pane; then click the Permissions tab.

5. Right-click a blank area of the Permissions tab and select Add Permission.

6. In the Assign Permissions dialog box, click the Add button.

7. From the Domain drop-down box, select the Active Directory domain.

8. Find the user or group to add, click the Add button, and then click OK.

   I recommend against using a specific user account here; instead, leverage a security group within Active Directory. Recall that ESXi integration into Active Directory requires a security group called ESX Admins; you might want to leverage that group here as well.

9. In the Assign Permissions dialog box, select Administrator from the Assigned Role drop-down list, and make sure that Propagate To Child Objects is selected.

   This ensures that the selected Active Directory users and/or groups have the Administrator role within the vCenter Server virtual appliance. By default, only the pre-defined root account has this role.

10. Click OK to return to the vSphere Client.

After completing this process, you'll now be able to log into the vCenter Server virtual appliance with the vSphere Client using an Active Directory username and password. You're all set — the vCenter Server virtual appliance is configured to use Active Directory.

Before I move on to the topic of managing permissions within vCenter Server, one quick item that I'd like to discuss pertains to how vCenter Server interacts with ESXi hosts. I think it's important to understand how vCenter Server uses a special user account as a proxy account for managing your ESXi hosts.

Understanding the vpxuser Account

In the first section of this chapter, I showed you how the ESXi security model employs users, groups, roles, privileges, and permissions. I also showed you how to manage local users and groups or to integrate your ESXi hosts with Active Directory.

As you'll see in the section "Managing vCenter Server Permissions," vCenter Server uses the same user/group-role-privilege-permission security model. When vCenter Server is present, all activities are funneled through vCenter Server using Windows accounts that have been assigned a role that has, in turn, been assigned to one or more inventory objects as a permission. This combination of Windows account, role, and inventory object creates a permission that allows (or disallows) the user to perform certain functions. The user accounts exist in Active Directory (or on the vCenter Server computer itself), not on the ESXi hosts, and the permissions and roles are defined within vCenter Server, not on the ESXi hosts. Because the user doesn't log into the ESXi host directly, this minimizes the need for many local user accounts on the ESXi host and thus provides better security. Alas, there still is a need, however small or infrequent, for local accounts on an ESXi host used primarily for administration, which is why I talked earlier about managing local users and groups and integrating ESXi authentication into Active Directory.

Because the user accounts exist outside the ESXi hosts, and because the roles, privileges, and permissions are defined outside the ESXi hosts, when you use vCenter Server to manage your virtual infrastructure, you are really only creating a task and not directly interacting with the ESXi hosts or the VMs. This is true for any user using vCenter Server to manage hosts or VMs. For instance, Shane, an administrator, wants to log into vCenter Server and create a new VM. Shane first needs the proper role — perhaps a custom role you created specifically for the purpose of creating new VMs — assigned to the proper inventory object or objects within vCenter Server.

Assuming the correct role has been assigned to the correct inventory objects — let's say it's a resource pool — Shane has what he needs to create, modify, and monitor VMs. But does Shane's user account have direct access to the ESXi hosts when he's logged into vCenter Server? No, it does not. In fact, a proxy account is used to communicate Shane's tasks to the appropriate ESXi host or VM. This account, vpxuser, is the only account that vCenter Server stores and tracks in its backend database.

VPXUSER SECURITY

The vpxuser account and password are stored in the vCenter Server database and on the ESXi hosts. The vpxuser account is used to communicate from a vCenter Server computer to an ESXi host. The vpxuser password consists of 32 (randomly selected) characters, is encrypted using SHA1 on an ESXi host, and is obfuscated on vCenter Server. Each vpxuser password is unique to the ESXi host being managed by vCenter Server.

No direct administrator intervention is warranted or advised for this account because that would break vCenter Server functions needing this account. The account and password are never used by humans, and they do not have shell access on any ESXi hosts. Thus, it isn't necessary to manage this account or include it with normal administrative and regular user account security policies.

Anytime vCenter Server polls an ESXi host or an administrator creates a task that needs to be communicated to an ESXi host, the vpxuser account is used. On the ESXi hosts that are managed by vCenter Server, the vpxuser account exists (it's created automatically by vCenter Server; this is why vCenter Server asks you for the root password when adding a host to the inventory) and is assigned the Administrator role. This gives the vpxuser account the ability to perform whatever tasks are necessary on the individual ESXi hosts managed by vCenter Server. When a user logs into vCenter Server, vCenter Server applies its security model (roles, privileges, and permissions) to that user, ensuring that the user is only permitted to perform the tasks for which they are authorized. On the backend, though, all these tasks are proxied onto the individual ESXi hosts as vpxuser.

You should now have a good idea of what's involved in vCenter Server authentication. I'd like to focus now on vCenter Server permissions, which control what users are allowed to do after they've authenticated to vCenter Server.

Managing vCenter Server Permissions

The security model for vCenter Server is identical to that explained in the previous section for an ESXi host: take a user or group and assign them to a role (which has one or more privileges assigned) for a specific inventory object. The key difference is that vCenter Server enables new objects in the inventory hierarchy that aren't possible with individual ESXi hosts. This would include objects like clusters and folders (both of which I discussed in Chapter 3). vCenter Server also supports resource pools (which I introduced in the section "Using Resource Pools to Assign Permissions" and which I'll discuss in greater detail in Chapter 11). vCenter Server also allows you to assign permissions in different ways; for example, an ESXi host has only one inventory view, while vCenter Server has the Hosts And Clusters inventory view, VMs And Templates inventory view, Datastores And Datastore Clusters inventory view, and Networking inventory view. Permissions — the assignment of a role to one or more inventory objects — can occur in any of these views.

As you can see, this means that vCenter Server allows vSphere administrators to create much more complex permissions hierarchies than you could create using only ESXi hosts.

Recall that a key part of the security model is the role — the grouping of privileges that you assign to a user or group in a permission. Let's take a closer look at the predefined roles that come with vCenter Server.

REVIEWING VCENTER SERVER'S ROLES

Where the ESXi host is quite limited in its default roles, vCenter Server provides more default roles, thereby offering a much greater degree of flexibility in constructing access control. Although both security models offer the flexibility of creating custom roles, ESXi includes three default roles, while vCenter Server provides nine default roles, including the same three offered in ESXi. Figure 8.15 details the default vCenter Server roles. These roles are visible from within the vSphere Client by selecting View ➢ Administration ➢ Roles.

As you can see, VMware provides a large number of roles in a default vCenter Server installation. Remember, just like the default ESXi roles, vCenter Server will prevent you from modifying the No Access, Read-Only, and Administrator roles — you must clone them in order to customize them. Once you clone one of the built-in roles, you can customize the privileges assigned to that role to meet your specific needs.

FIGURE 8.15
The vCenter Server default roles offer much more flexibility than an individual ESXi host.

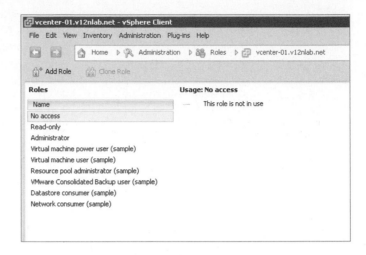

The key to using these roles effectively is to understand the functions of each of the roles that VMware provides:

No Access   This role is just what it sounds like — it permits a user or group no access. But why do you need it? The idea behind this role is to prevent a user or group that has permissions at some point higher in the hierarchy from having permissions on the object to which this role is assigned. For instance, you may have granted Eileen the Virtual Machine User role at the datacenter level, which would allow her to administer all of the VMs in the datacenter, but there is a security concern about her having access to one of the accounting VMs in that datacenter. You could assign Eileen to the No Access role on the Accounting VM, which would effectively supersede her Virtual Machine User privileges.

Read-Only   Read-Only allows users to see the vCenter Server inventory. It does not allow them to interact with any of the VMs in any way through the vSphere Client or the web client except to see the power status of each VM in the inventory where they have the Read-Only role applied.

Administrator   A user assigned to an object with the Administrator role will have full administrative capabilities over that object in vCenter Server. Note that this does *not* grant *any* privileges within the guest OSes installed inside the VMs. For instance, a user assigned the Administrator role for a VM may be able to change the RAM assigned to the VM and alter its performance parameters (Shares, Reservations, and Limits) but may not even have the permissions to log into that VM unless that user has been granted that right from within the guest OS.

The Administrator role can be granted at any object level in the hierarchy, and the user or group that is assigned the role at that level will have vCenter Server administrative privileges over that object and (if the inheritance box is selected) any child objects in the hierarchy.

Aside from the No Access, Read-Only, and Administrator roles, the rest of the roles are sample roles. These are intended to provide vSphere administrators with an idea of how to structure roles and permissions to model the appropriate administrative structure.

Virtual Machine Power User (Sample)   The Virtual Machine Power User sample role assigns permissions to allow a user to perform most functions on VMs. This includes tasks such as configuring CD and floppy media, changing the power state, taking and deleting snapshots, and modifying the configuration. These permissions apply only to VMs. The idea here is, as an example, if users are granted this role at a datacenter level, they would only be able to manage VMs in that datacenter and would not be able to change settings on objects such as resource pools in that datacenter.

Virtual Machine User (Sample)   The Virtual Machine User sample role grants the user the ability to interact with a VM but not the ability to change its configuration. Users can operate the VM's power controls and change the media in the virtual CD-ROM drive or floppy drive as long as they also have access to the media they want to change. For instance, a user who is assigned this role for a VM will be able to change the CD media from an ISO image on a shared storage volume to their own client system's physical CD-ROM drive. If you want them to have the ability to change from one ISO file to another (both stored on a Virtual Machine File System [VMFS] volume or Network File System [NFS] volume), they will also need to be granted the Browse Datastore permission at the parent of the datastore object in the vCenter Server hierarchy — usually the datacenter that the ESX/ESXi host is located in.

Resource Pool Administrator (Sample)   The Resource Pool Administrator sample role grants the user the ability to manage and configure resources with a resource pool including VMs, child pools, scheduled tasks, and alarms.

VMware Consolidated Backup User (Sample)   As the role name suggests, the VMware Consolidated Backup sample role grants the user the privileges required for performing a backup of a VM using VCB.

Datastore Consumer (Sample)   The Datastore Consumer sample role is targeted at users who need only a single permission: the permission to allocate space from a datastore. Clearly, this role is very limited.

Network Consumer (Sample)   Similar to the Datastore Consumer role, the Network Consumer sample role has only a single permission, and that is the permission to assign networks.

These default roles provide a good starting point, but they won't meet every company's needs. If you need something more than what is provided by default, you'll need to create a custom role. I describe this process in the next section.

WORKING WITH VCENTER SERVER ROLES

What if the default roles supplied with vCenter Server don't provide you with the necessary functionality for a particular grouping of users? Well, it depends on what the problem is. Let's take the most basic problem. You've chosen a best-fit role to assign a user privileges, but the role you've selected lacks a key permission, or perhaps the role you've selected grants a few permissions that you don't want included. To get the exact fit you need, you can simply clone the role and then customize the cloned role.

Perform the following steps to clone a role in vCenter Server:

1. Launch the vSphere Client if it is not already running, and connect to a vCenter Server instance.

2. Navigate to the Roles area using the menu, the navigation bar, or the keyboard shortcut.

3. Right-click the role that you want to clone, and select Clone from the context menu.

After you've cloned the role, you can add or remove privileges as needed. I described the process of editing a role in the section "Editing and Removing Roles."

LEAVE THE BUILT-IN ROLES INTACT

I recommend leaving all of the built-in roles intact and unmodified. vCenter Server prevents you from modifying the No Access, Read-Only, and Administrator roles but does not prevent you from modifying the rest of the roles. To help avoid confusion among multiple administrators, I recommend leaving the built-in roles intact and cloning them to a new custom role instead.

UNDERSTANDING VCENTER SERVER PRIVILEGES

Roles are very useful, but now that you've started to peek into the properties of the roles and how to edit roles, you also need to understand each of the privileges and what they do for you in terms of customizing roles. Remember that privileges are individual tasks that are assigned to roles. Without privileges assigned, roles are useless, so it's important to understand the privileges available within vCenter Server.

This is a rather long list of privileges, but it's broken down into some general categories, so let's look at what each of the categories means in general terms:

Alarms   Controls the ability to create, modify, delete, disable, and acknowledge vCenter Server alarms.

Auto Deploy   Controls the ability to use vSphere Auto Deploy for dynamically provisioning ESXi hosts at boot time.

Datacenter   Controls the ability to create, delete, move, and rename datacenters inside vCenter Server. The privilege for working with an IP pool is also found in the Datacenter category.

Datastore Controls who can access files stored on an ESXi attached volume. This permission needs to be assigned at the parent object of the ESXi host itself — for instance, a datacenter, an ESXi cluster, or a folder that contains ESXi hosts.

Datastore Cluster Controls who is permitted to configure a datastore cluster (used with profile-based storage and Storage DRS).

Distributed Virtual Port (dvPort) Group Controls who can create, delete, or modify distributed virtual port groups on distributed virtual switches.

ESX Agent Manager Controls the ability to view, configure, or modify ESX host agents.

Extension Controls the ability to register, update, or unregister extensions in vCenter Server. An example of an extension is vSphere Update Manager (VUM).

Folder Controls the creation, deletion, and general manipulation of folders in the vCenter Server hierarchy.

Global Includes the ability to manage vCenter Server license settings and server settings such as SNMP and SMTP.

Host Controls what users can do with ESXi hosts in the inventory. This includes tasks such as adding and removing ESXi hosts from the inventory, changing the host's memory configuration, or changing the firewall settings.

Host Profile Controls creating, editing, deleting, or viewing host profiles.

Inventory Service Controls who can access the tagging capabilities of the vCenter Inventory Service.

Network Controls the configuration or removal of networks from the vCenter Server inventory.

Performance Controls the ability of users to modify the intervals at which the performance chart information is displayed on the Performance tab of an object.

Permissions Controls who has the ability to modify the permissions assigned to a role and who can manipulate a role/user combination for a particular object.

Profile-Driven Storage Controls who can view and update profile-driven storage.

Resource Controls resource pool manipulation, including creating, deleting, or renaming the pool; also controls migration by using vMotion and applying DRS recommendations.

Scheduled Task Controls the configuration of tasks and the ability to run a task that is scheduled inside vCenter Server.

Sessions Controls the ability to view and disconnect vSphere Client sessions connected to vCenter Server and to send a global message to connected vSphere Client users.

Storage Views Controls changing the server configuration and looking at storage views.

Tasks Controls the ability to create or update tasks.

vApp Controls the configuration and management of vApps, such as the ability to add VMs to a vApp; clone, create, delete, export, or import a vApp; power on or power off the vApp; or view the Open Virtualization Format (OVF) environment.

Virtual Machine Controls the manipulation of VMs in the vCenter Server inventory, including the ability to create, delete, or connect to the remote console of a VM; controls the power state of a VM; controls the ability to change floppy and CD media and to manipulate templates, among other privileges.

VRMPolicy Controls settings around virtual rights management (VRM). VRM centers on the management of security policies and access controls for VMs.

vService Controls the ability to create, remove, or modify vService dependencies with vApps.

vSphere Distributed Switch Controls the right to create, delete, modify, or move vSphere Distributed Switches; add or remove ESXi hosts; and configure ports on a distributed virtual switch.

How these various privileges are assigned to roles is what really matters. As you saw earlier, vCenter Server ships with some default roles already defined. Some of these — namely, the No Access, Read-Only, and Administrator roles — are fairly well understood and cannot be modified. The other predefined roles are listed in Table 8.1 along with the privileges that are assigned to each role by default.

TABLE 8.1: TABLE OF PRIVILEGES FOR DEFAULT ROLES

PREDEFINED ROLE	ASSIGNED PRIVILEGES
	Datastore ➤ Browse Datastore
	Global ➤ Cancel Task
	Scheduled Task ➤ Create Tasks, Modify Task, Remove Task, Run Task
Virtual Machine Power User	Virtual Machine ➤ Configuration ➤ Add Existing Disk, Add New Disk, Add or Remove Device, Advanced, Change CPU Count, Change Resource, Disk Lease, Memory, Modify Device Settings, Remove Disk, Rename, Reset Guest Information, Settings, Upgrade Virtual Hardware
	Virtual Machine ➤ Interaction ➤ Acquire Guest Control Ticket, Answer Question, Configure CD Media, Configure Floppy Media, Console Interaction, Device Connection, Power Off, Power On, Reset, Suspend, VMware Tools Install
	Virtual Machine ➤ State ➤ Create Snapshot, Remove Snapshot, Rename Snapshot, Revert To Snapshot
	Global ➤ Cancel Task
	Scheduled Task ➤ Create Tasks, Modify Task, Remove Task, Run Task
Virtual Machine User	Virtual Machine ➤ Interaction ➤ Answer Question, Configure CD Media, Configure Floppy Media, Console Interaction, Device Connection, Power Off, Power On, Reset, Suspend, VMware Tools Install

TABLE 8-1: Table of privileges for default roles *(CONTINUED)*

PREDEFINED ROLE	ASSIGNED PRIVILEGES
Resource Pool Administrator	Alarms ➤ Create Alarm, Modify Alarm, Remove Alarm
	Datastore ➤ Browse Datastore
	Folder ➤ Create Folder, Delete Folder, Move Folder, Rename Folder
	Global ➤ Cancel Task, Log Event, Set Custom Attribute
	Permissions ➤ Modify Permissions
	Resource ➤ Assign Virtual Machine To Resource Pool, Create Resource Pool, Migrate, Modify Resource Pool, Move Resource Pool, Query vMotion, Relocate, Remove Resource Pool, Rename Resource Pool
	Scheduled Task ➤ Create Tasks, Modify Task, Remove Task, Run Task
	Virtual Machine ➤ Configuration ➤ Add Existing Disk, Add New Disk, Add Or Remove Device, Advanced, Change CPU Count, Change Resource, Disk Lease, Memory, Modify Device Settings, Raw Device, Remove Disk, Rename, Reset Guest Information, Settings, Upgrade Virtual Hardware
	Virtual Machine ➤ Interaction ➤ Answer Question, Configure CD Media, Configure Floppy Media, Console Interaction, Device Connection, Power Off, Power On, Reset, Suspend, VMware Tools Install
	Virtual Machine ➤ Inventory ➤ Create From Existing, Create New, Move, Register, Remove, Unregister
	Virtual Machine ➤ Provisioning ➤ Allow Disk Access, Allow Read-Only Disk Access, Allow Virtual Machine Download, Allow Virtual Machine Files Upload, Clone Template, Clone Virtual Machine, Create Template From Virtual Machine, Customize, Deploy Template, Mark As Template, Mark As Virtual Machine, Modify Customization Specification, Read Customization Specifications
	Virtual Machine ➤ State ➤ Create Snapshot, Remove Snapshot, Rename Snapshot, Revert To Snapshot
VMware Consolidated Backup User	Virtual Machine ➤ Configuration ➤ Disk Lease
	Virtual Machine ➤ Provisioning ➤ Allow Read-Only Disk Access, Allow Virtual Machine Download
	Virtual Machine ➤ State ➤ Create Snapshot, Remove Snapshot
Datastore Consumer	Datastore ➤ Allocate Space
Network Consumer	Network ➤ Assign Network

As you can see, vCenter Server is very specific about the privileges you can assign to roles. Because these privileges are specific, this can sometimes complicate the process of granting users the ability to perform seemingly simple tasks within vCenter Server. Let's review a couple of examples of how privileges, roles, and permissions combine in vCenter Server.

DELEGATING THE ABILITY TO CREATE VIRTUAL MACHINES AND INSTALL A GUEST OS

One common access control delegation in a virtual infrastructure is to give a group of users the rights to create VMs. After just browsing through the list of available privileges, it might seem simple to accomplish this. It is, however, more complex than meets the eye. Providing a user with the ability to create a VM involves assigning a combination of privileges at multiple levels throughout the vCenter Server inventory.

COMBINING PRIVILEGES, ROLES, AND PERMISSIONS IN vCENTER SERVER

So far, I've shown you all the pieces you need to know in order to structure vCenter Server to support your company's management and operational requirements. How these pieces fit together, though, can sometimes be more complex than you might expect. In the next few paragraphs, I will walk you through an example of how these pieces fit together.

Here's the scenario. Within your IT department, one group handles building all Windows servers. Once the servers are built, operational control of the servers is handed off to a separate group. Now that you have virtualized your datacenter, this same separation of duties needs to be re-created within vCenter Server. Sounds simple, right? You just need to configure vCenter Server so that this group has the ability to create VMs. This group is represented within Active Directory with a group object (this Active Directory group is named IT-Provisioning), and you'd like to leverage the Active Directory group membership to control who is granted these permissions within vCenter Server.

In the following steps, I've deliberately kept some of the items at a high level. For example, I don't go into how to create a role or how to assign that role to an inventory object as a permission because those tasks are covered elsewhere in this chapter.

Perform the following steps to allow a Windows-based group to create VMs:

1. Use the vSphere Client to connect to a vCenter Server instance. Log in with a user account that has been assigned the Administrator role within vCenter Server.

2. Create a new role called **VMCreator**.

3. Assign the following privileges to the VMCreator role:

   Datastore ➤ Allocate Space
   Virtual Machine ➤ Inventory ➤ Create New
   Virtual Machine ➤ Configuration ➤ Add New Disk
   Virtual Machine ➤ Configuration ➤ Add Existing Disk
   Virtual Machine ➤ Configuration ➤ Raw Device
   Resource ➤ Assign Virtual Machine To Resource Pool

   These permissions only allow the VMCreator role to create new VMs, not clone existing VMs or deploy from templates. Those actions would require additional privileges. For example, to allow this role to create new VMs from existing VMs you would add the following privileges to the VMCreator role:

Virtual Machine ➤ Inventory ➤ Create From Existing
Virtual Machine ➤ Provisioning ➤ Clone Virtual Machine
Virtual Machine ➤ Provisioning ➤ Customize

4. Add a permission on a folder, datacenter, cluster, or host for the Windows-based group (IT-Provisioning in my example) with the VMCreator role.

If you don't assign the role to a datacenter object, then you'll need to assign the role separately to a folder in the VMs And Templates view. Otherwise, you'll run into an error when trying to create the VM.

Similarly, if you don't assign the role to the datacenter object, then the group won't have permission on any datastore objects. Datastore objects are children of the datacenter object, so permissions applied to a datacenter object will, by default, propagate to the datastores. Without permissions on at least one datastore object (either via propagation or via direct assignment), you'll end up unable to create a new VM because you can't choose a datastore in which to store the VM.

5. If you want or need the Windows-based group to see other objects within the vCenter Server hierarchy, then assign the group the Read-Only role on the applicable objects.

For example, if the group should see all objects within the datacenter, add the Read-Only role on the datacenter object.

At this point, the privileges for creating a VM are complete; however, the IT-Provisioning group does not have the rights to mount a CD/DVD image and therefore cannot install a guest OS. Therefore, more permissions are required in order to allow the IT-Provisioning group to not only create the VMs and put them in the right place within vCenter Server but also to install the guest OS within those VMs.

Perform the following steps to allow the Windows-based IT-Provisioning group to install a guest OS from a CD/DVD image file:

1. Use the vSphere Client to connect to a vCenter Server instance. Log in with a user account that has been assigned the Administrator role within vCenter Server.

2. Create a new role named **GOS-Installers**.

3. Assign the following privileges to the GOS-Installers role:

Datastore ➤ Browse Datastore
Virtual Machine ➤ Configuration
Virtual Machine ➤ Interaction

4. Assign the desired Windows-based group (IT-Provisioning in my example) the GOS-Installers role on the datacenter, folder, cluster, or host, as applicable.

Keep in mind that you can't have the same user or group with two different roles on the same object.

As you can see, the seemingly simple task of creating a VM actually involves a couple of different roles and a number of permissions. This is only a single example; there are obviously an almost infinite number of other configurations where you can create roles and assign permissions to the various objects within ESXi and vCenter Server.

VCENTER SERVER PERMISSIONS INTERACTION

In organizations, both large and small, users often belong to multiple groups, and those groups are assigned different levels of permissions on different objects. Let's look at the effects of multiple group memberships and multiple permission assignments in the virtual infrastructure.

In one scenario, let's look at the effective permissions when a user belongs to multiple groups that have different permissions on objects at different levels in the inventory. In the example, a user named Rick Avsom is a member of the Res_Pool_Admins and VM_Auditors Windows groups. The Res_Pool_Admins group is assigned membership in the Resource Pool Admins vCenter Server role, and the permission is set at the Production resource pool. The VM_Auditors group is assigned membership in the Read-Only vCenter Server role, and the permission is set at the Win2008-02 VM. The Win2008-02 VM resides within the Production resource pool.

When the user is logged on to the vCenter Server computer as Rick Avsom, the inventory reflects only the objects available to him through his permissions. Based on the permission assignment described, Rick Avsom will be able to manage the Production resource pool and will have full privileges over the Win2008-01 VM to which the Resource Pool Admin privileges are propagating. However, Rick Avsom will not be able to manage the Win2008-02 VM for which he is limited to Read-Only privileges. The outcome of this example is that users in multiple groups with conflicting permissions on objects lower in the inventory are granted only the permissions configured directly on the object.

Another common scenario is the effective permissions when a user belongs to multiple groups that have different permissions on the same objects. In this example, a user named Sue Rindlee is a member of the VM_Admins and VM_Auditors Windows groups. The VM_Admins group has been assigned membership in the Virtual Machine Power User vCenter Server role, and the VM_Auditors group is assigned membership in the Read-Only vCenter Server role. Both of these roles have been assigned permissions on the Production resource pool.

When the user is logged on to the vCenter Server computer as Sue Rindlee, the inventory reflects only the objects available to her through her permissions. Based on the permission assignment described, Sue Rindlee will be able to modify all of the VMs in the Production resource pool. This validates that Sue's Virtual Machine Power User status through membership in the VM_Admin group prevails over the Read-Only status obtained through her membership in the VM_Auditors group.

The outcome of this scenario is that the effective permission is a cumulative permission when a user belongs to multiple groups with different permissions on the same object. Even if Sue Rindlee belonged to a group that had been assigned to the No Access vCenter Server role, her Virtual Machine Power User role would prevail. However, if Sue Rindlee's user account was added directly to a vCenter Server object and assigned the No Access role, then she would not have access to any of the objects to which that permission has propagated.

Even with a good understanding of permission propagation, you should always proceed with caution and always maintain the principle of least privilege to ensure that no user has been extended privileges beyond those that are needed as part of a job role.

When delegating authority, it is always better to err on the side of caution. Do not provide more permissions than are necessary for the job at hand. Just as in any other information systems environment, your access-control implementation is a living object that will consistently require consideration and revision. Manage your permissions carefully, be flexible, and expect that users and administrators alike are going to be curious and will push their access levels to the limits. Stay a step ahead, and always remember the principle of least privilege.

I'll conclude the section of vCenter Server security with a quick look at vCenter Server logging.

Examining vCenter Server Logging

As I mentioned in the section "Configuring ESXi Host Logging," logging is an important part of security, as well as an extremely useful tool in troubleshooting. You've seen how to handle logging for ESXi; now let's take a quick look at vCenter Server logging.

vCenter Server does not, unfortunately, have the ability to forward its logs to a centralized syslog server. However, the vSphere Client does provide a way to view the logs that vCenter Server generates. From the home screen of the vSphere Client, select System Logs under the Administration section to examine the logs. Figure 8.16 shows this section of the vSphere Client.

FIGURE 8.16
vCenter Server's logs are visible from within the Administration section of the vSphere Client.

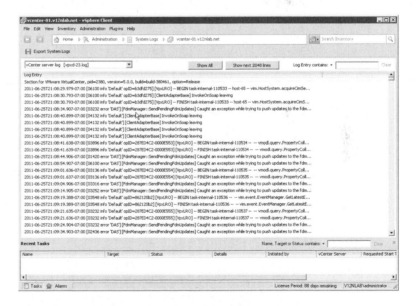

This screen allows you to review the vCenter Server logs for additional information on tasks performed, actions requested, and configuration changes made.

From this screen, you can also export the system logs, a task I described earlier in Chapter 3.

In the next section of this chapter, I'll shift the focus to securing the third and final component of your vSphere environment: the VMs.

Securing Virtual Machines

As with vCenter Server, any discussion of how to secure a VM is really a discussion of how to secure the guest OS within that VM. Entire books have been and are being written about how to secure Windows, Linux, Solaris, and the other guest OSes vSphere supports, so I won't attempt to cover that sort of material here. I will provide two recommendations around securing VMs. One of these is specific to the vSphere virtualized environment, whereas the other is broader and more general.

First, I want to call your attention to the vSphere network security policies.

Configuring Network Security Policies

vSphere provides some outstanding virtual networking functionality, particularly with the addition of the vSphere Distributed Switch and the Cisco Nexus 1000V third-party distributed virtual switch. These virtual switches provide several different security-related policies you can set to help ensure that the security of your VMs is maintained. I discussed all these settings in Chapter 5, "Creating and Configuring Virtual Networks."

The key security-related network security policies you can set in the vSphere virtual networking environment are as follows:

- Promiscuous mode

- MAC address changes

- Forged transmits

VMware recommends keeping all of these policies set to Reject. If there is a valid business need for one of these features to be allowed, you can use per-port group settings to enable the appropriate feature only for the specific VM or machines that require such functionality. One example I've used before is a network-based intrusion detection/intrusion prevention system (IDS/IPS). Rather than allowing promiscuous mode — required for most IDS/IPS to work — on the entire vSwitch, create a separate port group just for that VM and allow promiscuous mode on that port group only.

When considering the security of your VMs, be sure to keep these network security policies in mind, and be sure that they are configured for the correct balance of functionality versus security.

My next recommendation with regard to securing VMs is much more general but still a valid recommendation nevertheless.

Keeping VMs Patched

As with your ESXi hosts and your vCenter Server computer, it's imperative to keep the guest OSes in your VMs properly patched. My experience has shown me that many security problems could have been avoided with a proactive patching strategy for the guest OSes in the VMs.

In vSphere 4.x, you could use vSphere Update Manager (then called vCenter Update Manager) to patch the guest OSes inside your VMs. In vSphere 5, this functionality has been removed, and vSphere Update Manager — covered in detail in Chapter 4 — focuses on keeping your ESXi hosts patched and up to date. It's important, therefore, to deploy some sort of guest OS patching solution that will help you ensure your guest OSes remain patched and current with all vendor-supplied security fixes and updates. In the next chapter, I'll delve into the process of creating and configuring VMs.

The Bottom Line

Configure and control authentication to vSphere. Both ESXi and vCenter Server have authentication mechanisms, and both products have the ability to utilize local users and groups or users and groups defined in Active Directory. Authentication is a basic tenet of security; it's important to verify that users are who they claim to be. You can manage local users and groups on your ESXi hosts using either the vSphere Client or the command-line interface (such as the vSphere Management Assistant). Both the Windows-based and the Linux-based virtual appliance versions of vCenter Server can leverage Active Directory for authentication as well.

> **Master It** You've asked an administrator on your team to create some accounts on an ESXi host. The administrator is uncomfortable with the command line and is having a problem figuring out how to create the users. Is there another way for this administrator to perform this task?

Manage roles and access controls. Both ESXi and vCenter Server possess a role-based access control system that combines users, groups, privileges, roles, and permissions. vSphere administrators can use this role-based access control system to define very granular permissions that define what users are allowed to do with the vSphere Client against an ESXi host or a vCenter Server instance. For example, vSphere administrators can limit users to specific actions on specific types of objects within the vSphere Client. vCenter Server ships with some sample roles that help provide an example of how you can use the role-based access control system.

> **Master It** Describe the differences between a role, a privilege, and a permission in the ESXi/vCenter Server security model.

Control network access to services on ESXi hosts. ESXi provides a network firewall that you can use to control network access to services on your ESXi hosts. This firewall can control both inbound and outbound traffic, and you have the ability to further limit traffic to specific source IP addresses or subnets.

> **Master It** Describe how you can use the ESXi firewall to limit traffic to a specific source IP address.
>
> **Master It** List a limitation of the built-in ESXi firewall.

Integrate with Active Directory. All the major components of vSphere — the ESXi hosts, vCenter Server (both the Windows Server–based version and the Linux-based virtual appliance), as well as the vSphere Management Assistant — all support integration into Microsoft Active Directory. This gives vSphere administrators the option of using Active Directory as their centralized directory service for all major components of vSphere 5.

> **Master It** You've just installed a new ESXi host into your vSphere environment and you are trying to configure the host to enable integration with your Active Directory environment. For some reason, though, it doesn't seem to work. What could be the problem?

## Chapter 9

Creating and Managing Virtual Machines

The VMware ESXi hosts are installed, vCenter Server is running, the networks are blinking, the SAN is carved, and the VMFS volumes are formatted…let the virtualization begin! With the virtual infrastructure in place, you as the administrator must shift your attention to deploying the virtual machines.

In this chapter, you will learn to:

- ◆ Create a virtual machine
- ◆ Install a guest operating system
- ◆ Install VMware Tools
- ◆ Manage virtual machines
- ◆ Modify virtual machines

Understanding Virtual Machines

It is common for IT professionals to refer to a Windows or Linux system running on an ESXi host as a *virtual machine* (VM). Strictly speaking, this phrase is not 100 percent accurate. Just as a physical machine is a physical machine before the installation of an operating system, a VM is a VM before the installation of a guest operating system (the phrase "guest operating system" is used to denote an operating system instance installed into a VM). From an everyday usage perspective, though, you can go on calling the Windows or Linux system a VM. Any references you see to "guest operating system" (or "guest OS") are instances of Windows, Linux, or Solaris—or any other supported operating system—installed in a VM.

If a VM is not an instance of a guest OS running on a hypervisor, then what is a VM? The answer to that question depends on your perspective. Are you "inside" the VM, looking out? Or are you "outside" the VM, looking in?

Examining Virtual Machines from the Inside

From the perspective of software running inside a VM, a VM is really just a set of virtual hardware selected for the purpose of running a guest OS instance.

So, what kind of virtual hardware makes up a VM? By default, VMware ESXi presents the following fairly generic hardware to the VM:

◆ Phoenix BIOS

◆ Intel motherboard

◆ Intel PCI IDE controller

◆ IDE CD-ROM drive

◆ BusLogic parallel SCSI, LSI Logic parallel SCSI, or LSI Logic SAS controller

◆ AMD or Intel CPU, depending upon the physical hardware

◆ Intel e1000 or AMD PCnet NIC

◆ Standard VGA video adapter

VMware selected this generic hardware to provide the broadest level of compatibility across the entire supported guest OSes. As a result, it's possible to use commercial off-the-shelf drivers when installing a guest OS into a VM. Figure 9.1 shows a couple of examples of VMware vSphere providing virtual hardware that looks like standard physical hardware. Both the network adapter and the storage adapter—identified as an Intel Pro/1000MT and an LSI SAS 3000 series adapter, respectively—have corresponding physical counterparts, and drivers for these devices are available in many modern guest OSes.

FIGURE 9.1
VMware ESXi provides both generic and virtualization-optimized hardware for VMs.

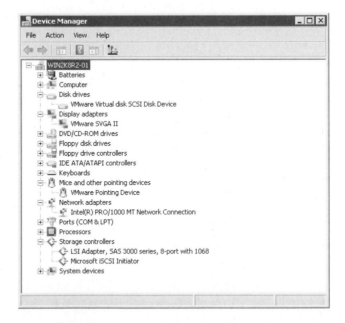

However, VMware vSphere may also present virtual hardware that is unique to the virtualized environment. Look back at the display adapter in Figure 9.1. There is no such physical card as a VMware SVGA II display adapter; this is a device that is unique to the virtualized

environment. These virtualization-optimized devices, also known as paravirtualized devices, are designed to operate efficiently within the virtualized environment created by the vSphere hypervisor. Because these devices have no corresponding physical counterpart, guest OS–specific drivers have to be provided. VMware Tools, described later in this chapter in the section titled "Installing VMware Tools," satisfies this function and provides virtualization-optimized drivers to run these devices.

Just as a physical machine might have a certain amount of memory installed, a certain number of network adapters, or a particular number of disk devices, the same goes for a VM. A VM can include the following types and numbers of virtual hardware devices:

- Processors: Between one and 32 processors with vSphere Virtual SMP (the number of processors depends on your vSphere licenses)

- Memory: Maximum of 1 TB of RAM

- SCSI adapter: Maximum of four SCSI adapters with 15 devices per adapter for a total of 60 SCSI devices per VM; it's possible to boot only from one of the first eight

- Network adapter: Maximum of 10 network adapters

- Parallel port: Maximum of three parallel ports

- Serial port: Maximum of four serial ports

- CD/DVD: Maximum of four CD/DVD drives (up to four IDE devices per VM, in any combination of CD/DVD drives or IDE hard drives)

- Floppy drive: Maximum of two floppy disk drives on a single floppy disk controller

- A single USB controller with up to 20 USB devices connected

- Keyboard, video card, and mouse

Hard drives are not included in the previous list because VM hard drives are generally added as SCSI devices. With up to four SCSI adapters and 15 SCSI devices per adapter, it is possible to attach 60 hard drives to a VM. If you are using IDE hard drives, then the VM is subject to the limit of four IDE devices per VM, as mentioned previously.

SIZE LIMITS FOR VIRTUAL HARD DRIVES

The maximum size for any virtual hard drive presented to a VM is just shy of 2 TB. More precisely, it is 2 TB minus 512 B. That's a lot of storage for just one VM!

There's another perspective on VMs besides what the guest OS instance sees. There's also the external perspective—what does the hypervisor see?

Examining Virtual Machines from the Outside

To better understand what a VM is, you must not just consider how a VM appears from the perspective of the guest OS instance (for example, from the "inside"), as I've just done. You must also consider how a VM appears from the "outside." In other words, you must consider how the VM appears to the ESXi host running the VM.

From the perspective of an ESXi host, a VM consists of several types of files stored on a supported storage device. The two most common files that compose a VM are the configuration file and the virtual hard disk file. The configuration file—hereafter referred to as the VMX file—is a plain-text file identified by a .vmx extension, and it functions as the structural definition of the VM. The VMX file defines the virtual hardware that resides in the VM. The number of processors, the amount of RAM, the number of network adapters, the associated MAC addresses, the networks to which the network adapters connect, and the number, names, and locations of all virtual hard drives are stored in the configuration file.

Listing 9.1 shows a sample VMX file for a VM named win2k8r2-02.

LISTING 9.1:   Example virtual machine configuration (VMX) file

```
.encoding = "UTF-8"
config.version = "8"
virtualHW.version = "8"
pciBridge0.present = "TRUE"
pciBridge4.present = "TRUE"
pciBridge4.virtualDev = "pcieRootPort"
pciBridge4.functions = "8"
pciBridge5.present = "TRUE"
pciBridge5.virtualDev = "pcieRootPort"
pciBridge5.functions = "8"
pciBridge6.present = "TRUE"
pciBridge6.virtualDev = "pcieRootPort"
pciBridge6.functions = "8"
pciBridge7.present = "TRUE"
pciBridge7.virtualDev = "pcieRootPort"
pciBridge7.functions = "8"
vmci0.present = "TRUE"
hpet0.present = "TRUE"
nvram = "win2k8r2-02.nvram"
virtualHW.productCompatibility = "hosted"
powerType.powerOff = "soft"
powerType.powerOn = "hard"
powerType.suspend = "hard"
powerType.reset = "soft"
displayName = "win2k8r2-02"
extendedConfigFile = "win2k8r2-02.vmxf"
floppy0.present = "TRUE"
scsi0.present = "TRUE"
scsi0.sharedBus = "none"
scsi0.virtualDev = "lsisas1068"
memsize = "4096"
scsi0:0.present = "TRUE"
```

```
scsi0:0.fileName = "win2k8r2-02.vmdk"
scsi0:0.deviceType = "scsi-hardDisk"
ide1:0.present = "TRUE"
ide1:0.clientDevice = "TRUE"
ide1:0.deviceType = "cdrom-raw"
ide1:0.startConnected = "FALSE"
floppy0.startConnected = "FALSE"
floppy0.fileName = ""
floppy0.clientDevice = "TRUE"
ethernet0.present = "TRUE"
ethernet0.virtualDev = "e1000"
ethernet0.networkName = "VLAN19"
ethernet0.addressType = "vpx"
ethernet0.generatedAddress = "00:50:56:81:71:92"
disk.EnableUUID = "TRUE"
guestOS = "windows7srv-64"
uuid.bios = "42 01 8b cd d8 fa 79 09-b0 1e a6 66 e2 9f e3 2e"
vc.uuid = "50 01 d4 dc cc 97 66 3e-d3 92 07 d2 47 4d 2d a7"
```

Reading through the win2k8r2-01.vmx file, you can determine the following facts about this VM:

◆ From the guestOS line, you can see the VM is configured for a guest OS referred to as "windows7srv-64"; this corresponds to Windows Server 2008 R2 64-bit.

◆ Based on the memsize line, you know the VM is configured for 4 GB of RAM.

◆ The scsi0:0.fileName line tells you the VM's hard drive is located in the file win2k8r2-02.vmdk.

◆ The VM has a floppy drive configured, based on the presence of the floppy0 lines, but it does not start connected (see floppy0.startConnected).

◆ The VM has a single network adapter configured to the VLAN19 port group, based on the ethernet0 lines.

◆ Based on the ethernet0.generatedAddress line, the VM's single network adapter has an automatically generated MAC address of 00:50:56:81:71:92.

While the VMX file is important, it is only the structural definition of the virtual hardware that composes the VM. It does not store any actual data from the guest OS instance running inside the VM. A separate type of file, the virtual hard disk file, performs that role.

The virtual hard disk file, identified by a .vmdk extension and hereafter referred to as the VMDK file, holds the actual data stored by a VM. Each VMDK file represents a hard drive. For a VM running Windows, the first VMDK file would typically be the storage location for the C: drive. For a Linux system, it would typically be the storage location for the root, boot, and a few other partitions. Additional VMDK files can be added to provide additional storage locations for the VM, and each VMDK file would appear as a physical hard drive to the VM.

While I refer to a virtual hard disk file as "a VMDK file," in reality there are two different files that compose a virtual hard disk. Both of them use the .vmdk extension, but each performs a very different role. One of these files is the VMDK header file, and the other is the VMDK flat file. There's a good reason why I—and others in the virtualization space—refer to a virtual hard disk file as "a VMDK file," though, and Figure 9.2 helps illustrate why.

FIGURE 9.2
The Datastore Browser in the vSphere Client shows only a single VMDK file.

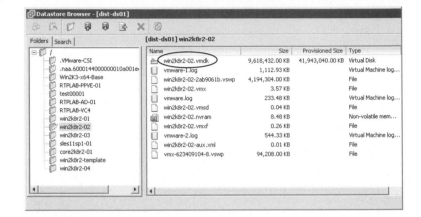

Looking closely at Figure 9.2, you'll see only a single VMDK file listed. In actuality, though, there are two files, but to see them you must go to a command-line interface. From there, as shown in Figure 9.3, you'll see the two different VMDK files: the VMDK header (the smaller of the two) and the VMDK flat file (the larger of the two and the one that has −flat in the filename).

FIGURE 9.3
There are actually two different VMDK files for every virtual hard disk in a VM, even though the vSphere Client shows only a single file.

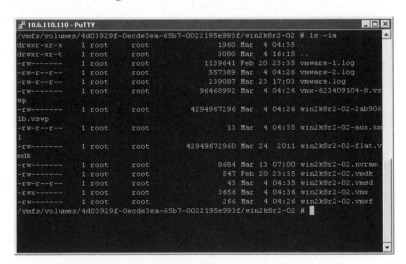

Of these two files, the VMDK header file is a plain-text file and is human-readable; the VMDK flat file is a binary file and is not human-readable. The VMDK header file contains only configuration information and pointers to the flat file; the VMDK flat file contains the actual data for the virtual hard disk. Naturally, this means that the VMDK header file is typically very small in size, while the VMDK flat file could be as large as the size of the configured virtual hard disk in the VMX. So, a 40 GB virtual hard disk could mean a 40 GB VMDK flat file, depending on other configuration settings you'll see later in this chapter.

Listing 9.2 shows the contents of a sample VMDK header file.

LISTING 9.2:   Example VMDK header file

```
# Disk DescriptorFile
version=1
encoding="UTF-8"
CID=d68134bc
parentCID=ffffffff
isNativeSnapshot="no"
createType="vmfs"

# Extent description
RW 83886080 VMFS "win2k8r2-02-flat.vmdk"

# The Disk Data Base
#DDB

ddb.adapterType = "lsilogic"
ddb.thinProvisioned = "1"
ddb.geometry.sectors = "63"
ddb.geometry.heads = "255"
ddb.geometry.cylinders = "5221"
ddb.uuid = "60 00 C2 92 fa bc c8 84-36 c7 b2 4a d1 d4 3d 9a"
ddb.longContentID = "446c3e35b2b8ccb9167deccad68134bc"
ddb.toolsVersion = "8352"
ddb.virtualHWVersion = "8"
ddb.deletable = "true"
```

There are several other types of files that make up a VM. For example, when the VM is running there will most likely be a VSWP file, which is a VMkernel swap file. You'll learn more about VMkernel swap files in Chapter 11, "Managing Resource Allocation." There will also be an NVRAM file, which stores the VM's BIOS settings.

Now that you have a feel for what makes up a VM, let's get started creating some VMs.

Creating a Virtual Machine

Creating VMs is a core part of using VMware vSphere, and VMware has made the process as easy and straightforward as possible. Let's walk through the process, and I will explain the steps along the way.

Perform the following steps to create a VM:

1. If it's not already running, launch the vSphere Client, and connect to a vCenter Server instance or an individual ESXi host.

2. In the inventory tree, right-click the name of a cluster, resource pool, or an individual ESXi host, and select the New Virtual Machine option, as shown in Figure 9.4. Alternatively, use the File menu or the Ctrl+N keyboard shortcut to launch the wizard.

FIGURE 9.4
You can launch the Create New Virtual Machine wizard from the context menu of an ESXi cluster or an individual ESXi host.

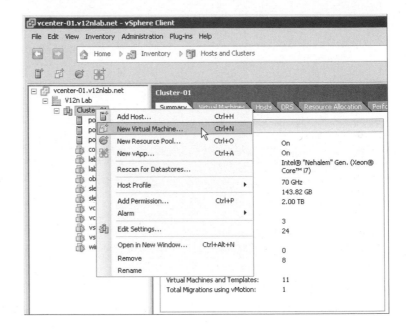

3. When the Create New Virtual Machine wizard opens, select the Custom radio button, shown in Figure 9.5, and then click Next.

   The Custom selection exposes a much greater set of options when creating a VM, such as the VM version, RAM, number of virtual CPUs, SCSI controller type, and more VM disk options. Once you've created several VMs and have a good understanding of the default values used and how to modify those values, you can use Typical instead of Custom. In the beginning, though, I recommend selecting Custom.

4. Type a name for the VM, select a location in the inventory where the VM should reside, and click Next.

5. If you selected a cluster without vSphere DRS enabled or you are running vSphere DRS in manual mode, you'll need to select a specific host within the cluster on which to create the VM. Select an ESXi host from the list then click Next.

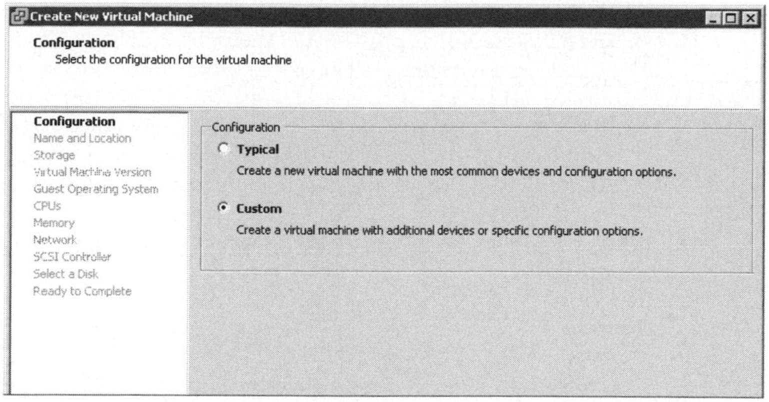

FIGURE 9.5
The Custom option exposes more configuration options to users when creating new VMs.

FIGURE 9.6
The logical folder structure selected here does not correspond to where the VM files (for example, VMX and VMDK) are located on the selected datastore.

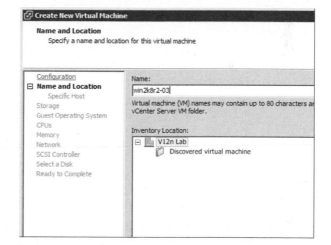

LOGICAL INVENTORY AND PHYSICAL INVENTORY

The inventory location you select when you create a new VM, as shown in Figure 9.6, is a logical location. This inventory location does not correspond to the server on which that VM will run or the datastore on which that VM will be stored. This logical inventory displays in the vSphere Client when you select VMs And Templates as the Inventory view.

---

6. Select a datastore where the VM files will be located.

As you can see in Figure 9.7, the vSphere Client shows a fair amount of information about the datastores (size, provisioned space, free space, type of datastore, VMFS version). However, the vSphere Client doesn't show information such as IOPS capacity or other performance statistics. In Chapter 6, "Creating and Configuring Storage Devices," I discussed profile-driven storage, which allows you to create VM storage profiles based on storage attributes provided to vCenter Server by the storage vendor (as well as user-defined storage attributes created and assigned by the vSphere administrator). In Figure 9.7, you can see the VM Storage Profile drop-down list, which lists the currently defined VM storage profiles. If no profiles are defined or if VM storage profiles are not enabled, this drop-down list will be disabled.

FIGURE 9.7

You can use VM storage profiles to help automate VM storage placement decisions when you create a new VM.

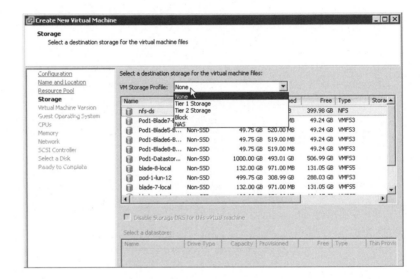

When you select a VM storage profile, the datastore listing will separate into two groups: compatible and incompatible. Compatible datastores are datastores whose attributes satisfy the VM storage profile; incompatible datastores are datastores whose attributes do not meet the criteria specified in the VM storage profile. Figure 9.8 shows a VM storage profile selected and a compatible datastore selected for this VM's storage.

The use of VM storage profiles helps automate the process of incorporating the capabilities of the underlying storage arrays into VM storage placement decisions. This makes VM storage profiles extremely powerful and useful. For more information on VM storage profiles, refer to Chapter 6.

After you select a datastore, click Next.

7. Select a VMware VM version. vSphere 5.0 introduces a new VM hardware version, version 8. As with earlier versions of vSphere, previous VM hardware versions are also supported. If the VM you are creating will be shared with ESXi hosts running both version 4.1 and version 5, then choose version 7. If the VM you are creating will be used only with vSphere 5, then choose version 8. Click Next.

FIGURE 9.8
When using VM
storage profiles,
select a compatible
datastore to ensure
that the VM's
storage needs are
properly satisfied.

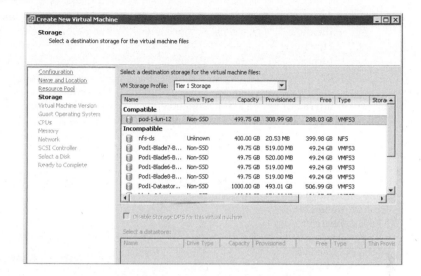

RUNNING VMs FROM PREVIOUS VERSIONS OF ESXI

Unlike upgrades from previous major versions of ESX/ESXi, version 5 allows you to run VMs created in earlier versions of ESXi without any sort of upgrade process. Some readers may recall that the upgrade from ESX 2.*x* to ESX 3.*x*, for example, required a "DMotion" upgrade process or significant downtime for the VMs.

This is not to say that there won't be any downtime for VMs when upgrading from earlier versions to vSphere 5, just that the downtime isn't required to occur during the upgrade of the hosts themselves. Instead, the tasks that do require VM downtime—upgrading VMware Tools and upgrading the virtual hardware from version 4 or version 7 to version 8—can be scheduled and performed at a later date.

---

8. Select the radio button that corresponds to the operating system vendor, select the correct operating system version, and then click Next. As you'll see shortly, this helps the vSphere Client provide recommendations for certain values later in the wizard. When you use the Typical setting instead of Custom, the selection of the guest OS drives many of the default decisions that the vSphere Client makes along the way.

9. Select the number of virtual CPUs to include in the VM.

You can select between 1 and 32 virtual CPU sockets, depending on your vSphere license. Additionally, you can choose the number of cores per virtual CPU socket. The total number of cores supported per VM with VM hardware version 8 is 32, and the maximum number of cores per VM for VM hardware version 7 is 8. Therefore, the number of cores available per virtual CPU socket will change based on the number of virtual CPU sockets selected. Table 9.1 shows the CPU socket/CPU cores available for VM version 8; Table 9.2 shows the same values for VM hardware version 7.

TABLE 9.1: Number of CPU cores available with VM version 8

VIRTUAL CPU SOCKETS SELECTED	NUMBER OF CPU CORES AVAILABLE	MAXIMUM CPU CORES POSSIBLE
1	1–16	16
2	1–16	32
3	1–10	30
4	1–8	32
5	1–6	30
6	1–5	30
7	1–4	28
8	1–4	32
9	1–3	27
10	1–3	30
11–16	1–2	32 (with 16 virtual CPU sockets)
17–32	1	32 (with 32 virtual CPU sockets)

TABLE 9.2: Number of CPU cores available with VM version 7

VIRTUAL CPU SOCKETS SELECTED	NUMBER OF CPU CORES AVAILABLE	MAXIMUM CPU CORES POSSIBLE
1	1–2	8
2	1–4	8
3	1–2	6
4	1–2	8
5 or more	1	8 (with 8 virtual CPU sockets)

Keep in mind that the operating system you will install into this VM must support the selected number of virtual CPUs. Also keep in mind that more virtual CPUs doesn't necessarily translate into better performance, and in some cases larger values may negatively impact performance.

When you finish configuring virtual CPUs, click Next to continue.

10. Configure the VM with the determined amount of RAM by clicking the up and down arrows or typing the value, as shown in Figure 9.9.

FIGURE 9.9
Based on guest OS selection, the vSphere Client provides some basic guidelines on the amount of memory you should configure for the VM.

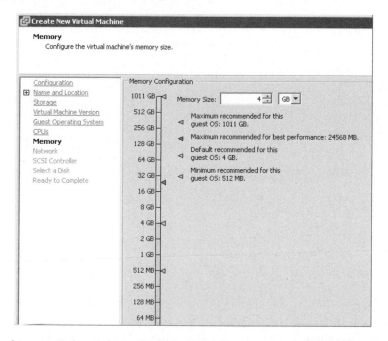

As I mentioned in step 7, the vSphere Client displays recommendations about the minimum and recommended amounts of RAM based on the earlier selection of operating system and version. This is one of the reasons why the selection of the correct guest OS is important when creating a VM.

The amount of RAM configured on this page is the amount of RAM the guest OS reflects in its system properties, and it is the maximum amount that a guest OS will ever be able to use. Think of it as the virtual equivalent of the amount of physical RAM installed in a system. Just as a physical machine cannot use more memory than is physically installed in it, a VM cannot access more memory than it is configured to use.

When you've selected the amount of RAM you want allocated to the VM, click Next.

DO YOU KNOW WHERE YOUR MEMORY IS?

The setting on this page is not a guarantee that physical memory will be used to achieve the configured value. As I discuss in later chapters, memory for a VM might be physical RAM, VMkernel swap file space, or some combination of the two.

11. Select the number of network adapters, the type of each network adapter, and the network to which each adapter will connect. Although you can ultimately add up to 10 virtual NICs to a VM, only four can be configured when you are creating the VM. Figure 9.10 shows a screenshot of configuring virtual NICs, and Table 9.3 provides additional information about the different types of virtual NICs.

FIGURE 9.10

You can configure a VM with up to four network adapters, of the same or different types, that reside on the same or different networks as needed.

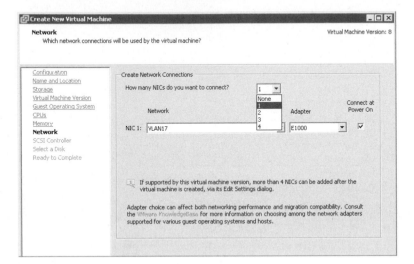

TABLE 9.3: Virtual NIC types in vSphere 5

VIRTUAL NIC TYPE	VM HARDWARE VERSIONS SUPPORTED	DESCRIPTION
E1000	4, 7, 8	This virtual NIC emulates the Intel 82545EM Gigabit Ethernet NIC. The driver for this NIC is found in many modern guest OSes, but some older guest OSes might not have a driver.
Flexible	4, 7, 8	This virtual NIC identifies itself as a Vlance adapter, an emulated form of the AMD 79C970 PCnet32 10 Mbps NIC. Drivers for this NIC are available in most 32-bit guest OSes. Once VMware Tools is installed (I'll discuss VMware Tools later in this chapter), this virtual NIC changes over to the higher-performance VMXNET adapter. The Flexible virtual NIC type is available for use only with certain 32-bit guest OSes. For example, you can't select the Flexible virtual NIC type for VMs running 32-bit versions of Windows Server 2008, but it is an option for 32-bit versions of Windows Server 2003.

TABLE 9.3:   Virtual NIC types in vSphere 5   *(CONTINUED)*

VIRTUAL NIC TYPE	VM HARDWARE VERSIONS SUPPORTED	DESCRIPTION
VMXNET 2 (Enhanced)	4, 7, 8	This virtual NIC type is based on the VMXNET adapter but provides additional high-performance features like jumbo frames and hardware offload. It's supported only for a limited set of guest OSes.
VMXNET 3	7, 8	The VMXNET 3 virtual NIC type is the latest version of a para-virtualized driver designed for performance. It offers all the features of VMXNET 2 plus additional features like multi-queue support, IPv6 offloads, and MSI/MSI-X interrupt delivery. It's supported only for VM hardware version 7 or later and for a limited set of guest OSes.

MORE INFORMATION ON VIRTUAL NIC ADAPTERS

VMware has detailed descriptions of the virtual NIC adapter types and the support requirements for each on its website at `http://kb.vmware.com/kb/1001805`.

After you select the best virtual NIC type for your new VM, click Next to move on to selecting a SCSI controller type and virtual disk properties.

12. Select the radio button that corresponds to the appropriate SCSI adapter for the operating system selected on the Guest Operating System page of the Create New Virtual Machine wizard.

The correct default driver should already be selected based on the previously selected operating system. For example, the LSI Logic parallel adapter is selected automatically when Windows Server 2003 is selected as the guest OS, but the LSI Logic SAS adapter is selected when Windows Server 2008 is chosen as the guest OS. I provided some additional details on the different virtual SCSI adapters in Chapter 6, "Creating and Configuring Storage Devices."

VIRTUAL MACHINE SCSI CONTROLLERS

Windows 2000 has built-in support for the BusLogic parallel SCSI controller, while Windows Server 2003 and later operating systems have built-in support for the LSI Logic parallel SCSI controller. Additionally, Windows Server 2008 has support for the LSI Logic SAS controller. Windows XP doesn't have built-in support for any of these, requiring a driver disk during installation. Choosing the wrong controller will result in an error during the operating system installation. The error states that hard drives cannot be found. Choosing the wrong SCSI controller during a physical-to-virtual (P2V) operation will result in a "blue screen error" for a Windows guest OS inside the VM, and the Windows installation will fail to boot.

13. Click Next, and then select the appropriate radio button for the virtual disk to be used, as shown in Figure 9.11. There are four options:

◆ The Create A New Virtual Disk option allows the user to create a new virtual disk (a VMDK file) that will house the guest OS's files and data. In most cases, when you are creating a new VM you will use this option.

◆ The Use An Existing Virtual Disk option allows a VM to be created using a virtual disk that is already configured with a guest OS and that resides in an available datastore.

◆ The Raw Device Mappings option allows a VM to have raw SAN LUN access. RDMs are discussed in a bit more detail in Chapter 6 and Chapter 7.

◆ The Do Not Create Disk option allows you to create a VM without creating an associated virtual disk. The use cases for this option are fairly rare, but there could be instances where you would need to create a VM but not create a VMDK at the same time. Use this option for those circumstances.

FIGURE 9.11
You can create a new virtual disk when a new VM is created, or you can use an existing virtual disk.

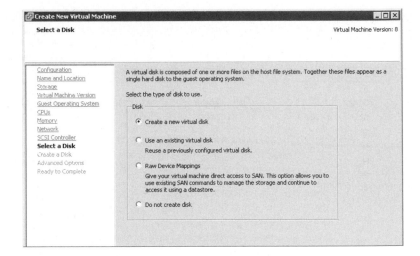

Select the Create A New Virtual Disk option, and click Next.

ADDING EXISTING DISKS

The existing virtual disk doesn't have to contain an instance of the guest OS; it can contain data that perhaps will serve as a secondary drive inside the VM. The ability to add existing disks with data makes virtual hard drives extremely portable, generally allowing users to move them from VM to VM without repercussions. You will obviously need to address any guest OS–specific issues such as partitions, filesystem type, or permissions.

14. When the Create A New Virtual Disk option is selected, options are available for the creation of the new virtual disk, as shown in Figure 9.12. First, configure the desired disk size for the VM hard drive. The maximum size will be determined by the format of the datastore on which the virtual disk is stored. Next, select the appropriate Disk Provisioning option:

◆ To create a virtual disk with all space allocated at creation but not pre-zeroed, select Thick Provision Lazy Zeroed. In this case, the VMDK flat file will be the same size as the specified virtual disk size. A 40 GB virtual disk means a 40 GB VMDK flat file.

◆ To create a virtual disk with all space allocated at creation and pre-zeroed, select Thick Provision Eager Zeroed. This option is required in order to support vSphere Fault Tolerance. This option also means a "full-size" VMDK flat file that is the same size as the size of the virtual hard disk.

◆ To create a virtual disk with space allocated on demand, select the Thin Provision option. In this case, the VMDK flat file will grow depending on the amount of data actually stored in it, up to the maximum size specified for the virtual hard disk.

Depending on your storage platform, storage type, and storage vendor's support for vSphere 5's storage integration technologies like VAAI or VASA, some of these options might be grayed out. For example, an NFS datastore that does not support the VAAIv2 extensions will have these options grayed out, as only thin provisioned VMDKs are supported. (VAAI and VASA are discussed in greater detail in Chapter 6.)

FIGURE 9.12
vSphere 5 offers a number of different Disk Provisioning options when creating new virtual disks.

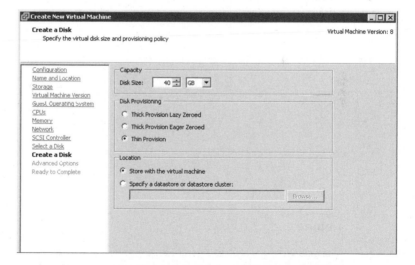

There are two options for the location of the new virtual disk. Keep in mind that these options control physical location, not logical location; these options will directly affect the datastore and/or directory where files are stored for use by the hypervisor.

◆ The option Store With The Virtual Machine will place the file in the same subdirectory as the configuration file and the rest of the VM files. This is the most commonly selected option and makes managing the VM files easier.

◆ The option Specify A Datastore Or Datastore Cluster allows you to store the VM file separately from the rest of the files. You'd typically select this option when adding new virtual hard disks to a VM or when you need to separate the operating system virtual disk from a data virtual disk.

When you've finished configuring the size, provisioning options, and location, click Next.

15. The Advanced Options page lets you specify the SCSI node or IDE controller to which the virtual disk is connected and also allows you to configure a virtual disk in Independent mode, as shown in Figure 9.13. As noted in the wizard, this page is normally not altered, and you can accept the default setting by clicking Next.

◆ The Virtual Device Node drop-down list reflects the 15 different SCSI nodes available on each of the four SCSI adapters a VM supports. When using an IDE controller, this drop-down list shows the four different IDE nodes that are available.

◆ By not selecting the Independent mode option, you ensure that the virtual disk remains in the default state that allows VM snapshots to be created. If you select the Independent check box, you can configure the virtual disk as a persistent disk, in which changes are written immediately and permanently to the disk, or as a nonpersistent disk, which discards all changes when the VM is turned off.

FIGURE 9.13
You can configure the virtual disk on a number of different SCSI adapters and SCSI IDs, and you can configure it as an independent disk.

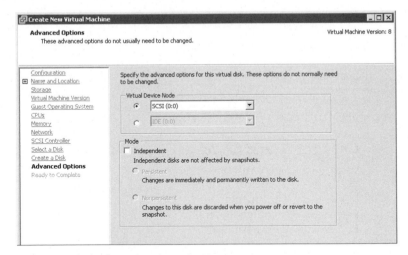

16. Complete a final review of the VM configuration. If anything is incorrect, go back and make changes to the configuration. As you can see in Figure 9.14, the steps in the left side of the wizard are hyperlinks that allow you to jump directly to an earlier point in the wizard and make changes.

When everything is correct, click Finish.

As you can see, the process for creating a VM is pretty straightforward. What's not so straightforward, though, are some of the values that should be used when creating new VMs. What are the best values to use?

FIGURE 9.14
Reviewing the configuration of the Create New Virtual Machine wizard ensures the correct settings for the VM and prevents mistakes that require deleting and re-creating the VM.

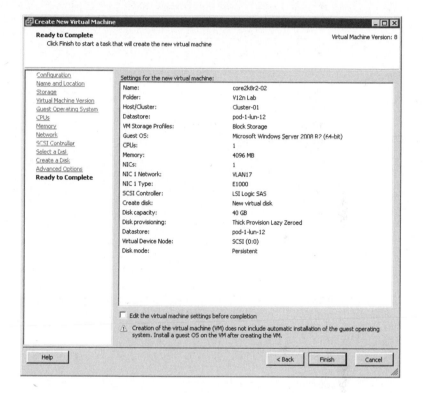

Choosing Values for Your New Virtual Machine

Choosing the right values to use for the number of virtual CPUs, the amount of memory, or the number or types of virtual NICs when creating your new VM can be difficult. Fortunately, there's lots of documentation out there on CPU and RAM sizing as well as networking for VMs, so my only recommendation there will be to right-size the VMs based on your needs (see the Real-World Scenario sidebar later in this chapter).

VIRTUAL MACHINE SIZING CAN HAVE AN IMPACT

Determining the right size for your VMs is a crucial part of your overall vSphere design, and it can impact a number of different areas. For more information on how right-sizing VMs impacts other areas of your vSphere design, refer to *VMware vSphere Design*, also by Sybex.

For other areas besides these, the guidance isn't quite so clear. Out of all the options available during the creation of a new VM, two areas tend to consistently generate questions from both new and experienced users alike:

◆ How should I handle naming my VMs?

◆ How big should I make the virtual disks?

Let's talk about each of these questions in a bit more detail.

Naming Virtual Machines

Choosing the display name for a VM might seem like a trivial assignment, but you must ensure an appropriate naming strategy is in place. I recommend making the display names of VMs match the hostnames configured in the guest OS being installed. For example, if the intention is to use the name Server1 in the guest OS, then the VM display name should match Server1. If spaces are used in the virtual display name—which is allowed—then using command-line tools to manage VMs becomes a bit tricky because the spaces will have to be quoted out on the command line. In addition, since DNS hostnames cannot include spaces, using spaces in the VM name would create a disparity between the VM name and the guest OS hostname. Ultimately, this means you should avoid using spaces and special characters that are not allowed in standard DNS naming strategies to ensure similar names both inside and outside the VM. Aside from whatever policies might be in place from your organization, this is usually a matter of personal preference.

The display name assigned to a VM also becomes the name of the folder in the VMFS volume where the VM files will live. At the file level, the associated configuration (VMX) and virtual hard drive (VMDK) files will assume the name supplied in the display name text box during VM creation. Refer to Figure 9.2 and Figure 9.15, where you can see the user-supplied name of win2k8r2-02 is reused for both the folder name and the filenames for the VM.

FIGURE 9.15
The display name assigned to a VM is used in a variety of places.

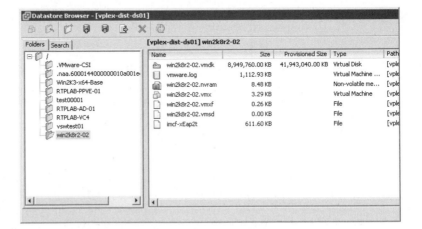

Sizing Virtual Machine Hard Disks

The answer to the second question—how big to make the hard disks in your VM—is a bit more complicated. There are many different approaches, but some best practices facilitate the management, scalability, and backup of VMs. First and foremost, it's generally recommended that you create VMs with multiple virtual disk files as a means of separating the operating system from the custom user/application data. Separating the system files and the user/application data will make it easier to increase the number of data drives in the future and will allow for a more practical backup strategy. A system drive of 25 GB to 30 GB, for example, usually provides ample room for the initial installation and continued growth of the operating system. The data drives across different VMs will vary in size because of underlying storage system capacity and functionality, the installed applications, the function of the system, and the number of users who connect to the computer. However, because the extra hard drives are not operating system data, it will be easier to make adjustments to those drives when needed.

Keep in mind that additional virtual hard drives will pick up on the same naming scheme as the original virtual hard drive. For example, a VM named Server1 that has an original virtual hard disk file named `win2k8r2-02.vmdk` will name the new virtual hard disk file `win2k8r2-02_1.vmdk`. Each additional file will increment the last number, making it administratively easy to identify all virtual disk files related to a particular VM. Figure 9.16 shows a VM with two virtual hard disks so that you can see how vSphere handles the naming for additional virtual hard disks.

FIGURE 9.16
vSphere automatically appends a number to the filename for additional virtual hard disks.

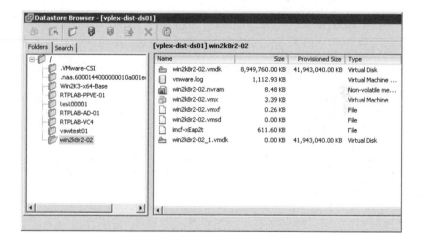

In the next chapter, "Using Templates and vApps," you'll revisit the process of creating VMs to see how to use templates to implement and maintain an optimal VM configuration that separates the system data from the user/application data. At this point, though, now that you've created a VM, you're ready to install the guest OS into the VM.

Real World Scenario

PROVISIONING VIRTUAL MACHINES IS NOT THE SAME AS PROVISIONING PHYSICAL MACHINES

You need to approach provisioning VMs differently from the way you provisioned physical machines in the past. After all, isn't it underutilized and overprovisioned servers that have led you to use virtualization to consolidate your workloads?

In the physical world, you provision servers based on the maximum you think that server might ever need throughout its lifetime. Because the intended workload for a server might shift over that lifetime, you probably provision the physical server with more CPU resources and more RAM than it really needs.

In the virtual environment, though, VMs should be provisioned only with the resources they really need. Additional resources can be added later should the workload need them, sometimes with no downtime required.

In the event that you don't make this shift in thinking, you'll end up much like a client of mine who had the same problem. During the early phases of the client's consolidation project, they provisioned VMs with the same level of resources given to physical machines. It wasn't until they ran out of resources in the virtual environment and had a far lower consolidation ratio than anticipated that I was able to convince them to change their provisioning practices. Once the provisioning practices were changed, the client was able to improve their consolidation ratio without negatively impacting the level of service they were able to provide. Right-sizing your VMs is a good thing!

Installing a Guest Operating System

A new VM is analogous to a physical computer with an empty hard drive. All the components are there but without an operating system. After creating the VM, you're ready to install a supported guest OS. Some of the more commonly installed guest OSes supported by ESXi include the following (this is not a comprehensive list):

- Windows 7 (32-bit and 64-bit)
- Windows Vista (32-bit and 64-bit)
- Windows Server 2008 R2 (64-bit)
- Windows Server 2008 (32-bit and 64-bit)
- Windows Server 2003 (32-bit and 64-bit)
- Windows Small Business Server 2003
- Windows XP Professional (32-bit and 64-bit)
- Red Hat Enterprise Linux 3/4/5/6 (32-bit and 64-bit)
- CentOS 4/5 (32-bit and 64-bit)

- SUSE Linux Enterprise Server 8/9/10/11 (32-bit and 64-bit)
- Ubuntu Linux (32-bit and 64-bit)
- NetWare 5.1/6.x
- Sun Solaris 10 (32-bit and 64-bit)
- FreeBSD (32-bit and 64-bit)

VIRTUAL MAC SERVERS?

VMware vSphere 5 adds support for some new guest OSes. Notably, vSphere 5 adds support for Apple Mac OS X Server 10.5 and 10.6. This allows you to run Mac OS X Server VMs on your VMware ESXi hosts. However, it's critically important to note that this is supported only when running ESXi on specific models of the Apple Xserve servers.

Installing any of these supported guest OSes follows the same common order of steps for installation on a physical server, but the nuances and information provided during the install of each guest OS might vary greatly. Because of the differences involved in installing different guest OSes or different versions of a guest OS, I won't go into any detail on the actual guest OS installation process. I'll leave that to the guest OS vendor. Instead, I'll focus on guest OS installation tasks that are specific to a virtualized environment.

Working with Installation Media

One task that is greatly beneficial in a virtual environment but that isn't typically required in a virtual environment concerns guest OS installation media. In the physical world, administrators would typically put the OS installation media in the physical server's optical drive, install the OS, and then be done with it. Well, in a virtual world, the process is similar, but here's the issue—where do you put the CD when the server is virtual? There are a couple of different ways to handle it. One way is quick and easy, and the second way takes a bit longer but pays off later.

VMs have a few different ways to access data stored on optical disks. As shown in Figure 9.17, VMs can access optical disks in one of three different ways:

Client Device   This option allows an optical drive local to the computer running the vSphere Client to be mapped into the VM. For example, if you are using the vSphere Client on your corporate-issued HP laptop, you have the option of simply inserting a CD/DVD into your local optical drive and mapping that into the VM with this option.

Host Device   This option maps the ESXi host's optical drive into the VM. VMware administrators would have to insert the CD/DVD into the server's optical drive in order for the VM to have access to the disk.

Datastore ISO File   This last option maps an ISO image (see the "ISO Image Basics" sidebar) into the VM. Although using an ISO image typically requires an additional step—creating the ISO image from the physical disk—more and more software is being distributed as an ISO image that can be leveraged directly from within your vSphere environment.

FIGURE 9.17

VMs can access optical disks physically located on the vSphere Client system, located on the ESXi host, or stored as an ISO image.

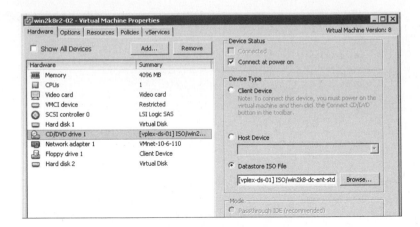

ISO IMAGE BASICS

An ISO image is an archive file of an optical disk. The name is derived from the International Organization for Standardization (ISO) 9660 file system standard used with CD-ROM media, and the ISO format is widely supported by many different software vendors. A variety of software applications can work with ISO images. In fact, most CD-burning software applications for Windows, Linux, and Mac OS X can create ISO images from existing physical disks or burn ISO images to a physical disk.

ISO images are the recommended way to install a guest OS because they are faster than using an actual optical drive and can be quickly mounted or dismounted with very little effort.

Before you can use an ISO image to install the guest OS, though, you must first put it in a location that ESXi can access. Generally, this means uploading it into a datastore accessible to your ESXi hosts.

Perform these steps to upload an ISO image into a datastore:

1. Use the vSphere Client to connect to a vCenter Server instance or an individual ESXi host.

2. From the vSphere Client menu bar, select View ➢ Inventory ➢ Datastores.

3. Right-click the datastore to which you want to upload the ISO image and select Browse Datastore from the context menu. The Datastore Browser window opens.

4. Select the destination folder in the datastore where you want to store the ISO image. Use the new Folder button (it looks like a folder with a green plus symbol) if you need to create a new folder in which to store the ISO image.

5. From the toolbar in the Datastore Browser window, click the Upload button (it looks like a disk with a green arrow pointing into the disk). From the pop-up menu that appears, select Upload File, as shown in Figure 9.18.

FIGURE 9.18
Use the Upload
File command
in the Datastore
Browser to upload
ISO images for use
when installing
guest OSes.

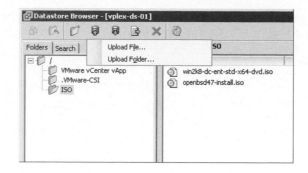

6. In the Upload Items dialog box, navigate to the location where the ISO image is stored. Select the ISO image, and then click Open.

7. The vSphere Client displays the Upload/Download Operating Warning dialog box, letting you know that any file or folder with the same name in the destination location will be replaced. Click Yes to continue.

8. The vSphere Client uploads the file into the selected folder in that datastore.

After the ISO image is uploaded to an available datastore, you're ready to actually install a guest OS using that ISO image.

Using the Installation Media

Once you have the installation media in place—either using the local CD-ROM drive on the computer where you are running the vSphere Client, using the physical server's optical drive, or by creating and uploading an ISO image into a datastore—you're ready to actually use that installation media to install a guest OS into the VM.

Perform the following steps to install a guest OS using an ISO file on a shared datastore:

1. Use the vSphere Client to connect to a vCenter Server instance or an individual ESXi host where a VM has been created.

2. If you're not already in the Hosts And Clusters or VMs And Templates view, use the menu bar to select View ➤ Inventory ➤ Hosts And Clusters or View ➤ Inventory ➤ VMs And Templates.

3. In the inventory tree, right-click the new VM, and select the Edit Settings menu option. The Virtual Machine Properties window opens.

4. Select the CD/DVD Drive 1 hardware option.

5. Select the Datastore ISO File radio button, and select the Connect At Power On check box. If you fail to select the Connect At Power On check box, the VM will not boot from the selected ISO image.

6. Click the Browse button to browse a datastore for the ISO file of the guest OS.

7. Navigate through the available datastores until you find the ISO file of the guest OS to be installed. After you select the ISO file, the properties page is configured similar to the screenshot shown previously in Figure 9.17.

8. Right-click the VM, and select the Open Console option. Alternatively, you can use the console in the details pane of the vSphere Client application.

9. Click the green Power On button from the toolbar of the console session. Alternatively, you can use the menu bar and select VM ➢ Power ➢ Power On. You can also use the Ctrl+B keyboard shortcut. The VM boots from the mounted ISO image and begins the installation of the guest OS.

10. Follow the on-screen instructions to complete the guest OS installation. These will vary depending on the specific guest OS you are installing; refer to the documentation for that guest OS for specific details regarding installation.

> **VIRTUAL MACHINE GUEST OSES**
>
> For a complete list of guest OSes and all respective information regarding installation notes and known issues, refer to the PDF available on the VMware website at www.vmware.com/pdf/GuestOS_guide.pdf (note that this URL is case sensitive).

Working in the Virtual Machine Console

Working within the VM console is like working at the console of a physical system. From here, you can do anything you need to do to the VM: you can access the VM's BIOS and modify settings, you can turn the power to the VM off (and back on again), and you can interact with the guest OS you are installing or have already installed into the VM. I'll describe most of these functions later in this chapter in the sections titled "Managing Virtual Machines" and "Modifying Virtual Machines," but there is one thing that I want to point out now.

The vSphere Client has to have a way to know if the keystrokes and mouse clicks you're generating go to the VM or if they should be processed by the vSphere Client itself. To do this, it uses the concept of *focus*. When you click within a VM console, that VM will have the focus: all of the keystrokes and the mouse clicks will be directed to that VM. Until you have the VMware Tools installed—a process I'll describe in the very next section, titled "Installing VMware Tools"—you'll have to manually tell the vSphere Client when you want to shift focus out of the VM. To do this, the vSphere Client uses a special keystroke: Ctrl+Alt. When you press Ctrl+Alt, the vSphere Client causes the VM that currently has control of the mouse and keyboard to relinquish control and return that control to the vSphere Client. Keep that in mind when you are trying to use your mouse and it won't travel beyond the confines of the VM console window. Just press Ctrl+Alt, and the VM will release control.

Once you've installed the guest OS, you should then install and configure VMware Tools. I discuss VMware Tools installation and configuration in the next section.

🌐 Real World Scenario

Microsoft Licensing and Windows Activation for Virtual Machines

As the virtualization market has matured, Microsoft has adjusted its licensing practices to reflect that market. In spite of those adjustments—or perhaps because of them—there is still confusion about the virtualization licensing available for the Windows Server operating system. The following list of licensing data is a combination of information from both Microsoft and VMware:

◆ Microsoft Windows Server licenses are attached to the physical machine, not to the VM.

◆ A licensed copy of Windows Server 2008 Datacenter Edition entitles a user to install and run an unlimited number of virtual Windows instances on the physical server to which that license is assigned.

◆ Similarly, a licensed copy of Windows Server 2008 Enterprise Edition grants the user the right to install and run up to four Windows instances on the physical server to which the license is assigned.

◆ A license for Windows Server 2008 Standard Edition allows the user to run a single virtual Windows instance on the physical server to which the license is assigned.

◆ Downgrade rights exist so that a physical server licensed with Windows Server 2008 Datacenter Edition can run unlimited VMs running Datacenter Edition, Enterprise Edition, Standard Edition, or any mix of the three. This also applies to running previous versions of Windows Server.

◆ vMotion, which moves a running VM to a new host, does not violate a Microsoft licensing agreement as long as the target ESXi host is licensed for the post-vMotion number of VMs. For example, if an ESXi host named ESXi01 has four running instances of Windows in VMs, a second ESXi host named ESXi02 has three running instances of Windows in VMs, and each of the physical systems has been assigned a Windows Server 2008 Enterprise Edition license, then it is within the licensing agreement to perform a vMotion move of one VM from ESXi01 to ESXi02. However, a vMotion move from ESXi02 to ESXi01 would violate the licensing agreement because ESXi01 is licensed to run only up to four instances of Windows at a time.

Because Microsoft requires Windows Server licenses to be attached to physical hardware, many organizations are choosing to license their physical hardware with Windows Server 2008 Datacenter Edition. This gives the organization the ability to run an unlimited number of Windows Server instances on that hardware, and downgrade or previous version rights allow the organization to use Standard, Enterprise, or Datacenter Edition of Windows Server 2003 or Windows Server 2008.

Activation is another area requiring a bit of planning. If your licensing structure for a Windows Server guest OS does not fall under the umbrella of a volume licensing agreement, you will be required to activate the operating system with Microsoft within 60 days of installation. Activation can be done automatically over the Internet or by calling the provided regional phone number. With Windows Server operating systems specifically, the activation algorithm takes into account the hardware specifications of the server. In light of this, when enough hardware changes have been made to significantly change the operating system, Windows requires reactivation. To facilitate the activation process and especially to reduce the possibility of reactivation, you should make adjustments to memory and processors, and install VMware Tools prior to performing the activation.

Installing VMware Tools

Although VMware Tools is not installed by default, the package is an important part of a VM. VMware Tools offers several great benefits without any detriments. Recall from the beginning of this chapter that VMware vSphere offers certain virtualization-optimized (or *paravirtualized*) devices to VMs in order to improve performance. In many cases, these paravirtualized devices do not have device drivers present in a standard installation of a guest OS. The device drivers for these devices are provided by VMware Tools, which is just one more reason why VMware Tools are an essential part of every VM and guest OS installation.

In other words, installing VMware Tools should be standard practice and not a debatable step in the deployment of a VM. The VMware Tools package provides the following benefits:

◆ Optimized SCSI driver

◆ Enhanced video and mouse drivers

◆ VM heartbeat

◆ VM quiescing for snapshots and backups

◆ Enhanced memory management

VMware Tools also helps streamline and automate the management of VM focus, so that you are able to move into and out of VM consoles easily and seamlessly without having to constantly use the Ctrl+Alt keyboard command.

The VMware Tools package is available for Windows, Linux, NetWare, Solaris, and FreeBSD; however, the installation methods vary because of the differences in the guest OSes. In all cases, the installation of VMware Tools starts when you select the option to install VMware Tools from the vSphere Client. Do you recall our discussion earlier about ISO images and how ESXi uses them to present CDs/DVDs to VMs? That's exactly the functionality that is being leveraged in this case. When you select to install VMware Tools, vSphere will mount an ISO as a CD/DVD for the VM, and the guest OS will reflect a mounted CD-ROM that has the installation files for VMware Tools.

WHERE ARE THE VMWARE TOOLS ISOS FOUND?

In the event you're curious, you'll find the VMware Tools ISO images located in the /vmimages/tools-isoimages directory on an ESXi host. This directory is visible only if you enable the ESX Shell on your ESXi hosts and then open an SSH connection to the host; it is not visible from the vSphere Client. The ISO images are placed there automatically during installation; you do not have to download them or obtain them from the installation CD-ROM, and you do not need to do anything to manage or maintain them.

As I mentioned previously, the exact process for installing the VMware Tools will depend upon the guest OS. Because Windows and Linux make up the largest portion of VMs deployed on VMware vSphere in most cases, those are the two examples I'll discuss in this section. First, I'll walk you through installing VMware Tools into a Windows-based guest OS.

Installing VMware Tools in Windows

Perform these steps to install VMware Tools into Windows Server 2008 R2 running as a guest OS in a VM (the steps for other versions of Windows are similar):

1. Use the vSphere Client to connect to a vCenter Server instance or an individual ESXi host.

2. If you aren't already in the Hosts And Clusters or VMs And Templates inventory view, use View ➤ Inventory ➤ Hosts And Clusters or View ➤ Inventory ➤ VMs And Templates to navigate to one of these views.

3. Right-click the VM in the inventory tree and select Open Console. You can also use the Launch Virtual Machine Console button on the toolbar in the vSphere Client.

4. If you aren't already logged into the guest OS in the VM, select VM ➤ Guest ➤ Send Ctrl-Alt-Delete and log into the guest OS.

5. From the menu, select VM ➤ Guest ➤ Install/Upgrade VMware Tools. A dialog box providing additional information appears. Click OK to dismiss the dialog box.

HOW DO I GET OUT OF HERE AGAIN?

Remember that before VMware Tools is installed into a guest OS, the ability to seamlessly move into and out of the guest OS in the console doesn't exist. Instead, you must click into the VM console in order to interact with the guest OS. When you are finished, you must press Ctrl+Alt to release the mouse and keyboard. After VMware Tools is installed, this happens automatically for you.

---

6. An AutoPlay dialog box appears, prompting the user for action. Select the option Run Setup64.exe.

   If the AutoPlay dialog box does not appear, open Windows Explorer, and double-click the CD/DVD drive icon. The AutoPlay dialog box should then appear.

7. Click Next on the Welcome To The Installation Wizard For VMware Tools page.

8. Select the appropriate setup type for the VMware Tools installation, and click Next.

   The Typical radio button will suffice for most situations. The Complete installation option installs all available features, while the Custom installation option allows for the greatest level of feature customization.

9. Click Install.

   During the installation, you may be prompted one or more times to confirm the installation of third-party device drivers; select Install for each of these prompts.

   If the AutoRun dialog box appears again, simply close the dialog box and continue with the installation.

10. After the installation is complete, click Finish.

11. Click Yes to restart the VM immediately, or click No to manually restart the VM at a later time.

Newer versions of Windows, such as Windows Server 2008, use a different mechanism—a different video driver—to improve the graphical performance of a console session.

Perform the following steps to install this different video driver and improve the graphical console performance:

1. From the Start menu, select Run. In the Run dialog box, type **devmgmt.msc** and click OK. This will launch the Device Manager console.

2. Expand the Display Adapters entry.

3. Right-click the Standard VGA Graphics Adapter or VMware SVGA II item, and select Update Driver Software.

4. Click Browse My Computer For Driver Software.

5. Using the Browse button, navigate to `C:\Program Files\Common Files\VMware\Drivers\wddm_video` and then click Next.

6. After a moment, Windows will report that it has successfully installed the driver for the VMware SVGA 3D (Microsoft Corporation – WDDM) device. Click Close.

7. Restart the VM when prompted.

After Windows restarts in the VM, you should notice improved performance when using the graphical console.

For older versions of Windows, such as Windows Server 2003, you can improve the responsiveness of the VM console by configuring the hardware acceleration setting. It is, by default, set to None; setting this to Maximum provides a much smoother console session experience. The VMware Tools installation routine reminds the user to set this value at the end of the installation, but if the user chooses not to set hardware acceleration at that time, it can easily be set later. This is highly recommended to optimize the graphical performance of the VM's console. (Note that Windows XP has this value set to Maximum by default.)

Perform the following steps to adjust the hardware acceleration in a VM running Windows Server 2003 (or Windows XP, in case the value has been changed from the default):

1. Right-click an empty area of the Windows desktop, and select the Properties option.

2. Select the Settings tab, and click the Advanced button.

3. Select the Troubleshooting tab.

4. Move the Hardware Acceleration slider to the Full setting on the right, as shown in Figure 9.19.

Now that the VMware Tools installation is complete and the VM is rebooted, the system tray displays the VMware Tools icon, a small gray box with the letters *VM* in the box (Windows taskbar settings might hide the icon). The icon in the system tray indicates that VMware Tools is installed and operational.

By double-clicking the VMware Tools icon in the system tray, you open the VMware Tools Properties dialog box, shown in Figure 9.20. Here you can configure time synchronization, show or hide VMware Tools from the taskbar, and select scripts to suspend, resume, shut down, or turn on a VM (that last option is found on the Scripts tab).

FIGURE 9.19
Adjusting the
hardware accel-
eration feature
of a Windows
guest OS is a com-
mon and helpful
adjustment for
improving mouse
performance.

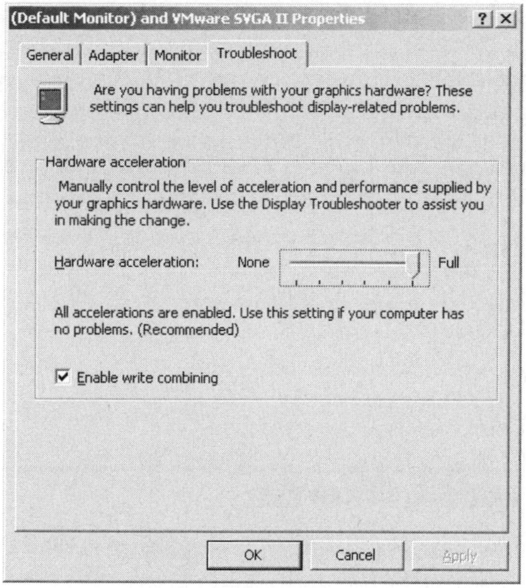

FIGURE 9.20
Use VMware Tools
Properties to
configure time
synchronization
with the host,
among other things.

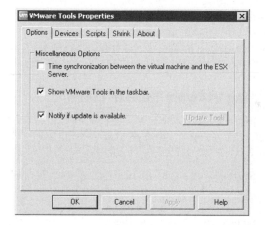

As you can see from Figure 9.20, time synchronization between the guest OS and the host is disabled by default. You'll want to use caution when enabling time synchronization between the guest OS and the ESXi host because Windows domain members rely on Kerberos for authentication and Kerberos is sensitive to time differences between computers. A Windows-based guest OS that belongs to an Active Directory domain is already configured with a native time synchronization process against the domain controller in its domain that holds the PDC Emulator operations master role. If the time on the ESXi host is different from the PDC Emulator operations master domain controller, the guest OS could end up moving outside the 5-minute window allowed by Kerberos. When the 5-minute window is exceeded, Kerberos will experience errors with authentication and replication.

You can take a few different approaches to managing time synchronizations in a virtual environment. The first approach involves not using VMware Tools time synchronization and relying instead on the W32Time service and a PDC Emulator with a Registry edit that configures synchronization with an external time server. Another approach involves disabling the native time synchronization across the Windows domain and then relying on the VMware Tools feature. A third approach might be to synchronize the VMware ESXi hosts and the PDC Emulator operations master with the same external time server and then to enable the VMware Tools option for synchronization. In this case, both the native W32Time service and VMware Tools should be adjusting the time to the same value.

VMware has a couple of Knowledge Base articles that contain the latest recommendations for timekeeping. For Windows-based guest OS installations, refer to `http://kb.vmware.com/kb/1318` or refer to the "Timekeeping in Virtual Machines" document at `www.vmware.com/files/pdf/Timekeeping-In-VirtualMachines.pdf`.

CONFIGURING NTP ON ESXI

If you do choose to synchronize the guest OS to the ESXi host using VMware Tools, be sure to synchronize the ESXi host to an authoritative time source using NTP. Refer to Chapter 2, "Planning and Installing VMware ESXi" for more information on how to configure ESXi to synchronize with an NTP-based time server.

I've shown you how to install the VMware Tools into a Windows-based guest operation system, so now I'd like to walk through the process for a Linux-based guest OS.

Installing VMware Tools in Linux

There are a number of different versions (or distributions) of Linux available and supported by VMware vSphere, and while they are all called "Linux," they do have subtle differences from one distribution to another that make it difficult to provide a single set of steps that would apply to all Linux distributions. In this section, I'll use Novell SuSE Linux Enterprise Server (SLES) version 11, a popular enterprise-focused distribution of Linux, as the basis for describing how to install VMware Tools in Linux.

Perform the following steps to install VMware Tools into a VM running the 64-bit version of SLES 11 as the guest OS:

1. Use the vSphere Client to connect to a vCenter Server instance or an individual ESXi host.

2. You will need access to the console of the VM onto which you're installing VMware Tools. Right-click the VM and select Open Console.

3. Log into the Linux guest OS using an account with appropriate permissions. This will typically be the root account or an equivalent (some Linux distributions, including Ubuntu, disable the root account but provide an administrative account you can use).

4. From the console's VM menu, select Guest ➢ Install/Upgrade VMware Tools. Click OK to the dialog box that pops up.

5. Assuming that you have a graphical user environment running in the Linux VM, a file-system browser window will open to display the contents of the VMware Tools ISO that was automatically mounted behind the scenes.

6. Open a Linux terminal window. In many distributions, you can right-click a blank area of the filesystem browser window and select Open In Terminal.

7. If you are not already in the same directory as the VMware Tools mount point, change directories to the location of the VMware Tools mount point using the following command (the exact path may vary from distribution to distribution and from version to version; this is the path for SLES 11):

```
cd /media/VMware\ Tools
```

8. Extract the compressed TAR file (with the `.tar.gz` extension) to a temporary directory, and then change to that temporary directory using the following commands:

```
tar -zxf VMwareTools-8.3.2-257589.tar.gz —C /tmp
cd /tmp/vmware-tools-distrib
```

9. In the `/tmp/vmware-tools-distrib` directory, use the `sudo` command to run the `vmware-install.pl` Perl script with the following command:

```
sudo ./vmware-install.pl
```

Enter the current account's password when prompted.

10. The installer will provide a series of prompts for information such as where to place the binary files, where the init scripts are located, and where to place the library files. Default answers are provided in brackets; you can just press Enter unless you need to specify a different value that is appropriate for this Linux system.

11. After the installation is complete, the VMware Tools ISO will be unmounted automatically. You can remove the temporary installation directory using these commands:

```
cd
rm -rf /tmp/vmware-tools-distrib
```

12. Reboot the Linux VM for the installation of VMware Tools to take full effect.

The steps described here were performed on a VM running Novell SLES 11 64-bit. Because of variations within different distributions of Linux, the commands you may need to install VMware Tools within another distribution may not match what I've listed here. However, these steps do provide a general guideline of what the procedure looks like.

VMWARE TOOLS FOR LINUX

When installing VMware Tools to a Linux guest OS, the path to the TAR file and the numbers in the TAR filename will vary. Depending upon your Linux distribution, the VMware Tools installer may also provide instructions on replacing the Ethernet driver with an updated VMXNet driver. Typically, these instructions involve unloading the older drivers, scanning for new devices, loading the new VMXNet driver, and then bringing the network interfaces back up.

After VMware Tools is installed, the Summary tab of a VM object identifies the status of VMware Tools as well as other information such as operating system, CPU, memory, DNS (host) name, IP address, and current ESXi host. Figure 9.21 shows a screenshot of this information for the SLES VM into which I just installed VMware Tools.

FIGURE 9.21
You can view details about VMware Tools, DNS name, IP address, and so forth from the Summary tab of a VM object.

In the event you are upgrading to vSphere 5 from a previous version of VMware vSphere, you will almost certainly have outdated versions of VMware Tools running in your guest OSes. You'll want to upgrade these in order to get the latest drivers. In Chapter 4, "Installing and Configuring vSphere Update Manager," I discuss the use of vSphere Update Manager to assist in this process, but you can also do it manually.

For Windows-based guest OSes, the process of upgrading VMware Tools is as simple as right-clicking a VM and selecting Guest ➤ Install/Upgrade VMware Tools. Select the option labeled Automatic Tools Upgrade, and click OK. vCenter Server will install the updated VMware Tools and automatically reboot the VM, if necessary.

For other guest OSes, upgrading VMware Tools typically means running through the install process again. You can refer to the instructions for installing VMware Tools on SLES previously in this chapter, for example, for information on upgrading VMware Tools in a Linux VM.

Creating VMs is just one aspect of managing VMs. In the next section I look at some additional VM management tasks.

Managing Virtual Machines

In addition to creating VMs, there is a range of other tasks that vSphere administrators will need to perform. While most of these tasks are relatively easy to figure out, I include them here for completeness.

Adding or Registering Existing VMs

Creating VMs from scratch, as I described in the previous section, is only one way of getting VMs into the environment. It's entirely possible that you, as a vSphere administrator, might receive pre-created VMs from another source. Suppose you receive the files that compose a VM—notably, the VMX and VMDK files—from another administrator and you need to put that VM to use in your environment. You've already seen how to use the Datastore Browser to upload files into a datastore, but what needs to happen once it's in the datastore? In this case, you need to register the VM. The process of registering the VM adds it to the vCenter Server (or ESXi host) inventory and allows you to then manage the VM.

Perform the following steps to add (or register) an existing VM into the inventory:

1. Use the vSphere Client to connect to a vCenter Server instance or an individual ESXi host.

2. Registering a VM can be done from a number of different views within the vSphere Client. The Datastores inventory view, though, is probably the most logical place to do it. Navigate to the Datastores inventory view using the menu bar, the navigation bar, or the Ctrl+Shift+D keyboard shortcut.

3. Right-click the datastore containing the VM you want to register. From the context menu, select Browse Datastore.

4. Use the Datastore Browser to navigate to the folder where the VMX file for the VM resides. Right-click the VMX file and select Add To Inventory. Figure 9.22 shows this process, which launches the Add To Inventory wizard.

FIGURE 9.22
You invoke the Add To Inventory wizard by right-clicking the VMX file for the VM you want to add to the inventory.

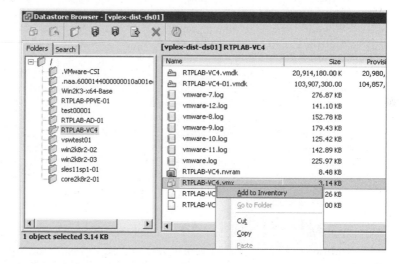

5. The Add To Inventory wizard prepopulates the VM Name field based on the contents of the VMX file. Accept the name or type a new one; then select a logical location within the inventory and click Next.

6. Choose the cluster on which you'd like to run this VM and click Next.

7. If you selected a cluster for which VMware DRS is not enabled or is set to Manual, you must also select the specific host on which the VM will run. Choose a specific host and click Next.

8. Review the settings. If everything is correct, click Finish; otherwise, use the hyperlinks on the left side of the wizard or the Back button to go back and make any necessary changes.

When the Add To Inventory wizard is finished, the VM will be added to the vSphere Client inventory. From here, you're ready to manipulate the VM in whatever fashion you need, such as powering it on.

Changing VM Power States

There are six different commands involved in changing the power state of a VM. Figure 9.23 shows these six commands on the context menu displayed when you right-click a VM and select Power.

FIGURE 9.23
The Power sub-menu allows you to power on, power off, suspend, or reset a VM, as well as interact with the guest OS if VMware Tools is installed.

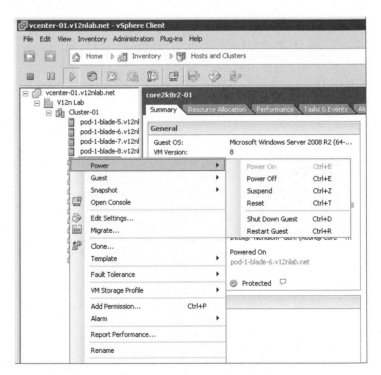

By and large, these commands are self-explanatory, but there are a few subtle differences in some of them:

Power On and Power Off These function exactly as their names suggest. They are equivalent to toggling the virtual power button on the VM without any interaction with the guest OS (if one is installed).

BE CAREFUL WITH POWER OFF

Although the behavior of the Power Off option can be configured in the Virtual Machine Properties dialog box—see the Options tab under VMware Tools—my testing showed that the default value of Power Off (Shut Down Guest) still did not behave in the same manner as the actual Shut Down Guest command. Instead, the Power Off command simply turned off power and did not invoke an orderly shutdown of the guest OS.

Suspend   This command suspends the VM. When you resume the VM, it will start back right where it was when you suspended it.

Reset   This command will reset the VM, which is not the same as rebooting the guest OS. This is the virtual equivalent of pressing the Reset button on the front of the computer.

Shut Down Guest   This command works only if VMware Tools is installed, and it works through VMware Tools to invoke an orderly shutdown of the guest OS. To avoid filesystem or data corruption in the guest OS instance, you should use this command whenever possible.

Restart Guest   Like the Shut Down Guest command, this command requires VMware Tools and initiates a reboot of the guest OS in an orderly fashion.

As you can see from Figure 9.23, keyboard shortcuts are available for all these commands.

Removing VMs

If you have a VM that you need to keep, but that you don't need listed in the VM inventory, you can remove the VM from the inventory. This keeps the VM files intact, and the VM can be re-added to inventory (i.e., registered) at any time later on using the procedure described earlier in the section titled "Adding or Registering Existing VMs."

To remove a VM, simply right-click a powered-off VM. From the context menu, select Remove From Inventory. Select Yes in the Confirm Remove dialog box, and the VM will be removed from the inventory. You can use the Datastore Browser to verify that the files for the VM are still intact in the same location on the datastore.

Deleting VMs

In the event you have a VM that you no longer need at all—meaning you don't need it listed in the inventory and you don't need the files maintained on the datastore—you can completely remove the VM. Be careful, though; this is not something that you can undo!

To delete a VM entirely, you only need to right-click a powered-off VM and select Delete From Disk from the context menu. The vSphere Client will prompt you for confirmation, reminding you that you are deleting the VM and its associated base disks (VMDK files). Click Yes to continue removing the files from both inventory and the datastore. Once the process is done, you can once again use the Datastore Browser to verify that the VM's files are gone.

Adding existing VMs, removing VMs from inventory, and deleting VMs are all relatively simple tasks. The task of modifying VMs, though, is significant enough to warrant its own section.

Modifying Virtual Machines

Just as physical machines require hardware upgrades or changes, a VM might require virtual hardware upgrades or changes to meet changing performance demands. Perhaps a new memory-intensive client-server application requires an increase in memory, or a new data-mining application requires a second processor or additional network adapters for bandwidth-heavy FTP traffic. In each of these cases, the VM requires a modification of the virtual hardware configured for the guest OS to use. Of course, this is only one task that an administrator charged with managing VMs could be responsible for completing. Other tasks might include leveraging vSphere's snapshot functionality to protect against a potential issue with the guest OS inside a VM. I describe both of these tasks in this section, starting with how to change the hardware of a VM.

Changing Virtual Machine Hardware

In most cases, modifying a VM requires that the VM be powered off. There are exceptions to this rule, as shown in Figure 9.24. You can hot-add a USB controller, an Ethernet adapter, a hard disk, or a SCSI device. Later in this section you'll see that some guest OSes also support the addition of virtual CPUs or RAM while they are powered on as well.

FIGURE 9.24

Users can add some types of hardware while the VM is powered on.

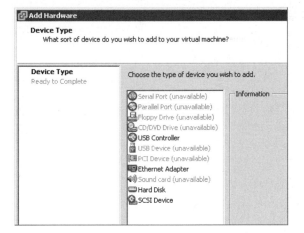

When adding new virtual hardware to a VM using the vSphere Client, the screens are similar to the screens used while creating a VM. For example, to add a new virtual hard disk to an existing VM, you would use the Add button at the top of the Virtual Machine Properties dialog box. You can see in Figure 9.24 that it is possible to add a virtual hard disk to a VM while it is powered on. From there, the vSphere Client uses the same steps shown in Figures 9.11, 9.12, and 9.13 earlier in this chapter. The only difference is that now you're adding a new virtual hard disk to an existing VM. As an example, I'll go through the steps to add an Ethernet adapter to a VM (the steps are the same regardless of whether the VM is actually running).

Perform the following steps to add an Ethernet adapter to a VM:

1. Launch the vSphere Client, and connect to a vCenter Server instance or an individual ESXi host.

2. If you aren't already in an inventory view that displays VMs, switch to the Hosts And Clusters or VMs And Templates view using the View ➢ Inventory menu.

3. Right-click the VM to which you want to add the Ethernet adapter, and select Edit Settings.

4. Click the Add button at the top of the Virtual Machine Properties dialog box.

5. Select Ethernet Adapter, and click Next.

6. Select the network adapter type, the network to which it should be connected, and whether the network adapter should be connected at power on, as shown in Figure 9.25. Click Next to continue.

FIGURE 9.25
To add a new network adapter, you must select the adapter type, the network, and whether it should be connected at power on.

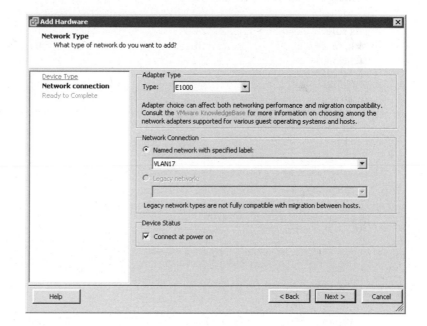

7. Review the settings, and click Finish.

Besides adding new virtual hardware, users can make other changes while a VM is powered on. For example, you can mount and unmount CD/DVD drives, ISO images, and floppy disk images while a VM is turned on. I described the process for mounting an ISO image as a virtual CD/DVD drive earlier in this chapter in the section titled "Installing a Guest Operating System." You can also assign and reassign adapters to virtual networks while a VM is running. All of these tasks are performed from the VM Properties dialog box, accessed by selecting Edit Settings from the Context menu for a VM.

DOES ANYONE STILL USE FLOPPY DRIVES?

New VMs created in a vSphere environment automatically come with a floppy drive, although in my experience it is rarely used. In fact, about the only time that it does get used is when a custom storage driver needs to be added during installation of a Windows-based guest OS. Unless you know you will need to use a floppy drive, it's generally safe to remove the floppy drive from the hardware list.

If you are running Windows Server 2008 or Windows Server 2008 R2 in the VM, then you also gain the ability to add virtual CPUs or RAM to a VM while it is running. At the time of writing, only Windows Server 2008 (and Windows Server 2008 R2) supported this hot-add functionality, but VMware disables the feature by default. In order to use this functionality, you'll have to first enable it. In a somewhat ironic twist, the VM for which you want to enable hot-add must be powered off.

To enable hot-add of virtual CPUs or RAM, perform these steps:

1. Launch the vSphere Client if it is not already running, and connect to a vCenter Server instance or an individual ESXi host.

2. Navigate to either the Hosts And Clusters or VMs And Templates inventory view.

3. If the VM for which you want to enable hot-add is currently running, right-click the VM and select Power ➢ Shut Down Guest. The VM must be shut down in order to enable hot-add functionality.

REMEMBER THE DIFFERENCE BETWEEN POWERING OFF AND SHUTTING DOWN THE GUEST

Recall from earlier in this chapter that the context menu of a VM contains two items that appear to do the same function.

The Power ➢ Power Off command does exactly that: it powers off the VM. It's like pulling out the power cord unexpectedly. The guest OS has no time to prepare for a shutdown.

The Power ➢ Shut Down Guest command issues a shutdown command to the guest OS so that the guest OS can shut down in an orderly fashion. This command requires that VMware Tools be already installed, and it ensures that the guest OS won't be corrupted or damaged by an unexpected shutdown.

In day-to-day operation, use the Shut Down Guest option. The Power Off option should be used only when it is absolutely necessary.

---

4. Right-click the VM and select Edit Settings.

5. Select the Options tab; then click Memory/CPU Hotplug.

6. To enable Memory Hot Add, select the radio button labeled Enable Memory Hot Add For This Virtual Machine.

7. To enable CPU Hot Plug, select the radio button labeled Enable CPU Hot Add Only For This Virtual Machine.

8. Click OK to save the changes to the VM.

Once this setting has been configured, you can add RAM or virtual CPUs to the VM when it is powered on. Figure 9.26 shows a powered-on VM that has memory hot-add enabled. Figure 9.27 shows a powered-on VM that has CPU hot-plug enabled; you can change the number of virtual CPU sockets, but you can't change the number of cores per virtual CPU socket.

FIGURE 9.26
The range of memory you can add is restricted when using memory hot-add.

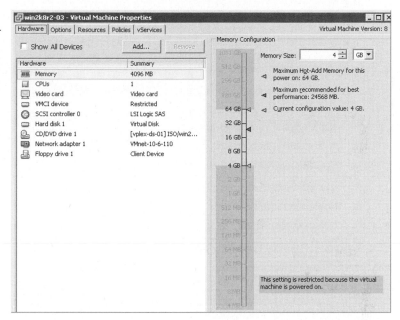

FIGURE 9.27
With CPU hot-plug enabled, more virtual CPU sockets can be configured, but the number of cores per CPU cannot be altered.

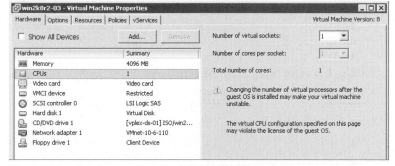

Aside from the changes described so far, configuration changes to a VM can take place only when the VM is in a powered-off state. When a VM is powered off, all the various configuration options are available to change: RAM, virtual CPUs, or adding or removing other hardware components such as CD/DVD drives or floppy drives.

ALIGNING VIRTUAL MACHINE FILESYSTEMS

In Chapter 6, I introduced the concept of aligning VMFS, and I suggested that the VM's filesystem should also be aligned. If you construct VMs with separate virtual hard drives for the operating system and data, then you are most concerned with the alignment of the filesystem for the data drive because the greatest amount of I/O occurs on that drive. For example, a VM with Disk 0 (that holds the operating system) and a blank disk called Disk 1 (that holds data that will incur significant I/O) should have Disk 1 aligned. The need to align the guest filesystem is applicable to almost all distributions of Linux and all but the most recent versions of Windows. For example, Windows 7 and Windows Server 2008 align themselves properly during installation, but earlier versions do not.

Perform the following steps to align Disk 1 of a VM running a version of Windows earlier than Windows Server 2008:

1. Log into the VM using an account with administrative credentials.

2. Open a command prompt, and type **Diskpart**.

3. Type **list disk**, and press Enter.

4. Type **select disk 1**, and press Enter.

5. Type **create partition primary align = 64**, and press Enter.

6. Type **assign letter = X**, where *X* is an open letter that can be assigned.

7. Type **list part** to verify the 64 KB offset for the new partition.

8. Format the partition.

Perhaps you are thinking that this seems like a tedious task to perform for all your VMs. It *is* a tedious task; however, the benefit of doing this is realized most when there is a significant I/O requirement.

As you can see, running your operating system in a VM offers advantages when it comes time to reconfigure hardware, even enabling such innovative features as CPU hot-plug. There are other advantages to using VMs, too; one of these advantages is a vSphere feature called snapshots.

Using Virtual Machine Snapshots

VM snapshots provide administrators with the ability to create point-in-time checkpoints of a VM. The snapshot captures the state of the VM at that specific point in time. VMware administrators can then revert to their pre-snapshot state in the event the changes made since the snapshot should be discarded. Or, if the changes should be preserved, the administrator can commit the changes and delete the snapshot.

This functionality can be used in a variety of ways. Suppose you'd like to install the latest vendor-supplied patch for the guest OS instance running in a VM, but you want to be able to recover in case the patch installation runs amok. By taking a snapshot before installing the patch, you can revert to the snapshot in the event the patch installation doesn't go well. You've just created a safety net for yourself.

OTHER FEATURES LEVERAGE SNAPSHOTS, TOO

Snapshots are leveraged by vSphere Update Manager and are also used by various VM backup frameworks.

Before starting to use snapshots, be aware that vSphere FT—discussed in Chapter 7, "Ensuring High Availability and Business Continuity"—does not support snapshots, so you can't take a snapshot of a VM that is protected with vSphere FT. Earlier versions of vSphere did not allow Storage vMotions to occur when a snapshot was present, but this limitation is removed in vSphere 5.

Perform the following steps to create a snapshot of a VM:

1. Use the vSphere Client to connect to a vCenter Server instance or an individual ESXi host.

2. Navigate to either the Hosts And Clusters or VMs And Templates inventory view. You can use the navigation bar, the View menu, or a keyboard shortcut (Ctrl+Shift+H to go to the Hosts And Clusters inventory view, for example).

3. Right-click the VM in the inventory tree, select Snapshot, and then select Take Snapshot.

4. Provide a name and description for the snapshot, and then click OK, as shown in Figure 9.28.

FIGURE 9.28
Providing names and descriptions for snapshots is an easy way to manage multiple historical snapshots.

As shown in Figure 9.28, there are two options when taking snapshots:

◆ The option labeled Snapshot The Virtual Machine's Memory specifies whether the RAM of the VM should also be included in the snapshot. When this option is selected, the current contents of the VM's RAM are written to a file ending in a .vmsn extension.

◆ The option labeled Quiesce Guest File System (Needs VMware Tools Installed) controls whether the guest filesystem will be quiesced—or quieted—so that the guest filesystem is considered consistent. This can help ensure that the data within the guest filesystem is intact in the snapshot.

When a snapshot is taken, depending on the previous options, some additional files are created on the datastore, as shown in Figure 9.29.

FIGURE 9.29
When a snapshot is taken, some additional files are created on the VM's datastore.

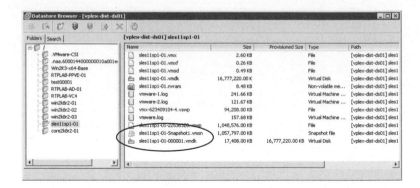

It is a common misconception for administrators to think of snapshots as full copies of VM files. As can be clearly seen in Figure 9.29, a snapshot is not a full copy of a VM. VMware's snapshot technology allows for minimal space consumption while still reverting to a previous snapshot by only allocating enough space to store the changes, rather than making a full copy.

To demonstrate snapshot technology and illustrate its behavior, I performed the following steps:

1. I created a VM with a default installation of Windows Server 2008 R2 with a single hard drive (recognized by the guest OS as drive C:). The virtual hard drive was thin provisioned on a VMFS volume with a maximum size of 40 GB.

2. I took a snapshot named FirstSnap.

3. I added approximately 2.7 GB of data to drive C:, represented as win2k8r2-02.vmdk.

4. I took a second snapshot named SecondSnap.

5. I once again added approximately 2.7 GB of data to drive C:, represented as win2k8r2-02.vmdk.

Review Table 9.4 for the results I recorded after each step.

TABLE 9.4: Snapshot demonstration results

	VMDK SIZE	NTFS SIZE	NTFS FREE SPACE
Start (pre-first snapshot)			
win2k8r2-02.vmdk (C:)	9.5 GB	40 GB	27.2 GB
First snapshot (pre-data copy)			
win2k8r2-02.vmdk (C:)	9.5 GB	40 GB	27.2 GB
win2k8r2-02-000001.vmdk	16.1MB		
First snapshot (post-data copy)			
win2k8r2-02.vmdk (C:)	9.5 GB	40 GB	24.5 GB

TABLE 9.4:   Snapshot demonstration results   *(CONTINUED)*

	VMDK SIZE	NTFS SIZE	NTFS FREE SPACE
`win2k8r2-02-000001.vmdk`	2.8 GB		
Second snapshot (pre-data copy)			
`win2k8r2-02.vmdk (C:)`	9.5 GB	40 GB	24.5 GB
`win2k8r2-02-000001.vmdk`	2.8 GB		
`win2k8r2-02-000002.vmdk`	16.1 MB		
Second snapshot (post-data copy)			
`win2k8r2-02.vmdk (C:)`	9.5 GB	40 GB	21.7 GB
`win2k8r2-02-000001.vmdk`	2.8 GB		
`win2k8r2-02-000002.vmdk`	2.8 GB		

As you can see from Table 9.4, the VM is unaware of the presence of the snapshot and the extra VMDK files that are created. ESXi, however, knows to write changes to the VM's virtual disk to the snapshot VMDK, properly known as a *delta disk* (or a *differencing disk*). These delta disks start small and over time grow to accommodate the changes stored within them.

Despite the storage efficiency that snapshots attempt to maintain, over time they can eat up a considerable amount of disk space. Therefore, use them as needed, but be sure to remove older snapshots on a regular basis. Also be aware there are performance ramifications to using snapshots. Because disk space must be allocated to the delta disks on demand, ESXi hosts must update the metadata files (.sf files) every time the differencing disk grows. To update the metadata files, LUNs must be locked, and this might adversely affect the performance of other VMs and hosts using the same LUN.

To view or delete a snapshot or revert to an earlier snapshot, you use the Snapshot Manager. Perform the following steps to access the Snapshot Manager:

1. Use the vSphere Client to connect to a vCenter Server instance or an individual ESXi host.

2. In the inventory tree, right-click the name of the VM, and from the context menu select Snapshot ➢ Snapshot Manager. Alternately, you can also click the Snapshot Manager button on the vSphere Client toolbar.

3. Select the appropriate snapshot to fall back to, and then click the Go To button, as shown in Figure 9.30.

To further illustrate the nature of snapshots, see Figure 9.31 and Figure 9.32. Figure 9.31 shows the filesystem of a VM running Windows Server 2008 R2 after data has been written into two new folders named `temp1` and `temp2`. Figure 9.32 shows the same VM but after reverting to a snapshot taken before that data was written. As you can see, it's as if the new folders never even existed. (And yes, I can assure you I didn't just delete the folders for these screenshots. Test it yourself!)

FIGURE 9.30
The Snapshot Manager can revert to previous snapshots, but all data written since that snapshot that hasn't been backed up elsewhere will be lost.

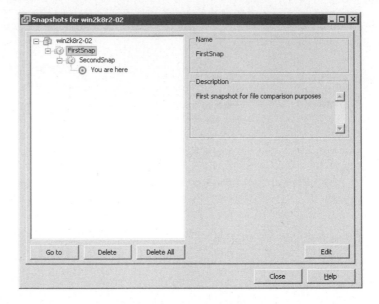

FIGURE 9.31
This VM running Windows Server 2008 R2 has had some data placed into two temporary folders.

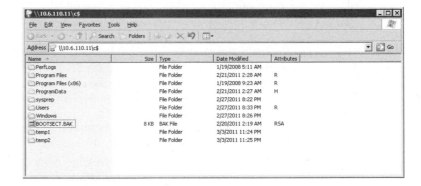

FIGURE 9.32
The same VM, after reverting to a snapshot taken before the temporary folders were created, no longer has any record of the data.

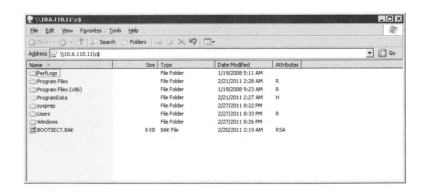

REVERTING TO A SNAPSHOT

Reverting to a snapshot incurs a loss of data. Any data that was written since the snapshot has occurred will no longer be available, along with any applications that were installed since the snapshot was taken. Therefore, revert to snapshots only if you have determined that the loss of data is acceptable or if the data is backed up elsewhere.

As you can see, snapshots are a great way to protect yourself against unwanted changes to the *data* stored in a VM. Snapshots aren't backups and should not be used in place of backups. However, they can protect you against misbehaving application installations or other processes that might result in data loss or corruption.

Snapshots cannot, though, protect the *configuration* of the VM. You've seen already how snapshots work by creating delta disks and redirecting data written in the guest OS instance into these delta disks. Snapshots don't protect the VMX file, which is where the configuration of the VM is defined and stored, so you can't use a snapshot to protect yourself against VM configuration changes. Be sure to keep that in mind.

There are additional VM management tasks that I'll discuss in other chapters. For example, you might want to migrate a VM from one ESXi host to another ESXi host using vMotion; this is covered in Chapter 12. Changing a VM's resource allocation settings is covered in Chapter 11.

In the next chapter, I'll move from creating and managing VMs to streamlining the VM provisioning process with templates, OVF templates, and vApps. While VMware makes the VM provisioning process pretty easy, I'll show you how using templates can simplify server provisioning even more while bringing some consistency to your VM and guest OS deployments.

The Bottom Line

Create a virtual machine. A VM is a collection of virtual hardware pieces, like a physical system—one or more virtual CPUs, RAM, video card, SCSI devices, IDE devices, floppy drives, parallel and serial ports, and network adapters. This virtual hardware is virtualized and abstracted from the underlying physical hardware, providing portability to the VM.

Master It Create two VMs, one intended to run Windows Server 2008 R2 and a second intended to run SLES 11 (64-bit). Make a list of the differences in the configuration that are suggested by the Create New Virtual Machine wizard.

Install a guest operating system. Just as a physical machine needs an operating system, a VM also needs an operating system. vSphere supports a broad range of 32-bit and 64-bit operating systems, including all major versions of Windows Server, Windows Vista, Windows XP, and Windows 2000, as well as various flavors of Linux, FreeBSD, Novell NetWare, and Solaris.

Master It What are the three ways in which a guest OS can access data on a CD/DVD, and what are the advantages of each approach?

Install VMware Tools For maximum performance of the guest OS, it needs to have virtualization-optimized drivers that are specially written for and designed to work with the ESXi hypervisor. VMware Tools provides these optimized drivers as well as other utilities focused on better operation in virtual environments.

Master It A fellow administrator contacts you and is having a problem installing VMware Tools. This administrator has selected the Install/Upgrade VMware Tools command, but nothing seems to be happening inside the VM. What could be the cause of the problem?

Manage virtual machines. Once a VM has been created, the vSphere Client makes it easy to manage the VM. Virtual floppy images and CD/DVD drives can be mounted or unmounted as necessary. vSphere provides support for initiating an orderly shutdown of the guest OS in a VM, although this requires that VMware Tools be installed. VM snapshots allow you to take a point-in-time "picture" of a VM so that administrators can roll back changes if needed.

Master It What are the three different ways an administrator can bring the contents of a CD/DVD into a VM?

Master It What is the difference between the Shut Down Guest command and the Power Off command?

Modify virtual machines. vSphere offers a number of features to make it easy to modify VMs after they have been created. Administrators can hot-add certain types of hardware, like virtual hard disks and network adapters, and some guest OSes also support hot-adding virtual CPUs or memory, although this feature must be enabled first.

Master It Which method is preferred for modifying the configuration of a VM—editing the VMX file or using the vSphere Client?

Master It Name the types of hardware that cannot be added while a VM is running.

## Chapter 10

Using Templates and vApps

Creating VMs manually and installing guest operating systems (guest OSes) into those VMs is fine on a small scale, but what if you need to deploy lots of VMs? What if you need to ensure that your VMs are consistent and standardized? Through vCenter Server, VMware vSphere offers a solution: VM cloning and templates. In this chapter, I'll show you how to use cloning, templates, and vApps to help streamline the deployment of VMs in your environment.

In this chapter, you will learn to

◆ Clone a VM

◆ Create a VM template

◆ Deploy new VMs from a template

◆ Deploy a VM from an Open Virtualization Format (OVF) template

◆ Export a VM as an OVF template

◆ Work with vApps

Cloning VMs

If you've ever wished there were a faster way to provision a new server into your environment, then VMware vSphere fulfills that wish in a big way. When you are using vCenter Server in your environment, you have the ability to clone a VM; that is, you can make a copy of the VM, including the VM's virtual disks. How does this help provision new VMs faster? Think about it: what takes the most time when creating a new VM? It's not the creation of the VM itself, because that takes only minutes. It's the installation of the guest OS — whether it be Windows Server, Linux, or some other supported guest OS — that takes up the bulk of the time needed to create a new VM. Using vCenter Server to clone a VM — which means also cloning the VM's virtual disks — keeps you from having to install the guest OS into the cloned VM. By cloning VMs, you eliminate the need to perform a guest OS installation into every new VM.

THE FIRST GUEST OS INSTALLATION IS STILL NEEDED

I mentioned in the text that cloning a VM eliminates the need to perform a guest OS installation into every new VM. That's true—assuming you actually installed the guest OS into the VM that you're cloning. As you consider using VM cloning to help provision new VMs, recognize that you still need to install the guest OS into your source VM. Some things just can't be eliminated!

However, there's a potential problem here: if you are making a clone of a guest OS installation, that means you'll now have two VMs with the same IP address, same computer name, same MAC address, and so forth. Not to worry, though: VMware built the ability to customize the guest OS installation in the cloned VM, so that you preserve the guest OS installation but create a new identity in the cloned VM. For Linux-based guest OSes, VMware leverages open source tools to customize the installation; for Windows-based guest OSes, vCenter Server will leverage Microsoft's well-known Sysprep tool. However, you must first install Sysprep on the vCenter Server computer.

Installing Sysprep on the vCenter Server

To customize Windows-based guest OS installations, vCenter Server leverages Microsoft's Sysprep tool. If you aren't familiar with Sysprep, the purpose of the tool is to allow for a single Windows installation to be cloned many times over, each time with a unique identity. This ensures that you have to install Windows only once, but you can reuse that Windows installation over and over again, each time using Sysprep to create a new computer name, new IP address, and new Security Identifier (SID).

In order for vCenter Server to use Sysprep, an administrator must first extract Sysprep and its associated files to a directory created during the installation of vCenter Server. If these files are not extracted before you deploy a VM, the ability to customize the guest OS will be unavailable for all versions of Windows prior to Windows Server 2008. (Windows Server 2008 does not require Sysprep to be installed on the vCenter Server computer). Figure 10.1 shows the Guest Customization page of the Deploy Template Wizard on a vCenter Server that has not had the Sysprep files extracted.

FIGURE 10.1
If the Sysprep files are not extracted and stored on the vCenter Server system, you might not be able to customize the guest OS when you clone a VM.

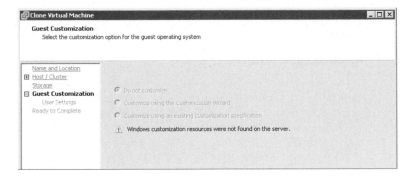

Perform these steps to allow guest OS customization of Windows Server 2003 x86 (32-bit) guest OS templates:

1. Insert the Windows Server 2003 x86 CD into the disk drive of the vCenter Server.

2. Navigate to the /support/tools/deploy.cab directory on the Windows Server 2003 CD.

3. If the vCenter Server computer is running Windows Server 2003, copy the `sysprep.exe` and `setupcl.exe` files to this directory:

`C:\Documents and Settings\All Users\Application Data\VMware\VMware VirtualCenter\sysprep\svr2003`

If the vCenter Server computer is running Windows Server 2008 or later, then the correct path to use is

`C:\ProgramData\VMware\VMware VirtualCenter\Sysprep\svr2003`

Repeat these steps for other platforms (use the `svr2003-64` folder for customizing 64-bit installations of Windows Server 2003 or the `xp` and `xp-64` folders for customizing installations of Windows XP and Windows XP 64-bit, respectively). As I mentioned previously, customizing installations of Windows Server 2008 does not require a version of Sysprep to be installed on the vCenter Server computer.

Once you've installed the Sysprep tools for the appropriate versions of Windows (where applicable), you're ready to start cloning and customizing VMs. Before you clone your first VM, though, I recommend that you take the time to create a customization specification, as I describe in the next section.

Creating a Customization Specification

vCenter Server's customization specification works hand-in-hand with the tools for customizing VM clones (Sysprep for VMs with a Windows-based guest OS, open source tools for a VM with a Linux-based guest OS). As you'll see later in this chapter in the section "Cloning a Virtual Machine," the administrator has to provide vCenter Server with the information necessary to give the cloned VM its own unique identity. This includes information such as the IP address, passwords, computer name, and licensing information. A customization specification allows an administrator to provide all the information only once and then apply it as needed when cloning a VM.

You can create a customization specification in the following two ways:

◆ During the process of cloning a VM

◆ By using the Customization Specification Manager in vCenter Server

I'll show you how to create a customization specification while cloning a VM in the section "Cloning a Virtual Machine." For now, I'll show you how to use the Customization Specifications Manager.

To access the Customization Specifications Manager, select View ➢ Management ➢ Customization Specifications Manager, or select the Customization Specifications Manager from the vSphere Client home page, as you can see in Figure 10.2.

After you're in the Customization Specifications Manager area of vCenter Server (note that the Navigation bar in the vSphere Client tells you the vCenter Server instance to which you are connected), you can create a new customization specification or edit an existing customization specification. The process is almost identical whether you are creating a new customization specification or editing an existing customization specification, and in both cases it involves the vSphere Client Guest Customization Wizard.

FIGURE 10.2
The Customization Specifications Manager is readily accessible from the home page of the vSphere Client in the Management tab.

Perform the following steps to create a new customization specification:

1. If the vSphere Client isn't already running, launch it and connect to a vCenter Server instance. (This functionality is available only when connecting to vCenter Server, not a stand-alone ESXi host.)

2. Navigate to the Customization Specifications Manager by selecting View ➢ Management ➢ Customization Specifications Manager, by using the navigation bar, or by using the Ctrl+Shift+U keyboard shortcut.

3. Click New to create a new customization specification. This opens the vSphere Client Windows Guest Customization wizard.

4. From the Target Virtual Machine OS drop-down box, select either Windows or Linux. Windows is the default.

5. Provide a name for the customization specification and, optionally, a description. Click Next to continue.

6. Supply a value for both Name and Organization (you won't be able to proceed until you supply both). Click Next to proceed.

7. Select an option for the computer name within the Windows guest OS installation.

There are four options from which to select:

◆ You can manually supply a name, but this option is useless without also selecting Append A Numeric Value To Ensure Uniqueness.

◆ Select Use The Virtual Machine Name to set the computer name within the guest OS installation to the same value as the name of the VM.

◆ Choose Enter A Name In The Deploy Wizard if you want to be prompted for a name when you use this customization specification.

◆ The fourth option uses a custom application configured with vCenter Server. Because there is no custom application configured with this instance of vCenter Server, it is currently disabled (grayed out).

I generally recommend selecting Use The Virtual Machine Name. This keeps the guest OS computer name matched up with the VM name, as I recommended when creating new VMs in Chapter 9. Figure 10.3 shows the four options.

FIGURE 10.3
The Guest Customization Wizard offers several different options for naming a cloned VM.

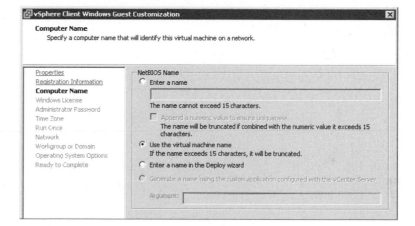

After you select the option you want to use in this customization specification, click Next.

8. Provide a Windows product key and select the appropriate server licensing mode (Per Seat or Per Server). Click Next.

9. Enter the password for the Windows Administrator account and then confirm the password.

If you'd like to log on automatically as the Administrator (perhaps to help with any auto-mated configuration scripts), select Automatically Log On As The Administrator and specify how many times to log on automatically. Click Next to continue.

10. Select the correct time zone and click Next.

11. If you have any commands you want to run the first time a user logs on, supply those commands at the Run Once screen of the vSphere Client Windows Guest Customization wizard. Click Next if you have no commands to run or when you are finished entering commands to run.

12. Choose the settings you'd like to apply to the network configuration:

   ◆ If you want to use DHCP to assign an IP address to the VM's network interfaces, select Typical Settings.

   ◆ If you want to assign a static IP address to any of the network interfaces, you'll need to select Custom Settings, and the wizard will prompt you to input that information.

   Many administrators don't want to use DHCP but still want to ensure that each VM has a unique IP address. To see how this can be done in the customization specification, select Custom Settings and click Next.

13. At the Network Interface Customizations screen, click the small button to the far right of the NIC1 line. Figure 10.4 has this button circled for your reference. This will open the Network Properties dialog box shown in Figure 10.5.

FIGURE 10.4
This small button allows you to customize the network interface settings.

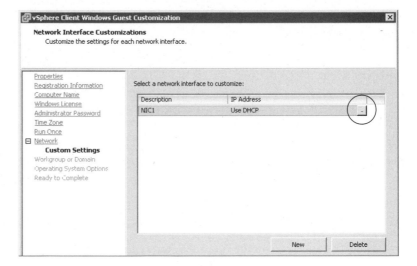

The key to assigning a static IP address to cloned VMs without having to modify the customization specification every time lies in the selection titled Prompt The User For An Address When The Specification Is Used. By selecting this, vCenter Server will prompt the user to supply a unique static IP address every time the specification is used when cloning a VM.

Select Prompt The User For An Address When The Specification Is Used. You must then supply a subnet mask, default gateway, and preferred and alternate DNS servers. Fill in these values, click OK, and then click Next.

FIGURE 10.5
The Network
Properties dialog
box has an option to
prompt the user for
an address.

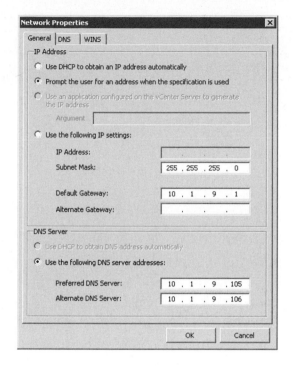

14. Select whether you want the Windows-based guest OS to join a workgroup or a domain.

    If the guest OS should join a workgroup, supply the workgroup name. If the guest should join a domain, supply the domain name and credentials to join the domain. Click Next.

15. Generally speaking, you will want to leave Generate New Security ID (SID) selected. Click Next.

16. Review the settings in the final screen of the vSphere Client Windows Guest Customization wizard to ensure you have the right values supplied.

    If you need to change anything, use the hyperlinks on the left or the Back button to go back and change the values. Otherwise, click Finish to complete the creation of the cus-tomization specification.

Because a customization specification for Windows usually contains product keys, you'll probably need to create multiple specifications for different versions or editions of Windows. Repeat the previous steps to create additional specifications.

Now that you have a customization specification in place and the Sysprep tools installed on the vCenter Server computer (if you are cloning a Windows version earlier than Windows Server 2008), all you need is a source VM with a guest OS installed and you're ready to clone and customize a VM.

CUSTOMIZATION SPECIFICATIONS AREN'T REQUIRED

You aren't required to create customization specifications. However, you will be required to supply the information found in a customization specification when you clone a VM. Because you have to enter the information anyway, why not do it only once by creating a customization specification?

Cloning a Virtual Machine

If you've performed all the steps in the previous two sections, then cloning a VM is actually simple.

Perform the following steps to clone a VM:

1. If the vSphere Client isn't already running, launch it and connect to an instance of vCenter Server. Cloning isn't possible when connecting directly to an ESXi host.

2. Navigate to either the Hosts And Clusters or VMs And Templates inventory view.

3. Right-click a VM and select Clone. This opens the Clone Virtual Machine wizard.

4. Supply a name for the VM and select a logical inventory location for the VM. Click Next.

5. Select the host or cluster on which the VM will run. Click Next.

6. If you selected a cluster for which DRS is not enabled or is configured in Manual mode, you must select the specific host on which to run the VM. Click Next.

7. If prompted, select the resource pool in which the VM should be placed. Click Next.

8. Select the desired virtual disk format and select a target datastore or datastore cluster. Use the Advanced button if you want or need to place the VM's configuration files in a different location than the virtual hard disks. Click Next to continue.

9. At this point the Clone Virtual Machine wizard is prompting you for guest customization options, as shown in Figure 10.6.

FIGURE 10.6
The Clone Virtual Machine Wizard offers several options for customizing the guest OS.

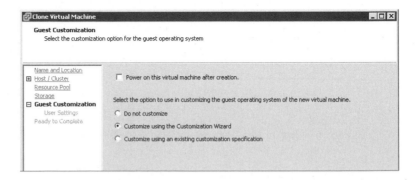

If you want to use a customization specification that you already created, you would select Customize Using An Existing Customization Specification. In this case, I want to show you how to create a specification while cloning the VM, so select Customize Using The Customization Wizard and click Next.

10. The vSphere Client Windows Guest Customization wizard opens.

This is the same wizard you used to create the customization specification in the section "Creating a Customization Specification." Refer back to that section for the specific details to use as you walk through the sections of this wizard.

11. At the end of the vSphere Client Windows Guest Customization wizard, you are prompted to save the specification for later use, as shown in Figure 10.7.

By selecting Save This Customization Specification For Later Use, you create a customization specification that you can use again later during the process of cloning a VM. You've now seen both ways to create a customization specification within the vSphere Client.

FIGURE 10.7
You can save guest OS customizations as a specification in the middle of the VM cloning wizard.

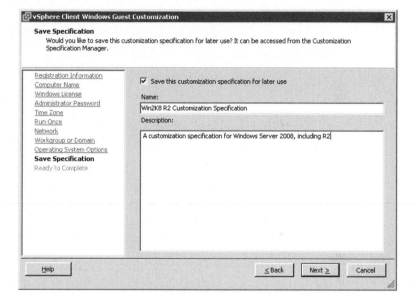

12. Click Finish to complete the guest customization process and return to the Clone Virtual Machine wizard.

13. Review the settings for cloning the VM. If any of the settings are incorrect, use the Back button or the hyperlinks on the left to go back to the appropriate section and make any desired changes. Otherwise, click Finish to start the VM cloning process.

When the VM cloning process kicks off, the vSphere Client will show a new active task in the Recent Tasks area, as shown in Figure 10.8. From here, you can monitor the progress of the cloning operation.

FIGURE 10.8
The cloning task in the vSphere Client provides feedback on the current status of the VM cloning operation.

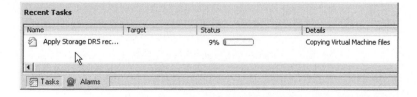

Once the cloning is complete, you can power on the VM. Note that guest OS customization won't begin until you power on the VM. After you power on the VM and the guest OS loads, the vSphere Client will kick in and start the guest customization process. Depending on the guest OS, it may take at least one reboot before the customization process is complete.

CLONING RUNNING VMs

It's possible to clone even powered-on VMs! The context menu of a VM provides a Clone option that allows you to make a copy of the VM. The Clone To New Virtual Machine option from the Commands list on a VM summary page accomplishes the same task. These commands are available for VMs that are powered off as well as VMs that are powered on. Keep in mind that unless you customize the guest OS, an exact copy of the original VM will be made. This could be especially useful when you're looking to create a test environment that mirrors a live production environment.

In fact, one very useful application of the ability to clone a live VM would be cloning your vCenter Server VM, assuming you have it running as a VM. This would make a live copy of a fairly critical part of your virtual data center.

As you can see, cloning VMs — which may take only a few minutes, depending upon the size of the VM and your infrastructure — is a much faster way of deploying new VMs than manually creating the VM and installing the guest OS.

Through the use of VM cloning, administrators can create a library of "gold VM images," master copies of VMs that have certain settings and a particular guest OS installed. The only problem with this approach is that these VMs, which are intended to serve as master copies and not be changed, can still be powered on and modified. This potential shortcoming is addressed through the use of VM templates within vCenter Server. I'll show you how templates work in the next section.

Creating Templates and Deploying Virtual Machines

In a vSphere environment, what would traditionally take several hours to do is now reduced to a matter of minutes. In this chapter, you've already seen how through the use of VM cloning and customization specifications you can quickly and easily spin up new VMs, complete with the guest OS already installed. The templates feature of vCenter Server builds on this functionality to help you roll out new VMs quickly and easily with limited administrative effort, while protecting the master VMs from inadvertent changes.

YOU'LL NEED VCENTER SERVER FOR THIS FEATURE

Because templates leverage cloning to deploy new VMs, it's possible to use templates only when you are using vCenter Server to manage your ESXi hosts.

---

vCenter Server offers two different options for creating templates: Clone To Template and Convert To Template. In both cases, you'll start with a VM that already has an instance of a guest OS installed. As the name suggests, the Clone To Template feature copies this initial VM to a template format, leaving the original VM intact. Similarly, the Convert To Template feature takes the initial VM and changes it to template format, thereby removing the ability to turn on the VM without converting back to VM format. Using either approach, once the VM is in template format, that template cannot be powered on or have its settings edited. It's now in a protected format that prevents administrators from inadvertently or unintentionally modifying the "gold image" from which other VMs are deployed.

When considering which VMs you should turn into templates, remember that the idea behind a template is to have a pristine system configuration that can be customized as needed for deployment to the target environment. Any information stored on a VM that becomes a template will become part of the new system that is deployed from that template. If you have VMs that are critical servers for production environments that have applications installed, those are not good candidates to become templates. The best VMs to use for templates are VMs that have a new, clean installation of the guest OS and any other base components.

In fact, I recommend creating a new VM specifically for use as a template or creating the template from a VM as soon after creation as possible. This ensures that the template is as pristine as possible and that all VMs cloned from that template will start out the same way.

You can convert a VM to a template using the context menu of the VM or the Convert To Template link in the Commands list. Figure 10.9 shows two ways an existing VM can be converted into a template format. Because templates cannot be modified, to make updates to a template you must first convert the template back to a VM, then update it, and finally convert it back to a template. Note that the Convert To Template command in Figure 10.9 is grayed out because the VM is currently powered on. To use the Convert To Template command, the VM must be powered off.

FIGURE 10.9
Users can either convert a VM to a template or clone the VM to a template.

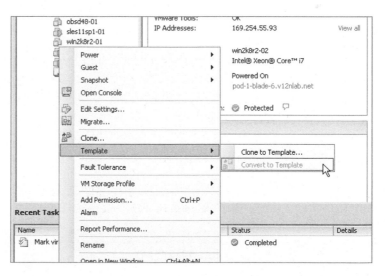

Cloning a Virtual Machine to a Template

The Clone To Template feature provides the same result as the conversion method in creating a template that can be deployed as a new VM, but it differs from the conversion method in that the original VM remains intact. By leaving the original VM in a format that can be turned on, the Clone To Template feature facilitates making updates to the template. This means you don't have to store the template object definition in the same datastore from which the VM was built.

Perform these steps to clone a VM into a template format:

1. Use the vSphere Client to connect to a vCenter Server instance. Cloning and templates are not supported when using the vSphere Client to connect directly to an ESXi host.

2. Navigate to the Hosts And Clusters or VMs And Templates inventory view.

   Either view allows you to clone to a template, but you'll only be able to see the template in the VMs And Templates inventory view.

3. Right-click the VM to be used as a template, and select Template ➢ Clone To Template.

4. Type a name for the new template in the Template Name text box, select a logical location in the inventory to store the template, and then click Next.

5. Select the host or cluster where the template should be hosted, and click Next.

6. If you selected a cluster for which DRS is disabled or is configured for Manual operation, you must select a specific host in the cluster. Click Next.

7. At the top of the next screen, shown in Figure 10.10, select the disk format for the template.

   Four options are available for the template's disk format:

   ◆ The Same Format As Source option keeps the template's virtual disks in the same format as the VM that is being cloned.

   ◆ Thick Provision Lazy Zeroed means that the space is fully allocated when the virtual disk is created, but the space is not zeroed out upon creation.

   ◆ Thick Provision Eager Zeroed also allocates all space on creation and also zeroes all the space out before it can be used. This format is required for use with vSphere FT.

   ◆ Thin Provision format commits space on demand, meaning that it will occupy only as much space as is currently used by the guest OS.

8. If you have defined any VM storage profiles, choose the appropriate storage profile from the VM Storage Profile drop-down list. If no VM storage profiles haven't been enabled or none are defined, this drop-down list is disabled (grayed out). Click Next to continue.

9. Review the template configuration information, and click Finish.

YOU DON'T CUSTOMIZE TEMPLATES

You'll note that you didn't have an option to customize the template. The guest OS customization occurs when you deploy VMs from a template, not when you create the template itself. Remember that templates can't be powered on, and guest OS customization requires that the VM be powered on.

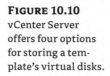

FIGURE 10.10
vCenter Server offers four options for storing a template's virtual disks.

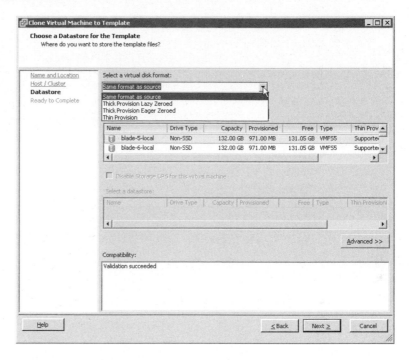

Templates have a different icon than the one used to identify a VM in the vCenter Server inventory. The template objects are available by clicking a datacenter object and then selecting the Virtual Machines tab or by adjusting the inventory view to the VMs And Templates view.

Deploying a Virtual Machine from a Template

After you have created a library of templates, provisioning a new VM is as simple as right-clicking the template you'd like to use as the base system image.

Perform these steps to deploy a VM from a template:

1. Use the vSphere Client to connect to a vCenter Server instance. Cloning and templates are not supported when using the vSphere Client to connect directly to an ESXi host.

2. Locate the template object to be used as the VM baseline. You will find the template object in the VMs And Templates inventory view.

3. Right-click the template object and select Deploy Virtual Machine From This Template. This launches the Deploy Template wizard.

4. Type a name for the new VM in the VM's Name text box, select a logical location in the inventory to store the VM, and then click Next.

5. Select the cluster or host on which the VM should run, and then click Next.

6. If you selected a cluster for which DRS is not enabled or is configured to operate in Manual mode, you must select the specific host on which to run the VM. Click Next.

7. If prompted, select the resource pool in which the VM should be located and click Next.

8. Select the desired virtual disk format for the VM to be created from the template.

9. If you have defined any VM storage profiles, choose the appropriate storage profile from the VM Storage Profile drop-down list, then select the destination datastore or datastore cluster. Use the Advanced button (shown in Figure 10.11 but not selected) if you need to place VM configuration files and virtual disks in separate locations.

FIGURE 10.11
Select a datastore for a new VM based on the vMotion, DRS, HA, and other constraints of your organization.

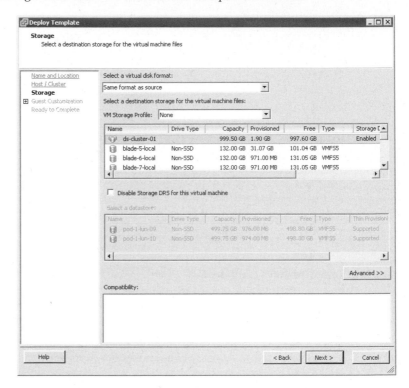

10. Select how you want to customize the guest OS.

You can use an existing customization specification by selecting Customize Using An Existing Customization Specification, or you can select Customize Using The Customization Wizard to supply the customization information interactively. I've shown you both options already. In this case, let's use the specification you created earlier, so select Customize Using An Existing Customization Specification and select the specification you created earlier. Click Next.

DON'T SELECT DO NOT CUSTOMIZE

I do not recommend selecting Do Not Customize. This will result in a VM that has the same guest OS settings as the original template. While this might not cause any problems the first time you deploy from this template, it will almost assuredly cause problems for future deployments.

The only instance in which selecting Do Not Customize is applicable is if you have already taken steps within the guest OS installation (such as running Sysprep in a VM with a Windows-based guest OS) before converting it to a template.

---

11. Because the customization specification you created earlier was created with the option to prompt the user for the static IP address to be assigned to the guest OS, the Deploy Template Wizard now prompts you for the IP address. Enter the IP address you want to assign to this VM and click Next. If the customization had been configured to use DHCP, the wizard would skip this step.

12. Review the template deployment information.

If there are changes you need to make, use the hyperlinks or the Back button to go back and make changes. Otherwise, click Finish to start the VM deployment from the template.

vCenter Server will proceed to copy all the files that compose the template into a new location on the selected datastore. The first time the new VM is powered on, vCenter Server will kick in and perform the customization according to the values stored in the customization specification or the values you entered in the Guest Customization wizard. Aside from those changes, the new VM will be an exact copy of the original template. By incorporating the latest patches and updates in your templates, you can thus be sure that your cloned VMs are up to date and consistent.

Templates are a great way to help standardize the configuration of your VMs while also speeding up the deployment of new VMs. Unfortunately, vCenter Server doesn't make it possible for you to transport a template between vCenter Server instances or between different installations of VMware vSphere. To help address that limitation, VMware helped develop a new industry standard: the Open Virtualization Format (OVF) standard.

Using OVF Templates

Open Virtualization Format (formerly called Open Virtual Machine Format) is a standard format for describing the configuration of a VM. While originally pioneered by VMware, other virtualization vendors now support OVF as well. VMware vSphere 5 provides OVF support in two different ways:

♦ Deploying new VMs from an OVF template (essentially, importing a VM in OVF format)

♦ Exporting a VM as an OVF template

Let's look first at deploying VMs from an OVF template.

Deploying a VM from an OVF Template

The first way to work with OVF templates is to deploy a VM from an OVF template by simply selecting File ➢ Deploy OVF Template. This initiates a wizard that walks you through deploying a new VM from the OVF template. Figure 10.12 shows that vCenter Server can deploy OVF templates stored locally as well as OVF templates that are stored remotely and are accessible with a URL.

Aside from selecting the source location of the OVF template, the process of deploying a VM from an OVF template is the same regardless of whether you are importing from a local set of files or downloading it across the Internet.

Perform the following steps to deploy a VM from an OVF template:

1. If it is not already running, launch the vSphere Client and connect to a vCenter Server instance or an ESXi host.

2. From within the vSphere Client, go to the File menu, and select Deploy OVF Template.

3. Select the source location of the OVF template — which must be provided in OVF or OVA format — and click Next.

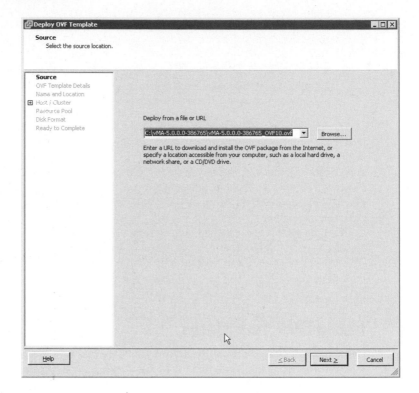

FIGURE 10.12
vCenter Server uses a wizard to deploy templates from OVF.

OVF OR OVA?

Later in this chapter in the section "Examining OVF Templates," I'll provide more information on the difference between OVF and OVA.

---

4. The OVF Template Details screen summarizes the information about the template. Click Next to continue.

5. Click the Accept button to accept the end user license agreement, and click Next.

6. Supply a name for the new VM you're deploying from the OVF template, and select a location within the vCenter Server inventory.

This is a logical location, not a physical location; you'll select the physical location (where the new VM will run and where the virtual hard disk files will be stored) in the next step.

7. Select a cluster, an ESXi host, or a resource pool where the new VM will run, and then click Next.

8. If you selected a cluster for which vSphere DRS is not enabled or is set to Manual, you must select a specific host on which to run the VM. Select an ESXi host and click Next.

9. Choose the datastore or datastore cluster where you want to store the new VM.

If you are unsure of how much space the new VM requires, the OVF Template Details screen, described in step 4, shows how much space the VM requires. Click Next after you've selected the datastore you want to use.

10. Select the virtual disk format you want to use for the new VM.

The Thick Provision Lazy Zeroed and Thick Provision Eagerly Zeroed options will allocate all space up front; the Thin Provision option will allocate space on an as-needed basis. Refer to the section "Creating a Virtual Machine" in Chapter 9 for more details on these options.

Click Next after selecting a disk format.

11. For each source network defined in the OVF template, map that source network to a destination network in vCenter Server.

The destination networks are port groups or dvPort groups, as you can see in Figure 10.13.

FIGURE 10.13
Source networks defined in the OVF template are mapped to port groups and dvPort groups in vCenter Server.

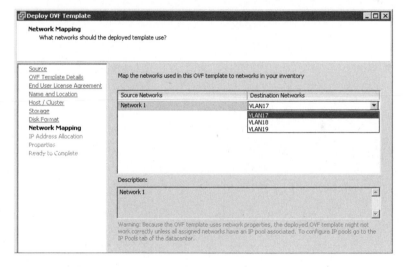

12. Some OVF templates will ask you to confirm how IP addresses should be assigned to the new VM, as you can see in Figure 10.14. Select the option you prefer (Fixed, Transient, or DHCP) and click Next.

SELECTING THE CORRECT IP ALLOCATION POLICY

Generally, you will select either Fixed or DHCP. The Transient option requires specific configurations within vCenter Server (IP pools created and configured) as well as support within the guest OS inside the OVF template. This support usually takes the form of a script or an executable application that sets the IP address.

FIGURE 10.14
vSphere
administrators have
different options
for controlling how
new VMs deployed
from OVF
templates are
assigned an IP
address.

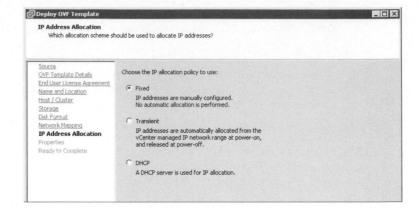

13. Some OVF templates will now prompt the user to input certain properties that will be used by the new VM.

For example, if you selected Fixed as the IP address allocation mechanism in step 12, you would be prompted to assign an IP address in this step as illustrated in Figure 10.15. Supply the correct value, and then click Next to continue.

FIGURE 10.15
The Deploy OVF
Template Wizard
provides a
warning if
properties have
invalid values
assigned.

14. The Ready To Complete screen summarizes the actions to be taken while deploying the new VM from the OVF template. If everything is correct, click Finish; if anything is incorrect, use the Back button to go back and make the correct selection.

Once the deployment of the new VM from the OVF template is complete, the new VM is treated like any other VM in the inventory. You can power it on, power it off, clone it, or snapshot it — refer to Chapter 9 for more details on these tasks.

The other way vCenter Server allows you to work with OVF is to export a VM as an OVF template.

Exporting a VM as an OVF Template

In addition to providing the ability to deploy new VMs from an OVF template, vCenter Server also provides the ability to export an existing VM as an OVF template. This functionality could be used in a number of different ways:

◆ Creating a template that could be transported between multiple vCenter Server instances

◆ Transporting a VM from one vSphere installation to another vSphere installation

◆ Allowing a software vendor to package its product as a VM and easily distribute it to customers

Whatever your reason for exporting a VM as an OVF template, the process is relatively straightforward.

Perform these steps to export a VM as an OVF template:

1. If it is not already running, launch the vSphere Client and connect to a vCenter Server instance or an ESXi host.

2. From within the vSphere Client, go to the File menu and select Export ➢ Export OVF Template. This opens the Export OVF Template dialog box.

3. Supply a name for the OVF template, select a directory where the OVF template will be stored, and choose the format:

◆ The Folder Of Files (OVF) format puts the separate components of an OVF template — the manifest (MF) file, the structural definition (OVF) file, and the virtual hard disk (VMDK) file — as separate files in a folder.

◆ The Single File (OVA) format combines the separate components into a single file. You might find this format easier to transport or distribute.

4. Supply a description for the OVF template.

5. When you are ready to begin the export, click OK.

6. The selected VM is exported to the chosen directory as an OVF template.

Figure 10.16 shows a VM that was exported as an OVF template in OVF (folder of files) format, so that you can see the different components.

FIGURE 10.16

Examining this VM
exported as an OVF
template shows the
different
components of an
OVF template.

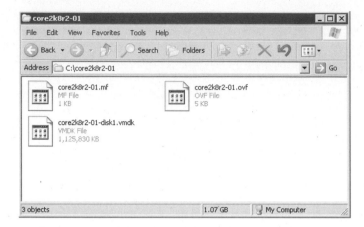

Once the VM has been successfully exported as an OVF template, you can use the steps in "Deploying a VM from an OVF Template" to import that VM back into a VMware vSphere implementation.

Before I move away from the topic of OVF templates, I want to take a quick look at the structure and components that make up an OVF template.

Examining OVF Templates

In Figure 10.16, I showed you the different files that make up an OVF template. In this example, three files make up the OVF template that you exported out of vCenter Server:

◆ The manifest file ends in .mf and contains SHA-1 digests of the other two files. This allows vCenter Server (and other applications that support the OVF specification) to verify the integrity of the OVF template by computing the SHA-1 digests of the other files in the package and comparing them against the SHA-1 digests in the manifest file. If the digests match, then the contents of the OVF template have not been modified.

WHAT PROTECTS THE MANIFEST?

The manifest contains SHA-1 digests to help an application verify that the components of the OVF template have not been modified. But what protects the manifest? The OVF specification allows for the use of an optional X.509 digital certificate that can verify the integrity of the manifest file as well.

◆ The OVF descriptor is an XML document, ending in .ovf, that contains information about the OVF template, such as product details, virtual hardware, requirements, licensing, a full list of file references, and a description of the content of the OVF template. Listing 10.1 shows the partial contents of the OVF descriptor for the VM I exported from vCenter Server in the previous section. (I've added backslashes (\) where a line has been manually wrapped to help with the readability of the OVF descriptor.)

◆ A virtual hard disk file, ending in .vmdk. The OVF specification supports multiple virtual hard disk formats, not just the VMDK files used by VMware vSphere, but obviously vCenter Server and VMware ESXi only natively support virtual hard disks in the VMDK format. Depending on the OVF template, it may contain multiple VMDK files, all of which would need to be referenced in the OVF descriptor file (refer to the DiskSection in the OVF descriptor file in Listing 10.1).

LISTING 10.1:   Partial contents of a sample OVF descriptor file:

```xml
<?xml version="1.0" encoding="UTF-8"?>
<!--Generated by VMware VirtualCenter Server, User: Administrator, \
    UTC time: 2011-04-05T00:37:32.238463Z-->
<Envelope vmw:buildId="build-380461" \
xmlns="http://schemas.dmtf.org/ovf/envelope/1" \
xmlns:cim="http://schemas.dmtf.org/wbem/wscim/1/common" \
xmlns:ovf="http://schemas.dmtf.org/ovf/envelope/1" \
xmlns:rasd="http://schemas.dmtf.org/wbem/wscim/1/cim-schema \
/2/CIM_ResourceAllocationSettingData"
xmlns:vmw="http://www.vmware.com/schema/ovf" \
xmlns:vssd="http://schemas.dmtf.org/wbem/wscim/1/cim-schema \
/2/CIM_VirtualSystemSettingData" \
xmlns:xsi="http://www.w3.org/2001/XMLSchema-instance">
  <References>
    <File ovf:href="core2k8r2-01-disk1.vmdk" ovf:id="file1" \
    ovf:size="1152849920" />
  </References>
  <DiskSection>
    <Info>Virtual disk information</Info>
    <Disk ovf:capacity="30" ovf:capacityAllocationUnits="byte * 2^30" \
    ovf:diskId="vmdisk1" ovf:fileRef="file1" \
    ovf:format="http://www.vmware.com/interfaces/specifications/vmdk.html# \
    streamOptimized" ovf:populatedSize="2744057856" />
  </DiskSection>
  <NetworkSection>
    <Info>The list of logical networks</Info>
    <Network ovf:name="VLAN19">
      <Description>The VLAN19 network</Description>
    </Network>
  </NetworkSection>
  <VirtualSystem ovf:id="core2k8r2-01">
    <Info>A virtual machine</Info>
    <Name>core2k8r2-01</Name>
    <OperatingSystemSection ovf:id="1" \
    vmw:osType="windows7Server64Guest">
      <Info>The kind of installed guest operating system</Info>
      <Description>Microsoft Windows Server 2008 R2 (64-bit) \
      </Description>
    </OperatingSystemSection>
    <VirtualHardwareSection>
      <Info>Virtual hardware requirements</Info>
      <System>
        <vssd:ElementName>Virtual Hardware Family</vssd:ElementName>
        <vssd:InstanceID>0</vssd:InstanceID>
        <vssd:VirtualSystemIdentifier>core2k8r2-01
        </vssd:VirtualSystemIdentifier>
        <vssd:VirtualSystemType>vmx-08</vssd:VirtualSystemType>
```

```
        </System>
      </VirtualHardwareSection>
    </VirtualSystem>
  </Envelope>
```

The OVF specification allows two different formats for OVF templates, which I've discussed briefly. OVF templates can be distributed as a set of files, like the OVF template I exported from vCenter Server in the previous section, "Exporting a VM as an OVF Template." In this case, it's easy to see the different components of the OVF template, but it's a bit more complicated to distribute unless you are distributing the OVF template as a set of files on a web server (keep in mind that vCenter Server and VMware ESXi can deploy VMs from an OVF template stored at a remote URL).

OVF templates can also be distributed as a single file. This single file ends in .ova and is in TAR format, and the OVF specification has strict requirements about the placement and order of components within the OVA archive. All the components that I've already described are still present, but because everything is stored in a single file, it's more difficult to view them independently of each other. However, using the OVA (single file) format does make it easier to move the OVF template between locations because there is only a single file with which to work.

WANT EVEN MORE DETAIL?

The full OVF specification as approved by the Desktop Management Task Force (DMTF) is available from the DMTF website at www.dmtf.org/standards/ovf. At the time this book was written, the latest version of the specification was version 1.1.0, published in January 2010.

The OVF specification also gives OVF templates another interesting ability: the ability to encapsulate multiple VMs inside a single OVF template. The OVF descriptor contains elements that specify whether the OVF template contains a single VM (noted by the VirtualSystem element, which you can see in Listing 10.1) or multiple VMs (noted by the VirtualSystemCollection element). An OVF template that contains multiple VMs would allow a vSphere administrator to deploy an entire collection of VMs from a single OVF template.

In fact, vSphere leverages this ability of an OVF template to encapsulate multiple VMs in a key feature known as vApps.

Working with vApps

vApps are a way for vSphere administrators to combine multiple VMs into a single unit. Why is this functionality useful? Increasingly, enterprise applications are no longer constrained to a single VM. Instead, enterprise applications may have components spread across multiple VMs. For example, a typical multitier application might have one or more front-end web servers, an application server, and a back-end database server. Although each of these servers is a discrete VM and could be managed as such, they are also part of a larger application that is servicing the organization. Combining these different VMs into a vApp allows the vSphere administrator to manage the different VMs as a single unit.

In this section, I'll show you how to work with vApps, including creating vApps and editing vApps. Let's start with creating a vApp.

Creating a vApp

Creating a vApp is a two-step process. First, you create the vApp container and configure any settings. Second, you add one or more VMs to the vApp, either by cloning existing VMs, deploying from a template, or creating a new VM from scratch in the vApp. You repeat adding VMs until you have all the necessary VMs contained in the vApp.

Perform these steps to create a vApp:

1. If it is not already running, launch the vSphere Client and connect to a vCenter Server instance or a stand-alone ESXi host.

2. Ensure that you are in an inventory view that will allow you to create a vApp by selecting View ➤ Inventory ➤ Hosts And Clusters or View ➤ Inventory ➤ VMs And Templates.

3. Right-click an existing host, resource pool, or cluster and select New vApp. This launches the New vApp Wizard.

LIMITATIONS ON CREATING NEW VAPPS

While you can create vApps inside other vApps, you can't create a vApp on a cluster that does not have vSphere DRS enabled.

---

4. Supply a name for the new vApp.

   If you are connected to vCenter Server, you must also select a location in the folder hierarchy in which to store the vApp. (This is logical placement, not physical placement.)

5. Click Next. This advances the New vApp Wizard to the Resource Allocation step. If you need to adjust the resource allocation settings for the vApp, you may do so here.

   By default, as shown in Figure 10.17, a new vApp is given normal priority, no reservation, and no limit on CPU or memory usage. It's important to note, however, that these default settings might not fit into your overall resource allocation strategy. Be sure to read Chapter 11, "Managing Resource Allocation," for more information on the impact of vApps on your resource allocation settings.

6. Click Next to proceed to the final step in the New vApp Wizard. From here, review the settings for the new vApp. If everything is correct, click Finish; otherwise, go back in the wizard to change what needs to be changed.

After the vApp is created, you can proceed with adding VMs to the vApp. There are a few different ways to add VMs to a vApp:

FIGURE 10.17

You will want to ensure these default resource allocation settings are appropriate for your specific environment.

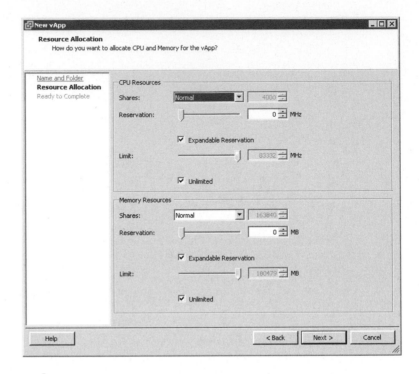

◆ You can clone an existing VM into a new VM inside the vApp. I described the process of cloning a VM earlier in this chapter in the section "Cloning a Virtual Machine"; that same procedure applies here. One interesting note: when cloning a VM into a vApp, the choice of logical folder location is ignored, as you can see in Figure 10.18.

FIGURE 10.18

Selecting a vApp as the destination for cloning an existing VM causes vCenter Server to ignore the logical folder location.

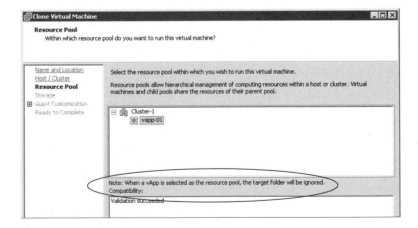

◆ You can deploy a new VM from a vCenter Server template and put the new VM into the vApp.

◆ You can create an entirely new VM from scratch inside the vApp. Because you are creating a new VM from scratch, this means that you will have to install the guest OS into the VM; cloning an existing VM or deploying from a template typically eliminates this task.

◆ You can drag and drop an existing VM and add it to a vApp.

Once the vApp is created and you've added one or more VMs to the vApp, you'll probably need to edit some of the vApp's settings.

Editing a vApp

Editing a vApp is a bit different because a vApp is a container, of sorts, and the vApp has properties and settings just as the VMs in that vApp have properties and settings. To help avoid confusion about where a setting should be set or edited, VMware has tried to make the vApp container as lean and simple as possible. There are really only a few settings that can be edited at the vApp level. I'll discuss these in the next few sections.

EDITING A VAPP'S RESOURCE ALLOCATION SETTINGS

To edit a vApp's resource allocation settings, right-click a vApp and select Edit Settings from the context menu. This will bring up the Edit vApp Settings dialog box, shown in Figure 10.19.

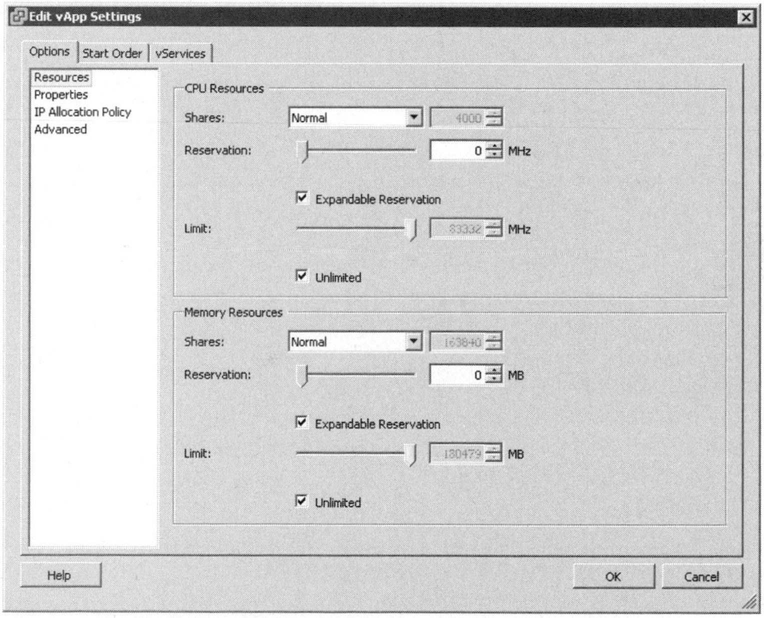

FIGURE 10.19
The Edit vApp Settings dialog box is where you can make any changes that need to be made to a vApp's configuration.

Selecting the Options tab and then the Resources option will expose the vApp's resource allocation settings. From here you can assign a higher or lower priority of access to resources, reserve resources for the vApp, or even limit the resources used by the vApp. If you don't understand what these settings mean or how they are used yet, don't worry; Chapter 11 provides complete details on using these settings in your VMware vSphere environment.

EDITING A VAPP'S IP ALLOCATION POLICY

On the Options tab of the Edit vApp Settings dialog box, the IP Allocation Policy option allows you to modify how IP addresses will be allocated to VMs contained within the vApp, as shown in Figure 10.20.

FIGURE 10.20
A vApp offers different options for assigning IP addresses to VMs inside a vApp.

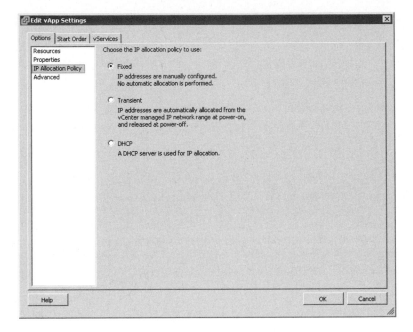

As you can see, the three possible settings are Fixed, Transient, and DHCP:

◆ When you use the Fixed option, the IP addresses must be manually set in the guest OS instance inside the VM.

◆ The Transient option leverages vCenter Server's ability to create and manage IP pools to assign IP addresses to the VMs inside a vApp. When the VMs are powered off, the IP addresses are automatically released.

◆ The DHCP option leverages an external DHCP server to assign IP addresses to the VMs in a vApp.

IP POOLS AREN'T THE SAME AS DHCP

You might initially think that using Transient with IP pools means that vCenter Server uses a DHCP-like mechanism to assign IP address to VMs inside a vApp without any further interaction from the user. Unfortunately, this is not the case. Using Transient with IP pools requires the guest OSes in the VMs in the vApp to have some sort of support for this functionality. This support is typically in the form of a script, executable, or other mechanism whereby an IP address is obtained from the IP pool, and it is assigned to the guest OS inside the VM. It is not the same as DHCP and it does not replace or supplant DHCP on a network segment.

When you first create a vApp, you will find that the only IP allocation policy that you can select here is Fixed. You will need to enable the other two options before you can select them. Enabling the other IP allocation options is done from the Advanced area of the Options tab by clicking the IP Allocation button. This activates the Advanced IP Allocation dialog box shown in Figure 10.21.

FIGURE 10.21

If you want to use the Transient (also called OVF Environment) or DHCP options, you must enable them in this dialog box.

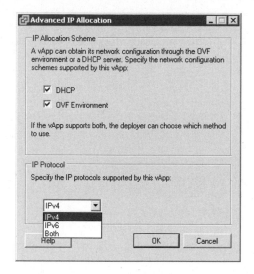

EDITING A VAPP'S ADVANCED SETTINGS

The Advanced area of the Edit vApp Settings dialog box is also where you can supply some additional metadata about the vApp, such as product name, product version, vendor name, or vendor URL. The values supplied here might be prepopulated, if you have a vApp that you received from a vendor, or you might populate these values yourself. Either way, the values set here show up on the Summary tab of the vApp in the vSphere Client. Figure 10.22 shows a vApp's metadata as it appears in the vSphere Client.

FIGURE 10.22

The vSphere Client displays the metadata in the General area of the Summary tab of a vApp object.

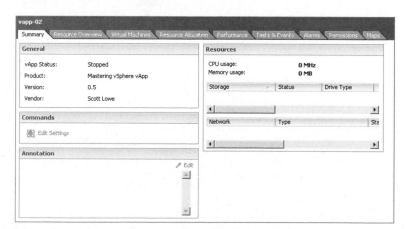

EDITING A VAPP'S POWER SETTINGS

One of the value propositions of a vApp is that you can power on or power off all the VMs in a vApp in one step. I'll show you how that's done in just a moment — although you probably have already figured it out — but first I want to cover the vApp's power settings.

The Start Order tab of the Edit vApp Settings dialog box is where you can set the startup order of the VMs and specify how much time will elapse between VMs booting up. Likewise, this is where you can set the shutdown action and timing.

For the most part, the only thing you'll really need to adjust here is the actual startup/shutdown order. Use the up/down arrows to move the order of the VMs so that the VMs boot up in the correct sequence. For example, you may want to ensure that the backend database VM comes up before the middle-tier application server, which should in turn come up before the frontend web server. You can control all this from the Start Order tab. Generally speaking, most of the defaults here are fine.

Note that I said "most of the defaults." There is one default setting that I would recommend you change. The Shutdown Action is, by default, set to Power Off. I recommend you change this to Guest Shutdown (which will require VMware Tools to be installed in the guest OS instance). You can set this on a per-VM basis, so if you have a VM that doesn't have the tools installed — not a recommended situation, by the way — then you can leave Shutdown Action set to Power Off.

Figure 10.23 shows the Shutdown Action for the VM named win2k8r2-04 set to Guest Shutdown instead of Power Off.

FIGURE 10.23
Using Guest Shutdown instead of Power Off will help avoid corruption in the guest OS instance.

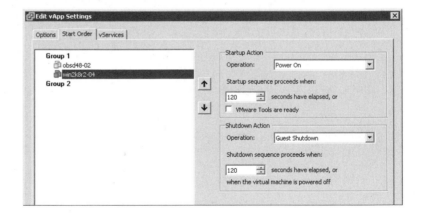

Changing a vApp's Power State

The process for powering on or powering off a vApp is the same as for a standard VM. You can select one of the following three methods to power on a vApp:

- The Power On button on the vSphere Client toolbar (looks like a green triangle)

- The Power On command in the Commands section of the Summary tab (these commands change to Power Off and Suspend when the vApp is powered on already, as shown in Figure 10.24)

- The Power On command from the vApp's context menu, accessible by right-clicking a vApp

FIGURE 10.24

The Commands section of the Summary tab for a vApp offers options to change the power state.

The Start Order tab in the vApp's properties controls what happens when the user tells vCenter Server to power on the vApp; you can see this in Figure 10.23. vCenter Server will power on all the VMs in a group, wait the specified period of time, then power on the VMs in the next group, wait the specified period of time, and so on. You can control the order in which VMs should be started as well as the waiting period between the groups by editing the settings shown in the Start Order tab.

Once the vApp is up and running, then you can suspend the vApp or power down the vApp just as you would suspend or power down a stand-alone VM. Depending on the settings on the Start Order tab, the VMs within a vApp can be configured in different ways to respond to a Power Off request to the vApp itself. As I recommended in the previous section, it's probably best to set Guest Shutdown as the action to take in response to a request to power off the vApp. Shutdown occurs in the reverse order from startup of the vApp.

Cloning a vApp

In much the same manner as cloning individual VMs, you can also clone a vApp.

Perform the following steps to clone a vApp:

1. If the vSphere Client is not already running, launch it and connect to a vCenter Server instance. You must connect to vCenter Server in order to clone a vApp.

2. Navigate to either the Hosts And Clusters or VMs And Templates inventory view; both of them show the vApp objects in the inventory.

3. Right-click the vApp and select Clone.

4. In the Clone vApp Wizard, select a host, cluster, or resource pool on which to run the new vApp. Because vApps require vSphere DRS, you cannot select a cluster on which vSphere DRS is not enabled. Click Next.

5. Supply a name for the new vApp, and select a logical inventory location for the vApp. Click Next to continue.

6. Select a target datastore or datastore cluster, and then click Next. Note that you do not have the option to select a VM storage profile. While member VMs can have VM storage profiles assigned, you can't assign a VM storage profile to the vApp itself.

7. Select the target virtual disk format. Click Next.

8. Select the correct mappings from the source networks to the destination networks. Click Next when you are finished with the network mappings.

9. If the vApp has specific properties defined, you will next have the option to edit those properties for the cloned vApp. Click Next when you are ready to continue.

10. Review the settings for the new vApp, and use the Back button or the hyperlinks on the left to go back and make changes if needed. If everything is correct, click Finish.

vCenter Server will clone the vApp container object and all VMs within the vApp. vCenter Server will not, however, customize the guest OS installations inside the VMs in the vApp; the administrator assumes the burden of ensuring that the VMs in the cloned vApp are customized appropriately.

So far in this chapter, you've seen how to clone VMs, customize cloned VMs, create templates, work with OVF templates, and work with vApps. In the last section of this chapter, I'll take a quick look at importing VMs from other environments into your VMware vSphere environment.

Importing Machines from Other Environments

Previous versions of VMware vSphere offered tools to help customers take OS installations on physical hardware and migrate them — using a process called a physical-to-virtual migration, or a P2V migration — into a virtualized environment running vSphere. Two tools, in particular, were included in previous versions of VMware vSphere:

◆ The vCenter Converter was a plug-in for vCenter Server that added P2V functionality directly in the vSphere Client. From within the vSphere Client, administrators could initiate P2V migrations.

◆ Guided Consolidation was a plug-in for vCenter Server that helped customers assess their physical systems to determine their suitability to run in a virtualized environment.

Unfortunately, vSphere 4.1 was the last version of VMware vSphere to include these tools. In vSphere 5, neither Guided Consolidation nor the vCenter Converter plug-in is available.

VMware does still offer a stand-alone product called VMware Converter. VMware Converter provides both P2V functionality as well as virtual-to-virtual (V2V) functionality. The V2V functionality allows VMs created on other virtualization platforms to be imported into VMware vSphere. Administrators can also use VMware Converter's V2V functionality to export VMs out of VMware vSphere to other virtualization platforms. This V2V functionality is particularly helpful in moving VMs between VMware's enterprise-class virtualization platform, VMware vSphere, and VMware's hosted virtualization platforms, such as VMware Workstation for Windows or Linux or VMware Fusion for Mac OS X. Although VMware created all these products, slight differences in the architecture of the products require the use of VMware Converter or a similar tool to move VMs between the products.

WHY NO VMWARE CONVERTER COVERAGE?

At the time this book was being written, a version of VMware Converter that was compatible with vSphere 5 had not yet entered beta testing, so it was impossible for me to provide any coverage of the tool in this book.

The Bottom Line

Clone a VM. The ability to clone a VM is a powerful feature that dramatically reduces the amount of time to get a fully functional VM with a guest OS installed and running. vCenter Server provides the ability not only to clone VMs but also to customize VMs, ensuring that each VM is unique. You can save the information to customize a VM as a customization specification and then reuse that information over and over again. vCenter Server can even clone running VMs.

Master It Where and when can customization specifications be created in the vSphere Client?

Master It A fellow administrator comes to you and wants you to help streamline the process of deploying Solaris x86 VMs in your VMware vSphere environment. What do you tell him?

Create a VM template. vCenter Server's templates feature is an excellent complement to the cloning functionality. With options to clone or convert an existing VM to a template, vCenter Server makes it easy to create templates. By creating templates, you ensure that your VM master image doesn't get accidentally changed or modified. Then, once a template has been created, vCenter Server can clone VMs from that template, customizing them in the process to ensure that each one is unique.

Master It Of the following tasks, which are appropriate to be performed on a VM running Windows Server 2008 that will eventually be turned into a template?

    A. Align the guest OS's file system to a 64 KB boundary.

    B. Join the VM to Active Directory.

    C. Perform some application-specific configurations and tweaks.

    D. Install all patches from the operating system vendor.

Deploy new VMs from a template. By combining templates and cloning, VMware vSphere administrators have a powerful way to standardize the configuration of VMs being deployed, protect the master images from accidental change, and reduce the amount of time it takes to deploy new guest OS instances.

Master It Another VMware vSphere administrator in your environment starts the wizard for deploying a new VM from a template. He has a customization specification he'd like to use, but there is one setting in the specification he wants to change. Does he have to create an all-new customization specification?

Deploy a VM from an OVF template. Open Virtualization Format (OVF, formerly Open Virtual Machine Format) templates provide a mechanism for moving templates or VMs between different instances of vCenter Server or even entirely different and separate installations of VMware vSphere. OVF templates combine the structural definition of a VM along with the data in the VM's virtual hard disk and can either exist as a folder of files or as a single file. Because OVF templates include the VM's virtual hard disk, OVF templates can contain an installation of a guest OS and are often used by software developers as a way of delivering their software preinstalled into a guest OS inside a VM.

Master It A vendor has given you a zip file that contains a VM they are calling a *virtual appliance*. Upon looking inside the zip file, you see several VMDK files and a VMX file. Will you be able to use vCenter Server's Deploy OVF Template functionality to import this VM? If not, how can you get this VM into your infrastructure?

Export a VM as an OVF template. To assist in the transport of VMs between VMware vSphere installations, you can use vCenter Server to export a VM as an OVF template. The OVF template will include both the configuration of the VM as well as the data found in the VM.

Master It You are preparing to export a VM to an OVF template. You want to ensure that the OVF template is easy and simple to transport via a USB key or portable hard drive. Which format is most appropriate, OVF or OVA? Why?

Work with vApps. vSphere vApps leverage OVF as a way to combine multiple VMs into a single administrative unit. When the vApp is powered on, all VMs in it are powered on, in a sequence specified by the administrator. The same goes for shutting down a vApp. vApps also act like a bit like resource pools for the VMs contained within them.

Master It Name two ways to add VMs to a vApp.

## Chapter 11

Managing Resource Allocation

The idea that we can take a single physical server and host many VMs has a great deal of value in today's dynamic datacenter environments, but let's face it: there are limits to how many VMs can run on a VMware ESXi host. The key to making the most of your virtualization platform is to understand how key resources — memory, processors, disks, and networks — are consumed by the VMs running on the host and how the host itself consumes resources. The method an ESXi host uses to arbitrate access to each resource is a bit different. This chapter discusses how an ESXi host allocates these resources and how you can change the way these resources are allocated.

In this chapter, you will learn to

◆ Manage VM memory allocation

◆ Manage CPU utilization

◆ Create and manage resource pools

◆ Control network and storage I/O utilization

Reviewing Virtual Machine Resource Allocation

One of the most significant advantages of server virtualization is the ability to allocate resources to a VM based on the machine's actual performance needs. In the traditional physical server environment, a server is often provided with more resources than it really needs because it was purchased with a specific budget in mind and the server specifications were maximized for the budget provided. For example, does a Dynamic Host Configuration Protocol (DHCP) server really need dual processors, 16 GB of RAM, and 146 GB mirrored hard drives? In most situations, the DHCP server will most certainly underutilize those resources. In the virtual world, you can create a VM better suited for the role of a DHCP server. For this DHCP server, then, you would assemble a VM with a more suitable 2 GB or 4 GB of RAM (depending on the guest OS), access to a single CPU, and 20 GB to 40 GB of disk space, all of which are provided by the ESXi host on which the VM is running. Then, you can create additional VMs with the resources they need to operate effectively without wasting valuable memory, CPU cycles, and disk storage. Correctly allocating resources based on the anticipated need of the guest OS and the applications inside a VM is the essence of *right-sizing* your VMs, which I discussed in Chapter 9, "Creating and Managing Virtual Machines." Right-sizing your VMs allows you to achieve greater efficiency and higher consolidation ratios (more VMs per physical server).

Even when you right-size your VMs, though, as you add more VMs, each VM places additional demand on the ESXi host, and the host's resources are consumed to support the VMs. At a certain point, the host will run out of resources. What does ESXi do when it runs out of resources? How does ESXi handle it when the VMs are asking for more resources than the physical host can actually provide? How can you guarantee that a guest OS and its applications get the resources they need without being starved by other guest OSes and their applications?

Fortunately, VMware vSphere offers a set of controls that are designed to do exactly that: to guarantee access to resources when necessary, to curb or control the use of resources, and to enable prioritized access to resources when available resources are low. Specifically, vSphere offers three controls for controlling or modifying resource allocation: reservations, limits, and shares.

While the behavior of these mechanisms varies based on the resource, the basic idea behind these mechanisms is as follows:

Reservations   Reservations serve to act as guarantees of a particular resource. You would use reservations when you want to ensure that, no matter what else is going on, a specific VM is absolutely assured to have access to a particular amount of a given resource.

Limits   Limits are, quite simply, a way to restrict the amount of a given resource that a VM can use. VMs already have some limits simply by how they are constructed — for example, a VM configured to have a single virtual CPU (vCPU) is limited to using only that single vCPU. The Limit feature within vSphere grants you even greater granularity over how resources are utilized. Depending on the resource to which the limit is being applied, the specific behavior of ESXi will change. I discuss this in detail later in this chapter under each resource's specific section.

Shares   Shares serve to establish priority. When an ESXi host comes under contention and must decide which VM gets access to which resources, shares are used to determine priority. VMs with higher shares assigned will have higher priority, and therefore greater access, to the ESXi host's resources.

Figure 11.1 shows these three mechanisms displayed in the properties of a VM.

FIGURE 11.1
Reservations, limits, and shares offer more fine-grained control over resource allocation.

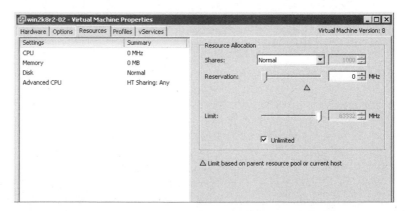

Throughout the rest of this chapter, I discuss how one or more of these three mechanisms — reservations, limits, and shares — are applied to control or modify resource allocation across all four major resources in a vSphere environment: memory, CPU, storage, and network.

THE GAME PLAN FOR GROWTH

One of the most challenging aspects of managing a virtual datacenter is managing growth without jeopardizing performance and without overestimating. For organizations of any size, it is critical to establish a plan for managing VM and ESXi host growth.

The easiest approach is to construct a resource consumption document that details the following:

◆ What is the standard configuration for a new VM to be added to the inventory? Be sure to specify critical configuration points such as the size of the operating system drive, the size of any data drives, and how much RAM is allocated. By establishing standards for VMs, you can increase efficiency and ensure VMs are right-sized.

◆ What are the decision points for creating a VM with specifications beyond the standard configuration? A standard configuration is great, but it won't address every single need in your organization. There are going to be exceptions, and you just need to document what drives an exception.

◆ How much of a server's resources can be consumed before availability and performance levels are jeopardized? This both affects and is affected by other design points like N+1 redundancy.

◆ At the point where the resources for an ESXi host (or an entire cluster) are consumed, do you add a single host or multiple hosts at one time?

◆ What is the maximum size of a cluster for your environment? When does adding another host (or set of hosts) constitute building a new cluster? This could affect operational considerations like how many hosts get added at a time. For example, if you have to start a new cluster, then you'll need at least two hosts, preferably three.

The first VM resource I'll examine is memory. In many instances, memory is the first resource to come under constraints, so taking a look at memory first is warranted.

Working with Virtual Machine Memory

Let's start with a discussion of how memory is allocated to a VM. Later in this section I'll discuss how you as an administrator can use reservations, shares, and limits to help control or modify how VMs consume memory.

When you create a new VM through the vSphere Client, the wizard asks you how much memory the VM should have, as shown in Figure 11.2. The vSphere Client suggests a default value based on the selected guest OS (the selected guest OS in this case is Windows Server 2008 R2).

The amount of memory you allocate on this screen is the amount the guest OS will see — in this example, it is 4,096 MB. This is the same as when you build a physical system and put a set of four 1,024 MB memory sticks into the system board. If you install Windows Server 2008 in this VM, Windows will report 4,096 MB of RAM installed. Ultimately, this is the amount of memory the VM "thinks" it has and the maximum amount of memory the guest OS will ever be able to access. Like a physical system with four 1,024 MB DIMMs installed, this VM will never be able to use more than 4,096 MB of RAM.

Let's assume you have an ESXi host with 16 GB of physical RAM available to run VMs (in other words, the hypervisor is using some RAM and there's 16 GB left over for the VMs). In the case of our new VM, it will comfortably run, leaving approximately 12 GB for other VMs (there is some additional overhead that I discuss later, but for now let's assume that the 12 GB is available to other VMs).

FIGURE 11.2
The memory configuration settings for a VM indicate the amount of RAM the VM "thinks" it has.

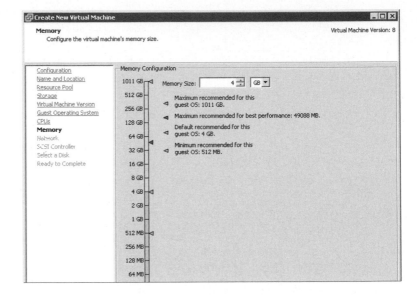

What happens when you run three more VMs, each configured with 4 GB of RAM? Each of the additional VMs will request 4 GB of RAM from the ESXi host. At this point, four VMs will be accessing the physical memory, and you will have allocated all 16 GB of memory to the VMs. ESXi has now run out of a critical resource (memory).

What happens when you launch a fifth VM? Will it run? The short answer is yes, and some of the key technologies that enable administrators to overcommit memory — that is, to allocate more memory to VMs than is actually installed in the VMware ESXi host — are quite advanced. Because these technologies are integral to understanding how memory allocation works with VMware ESXi, let's take a quick look at these technologies and how they work.

Understanding ESXi Advanced Memory Technologies

VMware ESXi is unique among hypervisors on the market today in that it supports a number of different technologies for advanced memory management. As a result of these advanced memory management technologies, at the time of this writing VMware ESXi is the only commercially available hypervisor on the market capable of performing memory overcommitment in a manner that is guest OS agnostic.

ESXi Does Not Require Guest OS Involvement

There are other commercially available hypervisors that offer the ability to overcommit memory, but these products support that functionality only for certain guest OSes.

VMware ESXi employs four different memory-management technologies to make sure that the physical server's RAM is utilized as efficiently as possible: transparent page sharing, ballooning, swapping, and memory compression.

For anyone interested in more in-depth and detailed information on these memory-management technologies, I strongly recommend reading "Memory Resource Management in VMware ESX Server," by Carl A. Waldspurger, available online at

http://www.waldspurger.org/carl/papers/esx-mem-osdi02.pdf

TRANSPARENT PAGE SHARING

The first memory-management technology VMware ESXi uses is *transparent page sharing*, in which identical memory pages are shared among VMs to reduce the total number of memory pages needed. The hypervisor computes hashes of the contents of memory pages to identify pages that contain identical memory. If a hash match is found, a full comparison of the matching memory pages is made in order to exclude a false positive. Once the pages are confirmed to be identical, the hypervisor will transparently remap the memory pages of the VMs so they are sharing the same physical memory page. This reduces overall host memory consumption. Advanced parameters are available to fine-tune the behavior of the page-sharing mechanisms.

Normally, ESXi works on 4 KB memory pages and will use transparent page sharing on all memory pages. However, when the hypervisor is taking advantage of hardware offloads available in the CPUs — such as Intel Extended Page Tables (EPT) Hardware Assist or AMD Rapid Virtualization Indexing (RVI) Hardware Assist — then the hypervisor uses 2 MB memory pages, also known as large pages. In these cases, ESXi will not share these large pages, but it will compute hashes for the 4 KB pages inside the large pages. In the event that the hypervisor needs to invoke swapping, the large pages will be broken into small pages, and having the hashes already computed allows the hypervisor to invoke page sharing before they are swapped out.

BALLOONING

I mentioned previously that ESXi's memory-management technologies are guest OS agnostic, meaning that the guest OS selection doesn't matter. This is true; any supported guest OS can take advantage of all of ESXi's memory-management functionality. However, these technologies are not necessarily guest OS independent, meaning that they operate without interaction from the guest OS. While transparent page sharing operates independently of the guest OS, ballooning does not.

Ballooning involves the use of a driver — referred to as the balloon driver — installed into the guest OS. This driver is part of VMware Tools and gets installed when VMware Tools are installed. Once installed into the guest OS, the balloon driver can respond to commands from the hypervisor to reclaim memory from that particular guest OS. The balloon driver does this by requesting memory from the guest OS — a process calling *inflating* — and then passing that memory back to the hypervisor for use by other VMs.

Because the guest OS can give up pages it is no longer using when the balloon driver requests memory, it's possible for the hypervisor to reclaim memory without any performance impact on the applications running inside that guest OS. If the guest OS is already under memory pressure — meaning the amount of memory configured for that VM is insufficient for the guest OS and its applications — it's very likely that inflating the balloon driver will invoke guest OS paging (or swapping), which will impair performance.

HOW DOES THE BALLOON DRIVER WORK?

The balloon driver is part of the VMware Tools, which I described in detail in Chapter 9. As such, it is a guest OS–specific driver, meaning that Linux VMs would have a Linux-based balloon driver, Windows VMs would have a Windows-based balloon driver, and so forth.

Regardless of the guest OS, the balloon driver works in the same fashion. When the ESXi host is running low on physical memory, the hypervisor will signal the balloon driver to grow. To do this, the balloon driver will request memory from the guest OS. This causes the balloon driver's memory footprint to grow, or to *inflate*. The memory that is granted to the balloon driver is then passed back to the hypervisor. The hypervisor can use these memory pages to supply memory for other VMs, reducing the need to swap and minimizing the performance impact of the memory constraints. When the memory pressure on the host passes, the balloon driver will *deflate*, or return memory to the guest OS.

The key advantage that ESXi gains from using a guest-OS-specific balloon driver in this fashion is that it allows the guest OS to make the decision about which pages can be given to the balloon driver process (and thus released to the hypervisor). In some cases, the inflation of the balloon driver can release memory back to the hypervisor without any degradation of VM performance because the guest OS is able to give the balloon driver unused or idle pages.

SWAPPING

There are two forms of swapping involved when you examine how memory is managed with VMware ESXi. There is *guest OS swapping*, in which the guest OS inside the VM swaps pages out to its virtual disk according to its own memory-management algorithms. This is generally due to higher memory requirements than available memory. In a virtualized environment, this would translate into a VM being configured with less memory than the guest OS and its applications require, such as trying to run Windows Server 2008 R2 in only 1 GB of RAM. Guest OS swapping falls strictly under the control of the guest OS and is not controlled by the hypervisor.

The other type of swapping involved is *hypervisor swapping*. In the event that none of the previously described technologies trim guest OS memory usage enough, the ESXi host will be forced to use hypervisor swapping. Hypervisor swapping means that ESXi is going to swap memory pages out to disk in order to reclaim memory that is needed elsewhere. ESXi's swapping takes place without any regard to whether the pages are being actively used by the guest OS. As a result, and due to the fact that disk response times are thousands of times slower than memory response times, guest OS performance is severely impacted if hypervisor swapping is invoked. It is for this reason that ESXi won't invoke swapping unless it is absolutely necessary.

The key thing to remember about hypervisor swapping is that you want to avoid it if at all possible; there is a significant and noticeable impact to performance.

MEMORY COMPRESSION

vSphere 4.1 and later, including vSphere 5, add another memory-management technology to the mix: memory compression. When an ESXi host gets to the point that hypervisor swapping is necessary, the VMkernel will attempt to compress memory pages and keep them in RAM in a compressed memory cache. Pages that can be successfully compressed by at least 50 percent are put into the compressed memory cache instead of being written to disk and can then be recovered much more quickly if the guest OS needs that memory page. Memory compression can dramatically reduce the number of pages that must be swapped to disk and thus can dramatically improve the performance of an ESXi host that is under strong memory pressure. Compression is invoked only when the ESXi host reaches the point that swapping is needed.

Although these advanced memory-management technologies allow ESXi to allocate more memory to VMs than there is actual RAM in the physical server, these memory-management technologies do not help guarantee memory or prioritize access to memory. Even with these advanced memory-management technologies, at some point it becomes necessary to exercise some control over how the VMs access and use the memory allocated to them. This is where a VMware vSphere administrator can use reservations, limits, and shares — the three mechanisms I described previously — to modify or control how resources are allocated. In the next section, I'll describe how these mechanisms are used to control memory allocation.

Controlling Memory Allocation

Like all physical resources, memory is a finite resource. The advanced memory-management technologies in ESXi help with the efficient use of this finite resource by making it go farther than it normally would go. For finer-grained control over how ESXi allocates memory, though, administrators must turn to the use of the three mechanisms I listed previously: reservations, shares, and limits. Figure 11.3 shows these three settings in the Virtual Machine Properties dialog box for a VM.

FIGURE 11.3
vSphere supports the use of reservations, shares, and limits for controlling memory allocation.

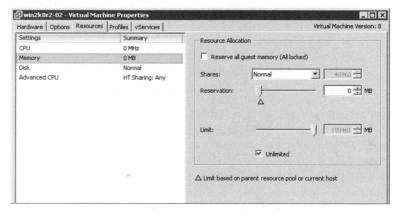

The steps for editing a Reservation, Limit, or Shares value for either memory or CPU are the same. Storage I/O and network I/O are handled a bit differently, so I'll discuss those in the appropriate sections later in this chapter. I cover storage I/O in the section "Controlling Storage I/O Utilization," and I discuss network I/O in the section "Regulating Network I/O Utilization." Perform the following steps to edit a VM's memory or CPU Reservation, Limit, or Shares:

1. Use the vSphere Client to connect to a vCenter Server instance or directly to an ESXi host.

2. Drill down through the inventory to find the VM to be edited.

3. Right-click the VM, and select the Edit Settings option.

4. Click the Resources tab.

5. On the Resources tab, select the CPU or Memory option from the Settings list on the left.

6. Adjust the Shares, Reservation, and Limit values as desired.

Now that you've seen how to adjust the Reservation, Limit, and Shares values, I'll take a detailed look at the specific behaviors of how these mechanisms apply to memory usage and allocation.

Using Memory Reservations

The memory reservation is an optional setting for each VM. You can see in Figure 11.3 that the default memory reservation is 0 MB (the equivalent of no memory reservation at all). You can use the slider to adjust this value, but what exactly does this value do? What impact does adjusting the memory reservation have?

The memory reservation amount specified on the Resources tab of the VM settings is the amount of actual, real physical memory that the ESXi host *must* provide to this VM for the VM to power on. A VM with a memory reservation is guaranteed the amount of RAM configured in its Reservation setting. As I mentioned, the default is 0 MB, or no reservation. In the previous example, the VM configured with 4 GB of RAM and the default reservation of 0 MB means the ESXi host is not required to provide the VM with any physical memory. If the ESXi host is not required to provide actual RAM to the VM, then where will the VM get its memory? In the absence of a reservation, the VMkernel has the option to provide VM memory from *VMkernel swap*.

VMkernel swap is the hypervisor swapping mechanism I referred to previously when discussing the various memory-management techniques that ESXi employs. VMkernel swap is implemented as a file with a `.vswp` extension that is created when a VM is powered on. These per-VM swap files created by the VMkernel reside, by default, in the same datastore location as the VM's configuration file and virtual disk files (although you do have the option of relocating the VMkernel swap). In the absence of a memory reservation — the default configuration — this file will be equal in size to the amount of RAM configured for the VM. Thus, a VM configured for 4 GB of RAM will have a VMkernel swap file that is also 4 GB in size and stored, by default, in the same location as the VM's configuration and virtual disk files.

In theory, this means a VM could get its memory allocation entirely from VMkernel swap — or disk — resulting in VM performance degradation because disk access time is several orders of magnitude slower than RAM access time.

THE SPEED OF RAM

How slow is VMkernel swap compared to RAM? If you make some basic assumptions regarding RAM access times and disk seek times, you can see that both appear fairly fast in terms of human abilities but that in relation to each other, RAM is much faster:

RAM access time = 10 nanoseconds (for example)

Disk seek time = 8 milliseconds (for example)

The difference between these is calculated as follows:

$$0.008 \div 0.00000001 = 800,000$$

RAM is accessed 800,000 times faster than disk. Or to put it another way, if RAM takes 1 second to access, then disk would take 800,000 seconds to access — or nine and a quarter days:

$$((800,000 \div 60 \text{ seconds}) \div 60 \text{ minutes}) \div 24 \text{ hours} = 9.259$$

As you can see, if VM performance is your goal, it is prudent to spend your money on enough RAM to support the VMs you plan to run. There are other factors, but this is a significant one. This incredible speed difference is also why adding memory compression to ESXi's arsenal of memory-management tools can make a big difference in performance; it helps avoid having to swap pages out to disk and keep them in memory instead.

Just because a VM without a reservation could potentially get all its memory from VMkernel swap, does this mean that a VM will actually get all of its memory from swap when ESXi host RAM is available? No. ESXi attempts to provide each VM with all the memory it requests, up to the maximum amount configured for that VM. Obviously, a VM configured with only 4,096 MB of RAM cannot request more than 4,096 MB of RAM. However, when an ESXi host doesn't have enough RAM available to satisfy the memory needs of the VMs it is hosting and when technologies such as transparent page sharing, the balloon driver, and memory compression aren't enough, the VMkernel is forced to page some of each VM's memory out to the individual VM's VMkernel swap file.

Is there a way you can control how much of an individual VM's memory allocation can be provided by swap and how much must be provided by real physical RAM? Yes. This is where a memory reservation comes into play. Recall that I said a memory reservation specifies the amount of real, physical RAM that the ESXi host must provide the VM. By default, a VM has a memory reservation of 0 MB, which means that ESXi is not required to provide any real, physical RAM. This means potentially all of the VM's memory could be paged out to the VMkernel swap file if necessary.

Let's look at what happens if you decide to set a memory reservation of 1,024 MB for this VM, shown in Figure 11.4. How does this change the way this VM gets memory?

FIGURE 11.4
This memory reservation guarantees 1,024 MB of RAM for the VM.

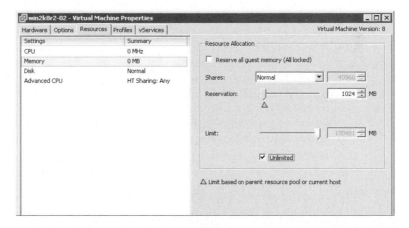

In this example, when this VM is started, the ESXi host must provide at least 1,024 MB of real RAM to support this VM's memory allocation. In fact, 1,024 MB of RAM is *guaranteed* for that VM. The host can provide the remaining 3,072 MB of RAM from either physical RAM or VMkernel swap, as shown in Figure 11.5. In this case, because some of the VM's RAM is guaranteed to come from physical RAM, ESXi reduces the size of the VMkernel swap file by the amount of the reservation. Therefore, the VMkernel swap file is reduced in size by 1,024 MB. This behavior is consistent with what I've shown you so far: with a reservation of 0 MB, the VMkernel swap file is the same size as the amount of configured memory. As the reservation increases, the size of the VMkernel swap file decreases in size correspondingly.

FIGURE 11.5
The memory reservation reduces the potential need for VMkernel swap space by the size of the reservation.

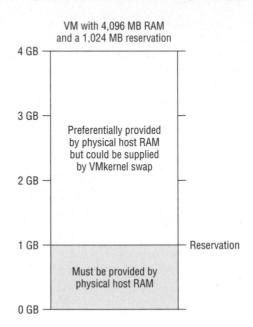

This behavior ensures that a VM has at least some high-speed memory available to it if the ESXi host is running more VMs than it has actual RAM to support, but there's also a downside. If you assume that each of the VMs you start on this host has a 1,024 MB reservation and you have 8 GB of available RAM in the host to run VMs, then you will be able to launch only eight VMs concurrently (8 × 1,024 MB = 8,192 MB). On a more positive note, if each VM is configured with an initial RAM allocation of 4,096 MB, then you're now running VMs that would need 32 GB of RAM on a host with only 8 GB. ESXi uses the technologies described previously — transparent page sharing, the balloon driver, memory compression, and finally VMkernel swap — to manage the fact that you, as the administrator, have allocated more RAM than is physically installed in the server.

There's one other side effect from using memory reservations that you must also understand. I mentioned previously in this section that using a memory reservation guarantees physical RAM for the VM. This is true, but only as the guest OS in the VM requests memory. If you have a VM with a 1,024 MB reservation configured, then the ESXi host will allocate RAM to the VM on an as-needed basis, and the first 1,024 MB of RAM allocated to that VM is part of the reservation. RAM is allocated on demand; the presence of a reservation doesn't change that behavior. Once allocated, though, because this RAM is part of the memory reservation, it's locked to this VM — it won't be reclaimed via the balloon driver, and it won't be swapped out to disk or compressed. In a way, that's good; it underscores the fact that this memory is guaranteed to this VM.

In a way, it's also bad, though, because the reserved memory, once allocated to a VM, can't be reclaimed for use by other VMs or for use by the hypervisor itself.

RESERVED MEMORY AND TRANSPARENT PAGE SHARING

While reserved memory won't be reclaimed by the hypervisor for use by other purposes — it is, after all, guaranteed for that VM — reserved memory can be shared via transparent page sharing. Transparent page sharing does not affect the availability of reserved memory because the page is still accessible to the VM.

Like all the mechanisms I describe in this chapter, this means that you'll want to use memory reservations carefully and with a full understanding of the impact on the ESXi host's behavior and operation.

USE MEMORY OVERCOMMITMENT WISELY

Although you can overcommit memory with VMware ESXi, be careful doing so. You must carefully weigh the performance considerations. Although VMware ESXi has advanced memory-management technologies such as transparent page sharing and idle page reclamation that help conserve memory, any workload that actually needs its memory might take a performance hit if that memory isn't available. In my experience, many workloads running in Windows-based VMs utilize only a portion of their configured memory.

In these sorts of environments, it's generally safe to overcommit memory by as much as 50 percent of the physical RAM installed in the server without seeing noticeable performance degradation. This means a server with 32 GB of RAM could potentially host VMs configured to use 48 GB of RAM. Larger overcommitment ratios are certainly very possible, and I've seen larger ratios in certain environments. However, the key to wisely using memory overcommitment to maximize the value of your vSphere deployment is knowing the needs of the VMs and how they consume resources.

USING MEMORY LIMITS

If you refer back to Figure 11.3, you will also see a setting for a memory limit. By default, all new VMs are created without a limit, which means that the initial RAM you assigned to it during creation is its effective limit. So, what exactly is the purpose of the Limit setting? It sets the actual limit on how much physical RAM may be utilized by that VM.

To see this behavior in action, let's now change the limit on this VM from the default setting of Unlimited to 2,048 MB.

So, what is the effective result of this configuration? Here's how it breaks down:

◆ The VM is configured with 4,096 MB of RAM, so the guest OS running inside that VM believes that it has 4,096 MB of RAM available to use.

◆ The VM has a reservation of 1,024 MB of RAM, which means that the ESXi host *must* allocate 1,024 MB of physical RAM to the VM. This RAM is guaranteed to this VM.

RESERVED MEMORY IS NOT SHARED

Remember that reserved memory — the memory specified by the Reservation setting — is not shared once it has been allocated to the VM. Once the hypervisor has, in fact, allocated RAM that is part of the reservation, the hypervisor will not reclaim that memory.

◆ Assuming the ESXi host has enough physical RAM installed and available, the hypervisor will allocate memory to the VM as needed up to 2,048 MB (the limit). Upon reaching 2,048 MB, the balloon driver kicks in to prevent the guest OS from using any more memory. When the guest OS's memory demands drop below 2,048 MB, the balloon driver deflates and returns memory to the guest. The effective result of this behavior is that the memory the guest OS uses remains below 2,048 MB (the limit).

◆ The 1,024 MB "gap" between the reservation and the limit could be supplied by either physical RAM or VMkernel swap space. ESXi will allocate physical RAM if it is available.

The key problem with the use of memory limits is that they are enforced without any guest OS awareness. If you have a VM configured for 4 GB of RAM, the guest OS inside that VM is going to think it has 4 GB of RAM with which to work, and it will behave accordingly. If you then place a 2 GB limit on that VM, the VMkernel will enforce that the VM only use 2 GB of RAM. Fine — but it will do so without the knowledge or cooperation of the guest OS inside that VM. The guest OS will continue to behave as if it has 4 GB of RAM, completely unaware of the limit that has been placed on it by the hypervisor. If the working set size of the guest OS and the applications running in it exceeds the memory limit, setting a memory limit will have a significant impact on the performance of the VM because the result is that the guest OS will constantly be forced to swap pages to disk (guest OS swapping, not hypervisor swapping).

In general, then, you should consider memory limits a temporary stop-gap measure when you need to reduce physical memory usage on an ESXi host and a negative impact to performance is acceptable. You wouldn't, generally speaking, want to overprovision a VM with RAM and constrain memory usage with a limit on a long-term basis. In that scenario, the VM will typically perform very poorly and would actually perform better with less RAM configured and no limit.

WHY USE MEMORY LIMITS?

You might be asking yourself, "Why should I even use limits? Why not just set the configured limit to whatever I want the VM to use?" That's a good question! Keeping in mind that memory limits are enforced by the VMkernel without any awareness by the guest OS of the configured limit, memory limits can, in many cases, negatively impact the performance of the VM.

However, there are times when you might need to use memory limits as a temporary measure to reduce physical memory usage in your hosts. Perhaps you need to perform maintenance on an ESXi host that is part of a cluster. You plan to use vMotion to migrate VMs to other hosts during the maintenance window, and you want to temporarily push down memory usage on less-important VMs so that you don't overcommit memory too heavily and negatively impact lots of VMs. Limits would help in this situation.

Knowing that memory limits can have negative impacts on performance, be sure to use them only when that negative performance impact is understood and acceptable.

Working together, an initial allocation of memory, a memory reservation, and a memory limit can be powerful tools in efficiently managing the memory available on an ESXi host. But there is still one more tool to examine, and that's memory shares.

USING MEMORY SHARES

In Figure 11.3, there is a third setting called Shares that I have not yet discussed. The two mechanisms that I described to you already, memory reservations and memory limits, help provide finer-grained controls over how ESXi should or should not allocate memory to a VM. These mechanisms are always in effect; that is, a Limit setting is enforced even if the ESXi host has plenty of physical RAM available for the VM to use.

Memory shares are very different. The share system in VMware is a proportional share system that provides administrators with a means of assigning resource priority to VMs, but shares are only used when the ESXi host is experiencing physical RAM contention. In other words, the VMs on an ESXi host are requesting more memory than the host is able to provide. If an ESXi host has plenty of memory available, shares will not play a role. However, when memory is scarce and ESXi has to make a decision about which VM should be given access to memory, shares are a way of establishing a priority setting for a VM requesting memory that is greater than the VM's reservation but less than its limit. (Recall that memory under the reservation is guaranteed to the VM, and memory over the limit would not be allocated. Shares, therefore, affect only the allocation of memory between the reservation and the limit.) In other words, if two VMs want more memory than their reservation limit and the ESXi host can't satisfy both of them using RAM, then you can set share values on each VM so that one gets higher-priority access to the RAM in the ESXi host than the other.

Some would say that you should just increase the reservation for that VM. Although that might be a valid technique, it might limit the total number of VMs that a host can run, as indicated previously in this chapter. Increasing the configured amount of RAM also requires a reboot of the VM to become effective (unless you are running a guest OS that supports hot-add of memory and that feature has been enabled for the VM, as described in Chapter 9), but shares can be dynamically adjusted while the VM remains powered on.

One key part I must repeat is that shares come into play only when the ESXi host cannot satisfy the requests for memory. If the ESXi host has enough free memory to satisfy the requests from the VMs for memory, then it doesn't need to prioritize those requests. It has enough to go around. It's only when the ESXi host doesn't have enough to go around that decisions have to be made on how that resource should be allocated.

For the sake of this discussion, let's assume you have two VMs (VM1 and VM2) each with a 1,024 MB reservation and a configured maximum of 4,096 MB, and both are running on an ESXi host with less than 2 GB of RAM available to the VMs. If the two VMs in question have an equal number of shares (let's assume it's 1,000 each; I'll show you actual values shortly), then as each VM requests memory above its reservation value, each VM will receive an equal quantity of RAM from the ESXi host. Furthermore, because the host cannot supply all of the RAM to both VMs, each VM will swap equally to disk (VMkernel swap file). This is assuming, of course, that ESXi cannot reclaim memory from other running VMs using the balloon driver or other memory-management technologies described previously. If you change VM1's Shares setting to 2,000, then VM1 now has twice the shares VM2 has assigned to it. This also means that when VM1 and VM2 are requesting the RAM above their respective Reservation values, VM1 gets two RAM pages for every one RAM page that VM2 gets. If VM1 has more shares, VM1 has a higher-priority access to available memory in the host. Because VM1 has 2,000 out of 3,000 shares allocated, it will get 67 percent; VM2 has 1,000 out of 3,000 shares allocated and therefore gets only 33 percent. This creates the two-to-one behavior I described previously. Each VM is allocated RAM pages based on the proportion of the total number of shares allocated across all VMs. Figure 11.6 illustrates this behavior.

FIGURE 11.6
Shares establish relative priority based on the number of shares assigned out of the total shares allocated.

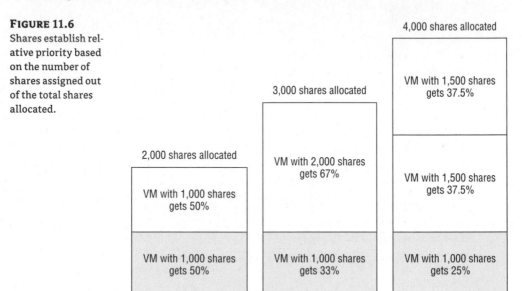

Even if you don't specifically assign shares to a VM, VMware vSphere automatically assigns shares to a VM when it is created. You can see the default shares value back in Figure 11.3; it is equal to 10 times the configured memory value. The VM shown in Figure 11.3 had 4,096 MB of RAM configured; therefore, its default memory shares value was 40960. This default allocation ensures that each VM is granted priority to memory on a measure that is directly proportional to the amount of memory configured for that VM.

It gets more difficult to predict the actual memory utilization and the amount of access each VM gets as more VMs run on the same ESXi host. Later in this chapter in the section titled "Using Resource Pools," I'll discuss more sophisticated methods of assigning memory limits, reservations, and shares to a group of VMs using resource pools.

I've talked about how VMware ESXi uses some advanced memory management technologies, but there is another aspect of virtualization that you must also consider: overhead. In the next section, I'll provide some information on the memory overhead figures when using ESXi.

EXAMINING MEMORY OVERHEAD

As they say, nothing in this world is free, and in the case of memory on an ESXi host, there is a cost. That cost is memory overhead. There are several basic processes on an ESXi host that will consume host memory. The VMkernel itself, various daemons (services) running on the ESXi host, and each VM that is running will cause the VMkernel to allocate some memory to host the VM above the initial amount that you assign to it. The amount of RAM allocated to host each VM depends on the configuration of each VM, as shown in Table 11.1. The values have been rounded to the nearest whole number.

TABLE 11.1: Virtual machine memory overhead

MEMORY ASSIGNED (MB)	1 vCPU	2 vCPUs	3 vCPUs	4 vCPUs	5 vCPUs	6 vCPUs	7 vCPUs	8 vCPUs
256	113	159	201	242	293	334	375	417
512	117	165	206	247	303	344	385	426
1,024	124	176	217	258	322	363	404	446
2,048	138	198	239	281	360	402	443	484
4,096	166	242	284	325	437	479	520	562
8,192	222	331	373	414	591	633	675	716
16384	335	508	550	592	900	943	986	1,028
32768	560	863	906	949	1,516	1,559	1,603	1,647
65536	1,011	1,572	1,616	1,660	2,746	2,792	2,838	2,884
131072	1,912	2,990	3,036	3,083	5,220	5,273	5,326	5,379
262144	3,714	5,830	5,885	5,938	10143	10205	10267	10329

Source: "vSphere Resource Management Guide" from VMware's website at www.vmware.com

As you go about planning the allocation of memory to your VMs, be sure to keep these memory overhead figures in mind. You will want to include these overhead values in your calculations of how memory will be assigned and used, especially if you plan on using VMs with large amounts of memory and a large number of virtual CPUs. As you can see in Table 11.1, the memory overhead in those situations is fairly substantial.

SUMMARIZING HOW RESERVATIONS, LIMITS, AND SHARES WORK WITH MEMORY

Because the specific behavior of reservations, shares, and limits is slightly different for each resource, here's a quick review of their behavior when used for controlling memory allocation:

◆ Reservations guarantee memory for a particular VM. Memory isn't allocated until requested by the VM, but the host must have enough free memory to satisfy the entire reservation before the VM can be powered on. Therefore — and this makes sense if you think about it — you cannot reserve more memory than the host physically has installed. Once allocated to a VM, reserved memory is not shared, swapped, or reclaimed by the ESXi host. It is locked to that VM.

◆ Limits enforce an upper ceiling on the usage of memory. Limits are enforced using the balloon driver (if VMware Tools are installed) and — depending on the VM's working set size — could have a dramatic negative impact on performance. As the VM approaches the limit (a limit of which the guest OS is not aware), the balloon driver will inflate to keep VM memory usage under the limit. This will cause the guest OS to swap out to disk, which will typically degrade performance noticeably.

◆ Shares apply only during periods of host RAM contention and serve to establish prioritized access to host RAM. VMs are granted priority based on percentage of shares allocated versus total shares granted. During periods when the host is not experiencing memory contention, shares do not apply and will not affect memory allocation or usage.

I'll provide a similar summary of the behavior of reservations, limits, and shares when used to control CPU usage, which is the topic of the next section.

Managing Virtual Machine CPU Utilization

When you create a new VM using the vSphere Client, the only two questions you are asked related to the CPU are "Number of virtual processors?" and "Number of cores per virtual CPU?" This CPU setting effectively lets the guest OS in the VM utilize between 1 and 32 virtual CPUs on the host system, depending upon the guest OS and the vSphere license.

When the VMware engineers designed the virtualization platform, they started with a real system board and modeled the VM after it — in this case it was based on the Intel 440BX chipset. The PCI bus was something the VM could emulate and could be mapped to input/output devices through a standard interface, but how could a VM emulate a CPU? The answer was "no emulation." Think about a virtual system board that has a "hole" where the CPU socket goes — and the guest OS simply looks through the hole and sees one of the cores in the host server. This allowed the VMware engineers to avoid writing CPU emulation software that would need to change each time the CPU vendors introduced new instruction sets. If there was an emulation layer, it would also add a significant quantity of overhead, which would limit the performance of the virtualization platform by adding more computational overhead.

So, how many CPUs should a VM have? Creating a VM to replace a physical DHCP server that runs at less than 10 percent CPU utilization at its busiest point in the day surely does not need more than one virtual CPU. As a matter of fact, if you give this VM two virtual CPUs (vCPUs), then you might limit the scalability of the entire host. Here's why.

The VMkernel simultaneously schedules CPU cycles for multi-vCPU VMs. This means that when a dual-vCPU VM places a request for CPU cycles, the request goes into a queue for the host to process, and the host has to wait until there are at least two cores or hyperthreads (if hyperthreading is enabled) with concurrent idle cycles to schedule that VM. A *relaxed co-scheduling* algorithm provides a bit of flexibility in allowing the cores to be scheduled on a slightly skewed basis, but even so, it can be more difficult for the hypervisor to find open time slots on at least two cores. This occurs even if the VM needs only a few clock cycles to do some menial task that could be done with a single processor. Here's an example: have you ever been stuck behind a truck with a wide load that takes up more than one lane? This one vehicle is occupying two different lanes at the same time. Normally traffic would be able to flow around this slow-moving vehicle, but now traffic is held up because both lanes are occupied.

On the other hand, if a VM needs two vCPUs because of the load it will be processing on a constant basis, then it makes sense to assign two vCPUs to that VM — but only if the host has four or more CPU cores total. If your ESX host is an older-generation dual-processor single-core system, then assigning a VM two vCPUs will mean that the VM owns all of the CPU processing power on that host every time it gets CPU cycles. You will find that the overall performance of the host and any other VMs will be less than stellar. Of course, in today's market of multicore CPUs, this particular consideration is less significant than it was in previous hardware generations, but it is something to keep in mind.

ONE (CPU) FOR ALL — AT LEAST TO BEGIN WITH

Every VM should be created with only a single virtual CPU so as not to create unnecessary contention for physical processor time. Only when a VM's performance level dictates the need for an additional CPU should one be allocated. Remember that multi-CPU VMs should be created only on ESXi hosts that have more cores than the number of virtual CPUs being assigned to the VM. A dual-vCPU VM should be created only on a host with two or more cores, a quad-vCPU VM should be created only on a host with four or more cores, and an eight-vCPU VM should be created only on a host with eight or more cores.

Default CPU Allocation

Like the memory settings I discussed previously, the Shares, Reservation, and Limit settings can be configured for CPU capacity as well.

When a new VM is created with a single vCPU, the total maximum CPU cycles for that VM equals the clock speed of the host system's core. In other words, if you create a new VM, it can see through the "hole in the system board," and it sees whatever the core is in terms of clock cycles per second — an ESXi host with 3 GHz CPUs in it will allow the VM to see one 3 GHz core.

Figure 11.7 shows the default settings for CPU Reservation, Limits, and Shares.

FIGURE 11.7
By default, vSphere provides no CPU reservation, no CPU limit, and 1000 CPU shares.

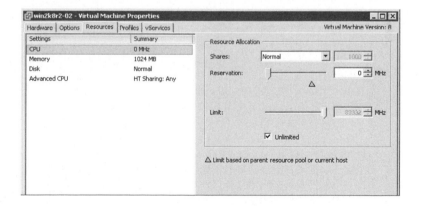

Setting CPU Affinity

In addition to shares, reservations, and limits, vSphere offers a fourth option for managing CPU usage: CPU affinity. CPU affinity allows an administrator to statically associate a VM to a specific physical CPU core. CPU affinity is generally not recommended; it has a list of rather significant drawbacks:

◆ CPU affinity breaks vMotion.

◆ The hypervisor is unable to load-balance the VM across all the processing cores in the server. This prevents the hypervisor's scheduling engine from making the most efficient use of the host's resources.

◆ Because vMotion is broken, you cannot use CPU affinities in a cluster where vSphere DRS isn't set to Manual operation.

Because of these limitations, most organizations don't use CPU affinity. However, if you find that you need to use CPU affinity in spite of these limitations, you can configure your VM to use CPU affinity.

Perform these steps to configure CPU affinity:

1. If it is not already running, launch the vSphere Client and connect to a vCenter Server instance or a stand-alone ESXi host.

2. Navigate to either the Hosts And Clusters or VMs And Templates inventory view.

3. Right-click the VM for which you'd like to configure CPU affinity and select Edit Settings.

4. Click the Resources tab.

5. Select Advanced CPU.

6. In the Scheduling Affinity section, supply a list of the CPU cores this VM is allowed to access.

   For example, if you wanted the VM to run on cores 1 through 4, you could type 1–4.

7. Click OK to save the changes.

Rather than trying to use CPU affinity to guarantee CPU resources, you're far better off using reservations.

Using CPU Reservations

As you saw in Figure 11.7, the default CPU reservation for a new VM is 0 MHz (no reservation). Recall that a reservation is a resource guarantee. Therefore, by default, a VM is not guaranteed any CPU activity by the VMkernel. This means that when the VM has work to be done, it places its CPU request into the CPU queue so that the VMkernel can handle the request in sequence along with all of the other VMs' requests. On a lightly loaded ESXi host, it's unlikely the VM will wait long for CPU time; however, on a heavily loaded host, the time this VM might have to wait could be significant.

If you were to set a 1,024 MHz reservation, as shown in Figure 11.8, this would effectively make that amount of CPU available instantly to this VM if there is a need for CPU cycles.

Using a CPU reservation has one notable impact on the behavior of the ESXi host, and in this regard CPU reservations and memory reservations behave identically. The ESXi *must be able* to satisfy the reservation by providing enough resources to meet the reservations. If each VM you create has a 1,024 MHz reservation and your host has 12000 MHz of CPU capacity, you can power on no more than 11 VMs (1,024 MHz × 11 = 11264 MHz), even if all of them are idle. Note that I said "power on" and not "create" — resources are allocated only when a VM is powered on, not created.

FIGURE 11.8

A VM configured with a 1,024 MHz reservation for CPU activity is guaranteed that amount of CPU capacity.

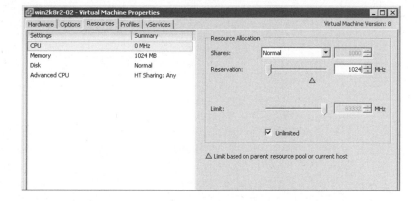

While a CPU reservation behaves like a memory reservation in this regard, a CPU reservation is very different than a memory reservation when it comes to "sharing" reserved CPU cycles. Recall from the previous section that reserved memory, once allocated to the VM, is never reclaimed, paged out to disk, or shared in any way. The same is not true of CPU reservations. Suppose you have a VM, creatively named VM1, that has a CPU reservation of 1,024 MHz. If VM1 is idle and not using its reserved CPU cycles, those cycles can be given to VM2. If VM1 suddenly needs cycles, VM2 doesn't get them anymore, and they are assigned to VM1.

So using a Reservation setting on CPU shares some similarity to using a Reservation setting with memory, but it is also very different. You saw previously that using a Limit setting with memory had some significant drawbacks; what about CPU limits?

Using CPU Limits

In addition to a CPU reservation, every VM also has an option that you can set to place a limit on the amount of CPU allocated. This effectively limits the VM's ability to see a maximum number of clock cycles per second, regardless of what the host has available. Keep in mind that VM with one single-core virtual CPU hosted on a 3 GHz, quad-processor ESXi host will see only a single 3 GHz core as its maximum, but as administrator you could alter the limit to hide the actual maximum core speed from the VM. For instance, you could set a 500 MHz limit on that DHCP server so that when it re-indexes the DHCP database, it won't try to take all of the 3 GHz on the processor that it can see. The CPU limit provides you with the ability to throttle the VM with less processing power than is available on a core on the physical host. Not every VM needs to have access to the entire processing capability of the physical processor core.

The key drawback to using a CPU Limit setting is the performance impact it will have on the guest OS and the applications running in that VM. The Limit setting is a true limit; the VM won't be scheduled to run on a physical CPU core more than the limit specifies, even if there are plenty of CPU cycles available. It's important, therefore, to understand the CPU processing needs of your VMs before arbitrarily setting CPU limits, or you could find yourself significantly impacting performance.

INCREASING CONTENTION IN THE FACE OF GROWTH

One of the most common problems administrators can encounter occurs when several VMs without limits are deployed on a new virtualized environment. The users get accustomed to stellar performance levels early in the environment life cycle, but as more VMs are deployed and start to compete for CPU cycles, the relative performance of the first VMs deployed will degrade.

One approach to this issue is to set a reservation of approximately 10 to 20 percent of a single core's clock rate and add approximately 20 percent to that value for a limit on the VM. For example, with 3 GHz CPUs in the host, each VM would start with a 300 MHz reservation and a 350 MHz limit. This would ensure that the VM performs similarly on both a lightly loaded ESXi host and on a more heavily loaded ESXi host. Consider setting these values on the VM that you use to create a template because these values will pass to any new VMs that were deployed from that template. Note that this is only a starting point. It is possible to limit a VM that really does need more CPU capabilities, and you should always actively monitor the VMs to determine whether they are using all of the CPU you are providing them.

If the numbers seem low, feel free to increase them as needed. The important concept is setting appropriate expectations for VM performance based on your knowledge of the workloads running in those VMs and the anticipated levels of performance.

Using CPU Shares

VMware vSphere's shares model, which provides a way to prioritize access to resources when resource content occurs, behaves similarly for both memory and CPU. The shares for CPU will determine how much CPU is provided to a VM in the face of contention with other VMs needing CPU activity. All VMs, by default, start with an equal number of shares, which means that if there is competition for CPU cycles on an ESXi host, each VM gets serviced with equal priority. Keep in mind that this share value affects only those CPU cycles that are greater than the reservation set for the VM, and the share value applies only when the ESXi host has more requests for CPU cycles than it has CPU cycles to allocate. In other words, the VM is granted access to its reservation cycles regardless of what else is happening on the host, but if the VM needs more — and there's competition — then the share values come into play. If there is no CPU contention on the host and it has enough CPU cycles to go around, the CPU shares value won't affect CPU allocation.

Several conditions have to be met for shares to even be considered for allocating CPU cycles. The best way to determine this is to consider several scenarios. For the scenarios I'll cover, assume the following details about the environment:

♦ The ESXi host includes dual, single-core, 3 GHz CPUs.

♦ The ESXi host has one or more VMs.

Scenario 1 The ESX host has a single VM running. The shares are set at the defaults for the running VMs. Will the Shares value have any effect in this scenario? No. There's no competition between VMs for CPU time.

Scenario 2 The ESX host has two idle VMs running. The shares are set at the defaults for the running VMs. Will the Shares values have any effect in this scenario? No. There's no competition between VMs for CPU time because both are idle.

Scenario 3 The ESX host has two equally busy VMs running (both requesting maximum CPU capacity). The shares are set at the defaults for the running VMs. Will the Shares values have any effect in this scenario? No. Again, there's no competition between VMs for CPU time, this time because each VM is serviced by a different core in the host.

CPU AFFINITY NOT AVAILABLE WITH CLUSTERS

If you are using a VSphere Distributed Resource Scheduler–enabled cluster configured in fully automated mode, CPU affinity cannot be set for VMs in that cluster. You must configure the cluster for manual or partially automated mode in order to use CPU affinity.

Scenario 4 To force contention, both VMs are configured to use the same CPU by setting the CPU affinity. The ESXi host has two equally busy VMs running (both requesting maximum CPU capacity). This ensures contention between the VMs. The shares are set at the defaults for the running VMs. Will the Shares values have any effect in this scenario? Yes! But in this case, because all VMs have equal Shares values, each VM has equal access to the host's CPU queue, so you don't see any effects from the Shares values.

Scenario 5 The ESXi host has two equally busy VMs running (both requesting maximum CPU capacity with CPU affinity set to the same core). The shares are set as follows: VM1 is set to 2,000 CPU shares, and VM2 is set to the default 1,000 CPU shares. Will the Shares values have any effect in this scenario? Yes. In this case, VM1 has double the number of shares that VM2 has. This means that for every clock cycle that VM2 is assigned by the host, VM1 is assigned two clock cycles. Stated another way, out of every three clock cycles assigned to VMs by the ESXi host, two are assigned to VM1, and one is assigned to VM2. The diagram in Figure 11.6 helps graphically reinforce how shares are allocated based on percentage of the total number of shares assigned to all VMs.

Scenario 6 The ESXi host has three equally busy VMs running (each requesting maximum CPU capabilities with CPU affinity set to the same core). The shares are set as follows: VM1 is set to 2,000 CPU shares, and VM2 and VM3 are set to the default 1,000 CPU shares. Will the Shares values have any effect in this scenario? Yes. In this case, VM1 has double the number of shares that VM2 and VM3 have assigned. This means that for every two clock cycles that VM1 is assigned by the host, VM2 and VM3 are each assigned a single clock cycle. Stated another way, out of every four clock cycles assigned to VMs by the ESXi host, two cycles are assigned to VM1, one is assigned to VM2, and one is assigned to VM3. You can see that this has effectively watered down VM1's CPU capabilities.

Scenario 7 The ESXi host has three VMs running. VM1 is idle while VM2 and VM3 are equally busy (each requesting maximum CPU capabilities, and all three VMs are set with the same CPU affinity). The shares are set as follows: VM1 is set to 2,000 CPU shares, and VM2 and VM3 are set to the default 1,000 CPU shares. Will the Shares values have any effect in this scenario? Yes. But in this case VM1 is idle, which means it isn't requesting any CPU cycles. This means that VM1's Shares value is not considered when apportioning the host CPU to the active VMs. In this case, VM2 and VM3 would equally share the host CPU cycles because their shares are set to an equal value.

> **AVOID CPU AFFINITY SETTINGS**
>
> You should avoid the CPU affinity setting at all costs. Even if a VM is configured to use a single CPU (for example, CPU1), it does not guarantee that it will be the only VM accessing that CPU, unless every other VM is configured not to use that CPU. At this point, vMotion capability will be unavailable for every VM. In short, don't do it. It's not worth losing vMotion. Use shares, limits, and reservations as an alternative.

Given these scenarios, if you were to extrapolate to an eight-core host with 30 or so VMs, it would be difficult to set Shares values on a VM-by-VM basis and to predict how the system will respond. The question then becomes, "Are shares a useful tool?" The answer is yes, but in large enterprise environments, you need to examine resource pools and the ability to set share parameters along with reservations and limits on collections of VMs. I'll introduce resource pools in the section "Using Resource Pools." First, though, I'll summarize the behavior of reservations, limits, and shares when used to control CPU allocation and usage.

Summarizing How Reservations, Limits, and Shares Work with CPUs

Some key behaviors and facts around the use of reservations, limits, and shares, when applied to controlling or modifying CPU usage, are as follows:

◆ Reservations set on CPU cycles provide guaranteed processing power for VMs. Unlike memory, reserved CPU cycles can and will be used by ESXi to service other requests when needed. As with memory, the ESXi host must have enough real, physical CPU capacity to satisfy a reservation in order to power on a VM. Therefore, you cannot reserve more CPU cycles than the host is actually capable of delivering.

◆ Limits on CPU usage simply prevent a VM from gaining access to additional CPU cycles even if CPU cycles are available to use. Even if the host has plenty of CPU processing power available to use, a VM with a CPU limit will not be permitted to use more CPU cycles than specified in the limit. Depending on the guest OS and the applications, this might or might not have an adverse effect on performance.

◆ Shares are used to determine CPU allocation when the ESXi host is experiencing CPU contention. Like memory, shares grant CPU access on a percentage basis calculated on the number of shares granted out of the total number of shares assigned. This means that the percentage of CPU cycles granted to a VM based on its Shares value is always relative to the number of other VMs and the total number of shares granted, and it is not an absolute value.

As you can see, there are some key differences as well as a number of similarities between how these mechanisms work for memory when compared to how they work for CPU.

So far I've discussed two of the four major resource types (memory and CPU). Before I can move on to the third resource type — networking — I need to discuss the concept of resource pools.

Using Resource Pools

The previously discussed settings for VM resource allocation (memory and CPU reservations, limits, and shares) are methods used to modify or control the allocation of resources to individual VMs or to modify the priority of a VM compared to other individual VMs also seeking access to resources. In much the same way as you assign users to groups and then assign permissions to the groups, you can leverage resource pools to make the allocation of resources to collections of VMs a less tedious and more effective process. In other words, instead of configuring reservations, limits, or shares on a per-VM basis, you can use a resource pool to set those values on a group of VMs all at once.

A *resource pool* is a special type of container object, much like a folder, in the Hosts And Clusters inventory view. You can create a resource pool on a stand-alone host or as a management object in a DRS-enabled cluster. Figure 11.9 shows the creation of a resource pool.

FIGURE 11.9
You can create resource pools on individual hosts and within clusters. A resource pool provides a management and performance configuration layer in the vCenter Server inventory.

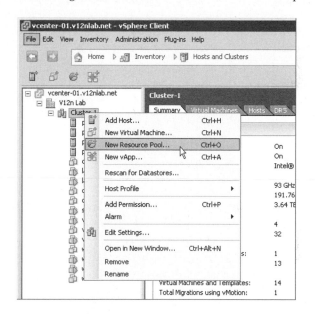

If you examine the properties of the resource pool, you'll see two sections: one for CPU settings (Reservation, Limit, and Shares) and another section with similar settings for memory. When you apply resource settings to a resource pool, those settings affect all the VMs found within that resource pool. This provides a scalable way to adjust the resource settings for groups of VMs. Setting CPU and memory shares, reservations, and limits on a resource pool is very much like setting these values on individual VMs. The behavior of these values, however, can be quite different on a resource pool than on an individual VM.

To illustrate how to set shares, reservations, and limits on a resource pool, as well as to explain how these values work when applied to a resource pool, I'll use an example of an ESXi host with two resource pools. The resource pools are named ProductionVMs and DevelopmentVMs. Figure 11.10 and Figure 11.11 show the values that have been configured for the ProductionVMs and DevelopmentVMs resource pools, respectively.

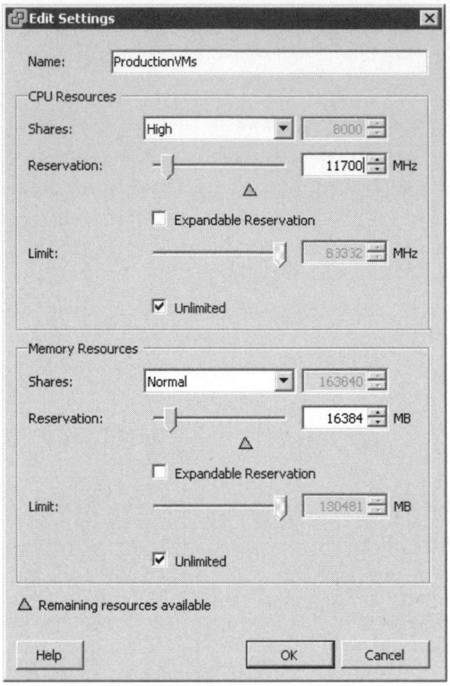

FIGURE 11.10
The ProductionVMs resource pool is guaranteed CPU and memory resources and higher-priority access to resources in the face of contention.

FIGURE 11.11
The Development VMs resource pool is configured for lower-priority access to CPU and memory in the event of resource contention.

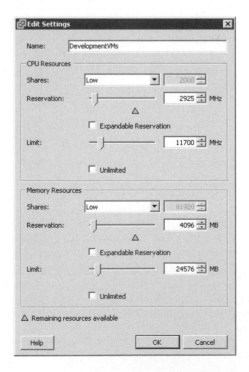

In the next two sections, refer to Figure 11.10 and Figure 11.11 as I explain how to configure resource pools and how resource pools handle resource allocation.

Configuring Resource Pools

Before I can show you how resource pools behave with regard to resource allocation, you must first create and configure the resource pools. Use the resource pools shown in Figure 11.10 and Figure 11.11 as examples for creating and configuring resource pools.

To create a resource pool, simply right-click either an individual ESXi host or a cluster of ESXi hosts, and select New Resource Pool. In the Create Resource Pool dialog box, you'll need to supply a name for the new resource pool and set the CPU Resources and Memory Resources values as desired.

After you create the resource pool, you must move the VMs into the appropriate resource pool by clicking the VM in the inventory panel and dragging it onto the appropriate resource pool. The result is a hierarchy similar to that shown in Figure 11.12.

FIGURE 11.12
VMs assigned to a resource pool consume resources allocated to the resource pool.

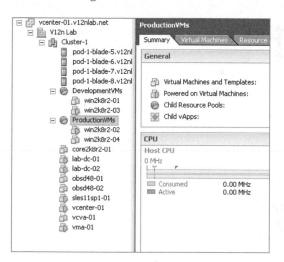

In this particular example, you have two classifications of servers: production and development. You've created a resource pool for each classification: ProductionVMs for the virtual servers classified as production and DevelopmentVMs for those virtual servers classified as development. The goal in this example is to ensure that if there's competition for a particular resource, the VMs in production should be assigned higher-priority access to that resource. In addition to that goal, you need to ensure that the VMs in development cannot consume more than 24 GB of physical memory with their running VMs. You don't care how many VMs run concurrently as part of the development group as long as they don't collectively consume more than 24 GB of RAM. Finally, you need to ensure that a minimum amount of resources are guaranteed for both groups of VMs.

To achieve your goal of guaranteeing resources for the production VMs, you will set the ProductionVMs resource pool to use the following settings (refer to Figure 11.10):

♦ CPU Resources area: Shares value of High.

♦ CPU Resources area: Reservation value of 11700 MHz.

◆ CPU Resources area: Expandable Reservation check box for CPU Reservation is deselected.

◆ CPU Resources area: no CPU limit (Unlimited check box is selected).

◆ Memory Resources area: Reservation of 16384 MB.

◆ Memory Resources area: Expandable Reservation check box under Reservation is deselected.

◆ Memory Resources area: No memory limit (Unlimited check box is selected).

Similarly, you will apply the following settings to the DevelopmentVMs resource pool (see Figure 11.11):

◆ CPU Resources area: Reservation value of 2,925 MHz.

◆ CPU Resources area: Expandable Reservation check box for Reservation is deselected.

◆ CPU Resources area: Limit value of 11700 MHz.

◆ Memory Resources area: Reservation value of 4,096 MB.

◆ Memory Resources area: Expandable Reservation check box under Reservation is deselected.

◆ Memory Resources area: Limit value of 24576 MB.

Again, setting the values on the DevelopmentVMs resource pool involves right-clicking the resource pool, selecting Edit Settings, and then setting the values you need.

Now that you have an example to work with, I'll explain what these settings will do to the VMs contained in each of the resource pools.

Understanding Resource Allocation with Resource Pools

In the previous section I walked you through creating a couple of resource pools called ProductionVMs and DevelopmentVMs. The values for these resource pools are illustrated in Figure 11.10 and Figure 11.11. The goal behind creating these resource pools and setting the values on them was to ensure that a certain level of resources would always be available to production VMs (those found in the ProductionVMs resource pool) and to limit the resources used by the development VMs (VMs found in the DevelopmentVMs resource pool). In this example, you used all three values — Shares, Reservation, and Limit — in an effort to accomplish your goal. Let's look at the behavior of each of these values when used on a resource pool.

MANAGING CPU USAGE WITH RESOURCE POOLS

First I'll examine the Shares value assigned to the resource pools for CPU usage. As you can see in Figure 11.10, the ProductionVMs resource pool's CPU shares are set to High (8,000). Figure 11.11 shows the DevelopmentVMs CPU shares set to Low (2,000). The effect of these two settings is similar to that of comparing two VMs' Shares values for CPU — except in this case, if there is any competition for CPU resources between VMs in the ProductionVMs and DevelopmentVMs resource pools, the entire ProductionVMs resource pool and all the VMs in it would have higher priority. Figure 11.13 shows how this would break down with two VMs in each resource pool.

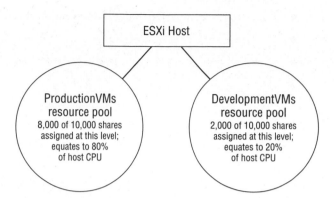

As you consider the information presented in Figure 11.13, keep in mind that the resource allocation occurs at each level. There are only two resource pools under the given ESXi host, so the CPU is allocated 80/20 according to its Shares value. This means that the ProductionVMs resource pool gets 80 percent of the CPU time while the DevelopmentVMs resource pool gets only 20 percent of the CPU time.

Now let's expand on Figure 11.13 and add the two VMs in each resource pool to get a more complete view of how Shares values would work with a resource pool. Within the resource pool the CPU Shares values assigned to the VMs, if any at all, come into play. Figure 11.14 shows how this works.

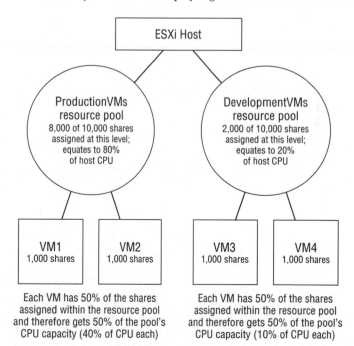

In Figure 11.14, there are no custom CPU shares assigned to the VMs, so they all use the default value of 1,000 CPU shares. With two VMs in the resource pool, this means each VM gets

50 percent of the resource available to the resource pool in which it is located (because each VM has 50 percent of the total number of shares assigned within the pool). In this example, this means 40 percent of the host CPU capacity will go to each of the two VMs in the ProductionVMs resource pool. If there were three VMs in each resource pool, then the CPU allocated to the parent resource pool would be split three ways. Similarly, if there were four VMs, then the CPU allocated to the parent resource pool would be split four ways. You can verify this breakdown of resource allocation using the Resource Allocation tab on the selected cluster, ESXi host, or resource pool. Figure 11.15 shows the Resource Allocation tab for a cluster with the ProductionVMs and DevelopmentVMs resource pools. The CPU button is selected, meaning that the vSphere Client is showing you the breakdown of CPU allocation for the selected cluster.

FIGURE 11.15

The Resource Allocation tab can verify the allocation of resources to objects within the vCenter Server hierarchy.

Name	Reservation - MHz	Limit - MHz	Shares	Shares Value	% Shares
lab-dc-02	0	Unlimited	Normal	1000	4
vma-01	0	Unlimited	Normal	1000	4
sles11sp1-01	0	Unlimited	Normal	1000	4
obsd48-01	0	Unlimited	Normal	1000	4
obsd48-02	0	Unlimited	Normal	1000	4
core2k8r2-01	0	Unlimited	Normal	1000	4
vcva-01	0	Unlimited	Normal	2000	9
vcenter-01	0	Unlimited	Normal	2000	9
lab-dc-01	0	Unlimited	Normal	1000	4
DevelopmentVMs	2925	11700	Low	2000	9
ProductionVMs	11700	Unlimited	High	8000	38

CPU — Total Capacity: 83332 MHz, Reserved Capacity: 31041 MHz, Available Capacity: 52291 MHz.
Memory — Total Capacity: 180481 MB, Reserved Capacity: 66012 MB, Available Capacity: 114469 MB.

Note that in the screenshot in Figure 11.15, there are both resource pools and VMs directly in the root of the cluster (which, for all intents and purposes, is a resource pool itself). In this case, the sum of all the Shares values — for both resource pools as well as VMs — is used to calculate the percentage of CPU allocated.

SHARES APPLY ONLY DURING ACTUAL RESOURCE CONTENTION

Remember that share allocations come into play only when VMs are fighting one another for a resource — in other words, when an ESXi host is actually unable to satisfy all the requests for a particular resource. If an ESXi host is running only eight VMs on top of two quad-core processors, there won't be contention to manage (assuming these VMs have only a single vCPU) and Shares values won't apply. Be sure to keep this in mind when reviewing the results of Shares allocations like those displayed in Figure 11.14.

Now that I've introduced you to the Resource Allocation tab, I need to discuss an important consideration about the use of resource pools. It's possible to use resource pools as a form of organization, like a folder. Some organizations and administrators have taken to using resource pools in this way to help keep VMs organized in a specific fashion. While this is possible, it's not recommended. The Resource Allocation tab helps show why.

Look at Figure 11.16, which shows the Resource Allocation tab for a cluster of ESXi hosts. In the root of this cluster are 12 VMs assigned a total of 14,000 shares. Because each of these VMs is using the default CPU Shares Value (1,000 shares per vCPU), they each get equal access to the host CPU capacity — in this case, 7 percent per vCPU (the VMs with 2,000 shares and 14% Shares have two vCPUs).

FIGURE 11.16
In the absence of custom CPU shares, CPU capacity is equally allocated to all VMs.

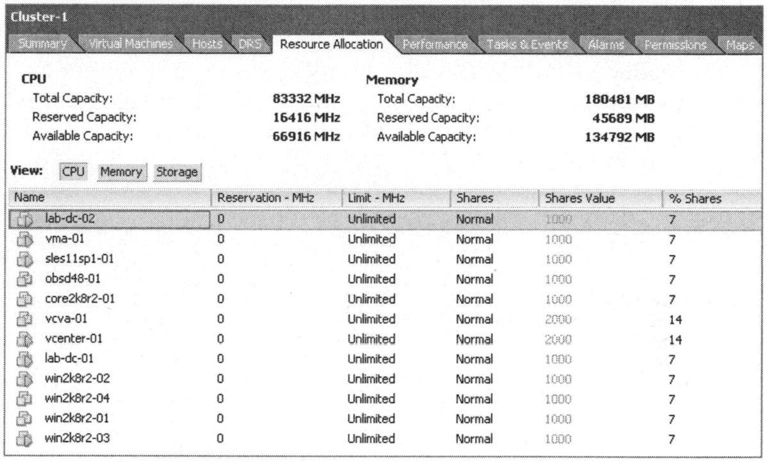

Now look at Figure 11.17. The only change here is that I've added a resource pool. I did not change any of the default values for the resource pool. Note that the resource pool has a default CPU Shares Value of 4,000, and note how the simple addition of this resource pool changes the default CPU allocation for the individual VMs from 7 percent per vCPU to only 5 percent per vCPU. The resource pool, on the other hand, now gets 22 percent. If you added a single VM to the resource pool, that one VM would get 22 percent of the host CPU capacity while other VMs only received 5 percent (or 11 percent for VMs with two vCPUs).

FIGURE 11.17
The addition of a resource pool will, by default, alter the resource allocation policy even if you don't set any custom values.

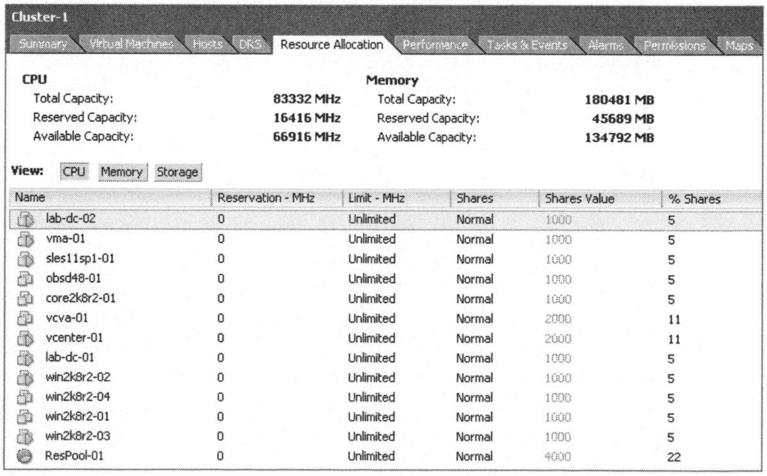

This unintended change on the resource allocation distribution is why I don't recommend using resource pools strictly for the purposes of organizing VMs. If you do insist on using resource pools in this way, be sure to understand the impact of configuring your environment in this manner.

The next setting in the resource pool properties to evaluate is CPU Reservation for the CPU. Continuing with the examples shown in Figure 11.10 and Figure 11.11, you can see a CPU Reservation value of 11700 MHz has been set on the ProductionVMs resource pool. The DevelopmentVMs pool has a CPU Reservation value of 2,925 MHz. (The ESXi hosts in the cluster hosting these resource pools have quad-core 2.93 GHz Intel Xeon CPUs, so this essentially reserves four cores on one server for the ProductionVMs resource pool and one core on one server for the DevelopmentVMs resource pool.) This setting ensures that at least 11700 MHz of CPU time is available for all the VMs located in the ProductionVMs resource pool (or 2,925 MHz of CPU for VMs in the DevelopmentVMs resource pool). Assuming that the ESXi host has a total of 23400 MHz CPU (8 × 2,925 MHz = 23400 MHz), this means 8,775 MHz of CPU time is available on that host for other reservations. If one more resource pool was created with a Reservation value of 8,775 MHz, then the cumulative reservations on the system have reserved all available host CPU capacity (5,850 MHz × 4 = 23400 MHz). This configuration means the administrator will not be able to create any additional resource pools or any individual VMs with Reservation values set. Remember that the ESXi host or cluster has to have enough resource capacity — CPU capacity, in this case — to satisfy all reservations. You can't reserve more capacity than the host actually has.

Part of the CPU Reservation setting is the option to make the reservation expandable. An expandable reservation (noted as such by selecting the Expandable Reservation check box) allows a resource pool to "borrow" resources from its parent host or parent resource pool in order to satisfy reservations set on individual VMs within the resource pool. Note that a resource pool with an expandable reservation would only "borrow" from the parent in order to satisfy reservations, not in order to satisfy requests for resources in excess of the reservations. Neither of the resource pools has expandable reservations, so you will be able to assign only 5,850 MHz of CPU capacity as reservations to individual VMs within each resource pool. Any attempt to reserve more than that amount will result in an error message explaining that you've exceeded the allowed limit.

Deselecting the Expandable Reservation check box does not limit the total amount of CPU capacity available to the resource pool; it limits only the total amount of CPU capacity that can be *reserved* within the resource pool. To set an upper limit on actual CPU usage, you'll need to use a CPU Limit setting.

CPU Limit is the third setting on each resource pool. The behavior of the CPU limit on a resource pool is similar to its behavior on individual VMs, except in this case the limit applies to all VMs in the resource pool. All VMs combined are allowed to consume up to this value. In the example, the ProductionVMs resource pool does not have a CPU limit assigned. In this case, the VMs in the ProductionVMs resource pool are allowed to consume as many CPU cycles as the ESXi hosts in the cluster are able to provide. The DevelopmentVMs resource pool, on the other hand, has a CPU Limit setting of 11700 MHz, meaning that all the VMs in the DevelopmentVMs resource pool are allowed to consume a maximum of 11700 MHz of CPU capacity. With 2.93 GHz Intel Xeon CPUs, this is the approximate equivalent of one quad-core CPU.

For the most part, CPU shares, reservations, and limits behave similarly on resource pools to the way they do on individual VMs. The same is also true for memory shares, reservations, and limits, as you'll see in the next section.

MANAGING MEMORY USAGE WITH RESOURCE POOLS

In the memory portion of the resource pool settings, the first setting is the Shares value. This setting works in much the same way as memory shares worked on individual VMs. It determines which group of VMs will be the first to give up memory via the balloon driver — or if memory pressure is severe enough, activate memory compression or swap out to disk via hypervisor swapping — in the face of contention. However, this setting is used to set a priority value for all VMs in the resource pool when competing for resources with VMs in other resource pools. Looking at the memory share settings in our example (ProductionVMs = Normal and DevelopmentVMs = Low), this means that if host memory is limited, VMs in the DevelopmentVMs resource pool that need more memory than their reservation would have a lower priority than an equivalent VM in the ProductionVMs resource pool. Figure 11.14, which I used previously to help explain CPU shares on resource pool, applies here as well. As with CPU shares, you can also use the Resource Allocation tab to explore how memory resources are being assigned to resource pools or VMs within resource pools.

The second setting is the resource pool's memory Reservation. The memory Reservation value will reserve this amount of host RAM for VMs in this resource pool, which effectively ensures that there is some actual RAM that is guaranteed to the VMs in this resource pool. As I explained in the discussion on CPU reservations, the Expandable Reservation check box does not limit how much memory the resource pool can use but rather how much memory you can reserve within the resource pool.

The memory Limit value is how you would set a limit on how much host RAM a particular group of VMs can consume. If administrators have been given the Create Virtual Machines permission in the DevelopmentVMs resource pool, then the memory Limit value would prevent those administrators from running VMs that will consume more than that amount of actual host RAM. In our example, the memory Limit value on the DevelopmentVMs resource pool is set to 24576 MB. How many VMs can administrators in development create? They can create as many as they want.

Although this setting does nothing to limit creating VMs, it will place a limit on running VMs. So, how many can they run? The cap placed on memory use is not a per VM setting but a cumulative setting. They might be able to run only one VM with all the memory or multiple VMs with lower memory configurations. Assuming that each VM is created without an individual memory Reservation value, the administrator can run as many VMs concurrently as he or she wants! The problem will be that once the VMs consume 24576 MB of host RAM, the hypervisor is going to step in and prevent the VMs in the resource group from using any additional memory. Refer back to my discussion of memory limits in the section titled "Using Memory Limits" for the techniques that the VMkernel will use to enforce the memory limit. If the administrator builds six VMs with 4,096 MB as the initial memory amount, then all four VMs will consume 24576 MB (assuming no overhead, which I've already shown you isn't the case) and will run in real RAM. If an administrator tried to run 20 VMs configured for 2,048 MB of RAM, then all 20 VMs will share the 24576 MB of RAM, even though their requirement is for 40960 MB (20 × 2,048 MB) — the remaining amount of RAM would most likely be provided by VMkernel swap. At this point, performance would be noticeably slow.

If you want to clear a limit, select the Unlimited check box. This is true for both CPU limits as well as memory limits. By now you should have a pretty fair idea of how ESXi allocates resources to VMs, as well as how you can tweak those settings to meet your specific demands and workloads.

As you can see, if you have groups of VMs with similar resource demands, using resource pools is an excellent way of ensuring consistent resource allocation. As long as you understand the hierarchical nature of resource pools — that resources are allocated first to the pool at its level in the hierarchy, and then those resources are allocated to the VMs in the pool — then you should be able to use resource pools effectively.

So far you've seen how to control the use of CPU and memory, but those are only two of the four major resources consumed by VMs. In the next section, you'll see how to control network traffic through the use of network resource pools.

Regulating Network I/O Utilization

The resource pools I've shown you so far can only be used to control CPU and memory usage. However, vSphere offers another type of resource pool, a *network resource pool* that allows you to control network utilization. Using network resource pools — to which are assigned shares and limits — you can control outgoing network traffic. This feature is referred to as vSphere Network I/O Control (NetIOC).

OUTGOING TRAFFIC ONLY, AND ONLY ON A DISTRIBUTED SWITCH

vSphere Network I/O Control applies only to outgoing network traffic and is available only on a vSphere Distributed Switch (vDS) version 4.1.0 or later. Refer to Chapter 5 for more information on setting up or configuring a vDS.

When you enable vSphere NetIOC, vSphere activates six predefined network resource pools:

- Fault Tolerance (FT) Traffic
- iSCSI Traffic
- Management Traffic
- NFS Traffic
- Virtual Machine Traffic
- vMotion Traffic

For version 5.0.0 vSphere Distributed Switches, a seventh predefined network resource pool is also available: Host Based Replication (HBR) Traffic.

All of these network resource pools are visible on the Resource Allocation tab of the vDS, as you can see in Figure 11.18.

Two steps are involved in setting up and using NetIOC. First, you must enable NetIOC on that particular vDS. Second, you must create and configure network resource pools as necessary.

Perform the following steps to enable NetIOC on a vDS:

1. If it is not already running, launch the vSphere Client and connect to a vCenter Server instance. Because NetIOC relies on vDS and vDS is only available with vCenter, NetIOC cannot be used when connected directly to an ESXi host.

2. Navigate to the Networking Inventory view using the View menu, the navigation bar, or the home screen.

3. Select the vDS for which you want to enable NetIOC.

4. Click the Resource Allocation tab for that vDS.

5. Click Properties.

6. In the Resource Allocation Properties dialog box, check Enable Network I/O Control On This vSphere Distributed Switch, and then click OK.

dvSwitch-02
Summary
Networks
Ports
Resource Allocation
Configuration
Virtual Machines
Hosts
Tasks & Events
Alarms
Permissions
Summary
Total number of physical adapters: --
Total network bandwidth capacity: --
Network I/O Control: Disabled
New Network Resource Pool...
Manage Port Groups...
Properties...
Network resource pool
Host limit - Mbps
Physical adapter shares
Shares value
QoS priority tag
System network resource pools
Fault Tolerance (FT) Traffic Unlimited Normal 50 --
Host Based Replication (HBR) Traffic Unlimited Normal 50 --
iSCSI Traffic Unlimited Normal 50 --
Management Traffic Unlimited Normal 50 --
NFS Traffic Unlimited Normal 50 --
Virtual Machine Traffic Unlimited High 100 --
vMotion Traffic Unlimited Normal 50 --
User-defined network resource pools

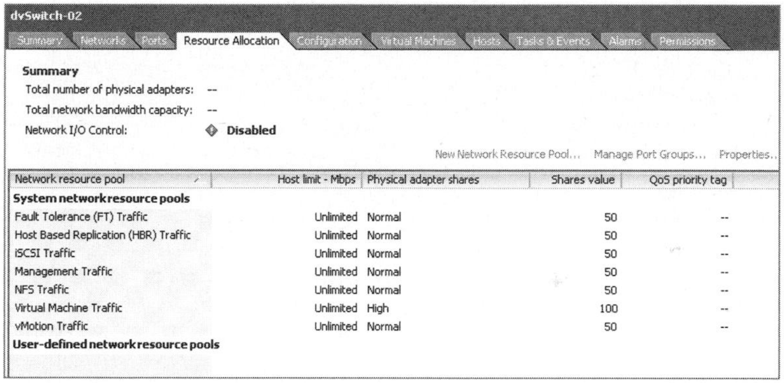

FIGURE 11.18 Network resource pools on a vDS provide granular control of network traffic.

This enables NetIOC on this vDS. The Resource Allocation tab of the vDS object will note that NetIOC is enabled, as shown in Figure 11.19.

dvSwitch-02
Summary
Networks
Ports
Resource Allocation
Configuration
Summary
Total number of physical adapters: --
Total network bandwidth capacity: --
Network I/O Control: Enabled

FIGURE 11.19 vCenter Server provides a clear indication that NetIOC is enabled for a vDS.

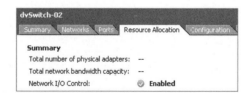

Along with actually enabling NetIOC, you can also modify existing network resource pools or create new resource pools, if you are using a vDS version 5.0. For a version 4.1.0 vDS, you can neither create new network resource pools nor edit the existing network resource pools.

A network resource pool consists of three basic settings:

- The first value is *Physical Adapter Shares*. Like the shares you used to prioritize access to CPU or RAM when there was contention, physical adapter shares in a network resource pool establish priority for access to the physical network adapters when there is network contention. As with other types of shares, this value does not apply when there is no contention.

  You can set this value to one of three predefined values, or you can set a Custom value of up to 100. For the predefined values, Low translates to 25 shares, Normal equates to 50 shares, and High equals 100 shares.

◆ The second value is the *Host Limit*. This value specifies an upper limit on the amount of network traffic, in Mbps, that this network resource pool is allowed to consume. Leaving Unlimited selected means that only the physical adapters themselves limit the network resource pool.

◆ The third value is the *QoS Priority Tag*. The QoS (Quality of Service) priority tag is an 802.1p tag that is applied to all outgoing packets. Upstream network switches that are configured to recognize the 802.1p tags can further enhance and enforce the QoS beyond just the ESXi host.

Figure 11.20 shows all three of the values for one of the predefined network resource pools, the Fault Tolerance (FT) Traffic network resource pool.

FIGURE 11.20
vSphere does allow an administrator to modify the predefined network resource pools.

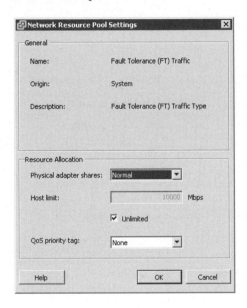

Administrators have the option of editing the predefined network resource pools or creating their own network resource pools.

Perform the following steps to edit an existing network resource pool:

1. If it is not already running, launch the vSphere Client and connect to a vCenter Server instance.

2. Navigate to the Networking inventory view.

   You can use the navigation bar, use the keyboard shortcut (Ctrl+Shift+N), or select View ➤ Inventory ➤ Networking.

3. Select the vDS that contains the network resource pool you want to modify.

4. Click the Resource Allocation tab.

5. Right-click the network resource pool you want to edit and select Edit Settings.

You can also click the Edit Setting hyperlink found just below the list of network resource pools.

6. From the Network Resource Pool Settings dialog box, modify the Physical Adapter Shares, Host Limit, or QoS Priority Tag values as desired.

7. Click OK to save the changes to the network resource pool.

You might prefer to leave the predefined network resource pools intact and create your own. Perform the following steps to create a new network resource pool:

1. If it is not already running, launch the vSphere Client and connect to a vCenter Server instance.

2. Navigate to the Networking inventory view. You can use the navigation bar, use the keyboard shortcut (Ctrl+Shift+N), or select View ➤ Inventory ➤ Networking.

3. Select the vDS on which you want to create the new network resource pool.

4. Click the Resource Allocation tab.

5. Click the New Network Resource Pool hyperlink. The Network Resource Pool Settings dialog box appears, as shown in Figure 11.21.

FIGURE 11.21
Administrators have the option of creating new network resource pools for custom network traffic control.

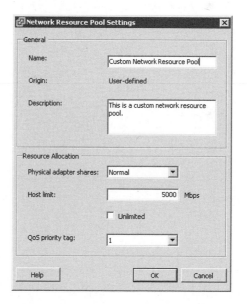

6. Supply a name and description for the new network resource pool.

7. For Physical Adapter Shares, select a predefined option (Low, Normal, or High), or select Custom and enter a value from 1 to 100.

8. To set a limit, select the Unlimited check box (to uncheck it) and then enter a value for Host Limit. This value is entered in Mbps (megabits per second).

9. If you want to apply a QoS priority tag, select the value from the drop-down list.

10. Click OK to create the new network resource pool with the values you specified.

After you have at least one user-defined network resource pool, you have the option of mapping port groups to your network resource pool.

CAN'T MAP PORT GROUPS TO SYSTEM POOLS

Port groups can only be mapped to user-defined network resource pools, not system network resource pools.

Perform the following steps to assign a port group to a user-defined network resource pool:

1. Launch the vSphere Client if it is not already running, and connect to a vCenter Server instance.

2. Switch to the Networking inventory view.

3. Select the vDS that hosts the network resource pool you'd like to map to a port group.

4. Click the Resource Allocation tab.

5. Click the Manage Port Groups hyperlink. This opens the Manage Port Groups dialog box shown in Figure 11.22.

FIGURE 11.22
Users can map a port group to any user-defined network resource pool, and multiple port groups can be associated to a single network resource pool.

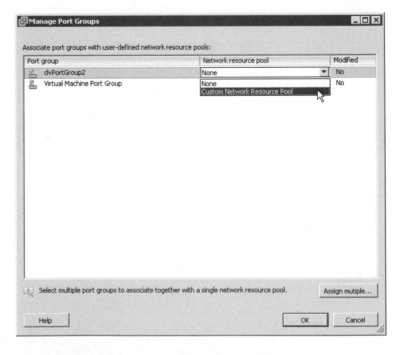

6. Click OK to save the changes and return to the Resource Allocation tab.

In large environments with lots of port groups, it might be a bit tedious to try to determine which port groups are mapped to which network resource pools. To help ease this administrative burden, vCenter Server offers an easy way to show all the port groups linked to a particular network resource pool. With a network resource pool selected, simply click the Port Groups button near the bottom of the screen. The view will shift to show you the specific port groups associated with the selected network resource pool. You can see this displayed in Figure 11.23, which shows the port groups associated with the user-defined network resource pool named Custom Network Resource Pool. You'll notice that a fair amount of networking-specific detail — like VLAN ID, port binding, number of attached VMs, and so forth — is also included in this display for ease of use.

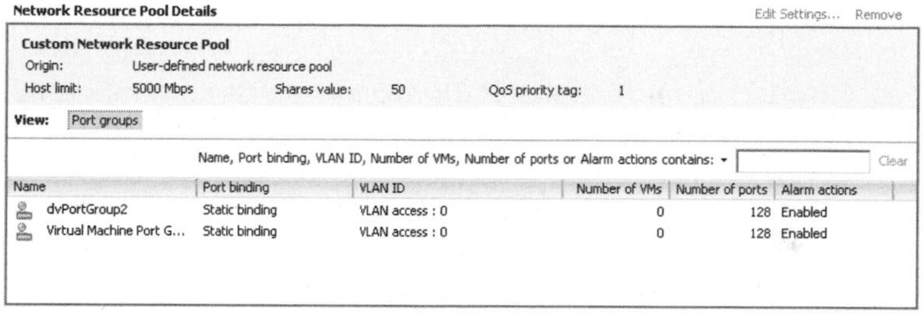

FIGURE 11.23
The vSphere Client provides a consolidated view of all the port groups associated with a network resource pool for reduced administrative overhead.

NetIOC offers a powerful way to help ensure that all the various types of network traffic present in a VMware vSphere environment will coexist properly, especially as organizations move toward 10 Gigabit Ethernet and away from Gigabit Ethernet. Fewer faster connections means more consolidated traffic and therefore a greater need for controlling how that traffic coexists on the same physical medium.

I've taken you through three of the four major resources and shown you how VMware vSphere offers controls for managing the use of and access to that resource. Only one resource remains: storage.

Controlling Storage I/O Utilization

For vSphere, controlling memory or CPU allocation and utilization is relatively easy. The hypervisor can easily determine how busy the CPU is and if physical memory has been depleted. When conditions of resource contention occur for these resources, not only is it easy to detect, but it's also easy to correct. If the CPU is too busy and there aren't enough CPU cycles to go around, then don't schedule cycles for lower-priority VMs and assign more cycles to higher-priority VMs. And how is this priority determined? Remember that Shares values are the mechanism that vSphere uses to determine priority. Likewise, if RAM becomes constrained, invoke the balloon drivers in the guest OSes and reclaim some memory, or slow down the rate of allocation to lower-priority VMs and increase the rate of allocation to higher-priority VMs. Not only does the hypervisor have complete visibility into the utilization of these resources, but the hypervisor also has complete control over the resources. Nothing gets scheduled on the CPU without going through the hypervisor, and nothing gets stored in RAM without the hypervisor knowing about it. This complete control is what enables vSphere to not only offer shares as a way of establishing priority, but also to offer reservations (guaranteed access to resources) and limits (caps on the usage of a resource). You read and learned about these mechanisms in previous parts of this chapter.

When you get to network utilization, things begin to change a little. The hypervisor has some visibility into the network; it can see how many Mbps are being generated and by which VMs. However, the hypervisor does not have complete control over network utilization; it can only control outbound traffic. Traffic generated somewhere else in the network really can't be controlled. Given the nature of networking, it's pretty much a given that other workloads outside the control of VMware vSphere are going to be present, and vSphere isn't going to be able to control or influence them in any way. Even so, the level of control that vSphere has enables it to offer shares (to establish priority) as well as limits (to enforce a cap on the amount of network bandwidth a VM can consume). This is Network I/O Control, and I discussed it in the previous section.

With regard to resource allocation and utilization, storage is similar in many ways to networking. It is very likely that other workloads will be present on the shared storage that is required by vSphere for so many features. These other workloads are going to be external to vSphere and can't be controlled or influenced in any way, and therefore vSphere isn't going to have complete control over the resource. It's also generally true that the hypervisor won't have as much visibility into the storage as it does with CPU and memory, making it more difficult to detect and adjust the utilization of storage resources. There is a metric, however, that vSphere can use to help determine the utilization of storage. That metric is latency. Using latency as the metric to detect contention, vSphere can offer shares (to establish priority when contention occurs) as well as limits (to ensure a VM doesn't consume too many storage resources). The feature that enables this functionality is called Storage I/O Control, or SIOC.

STORAGE I/O CONTROL FIRST APPEARED IN vSPHERE 4.1

Storage I/O Control first appeared in VMware vSphere 4.1 and supported only Fibre Channel and iSCSI datastores. In vSphere 5, SIOC adds support for NFS as well.

Longtime users of VMware vSphere (and VMware Infrastructure before that) are probably aware that you've been able to assign Shares values to disks for quite some time. The difference between that functionality and what SIOC offers is a matter of scope. Without SIOC, enabling shares on a VM's virtual disk is only effective for that specific host; the ESX/ESXi hosts did not exchange information about how many shares each VM was allocated or how many shares were assigned in total. This meant it was impossible to properly align the Shares values with the correct ratios of access to storage resources across multiple hosts.

SIOC addresses this by extending shares assignments across all hosts accessing a particular datastore. Using vCenter Server as the central information store, SIOC combines all the assigned shares across all the VMs on all the hosts and allocates storage I/O resources in the proper ratios according to the shares assignment.

In order to make this work, SIOC has a few requirements you must meet:

◆ All datastores that are SIOC-enabled have to be under the management of a single vCenter Server instance. vCenter Server is the "central clearinghouse" for all the shares assignments, so it makes sense that all the datastores and hosts have to be managed by a single vCenter Server instance.

◆ SIOC is supported on VMFS datastores connected via Fibre Channel (including FCoE) and iSCSI. NFS datastores are also supported. Raw Device Mappings (RDMs) are not supported.

◆ Datastores must have only a single extent. Datastores with multiple extents are not supported.

STORAGE I/O CONTROL AND ARRAY AUTO-TIERING

If your storage array supports auto-tiering — the ability for the array to seamlessly and transparently migrate data between different tiers (SSD, FC, SAS, SATA) of storage, be sure to double-check the VMware Hardware Compatibility List (HCL) to verify that your array's auto-tiering functionality has been certified to be compatible with SIOC.

Assuming that your environment meets the requirements, then you can take advantage of SIOC. Configuring SIOC is a two-step process. First, enable SIOC on one or more datastores. Second, assign shares or limits to storage I/O resources on individual VMs.

Let's look first at enabling SIOC for a particular datastore.

Enabling Storage I/O Control

SIOC is enabled on a per-datastore basis. By default, SIOC is disabled for a datastore, meaning that you have explicitly enabled SIOC if you want to take advantage of its functionality.

DATASTORES VERSUS DATASTORE CLUSTERS

While SIOC is disabled by default for individual datastores, it is *enabled* by default for Storage DRS–enabled datastore clusters that have I/O metrics enabled for Storage DRS. Refer to "Introducing and Working with Storage Distributed Resource Scheduler" in Chapter 12 for more information on Storage DRS.

Perform the following steps to enable SIOC for a datastore:

1. Launch the vSphere Client, if it is not already running, and connect to a vCenter Server instance.

   SIOC is available only when connected to vCenter Server, not when you are connected to an individual ESXi host.

2. Navigate to the Datastores And Datastore Clusters inventory view.

   You can use the navigation bar, use the Ctrl+Shift+D keyboard shortcut, or select View ➢ Inventory ➢ Datastores And Datastore Clusters.

3. Select the datastore for which you want to enable SIOC.

4. Click the Configuration tab.

5. Select the Properties hyperlink. Figure 11.24 shows the location of this hyperlink just below the list of hosts connected to the selected datastore.

6. In the Datastore Name Properties dialog box, select Enabled under Storage I/O Control.

7. Click Close.

SIOC is now enabled for the selected datastore; this is reflected in the Datastore Details pane of the vSphere Client under the Storage I/O Control heading, as you can see in Figure 11.25.

FIGURE 11.24
This Properties
hyperlink allows
you to manage the
configuration of a
specific datastore,
including enabling
SIOC.

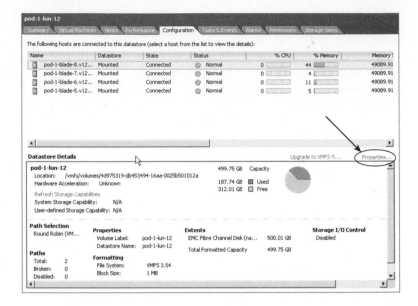

FIGURE 11.25
The status of SIOC
for a datastore is
displayed in the
vSphere Client for
easy reference.

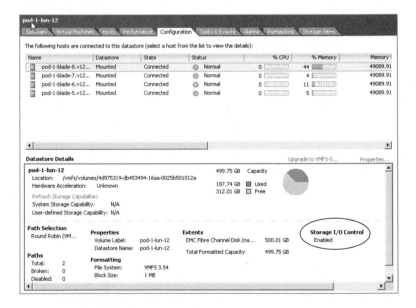

Generally speaking, enabling SIOC using these steps is all that is required to get started using SIOC to control the utilization of storage I/O resources.

However, in some cases, you might find it necessary to adjust the configuration of SIOC in order to make it function properly for your specific array and array configuration. Previously in this section, I mentioned that vSphere had a metric that could be used to detect contention: latency. SIOC uses latency as the threshold to determine when it should activate and enforce

Shares values for access to storage I/O resources. Specifically, when vSphere detects latency in excess of a specific threshold value (measured in milliseconds), SIOC is activated. Because of the vast differences in array architectures and array performance, VMware recognized that users might need to adjust this default congestion threshold values for SIOC. After all, a certain latency measurement might indicate congestion (or contention) on some arrays and configurations, but not on others. Making the congestion threshold adjustable allows vSphere administrators to fine-tune the behavior of SIOC to best match their particular array and configuration.

Perform the following steps to adjust the congestion threshold setting for SIOC on a particular datastore:

1. If it is not already running, launch the vSphere Client and connect to a vCenter Server instance.

2. Navigate to the Datastores And Datastore Clusters inventory view.

3. Select the desired datastore from the inventory tree.

4. Click the Configuration tab; then click the Properties hyperlink.

5. Click the Advanced button. A warning dialog box appears, letting you know that improperly adjusting the congestion threshold settings could impede the performance of a datastore. Click OK to dismiss the warning dialog box.

6. The Edit Congestion Threshold dialog box appears. Enter the desired congestion threshold setting, in milliseconds, and then click OK.

7. Click Close to return to the Datastores And Datastore Clusters inventory view.

WHAT VALUES SHOULD I USE?

When adjusting the congestion threshold setting, it is imperative that you set it properly based on your specific array, array configuration, and array vendor's recommendations. These recommendations will vary from vendor to vendor and depend on the number of drives in the array, the types of drives in the array, and whether features like array auto-tiering are enabled. In general, though, the following settings are considered reasonable guidelines for the congestion threshold:

◆ For datastores composed of SSDs, decrease to 10 ms.

◆ For datastores composed of 10K/15K FC and SAS, leave at 30 ms.

◆ For datastores composed of 7.2K SATA/NL-SAS, increase to 50 ms.

◆ For auto-tiered datastores with multiple drive types, leave at 30 ms.

While these are reasonable guidelines, I strongly urge you to consult your specific vendor's documentation on the recommended values to use as the congestion threshold when using SIOC in conjunction with their products.

Once you have enabled SIOC on one or more datastores and you have (optionally) adjusted the congestion threshold per your storage vendor's recommended values, you can start setting storage I/O resource values on your VMs.

Configuring Storage Resource Settings for a Virtual Machine

SIOC provides two mechanisms for controlling the use of storage I/O by VMs: shares and limits. These mechanisms operate in exactly the same way here as with other resources; the Shares value establishes a relative priority as a ratio of the total number of shares assigned, while the Limit value defines the upper ceiling on the number of I/O operations per second (IOPS) that a given VM may generate. As with memory, CPU, and network I/O, vSphere provides default settings for disk shares and limits. By default, every VM you create is assigned 1,000 disk shares per virtual disk and no IOPS limits.

If you need different settings than the default values, you can easily modify either the assigned storage I/O shares or the assigned storage I/O limit.

ASSIGNING STORAGE I/O SHARES

Modifying the default storage I/O Shares value is done on the Resources tab of the VM's properties dialog box, just as it's done for modifying memory allocation or CPU utilization. Figure 11.26 shows the Resources tab for a VM.

FIGURE 11.26
Modifying storage I/O shares is done from the same area as modifying other resource allocation settings.

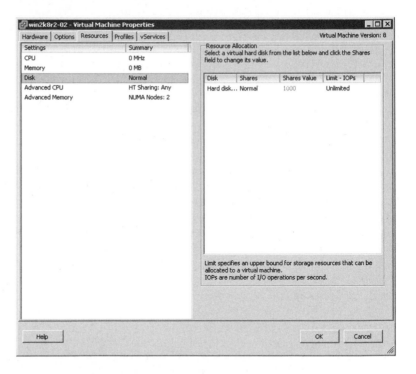

Perform the following steps to modify the storage I/O Shares value for a VM:

1. Launch the vSphere Client, if it is not already running, and connect to a vCenter Server instance.

2. Navigate to either the Hosts And Clusters or VMs And Templates inventory view.

3. Right-click the specific VM for which you'd like to change the storage I/O settings and select Edit Settings from the context menu.

4. Click the Resources tab. This displays the dialog box shown previously in Figure 11.26.

5. Select Disk from the list of resources on the left.

6. A list of virtual disks assigned to this VM will appear in the list on the right. For each virtual disk, click in the Shares column to change the setting from Normal to Low, High, or Custom, as shown in Figure 11.27.

FIGURE 11.27
You must change the setting to Custom if you want to assign an arbitrary storage I/O Shares value.

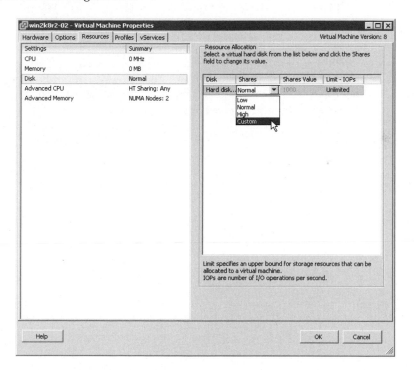

7. If you selected Custom in step 6, click in the Shares value column and supply a custom storage I/O Shares value.

8. Repeat steps 6 and 7 for each virtual disk associated with this VM.

9. Click OK to save the changes and return to the vSphere Client.

The selected virtual disks belonging to this VM will now receive a proportional allocation of storage I/O resources based on the Shares value whenever SIOC detects contention (or congestion) on the datastore. (Keep in mind that vSphere uses latency, as specified in the congestion threshold I described previously, as the trigger for activating SIOC.) Like all other Shares values, SIOC enforces Shares values only when contention for storage I/O resources is detected. If there is no contention — as indicated by low latency values for that datastore or datastore cluster — then SIOC will not activate.

SHARES ACTIVATE ONLY ON RESOURCE CONTENTION

Shares are applicable only when there is resource contention. This is true for all the different Shares values I've shown you throughout this chapter. Regardless of whether you are setting Shares values for memory, CPU, network, or storage, vSphere will not step in and enforce those shares until the hypervisor detects contention for that particular resource. Shares aren't guarantees or absolute values; they establish relative priority when the hypervisor isn't able to meet all the demands of the VMs.

CONFIGURING STORAGE I/O LIMITS

You can also set a limit on the number of IOPS that a VM is allowed to generate. By default, as I stated previously, this value is unlimited. However, if you feel that you need to set an IOPS limit, you can set the IOPS limit in the same place you would set storage I/O shares.

Perform these steps to set a storage I/O limit on IOPS:

1. If it is not already running, launch the vSphere Client and connect to a vCenter Server instance.

2. Navigate to the Hosts And Clusters or VMs And Templates inventory view.

3. Right-click a VM and select Edit Settings.

4. Select the Resources tab and then click Disk from the list of resources on the left.

5. Select the virtual disk for which you'd like to set an IOPS limit from the list of virtual disks on the right.

6. Click in the Limit – IOPS column and type in a value for the maximum number of IOPS that this VM will be allowed to generate against this virtual disk.

7. Repeat step 5 and step 6 for each virtual disk assigned to this VM.

8. Click OK to save the changes and return to the vSphere Client.

BE CAREFUL WITH IOPS LIMITS

Setting an improper IOPS limit can have a severe performance impact on a VM. Be sure that you have a clear understanding of the IOPS requirements of the guest OS and the applications installed in that guest OS before assigning an IOPS limit.

Like the limits you apply to memory, CPU, or network I/O, the storage I/O limits are absolute values. The hypervisor will enforce the assigned storage I/O limit, even when there is plenty of storage I/O available.

Setting these storage I/O resource values on a per-VM basis is fine, but what about when you need to have some sort of consolidated view of what settings have been applied to all the VMs on a datastore? Fortunately, vCenter Server and the vSphere Client provide a way to easily see a summary of the various settings.

VIEWING STORAGE I/O RESOURCE SETTINGS FOR VIRTUAL MACHINES

In the Datastores And Datastore Clusters inventory view, you can view a list of all the datastores managed by a particular vCenter Server instance. It was in this view that you enabled SIOC previously in the section "Enabling Storage I/O Control," and it's in this view that you can get a consolidated view of all the storage I/O settings applied to the VMs on a datastore.

On the Virtual Machines tab of a selected datastore in the Datastores And Datastore Clusters inventory view, vCenter Server provides a list of all the VMs on that datastore. If you scroll to the right using the scroll bar at the bottom of the vSphere Client window, you will see three SIOC-specific columns:

- ◆ Shares Value

- ◆ Limit – IOPs

- ◆ Datastore % Shares

Figure 11.28 shows these three columns on a datastore for which SIOC has been enabled. Note that the default values for the VMs on the selected SIOC-enabled datastore have not been modified.

FIGURE 11.28
The Virtual Machines tab of a datastore provides a useful summary view of storage-related information for all the VMs on that datastore.

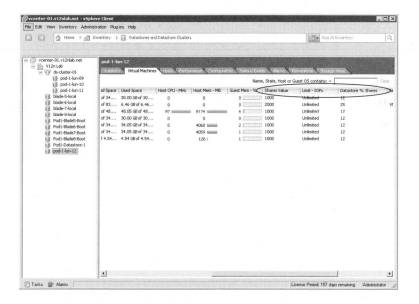

As you can see in Figure 11.28, vCenter Server has used the assigned Shares values to establish relative percentages of access to storage I/O resources in the event of contention. This consistent behavior makes the complex task of managing resource allocation a bit easier for vSphere administrators.

STORAGE I/O CONTROL AND EXTERNAL WORKLOADS

Storage I/O Control operates on the basis that only VMware vSphere is utilizing the storage I/O resources being managed by vCenter Server. However, this is often not the case. Because of the way that many modern arrays are structured, there may be many different workloads that are all running on the same physical disks that support an SIOC-enabled datastore.

In such cases, SIOC has the ability to detect "external workloads" and will automatically stop throttling. However, at the next latency evaluation period (4 seconds), SIOC will again check the latency of the datastore against the congestion threshold and see if it needs to start throttling again, and the cycle starts again.

To resolve this issue, VMware recommends that you avoid sharing physical disks across both virtual and non-virtual workloads. Because of the architecture of some arrays, this may be difficult, so check with your storage vendor for their recommendations and best practices.

Throughout this chapter, I've shown you how to use reservations, shares, and limits to modify the resource allocation and resource utilization behaviors of VMware vSphere. In the next chapter, I'll show you some additional tools for balancing resource utilization across groups of servers.

The Bottom Line

Manage virtual machine memory allocation. In almost every virtualized datacenter, memory is the resource that typically comes under contention first. Most organizations run out of memory on their VMware ESXi hosts before other resources become constrained. Fortunately, VMware vSphere offers both advanced memory-management technologies as well as extensive controls for managing the allocation of memory and utilization of memory by VMs.

Master It To guarantee certain levels of performance, your IT director believes that all VMs must be configured with at least 8 GB of RAM. However, you know that many of your applications rarely use this much memory. What might be an acceptable compromise to help ensure performance?

Manage CPU utilization. In a VMware vSphere environment, the ESXi hosts control VM access to physical CPUs. To effectively manage and scale VMware vSphere, administrators must understand how to allocate CPU resources to VMs, including how to use reservations, limits, and shares. Reservations provide guarantees to resources, limits provide a cap on resource usage, and shares help adjust the allocation of resources in a constrained environment.

Master It A fellow VMware administrator is a bit concerned about the use of CPU reservations. She is worried that using CPU reservations will "strand" CPU resources, preventing those reserved but unused resources from being used by other VMs. Are this administrator's concerns founded?

Create and manage resource pools. Managing resource allocation and usage for large numbers of VMs creates too much administrative overhead. Resource pools provide a mechanism for administrators to apply resource allocation policies to groups of VMs all at the same time. Resource pools use reservations, limits, and shares to control and modify resource allocation behavior, but only for memory and CPU.

Master It   Your company runs both test/development workloads and production workloads on the same hardware. How can you help ensure that test/development workloads do not consume too many resources and impact the performance of production workloads?

Control network and storage I/O utilization.   Along with memory and CPU, network I/O and storage I/O make up the four major resource types that VMware vSphere administrators must effectively manage in order to have an efficient virtualized datacenter. By applying controls to network I/O and storage I/O, administrators can help ensure consistent performance, meet service-level objectives, and prevent one workload from unnecessarily consuming resources at the expense of other workloads.

Master It   Name two limitations of Network I/O Control.

Master It   What are the requirements for using Storage I/O Control?

## Chapter 12

Balancing Resource Utilization

Virtualization with VMware vSphere is, among other things, about getting better utilization of your computing resources. This means utilization of resources within a single physical host, which vSphere accomplishes by allowing you to run multiple guest operating system instances on a single physical host. However, it's also about getting better resource utilization across multiple physical hosts, and that means the ability to shift workloads between hosts in order to balance the resource utilization. vSphere offers a number of powerful tools for helping administrators balance resource utilization.

In this chapter, you will learn to

♦ Configure and execute vMotion

♦ Ensure vMotion compatibility across processor families

♦ Configure and manage vSphere Distributed Resource Scheduler

♦ Use Storage vMotion

♦ Configure and manage Storage DRS

Comparing Utilization with Allocation

The fundamental but subtle difference between allocation and utilization can be difficult to understand at times. *Allocation* is about how a resource is assigned; so in a vSphere environment, allocation is about how CPU cycles, memory, storage I/O, and network bandwidth are allocated to a particular VM or group of VMs. *Utilization*, on the other hand, is about how resources are used after they are allocated. vSphere provides three mechanisms for affecting allocation: reservations (guaranteed allocations of resources), limits (bounds on the maximum allocation of resources), and shares (prioritized access to resource allocation). While these mechanisms are powerful and useful — as you saw in Chapter 11, "Managing Resource Allocation" — they do have their limits (no pun intended). What about situations when a resource is highly utilized on one host and lightly utilized on another host? None of the three mechanisms I've shown you so far will help balance the *utilization* of resources among ESXi hosts; they will only control the *allocation* of resources. This difference between allocation and utilization is the difference between what I showed you in Chapter 11 and what I'm going to discuss in this chapter.

VMware vSphere helps balance the utilization of resources in the following four ways:

vMotion   vMotion, also generically known as *live migration*, is used to manually balance resource utilization between two ESXi hosts.

vSphere Distributed Resource Scheduler   vSphere Distributed Resource Scheduler (DRS) is used to automatically balance resource utilization among two or more ESXi hosts.

Storage vMotion   Storage vMotion is the storage equivalent of vMotion, and it is used to manually balance storage utilization between two datastores.

Storage DRS   Just as Storage vMotion is the storage equivalent of vMotion, Storage DRS is the storage equivalent of DRS, and it is used to automatically balance storage utilization among two or more datastores.

Along the way of introducing and explaining each of these four mechanisms for balancing resource utilization, I'll also introduce or review a few other related features of vSphere, such as clusters and VMware Enhanced vMotion Compatibility (EVC).

Let's start with vMotion.

Exploring vMotion

I've defined the vMotion feature as a way to manually balance resource utilization between two ESXi hosts. What does that mean, exactly? vMotion provides the ability to perform a live migration of a VM from one ESXi host to another ESXi host without service interruption. This is a no-downtime operation; network connections are not dropped and applications continue running uninterrupted. In fact, the end users do not know and are not aware that the VM has been migrated between physical ESXi hosts. When you use vMotion to migrate a VM from one ESXi host to another ESXi host, this means you also migrate the resource allocation — CPU and memory — from one host to another. This makes vMotion an extremely effective tool for manually load-balancing VMs across ESXi hosts and eliminating "hot spots" — heavily utilized ESXi hosts — within your virtualized datacenter.

In addition to manually balancing VM loads among ESXi hosts, vMotion brings other benefits, too. If an ESXi host needs to be powered off for hardware maintenance or some other function that would take it out of production, you can use vMotion to migrate all active VMs from the host going offline to another host without waiting for a hardware maintenance window. Because vMotion is a live migration — no interruption in service and no downtime — the VMs will remain available to the users who need them.

While it sounds like magic, the basic premise of vMotion is relatively straightforward. vMotion works by copying the contents of VM memory from one ESXi host to another ESXi host and then transferring control of the VM's disk files to the target host.

Let's take a closer look. vMotion operates in the following sequence:

1. An administrator initiates a migration of a running VM (VM1) from one ESXi host (pod-1-blade-5) to another (pod-1-blade-7), shown in Figure 12.1.

2. The source host (pod-1-blade-5) begins copying the active memory pages VM1 has in host memory to the destination host (pod-1-blade-7) across a VMkernel interface that has been enabled for vMotion. This is called *preCopy*. During this time, the VM still services clients on the source (pod-1-blade-7). As the memory is copied from the source host to the target, pages in memory could be changed. ESXi handles this by keeping a log of changes that occur in the memory of the VM on the source host after that memory address has been copied to the target host. This log is called a *memory bitmap*. See Figure 12.2. Note that this process occurs iteratively, repeatedly copying over memory contents that have changed.

FIGURE 12.1
Step 1 in a vMotion migration is invoking a migration while the VM is powered on.

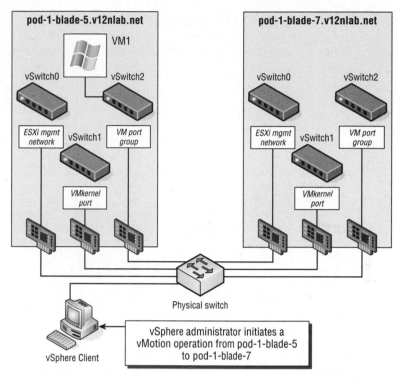

FIGURE 12.2
Step 2 in a vMotion migration is starting the memory copy and adding a memory bitmap.

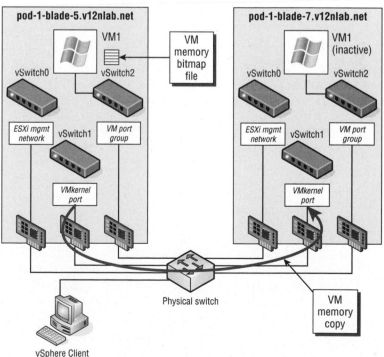

---

vMotion Can Now Leverage Multiple NICs

As of vSphere 5, vMotion can take advantage of multiple NICs to assist with transferring memory data between hosts.

---

3. After the entire contents of RAM for the VM being migrated have been transferred to the target host (pod-1-blade-7), then VM1 on the source ESXi host (pod-1-blade-5) is *quiesced*. This means that it is still in memory but is no longer servicing client requests for data. The memory bitmap file is then transferred to the target (pod-1-blade-7). See Figure 12.3.

The Memory Bitmap

The memory bitmap does not include the contents of the memory address that has changed; it simply includes the addresses of the memory that has changed — often referred to as the *dirty memory*.

FIGURE 12.3
Step 3 in a vMotion migration involves quiescing VM1 and transferring the memory bitmap file from the source ESXi host to the destination ESXi host.

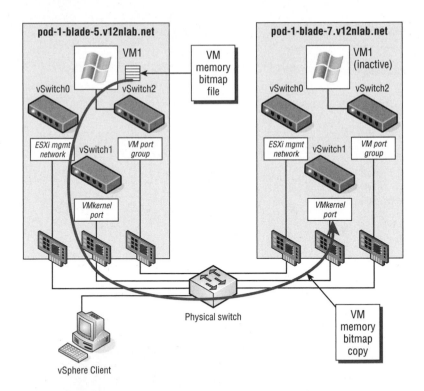

4. The target host (pod-1-blade-7) reads the addresses in the memory bitmap file and requests the contents of those addresses from the source (pod-1-blade-5). See Figure 12.4.

FIGURE 12.4
In step 4 in a vMotion migration, the actual memory listed in the bitmap file is fetched from the source to the destination (dirty memory).

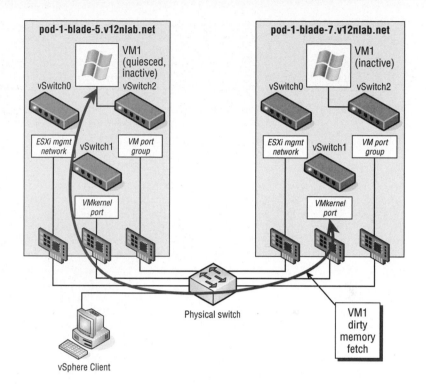

5. After the contents of the memory referred to in the memory bitmap file have been transferred to the target host, the VM starts on that host. Note that this is not a reboot — the VM's state is in RAM, so the host simply enables it. At this point a Reverse Address Resolution Protocol (RARP) message is sent by the host to register its MAC address against the physical switch port to which the target ESXi host is connected. This process enables the physical switch infrastructure to send network packets to the appropriate ESXi host from the clients that are attached to the VM that just moved.

6. After the VM is successfully operating on the target host, the memory the VM was using on the source host is deleted. This memory becomes available to the VMkernel to use as appropriate, as shown in Figure 12.5.

TRY IT WITH *ping -t*

Following the previous procedure carefully, you'll note there will be a time when the VM being moved is not running on either the source host *or* the target host. This is typically a short period of time. Testing has shown that a continuous ping (ping -t) of the VM being moved might, on a bad day, result in the loss of one ping packet. Most client-server applications are built to withstand the loss of more than a packet or two before the client is notified of a problem.

FIGURE 12.5
In step 6 in a vMotion migration, vCenter Server deletes the VM from the source ESXi host.

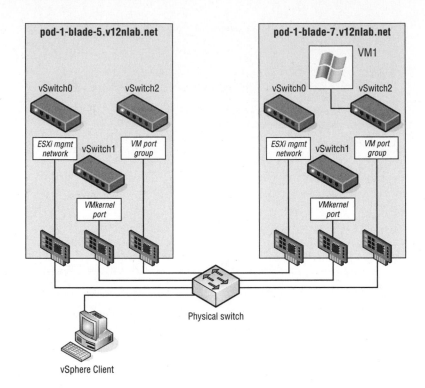

Examining vMotion Requirements

The vMotion migration is pretty amazing, and when users see it work for the first time in a live environment, they are extremely impressed. However, detailed planning is necessary for this procedure to function properly. The hosts involved in the vMotion process have to meet certain requirements, along with the VMs being migrated.

Each of the ESXi hosts that are involved in vMotion must meet the following requirements:

- Shared storage for the VM files (a VMFS or NFS datastore) that is accessible by both the source and target ESXi host.

- A Gigabit Ethernet or faster network interface card (NIC) with a VMkernel port defined and enabled for vMotion on each ESXi host.

This VMkernel port can be on a vSphere Standard Switch, on a vSphere Distributed Switch, or on a third-party distributed virtual switch like the Cisco Nexus 1000V, but it must be enabled for vMotion. The Gigabit Ethernet or faster NIC should preferably be dedicated to vMotion traffic, although it is acceptable to share this NIC with other traffic types if necessary.

In Chapter 5, "Creating and Configuring Virtual Networks," I provided the steps for creating a VMkernel port on a vSwitch. I included instructions for creating a VMkernel port on either a vSphere Standard Switch or a vSphere Distributed Switch. I'll review the steps for creating a VMkernel port on a vSphere Distributed Switch again just for convenience.

Perform the following steps to create a VMkernel port on an existing vSphere Distributed Switch:

1. Launch the vSphere Client if it is not already running, and connect to an instance of vCenter Server.

2. Navigate to the Hosts And Clusters inventory view.

3. From the inventory list on the left, select an ESXi host that is already participating in the vSphere Distributed Switch.

4. Select the Configuration tab from the contents pane on the right.

5. Click Networking to display the host's networking configuration.

6. Switch the view to vSphere Distributed Switch using the buttons just below the tab bar.

7. Click the Manage Virtual Adapters link.

8. In the Manage Virtual Adapters dialog box, click the link to add a new virtual adapter.

9. In the Add Virtual Adapter dialog box, select New Virtual Adapter, and click Next.

10. Select VMkernel and click Next.

11. Choose the correct port group from the drop-down list, and then be sure to select the box Use This Virtual Adapter For vMotion. Click Next.

12. Specify an IP address and network mask for this VMkernel interface.

    If the vMotion network is nonroutable, leave the default gateway blank, or simply use the default gateway assigned for the management network. Click Next.

13. Review the graphical diagram that shows the pending changes to the distributed switch.

    If everything is correct, click Finish to complete adding the VMkernel interface. Otherwise, use the Back button to change the settings accordingly.

In addition to the configuration requirements I just outlined (shared storage and a vMotion-enabled VMkernel port), a successful vMotion migration between two ESXi hosts also relies on all of the following conditions being met:

◆ Both the source and destination hosts must be configured with identical virtual switches that are correctly configured, vMotion-enabled VMkernel ports. If you are using vSphere Distributed Switches, both hosts must be participating in the same vSphere Distributed Switch.

◆ All port groups to which the VM being migrated is attached must exist on both of the ESXi hosts. Port group naming is case sensitive, so create identical port groups on each host, and make sure they plug into the same physical subnets or VLANs. A virtual switch named Production is not the same as a virtual switch named PRODUCTION. Remember that to prevent downtime the VM is not going to change its network address as it is moved. The VM will retain its MAC address and IP address so clients connected to it don't have to resolve any new information to reconnect.

◆ Processors in both hosts must be compatible. When a VM is transferred between hosts, the VM has already detected the type of processor it is running on when it booted. Because the VM is not rebooted during a vMotion, the guest assumes the CPU instruction set on the target host is the same as on the source host. You can get away with slightly dissimilar processors, but in general the processors in two hosts that perform vMotion must meet the following requirements:

◆ CPUs must be from the same vendor (Intel or AMD).

◆ CPUs must be from the same CPU family (Xeon 55xx, Xeon 56xx, or Opteron).

◆ CPUs must support the same features, such as the presence of SSE2, SSE3, and SSE4, and NX or XD (see the sidebar "Processor Instruction").

◆ For 64-bit VMs, CPUs must have virtualization technology enabled (Intel VT or AMD-v).

I'll talk more about processor compatibility in the section "Ensuring vMotion Compatibility."

PROCESSOR INSTRUCTION

Streaming SIMD Extensions 2 (SSE2) was an enhancement to the original Multimedia Extension (MMX) instruction set found in the PIII processor. The enhancement was targeted at the floating-point calculation capabilities of the processor by providing 144 new instructions. SSE3 instruction sets are an enhancement to the SSE2 standard targeted at multimedia and graphics applications. The new SSE4 extensions target both the graphics and the application server.

AMD's Execute Disable (XD) and Intel's NoExecute (NX) are features of processors that mark memory pages as data only, which prevents a virus from running executable code at that address. The operating system needs to be written to take advantage of this feature, and in general, versions of Windows starting with Windows 2003 SP1 and Windows XP SP2 support this CPU feature.

The latest processors from Intel and AMD have specialized support for virtualization. The AMD-V and Intel Virtualization Technology (VT) must be enabled in the BIOS in order to create 64-bit VMs.

In addition to the vMotion requirements for the hosts involved, the VM must meet the following requirements to be migrated:

◆ The VM must not be connected to any device physically available to only one ESXi host. This includes disk storage, CD/DVD drives, floppy drives, serial ports, or parallel ports. If the VM to be migrated has one of these mappings, simply deselect the Connected check box beside the offending device. For example, you won't be able to migrate a VM with a CD/DVD drive connected; to disconnect the drive and allow vMotion, deselect the Connected box.

◆ The VM must not be connected to an internal-only virtual switch.

◆ The VM must not have its CPU affinity set to a specific CPU.

◆ The VM must have all disk, configuration, log, and nonvolatile random access memory (NVRAM) files stored on a VMFS or NFS datastore accessible from both the source and the destination ESXi hosts.

If you start a vMotion migration and vCenter Server finds an issue that is considered a violation of the vMotion compatibility rules, you will see an error message. In some cases, a warning, not an error, will be issued. In the case of a warning, the vMotion migration will still succeed. For instance, if you have cleared the check box on the host-attached floppy drive, vCenter Server will tell you there is a mapping to a host-only device that is not active. You'll see a prompt asking whether the migration should take place anyway.

VMware states that you need a Gigabit Ethernet NIC for vMotion; however, it does not have to be dedicated to vMotion. When you're designing the ESXi host, dedicate a NIC to vMotion if possible. You thus reduce the contention on the vMotion network, and the vMotion process can happen in a fast and efficient manner.

Now that I've reviewed all the various prerequisites, both for ESXi hosts and VMs, let's actually perform a vMotion migration.

Performing a vMotion Migration

After you've verified the ESXi host requirements as well as the VM requirements, you are ready to perform a vMotion migration.

Perform the following steps to conduct a vMotion migration of a running VM:

1. Launch the vSphere Client if it is not already running, and connect to a vCenter Server instance.

   vMotion requires vCenter Server.

2. Navigate to either the Hosts And Clusters or VMs And Templates inventory view.

3. Select a powered-on VM in your inventory, right-click the VM, and select Migrate.

4. Select Change Host, and then click Next.

5. Choose the target host.

   Figure 12.6 shows a target host that produces validation errors; that is, vCenter Server has found errors that would prevent a successful vMotion operation. Figure 12.7 shows a compatible and properly configured target host selected.

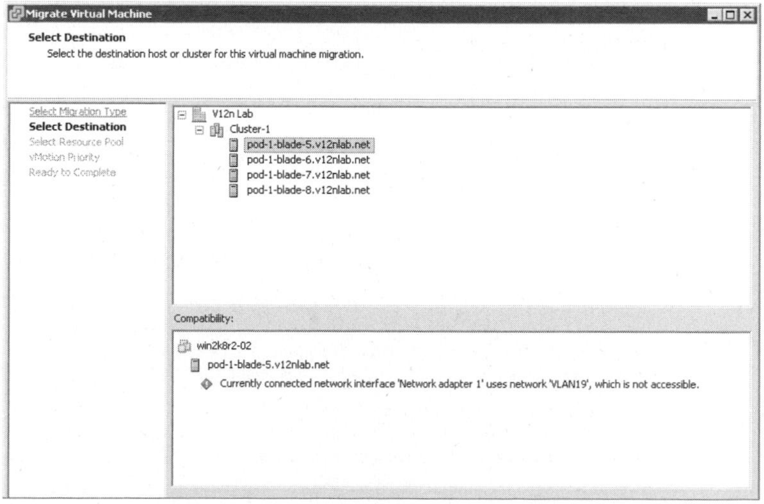

FIGURE 12.6
vCenter Server will show you errors found during validation of the selected target host in a vMotion operation.

FIGURE 12.7
If vCenter Server
does not show any
validation errors,
then the vMotion
operation is allowed
to proceed.

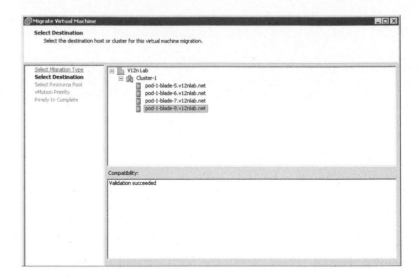

After you've selected the correct target host, click Next.

6. If you have any resource pools defined on the target host or target cluster, you'll need to select the target resource pool (or cluster). You also have the option of selecting a vApp as your target resource pool; I introduced the concept of vApps in Chapter 10, "Using Templates and vApps."

   Most of the time the same resource pool (or cluster) that the VM currently resides in will suffice. As of vSphere 5, the resource pool where the VM currently resides is automatically selected as the target resource pool. Keep in mind that choosing a different resource pool might change that VM's priority access to resources. Refer to Chapter 11, "Managing Resource Allocation," for a more in-depth discussion of how resource allocation is affected by placement into a resource pool. If no resource pool is defined on the target host, then vCenter Server skips this step entirely.

7. Select the priority that the vMotion migration needs to proceed with.

   In vSphere 5, this setting controls the share of reserved resources allocated for migrations with vMotion. Migrations marked as High Priority receive a higher share of CPU resources than migrations marked as Standard Priority. Migrations will proceed regardless of the resources reserved. This behavior is different than in earlier versions; see the sidebar "Migration Priority in Earlier Versions of vSphere." Generally, you will select High Priority (Recommended). Click Next to continue.

MIGRATION PRIORITY IN EARLIER VERSIONS OF VSPHERE

The behavior of the High Priority and Standard Priority settings for vMotion changed in vSphere 4.1; this behavior carries forward to vSphere 5 as described in the text. For vSphere 4, however, the behavior of these options is different. For vSphere 4, high-priority migrations do not proceed if resources are unavailable to be reserved for the migration, whereas standard priority migrations will proceed. However, standard priority migrations might proceed more slowly and might even fail to complete if enough resources are not available.

8. Review the settings, and click Finish if all the information is correct.

   If there are any errors, use the Back button or the hyperlinks on the left to go back and correct the errors.

9. The VM should start to migrate. Often, the process will pause at about 10 percent in the progress dialog box and then again at 90 percent.

   The 10 percent pause occurs while the hosts in question establish communications and gather the information for the pages in memory to be migrated; the 90 percent pause occurs when the source VM is quiesced and the dirty memory pages are fetched from the source host, as shown in Figure 12.8.

FIGURE 12.8
The Recent Tasks pane of the vSphere Client shows the progress of the vMotion operation.

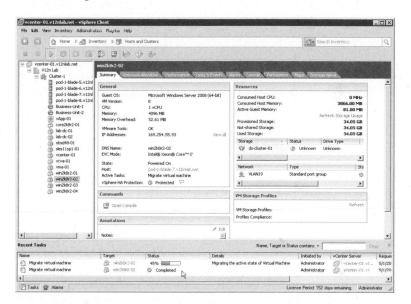

VMOTION IS NOT A HIGH-AVAILABILITY FEATURE

vMotion is a great feature, but it is not a high-availability feature. Yes, it can be used to improve uptime by preventing downtime because of planned outages, but vMotion will not provide any protection in the event of an unplanned host failure. For that functionality, you'll need vSphere High Availability (HA) and vSphere Fault Tolerance (FT), two features that are discussed in Chapter 7, "Ensuring High Availability and Business Continuity."

---

vMotion is an invaluable tool for virtual administrators. Once you've managed a datacenter with vMotion, you'll wonder how you managed without it.

Over time, though, you could find yourself in a situation where you are without vMotion. As hardware manufacturers such as Intel and AMD introduce new generations of CPUs, you could find yourself in a situation where some of your ESXi hosts have one generation of CPUs and others have a newer generation of CPUs. Remember that one of the requirements for vMotion is compatible CPUs. So what happens when you need to refresh some of your hardware and you have to start using a new generation of CPUs? vSphere addresses this potential problem with a feature called VMware Enhanced vMotion Compatibility (EVC).

Ensuring vMotion Compatibility

In the section "Examining vMotion Requirements," I discussed some of the prerequisites needed to perform a vMotion operation. In particular, I mentioned that vMotion has some fairly strict CPU requirements. Specifically, the CPUs must be from the same vendor, must be in the same family, and must share a common set of CPU instruction sets and features.

In a situation where two physical hosts exist in a cluster and there are CPU differences between the two hosts, vMotion will fail. I often refer to this issue as a *vMotion boundary*. Until later versions of ESXi 3.*x* and appropriate support from Intel and AMD in their processors, there was no fix for this issue — it was something that virtual datacenter administrators and architects simply had to endure.

However, in later versions of VMware Virtual Infrastructure 3.*x* and continuing into VMware vSphere 4.*x* and 5, VMware supports hardware extensions from Intel and AMD to help mitigate these CPU differences. In fact, vSphere provides two ways to address this issue, either in part or in whole.

Using Per–Virtual Machine CPU Masking

vCenter Server offers the ability to create custom CPU masks on a per-VM basis. Although this can offer a tremendous amount of flexibility in enabling vMotion compatibility, it's also important to note that, with one exception, this is *completely unsupported by VMware*.

What is the one exception? On a per-VM basis, you'll find a setting that tells the VM to show or mask the No Execute/Execute Disable (NX/XD) bit in the host CPU, and this specific instance of CPU masking is fully supported by VMware. Masking the NX/XD bit from the VM tells the VM that there's no NX/XD bit present. This is useful if you have two otherwise compatible hosts with an NX/XD bit mismatch. If the VM doesn't know there's an NX or XD bit on one of the hosts, it won't care if the target host has or doesn't have that bit if you migrate that VM using vMotion. The greatest vMotion compatibility is achieved by masking the NX/XD bit. If the NX/XD bit is exposed to the VM, as shown in Figure 12.9, the BIOS setting for NX/XD must match on both the source and destination ESXi hosts.

FIGURE 12.9
The option for masking the NX/XD bit is controlled on a per-VM basis.

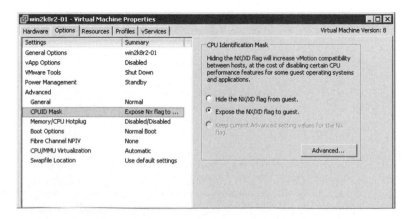

For features other than the NX/XD bit, you would have to delve into custom CPU masks. This is where you will step outside the bounds of VMware support. Looking at the dialog box in Figure 12.9, you'll note the Advanced button. Clicking the Advanced button opens the CPU Identification Mask dialog box, shown in Figure 12.10.

FIGURE 12.10

The CPU Identification Mask dialog box allows you to create custom CPU masks.

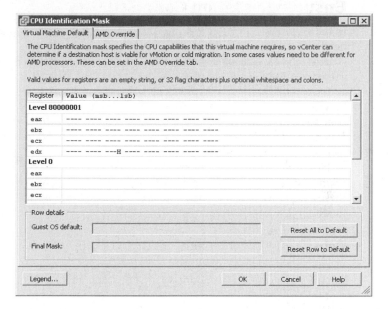

In this dialog box, you can create custom CPU masks to mark off specific bits within the CPU ID value. I won't go into great detail here because all of this is unsupported by VMware. However, refer to the sidebar "More Information on CPU Masking" for two URLs that provide additional information.

🌐 Real World Scenario

MORE INFORMATION ON CPU MASKING

Creating custom CPU masks is one way to ease potential vMotion incompatibilities. Remember, though, that this is completely unsupported by VMware, so it's useful only in test and development environments where you are not running production workloads and don't need the full support of VMware behind you.

If your test lab is anything like my test lab used to be, it's full of older hardware that's been cycled out of production. This often creates the exact kind of environment where vMotion does not work as expected because of differences in the underlying CPUs. As a result, I had to create some custom CPU masks to allow vMotion between some old Pentium III servers (OK, so they were *really* old servers) and some newer Pentium 4 servers. At that time, VMware did not have anything like EVC, and the hardware vendors didn't have anything like the current hardware virtualization extensions. I had to use an ISO image that VMware included on the ESX 3.0.*x* installation disc. This bootable ISO image, which does not appear to be included on the vSphere 4 ESX installation media, provided output on the CPUID response from the CPUs. The hexadecimal output from that disc had to be converted to binary and compared in order to find which bits had to be masked in a custom CPU mask.

I documented all the steps and the techniques involved in creating these custom CPU masks on my website. If you are interested in getting more information on custom CPU masks, you can review the following web pages:

http://blog.scottlowe.org/2006/09/25/sneaking-around-vmotion-limitations/

http://blog.scottlowe.org/2007/06/19/more-on-cpu-masking/

Both of these web pages provide in-depth details from the real-life work that I did creating custom CPU masks in my own test lab.

Fortunately, there's an easier — and fully supported — way of handling this issue, and it's called VMware Enhanced vMotion Compatibility (EVC).

Using VMware Enhanced vMotion Compatibility

Recognizing that potential compatibility issues with vMotion could be a significant problem, VMware worked closely with both Intel and AMD to craft functionality that would address this issue. On the hardware side, Intel and AMD put functions in their CPUs that would allow them to modify the CPU ID value returned by the CPUs. Intel calls this functionality FlexMigration; AMD simply embedded this functionality into their existing AMD-V virtualization extensions. On the software side, VMware created software features that would take advantage of this hardware functionality to create a common CPU ID baseline for all the servers within a cluster. This functionality, originally introduced in VMware ESX/ESXi 3.5 Update 2, is called VMware Enhanced vMotion Compatibility.

EVC is enabled at the cluster level. Figure 12.11 shows the EVC controls for a cluster.

FIGURE 12.11
VMware EVC is enabled and disabled at the cluster level.

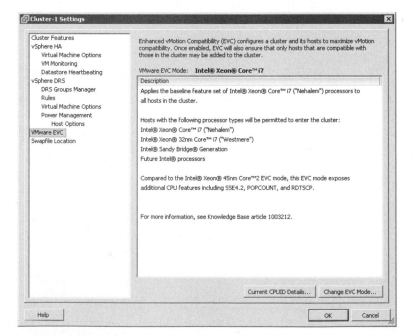

As you can see in Figure 12.11, EVC is currently enabled on this cluster. This cluster contains servers with Intel Xeon processors, so EVC is using an Intel Xeon Core i7 baseline. To change the baseline that EVC is using, click the Change EVC Mode button. This opens a dialog box that allows you to disable EVC or to change the EVC baseline, as illustrated in Figure 12.12.

FIGURE 12.12

You can enable or disable EVC, as well as change the processor baseline EVC uses.

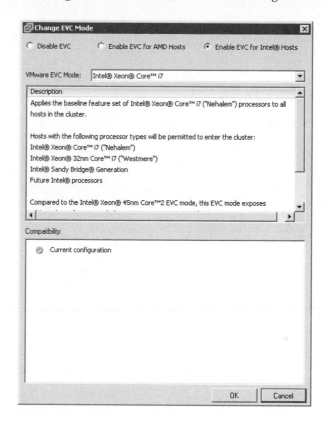

vCenter Server performs some validation checks to ensure that the physical hardware is capable of supporting the selected EVC mode and processor baseline. If you select a setting that the hardware cannot support, the Change EVC Mode dialog box will reflect the incompatibility. Figure 12.13 shows an incompatible EVC mode selected.

When you enable EVC and set the processor baseline, vCenter Server then calculates the correct CPU masks that are required and communicates that information to the ESXi hosts. The ESXi hypervisor then works with the underlying Intel or AMD processors to create the correct CPU ID values that would match the correct CPU mask. When vCenter Server validates vMotion compatibility by checking CPU compatibility, the underlying CPUs will return compatible CPU masks and CPU ID values. However, vCenter Server and ESXi cannot set CPU masks for VMs that are currently powered on. (You can verify this by opening the properties of a running VM and going to the CPUID Mask area on the Resources tab. You'll find all the controls there are disabled.)

Consequently, if you attempt to change the EVC mode on a cluster that has powered-on VMs, vCenter Server will prevent you from making the change, as you can see in Figure 12.14 (note the warning and note that the OK button is disabled). You'll have to power down the VMs in order to change the cluster's EVC mode.

FIGURE 12.13
vCenter Server
ensures that the
selected EVC mode
is compatible with
the underlying
hardware.

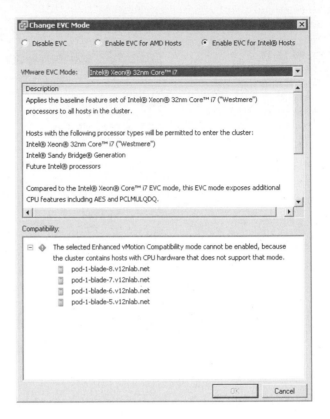

When setting the EVC mode for a cluster, keep in mind that some CPU-specific features — such as newer multimedia extensions or encryption instructions, for example — could
be disabled when vCenter Server and ESXi disable them via EVC. VMs that rely on these
advanced extensions might be affected by EVC, so be sure that your workloads won't be
adversely affected before setting the cluster's EVC mode.

EVC is a powerful feature that assures vSphere administrators that vMotion compatibility
will be maintained over time, even as hardware generations change. With EVC, you won't have
to remember what life's like without vMotion.

But vMotion is a *reactive* tool; an administrator has to manually initiate vMotion. How
much more powerful would vMotion be if vSphere used vMotion *proactively*? That is the basis
for vSphere Distributed Resource Scheduler (DRS), a feature that you can enable on ESXi
clusters.

FIGURE 12.14
vCenter Server informs the user which ESXi hosts in the cluster have powered-on or suspended VMs that are preventing the change to the cluster's EVC mode.

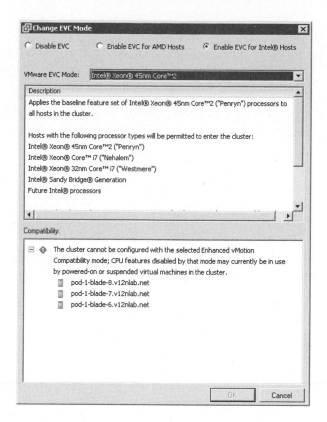

Exploring vSphere Distributed Resource Scheduler

When I introduced you to vMotion, I said that vMotion was a way of manually balancing loads across VMware ESXi hosts. vSphere Distributed Resource Scheduler (DRS) builds on the idea of manually balancing loads across ESXi hosts and turns it into a way of *automatically* balancing load across groups of ESXi hosts. The groups are clusters, which I introduced in Chapter 3 and discussed again in Chapter 7.

vSphere DRS is a feature of vCenter Server on the properties of a cluster that balances a load across multiple ESXi hosts. It has the following two main functions:

◆ To decide which node of a cluster should run a VM when it's powered on, a function often referred to as *intelligent placement*

◆ To evaluate the load on the cluster over time and either make recommendations for migrations or use vMotion to automatically move VMs to create a more balanced cluster workload

vSphere DRS runs as a process within vCenter Server, which means that you must have vCenter Server in order to use vSphere DRS. By default, DRS checks every five minutes (or 300 seconds) to see if the cluster's workload is balanced. DRS is also invoked by certain actions within the cluster, such as adding or removing an ESXi host or changing the resource settings of a VM. When DRS is invoked, it will calculate the imbalance of the cluster, apply any resource controls (such as reservations, shares, and limits), and, if necessary, generate recommendations for migrations of VMs within the cluster. Depending on the configuration of vSphere DRS, these recommendations could be applied automatically, meaning that VMs will automatically be migrated between hosts by DRS in order to maintain cluster balance (or, put another way, to minimize cluster imbalance).

---

vSphere Distributed Resource Scheduler Enables Resource Pools

As I mentioned in the previous section of this chapter, vSphere DRS enables the use of resource pools when clustering ESXi hosts.

Fortunately, if you like to retain control, you can set how aggressively DRS will automatically move VMs around the cluster.

If you start by looking at the DRS properties — you can view these properties by right-clicking a DRS-enabled cluster, selecting Edit Settings, and then clicking the vSphere DRS heading on the left — you will see there are three selections regarding the automation level of the DRS cluster: Manual, Partially Automated, and Fully Automated. The slider bar affects only the actions of the Fully Automated setting on the cluster. These settings control the initial placement of a VM and the automatic movement of VMs between hosts. I'll examine the behavior of these automation levels in the next three sections.

Understanding Manual Automation Behavior

When a DRS cluster is set to Manual, every time you power on a VM, the cluster prompts you to select the ESXi host on which that VM should be hosted. The dialog box rates the available hosts according to suitability at that moment: the lower the priority, the better the choice, as shown in Figure 12.15.

Figure 12.15
A DRS cluster set to Manual requires you to specify where the VM should be powered on.

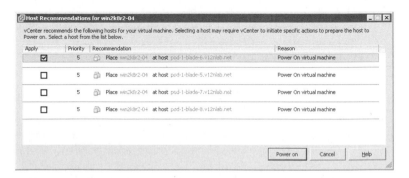

The Manual setting also suggests vMotion migrations when DRS detects an imbalance between ESXi hosts in the cluster. This is an averaging process that works over longer periods of time than many of us are used to in the IT field. It is unusual to see DRS make any recommendations unless an imbalance has existed for longer than five minutes. The recommended list of migrations is available by selecting the cluster in the inventory and then selecting the DRS tab.

From the DRS tab, the Apply Recommendations button allows you to agree with any pending DRS recommendations and initiate a migration. vMotion handles the migration automatically. Figure 12.16 shows some pending recommendations displayed on the DRS tab of a cluster set for Manual DRS automation.

FIGURE 12.16
vMotion operations must be approved by an administrator when DRS is set for Manual automation.

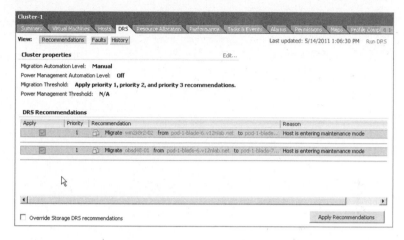

Reviewing Partially Automated Behavior

If you select the Partially Automated setting on the DRS properties, DRS will make an automatic decision about which host a VM should run on when it is initially powered on (without prompting the user who is performing the power-on task) but will still prompt for all migrations on the DRS tab. Thus, initial placement is automated, but migrations are still manual.

Examining Fully Automated Behavior

The third setting for DRS is Fully Automated. This setting makes decisions for initial placement without prompting and also makes automatic vMotion decisions based on the selected automation level (the slider bar).

There are five positions for the slider bar on the Fully Automated setting of the DRS cluster. The values of the slider bar range from Conservative to Aggressive. Conservative automatically applies recommendations ranked as priority 1 recommendations. Any other migrations are listed on the DRS tab and require administrator approval. If you move the slider bar from the most conservative setting to the next stop to the right, then all priority 1 and priority 2 recommendations are automatically applied; recommendations higher than priority 2 will wait for administrator approval. With the slider all the way over to the Aggressive setting, any imbalance in the cluster that causes a recommendation is automatically approved (apply even priority 5 recommendations). Be aware that this can cause additional stress in your ESXi host environment, because even a slight imbalance will trigger a migration.

Calculations for migrations can change regularly. Assume that during a period of high activity DRS makes a priority 3 recommendation, and the automation level is set so priority 3 recommendations need manual approval, but the recommendation is not noticed (or an administrator is not even in the office). An hour later, the VMs that caused the recommendation in the first place have settled down and are now operating normally. At this point, the DRS tab no longer reflects the recommendation. The recommendation has since been withdrawn. This behavior occurs because if the migration was still listed, an administrator might approve it and cause an imbalance where one did not exist.

In many cases, priority 1 recommendations have little to do with load on the cluster. Instead, priority 1 recommendations are generally the result of one of two conditions. The first condition that causes a priority 1 recommendation is when you put a host into maintenance mode, as shown in Figure 12.17.

FIGURE 12.17
An ESXi host put into maintenance mode cannot power on new VMs or be a target for vMotion.

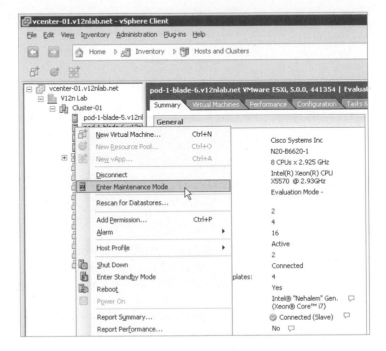

Maintenance mode is a setting on a host that prevents the ESXi host from performing any VM-related functions. VMs currently running on a host being put into maintenance mode must be shut down or moved to another host before the host will actually enter maintenance mode. This means that an ESXi host in a DRS-enabled cluster will automatically generate priority 1 recommendations to migrate all VMs to other hosts within the cluster. Figure 12.16 shows priority 1 recommendations generated as the result of an ESXi host being placed into maintenance mode.

The second condition that could cause a priority 1 recommendation is when DRS affinity rules come into play. This leads us to a discussion of DRS affinity rules.

A QUICK REVIEW OF DISTRIBUTED RESOURCE SCHEDULER CLUSTER PERFORMANCE

Monitoring the detailed performance of a cluster is an important task for any virtual infrastructure administrator, particularly monitoring the CPU and memory activity of the whole cluster as well as the respective resource utilization of the VMs within the cluster. The Summary tab of the details pane for a cluster object includes information on the configuration of the cluster as well as statistics regarding the current load distribution. Additionally, the View Resource Distribution Chart link allows you to open a graphical chart that shows the current resource distribution of the ESXi hosts in the cluster. While resource allocation and distribution isn't necessarily a direct indicator of performance, it can be a helpful metric nevertheless.

Working with Distributed Resource Scheduler Rules

To further allow an administrator to customize the behavior of vSphere DRS for their specific environment, vSphere offers the ability to create DRS rules. vSphere DRS supports three types of DRS rules:

♦ VM affinity rules, referred to as Keep Virtual Machines Together in the vSphere Client

♦ VM anti-affinity rules, referred to as Separate Virtual Machines in the vSphere Client

♦ Host affinity rules, referred to as Virtual Machines To Hosts in the vSphere Client

Figure 12.18 shows these three types of rules in the dialog box for creating new DRS rules.

FIGURE 12.18
DRS supports VM affinity, VM anti-affinity, and host affinity rules.

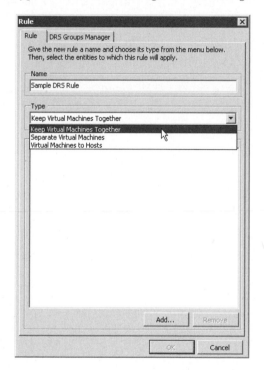

Recall from the previous section that DRS rules are the second of two conditions that will trigger a priority 1 recommendation (the other is maintenance mode). When DRS detects that VMs will violate DRS rules, it generates a priority 1 recommendation to migrate one or more VMs in order to satisfy the constraint expressed in the DRS rule.

vSphere's DRS rule functionality gives vSphere administrators the power to model the complex relationships that often exist in today's datacenters. Let's take a closer look at each of these three types of DRS rules.

CREATING VM AFFINITY RULES

Affinity rules keep VMs together on the same host. Consider a multitier application where you have a web application server and a backend database server that frequently communicate with each other, and you'd like that communication to take advantage of the high-speed bus within a single server rather than going across the network. In that case, you could define an affinity rule (Keep Virtual Machines Together) that would ensure these two VMs stay together in the cluster.

Perform the following steps to create a DRS affinity rule:

1. Launch the vSphere Client if it is not already running, and connect to a vCenter Server instance.

   DRS and DRS rules cannot be managed when connected to a specific ESXi host; you must connect to a vCenter Server instance.

2. Navigate to the Hosts And Clusters inventory view.

3. Right-click the DRS cluster where the rules need to exist, and select the Edit Settings option.

4. Click the Rules option.

5. Click the Add button near the bottom of the dialog box.

6. Type a name for the rule, and select Keep Virtual Machines Together for the type of rule to create.

7. Click the Add button to include the necessary VMs in the rule.

   Simply select the check box for the VMs you want to include in the DRS rule.

8. Click OK.

9. Review the new rule configuration to ensure it is correct.

10. Click OK.

VM affinity rules let you specify VMs that should always stay together, but what about VMs that should always stay separate? DRS offers that functionality with VM anti-affinity rules.

Creating VM Anti-Affinity Rules

Consider an environment with two mail server VMs. In all likelihood, administrators would not want both mail servers to reside on the same ESXi host. Instead, the administrators would want the mail servers split onto two different ESXi hosts in the cluster, so that the failure of one host would affect only one of the two mail servers. In this sort of situation, a VM anti-affinity rule is the right tool to use.

Perform the following steps to create a DRS anti-affinity rule:

1. Launch the vSphere Client if it is not already running, and connect to a vCenter Server instance. Recall that DRS and DRS rules are available only with vCenter Server.

2. Navigate to the Hosts And Clusters inventory view.

3. Right-click the DRS cluster where the rules need to exist, and select the Edit Settings option.

4. Click the Rules option.

5. Click the Add button near the bottom of the dialog box.

6. Type a name for the rule, and select Separate Virtual Machines as the type of rule to create.

7. Click the Add button to include the necessary VMs in the rule. Simply select the check box for the VMs you want to include in the DRS rule.

8. Click OK.

9. Review the new rule configuration to ensure it is correct.

10. Click OK.

With both VM affinity and VM anti-affinity rules, it is possible to create fallible rules, such as building a Separate Virtual Machines rule that has three VMs in it on a DRS cluster that has only two hosts. In this situation, vCenter Server will generate report warnings because DRS cannot satisfy the requirements of the rule.

So far you've seen how to instruct DRS to keep VMs together or to keep VMs separate, but what about situations where you want to constrain VMs to a group of hosts within a cluster? This is where host affinity rules come into play.

HOST AFFINITY RULES FIRST APPEARED IN VSPHERE 4.1

VMware introduced host affinity rules in vSphere 4.1. Host affinity rules were not available in earlier versions.

WORKING WITH HOST AFFINITY RULES

In addition to VM affinity and VM anti-affinity rules, vSphere DRS supports a third type of DRS rule: the host affinity rule. Host affinity rules are used to govern the relationships between VMs and the ESXi hosts in a cluster, giving administrators control over which hosts in a cluster are allowed to run which VMs. When combined with VM affinity and VM anti-affinity rules, administrators have the ability to create very complex rule sets to model the relationships between applications and workloads in their datacenter.

Before you can start creating a host affinity rule, you have to create at least one VM DRS group and at least one host DRS group. There are a couple of different places to manage DRS groups; one of the easiest ways is via the DRS Groups Manager, found in the Settings dialog box for a DRS-enabled cluster. Figure 12.19 shows the DRS Groups Manager. As you can see, a few groups have already been defined.

Perform the following steps to create a VM or host DRS group:

1. Launch the vSphere Client, if it is not already running, and connect to a vCenter Server instance.

2. Navigate to the Hosts And Clusters inventory view.

3. Right-click the DRS-enabled cluster and select Edit Settings.

4. From the Settings dialog box, click DRS Groups Manager.

5. To create a VM DRS group, click the Add button under the section Virtual Machines DRS Groups; to create a host DRS group, click the Add button in the section Host DRS Groups.

   You'll note that the steps and the dialog boxes are almost identical between the two different types of groups.

6. Supply a name for the new DRS group.

7. For a VM DRS group, select one or more VMs that you want to add to the group, and use the double-arrow button in the middle of the dialog box to move them into the group.

Figure 12.20 shows where I have added four VMs to a new VM DRS group and have another VM selected to add.

FIGURE 12.19
The DRS Groups Manager allows you to create and modify VM DRS groups and host DRS groups.

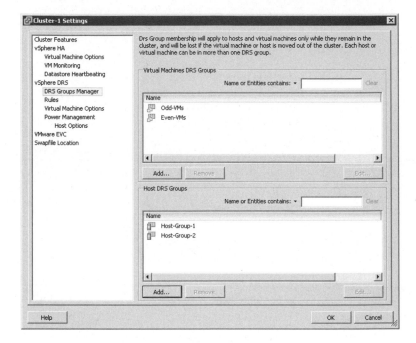

FIGURE 12.20
Use the double-arrow buttons to add or remove VMs or hosts from a DRS group. This screenshot shows adding VMs to a DRS group.

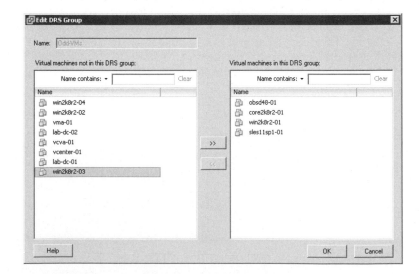

8. Click OK when you finish adding or removing VMs or hosts from the DRS group.

9. Click OK in the cluster Settings dialog box to save the DRS groups and return to the vSphere Client.

The previous steps are the same for both VM DRS groups and host DRS groups, and you'll need to have at least one of each group defined before you can create the rule.

After you've defined your VM DRS groups and host DRS groups, you're ready to actually define the host affinity rule. The host affinity rule brings together a VM DRS group and a host DRS group along with the preferred rule behavior. There are four host affinity rule behaviors:

◆ Must Run On Hosts In Group

◆ Should Run On Hosts In Group

◆ Must Not Run On Hosts In Group

◆ Should Not Run On Hosts In Group

These rules are, for the most part, self-explanatory. Each rule is either mandatory ("Must") or preferential ("Should") plus affinity ("Run On") or anti-affinity ("Not Run On"). Mandatory host affinity rules — those with "Must" — are honored not only by DRS but also by vSphere HA and vSphere DPM. For example, vSphere HA will not perform a failover if the failover would violate a required host affinity rule. Preferred rules, on the other hand, might be violated. Administrators have the option of creating an event-based alarm to monitor for the violation of preferred host affinity rules. You'll learn about alarms in Chapter 13.

Figure 12.21 shows a host affinity rule coming together with a selected VM DRS group, a rule behavior, and a selected host DRS group.

FIGURE 12.21
This host affinity rule specifies that the selected group of VMs must run on the selected group of ESXi hosts.

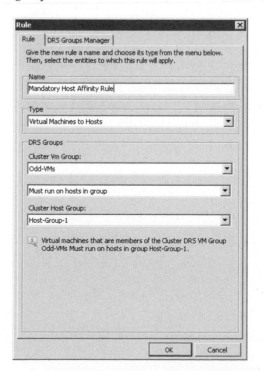

Be careful when defining host affinity rules, especially mandatory host affinity rules like the one shown in Figure 12.21. vCenter doesn't perform any checking to ensure that the rules can be satisfied. If you were to create two required host affinity rules that affected a single VM, that VM would be able to run only on hosts that were members of both groups. This is illustrated in Figure 12.22.

FIGURE 12.22
Administrators should ensure that using multiple required host affinity rules creates the desired results.

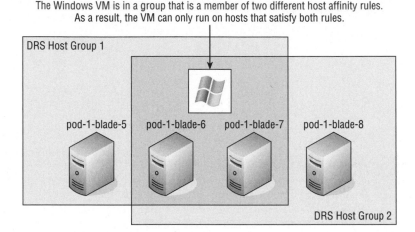

In the event of a rule conflict with DRS host affinity rules, the older rule prevails and the newer rule is automatically disabled. Disabled rules are ignored by DRS.

In fact, if you need to, you can temporarily disable DRS rules by deselecting the check box next to the rule. This might be useful in a troubleshooting scenario or in any situation where you need DRS to temporarily ignore the rule.

While the different sorts of rules that DRS supports provide lots of flexibility, there might be times when you need an even greater granularity. To satisfy that need for granularity, you can modify or disable DRS on individual VMs in the cluster.

Configuring Per-VM Distributed Resource Scheduler Settings

Although most VMs should be allowed to take advantage of the DRS balancing act, it's possible there will be enterprise-critical VMs that administrators are adamant about not being vMotion candidates. However, the VMs should remain in the cluster to take advantage of high-availability features provided by vSphere HA. In other words, VMs will take part in HA but not DRS despite both features being enabled on the cluster. As shown in Figure 12.23, VMs in a cluster can be configured with individual DRS compatibility levels. Figure 12.23 also shows that the ability to set automation levels on specific VMs can be disabled by deselecting the Enable Individual Virtual Machine Automation Levels check box.

This dialog box lists the VMs that are part of the cluster and their default automation levels. In this case, all VMs are set at Fully Automated because that's how the automation level of the cluster was set. The administrator can then selectively choose VMs that are not going to be acted on by DRS in the same way as the rest in the cluster. The automation levels available include the following:

◆ Fully Automated

◆ Manual

◆ Partially Automated

◆ Disabled

◆ Default (inherited from the cluster setting)

FIGURE 12.23
Individual VMs can
be prevented from
participating in
DRS.

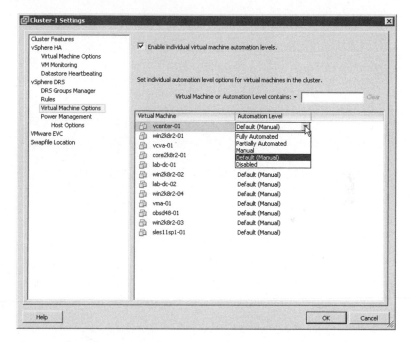

The first three options work as discussed previously in this chapter, in the sections
"Understanding Manual Automation Behavior," "Reviewing Partially Automated Behavior,"
and "Examining Fully Automated Behavior." The Disabled option turns off DRS, including the
automatic host selection at startup and the migration recommendations. The Default option configures the VM to accept the automation level set at the cluster.

AT LEAST BE OPEN TO CHANGE

Even if a VM or several VMs have been chosen not to participate in the automation of DRS, it is best
not to set VMs to the Disabled option because recommendations will not be provided. It is possible
that a priority 2 recommendation could be provided that suggests moving a VM an administrator thought was best on a specific host. Yet the migration might suggest a different host. For this
reason, the Manual option is better. At least be open to the possibility that a VM might perform
better on a different host.

VMware vSphere provides a number of tools for administrators to make their lives easier as
long as the tools are understood and set up properly. It might also be prudent to monitor the
activities of these tools to see whether a change to the configuration might be warranted over
time as your environment grows. Monitoring and alarms are discussed in detail in Chapter 13.

DRS is a valuable and useful part of vSphere, and it builds on vMotion to enable vSphere administrators to be more proactive about managing their environments. However, both vMotion and vSphere DRS help only with balancing CPU and memory load. In the next section, we'll discuss a method for manually balancing storage load.

Using Storage vMotion

vMotion and Storage vMotion are like two sides of the same coin. vMotion migrates a running VM from one physical host to another, moving CPU and memory usage between hosts but leaving the VM's storage unchanged. This allows you to manually balance the CPU and memory load by shifting VMs from host to host. Storage vMotion, on the other hand, migrates a running VM's virtual disks from one datastore to another datastore but leaves the VM executing — and therefore using CPU and memory resources — on the same ESXi host. This allows you to manually balance the "load" or utilization of a datastore by shifting a VM's storage from one datastore to another. Like vMotion, Storage vMotion is a live migration; the VM does not incur any outage during the migration of its virtual disks from one datastore to another.

So how does Storage vMotion work? The process is relatively straightforward:

1. First, vSphere copies over the nonvolatile files that make up a VM: the configuration file (VMX), VMkernel swap, log files, and snapshots.

2. Next, vSphere starts a ghost or shadow VM on the destination datastore. Because this ghost VM does not yet have a virtual disk (that hasn't been copied over yet), it sits idle waiting for its virtual disk.

3. Storage vMotion first creates the destination disk. Then a mirror device — a new driver that mirrors I/Os between the source and destination — is inserted into the data path between the VM and the underlying storage.

SVM Mirror Device Information in the Logs

If you review the vmkernel log files on an ESXi host during and after a Storage vMotion operation, you will see log entries prefixed with "SVM" that show the creation of the mirror device and that provide information about the operation of the mirror device.

---

4. With the I/O mirroring driver in place, vSphere makes a single-pass copy of the virtual disk(s) from the source to the destination. As changes are made to the source, the I/O mirror driver ensures those changes are also reflected at the destination.

5. When the virtual disk copy is complete, vSphere quickly suspends and resumes in order to transfer control over to the ghost VM created on the destination datastore earlier. This generally happens so quickly that there is no disruption of service, like with vMotion.

6. The files on the source datastore are deleted.

It's important to note that the original files aren't deleted until it's confirmed that the migration was successful; this allows vSphere to simply fall back to its original location if an error occurs. This helps prevent data loss situations or VM outages because of an error during the Storage vMotion process.

Perform these steps to migrate a VM's virtual disks using Storage vMotion:

1. Launch the vSphere Client if it is not already running, and connect to a vCenter Server instance. Storage vMotion is available only when you are working with vCenter Server.

2. Navigate to the Hosts And Clusters or VMs And Templates inventory view.

3. Select the VM whose virtual disks you want to migrate from the inventory tree on the left, and then select Migrate from the Commands section on the Summary tab on the right.

   You can also right-click the VM and select Migrate. This opens the Migrate Virtual Machine dialog box, the same dialog box used to initiate a vMotion operation.

4. Select Change Datastore and click Next.

5. Select the desired virtual disk format (Same Format As Source, Thick Provision Lazy Zeroed, Thick Provision Eager Zeroed, or Thin Provision).

Storage vMotion allows you to change the disk format during the actual disk-migration process, so you can switch from Thick Provision Lazy Zeroed to Thin Provision, for example.

STORAGE VMOTION WITH RAW DEVICE MAPPINGS

Be careful when using Storage vMotion with Raw Device Mappings (RDMs). If you want to migrate only the VMDK mapping file, be sure to select Same Format As Source for the virtual disk format. If you select a different format, virtual mode RDMs will be converted into VMDKs as part of the Storage vMotion operation (physical mode RDMs are not affected). Once an RDM has been converted into a VMDK, it cannot be converted back into an RDM again.

---

6. If you have a storage provider installed in vCenter Server and have defined a VM storage profile, select the desired profile from the VM Storage Profile drop-down box.

7. Select a destination datastore or datastore cluster. (You'll learn more about datastore clusters in the section " Introducing and Working with Storage DRS.")

8. If you need to migrate the VM's configuration file and virtual hard disks separately or to separate destinations, click the Advanced button.

   Figure 12.24 shows the Advanced view of the Storage step of the Migrate Virtual Machine Wizard and how you can choose the destination and disk format individually for different components of the VM.

FIGURE 12.24
Use the Advanced view of the Migrate Virtual Machine Wizard to migrate a VM's configuration files and virtual disks independently.

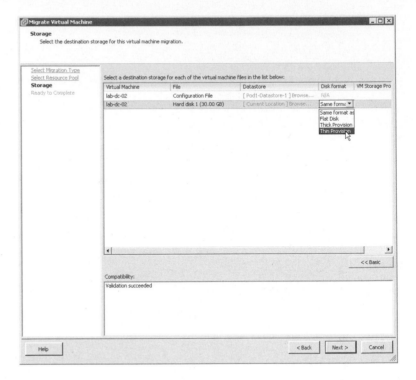

9. When you have finished making selections on the Storage screen, click Next to continue with the Migrate Virtual Machine Wizard.

10. Review the settings for the Storage vMotion to ensure that everything is correct.

   If you need to make changes, use the hyperlinks on the left or the Back button to go back and make any changes.

Once you initiate the Storage vMotion operation, the vSphere Client will show the progress of the migration in the Tasks pane, as you've seen for other tasks (such as vMotion).

Like vMotion, Storage vMotion is great for manually adjusting the load or utilization of resources. vSphere DRS leverages vMotion to bring a level of automation to this process. New in vSphere 5, Storage DRS does the same thing for storage — brings a level of automation and leverages Storage vMotion to help balance storage utilization across datastores.

Introducing and Working with Storage DRS

Storage DRS is a feature that is new to vSphere 5. Building on the functionality that VMware introduced in earlier versions — specifically, building on Storage I/O Control and Storage vMotion — SDRS introduces the ability to perform automated balancing of storage utilization. SDRS can perform this automated balancing not only on the basis of space utilization but also on the basis of I/O load balancing.

Like vSphere DRS, SDRS is built on some closely related concepts and terms:

◆ Just as vSphere DRS uses clusters as a collection of hosts on which to act, SDRS uses data store clusters as collections of datastores on which it acts.

◆ Just as vSphere DRS can perform both initial placement and manual and ongoing balancing, SDRS also performs initial placement of VMDKs and ongoing balancing of VMDKs. The initial placement functionality of SDRS is especially appealing because it helps simplify the VM provisioning process for vSphere administrators.

◆ Just as vSphere DRS offers affinity and anti-affinity rules to influence recommendations, SDRS offers VMDK affinity and anti-affinity functionality.

As I just mentioned, SDRS uses the idea of a *datastore cluster* — a group of datastores treated as shared storage resources — in order to operate. Before you can enable or configure SDRS, you must create a datastore cluster. However, you can't just arbitrarily combine datastores into a datastore cluster; there are some guidelines you need to follow.

Specifically, VMware provides the following guidelines for datastores that are combined into datastore clusters:

◆ Datastores of different sizes and I/O capacities can be combined in a datastore cluster. Additionally, datastores from different arrays and vendors can be combined into a datastore cluster. However, you cannot combine NFS and VMFS datastores in a datastore cluster.

◆ You cannot combine replicated and nonreplicated datastores into an SDRS-enabled datastore cluster.

◆ All hosts attached to a datastore in a datastore cluster must be running ESXi 5 or later. ESX/ESXi 4.*x* and earlier cannot be connected to a datastore that you want to add to a datastore cluster.

◆ Datastores shared across multiple datacenters are not supported for SDRS.

WHAT ABOUT MIXED HARDWARE ACCELERATION SUPPORT?

Hardware acceleration as a result of support for the vSphere Storage APIs for Array Integration (more commonly known as VAAI) is another factor to consider when creating datastore clusters. As a best practice, VMware recommends against mixing datastores that do support hardware acceleration with datastores that don't support hardware acceleration. All the datastores in a datastore cluster should be homogeneous with regard to hardware acceleration support in the underlying array(s).

In addition to these general guidelines from VMware, I'd recommend you consult your specific storage array vendor for any additional recommendations that are particular to your specific array. Your storage vendors may have additional recommendations on what array-based features are or are not supported in conjunction with SDRS.

In the next section, I'll show you how to create and work with datastore clusters in preparation for a more in-depth look at configuring SDRS.

Creating and Working with Datastore Clusters

Now you're ready to create a datastore cluster and begin exploring SDRS in greater detail. Perform these steps to create a datastore cluster:

1. If it is not already running, launch the vSphere Client and connect to an instance of vCenter Server.

   Storage DRS and datastore clusters are possible only when you are using vCenter Server in your environment.

2. Navigate to the Datastores And Datastore Clusters inventory view by selecting View ➢ Inventory ➢ Datastores And Datastore Clusters.

   You can also use the navigation bar or the keyboard shortcut (Ctrl+Shift+D).

3. Right-click the datastore object where you want to create a new datastore cluster. From the context menu that appears, select New Datastore Cluster. This launches the New Datastore Cluster Wizard.

4. Supply a name for the new datastore cluster.

5. If you want to enable Storage DRS for this datastore, select Turn On Storage DRS. Click Next.

6. Storage DRS can operate in a manual mode, where it will make recommendations only, or in Fully Automated mode, where it will actually perform storage migrations automatically. Select Fully Automated and click Next.

7. If you want Storage DRS to include I/O metrics along with space utilization as part of its recommendations or migrations, select Enable I/O Metric For Storage DRS Recommendations.

   Configuring SDRS to include I/O metrics in this manner will automatically enable Storage I/O Control on the datastores that are a part of this cluster.

8. You can adjust the thresholds that Storage DRS uses to control when it recommends or performs migrations (depending on whether Storage DRS is configured for manual or fully automated operation).

   The default utilized space threshold is 80 percent; this means when the datastore reaches 80 percent full, Storage DRS will recommend or perform a storage migration. The default setting for I/O latency is 15 ms; you should adjust this based on recommendations from your storage vendor. Figure 12.25 shows the default settings for the SDRS runtime rules. When you are finished adjusting these values, click Next.

STORAGE I/O CONTROL AND STORAGE DRS LATENCY THRESHOLDS

In Chapter 11 in the section "Controlling Storage I/O Utilization," I discussed adjusting storage latency as the threshold for Storage I/O Control (SIOC). You'll note that the default I/O latency threshold for SDRS (15 ms) is well below the default for SIOC (30 ms). The idea behind these default settings is that SDRS can make a migration to balance the load (if fully automated) before throttling becomes necessary.

Just as I recommended you check with your storage vendor for specific recommendations on SIOC latency values, you should also check with your array vendor to see if that vendor offers recommendations for SDRS latency values.

FIGURE 12.25
The default settings
for SDRS include
I/O metrics
and settings for
utilized space and
I/O latency.

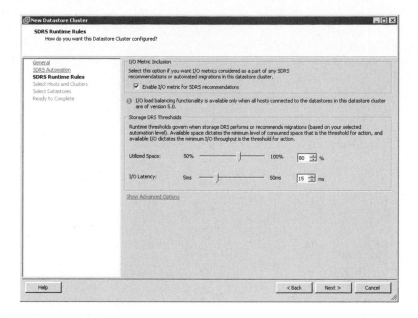

9. Place a check in the check box next to the ESXi hosts and/or clusters to which this new datastore cluster should be added; then click Next.

10. Select the available datastores you'd like to add to the new datastore cluster.

    Because of the nature of Storage DRS, you'll want to leave the Show Datastores drop-down box at the default setting of Connected To All Hosts, so that any datastores listed here are accessible from the hosts and/or clusters you selected in the previous step. Place a check in the check box next to each datastore you want added to the datastore cluster. Click Next.

11. Review the settings in the final screen of the New Datastore Cluster Wizard.

    If any of the settings are incorrect or if you need to make any changes, use the hyperlinks on the left or the Back button to go back. Otherwise, click Finish.

The newly created datastore cluster will appear in the Datastores And Datastore Clusters inventory view. The Summary tab of the datastore cluster, shown in Figure 12.26, will display the aggregate statistics about the datastores in the datastore cluster.

Once you've created a datastore cluster, you can add capacity to the datastore cluster by adding more datastores, much in the same way you would add capacity to a vSphere DRS cluster by adding new ESXi hosts.

To add a datastore to a datastore cluster, just right-click an existing datastore cluster and select Add Storage from the pop-up context menu. This opens the Add Storage dialog box, where you can select additional datastores to add to the datastore cluster. Figure 12.27 shows the Add Storage dialog box, where you can see that some datastores cannot be added because all necessary ESXi hosts aren't connected. This ensures that you don't inadvertently add a datastore to a datastore cluster and then find that an SRDS migration renders that VMDK unreachable by one or more ESXi hosts.

FIGURE 12.26
The Summary tab of a datastore cluster provides overall information about total capacity, total used space, total free space, and largest free space.

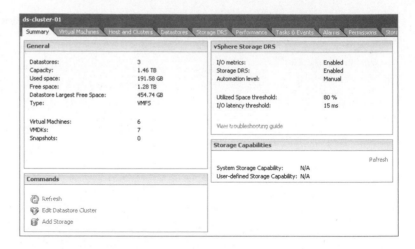

FIGURE 12.27
To add a datastore to a datastore cluster, the new datastore must be connected to all the hosts currently connected to the datastore cluster.

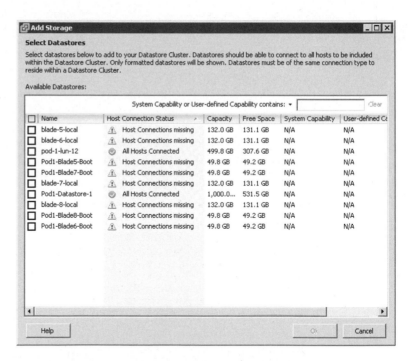

SDRS also offers a maintenance mode option for datastores, just as vSphere DRS offers a maintenance mode option for ESXi hosts. To place a datastore into SDRS maintenance mode, right-click the datastore and select Enter SDRS Maintenance Mode. If there are any registered VMs currently on that datastore, SDRS will immediately generate migration recommendations, as Figure 12.28 shows. If you select Cancel in the SDRS Maintenance Mode Migration Recommendations dialog box, you will cancel the SDRS maintenance mode request, and the datastore will not go into SDRS maintenance mode.

FIGURE 12.28
Putting a
datastore into SDRS
maintenance mode
generates SDRS
recommendations
to evacuate the
datastore.

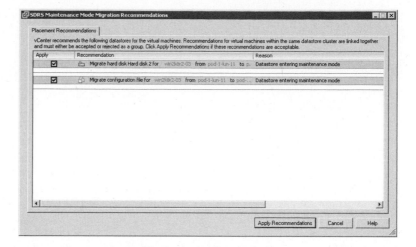

> **STORAGE DRS MAINTENANCE MODE DOESN'T AFFECT TEMPLATES AND ISOS**
>
> When you enable SDRS maintenance mode for a datastore, recommendations are generated for registered VMs. However, SDRS maintenance mode will not affect templates, unregistered VMs, or ISOs stored on that datastore.

You'd need to put a datastore into SDRS maintenance mode in order to remove the datastore from the datastore cluster. (Again, this is eerily similar to how you place hosts into maintenance mode in order to remove them from a vSphere DRS-enabled cluster. You might even think that VMware planned it that way!)

Once a datastore is in SDRS maintenance mode, you can simply use drag and drop to move the datastore out of the datastore cluster. In addition to using the Add Storage dialog box I showed you earlier in this section, you can use drag and drop to add a datastore to an existing datastore cluster as well. Note, however, that drag and drop won't warn you that you're adding a datastore that doesn't have connections to all the hosts that are currently connected to the datastore cluster, so I generally recommend using the Add Storage dialog box shown in Figure 12.27.

Let's now take a more in-depth look at configuring SDRS to work with the datastore cluster(s) that you've created.

Configuring Storage DRS

All of the configuration for SDRS is done from the Edit Cluster dialog box. You'll open the Edit Cluster dialog box by right-clicking a datastore cluster and selecting Edit Settings or by clicking the Edit Settings command on the Summary tab of a datastore cluster. Both methods will give you the same result.

From the Edit Cluster dialog box, you can accomplish the following tasks:

◆ Enable or disable SDRS

◆ Configure the SDRS automation level

- ◆ Change or modify the SDRS runtime rules
- ◆ Configure or modify custom SDRS schedules
- ◆ Create SDRS rules to influence SDRS behavior
- ◆ Configure per-VM SDRS settings

The following sections examine each of these areas in more detail.

ENABLING OR DISABLING STORAGE DRS

From the General area of the Edit Cluster dialog box, you can easily enable or disable SDRS. Figure 12.29 shows this area of the Edit Cluster dialog box. From here, you can enable SDRS by selecting Turn On Storage DRS. If Storage DRS is already enabled, you can deselect Turn On Storage DRS to disable it. If you disable SDRS, the SDRS settings are preserved. If SDRS is later reenabled, the configuration is returned to the point where it was when it was disabled.

FIGURE 12.29
In addition to enabling or disabling Storage DRS, you can rename the datastore cluster from this dialog box.

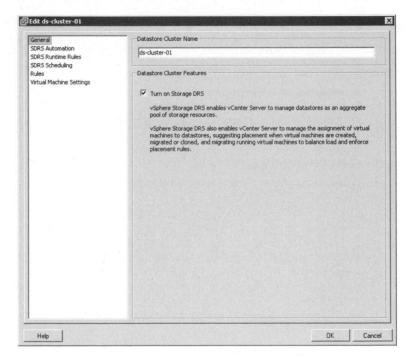

CONFIGURING STORAGE DRS AUTOMATION

SDRS offers two predefined automation levels, as you can see in Figure 12.30: No Automation (Manual Mode) and Fully Automated.

When the SDRS automation level is set to No Automation (Manual Mode), SDRS will generate recommendations for initial placement as well as recommendations for storage migrations based on the configured space and I/O thresholds. Initial placement recommendations are generated when you create a new VM (and thus a new virtual disk), add a virtual disk to a VM, or clone a VM or template. Initial placement recommendations take the form of a pop-up window, like the one shown in Figure 12.31.

FIGURE 12.30
Storage DRS offers both Manual and Fully Automated modes of operation.

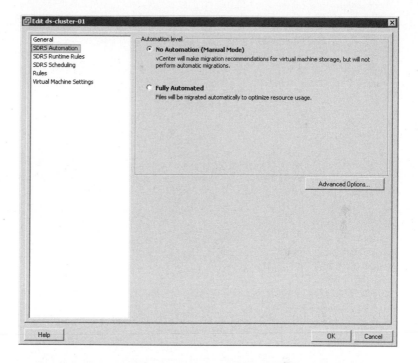

FIGURE 12.31
Storage DRS presents a list of initial placement recommendations whenever a new virtual disk is created.

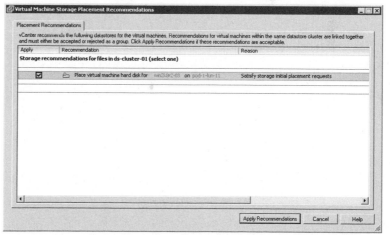

Recommendations for storage migrations are noted in two different ways. First, an alarm is generated to note that an SDRS recommendation is present. You can view this alarm on the Alarms tab of the datastore cluster in Datastores And Datastore Clusters inventory view, as shown in Figure 12.32.

FIGURE 12.32
This alarm on the datastore cluster indicates that an SDRS recommendation is present.

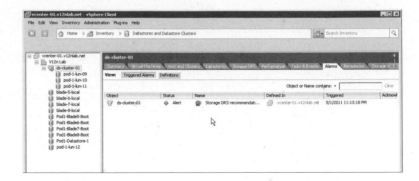

In addition, the Storage DRS tab of the datastore cluster (visible in Datastores And Datastore Clusters inventory view, as shown in Figure 12.33) will list the current SDRS recommendations and give you the option to apply those recommendations — that is, initiate the suggested Storage vMotion migrations.

FIGURE 12.33
Select Apply Recommendations in the Storage DRS tab to initiate the storage migrations suggested by SDRS.

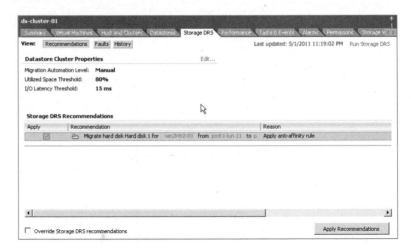

When SDRS is configured for Fully Automated mode, SDRS will automatically initiate Storage vMotion migrations instead of generating recommendations for the administrator to approve. In this instance, you can use the Storage DRS tab of the datastore cluster to view the history of SDRS actions by selecting the History button at the top of the Storage DRS tab. Figure 12.34 shows the SDRS history for the selected datastore cluster.

FIGURE 12.34
On the Storage DRS tab of a datastore cluster, use the History button to review the SDRS actions that have taken place when running in Fully Automated mode.

To modify how aggressive SDRS is when running in Fully Automated mode, you'll need to switch over to the SDRS Runtime Rules section of the Edit Cluster dialog box, described in the next section.

MODIFYING THE STORAGE DRS RUNTIME BEHAVIOR

In the SDRS Runtime Rules section of the Edit Cluster dialog box, you have several options for modifying the behavior of SDRS.

First, if you'd like to tell SDRS to operate only on the basis of space utilization and not I/O utilization, simply deselect Enable I/O Metric For SDRS Recommendations. This will tell SDRS to recommend or perform (depending on the automation level) migrations based strictly on space utilization.

Second, the Storage DRS Thresholds area allows you to adjust the thresholds that SDRS uses to recommend or perform migrations. By default, the Utilized Space setting is 80 percent, meaning that SDRS will recommend or perform a migration when a datastore reaches 80 percent full. The default I/O Latency setting is 15 ms; when latency measurements exceed 15 ms for a given datastore in a datastore cluster and I/O metrics are enabled, then SDRS will recommend or perform a storage migration to another datastore with a lower latency measurement.

If you click the Show Advanced Options hyperlink, you can further fine-tune the runtime behavior of SDRS:

◆ The first slider bar, labeled "No recommendations until utilization difference between source and destination is," allows you to specify how much of an improvement SDRS should look for before making a recommendation or performing a migration. The setting defaults to 5 percent. This means that if the destination's values are 5 percent lower than the source's values, SDRS will make the recommendation or perform the migration.

◆ The Evaluate I/O Load Every option allows you to control how often SDRS evaluates the I/O or space utilization in order to make a recommendation or perform a migration.

◆ Finally, the I/O Imbalance Threshold controls the aggressiveness of the SDRS algorithm. As the slider is moved toward Aggressive and the counter increases, this moves up the priority of the recommendation that will be automatically acted on when SDRS is running in Fully Automated mode.

In addition to the rudimentary schedule control that controls how often SDRS evaluates I/O and space utilization, you also have the ability to create more complex scheduling settings.

CONFIGURING OR MODIFYING THE STORAGE DRS SCHEDULE

The SDRS Scheduling area of the Edit Cluster dialog box allows you to create custom schedules. These custom schedules enable vSphere administrators to specify times when the SDRS behavior should be different. For example, are there times when SDRS should be running in No Automation (Manual Mode)? Are there times when the space utilization or I/O latency thresholds should be different? If so, and you need SDRS to adjust to these recurring differences, you can accommodate that through custom SDRS schedules.

Let's look at an example. Let's say that you normally have SDRS running in Fully Automated mode, and it works fine. However, at night, when backups are running, you want SDRS not to automatically perform storage migrations. Using a custom SDRS schedule, you can tell SDRS to switch into manual mode during certain times of the day and days of the week and then return into Fully Automated mode when that day/time period is over.

Perform the following steps to create a custom SDRS schedule:

1. If it's not already running, launch the vSphere Client and log into a vCenter Server instance.

   SDRS is available only when you're using vCenter Server.

2. Navigate to the Datastore And Datastore Clusters inventory view.

3. Right-click a datastore cluster and select Edit Settings.

4. Select SDRS Scheduling from the list of areas on the left.

5. Click Add. This opens the Create SDRS Schedule Task Wizard.

6. Specify the start and end times and the days of the week when this custom schedule task should be active.

   For example, if you needed to change SDRS behavior while backups are running in the middle of the night, you could set the Start to 10:00 PM and the End to 5:30 AM. Click Next to continue.

7. Provide a description and then select the SDRS settings that should go into effect at the start of the days and times you specified in the previous step.

   For example, you could set Automation Level to Manual and deselect Enable I/O Metric For SDRS Recommendations. Click Next when you've set the desired values.

8. Provide another description and select the SDRS settings you want to go into effect at the end of the days and times you selected in step 6.

   To make it easier to go back to the original settings, VMware has included a check box labeled Restore Settings To The Original Configuration. Select that option and then click Next.

9. Review the settings. Click Finish if they are correct; otherwise, use the Back button or the hyperlinks on the left to go back and make any desired changes.

After you complete the Create SDRS Schedule Task Wizard, a new set of entries appears in the list of SDRS Scheduling, as illustrated in Figure 12.35.

The ability to have SDRS be configured differently at different times or on different days is a powerful feature that will let vSphere administrators customize SDRS behaviors to best suit their environments. SDRS rules are another tool that provide administrators with more control over how SDRS handles VMs and virtual disks, as you'll see in the next section.

FIGURE 12.35
SDRS scheduling
entries allow you
to automatically
change the settings
for SDRS on certain
days and at certain
times.

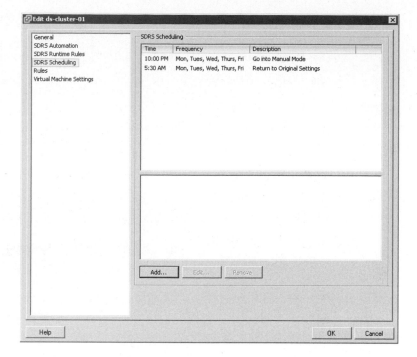

CREATING STORAGE DRS RULES

Just as vSphere DRS has affinity and anti-affinity rules, SDRS offers vSphere administrators the ability to create VMDK anti-affinity and VM anti-affinity rules. These rules modify the behavior of SDRS to ensure that specific VMDKs are always kept separate (VMDK anti-affinity rule) or that all the virtual disks from certain VMs are kept separate (VM anti-affinity rule).

Perform these steps to create an SDRS VMDK anti-affinity or SDRS VM anti-affinity rule:

1. In the vSphere Client, navigate to the Datastores And Datastore Clusters inventory view.

2. Right-click a datastore cluster and select Edit Settings.

   You can also use the Edit Settings command on the Summary tab of the datastore cluster.

3. Select Rules.

4. Click Add to add a rule.

5. In the Rule dialog box, supply a name for the rule you are creating.

6. From the Type drop-down box, select VMDK Anti-Affinity or VM Anti-Affinity, depending on which type of rule you want to create.

For the purposes of this procedure, select VMDK Anti-Affinity Rule.

7. Click Add to select the virtual disks that you want to include in this rule.

8. To select the virtual disks in this rule, you must first select a VM.

In the Virtual Disks dialog box, click Select Virtual Machine and select the specific VM that has at least two virtual disks you want to keep on separate datastores. After selecting the desired VM in the Virtual Machines dialog box, click OK to return to the Virtual Disks dialog box.

9. In the Virtual Disks dialog box, select the specific virtual disks that you want included in the rule, as shown in Figure 12.36, and then click OK.

FIGURE 12.36
An SDRS VMDK anti-affinity rule allows you to specify particular virtual disks for a VM that should be kept on separate datastores in a datastore cluster.

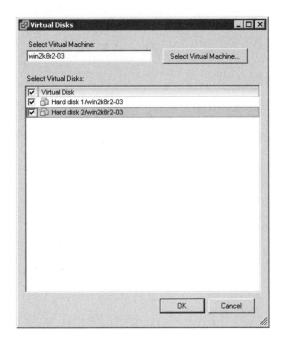

10. Click OK in the Rule dialog box to complete the creation of the SDRS anti-affinity rule.

You might receive a warning dialog box, like the one shown in Figure 12.37, letting you know that the anti-affinity rule you are creating will override the values in the Virtual Machine Settings area (see the section "Setting Storage DRS Virtual Machine Settings" for more information).

Normally, Storage DRS runs an evaluation every eight hours (this can be adjusted; refer back to the "Modifying the Storage DRS Runtime Behavior" section). At the next evaluation, Storage DRS will include the new anti-affinity rule in the evaluation. If you want to invoke

SDRS immediately, the Storage DRS tab of the datastore cluster, shown in Figure 12.38, offers the option to invoke SDRS immediately using the Run Storage DRS link in the upper-right corner.

FIGURE 12.37
This warning indicates that the rule you've created will override per-VM SDRS settings.

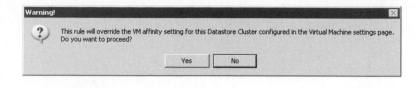

FIGURE 12.38
Use the Run Storage DRS link to invoke SDRS on demand.

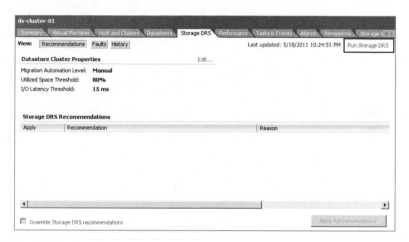

You might have noticed that there is no user interface for creating affinity rules; for example, rules to keep VMs or VMDKs on the same datastore. There is a way to configure this, but it's configured in a different area of the Storage DRS configuration, as you'll see in the next section.

SETTING STORAGE DRS VIRTUAL MACHINE SETTINGS

Administrators can use anti-affinity rules to keep VMs or VMDKs on separate datastores, but as you've already seen, there is no way to create affinity rules. Instead of requiring you to create affinity rules to keep the virtual disks for a VM together, vSphere offers a simple check box in the Virtual Machine Settings area of the datastore cluster properties.

Figure 12.39 shows the Virtual Machine Settings area for a datastore cluster. To configure Storage DRS to keep all disks for a VM together, check the boxes in the Keep VMDKs Together column. You'll note in Figure 12.39 that one VM (win2k8r2-03) is unchecked; this is the VM for which we configured an anti-affinity rule. Because we configured a VMDK anti-affinity rule, that rule overrides the setting here in the Virtual Machine Settings area. This is the result of the warning shown to you in Figure 12.37.

As you can see, SDRS has a tremendous amount of flexibility built into it to allow vSphere administrators to harness the power of SDRS by tailoring its behavior to best suit their specific environments.

In the next chapter, I'll move into a review and discussion of monitoring and alarms and show what tools or features VMware vSphere offers administrators in the realm of performance monitoring.

FIGURE 12.39
The Virtual Machine Settings area shows which VMs will have their VMDKs kept together by SDRS.

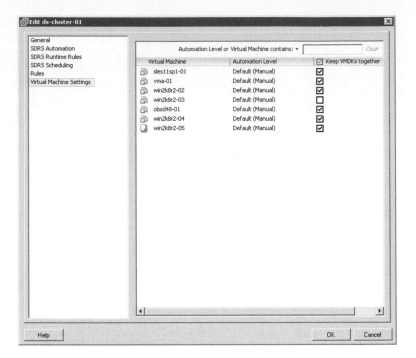

The Bottom Line

Configure and execute vMotion. vMotion is a feature that allows running VMs to be migrated from one physical ESXi host to another physical ESXi host with no downtime to end users. To execute vMotion, both the ESXi hosts and the VMs must meet specific configuration requirements. In addition, vCenter Server performs validation checks to ensure that vMotion compatibility rules are observed.

Master It A certain vendor has just released a series of patches for some of the guest OSes in your virtualized infrastructure. You request an outage window from your supervisor, but your supervisor says to just use vMotion to prevent downtime. Is your supervisor correct? Why or why not?

Master It Is vMotion a solution to prevent unplanned downtime?

Ensure vMotion compatibility across processor families. vMotion requires compatible CPU families on the source and destination ESXi hosts in order to be successful. To help alleviate any potential problems resulting from changes in processor families over time, vSphere offers Enhanced vMotion Compatibility (EVC), which can mask differences between CPU families in order to maintain vMotion compatibility.

Master It Can you change the EVC level for a cluster while there are VMs running on hosts in the cluster?

Configure and manage vSphere Distributed Resource Scheduler.   VMware Distributed Resource Scheduler enables vCenter Server to automate the process of conducting vMotion migrations to help balance the load across ESXi hosts within a cluster. DRS can be as automated as desired, and vCenter Server has flexible controls for affecting the behavior of DRS as well as the behavior of specific VMs within a DRS-enabled cluster.

Master It   You want to take advantage of vSphere DRS to provide some load balancing of virtual workloads within your environment. However, because of business constraints, you have a few workloads that should not be automatically moved to other hosts using vMotion. Can you use DRS? If so, how can you prevent these specific workloads from being affected by DRS?

Use Storage vMotion.   Just as vMotion is used to migrate running VMs from one ESXi host to another, Storage vMotion is used to migrate the virtual disks of a running VM from one datastore to another. You can also use Storage vMotion to convert between thick and thin virtual disk types.

Master It   A fellow administrator is trying to migrate a VM to a different datastore and a different host, but the option is disabled (grayed out). Why?

Master It   Name two features of Storage vMotion that would help administrators cope with storage-related changes in their vSphere environment.

Configure and manage Storage DRS.   Building on Storage vMotion just as vSphere DRS builds on vMotion, Storage DRS brings automation to the process of balancing storage capacity and I/O utilization. Storage DRS uses datastore clusters and can operate in manual or Fully Automated mode. Numerous customizations exist — such as custom schedules, VM and VMDK anti-affinity rules, and threshold settings — to allow administrators to fine-tune the behavior of Storage DRS for their specific environments.

Master It   Name the two ways in which an administrator is notified that a Storage DRS recommendation has been generated.

Master It   What is a potential disadvantage of using drag and drop to add a datastore to a datastore cluster?

## Chapter 13

Monitoring VMware vSphere Performance

The monitoring of VMware vSphere should be a combination of proactive benchmarking and reactive alarm-based actions. vCenter Server provides both methods to help the administrator keep tabs on each of the VMs and hosts as well as the hierarchical objects in the inventory. Using both methods ensures that the administrator is not caught unaware of performance issues or lack of capacity.

vCenter Server provides some exciting new features for monitoring your VMs and hosts, such as expanded performance views and charts, and it greatly expands the number and types of alarms available by default. Together, these features make it much easier to manage and monitor VMware vSphere performance.

In this chapter, you will learn to

- ◆ Use alarms for proactive monitoring

- ◆ Work with performance graphs

- ◆ Gather performance information using command-line tools

- ◆ Monitor CPU, memory, network, and disk usage by ESXi hosts and VMs

Overview of Performance Monitoring

Monitoring performance is a key part of every vSphere administrator's job. Fortunately, vCenter Server provides a number of ways to get insight into the behavior of the vSphere environment and the VMs running within that environment.

The first tool vCenter Server provides is its alarms mechanism. Alarms can be attached to just about any object within vCenter Server and provide an ideal way to proactively alert the vSphere administrator about potential performance concerns or resource usage. I'll discuss alarms in detail in the section "Using Alarms."

Another tool that vCenter Server provides is the Resources pane on the Summary tab of ESXi hosts and VMs. The Resources pane provides quick "at-a-glance" information on resource usage. This information can be useful as a quick barometer of performance, but for more detailed performance information, you will have to dive deeper into the vCenter tools that I'll discuss later in this chapter.

Another tool that provides an at-a-glance performance summary is the Virtual Machines tab, found on vCenter Server objects, datacenter objects, cluster objects, and ESXi hosts. Figure 13.1 shows the Virtual Machines tab of a cluster object. This tab provides an overview of general performance and resource usage. This information includes CPU utilization, memory usage, and storage space utilized. As with the Resources pane, this information can be useful, but it is quite limited. However, keep in mind that a quick trip here might help you isolate the one VM that could be causing performance issues for the ESXi host on which it is running.

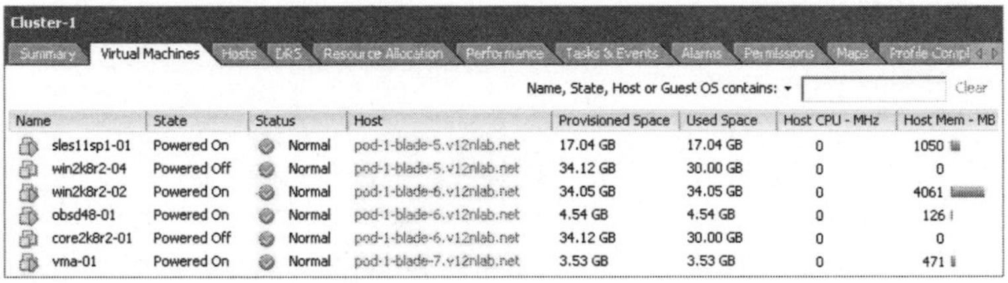

FIGURE 13.1

The Virtual Machines tab of a cluster object offers a quick look at VM CPU and memory usage.

For ESXi clusters, resource pools and VMs, another tool you can use is the Resource Allocation tab. The Resource Allocation tab provides a picture of how CPU and memory resources are being used for the entire pool. This high-level method of looking at resource usage is useful for analyzing overall infrastructure utilization. This tab also provides an easy way of adjusting individual VMs or resource pool reservations, limits, and/or shares without editing each object independently.

vCenter Server also offers a powerful, in-depth tool found on the Performance tab that provides a mechanism for creating graphs that depict the actual resource consumption over time for a given ESXi host or VM. The graphs provide historical information and can be used for trend analysis. vCenter Server provides many objects and counters to analyze the performance of a single VM or host for a selected interval. The Performance tab and the graphs are powerful tools for isolating performance considerations, and I discuss them in greater detail in the section "Working with Performance Graphs."

VMware also provides `resxtop` for an in-depth view of all the counters available in vSphere to help isolate and identify problems in the hypervisor. `resxtop` runs only inside the vSphere Management Assistant (vMA). I'll take a look at `resxtop` later in this chapter in the section "Working with `resxtop`."

Finally, I'll take the various tools that I've discussed and show how to use them to monitor the four major resources in a vSphere environment: CPU, memory, network, and storage.

Let's get started with a discussion of alarms.

Using Alarms

In addition to using the graphs and high-level information tabs, the administrator can create alarms for VMs, hosts, networks, and datastores based on predefined triggers provided with vCenter Server. Depending on the object, these alarms can monitor resource consumption or the state of the object and alert the administrator when certain conditions have been met, such as high resource usage or even low resource usage. These alarms can then provide an action that informs the administrator of the condition by email or SNMP trap. An action can also automatically run a script or provide other means to correct the problem the VM or host might be experiencing.

In vSphere 4 the number of alarms had been extended considerably compared to earlier versions. In vSphere 5 only a few alarms and condition checks have been added. As you can see in Figure 13.2, the alarms that come with vCenter Server are defined at the topmost object, the vCenter Server object.

FIGURE 13.2
The default alarms for objects in vCenter Server are defined on the vCenter Server object itself.

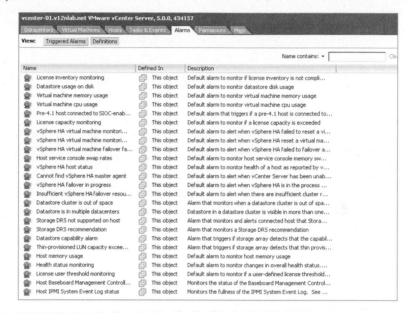

These default alarms are usually generic in nature. Some of the predefined alarms alert the administrator if any of the following situations occur:

◆ A host's storage status, CPU status, voltage, temperature, or power status changes

◆ A cluster experiences a vSphere High Availability (HA) error

◆ A datastore runs low on free disk space

◆ A VM's CPU usage, memory usage, disk latency, or even fault tolerance status changes

In addition to the small sampling of predefined alarms I've just described, there are many more, and VMware has enabled users to create alarms on just about any object within vCenter Server. This greatly increases the ability of vCenter Server to proactively alert administrators to changes within the virtual environment before a problem develops.

Because the default alarms are likely too generic for your administrative needs, creating your own alarms is often necessary. Before showing you how to create an alarm, though, I need to first discuss the concept of alarm scopes. Once I've discussed alarm scopes, I'll walk you through creating a few alarms.

Understanding Alarm Scopes

When you create alarms, one thing to keep in mind is the *scope* of the alarm. In Figure 13.2, you saw the default set of alarms that are available in vCenter Server. These alarms are defined at the vCenter Server object and thus have the greatest scope — they apply to all objects managed by that vCenter Server instance. It's also possible to create alarms at the datacenter level, the cluster level, the host level, or even the VM level. This allows you, the vSphere administrator, to create specific alarms that are limited in scope and are intended to meet specific monitoring needs.

When you define an alarm on an object, that alarm applies to all objects beneath that object in the vCenter Server hierarchy. The default set of alarms that VMware provides with vCenter Server is defined at the vCenter Server object and therefore applies to all objects — datacenters, hosts, clusters, datastores, networks, and VMs — managed by that instance of vCenter Server. If you were to create an alarm on a resource pool, then the alarm would apply only to VMs found in that resource pool. Similarly, if you were to create an alarm on a specific VM, that alarm would apply only to that specific VM.

Alarms are also associated with specific types of objects. For example, some alarms apply only to VMs, while other alarms apply only to ESXi hosts. You'll want to use this filtering mechanism to your advantage when creating alarms. For example, if you needed to monitor a particular condition on all ESXi hosts, you could define a host alarm on the datacenter or vCenter Server object, and it would apply to all ESXi hosts but not to any VMs.

It's important that you keep these scoping effects in mind when defining alarms so that your new alarms work as expected. You don't want to inadvertently exclude some portion of your vSphere environment by creating an alarm at the wrong point in your hierarchy or by creating the wrong type of alarm.

Now you're ready to look at actually creating alarms.

Creating Alarms

As you've already learned, there are many different types of alarms that administrators might want to create. These could be alarms that monitor resource consumption — such as how much CPU time a VM is consuming or how much RAM an ESXi host has allocated — or these alarms could monitor for specific events, such as whenever a specific distributed virtual port group is modified. In addition, you've already learned that alarms can be created on a variety of different objects within vCenter Server. Regardless of the type of alarm or the type of object to which that alarm is attached, the basic steps for creating an alarm are the same. In the following sections, I'll walk you through creating a couple of different alarms so that you have the opportunity to see the options available to you.

CREATING A RESOURCE CONSUMPTION ALARM

First, let's create an alarm that monitors resource consumption. As I discussed in Chapter 9, "Creating and Managing Virtual Machines," vCenter Server supports VM snapshots. These snapshots capture a VM at a specific point in time, allowing you to roll back (or revert) to that state later. However, snapshots require additional space on disk, and monitoring disk space usage by snapshots is an important task. In vSphere, vCenter Server offers the ability to create an alarm that monitors VM snapshot space.

Before you create a custom alarm, though, you should ask yourself a couple of questions. First, is there an existing alarm that already handles this task for you? Browsing the list of predefined alarms available in vCenter Server shows that although some storage-related alarms are present, there is no alarm that monitors snapshot disk usage. Second, if you're going to create a new alarm, where is the appropriate place within vCenter Server to create that alarm? This refers to the earlier discussion of scope: on what object should you create this alarm so that it is properly scoped and will alert you only under the desired conditions? In this particular case, you'd want to be alerted to any snapshot space usage that exceeds your desired threshold, so a higher-level object such as the datacenter object or even the vCenter Server object would be the best place to create the alarm.

Perform the following steps to create an alarm that monitors VM snapshot disk space usage for all VMs in a datacenter:

1. Launch the vSphere Client if it is not already running, and connect to a vCenter Server instance.

YOU MUST USE vCENTER SERVER FOR ALARMS

You can't create alarms by connecting directly to an ESXi host; vCenter Server provides the alarm functionality. You must connect to a vCenter Server instance in order to work with alarms.

2. Navigate to an inventory view, such as Hosts And Clusters or VMs And Templates.

   You can use the menu bar, the navigation bar, or the appropriate keyboard shortcut.

3. Right-click the datacenter object and select Alarm ➢ Add Alarm.

4. On the General tab in the Alarm Settings dialog box, enter an alarm name and alarm description.

5. Select Virtual Machine from the Monitor drop-down list.

6. Be sure that the radio button marked Monitor For Specific Conditions Or State, For Example, CPU Usage, Power State is selected.

7. On the Triggers tab, click the Add button to add a new trigger.

8. Set Trigger Type to VM Snapshot Size (GB). For this alarm, you're interested in snapshot size only, but these other triggers are available:

   ◆ VM Memory Usage (%)

   ◆ VM Network Usage (kbps)

   ◆ VM State

   ◆ VM Heartbeat

   ◆ VM Snapshot Size (GB)

   ◆ VM CPU Ready Time (ms)

9. Ensure that the Condition column is set to Is Above.

10. Set the value in the Warning column to 1.

11. Set the value in the Alert column to 2.

   Figure 13.3 shows the Triggers tab after changing the Warning and Alert values.

FIGURE 13.3
On the Triggers tab, define the conditions that cause the alarm to activate.

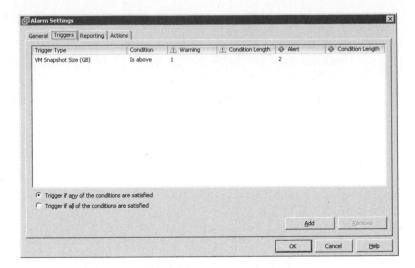

12. On the Reporting tab, leave both the Range value at 0 and the Frequency value at 0.

    This ensures that the alarm is triggered at the threshold values you've specified and instructs vCenter Server to alert you every time the thresholds are exceeded.

CAUTION: COUNTER VALUES WILL VARY!

The Is Above condition is selected most often for identifying a VM, host, or datastore that exceeds a certain threshold. The administrator decides what that threshold should be and what is considered abnormal behavior (or at least interesting enough behavior to be monitored). For the most part, monitoring across ESXi hosts and datastores will be consistent. For example, administrators will define a threshold that is worthy of being notified about — such as CPU, memory, or network utilization — and configure an alarm across all hosts for monitoring that counter. Similarly, administrators may define a threshold for datastores, such as the amount of free space available, and configure an alarm across all datastores to monitor that metric.

However, when looking at VM monitoring, it might be more difficult to come up with a single baseline that works for all VMs. Specifically, think about enterprise applications that must perform well for extended periods of time. For these types of scenarios, administrators will want custom alarms for earlier notifications of performance problems. This way, instead of reacting to a problem, administrators can proactively try to prevent problems from occurring.

For VMs with similar functions like domain controllers and DNS servers, it might be possible to establish baselines and thresholds covering all such infrastructure servers. In the end, the beauty of vCenter Server's alarms is in the flexibility to be as customized and as granular as each individual organization needs.

---

13. On the Actions tab, specify any additional actions that should be taken when the alarm is triggered.

Some of the actions that can be taken include the following:

◆ Send a notification email.

◆ Send a notification trap via SNMP.

◆ Change the power state on a VM.

◆ Migrate a VM.

If you leave the Actions tab empty, then the alarm will alert administrators only within the vSphere Client. For now, leave the Actions tab empty.

CONFIGURING VCENTER SERVER FOR EMAIL AND SNMP NOTIFICATIONS

To have vCenter Server send an email for a triggered alarm, you must configure vCenter Server with an SMTP server. To configure the SMTP server, from the vSphere Client choose the Administration menu, and then select vCenter Server Settings. Click Mail in the list on the left, and then supply the SMTP server and the sender account. I recommend using a recognizable sender account so that when you receive an email, you know it came from the vCenter Server computer. You might use something like vcenter-alerts@v12nlab.net

Similarly, to have vCenter Server send an SNMP trap, you must configure the SNMP receivers in the same vCenter Server Settings dialog box under SNMP. You may specify from one to four management receivers to monitor for traps.

---

14. Click OK to create the alarm.

The alarm is now created. To view the alarm you just created, select the datacenter object from the inventory tree on the left, and then click the Alarms tab on the right. Select Definitions instead of Triggered Alarms, and you'll see your new alarm listed, as shown in Figure 13.4.

USING RANGE AND FREQUENCY WITH ALARMS

Let's create another alarm. This time you'll create an alarm that takes advantage of the Range and Frequency parameters on the Reporting tab. With the VM snapshot alarm, these parameters didn't really make any sense; all you really needed was just to be alerted when the snapshot exceeded a certain size. With other types of alarms, it may make sense to take advantage of these parameters.

The Range parameter specifies a tolerance percentage above or below the configured threshold. For example, the built-in alarm for VM CPU usage specifies a warning threshold of 75 percent but specifies a range of 0. This means that the trigger will activate the alarm at exactly 75 percent. However, if the Range parameter were set to 5 percent, then the trigger would not activate the alarm until 80 percent (75 percent threshold + 5 percent tolerance range). This helps prevent alarm states from transitioning because of false changes in a condition by providing a range of tolerance.

The Frequency parameter controls the period of time during which a triggered alarm is not reported again. Using the built-in VM CPU usage alarm as our example, the Frequency parameter is set, by default, to five minutes. This means that a VM whose CPU usage triggers the activation of the alarm won't get reported again — assuming the condition or state is still true — for five minutes.

FIGURE 13.4
The Defined In column shows where an alarm was defined.

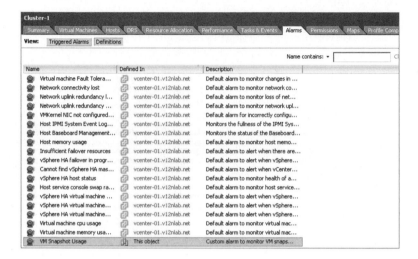

With that information in mind, let's walk through another example of creating an alarm. Perform the following steps to create an alarm that is triggered based on VM network usage:

1. Launch the vSphere Client if it is not already running, and connect to a vCenter Server instance.

2. Navigate to an inventory view, such as Hosts And Clusters or VMs And Templates.

3. Select the datacenter object from the inventory tree on the left.

4. Select the Alarms tab from the content pane on the right.

5. Select the Definitions button just below the tab bar to show alarm definitions instead of triggered alarms.

6. Right-click a blank area of the content pane on the right, and select New Alarm.

7. Supply an alarm name and description.

8. Set the Monitor drop-down list to Virtual Machines.

9. Select the radio button marked Monitor For Specific Conditions Or State, For Example, CPU Usage, Power State.

10. On the Triggers tab, click Add to add a new trigger.

11. Set the Trigger Type column to VM Network Usage (kbps).

12. Set Condition to Is Above.

13. Set the value of the Warning column to 500, and leave the Condition Length setting at five minutes.

14. Set the value of the Alert column to 1000, and leave the Condition Length setting at five minutes.

15. On the Reporting tab, set Range to 10 percent, and set the Frequency parameter to five minutes.

16. Don't add anything on the Actions tab. Click OK to create the alarm.

ALARMS ON OTHER vCENTER SERVER OBJECTS

Although the two alarms you've created so far have been specific to VMs, the process is similar for other types of objects within vCenter Server.

Alarms can have more than just one trigger condition. The alarms you've created so far had only a single trigger condition. For an example of an alarm that has more than one trigger condition, look at the built-in alarm for monitoring host connection and power state. Figure 13.5 shows the two trigger conditions for this alarm. Note that the radio button marked Trigger If All Of The Conditions Are Satisfied is selected; it ensures that only powered-on hosts that are not responding will trigger the alarm.

FIGURE 13.5
You can combine multiple triggers to create more complex alarms.

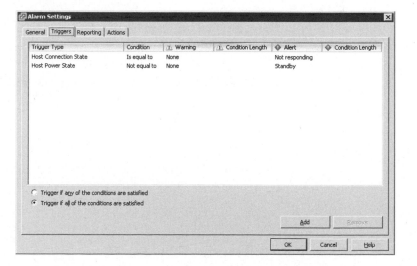

DON'T MODIFY BUILT-IN ALARMS

Instead of modifying one of the built-in alarms, disable the built-in alarm (using the Enable This Alarm check box at the bottom of the General tab), and create a custom alarm that meets your needs.

It might seem obvious, but it's important to note that you can have more than one alarm for an object.

As with any new alarm, testing its functionality is crucial to make sure you get the desired results. You might find that the thresholds you configured are not optimized for your environment and either are not activating the alarm when they should or are activating the alarm when they shouldn't. In these cases, edit the alarm to set the thresholds and conditions appropriately. Or, if the alarm is no longer needed, right-click the alarm, and choose Remove to delete the alarm.

You'll be able to edit or delete alarms only if two conditions are met. First, the user account with which you've connected to vCenter Server must have the appropriate permissions granted in order to edit or delete alarms. Second, you must be attempting to edit or delete the alarm from the object on which it was defined. Think back to my discussion on alarm scope, and this makes sense. You can't delete an alarm from the datacenter object when that alarm was defined on the vCenter Server object. You must go to the object where the alarm was defined in order to edit or delete the alarm.

Now that you've seen some examples of creating alarms — and keep in mind that creating alarms for other objects within vCenter Server follows the same basic steps — let's take a look at managing alarms.

Managing Alarms

Several times so far in this chapter I've directed you to the Alarms tab within the vSphere Client. Up until now, you've been working with the Definitions view of the Alarms tab, looking at defined alarms. There is, however, another view to the Alarms tab, and that's the Triggered Alarms view. Figure 13.6 shows the Triggered Alarms view, which you access using the Triggered Alarms button just below the tab bar.

FIGURE 13.6
The Triggered Alarms view shows the alarms that vCenter Server has activated.

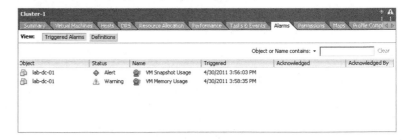

> **GETTING TO THE TRIGGERED ALARMS VIEW QUICKLY**
>
> The vSphere Client provides a handy shortcut to get to the Triggered Alarms view for a particular object quickly. When an object has at least one triggered alarm, small icons appear in the upper-right corner of the content pane for that object. You can see these icons in Figure 13.6. Clicking these icons takes you to the Triggered Alarms view for that object.

The Triggered Alarms view shows all the activated alarms for the selected object and all child objects. In Figure 13.6, the datacenter object was selected, so the Triggered Alarms view shows all activated alarms for all the objects under the datacenter. In this instance, the Triggered Alarms view shows four alarms: one host alarm and three VM alarms.

However, if only the VM had been selected, the Triggered Alarms view on the Alarms tab for that VM would show only the two activated alarms for that particular VM. This makes it easy to isolate the specific alarms you need to address.

After you are in Triggered Alarms view for a particular object, a couple of actions are available to you for each of the activated alarms. For alarms that monitor resource consumption (that is, the alarm definition uses the Monitor For Specific Conditions Or State, For Example, CPU Usage, Power State setting selected under Alarm Type on the General tab), you have the option to acknowledge the alarm. To acknowledge the alarm, right-click the alarm and select Acknowledge Alarm.

When an alarm is acknowledged, vCenter Server records the time the alarm was acknowledged and the user account that acknowledged the alarm. As long as the alarm condition persists, the alarm will remain in the Triggered Alarms view but is grayed out. When the alarm condition is resolved, the activated alarm disappears.

For an alarm that monitors events (this would be an alarm that has the Monitor For Specific Events Occurring On This Object, For Example, VM Powered On option selected under Alarm Type on the General tab), you can either acknowledge the alarm, as described previously, or reset the alarm status to green by selecting the "clear" option. Figure 13.7 illustrates this option.

FIGURE 13.7
For event-based alarms, you also have the option to reset the alarm status to green.

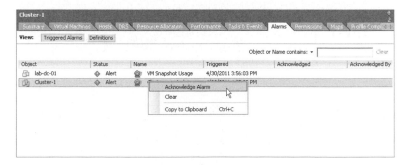

Resetting an alarm to green removes the activated alarm from the Triggered Alarms view, even if the underlying event that activated the alarm hasn't actually been resolved. This behavior makes sense if you think about it. Alarms that monitor events are merely responding to an event being logged by vCenter Server; whether the underlying condition has been resolved is unknown. So, resetting the alarm to green just tells vCenter Server to act as if the condition has been resolved. Of course, if the event occurs again, the alarm will be triggered again.

Now that we've looked at alarms for proactive performance monitoring, let's move on to using vCenter Server's performance graphs to view even more information about the behavior of VMs and ESXi hosts in your vSphere environment.

Working with Performance Graphs

Alarms are a great tool for alerting administrators of specific conditions or events, but alarms don't provide the detailed information that administrators sometimes need. This is where vCenter Server's performance graphs come in. vCenter Server has many new and updated features for creating and analyzing graphs. Without these graphs, analyzing the performance of a VM would be nearly impossible. Installing agents inside a VM will not provide accurate details about the server's behavior or resource consumption. The reason for this is elementary: a VM is configured only with virtual devices. Only the VMkernel knows the exact amount of resource consumption for any of those devices because it acts as the arbitrator between the virtual hardware and the physical hardware. In most virtual environments, the VM's virtual devices can outnumber the actual physical hardware devices, necessitating the complex sharing and scheduling abilities in the VMkernel.

By clicking the Performance tab for a datacenter, cluster, host, or VM, you can learn a wealth of information. Before you use these graphs to help analyze resource consumption, we need to talk about performance graphs and legends. I'll start by covering the two different layouts available in performance graphs: the Overview layout and the Advanced layout.

Overview Layout

The Overview layout is the default view when you access the Performance tab. Figure 13.8 shows you the Overview layout of the Performance tab for an ESXi host. Note the horizontal and vertical scrollbars; there's a lot more information here than the vSphere Client can fit in a single screen.

At the top of the Overview layout are options to change the view or to change the time range. The contents of the View drop-down list change depending on the object you select in the vSphere Client. Table 13.1 lists the different options available, depending on what type of object you select in the vSphere Client.

Next to the View drop-down list is an option to change the time range for the data currently displayed in the various performance graphs. This allows you to set the time range to a day, a week, a month, or a custom value.

FIGURE 13.8
The Overview layout provides information on a range of performance counters.

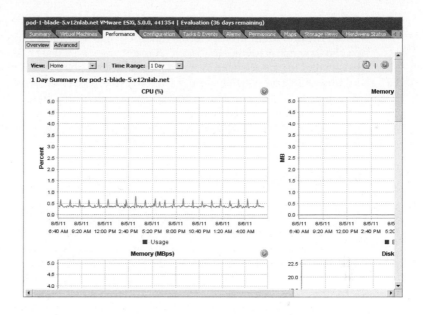

TABLE 13.1: View options on the Performance tab

IF YOU ARE VIEWING THE PERFORMANCE TAB FOR THIS KIND OF OBJECT...	THE VIEW DROP-DOWN LIST CONTAINS THESE OPTIONS:
Datacenter	Clusters, Storage
Cluster	Home, Resource Pools & Virtual Machines, Hosts
Resource Pool	Home, Resource Pools & Virtual Machines
Host	Home, Virtual Machines
Virtual Machine	Home, Storage

In the upper-right corner of the Overview layout, you'll see a button for refreshing the display and a button for getting help.

Below the gray title bar (where you'll find the View and Time Range drop-down lists, the Refresh button, and the Help button) are the actual performance graphs. The layout and the graphs that are included vary based on the object selected and the option chosen in the View drop-down list. I don't have the room here to list all of them, but a couple of them are shown in Figure 13.9 and Figure 13.10. I encourage you to explore a bit and find the layouts that work best for you.

FIGURE 13.9

The Virtual Machines view of the Performance tab for an ESXi Host in Overview layout offers both per-VM and summary information.

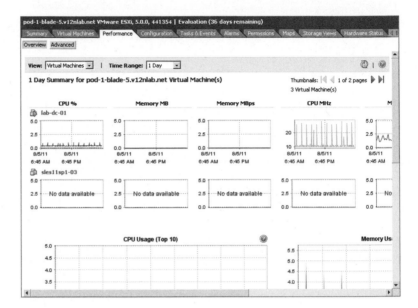

FIGURE 13.10

The Storage view of the Performance tab for a VM in Overview layout displays a breakdown of storage utilization.

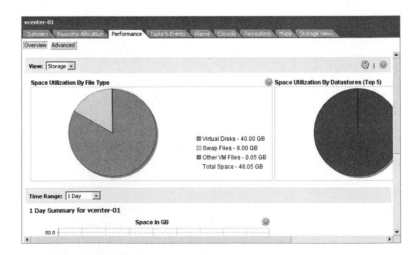

The Overview layout works well if you need a broad overview of the performance data for a datacenter, cluster, resource pool, host, or VM. But what if you need more specific data in a more customizable format? The Advanced layout is the answer, as you'll see in the next section.

Advanced Layout

Figure 13.11 shows the Advanced layout of the Performance tab for a cluster of ESXi hosts. Here, in the Advanced layout, is where the real power of vCenter Server's performance graphs is made available to you.

FIGURE 13.11
The Advanced layout of the Performance tab provides much more extensive controls for viewing performance data.

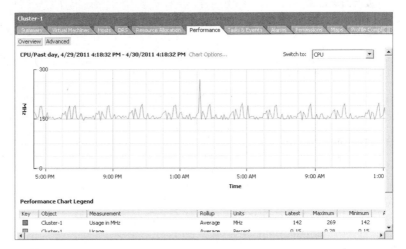

Starting from the top left, you'll see the name of the object being monitored. Just below that is the type of the chart and the time range. The Chart Options link provides access to customize settings for the chart. To the right, you'll find a drop-down list to quickly switch graph settings, followed by buttons to print the chart, refresh the chart, save the chart, or view the chart as a pop-up chart. The Print button allows you to print the chart; the Save button allows you to export the chart as a JPEG, BMP, GIF, PNG graphic, or XLS document. I'll discuss this functionality in the section "Saving Performance Graphs." The Refresh button refreshes the data. The Pop-up button opens the chart in a new window. This allows you to navigate elsewhere in the vSphere Client while still keeping a performance graph open in a separate window. Pop-up charts also make it easy to compare one ESXi host or VM with another host or VM. On each side of the graph are units of measurement. In Figure 13.11, the counters selected are measured in percentages and megahertz. Depending on the counters chosen, there may be only one unit of measurement but no more than two. Next, on the horizontal axis, is the time interval. Below that, the Performance Chart Legend provides color-coded keys to help the user find a specific object or item of interest. This area also breaks down the graph into the object being measured; the measurement being used; the units of measure; and the Latest, Maximum, Minimum, and Average measurements recorded for that object.

Hovering the mouse pointer over the graph at a particular recorded interval of interest displays the data points at that specific moment in time.

Another nice feature of the graphs is the ability to emphasize a specific object so that it is easier to pick out this object from the other objects. By clicking the specific key at the bottom, the key and its color representing a specific object will be emphasized, while the other keys and their respective colors become lighter and less visible. For simple charts such as the one shown previously in Figure 13.11, this might not be very helpful. For busier charts with many performance counters, this feature is very useful.

Now that you have a feel for the Advanced layout, take a closer look at the Chart Options link. This link exposes vCenter Server's functionality in creating highly customized performance graphs. Figure 13.12 shows the Customize Performance Chart dialog box. This dialog box is the central place where you will come to customize vCenter Server's performance graphs. From here, you select the counters to view, the time ranges, and the kind of graph (line graph or stacked graph) to display.

FIGURE 13.12
The Customize Performance Chart dialog box offers tremendous flexibility to create exactly the performance graph you need.

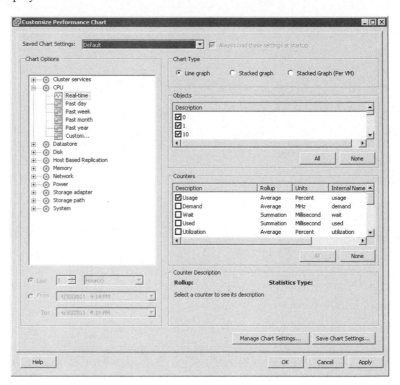

Because there is so much information available in the Customize Performance Chart dialog box, I've grouped the various options and types of information into the sections that follow.

CHOOSING A RESOURCE TYPE

On the left side of the Customize Performance Chart dialog box (shown in Figure 13.12), you can choose which resource (Cluster Services, CPU, Datastore, Disk, Host Based Replication, Memory, Network, Power, Storage Adapter, Storage Path, or System) VM to monitor or analyze. The actual selections available in this area change depending on the type of object that you have selected in vCenter Server. That is, the options available when viewing the Performance tab for an ESXi host are different from the options available when viewing the Performance tab of a VM, a cluster, or a datacenter.

Within each of these resources, different objects and counters are available. Be aware that other factors affect what objects and counters are available to view; for example, in some cases the real-time interval shows more objects and counters than other intervals. The next few sections list the various counters that are available for the different resource types in the Customize Performance Chart dialog box.

If a particular counter is new to you, click it to highlight the counter. At the bottom of the dialog box, in a section called Counter Description, you'll see a description of the counter. This can help you determine which counters are most applicable in any given situation.

SETTING A CUSTOM INTERVAL

Within each of the resource types, you have a choice of intervals to view. Some objects offer a Real-Time option; this option shows what is happening with that resource right now. The others are self-explanatory. The Custom option allows you to specify exactly what you'd like to see on the performance graph. For example, you could specify that you'd like to see performance data for the last eight hours. Having all of these interval options allows you to choose exactly the right interval necessary to view the precise data you're seeking.

VIEWING CPU PERFORMANCE INFORMATION

If you select the CPU resource type in the Chart Options section of the Customize Performance Chart dialog box, you can choose what specific objects and counters you'd like to see in the performance graph. Note that the CPU resource type is not available when viewing the Performance tab of a datacenter object (DC). It is available for clusters (CL), ESXi hosts (ESXi), resource pools (RP), and individual virtual machines (VMs).

Table 13.2 lists the most important objects and counters available for CPU performance information. A complete list of all CPU performance information can be found at www.sybex.com/go/masteringvsphere5.

TABLE 13.2:   Available CPU performance counters

COUNTER	DC	CL	ESXi	RP	VM
Max Limited					X
Ready			X		X
Run					X
Swap Wait			X		X
System					X
Total		X			
Usage In MHz		X	X	X	X
Used			X		X
Utilization			X		
Wait			X		X

Quite a bit of CPU performance information is available. In the section "Monitoring CPU Usage" I'll discuss how to use these CPU performance objects and counters to monitor CPU usage.

VIEWING MEMORY PERFORMANCE INFORMATION

If you select the Memory resource type in the Chart Options section of the Customize Performance Chart dialog box, different objects and counters are available for display in the performance graph. The Memory resource type is not available when viewing the Performance tab of a datacenter object. It is available for clusters, ESXi hosts, resource pools, and individual VMs.

Table 13.3 lists the most important objects and counters available for memory performance information. A complete list of all memory performance information can be found at www.sybex.com/go/masteringvsphere5.

TABLE 13.3:   Available Memory performance counters

COUNTER	DC	CL	ESXi	RP	VM
Active			X		X
Compressed			X		X
Consumed		X	X	X	X
Swap In			X		X
Swap Out			X		X
Swap Used			X		
Usage		X	X		X
Balloon Target					X
Zipped Memory					X
Memory Saved By Zipping					X

In the section "Monitoring Memory Usage" you'll get the opportunity to use these different objects and counters to monitor how ESXi and VMs are using memory.

VIEWING DISK PERFORMANCE INFORMATION

Disk performance is another key area that vSphere administrators need to monitor. Table 13.4 shows you the most important objects and counters available for disk performance information. A complete list of all disk performance information can be found at www.sybex.com/go/masteringvsphere5.

Note that these counters aren't supported for datacenters, clusters, and resource pools, but they are supported for ESXi hosts and VMs. Not all counters are visible in all display intervals.

TABLE 13.4:   Available Disk performance counters

COUNTER	DC	CL	ESXI	RP	VM
Disk Bus Resets			X		
Disk Commands Terminated			X		
Disk Kernel Command Latency			X		
Disk Kernel Read Latency			X		
Disk Kernel Write Latency			X		
Disk Maximum Queue Depth			X		
Disk Command Latency			X		
Disk Read Latency			X		
Disk Write Latency			X		
Disk Queue Command Latency			X		

You'll use these counters in the section "Monitoring Disk Usage," later in this chapter.

VIEWING NETWORK PERFORMANCE INFORMATION

To monitor network performance, the vCenter Server performance graphs cover a wide collection of performance counters. Network performance counters are available only for ESXi hosts and VMs; they are not available for datacenter objects, clusters, or resource pools.

Table 13.5 shows the most important objects and counters available for network performance information. A complete list of all network performance information can be found at www.sybex.com/go/masteringvsphere5.

TABLE 13.5:   Available Network performance counters

COUNTER	DC	CL	ESXI	RP	VM
Data Receive Rate			X		X
Data Transmit Rate			X		X
Receive Packets Dropped			X		X
Transmit Packets Dropped			X		X
Packet Receive Errors			X		
Packet Transmit Errors			X		

TABLE 13-5 *(continued)*

COUNTER	DC	CL	ESXI	RP	VM
Packets Received			X		X
Packets Transmitted			X		X
Data Receive Rate			X		X
Data Transmit Rate			X		X
Usage			X		X

You'll use these network performance counters in the "Monitoring Network Usage" section later in this chapter.

VIEWING SYSTEM PERFORMANCE INFORMATION

ESXi hosts and VMs also offer some performance counters in the System resource type. Datacenters, clusters, and resource pools do not support any system performance counters.

Table 13.6 lists the most important objects and counters available for system performance information. A complete list of all system performance information can be found at www.sybex.com/go/masteringvsphere5.

TABLE 13.6: Available System performance counters

COUNTER	DC	CL	ESXI	RP	VM
Resource CPU Active (1 Min Average)			X		
Resource CPU Active (5 Min Average)			X		
Resource CPU Maximum Limited (1 Min)			X		
Resource CPU Maximum Limited (5 Min)			X		
Resource CPU Running (1 Min Average)			X		
Resource CPU Running (5 Min Average)			X		
Resource CPU Usage (Average)			X		

TABLE 13-6 *(continued)*

COUNTER	DC	CL	ESXi	RP	VM
Resource Memory Shared			X		
Resource Memory Swapped			X		
Uptime			X		X

The majority of these counters are valid only for ESXi hosts, and they all center on how resources are allocated or how the ESXi host itself is consuming CPU resources or memory.

VIEWING DATASTORE PERFORMANCE INFORMATION

Monitoring datastore performance allows you to see the performance of the whole datastore instead of using disk counters per VM. Datastore performance counters are available only for ESXi hosts and VMs; they are not available for datacenter objects, clusters, or resource pools.

Table 13.7 shows the most important objects and counters available for datastore performance information. A complete list of all datastore performance information can be found at www. sybex.com/go/masteringvsphere5.

TABLE 13.7:   Available Datastore performance counters

COUNTER	DC	CL	ESXi	RP	VM
Storage I/O Control Aggregated IOPS			X		
Storage I/O Control Datastore Maximum Queue Depth			X		
Storage DRS Datastore Normalized Read Latency			X		
Storage DRS Datastore Normalized write latency			X		
Highest Latency			X		X
Average Read Requests Per Second			X		X
Average Write Requests Per Second			X		X
Storage I/O Control Normalized Latency			X		
Read Latency			X		X
Write Latency			X		X

VIEWING STORAGE PATH PERFORMANCE INFORMATION

Storage Path performance is one of the new sections with performance counters that help you troubleshoot storage path problems. Storage Path counters are available only for ESXi; they are not available for datacenter objects, clusters, VMs or resource pools.

Table 13.8 shows the objects and counters available for storage path performance information.

TABLE 13.8: Available Storage Path performance counters

COUNTER	DC	CL	ESXi	RP	VM
Average Commands Issued Per Second			X		
Highest Latency			X		
Average Read Requests Per Second			X		
Average Write Requests Per Second			X		
Read Rate			X		
Storage Path Throughput Usage			X		
Read Latency			X		
Write Latency			X		
Write Rate			X		

VIEWING OTHER PERFORMANCE COUNTERS

These are the other available performance counter types:

◆ ESXi hosts participating in a cluster also have a resource type of Cluster Services, with two performance counters: CPU Fairness and Memory Fairness. Both of these counters show the distribution of resources within a cluster.

◆ The datacenter object contains a resource type marked as Virtual Machine Operations. This resource type contains performance counters that simply monitor the number of times a particular VM operation has occurred. These include VM Power-On Events, VM Power-Off Events, VM Resets, vMotion Operations, and Storage vMotion Operations.

MANAGING CHART SETTINGS

There's one more area of the Customize Performance Chart dialog box that I'll discuss, and that's the Manage Chart Settings and Save Chart Settings buttons in the lower-right corner.

After you've gone through and selected the resource type, display interval, objects, and performance counters that you'd like to see in the performance graph, you can save that collection of chart settings using the Save Chart Settings button. vCenter Server prompts you to enter a name for the saved chart settings. After a chart setting is saved, you can easily access it again from the drop-down list at the top of the performance graph Advanced layout.

Figure 13.13 shows the Switch To drop-down list, where two custom chart settings — VM Activity and Cluster Resources — are shown. By selecting either of these from the Switch To drop-down list, you can quickly switch to those settings. This allows you to define the performance charts that you need to see and then quickly switch between them.

FIGURE 13.13
You can access saved chart settings from the Switch To drop-down list.

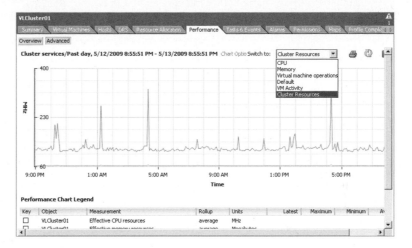

The Manage Chart Settings button allows you to delete chart settings you've saved but no longer need.

In addition to offering you the option of saving the chart settings, vCenter Server also allows you to save the graph.

SAVING PERFORMANCE GRAPHS

When I first introduced you to the Advanced layout view of the Performance tab, I briefly mentioned the Save button. This button, found in the upper-right corner of the Advanced layout, allows you to save the results of the performance graph to an external file for long-term archiving, analysis, or reporting.

When you click the Save button, a standard Windows Save dialog box appears. You have the option of choosing where to save the resulting file as well as the option of saving the chart either as a graphic file or as a Microsoft Excel spreadsheet. If you are going to perform any additional analysis, the option to save the chart data as an Excel spreadsheet is quite useful. The graphics options are useful when you need to put the performance data into a report of some sort.

There's a lot of information exposed via vCenter Server's performance graphs. I'll revisit the performance graphs again in the sections on monitoring specific types of resources later in this chapter. First I'll introduce you to `resxtop`, your most important tool in gathering performance information.

Working with `resxtop`

In addition to alarms and performance graphs, VMware also provides `resxtop` to help with monitoring performance and resource usage. In early ESX versions a number of tools were available on the service console command line. Later VMware released ESXi and limited the number of commands available directly on the host but developed a special virtual appliance that provides a command-line interface for managing ESX and ESXi hosts called the vSphere Management Assistant (vMA). You can use the vMA to run commands against the ESXi host as if they were run on the console. In ESXi 3.*x* and ESXi 4.0, getting access to the console was unsupported. With ESXi 4.1 VMware made the console supported, but it is locked and not accessible by default. More commands are available on the console than previous ESXi versions; however, VMware still advises using the vMA for running commands against ESXi hosts.

Using resxtop

You can also monitor VM performance using a command-line tool named resxtop. A great reason to use resxtop is the immediate feedback it gives you. Using resxtop, you can monitor all four major resource types (CPU, disk, memory, and network) on a particular ESXi host. Figure 13.14 shows some sample output from resxtop.

The resxtop command is included with the vMA. Before you can actually view real-time performance data, though, you first have to tell resxtop which remote server you want to use. To launch resxtop and connect to a remote server, enter this command:

```
resxtop --server pod-1-blade-7.v12nlab.net
```

You'll want to replace pod-1-blade-7.v12nlab.net with the appropriate hostname or IP address of the ESXi host to which you want to connect. When prompted, supply a username and password, and then resxtop will launch. Once resxtop is running, you can use single-letter commands to switch among the various views.

FIGURE 13.14
resxtop shows real-time information on CPU, disk, memory, and network utilization.

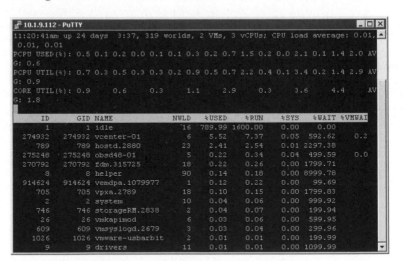

---

esxtop **Is Only for VMware ESXi Shell**

It is still possible to run esxtop, which you might know from former ESX versions, in the VMware ESXi shell, but it is highly recommended to use only the VMware vMA.

Upon launch, `resxtop` defaults to showing CPU utilization, as illustrated in Figure 13.14. At the top of the screen are summary statistics; below that are statistics for specific VMs and VMkernel processes. To show only VMs, press V. Be aware that `resxtop`, like many Linux commands, is case sensitive, so you'll need to be sure to use an uppercase V in order to toggle the display of VMs only.

Two CPU counters of interest to view with `resxtop` are the CPU Used (%USED) and Ready Time (%RDY). You can also see these counters in the VM graphs, but with `resxtop` they are calculated as percentages. The %RDY counter is also helpful in determining whether you have overallocated CPU resources to the VM. This might be the case if, for example, you've allocated two vCPUs to a VM that really needs only a single vCPU. While in CPU mode, you can also press lowercase e to expand a VM's CPU statistics so that you can see the different components that are using CPU time on behalf of a VM. This is quite useful in determining what components of a VM may be taking up CPU capacity.

If you switch away to another resource, press C (uppercase or lowercase) to come back to the CPU counters display. At any time when you are finished with `resxtop`, you can simply press q (lowercase only) to exit the utility and return to the vMA command prompt.

`resxtop` **Shows Single Hosts Only**

Remember, `resxtop` shows only a single ESXi host. In an environment where vMotion, vSphere Distributed Resource Scheduler (DRS), and vSphere High Availability (HA) have been deployed, VMs may move around often. It is possible that while you are monitoring a VM it is suddenly moved off the host by a vMotion action. Also be aware of this when capturing performance in batch mode.

Monitoring Memory Usage with m   Memory is one of the most important components of your ESXi host, because this resource is usually one of the first to get exhausted.

To monitor memory usage with `resxtop,` press m (lowercase only). This gives you real-time statistics about the ESXi host's memory usage in the top portion and the VM's memory usage in the lower section. As with CPU statistics, you can press V (uppercase only) to show only VMs. This helps you weed out VMkernel resources when you are trying to isolate a problem with a VM. The %ACTV counter, which shows current active guest physical memory, is a useful counter, as are the %ACTVS (slow-moving average for long-term estimates), %ACTVF (fast-moving average for short-term estimates), %ACTVN (prediction of %ACTV at next sampling), and SWCUR (current swap usage) counters.

Monitoring Network Statistics with n   Networking in a vSphere environment is often taken for granted, but while your environment grows, you'll learn that keeping an eye on network performance is essential.

To monitor network statistics about the vmnics, individual VMs, or VMkernel ports used for iSCSI, VMotion, and NFS, press n (lowercase only). The columns showing network usage include packets transmitted and received and megabytes transmitted and received for each vmnic or port. Also shown in the DNAME column are the vSwitches or dvSwitches and, to the left, what is plugged into them, including VMs, VMkernel, and Service Console ports. If a particular VM is monopolizing the vSwitch, you can look at the amount of network traffic on a specific switch and the individual ports to see which VM is the culprit. Unlike other resxtop views, you can't use V (uppercase only) here to show only VMs.

Monitoring Disk I/O Statistics with d   Memory and disk are considered the most important components in your vSphere environment. Where memory is important because it gets exhausted first, disk I/O is often overlooked even though bad disk performance will directly impact the VMs performance.

To monitor disk I/O statistics about each of the disk adapters, press d (lowercase only) and press u (lowercase only) for disk devices and v (lowercase only) for disk VM. Like some other views, you can press V (uppercase only) to show only VMs. The columns labeled READS/s, WRITES/s, MBREAD/s, and MBWRTN/s are most often used to determine disk loads. Those columns show loads based on reads and writes per second and megabytes read and written per second.

The resxtop command also lets you view CPU interrupts by pressing i. This command will show you the device(s) using the interrupt and is a great way to identify VMkernel devices, such as a vmnic, that might be sharing an interrupt with the Service Console. This sort of interrupt sharing can impede performance.

Capturing and Playing Back Performance Data with resxtop

Another great feature of resxtop is the ability to capture performance data for a short period of time and then play back that data. Using the command vm-support, you can set an interval and duration for the capture.

Perform the following steps to capture data to be played back on resxtop:

1. Using PuTTY (Windows) or a terminal window (Mac OS X or Linux), open an SSH session to an ESXi host. Note that this requires enabling the ESXi Shell and SSH, both of which are disabled by default.

2. Enter the **su** – command to assume root privileges.

3. While logged in as root or after switching to the root user, change your working directory to /tmp by issuing the command **cd /tmp**.

4. Enter the command **vm-support -p -i 10 -d 180**. This creates a resxtop snapshot, capturing data every 10 seconds, for the duration of 180 seconds.

5. The resulting file is a tarball and is compressed with gzip. You must extract it with the command **tar -xzf esx*.tgz**. This creates a vm-support directory that is called in the next command.

6. Run **resxtop -R /vm-support*** to replay the data for analysis.

Now that I've shown you the various tools (alarms, performance graphs, and resxtop) that you will use to monitor performance in a vSphere environment, let's go through the four major resources — CPU, RAM, network, and disk — and see how to monitor the usage of these resources.

Monitoring CPU Usage

When monitoring a VM, it's always a good starting point to keep an eye on CPU consumption. Many VMs started out in life as underperforming physical servers. One of VMware's most successful sales pitches is being able to take all those lackluster physical boxes that are not busy and convert them to VMs. Once they are converted, virtual infrastructure managers tend to think of these VMs as simple, lackluster, and low-utilization servers with nothing to worry over or monitor. The truth, though, is quite the opposite.

When the server was physical, it had an entire box to itself. Now it must share its resources with many other workloads. In aggregate, they represent quite a load, and if some or many of them become somewhat busy, they contend with each other for the finite capabilities of the ESXi host on which they run. Of course, they don't know they are contending for resources, since the VMkernel tries to make sure they get the resources they need. Virtual CPUs need to be scheduled, and ESXi does a remarkable job given that there are more VMs than physical processors most of the time. Still, the hypervisor can do only so much with the resources it has, and invariably there comes a time when the applications running in that VM need more CPU time than the host can give.

When this happens, it's usually the application owner who notices first and raises the alarm with the system administrators. Now the vSphere administrators have the task of determining why this VM is underperforming. Fortunately, vCenter Server provides a number of tools that make monitoring and analysis easier. These are the tools you've already seen: alarms, performance graphs, and `resxtop`.

Let's begin with a hypothetical scenario. A help desk ticket has been submitted indicating that an application owner isn't getting the expected level of performance on a particular server, which in this case is a VM. As the vSphere administrator, you need to first delve deeper into the problem and ask as many questions as necessary to discover what the application owner needs to be satisfied with performance. Some performance issues are subjective, meaning some users might complain about the slowness of their applications, but they have no objective benchmark for such a claim. Other times, this is reflected in a specific benchmark, such as the number of transactions by a database server or throughput for a web server. In this case, our issue revolves around benchmarking CPU usage, so our application is CPU intensive when it does its job.

ASSESSMENTS, EXPECTATIONS, AND ADJUSTMENTS

If an assessment was done prior to virtualizing a server, there might be hard numbers to look at to give some details as to what was expected with regard to minimum performance or a service-level agreement (SLA). If not, the vSphere administrator needs to work with the application's owner to make more CPU resources available to the VM when needed.

---

vCenter Server's graphs, which you have explored in great detail, are the best way to analyze usage, both short and long term. In this case, let's assume the help desk ticket describes a slowness issue in the last hour. As you've already seen, you can easily create a custom performance graph to show CPU usage over the last hour for a particular VM or ESXi host.

Perform the following steps to create a CPU graph that shows data for a VM from the last hour:

1. Connect to a vCenter Server instance with the vSphere Client.

2. Navigate to the Hosts And Clusters or VMs And Templates inventory view.

3. In the inventory tree, select a virtual machine.

4. Select the Performance tab from the content pane on the right, and then change the view to Advanced.

5. Click the Chart Options link.

6. In the Customize Performance Chart dialog box, select CPU from the resource type list. Select the Custom interval.

7. Near the bottom of the Chart Options section, change the interval to Last 1 Hour(s).

8. Set the chart type to Line graph.

9. Select the VM itself from the list of objects.

10. From the list of counters, select CPU Usage In MHz (Average) and CPU Ready.

11. Click OK to apply the chart settings.

CPU READY

CPU Ready shows how long a VM is waiting to be scheduled on a physical processor. A VM waiting many thousands of milliseconds to be scheduled on a processor might indicate that the ESXi host is overloaded, a resource pool has too tight a limit, or the VM has too few CPU shares (or, if no one is complaining, nothing at all). Be sure to work with the server or application owner to determine an acceptable amount of CPU Ready for any CPU-intensive VM.

This graph shows CPU utilization for the selected VM, but it won't necessarily help you get to the bottom of why this particular VM isn't performing as well as expected. In this scenario, I would fully expect the CPU Usage In MHz (Average) counter to be high; this simply tells you that the VM is using all the CPU cycles it can get. Unless the CPU Ready counters are also high, indicating that the VM is waiting on the host to schedule it onto a physical processor, you still haven't uncovered the cause of the slowness that triggered the help desk ticket. Instead, you'll need to move to monitoring host CPU usage.

Monitoring a host's overall CPU usage is fairly straightforward. Keep in mind that other factors usually come into play when looking at spare CPU capacity. Add-ons such as vMotion, vSphere DRS, and vSphere HA directly impact whether there is enough spare capacity on a server or a cluster of servers. Compared to previous versions of ESX, the VMkernel will usually not be as competitive for processor 0 because there are fewer processes to consume CPU time.

VMKERNEL STUCK ON 0

In older ESX versions, the Service Console was stuck to processor 0 only. It wouldn't get migrated to other processors even in the face of heavy contention. In ESXi there is no Service Console anymore, but the VMkernel process is still stuck on processor 0.

Perform the following steps to create a real-time graph for a host's CPU usage:

1. Launch the vSphere Client if it is not already running, and connect to a vCenter Server instance.

2. Navigate to the Hosts And Clusters or VMs And Templates inventory view.

3. In the Inventory tree, select a host.

   This shows you the Summary tab.

4. Click the Performance tab, and switch to Advanced view.

5. Click the Chart Options link.

6. In the Customize Performance Chart dialog box, select the CPU resource type and the Real-Time display interval.

7. Set Chart Type to Stacked Graph (Per VM).

8. Select all objects.

   You should see a separate object for each VM hosted on the selected ESXi host.

9. Select the CPU Usage (Average) performance counter.

10. Click OK to apply the chart settings and return to the Performance tab.

This chart shows the usage of all the VMs on the selected ESXi host in a stacked fashion. From this view, you should be able to determine whether there is a specific VM or group of VMs that are consuming abnormal amounts of CPU capacity.

VMkernel Balancing Act

Always remember that on an oversubscribed ESXi host the VMkernel will load balance the VMs based on current loads, reservations, and shares represented on individual VMs and/or resource pools.

In this scenario, I identified the application within the VM as CPU bound, so these two performance charts should clearly identify why the VM isn't performing well. In all likelihood, the ESXi host on which the VM is running doesn't have enough CPU capacity to satisfy the requests of all the VMs. Your solution, in this case, would be to use the resource allocation tools described in Chapter 11, "Managing Resource Allocation," to ensure that this specific application receives the resources it needs to perform at acceptable levels.

Monitoring Memory Usage

Monitoring memory usage, whether on a host or a VM, can be challenging. The monitoring itself is not difficult; it's the availability of the physical resource that can be a challenge. Of the four resources, memory can be oversubscribed without much effort. Depending on the physical form factor chosen to host VMware ESXi, running out of physical RAM is easy to do. Although the blade form factor creates a very dense consolidation effort, the blades are sometimes constrained by the amount of physical memory and network adapters that can be installed. But even with other regular form factors, having enough memory installed comes down to how much the physical server can accommodate and your budget.

If you suspect that memory usage is a performance issue, the first step is to isolate whether this is a memory shortage affecting the host (you've oversubscribed physical memory and need to add more memory) or whether this is a memory limit affecting only that VM (meaning you need to allocate more memory to this VM or change resource allocation policies). Normally, if the ESXi host is suffering from high memory utilization, the predefined vCenter Server alarm will trigger and alert the vSphere administrator. However, the alarm doesn't allow you to delve deeper into the specifics of how the host is using memory. For that, you'll need a performance graph.

Perform the following steps to create a real-time graph for a host's memory usage:

1. Connect to a vCenter Server instance with the vSphere Client.

2. Navigate to the Hosts And Clusters inventory view.

3. In the inventory tree, click an ESXi host. This shows you the Summary tab.

4. Click the Performance tab, and switch to Advanced view.

5. Click the Chart Options link.

6. In the Customize Performance Chart dialog box, select the Memory resource type and the Real-Time display interval.

7. Select Line Graph as the chart type. The host will be selected as the only available object.

8. In the Counters area, select the Memory Usage (Average), Memory Overhead (Average), Memory Active (Average), Memory Consumed (Average), Memory Used by VMkernel, and Memory Swap Used (Average).

   This should give you a fairly clear picture of how much memory the ESXi host is using.

9. Click OK to apply the chart options and return to the Performance tab.

COUNTERS, COUNTERS, AND MORE COUNTERS

As with VMs, a plethora of counters can be utilized with a host for monitoring memory usage. Which ones you select will depend on what you're looking for. Straight memory usage monitoring is common, but don't forget that there are other counters that could be helpful, such as Ballooning, Unreserved, VMkernel Swap, and Shared, just to name a few. The ability to assemble the appropriate counters for finding the right information comes with experience and depends on what is being monitored.

These counters, in particular the Memory Swap Used (Average) counter, will give you an idea of whether the ESXi host is under memory pressure. If the ESXi host is not suffering from memory pressure and you still suspect a memory problem, then the issue likely lies with the VM.

Perform the following steps to create a real-time graph for a VM's memory usage:

1. Use the vSphere client to connect to a vCenter Server instance.

2. Navigate to either the Hosts And Clusters or the VMs And Templates inventory view.

3. In the inventory tree, click a virtual machine. This shows you the Summary tab.

4. Click the Performance tab, and switch to the Advanced view.

5. Click the Chart Options link.

6. In the Customize Performance Chart dialog box, select the Memory resource type and the Real-Time display interval.

7. Select Line Graph as the chart type.

8. In the list of counters, select to show the Memory Usage (Average), Memory Overhead (Average), Memory Consumed (Average), and Memory Granted (Average) counters. This shows memory usage, including usage relative to the amount of memory configured for the VM.

9. Click OK to apply the chart options and return to the Performance tab.

From this performance graph, you will be able to tell how much of the memory configured for the VM is actually being used. This might reveal to you that the applications running inside that VM need more memory than the VM has been assigned and that adding more memory to the VM — assuming that there is sufficient memory at the host level — might improve performance.

Memory, like CPU, is just one of several different factors that can impact VM performance. Network usage is another area that can impact performance, especially perceived performance.

Monitoring Network Usage

vCenter Server's graphs provide a wonderful tool for measuring a VM's or a host's network usage.

Monitoring network usage requires a slightly different approach than monitoring CPU or memory. With either CPU or memory, reservations, limits, and shares can dictate how much of these two resources can be consumed by any one VM. Network usage cannot be constrained by these mechanisms. Because VMs plug into a VM port group, which is part of a vSwitch on a single host, how the VM interacts with the vSwitch can be manipulated by the virtual switch's or port group's policy. For instance, if you need to restrict a VM's overall network output, you would configure traffic shaping on the port group to restrict the VM to a specific amount of outbound bandwidth. Unless you are using vSphere Distributed Switches or the Nexus 1000V third-party distributed virtual switch, there is no way to restrict VM inbound bandwidth on ESXi hosts.

VM ISOLATION

Certain VMs may indeed need to be limited to a specific amount of outbound bandwidth. Servers such as FTP, file and print, or web and proxy servers, or any server whose main function is to act as a file repository or connection broker, may need to be limited or traffic shaped to an amount of bandwidth that allows it to meet its service target but not monopolize the host it runs on. Isolating any of these VMs to a vSwitch of its own is more likely a better solution, but it requires the appropriate hardware configuration.

To get an idea of how much network traffic is actually being generated, you can measure a VM's or a host's output or reception of network traffic using the graphs in vCenter Server. The graphs can provide accurate information on the actual usage or ample information that a particular VM is monopolizing a virtual switch, especially using the Stacked Graph chart type.

Perform the following steps to create a real-time graph for a stacked graph of transmitted network usage by each VM on an ESXi host:

1. Launch the vSphere Client if it is not already running, and connect to a vCenter Server instance.

2. Navigate to either the Hosts And Clusters inventory view or the VMs And Templates inventory view.

3. In the inventory tree, click an ESXi host. This shows you the Summary tab.

4. Click the Performance tab, and switch to Advanced view.

5. Click the Chart Options link.

6. From the Customize Performance Chart dialog box, select the Network resource type and the Real-Time display interval in the Chart Options area.

7. Select a chart type of Stacked Graph (Per VM).

8. In the objects list, be sure all the VMs are selected.

9. In the list of counters, select the Network Data Transmit Rate counter.

   This gives you an idea of how much network bandwidth each VM is consuming outbound on this ESXi host.

10. Click OK to apply the changes and return to the Performance tab.

What if you wanted a breakdown of traffic on each of the network interface cards (NICs) in the ESXi host, instead of by VM? That's fairly easily accomplished by another trip back to the Customize Performance Chart dialog box.

Perform the following steps to create a real-time graph for a host's transmitted network usage by NIC:

1. Connect to a vCenter Server instance with the vSphere Client.

2. Navigate to the Hosts And Clusters inventory view.

3. In the inventory tree, select an ESXi host. This will show you the Summary tab in the Details section on the right.

4. Select the Performance tab, and switch to Advanced view.

5. Click the Chart Options link.

6. Under Chart Options in the Customize Performance Chart dialog box, select the Network resource type and the Real-Time display interval.

7. Set the chart type to Line Graph.

8. In the objects list, select the ESXi host as well as all the specific NICs.

9. Select the Network Data Transmit Rate and Network Packets Transmitted counters.

10. Click OK to apply the changes and return to the Performance tab.

Very much like the previous example for a VM, these two counters will give you a window into how much network activity is occurring on this particular host in the outbound direction for each physical NIC. This is especially relevant if you want to see different rates of usage for each physical network interface, which, by definition, represent different virtual switches.

Now that you've examined how to monitor CPU, memory, and network usage, there's only one major area left: monitoring disk usage.

Monitoring Disk Usage

Monitoring a host's controller or VM's virtual disk usage is similar in scope to monitoring network usage. This resource, which represents a controller or the storing of a VM's virtual disk on a type of supported storage, isn't restricted by CPU or memory mechanisms like reservations, limits, or shares. The only way to restrict a VM's disk activity is to assign shares on the individual VM, which in turn may have to compete with other VMs running from the same storage volume. vCenter Server's graphs come to our aid again in showing actual usage for both ESXi hosts and VMs.

Perform the following steps to create a host graph showing disk controller utilization:

1. Use the vSphere Client to connect to a vCenter Server instance.

2. Navigate to the Hosts And Clusters inventory view.

3. In the inventory tree, select an ESXi host.

   This shows you the Summary tab in the Details section on the right.

4. Select the Performance tab, and switch to the Advanced view.

5. Click the Chart Options link. This opens the Customize Performance Chart dialog box.

6. Under Chart Options, choose the Real-Time display interval for the Disk resource type.

7. Set the chart type to Line Graph.

8. Selecting an object or objects — in this case a controller — and a counter or counters lets you monitor for activity that is interesting or necessary to meet service levels. Select the objects that represent the ESXi host and one of the disk controllers.

9. In the counters list, select Disk Read Rate, Disk Write Rate, and Disk Usage (Average/Rate) to get an overall view of the activity for the selected controller.

10. Click OK to return to the Performance tab.

This performance graph will give you an idea of the activity on the selected disk controller. But what if you want to see disk activity for the entire host by each VM? In this case, a Stacked Graph view can show you what you need.

STACKED VIEWS

A stacked view is helpful in identifying whether one particular VM is monopolizing a volume. Whichever VM has the tallest stack in the comparison may be degrading the performance of other VMs' virtual disks.

Now let's switch to the virtual machine view. Looking at individual VMs for insight into their disk utilization can lead to some useful conclusions. File and print VMs, or any server that provides print queues or database services, will generate some disk-related I/O that needs to be monitored. In some cases, if the VM is generating too much I/O, it may degrade the performance of other VMs running out of the same volume. Let's take a look at a VM's graph.

Perform the following steps to create a VM graph showing real-time disk controller utilization:

1. Launch the vSphere Client if it is not already running, and connect to a vCenter Server instance.

2. Navigate to either the Hosts And Clusters view or the VMs And Templates inventory view.

3. In the inventory tree, click a virtual machine.

   This shows you the Summary tab in the Details section on the right.

4. Select the Performance tab, and switch to Advanced view.

5. Click the Chart Options link to open the Customize Performance Chart dialog box.

6. Under Chart Options, select the Virtual Disk resource type and the Real-Time display interval.

7. Set the chart type to Line Graph.

8. Set both objects listed in the list of objects.

9. In the list of counters, select Read Rate, Write Rate (Average/Rate).

10. Click OK to apply these changes and return to the Performance tab.

With this graph, you should have an informative picture of this VM's disk I/O behavior. This VM is busy generating reads and writes for its application. Does the graph show enough I/O to meet a service-level agreement, or does this VM need some help? The graphs allow administrators to make informed decisions, usually working with the application owners, so that any adjustments to improve I/O will lead to satisfied VM owners.

In addition, by looking at longer intervals of time to gain a historical perspective, you may find that a VM has become busier or fallen off its regular output. If the amount of I/O is just slightly impaired, then adjusting the VM's shares may be a way to prioritize its disk I/O ahead of other VMs sharing the volume. The administrator may be forced to move the VM's virtual disk(s) to another volume or LUN if share adjustments don't achieve the required results. You can use Storage VMotion, described in Chapter 6, "Creating and Configuring Storage Devices," to perform this sort of LUN-based load balancing without any disruption to the end users.

PERFORMANCE MONITORING FROM THE INSIDE AND THE OUTSIDE

It's important to remember that the very nature of how virtualization operates means that it is impossible to use performance metrics from within a guest OS as an indicator of overall resource utilization. Here's why.

In a virtualized environment, each guest OS "sees" only its slice of the hardware as presented by the VMkernel. A guest OS that reports 100 percent CPU utilization isn't reporting that it's using 100 percent of the physical server's CPU, but rather that it's using 100 percent of the *CPU capacity given to it by the hypervisor*. A guest OS that is reporting 90 percent RAM utilization is really only using 90 percent of the *RAM made available to it by the hypervisor*.

Does this mean that performance metrics gathered from within a guest OS are useless? No, but these metrics cannot be used to establish overall resource usage — only relative resource usage. You must combine any performance metrics gathered from within a guest OS with matching metrics gathered outside the guest OS. By combining the metrics from within the guest OS with metrics outside the guest OS, you can create a more complete view of how a guest OS is using a particular type of resource and therefore get a better idea of what steps to take to resolve any resource constraints.

For example, if a guest OS is reporting high memory utilization but the vCenter Server resource management tools are showing that the physical system has plenty of memory available, this tells you that the guest OS is using everything available to it and might perform better with more memory allocated to it.

Monitoring resources can be tricky, and it requires a good knowledge of the applications running in the VMs in your environment. If you are a new vSphere administrator, it's worth spending some time using vCenter Server's performance graphs to establish some baseline behaviors. This helps you become much more familiar with the normal operation of the VMs so that when something unusual or out of the ordinary does occur, you'll be more likely to spot it.

The Bottom Line

Use alarms for proactive monitoring.   vCenter Server offers extensive alarms for alerting vSphere administrators to excessive resource consumption or potentially negative events. You can create alarms on virtually any type of object found within vCenter Server, including datacenters, clusters, ESXi hosts, and VMs. Alarms can monitor for resource consumption or for the occurrence of specific events. Alarms can also trigger actions, such as running a script, migrating a VM, or sending a notification email.

> **Master It**   What are the questions a vSphere administrator should ask before creating a custom alarm?

Work with performance graphs.   vCenter Server's detailed performance graphs are the key to unlocking the information necessary to determine why an ESXi host or VM is performing poorly. The performance graphs expose a large number of performance counters across a variety of resource types, and vCenter Server offers functionality to save customized chart settings, export performance graphs as graphic figures or Excel workbooks, or view performance graphs in a separate window.

Master It   You find yourself using the Chart Options link in the Advanced view of the Performance tab to set up the same graph over and over again. Is there a way to save yourself some time and effort so that you don't have to keep re-creating the custom graph?

Gather performance information using command-line tools.   VMware supplies a few command-line tools that are useful in gathering performance information. For VMware ESXi hosts, `resxtop` provides real-time information about CPU, memory, network, or disk utilization. You should run `resxtop` from the VMware vMA. Finally, the `vm-support` tool can gather performance information that can be played back later using `resxtop`.

Master It   Know how to run `resxtop` from the VMware vMA command line.

Monitor CPU, memory, network, and disk usage by ESXi hosts and VMs.   Monitoring usage of the four key resources — CPU, memory, network, and disk — can be difficult at times. Fortunately, the various tools supplied by VMware within vCenter Server can lead the vSphere administrator to the right solution. In particular, using customized performance graphs can expose the right information that will help a vSphere administrator uncover the source of performance problems.

Master It   A junior vSphere administrator is trying to resolve a performance problem with a VM. You've asked this administrator to see whether it is a CPU problem, and the junior administrator keeps telling you that the VM needs more CPU capacity because the CPU utilization is high within the VM. Is the junior administrator correct, based on the information available to you?

Chapter 14

Automating VMware vSphere

As a VMware vSphere administrator, you'll need to perform lots of repetitive tasks. Examples include creating five new VMs from a template, changing the network configuration on 18 VMs, or creating a new port group on seven different ESXi hosts. All these examples are tasks where automation would help you complete the task more quickly, provide greater consistency, save you time, and ultimately save your organization money. Clearly, automation is an area that can benefit every vSphere administrator and every organization that adopts vSphere in their environment.

In this chapter, you will learn to

- ◆ Identify some of the tools available for automating vSphere
- ◆ Configure vCenter Orchestrator
- ◆ Use a vCenter Orchestrator workflow
- ◆ Create a PowerCLI script for automation
- ◆ Use vCLI to manage ESXi hosts from the command line
- ◆ Use vCenter in combination with vMA to manage all your hosts
- ◆ Employ the Perl toolkit and VMware SDK for virtual server operations from the command line

Why Use Automation?

The real question isn't "why use automation?" but "why not use automation?" As a former system administrator, I frequently looked for ways to automate tasks that I had to perform on a regular basis. Whether it was creating user accounts, rebuilding computers, deploying new applications, or querying the status of a remote server in another location, anything that saved me time and prevented me from having to repeat the same steps was a good thing. That also applies here: anything that can save you time and prevent you from performing the same steps repeatedly in your vSphere environment is a good thing.

You can provide automation in your vSphere environment in a number of ways. Depending on your programming skill level and your experience, there is likely a toolkit or automation tool that fits you and your needs:

- ◆ System administrators with some prior experience in JavaScript can use vCenter Orchestrator, an automation platform installed automatically with vCenter Server, to build workflows.

- ◆ vSphere administrators with knowledge or experience in Microsoft PowerShell can use PowerShell and PowerCLI to create PowerShell scripts that automate tasks within the vSphere environment.

◆ Administrators with experience in traditional Unix or Linux shell scripting can create shell scripts to automate some tasks by using vCLI from the vSphere Management Assistant (vMA).

◆ Administrators with experience in traditional Unix or Linux shell scripting can create shell scripts to automate some tasks from the vMA.

◆ System administrators with knowledge of Perl can use the vSphere Software Development Kit (SDK) for Perl, which provides Perl interfaces to the vSphere API.

As you can see, you have lots of options for bringing automation into your vSphere environment — and that's without taking into account any of the numerous third-party solutions available!

In this chapter, I'll discuss the first three tools that you can use for automation in your vSphere environment, and then I'll discuss using the vMA and SDK with Perl.

These solutions address the majority of the needs of most vSphere administrators. I'll start with vCenter Orchestrator.

Using Workflows with vCenter Orchestrator

vCenter Orchestrator (vCO) is a workflow automation product that allows you to build custom workflows that automate entire sequences of events. vCO provides access to the vCenter Server API and the more than 800 actions that are available within vCenter Server, allowing you to build workflows that address just about every conceivable need. To give you an idea of the versatility of the vCO product, keep in mind that the vCO engine ran underneath vCenter Lifecycle Manager. vCenter Lifecycle Manager was a separate product from VMware that provided automation around the entire VM life cycle, from provisioning all the way to decommissioning, and it was built entirely on vCO.

To help users harness the power of vCO in their environments, vCO is silently installed when vCenter Server is installed. Now I'd like to delve much deeper into vCO and show you how you can use it to provide some automation in your environment.

Although vCO is installed with vCenter Server, you must configure vCO separately after the installation is complete. In the next section, I'll walk you through configuring vCO so that it is ready for you to use.

Understanding vCenter Orchestrator Prerequisites

Because vCO is installed with vCenter Server, many of the prerequisites for vCO are the same as for vCenter Server. Like vCenter Server, vCO runs on any x64 Windows server. Also like vCenter Server, vCO requires a separate backend database. This backend database must be separate from the vCenter Server backend database.

These are the database servers that vCO supports for this backend database:

◆ Microsoft SQL Server 2005 SP3 (Standard or Enterprise), 32-bit or 64-bit.

◆ Microsoft SQL Server 2008 (SP1 or SP2) (Standard or Enterprise) , 32-bit or 64-bit.

◆ Oracle 10g (Standard or Enterprise) Release 2 (10.2.0.3.0), 32-bit, or 64-bit

◆ Oracle 11g (Standard or Enterprise) Release 1 (11.1.0.7), 32-bit, or 64-bit

MySQL and PostgreSQL are also supported but only for testing and evaluation purposes.

USE A SEPARATE PHYSICAL SERVER FOR THE ORCHESTRATOR DATABASE

Because of CPU and memory usage, VMware recommends placing the vCO database on a separate machine from the vCO server. These machines should reside in the same datacenter for high-speed LAN connectivity.

If you are planning on using an Oracle database, you must download the Oracle drivers and copy them to the appropriate locations; the vCO installer does not do this for you. For more complete information on exactly how this is accomplished, refer to the "vCO Installation and Configuration Guide" available from VMware's website at www.vmware.com/support/pubs/ orchestrator_pubs.html.

vCO also requires a working LDAP server in your environment. Supported LDAP servers include OpenLDAP, Novell eDirectory, Sun Java Directory Server, and Microsoft Active Directory.

After you verify that you meet all these prerequisites, you are ready to get started configuring vCenter Orchestrator.

Configuring vCenter Orchestrator

After you complete the installation of vCenter Server and, with it, vCenter Orchestrator, you can proceed with the configuration of vCO so that it is ready to use. The process of configuring vCO involves a number of steps, each of which I describe in detail in the following sections.

The vCO configuration process involves, at the very least, the following steps:

1. Start the vCO Configuration service.

2. Configure the vCO network connection.

3. Create and test a connection to a working Lightweight Directory Access Protocol (LDAP) server.

4. Set up the backend database.

5. Import or create a Secure Sockets Layer (SSL) certificate for vCenter Orchestrator.

6. Import the vCenter Server license.

7. Configure the default plug-ins.

I'll walk you through each of these steps in the following sections.

STARTING THE vCENTER ORCHESTRATOR CONFIGURATION SERVICE

The first step in configuring vCO is starting the vCO Configuration service. By default, this service is set for manual startup. In order to be able to access the web-based configuration interface, you must first start this service.

Perform the following steps to start the vCO Configuration service:

1. Log into the computer running vCenter Server, where vCenter Orchestrator was also installed automatically, as an administrative user.

2. From the Start menu, choose Run.

3. In the Run dialog box, type **services.msc**, and click OK.

4. When the Services window opens, scroll through the list of services in the pane on the right until you see the VMware vCenter Orchestrator Configuration service.

5. Right-click the VMware vCenter Orchestrator Configuration service and select Start.

6. Verify that the service started correctly by ensuring that the Status column for the VMware vCenter Orchestrator Configuration service lists Started.

After the service starts, you can access the vCO Web Configuration interface. There are two ways to access the interface:

◆ From the Start menu, select All Programs ➢ VMware ➢ vCenter Orchestrator Web Configuration.

◆ Open a web browser, and go to http://<computer IP address or DNS name>:8282.

VCENTER ORCHESTRATOR START MENU ICONS MIGHT BE MISSING

If you installed vCenter Server to run in the context of a dedicated user account — perhaps in order to support Windows authentication to a backend database running on Microsoft SQL Server — the vCenter Orchestrator Start menu icons are visible only to that user account. To make them visible to other user accounts, you must move them to the All Users portion of the Start menu.

You will log into the vCenter Orchestrator Web Configuration interface using the username *vmware* and the password *vmware*. Although you cannot change the default username, I highly recommend that you change the default password. There is an option for changing the default password in the vCenter Orchestrator Web Configuration interface.

You are now ready to proceed with configuring vCenter Orchestrator. Your first task is configuring the vCO network connection.

CONFIGURING THE NETWORK CONNECTION

When you first log into the vCO Configuration interface, you'll see a series of options along the left with red triangles, as shown in Figure 14.1. These red triangles, or status indicators, indicate that these options have not yet been configured. You need to ensure that all these status indicators are green circles before the vCO Server will start and operate.

Starting at the top of this list of status indicators, your first task is to configure the network connection.

FIGURE 14.1:
The vCenter
Orchestrator
Configuration inter-
face provides status
indicators to tell you
whether it is prop-
erly configured.

FIGURE 14.1:
The vCenter
Orchestrator
Configuration inter-
face provides status
indicators to tell you
whether it is prop-
erly configured.

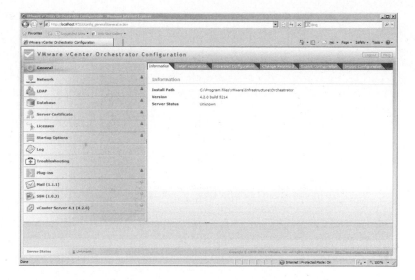

Perform the following steps to configure the network connection:

1. In the vCenter Orchestrator Configuration interface, click the Network tab on the left side of the window.

2. In the IP Address drop-down list, select the IP address on which you want the vCenter Orchestrator Server to listen.

3. Click Apply Changes. It is generally not necessary to change any of the default ports for vCenter Orchestrator.

The status indicator for Network should now change from a red triangle to a green circle. Next, you need to configure the LDAP connection.

CREATING AND TESTING THE LDAP CONNECTION

vCO requires a supported LDAP server. In many cases, you will use Active Directory as your supported LDAP server because vCenter Server also integrates with Active Directory. As I mentioned earlier, other LDAP servers are supported. Here I'll explain how to configure vCO to use Active Directory.

Perform the following steps to use an Active Directory domain controller as your LDAP server:

1. In the vCenter Orchestrator Configuration interface, click the LDAP tab on the left side of the web browser.

2. In the LDAP Client drop-down list, select Active Directory.

3. In the Primary LDAP Host text box, supply the fully qualified domain name (FQDN) of an Active Directory domain controller.

4. In the Secondary LDAP Host text box, supply the FQDN for a secondary Active Directory domain controller.

5. In the Root text box, supply the root DN for your Active Directory domain.

   For example, if your Active Directory domain name was v12nlab.net, the root DN would be dc=v12nlab,dc=net.

6. In the Username and Password text boxes, supply the username and password that vCenter Orchestrator will use to authenticate against Active Directory.

   Specify the username in DN format (cn=username,cn=Users,dc=domain,dc=com) or universal principal name (UPN) format (username@domain.com).

7. In the User Lookup Base text box, supply the base DN that vCenter Orchestrator should use when searching for user accounts.

   If you are unsure of what to use, specify the same value as the root DN.

8. In the Group Lookup Base text box, supply the base DN that vCenter Orchestrator should use when searching for groups.

   If you are unsure of what to use, specify the same value as the root DN.

9. In the vCO Admin Group text box, specify the DN of an Active Directory group that should receive vCenter Orchestrator administration rights.

   This should look something like cn=Administrators,cn=Builtin,dc=domain,dc=com.

10. Click the Apply Changes button.

The red triangle status indicator should change to a green circle. If it does not, double-check the LDAP configuration and try again.

Next, you are ready to set up the backend database.

SETTING UP THE BACKEND DATABASE

Like vCenter Server and vSphere Update Manager, vCenter Orchestrator requires a backend database in order to operate. You must configure the backend database and the vCenter Orchestrator database connection in order for vCenter Orchestrator to work. In this section, I'll walk you through setting up a database on Microsoft SQL Server and configuring vCenter Orchestrator to use that database.

Creating and configuring the backend database on Microsoft SQL Server is straightforward. Create the database, and specify the owner of the database to be either a Windows account or an SQL login. Be sure to note the owner of the database and the password for that owner, because both pieces of information will be necessary when you configure vCenter Orchestrator.

Perform the following steps to configure vCenter Orchestrator to use this backend database:

1. In the vCenter Orchestrator Configuration interface, select the Database tab from the left side of the web browser window.

2. In the Select/Change Database Type drop-down list, select SQL Server.

3. Supply the username, password, hostname, port, database name, instance name (if using named instances), and domain name in the applicable text boxes.

   If you are using SQL authentication, leave the domain name text box blank.

4. Click the Install Database link to install the database tables that vCenter Orchestrator needs.

5. Click the Apply Changes button.

The red triangle should change to a green circle to show that database connectivity has been successfully verified.

Next, you need to configure the server certificate.

CONFIGURING THE SERVER CERTIFICATE

vCenter Orchestrator requires that a valid SSL certificate be installed on the vCenter Orchestrator computer. The Server Certificate section of the vCenter Orchestrator Configuration interface allows you either to create your own self-signed certificate or to import an SSL certificate from an existing certificate authority. If you already have an existing public key infrastructure (PKI) set up within your environment, then I recommend leveraging that PKI and importing a valid SSL certificate from your PKI. Otherwise, you can create a self-signed SSL certificate using the Create A New Certificate Database And Server Certificate link.

Perform the following steps to create a new self-signed certificate for vCenter Orchestrator:

1. In the vCenter Orchestrator Configuration interface, click the Server Certificate tab on the left side of the interface.

2. Click the Create A New Certificate Database And Server Certificate link.

3. For Common Name, supply the FQDN of the vCenter Server computer.

4. For Organization and Organizational Unit, provide appropriate values for your environment.

5. Select the correct country in the Country drop-down list.

6. Click the Create button.

The vCenter Orchestrator Configuration service will generate a new SSL certificate and install it for use by vCenter Orchestrator. The red triangle will also change to a green circle, letting you know that this task has been completed. Next, you will import the vCenter Server license.

IMPORTING THE vCENTER SERVER LICENSE

Although it is installed with vCenter Server, vCenter Orchestrator does not automatically share the vCenter Server licensing information. To let vCenter Orchestrator know the type of vCenter Server license you have, you will need to import that license into the vCenter Orchestrator Configuration interface. You can do this by either entering the 25-digit serial number or by connecting to vCenter.

Perform the following steps to connect to vCenter:

1. In the vCenter Orchestrator Configuration interface, select the Licenses tab on the left side of the interface.

2. Enter the username and password for the vCenter Server, since the remaining defaults should work.

3. Click the Apply Changes button.

Perform the following steps to enter the serial number:

1. In the vCenter Orchestrator Configuration interface, select the Licenses tab on the left side of the interface.

2. Supply the 25-digit serial number of your vCenter Server license and the license owner.

3. Click the Apply Changes button.

Depending on the vCenter Server license that you own, vCenter Orchestrator will operate in one of two modes:

◆ For a vCenter Server Standard license, vCenter Orchestrator operates in Server mode. This provides full access to all Orchestrator elements and the ability to run and edit workflows.

◆ For a vCenter Server Foundation or vCenter Server Essentials license, vCenter Orchestrator runs in Player mode. You are granted read-only permission on Orchestrator elements, and you can run workflows, but you cannot edit them.

You're almost finished with the vCenter Orchestrator configuration. At this point, all of the status indicators except Startup Options and Plug-ins should be green. As long as the Startup Options status indicator is still red, you won't be able to start vCenter Orchestrator Server. The last task for you is to configure the plug-ins.

CONFIGURING THE PLUG-INS

vCenter Orchestrator uses a plug-in architecture to add functionality and connectivity to the base workflow engine. By default, vCenter Orchestrator comes with a default set of plug-ins, but you'll need to provide a username and password of an account with administrative permissions in vCenter Orchestrator to install them.

Perform the following steps to install the default set of plug-ins:

1. In the vCenter Orchestrator Configuration interface, click the Plug-Ins tab.

2. Specify the username and password of an account that is a member of the vCO Administration group.

   This is the group you specified previously when you configured the LDAP server.

3. Click Apply Changes.

The Plug-ins status indicator will change to a green circle and, assuming all the other status indicators are also green circles, the Startup Options status indicator will be also. However, there is one more essential task you need to complete, and that is adding a vCenter Server host with which vCenter Orchestrator will communicate.

ADDING A VCENTER SERVER HOST

If you scroll down to the bottom of the list of configuration tabs in the vCenter Orchestrator Configuration interface, you will see a plug-in named vCenter Server. That is the area where you will need to add a vCenter Server host with which vCenter Orchestrator will communicate. Without performing this task, vCenter Orchestrator will work, but it will not be able to automate tasks within vCenter Server — which kind of defeats its purpose.

Perform the following steps to add a vCenter Server host to vCenter Orchestrator:

1. At the bottom of the list of configuration tasks in the vCenter Orchestrator Configuration interface, select the tab labeled vCenter Server.

2. Click the New VirtualCenter Host tab.

3. From the Available drop-down list, select Enabled.

4. In the Host text box, supply the FQDN of the vCenter Server computer you are adding.

5. Under the heading Specify The User Credential For The Administrator Session, specify an administrative username and password for this vCenter Server instance.

6. Under the heading Specify Which Strategy Will Be Used For Managing The Users Logins, select Share A Unique Session, and then supply a username and password to be passed to vCenter Server.

7. Click Apply Changes.

You will note that after you click the Apply Changes button, the vCenter Server status indicator and the Startup Options status indicator change back to red. In order for vCenter Orchestrator to work with vCenter Server over an SSL connection, you must also import the vCenter Server SSL certificate.

Perform the following steps to import the vCenter Server SSL certificate:

1. Click the vCenter Server tab on the left side of the vCenter Orchestrator Configuration interface.

2. Click the Hosts tab.

3. Click the SSL Certificates link.

4. Because vCenter Orchestrator is installed by default on the same server as vCenter Server, you can import the SSL certificate from a local file. Click the Browse button.

5. Navigate to `C:\ProgramData\VMware\VMware VirtualCenter\SSL`, and select the `rui.crt` file.

6. Click the Open button in the Choose File dialog box.

7. Click the Import button to import the selected certificate.

8. Click the vCenter Server tab again on the left side of the vCenter Orchestrator Configuration interface.

9. Click the Restart The vCO Configuration Server link.

   This will log you out of the vCenter Orchestrator Configuration interface.

10. Log back into the vCenter Orchestrator Configuration interface.

   Now, you are finally ready to install and start the vCenter Orchestrator Server service.

INSTALLING AND STARTING THE vCENTER ORCHESTRATOR SERVER SERVICE

After you complete all the configuration steps, you can install and start the vCenter Orchestrator Server. Before you continue, ensure that all the status indicators in the vCenter Orchestrator Configuration interface show a green circle. If any of the status indicators do not have a green circle, you won't be able to start the vCenter Orchestrator Server.

Perform the following steps to install and start the vCenter Orchestrator Server:

1. In the vCenter Orchestrator Configuration interface, click the Startup Options tab.

2. Click the Install vCO Server As A Service link. The interface will change to show a spinning progress meter while the configuration service installs the server service.

3. When the interface returns and indicates success with a green message at the top of the Startup Options screen, click the Start Service link.

4. The vCenter Orchestrator Server service will attempt to start. It might take a few minutes for the service to start, so be patient. You can use the Services management console (select Start ➢ Run, and enter `services.msc`) to verify the status of the VMware vCenter Orchestrator Server service.

After the vCenter Orchestrator Server service is running, you're ready to start using vCenter Orchestrator workflows.

Using an Orchestrator Workflow

So far, you've only seen how to configure the vCenter Orchestrator Server, but now that the server is up and running, you are ready to launch the client and actually run a workflow. The vCenter Orchestrator Client is the application you will use to actually launch a workflow. You can launch the vCenter Orchestrator Client from the Start menu and then log in with the Active Directory credentials of an account in the vCO Administrators group (this is the group configured earlier when you set up the LDAP server connection for vCenter Orchestrator).

vCenter Orchestrator comes with a library of preinstalled workflows. To view these workflows in the vCenter Orchestrator Client, click the Workflows tab on the left side of the window, and then browse through the tree folder structure to see what workflows are already available for you to use. Figure 14.2 shows some of the preinstalled workflows in the vCenter Orchestrator Client.

To run any of the workflows in the vCenter Orchestrator Client, you just right-click the workflow and select Execute Workflow. Depending on the workflow, the vCenter Orchestrator Client prompts you for the information it needs to complete the workflow, such as the name of a VM or the name of an ESXi host. The information that the vCenter Orchestrator Client prompts you to supply will vary based on the workflow you have selected to run.

FIGURE 14.2:
The vCenter folder contains all the workflows that automate actions in vCenter Server.

CREATING WORKFLOWS IS MOSTLY A DEVELOPER'S TASK

Unfortunately, creating custom workflows is probably beyond the reach of most vSphere administrators. Creating workflows and actions requires expertise and experience with web development languages like JavaScript. If this is something with which you have some knowledge, then download the "vCenter Orchestrator Developer's Guide" from VMware's website at www.vmware.com/support/pubs/orchestrator_pubs.html. This developer's guide provides more detailed information on how to create Orchestrator workflows.

---

vCenter Orchestrator is a powerful tool that is capable of creating some complex and highly interactive workflows. However, vCenter Orchestrator doesn't give up its secrets easily, and creating workflows may be beyond the skills of many vSphere administrators. One automation tool that is much easier to learn and is rapidly gaining popularity in the VMware community, though, is Microsoft PowerShell. PowerShell and PowerCLI can be great tools for automating your vSphere environment, as you'll see in the next section.

Automating with PowerShell and PowerCLI

PowerShell is Microsoft's premier administrative automation language. Built on the .NET framework, PowerShell has access to the full breadth of Windows-based applications. If you do a search on PowerShell, you will find the full spectrum of what's possible. Everything from simple process manipulation to complex server deployments can be handled in a single PowerShell script. PowerShell also features a rich programming language and as such can be used to prototype .NET code or invoke native C libraries within Windows. For the purpose of PowerCLI, we will focus on the command line and what's possible using the PowerCLI PowerShell snap-in. First, we need to cover some terminology.

At the base of PowerShell is the *pipeline*. Those coming from a Unix background will be well versed in the concept of a pipeline. However, PowerShell took the traditional pipeline and kicked it up a notch. In the past, pipelines were a means to pass text from one command to another, simplifying the syntax of a given operation. In PowerShell, pipelines are a means to pass whole .NET objects from one cmdlet to another. This ability greatly increased the power of the pipeline while simplifying its ability to accomplish almost any administrative action. While PowerShell does contain a core scripting language, for the most part actions are performed by executing cmdlets.

Another term that needs defining is *cmdlets* (pronounced *command-lets*), which are compiled .NET classes that perform a single action on an object. They are named in the `<verb>-<singular noun>` format. This enables several things; for the most part cmdlets are simple to use because they don't attempt to do too much at once. Also, because there is an established naming convention, often you can find the cmdlet you need by simply guessing. For instance, to get all the VMs in vCenter you run `Get-VM` — intuitive by design.

Finally, PowerShell offers third parties the ability to extend the core set of 400+ cmdlets with snap-ins and modules. A *snap-in* is a compiled .`dll` that contains a set of cmdlets. A *module*, new to PowerShell V2, is the next generation of script packaging. A module can be either compiled or script and offers a private runspace for the module author. PowerCLI is a PowerShell snap-in, although by the time you read this I suspect there will be a module as well. The current version of PowerCLI contains 260+ cmdlets covering almost every aspect of vSphere.

The first step you take in order to use PowerCLI is to install it, as I'll show you in the next section.

Installing PowerCLI

Installing PowerCLI actually means installing two different components:

- PowerShell is a core component of Windows since Windows 7, but if you're running an older version of Windows, you'll need to install the Windows Management Framework, available for download from Microsoft's website at www.microsoft.com/download.

- PowerCLI is available for download from VMware's website at www.vmware.com/go/PowerCLI.

Perform the following steps to install PowerCLI:

1. Launch the PowerCLI installer that you downloaded from VMware's website.

2. If the installer displays a dialog box informing you that VMware VIX will be installed at the end of setup, click OK to continue.

3. If a message is displayed warning that the PowerShell execution policy is currently set to Restricted, click Continue. You will change this later.

4. On the first screen of the VMware vSphere PowerCLI Installation Wizard, click Next to start the installation.

5. Select the radio button marked I Accept The Terms In The License Agreement, and click Next.

6. Change the location where PowerCLI will be installed, or click Next to accept the default location.

7. Click Install.

8. After the installation is complete, deselect the box to launch PowerCLI, and click Finish.

Remember the warning about the PowerShell execution policy? Before you can use PowerCLI, you'll need to set the PowerShell execution policy to allow some of the PowerCLI components to execute.

Perform the following steps to set the PowerShell execution policy:

1. In the Start menu, select All Programs ➢ Accessories ➢ Windows PowerShell ➢ Windows PowerShell, right-click, and select Run As Administrator.

2. At the PowerShell prompt, enter the following command:

   `Set-ExecutionPolicy RemoteSigned`

3. To verify the setting, enter the following command:

   `Get-ExecutionPolicy`

The results of the `Get-ExecutionPolicy` command should be `RemoteSigned`.

WHAT HAPPENS IF YOU DON'T SET THE EXECUTION POLICY?

Because PowerCLI runs a few PowerShell scripts during startup to load the appropriate snap-ins, failing to set the execution policy to `RemoteSigned` means these scripts will not run properly. Errors will be returned when these scripts execute, and PowerCLI will not be correctly initialized.

Now you are ready to launch PowerCLI. When you launch PowerCLI, you are greeted with a few quick tips and the PowerCLI prompt, as shown in Figure 14.3.

If you are seeing this screen when you launch PowerCLI, then you're ready to start using PowerCLI to manage your VMware vSphere environment. First, though, I'll review the topic of objects and introduce you to a few useful objects in PowerCLI.

Working with Objects

Everything in PowerShell (and hence PowerCLI) is built on the idea of objects. For example, an ESXi host exists as an object in PowerCLI. A VM exists as an object in PowerCLI. A snapshot exists as an object. You will work with these objects in PowerCLI by modifying their properties, creating them, or deleting them.

FIGURE 14.3
The PowerCLI startup screen provides quick tips on a few useful commands.

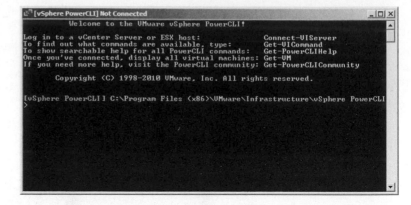

With PowerCLI specifically, you must first connect to the vSphere environment, either to a vCenter Server instance or to an ESXi host, before you can work with any of the objects available to you. You can connect to the vSphere environment using the following `Connect-VIServer` command:

```
Connect-VIServer -Server <vCenter Server hostname> -User <Username>
-Password <password>
```

GET-HELP IS YOUR FRIEND

The `Get-Help` cmdlet is invaluable as you explore PowerCLI. Anytime you are unsure of a command or its syntax, simply use `Get-Help` followed by the command or a portion of the command. If you are unsure how to use `Get-Help`, use `Get-Help Get-Help`.

After you connect, you are ready to work with some vSphere objects. Let's say you wanted to list all the ESXi hosts connected to your vCenter Server instance. You could do that with the following command, which would list all the ESXi hosts connected to the vCenter Server instances to which you connected with the `Connect-VIServer` command:

```
Get-VMHost
```

This command returns an object or set of objects, each of which represents an ESXi host.

Next, let's say that you wanted to list all the VMs currently running on one of those ESXi hosts. To do this, you would combine the `Get-VMHost` command in a pipeline (noted by the | symbol) with the `Get-VM` command, like this:

```
Get-VMHost <Hostname> | Get-VM
```

This command would return a list of objects. Each object returned represents a VM running on the specified ESXi host. You could now take this list of VM objects and combine the objects with another command to list all the virtual network interface cards (NICs) within each VM on the specified ESXi host:

```
Get-VMHost <Hostname> | Get-VM | Get-NetworkAdapter
```

This command would provide a list of objects, each of which represents a virtual network adapter within a VM. Because the output of this command is objects, you could then use the Select command to selectively filter the output, like this:

```
Get-VMHost <Hostname> | Get-VM | Get-NetworkAdapter | Select-Object NetworkName, Type
```

This would produce the output shown in Figure 14.4.

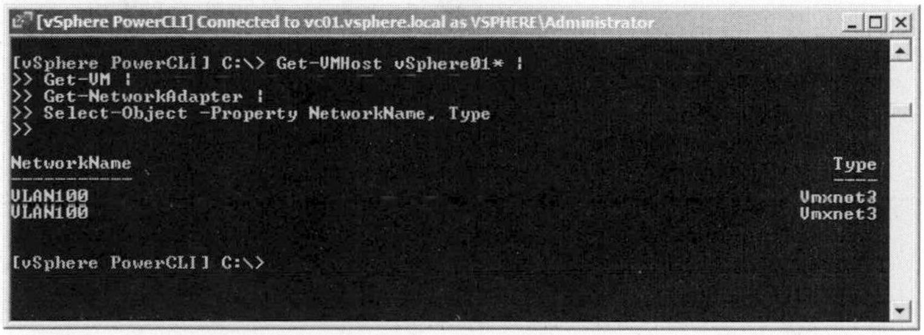

FIGURE 14.4
The Select statement filters the output from commands in PowerCLI.

These examples show you how PowerShell and PowerCLI work with objects and how commands can be combined in a pipeline to create more complex instructions. Because of the sheer number of cmdlets within the PowerCLI snap-in, I cannot cover them all. However, I will teach you how to make PowerShell work for you. PowerShell has a couple of built-in cmdlets that make discovering cmdlets easier.

PowerCLI itself ships with such a cmdlet. To quickly get a list of all the cmdlets contained within PowerCLI, run Get-VICommand. However, to perform a more powerful search you can use the Get-Command cmdlet. For instance, to find any cmdlet that interacts with a VM you can run:

```
Get-Command -Noun VM
```

Alternatively you could find all the Get cmdlets contained within PowerCLI by running:

```
Get-Command -Module VMware* -Verb Get
```

If you don't have any idea what the verb or noun may be, but you know the analog within VIC, you can leverage Get-Help to search through the help documents for a command. For instance, to find the cmdlet to mount a NFS datastore you would run:

```
Get-Help *NFS*
```

So now you know how to find a cmdlet once you've located that magical single unit of work. Most PowerCLI users will point to their cool scripts as examples, but you can use PowerCLI every day to automate every facet of your environment and never write a script. That's the beauty of the pipeline. The basic workflow works as such given a problem like "I need to find every VM in the Production resource pool where the VMware Tools are out of date." From here you simply start to convert the natural-language problem into a PowerShell pipeline. First, you need to get every VM in the Production resource pool:

```
Get-ResourcePool Production | Get-VM
```

Now you need to figure out how to determine if VMware Tools are up to date. For this you'll use two built-in cmdlets: Get-Member and Format-List. To see all the methods and properties associated with an object in PowerShell, simply pipe the object to Get-Member, as shown in Figure 14.5.

FIGURE 14.5
Get all the methods and properties of an object with Get-Member.

Get-Member uses .NET reflection to inspect an object and report any methods or properties associated with it. Pay attention to the definition of any properties. If they are a simple type, such as System.String, System.Int32, or System.Bool, then they contain information. If, however, they are not a simple type, such as VMware.VimAutomation.ViCore.Types.V1.Inventory.PowerState, then they contain an embedded object with more information. Objects are like a file system; sometimes to find what you're looking for, you need to traverse many levels. In this case, you save a single VM object to a variable to ease this discovery process:

```
$VM  = Get-VM SVR01
```

Now you can access any properties or methods by simply adding a dot. For example, to examine what exactly is contained within the PowerState object you would run

```
$VM.PowerState
```

After a little discovery you will find that the Tools status is reported by running

```
$VM.Guest.ExtensionData.ToolsStatus
```

Back to the original objective to get any VM in the Production resource pool where VMware Tools are out of date, you would run:

```
Get-ResourcePool Production | Get-VM | Where-Object
{ $_.Guest.ExtensionData.ToolsStatus -eq "ToolsOld"}
```

While this is undoubtedly still code, notice how close to the original problem your code reads, almost like an English sentence. Using the technique just covered you can work with PowerCLI every day and never write a single script. Instead, you can just leverage the pipeline to perform one simple action against any number of objects. But after a while you will grow tired of typing, and that's where scripts step in.

Running Some Simple PowerCLI Scripts

Scripts are nothing more than a series of PowerCLI cmdlets strung into a series of PowerShell pipelines saved to a text file with a .ps1 extension. With that in mind, we will cover a few examples where PowerCLI can make your life easier.

SCRIPT EXECUTION

By default, the running of scripts is disabled on a fresh install of PowerShell. However, you enabled them when you set the execution policy to remotesigned. To learn more about script signing, run Get-Help about_Signing.

MIGRATING ALL VIRTUAL MACHINES ON A HOST

In the first example, you'll build a simple pipeline using multiple PowerCLI cmdlets. By combining cmdlets in a pipeline, you can build more complex commands, such as the following:

```
Get-VMHost <FirstHost> | Get-VM | Move-VM -destination
(Get-VMHost <SecondHost>)
```

This command relocates all VMs on the ESXi host specified by FirstHost to the ESXi host represented by SecondHost. This includes both running VMs, which are moved with VMotion, as well as powered-off VMs.

MANIPULATING VIRTUAL MACHINE SNAPSHOTS

Let's look at a second example of how to use PowerCLI in your VMware vSphere environment. In this example, you'll use PowerCLI to work with VM snapshots.

Let's say that you need to create a snapshot for all the VMs on a particular ESXi host. This command would accomplish that for you:

```
Get-VMHost <Hostname> | Get-VM | New-Snapshot -Name "Target-Snapshot"
```

If you later needed to remove the snapshot you created, you could use the Remove-Snapshot cmdlet to delete that snapshot:

```
Get-VMHost <Hostname> | Get-VM | Get-Snapshot
-Name "Target-Snapshot" | Remove-Snapshot
```

Finally, you could use the Get-Snapshot cmdlet to list all snapshots so that you could be sure you had actually created or deleted the snapshots:

```
Get-VMHost <Hostname> | Get-VM | Get-Snapshot
```

This command would return a list of snapshot objects for all the VMs on the specified ESXi host.

Real World Scenario

AUTOMATION AS A WAY OF LIFE

As you scale out your virtual infrastructure you will quickly get to a point where your ability to manage your environment from the GUI is stretched. For instance when you have 120 virtual machines, changing a network setting on each VM would take days. Days of repetitive mundane work, the type of work that leads to mistakes and downtime. In these scenarios you'll need to employ a little automation. Not only to save time, but more importantly to reduce risk. A script or workflow doesn't mis-click or mis-type. A script can be counted on to perform an action without exception. A healthy environment can only be maintained at scale with the use of automation. Fortunately, VMware supports the whole gambit of automation frameworks available today, so employ whatever you're most comfortable with, but make sure automation is part of your toolkit. As a good general rule anything that will be done more than 10 times should be done via a script. The reason for selecting 10 as the demarcation point is due to the time investment. Generally speaking if you're going to do something at least 10 times your organization will actually gain time by you taking the time to script a solution. Yes, the script will take slightly longer to write the first time, but once written that script has no shelf life, and can be employed multiple times. Time spent manually performing a task can never be recuperated, and often leads to work having to be duplicated due to human error.

RECONFIGURING VIRTUAL MACHINE NETWORKING

In this third example, let's say that you want to move all the VMs currently connected to one port group to an entirely different port group. This is actually possible with a one-line command in PowerCLI:

```
Get-VM | Get-NetworkAdapter | ↵
Where-Object { $_.NetworkName -like "OldPortGroupName" } | ↵
Set-NetworkAdapter -NetworkName "NewPortGroupName" -Confirm:$false.
```

There are a few new ideas introduced here, so let me break it down a little bit:

◆ The Get-VM cmdlet retrieves VM objects.

◆ These VM objects are passed to the Get-NetworkAdapter cmdlet, which returns virtual NIC objects.

◆ These virtual NIC objects are parsed using the Where-Object cmdlet to include only those virtual NICs whose NetworkName property is like the "OldPortGroupName" string.

◆ The parsed list of virtual NICs is passed to the Set-NetworkAdapter cmdlet, which sets the NetworkName property to the "NewPortGroupName" value.

◆ The Confirm parameter instructs PowerShell not to ask the user for confirmation of each operation.

MOVING VIRTUAL MACHINES BETWEEN RESOURCE POOLS

In this last example, you'll use PowerCLI to move a group of VMs from one resource pool to another. However, you want to move only a subset of the VMs in this resource pool. Only the

VMs that are running a Microsoft Windows guest operating system (guest OS) should be moved to the new resource pool.

I'll build this example in steps. First, you've probably guessed that you can use the `Get-ResourcePool`, `Get-VM`, and `Get-VMGuest` cmdlets to create a list of VM guest OS objects in the resource pool:

```
Get-ResourcePool <ResourcePoolName> | Get-VM | Get-VMGuest
```

Next, you would need to filter the output to return only those objects identified as Microsoft Windows guest OSes. As you saw in a previous example, you can use the `Where-Object` cmdlet to filter the output list in a pipeline:

```
Get-ResourcePool <ResourcePoolName> | Get-VM | Get-VMGuest |
Where-Object { $_.OSFullName -match "^Microsoft Windows.*" }
```

This should do it, right? To finish the command, you should be able to add the `Move-VM` cmdlet and move the VMs to the destination resource pool. Unfortunately, that won't work. You're working with *objects* here, and a VM guest OS object — which is what is being returned by the `Get-VMGuest` cmdlet — isn't the kind of object that the `Move-VM` cmdlet will accept as input.

Instead, you'll have to use a multiline script for this, as shown in Listing 14.1.

LISTING 14.1:   A PowerCLI script to selectively move VMs to a new resource pool

```
$VMs = Get-VM -Location (Get-ResourcePool Infrastructure)
foreach ($vm in $VMs) {
$vmguest = Get-VMGuest -VM $vm
if ($vmguest.OSFullName -match "^Microsoft Windows.*") {
Move-VM -VM $vm -Destination (Get-ResourcePool "Windows VMs") } }
```

Again, I'll break down the script so that it is easier to understand:

◆ The first line uses the `Get-VM` and `Get-ResourcePool` cmdlets to retrieve a list of VM objects in the specified resource pool. That list of VM objects is stored in the `$VMs` variable.

◆ The second line creates a loop that operates for each of the objects in the `$VMs` variable. Each individual VM object is stored as `$vm`.

◆ The third line uses the `Get-VMGuest` cmdlet with the `$vm` variable to retrieve the guest OS object for that VM object and store the result in the `$vmguest` variable.

◆ The fourth line tests to see whether the `OSFullName` property of the `$vmguest` object matches a string starting with "Microsoft Windows."

◆ The fifth line executes only if the test on the fourth line was successful; if it executes, it uses the `Move-VM` and `Get-ResourcePool` cmdlets to move the VM object represented by the `$vm` variable to the resource pool named Windows VMs.

If you were to save the script in Listing 14.1 as `MoveWindowsVMs.ps1`, then you could run it in PowerCLI like this:

```
<Path to Script>\MoveWindowsVMs.ps1
```

There is so much more that you can do with PowerShell and PowerCLI; these simple examples barely scratch the surface. I encourage you to use the numerous PowerCLI resources available online to learn more about PowerCLI and PowerShell.

PowerShell and PowerCLI aren't the only scripting environments around, though; you can also use the vSphere Management Assistant to run standard shell scripts. I'll show how to use shell scripts in the next section.

Using vCLI from vSphere Management Assistant

VMware vSphere 5 completely removes VMware ESX and the traditional Linux-based Service Console. This means that a lot of vSphere administrators and organizations need to adapt to not having a Linux environment available on each host. However, the vSphere Management Assistant, lovingly referred to as the vMA, is fully capable of running configuration commands that historically could be done from the ESX Service Console. VMware also provides the vSphere CLI (vCLI) that implements the familiar console commands from the old ESX Service Console. The vMA comes pre-installed with the vCLI, giving vSphere administrators a familiar method for performing configuration tasks from the command line.

For example, adding a vSwitch to a host with the vCLI uses the exact same syntax as previously, with an added option to specify the host to which you need to connect:

```
esxcfg-vswitch --server <Hostname> --list
```

Alternatively, you can use the newer vCLI naming convention where the commands use the vicfg- prefix in place of esxcfg-. The esxcfg- prefix is kept for backward compatibility but will be phased out over time . Therefore, you can use either format.

```
vicfg-vswitch --server <Hostname> --list
esxcfg-vswitch --server <Hostname> --list
```

By using this set of commands you can do common tasks needed for basic host configuration that would previously be done from the bash Service Console. For instance, Listing 14.2 will perform the following:

◆ Create a new vSwitch named vSwitch1

◆ Add vmnic1 as an uplink to our new vSwitch

◆ Create a new VM portgroup

◆ Add a VLAN to our new vSwitch

LISTING 14.2:   Create a new vSwitch from vMA

```
# add a new vSwitch
vi-admin@vma01:~> vicfg-vswitch --server pod-1-blade-6.v12nlab.net -a vSwitch1

# add an uplink to the vSwitch
vi-admin@vma01:~> vicfg-vswitch --server pod-1-blade-6.v12nlab.net -L vmnic1 vSwitch1

# add a VM portgroup to the new vSwitch
```

```
vi-admin@vma01:~> vicfg-vswitch --server pod-1-blade-6.v12nlab.net -A "VM-Public"
vSwitch1

# set the VLAN for the new portgroup
vi-admin@vma01:~> vicfg-vswitch --server pod-1-blade-6.v12nlab.net -v 10 ↵
-p "VM-Public" vSwitch1
```

Executing these commands, however, becomes tedious very quickly because you must constantly enter the username and password to connect to the server. One workaround would be to wrap the commands in a bash script and pass the username and password as parameters. This is somewhat undesirable, however, because you are leaving credentials to your ESXi hosts available to anyone who can log into your server. This is where the benefit of using vMA over a standard host with the vCLI installed comes into play.

vMA has some additional functionality installed to it called *fastpass*. Fastpass allows you to securely add ESXi, and even vCenter, hosts to your vMA once and connect to them without a password during script execution. This allows you to treat the vMA's command line as you would the native host. First, you must initialize the host with fastpass:

```
vifp addserver <Hostname>
```

This command then prompts for the ESXi host's root password, connects to the host, and adds two users to the host, which are used for executing commands. Should you specify the "adauth" authpolicy, fastpass would use an Active Directory account for authentication to the host.

You can view any hosts that fastpass has been configured for using the vifp listservers command:

```
vi-admin@vma01:~> vifp listservers
vSphere01.vSphere.local ESXi
```

You can see that a single host is fastpass enabled, and it is an ESXi host.

Now that fastpass is aware of the host, you set the host as the current target using the vifptarget command:

```
vifptarget -s <Hostname>
```

After this you can execute ESXi configuration commands as though you are logged into the console of that host. The list of commands now looks like standard ESX configuration commands from the old Service Console. Note that you can still use the esxcfg- prefix for the commands, so existing scripts can be copied into place with minimal changes. For example, Listing 14.3 adds a vSwitch to the vSphere01 host using vMA fastpass.

LISTING 14.3:   Add a vSwitch using vMA fastpass

```
vi-admin@vma01:~> vifptarget -s vSphere01.vSphere.local
vi-admin@vma01:~[vSphere01.vSphere.local]> vicfg-vswitch -a vSwitch1
vi-admin@vma01:~[vSphere01.vSphere.local]> vicfg-vswitch -L vmnic1 vSwitch1
vi-admin@vma01:~[vSphere01.vSphere.local]> vicfg-vswitch -A "VM-Public" ↵
vSwitch1
vi-admin@vma01:~[vSphere01.vSphere.local]> vicfg-vswitch -v 10 -p ↵
"VM-Public" vSwitch1
```

By adding additional ESXi servers to fastpass, you can configure multiple hosts quickly using a simple bash loop. For example, Listing 14.4 will connect to each host and add the vm_nfs01 datastore.

LISTING 14.4:   Add an NFS datastore or multiple hosts by using vMA fastpass

```
for server in "vSphere01 vSphere02 vSphere03 vSphere04 vSphere05"; do
> vifptarget -s $server
> vicfg-nas -a -o FAS3210A.vSphere.local -s /vol/vm_nfs01 vm_nfs01
> vifptarget -c
> done
```

Using vSphere Management Assistant for Automation with vCenter

Leveraging the fastpass technology with vCenter allows you a simple luxury: you no longer have to add each host to fastpass. However, there is a caveat that you must specify an additional command-line parameter for each command.

This has both advantages and disadvantages. It's extremely convenient to no longer be concerned about whether the host you are manipulating has been initialized for fastpass. Scripts that are written can simply use the vCenter credentials to manipulate host settings, while still being logged in vCenter's task list. Additionally, all tasks executed through vCenter are logged in vCenter for auditing purposes. The downside is losing the ability to use legacy scripts that assume you are on the console of the host and have not had the additional parameter set.

Connecting vCenter to fastpass is the same as it is for hosts. vMA is kind enough to warn you that storing the vCenter credentials is a security risk, and we do recommend you use vCenter's role-based access to limit the permissions to the minimum needed. That being said, you should always protect your vMA as you would any other server in your environment and ensure that a sufficiently complex password is used for the vi-admin user to prevent unauthorized access. Keep in mind that should the vMA become compromised, all of the hosts that are fastpass enabled are also compromised. You should use the same command for vCenter as for your ESXi hosts:

```
vi-admin@vma01:~> vifp addserver vCenter01
Enter username for vCenter01: fp_admin
fp_admin@vCenter01's password:
This will store username and password in credential store which is
a security risk. Do you want to continue?(yes/no): yes
vi-admin@vma01:~> vifp listservers
vCenter01.vSphere.local    vCenter
vi-admin@vma01:~> vifptarget -s vCenter01
vi-admin@vma01:~[vCenter01.vSphere.local]>
```

Notice that you can set the fastpass target server to vCenter just like an ESXi host, and you can execute standard host commands against it as well:

```
vi-admin@vma01:~[vCenter01.vSphere.local]> vicfg-vswitch -l
The --vihost option must be specified when connecting to vCenter.
For a summary of command usage, type '/usr/bin/vicfg-vswitch --help'.
For documentation, type 'perldoc /usr/bin/vicfg-vswitch'.
```

But wait! There's an error. Notice that you must specify which ESXi host you want to actually execute the command against now that you are connecting to vCenter. Following the recommendation of the error message, you specify the host using the --vihost or -h option and execute the command:

```
vi-admin@vma01:~[vCenter01.vSphere.local]> vicfg-vswitch -h vSphere01 -l
Switch Name  Num Ports  Used Ports  Configured Ports  MTU   Uplinks
vSwitch0     128        3           128               1500  vmnic0

     PortGroup Name         VLAN ID  Used Ports     Uplinks
     VM Network             0        0              vmnic0
     Management Network     0        1              vmnic0
```

You can do the same management tasks as before, just using the extra -h switch when executing each one. For example, you can set advanced options and kernel module options on multiple hosts by running the following:

```
vi-admin@vma01:~> vifptarget -s vCenter01
vi-admin@vma01:~[vCenter01.vSphere.local]> for server in "vSphere01 ↵
vSphere02 vSphere03 vSphere04 vSphere05"; do
echo "$server is being configured..."
> # see http://kb.vmware.com/kb/1268 for more info on this setting
> vicfg-advcfg -h $server -s 64 Disk.SchedNumReqOutstanding
> # see http://kb.vmware.com/kb/1267 for more info on this setting
> vicfg-module -h $server -s ql2xmaxqdepth=128 qla2xxx
> done
vi-admin@vma01:~[vCenter01.vSphere.local]> vifptarget -c
```

VMware has been kind enough in this version of the vCLI to include the ability to enable vMotion on an interface from the command line. This makes it easy to configure a host almost entirely from the command line.

There are lots of ways this script could be improved; for example, there's no error checking to ensure that a matching port group and VMkernel interface are actually found by the first command.

Leveraging the Perl Toolkit with vSphere Management Assistant

vMA's fastpass with vCenter and the Perl SDK are a powerful combination. With a handful of helper scripts, you can administer a large number of hosts using the vCLI through vCenter.

Listing 14.5 is a Perl script that simply returns the hostnames in a cluster. This can be useful for configuring a cluster of ESXi hosts for a new datastore, a new vSwitch, or other items that you would want to match across all members of the cluster.

LISTING 14.5:   Get all hosts in a cluster by using the Perl SDK

```perl
#!/usr/bin/perl
#
# Script Name: ~/bin/getClusterHosts.pl
# Usage: getClusterHosts.pl --server vCenter.your.domain clusterName
# Result: a newline delimited list of ESXihosts in the cluster
#
use strict;
use warnings;

# include the standard VMware perl SDK modules
use VMware::VIRuntime;

# some additional helper functions
use VMware::VIExt;

# define the options we need for our script
my %opts = (
    # we can use the special _default_ so that we do not have
    # to provide a command line switch when calling our script.
    # The last parameter is assumed to be the clustername
    '_default_' => {
        # this parameter is a string
        type => "=s",

        # what is reported when the user passes the --help option
        help => "Name of the cluster to report hosts for",

        # boolean to determine if the option is mandatory
        required => 1
    }
);

# add the options to the standard VMware options
Opts::add_options(%opts);

# parse the options from the command line
Opts::parse();

# ensure valid input was passed
Opts::validate();
```

```perl
# the user should have passed, or been prompted for, a
# username and password as two of the standard VMware
# options.  connect using them now...
Util::connect();

# search the connected host (should be vCenter) for our cluster
my $clusterName = Opts::get_option('_default_');
my $clusterView = Vim::find_entity_view(
        view_type => 'ClusterComputeResource',
        filter => { name => qr/($clusterName)/i }
    );

# ensure that we found something
if (! $clusterView) {
    VIExt::fail("A cluster with name " . $clusterName . " was not found!");
}

# now we want to search for hosts inside the cluster we just
# retrieved a reference to
my $hostViews = Vim::find_entity_views(
        view_type => 'HostSystem',
        begin_entity => $clusterView,
        # limit the properties returned for performance
        properties => [ 'name' ]
    );

# print a simple newline delimited list of the found hosts
foreach my $host (@{$hostViews}) {
    print $host->name . "\n";
}

# and destroy the session with the server
Util::disconnect();
```

Executing our script, you see the following results:

```
vi-admin@vma01:~> getClusterHosts.pl --server vCenter01 cluster01
Enter username: administrator
Enter password:
vSphere01.vSphere.local
vSphere02.vSphere.local
```

Notice that we were prompted for the username and password. This is a feature of using the VIRuntime library. VMware has simplified things for developers by providing default options. These are the same as for all of the vCLI scripts, so --username and --password apply regardless of whether you are using an vCLI script or one that you created. If you pass the username and password arguments to the script via the command line, it will not prompt for them.

Alternatively, using fastpass will also eliminate the need for a username and password to be supplied.

You can now combine your Perl script with bash and fastpass to configure an entire cluster with a new portgroup quickly and efficiently.

```
vi-admin@vma01:~> vifptarget -s vCenter01
vi-admin@vma01:~[vCenter01.vSphere.local]> for server in ↵
`getClusterHosts.pl cluster01`; do
> echo "$server is being configured..."
> vicfg-vswitch -h $server -A VLAN100 vSwitch0
> vicfg-vswitch -h $server -v 100 -p VLAN100 vSwitch0
> done
vSphere01.vSphere.local is being configured...
vSphere02.vSphere.local is being configured...
vi-admin@vma01:~[vCenter01.get-admin.com]> vifptarget -c
```

This example is just a tiny portion of what can be done with the Perl toolkit. The vCLI does not include functionality for managing virtual servers; however, you can leverage the Perl toolkit and the SDK to manage VMs just like PowerCLI. Using the SDK, you can accomplish any task that can be done through the VI Client or PowerCLI; the difference is the level of effort required to get the same results. Additional sample Perl scripts can be found on vMA at /usr/lib/vmware-vcli/apps/ and /usr/share/doc/vmware-vcli/samples/.

Shell scripting is a fine art, and there is much, much more to writing shell scripts than the tiny snippets I've shown you here. Between shell scripts, vCenter Orchestrator workflows, and PowerCLI scripts, you should have all the tools you need at your disposal for automating your vSphere environment.

The Bottom Line

Identify some of the tools available for automating vSphere.   VMware offers a number of different solutions for automating your vSphere environment, including vCenter Orchestrator, PowerCLI, an SDK for Perl, an SDK for web service developers, and shell scripts in VMware ESXi. Each of these tools has its own advantages and disadvantages.

> **Master It**   VMware offers a number of different automation tools. What are some guidelines for choosing which automation tool to use?

Configure vCenter Orchestrator.   vCenter Orchestrator is installed silently with vCenter Server, but before you can use vCenter Orchestrator, you must configure it properly. The web-based vCenter Orchestrator Configuration interface allows you to configure various portions of vCenter Orchestrator.

> **Master It**   How can you tell whether some portion of the vCenter Orchestrator configuration is incomplete or incorrect?

Use a vCenter Orchestrator workflow.   After vCenter Orchestrator is configured and is running, you can use the vCenter Orchestrator Client to run a vCenter Orchestrator workflow. vCenter Orchestrator comes with a number of preinstalled workflows to help automate tasks.

> **Master It** An administrator in your environment configured vCenter Orchestrator and has now asked you to run a couple of workflows. However, when you log into the vCenter Server where vCenter Orchestrator is also installed, you don't see the icons for vCenter Orchestrator. Why?

Create a PowerCLI script for automation. VMware vSphere PowerCLI builds on the object-oriented PowerShell scripting language to provide administrators with a simple yet powerful way to automate tasks within the vSphere environment.

> **Master It** If you are familiar with other scripting languages, what would be the biggest hurdle in learning to use PowerShell and PowerCLI, other than syntax?

Use vCLI to manage ESXi hosts from the command line. VMware's remote command-line interface, or vCLI, is the new way of managing an ESXi host using the familiar `esxcfg-*` command set. By combining the features of fastpass with vCLI, you can seamlessly manage multiple hosts using the same command set from a single login.

> **Master It** Have you migrated management and configuration operations for which you currently use the ESXi command-line interface to vMA?

Use vCenter in combination with vMA to manage all your hosts. The new version of vMA can use vCenter as a target. This means that you can manage all of your hosts using vCLI without having to manually add each host to the fastpass target list.

> **Master It** Use a combination of shell scripting with vCLI commands to execute commands against a number of hosts.

Employ the Perl toolkit and VMware SDK for virtual server operations from the command line. The vCLI is designed for host management and consequently lacks tools for manipulating virtual servers. With the Perl toolkit, leveraged against the VMware SDK, any task that can be accomplished in the Virtual Infrastructure client can be done from the command line.

> **Master It** Browse the sample scripts and SDK documentation to discover the world of possibilities that are unlocked by using Perl, or any of the other supported languages, to accomplish management tasks.

Appendix A

The Bottom Line

Each of The Bottom Line sections in the chapters suggests exercises to deepen skills and understanding. Sometimes there is only one possible solution, but often you are encouraged to use your skills and creativity to create something that builds on what you know and lets you explore one of many possibilities.

Chapter 1: Introducing VMware vSphere 5

Identify the role of each product in the vSphere product suite.   The VMware vSphere product suite contains VMware ESXi and vCenter Server. ESXi provides the base virtualization functionality and enables features like Virtual SMP. vCenter Server provides management for ESXi and enables functionality like vMotion, Storage vMotion, vSphere Distributed Resource Scheduler (DRS), vSphere High Availability (HA), and vSphere Fault Tolerance (FT). Storage I/O Control (SIOC) and Network I/O Control (NetIOC) provide granular resource controls for VMs. The vStorage APIs for Data Protection (VADP) provide a backup framework that allows for the integration of third-party backup solutions into a vSphere implementation.

Master It   Which products are licensed features within the VMware vSphere suite?

Solution   Licensed features in the VMware vSphere suite are Virtual SMP, vMotion, Storage vMotion, vSphere DRS, vSphere HA, and vSphere FT.

Master It   Which two features of VMware ESXi and VMware vCenter Server together aim to reduce or eliminate downtime due to unplanned hardware failures?

Solution   vSphere HA and vSphere FT are designed to reduce (vSphere HA) and eliminate (vSphere FT) the downtime resulting from unplanned hardware failures.

Recognize the interaction and dependencies between the products in the vSphere suite   VMware ESXi forms the foundation of the vSphere product suite, but some features require the presence of vCenter Server. Features like vMotion, Storage vMotion, vSphere DRS, vSphere HA, vSphere FT, SIOC, and NetIOC require both ESXi as well as vCenter Server.

Master It   Name three features that are supported only when using vCenter Server along with ESXi.

Solution   All of the following features are available only with vCenter Server: vSphere vMotion, Storage vMotion, vSphere DRS, Storage DRS, vSphere HA, vSphere FT, SIOC, and NetIOC.

Master It Name two features that are supported without vCenter Server but with a licensed installation of ESXi.

Solution Features that are supported by VMware ESXi without vCenter Server include core virtualization features like virtualized networking, virtualized storage, vSphere vSMP, and resource allocation controls.

Understand how vSphere differs from other virtualization products. VMware vSphere's hypervisor, ESXi, uses a type 1 bare-metal hypervisor that handles I/O directly within the hypervisor. This means that a host operating system, like Windows or Linux, is not required in order for ESXi to function. Although other virtualization solutions are listed as "type 1 bare-metal hypervisors," most other type 1 hypervisors on the market today require the presence of a "parent partition" or "dom0," through which all VM I/O must travel.

Master It One of the administrators on your team asked whether he should install Windows Server on the new servers you purchased for ESXi. What should you tell him, and why?

Solution VMware ESXi is a bare-metal hypervisor that does not require the installation of a general-purpose host operating system. Therefore, it's unnecessary to install Windows Server on the equipment that was purchased for ESXi.

Chapter 2: Planning and Installing VMware ESXi

Understand the differences between ESXi Installable and ESXi Embedded. Although ESXi Installable and ESXi Embedded share the same core hypervisor technology and the same functionality, ESXi Embedded is an OEM solution that is designed to be preinstalled and integrated by equipment manufacturers; ESXi Installable (referred to just as ESXi in this chapter) is designed to be deployed and installed by customers.

Master It You're evaluating ESXi Installable and ESXi Embedded and trying to decide which to use for the vSphere deployment within your company. What are some of the factors that might lead you to choose ESXi Installable over ESXi Embedded or vice versa?

Solution Hardware/manufacturer support would be one factor to consider. ESXi Embedded is offered only by certain hardware manufacturers and only for certain models of their servers. In the event you are planning on using a supported model/manufacturer, then ESXi Embedded can make your deployment very easy. If you aren't planning on using a server supported for ESXi Embedded by the manufacturer, then you're better off with ESXi Installable. ESXi Installable also offers more flexible deployment options.

Understand ESXi compatibility requirements. Unlike traditional operating systems like Windows or Linux, ESXi has much stricter hardware compatibility requirements. This helps ensure a stable, well-tested product line that is able to support even the most mission-critical applications.

Master It   You'd like to run ESXi Embedded, but your hardware vendor doesn't have a model that includes ESXi Embedded. Should you go ahead and buy the servers anyway, even though the hardware vendor doesn't have a model with ESXi Embedded?

Solution   No. ESXi Embedded is intended to be deployed on a persistent storage device, such as firmware, within a server. Only servers found on the Hardware Compatibility List should be used.

Master It   You have some older servers onto which you'd like to deploy ESXi. They aren't on the Hardware Compatibility List. Will they work with ESXi?

Solution   They might, but they won't be supported by VMware. In all likelihood, the CPUs in these older servers don't support some of the hardware virtualization extensions or don't support 64-bit operation, both of which would directly impact the ability of ESXi to run on that hardware. You should choose only hardware that is on the Hardware Compatibility List.

Plan an ESXi deployment.   Deploying ESXi will affect many different areas of your organization — not only the server team but also the networking team, the storage team, and the security team. There are many issues to consider, including server hardware, storage hardware, storage protocols or connection types, network topology, and network connections. Failing to plan properly could result in an unstable and unsupported implementation.

Master It   Name three areas of networking that must be considered in a vSphere design.

Solution   Among other things, networking areas that must be considered include VLAN support, link aggregation, network speed (1 Gbps or 10 Gbps), load-balancing algorithms, and the number of NICs and network ports required.

Deploy ESXi.   ESXi can be installed onto any supported and compatible hardware platform. You have three different ways to deploy ESXi: you can install it interactively, you can perform an unattended installation, or you can use vSphere Auto Deploy to provision ESXi directly to the host memory of a server as it boots up. This last method is also referred to as a stateless configuration.

Master It   Your manager asks you to provide him with a copy of the unattended installation script that you will be using when you roll out ESXi using vSphere Auto Deploy. Is this something you can give him?

Solution   No. When using vSphere Auto Deploy, there is no installation script. The vSphere Auto Deploy server streams an ESXi image to the physical host as it boots up. Redeployment of an ESXi host with vSphere Auto Deploy can be as simple as a reboot.

Master It   Name two advantages and two disadvantages of using vSphere Auto Deploy to provision ESXi hosts.

Solution   Some advantages include fast provisioning, fast reprovisioning, and the ability to quickly incorporate new ESXi images or updates into the provisioning process. Some disadvantages include additional complexity and the need for additional configurations to address the stateless nature of the deployment.

Perform post-installation configuration of ESXi. Following the installation of ESXi, some additional configuration steps may be required. For example, if the wrong NIC is assigned to the management network, then the server won't be accessible across the network. You'll also need to configure time synchronization.

Master It You've installed ESXi on your server, but the welcome web page is inaccessible, and the server doesn't respond to a ping. What could be the problem?

Solution More than likely, the wrong NIC was selected for use with the management network. You'll need to use the Direct Console User Interface (DCUI) directly at the physical console of the ESXi host in order to reconfigure the management network and restore network connectivity.

Install the vSphere Client. ESXi is managed using the vSphere Client, a Windows-only application that provides the functionality to manage the virtualization platform. There are a couple different ways to obtain the vSphere Client installer, including running it directly from the VMware vCenter Installer or by downloading it using a web browser connected to the IP address of a vCenter Server instance.

Master It List two ways by which you can install the vSphere Client.

Solution Two ways are by downloading it from the Welcome To vSphere web page on a vCenter Server instance or by installing it from the vCenter Server installation media. You can also download the vSphere Client from VMware's website.

Chapter 3: Installing and Configuring vCenter Server

Understand the features and role of vCenter Server. vCenter Server plays a central role in the management of ESXi hosts and VMs. Key features such as vMotion, Storage vMotion, vSphere DRS, vSphere HA, and vSphere FT are all enabled and made possible by vCenter Server. vCenter Server provides scalable authentication and role-based administration based on integration with Active Directory.

Master It Specifically with regard to authentication, what are three key advantages of using vCenter Server?

Solution First, vCenter Server centralizes the authentication so that user accounts don't have to be managed on a per-host basis. Second, vCenter Server eliminates the need to share the root password for hosts or to use complex configurations to allow administrators to perform tasks on the hosts. Third, vCenter Server brings role-based administration for the granular management of hosts and VMs.

Plan a vCenter Server deployment. Planning a vCenter Server deployment includes selecting a backend database engine, choosing an authentication method, sizing the hardware appropriately, and providing a sufficient level of high availability and business continuity. You must also decide whether you will run vCenter Server as a VM or on a physical system. Finally, you must decide whether you will use the Windows Server–based version of vCenter Server or deploy the vCenter Server virtual appliance.

Master It   What are some of the advantages and disadvantages of running vCenter Server as a VM?

Solution   Some of the advantages include the ability to easily clone the VM for backup or disaster-recovery purposes, the ability to take snapshots to protect against data loss or data corruption, and the ability to leverage features such as vMotion or Storage vMotion. Some of the disadvantages include the inability to cold clone the vCenter Server VM, cold migrate the vCenter Server VM, or edit the virtual hardware of the vCenter Server VM.

Master It   What are some of the advantages and disadvantages of using the vCenter Server virtual appliance?

Solution   Some of the advantages include a potentially much easier deployment (just use the Deploy OVF Template and perform post-deployment configuration instead of install-ing Windows Server, installing prerequisites, and finally installing vCenter Server), more services available with a single deployment, and no Windows Server licensing require-ments. Disadvantages include a lack of support for linked mode groups and no support for external SQL Server databases.

Install and configure a vCenter Server database.   vCenter Server supports several enter-prise-grade database engines, including Oracle and Microsoft SQL Server. IBM DB2 is also supported. Depending on the database in use, there are specific configuration steps and spe-cific permissions that must be applied in order for vCenter Server to work properly.

Master It   Why is it important to protect the database engine used to support vCenter Server?

Solution   Although vCenter Server uses Microsoft Active Directory for authentication and Microsoft Active Directory application mode to store some replicated configuration data, the majority of the information managed by vCenter Server is stored in the backend database. The loss of the backend database would mean the loss of significant amounts of data that are crucial to the operation of vCenter Server. Organizations should take ad-equate steps to protect the backend database accordingly.

Install and configure vCenter Server.   vCenter Server is installed using the VMware vCen-ter Installer. You can install vCenter Server as a stand-alone instance or join a linked mode group for greater scalability. vCenter Server will use a predefined ODBC DSN to communi-cate with the separate database server.

Master It   When preparing to install vCenter Server, are there any concerns about which Windows account should be used during the installation?

Solution   With vCenter Server 5, no. The account just needs administrative permissions on the computer where vCenter Server is being installed. In previous versions, if you were using Microsoft SQL Server with Windows authentication, you had to log on to the computer that was going to run vCenter Server using the account that was previously configured with the appropriate permissions on the SQL Server and SQL database. This is because the earlier versions of the vCenter Server installer did not provide the ability to choose which account to use; it used the currently logged-on account. This is no longer the case with vCenter Server 5.

Use vCenter Server's management features. vCenter Server provides a wide range of management features for ESXi hosts and VMs. These features include scheduled tasks, topology maps, host profiles for consistent configurations, and event logging.

Master It Your manager has asked you to prepare an overview of the virtualized environment. What tools in vCenter Server will help you in this task?

Solution vCenter Server can export topology maps in a variety of graphics formats. The topology maps, coupled with the data found on the Storage Views, Hardware Status, and Summary tabs should provide enough information for your manager.

Chapter 4: Installing and Configuring vSphere Update Manager

Install VUM and integrate it with the vSphere Client. vSphere Update Manager (VUM) is installed from the VMware vCenter installation media and requires that vCenter Server has already been installed. Like vCenter Server, VUM requires the use of a backend database server. Finally, you must install a plug-in into the vSphere Client in order to access, manage, or configure VUM.

Master It You have VUM installed, and you've configured it from the vSphere Client on your laptop. One of the other administrators on your team is saying that she can't access or configure VUM and that there must be something wrong with the installation. What is the most likely cause of the problem?

Solution The most likely cause is that the VUM plug-in hasn't been installed in the other administrator's vSphere Client. The plug-in must be installed on each instance of the vSphere Client in order to be able to manage VUM from that instance.

Determine which ESX/ESXi hosts or VMs need to be patched or upgraded. Baselines are the "measuring sticks" whereby VUM knows whether an ESX/ESXi host or VM instance is up to date. VUM compares the ESX/ESXi hosts or guest OSes to the baselines to determine whether they need to be patched and, if so, what patches need to be applied. VUM also uses baselines to determine which ESX/ESXi hosts need to be upgraded to the latest version or which VMs need to have their VM hardware upgraded. VUM comes with some predefined baselines and allows administrators to create additional baselines specific to their environments. Baselines can be fixed — the contents remain constant — or they can be dynamic, where the contents of the baseline change over time. Baseline groups allow administrators to combine baselines and apply them together.

Master It In addition to ensuring that all your ESX/ESXi hosts have the latest critical and security patches installed, you also need to ensure that all your ESX/ESXi hosts have another specific patch installed. This additional patch is noncritical and therefore doesn't get included in the critical patch dynamic baseline. How do you work around this problem?

Solution   Create a baseline group that combines the critical patch dynamic baseline with a fixed baseline that contains the additional patch you want installed on all ESX/ESXi hosts. Attach the baseline group to all your ESX/ESXi hosts. When you perform re-mediation, VUM will ensure that all the critical patches in the dynamic baseline plus the additional patch in the fixed baseline are applied to the hosts.

Use VUM to upgrade VM hardware or VMware Tools.   VUM can detect VMs with out-dated VM hardware versions and guest OSes that have outdated versions of the VMware Tools installed. VUM comes with predefined baselines that enable this functionality. In addi-tion, VUM has the ability to upgrade VM hardware versions and upgrade the VMware Tools inside guest OSes to ensure that everything is kept up to date. This functionality is especially helpful after upgrading your ESX/ESXi hosts to version 5.0 from a previous version.

Master It   You've just finished upgrading your virtual infrastructure to VMware vSphere. What two additional tasks should you complete?

Solution   Upgrade the VMware Tools in the guest OSes and then the virtual machine hardware to version 8.

Apply patches to ESX/ESXi hosts.   Like other complex software products, VMware ESX and VMware ESXi need software patches applied from time to time. These patches might be bug fixes or security fixes. To keep your ESX/ESXi hosts up to date with the latest patches, VUM can apply patches to your hosts on a schedule of your choosing. In addition, to reduce downtime during the patching process or perhaps to simplify the deployment of patches to remote offices, VUM can also stage patches to ESX/ESXi hosts before the patches are applied.

Master It   How can you avoid VM downtime when applying patches (for example, re-mediating) to your ESX/ESXi hosts?

Solution   VUM automatically leverages advanced VMware vSphere features like Distributed Resource Scheduler (DRS). If you make sure that your ESX/ESXi hosts are configured in a DRS cluster, then VUM will leverage vMotion and DRS to move VMs to other ESX/ESXi hosts, avoiding downtime, in order to patch one host.

Apply patches to Windows guests.   VUM can check the compliance status of your ESXi hosts and your legacy ESX/ESXi hosts, your VM hardware, VMware Tools and certified virtual appliances. To ensure your software stack has all the available software patches and security fixes applied, you also need to consider the state of the guest OSes and applications running within the VMs.

Master It   You are having a discussion with another VMware vSphere administrator about keeping hosts and guests updated. The other administrator insists that you can use VUM to keep guest OSes updated as well. Is this accurate?

Solution   No, this is not accurate. Previous versions of VUM were capable of patch-ing select versions of Windows and Linux guest OSes and some guest application software, but this functionality was deprecated in VUM with the introduction of vSphere 5.0. Native patch-management tools such as Windows Update and WSUS for

Windows, apt and yum for Linux, or third-party software management tools should be employed.

Chapter 5: Creating and Configuring Virtual Networks

Identify the components of virtual networking.   Virtual networking is a blend of virtual switches, physical switches, VLANs, physical network adapters, virtual adapters, uplinks, NIC teaming, VMs, and port groups.

Master It   What factors contribute to the design of a virtual network and the components involved?

Solution   Many factors contribute to a virtual network design. The number of physical network adapters in each ESXi host, using vSwitches versus Distributed Virtual Switches, the presence or use of VLANs in the environment, the existing network topology, and the connectivity needs of the VMs in the environment are all factors that will play a role in the final network design. These are some common questions to ask while designing the network:

◆ Do you have or need a dedicated network for management traffic, such as for the management of physical switches?

◆ Do you have or need a dedicated network for vMotion traffic?

◆ Are you using 1 Gb Ethernet or 10 Gb Ethernet?

◆ Do you have an IP storage network? Is this IP storage network a dedicated network? Are you running iSCSI or NAS/NFS?

◆ Is there a need for extremely high levels of fault tolerance for VMs?

◆ Is the existing physical network composed of VLANs?

◆ Do you want to extend the use of VLANs into the virtual switches?

Create virtual switches (vSwitches) and distributed virtual switches (dvSwitches).   vSphere introduces a new type of virtual switch, the vSphere Distributed Virtual Switch, as well as continuing to support the host-based vSwitch (now referred to as the vSphere Standard Switch) from previous versions. vSphere Distributed Switches bring new functionality to the vSphere networking environment, including private VLANs and a centralized point of management for ESXi clusters.

Master It   You've asked a fellow vSphere administrator to create a vSphere Distributed Virtual Switch for you, but the administrator is having problems completing the task because he can't find the right command-line switches for vicfg-vswitch. What should you tell this administrator?

Solution   vSphere Distributed Virtual Switches can be created only by using the vSphere Client. Although the vicfg-vswitch command does have a few options for modifying an existing dvSwitch, creating a new dvSwitch will need to be done from the vSphere Client.

Install and perform basic configuration of the Cisco Nexus 1000V.   The Cisco Nexus 1000V is the first third-party Distributed Virtual Switch for vSphere. Running Cisco's NX-OS, the Nexus 1000V uses a distributed architecture that supports redundant supervisor modules and provides a single point of management. Advanced networking functionality like quality of service (QoS), access control lists (ACLs), and SPAN ports is made possible via the Nexus 1000V.

Master It   A vSphere administrator is trying to use the vSphere Client to make some changes to the VLAN configuration of a dvPort group configured on a Nexus 1000V, but the option to edit the settings for the dvPort group isn't showing up. Why?

Solution   The Cisco Nexus 1000V Virtual Supervisor Module (VSM) controls the creation, modification, and deletion of dvPort groups on the Virtual Ethernet Module (VEM) on each host. All changes to the dvPort groups must be made via the VSM; the dvPort groups cannot be modified in any way from the vSphere Client.

Create and manage NIC teaming, VLANs, and private VLANs.   NIC teaming allows for virtual switches to have redundant network connections to the rest of the network. Virtual switches also provide support for VLANs, which provide logical segmentation of the network, and private VLANs, which provide added security to existing VLANs while allowing systems to share the same IP subnet.

Master It   You'd like to use NIC teaming to bond multiple physical uplinks together for greater redundancy and improved throughput. When selecting the NIC teaming policy, you select Route Based On IP Hash, but then the vSwitch seems to lose connectivity. What could be wrong?

Solution   The Route Based On IP Hash load-balancing policy requires that the physical switch be also configured to support this arrangement. This is accomplished through the use of link aggregation, referred to as *EtherChannel* in the Cisco environment. Without an appropriate link aggregation configuration on the physical switch, using the IP hash load-balancing policy will result in a loss of connectivity. One of the other load-balancing policies, such as the default policy titled Route Based On Originating Virtual Port ID, may be more appropriate if the configuration of the physical switch cannot be modified.

Configure virtual switch security policies.   Virtual switches support security policies for allowing or rejecting Promiscuous Mode, allowing or rejecting MAC address changes, and allowing or rejecting forged transmits. All of the security options can help increase Layer 2 security.

Master It   You have a networking application that needs to see traffic on the virtual network that is intended for other production systems on the same VLAN. The networking application accomplishes this by using Promiscuous mode. How can you accommodate the needs of this networking application without sacrificing the security of the entire virtual switch?

Solution   Because port groups (or dvPort groups) can override the security policy settings for a virtual switch, and because there can be multiple port groups/dvPort groups that correspond to a VLAN, the best solution involves creating another port group that has all the same settings as the other production port group, including the same VLAN

ID. This new port group should allow Promiscuous mode. Assign the VM with the networking application to this new port group, but leave the remainder of the VMs on a port group that rejects Promiscuous mode. This allows the networking application to see the traffic it needs to see without overly compromising the security of the entire virtual switch.

Chapter 6: Creating and Configuring Storage Devices

Differentiate and understand the fundamentals of shared storage, including SANs and NAS. vSphere depends on shared storage for advanced functions, cluster-wide availability, and the aggregate performance of all the VMs in a cluster. Designing high-performance and highly available shared storage infrastructure is possible on Fibre Channel, FCoE, and iSCSI SANs and is possible using NAS; in addition, it's available for midrange to enterprise storage architectures. Always design the storage architecture to meet the performance requirements first, and then ensure that capacity requirements are met as a corollary.

> **Master It** Identify examples where each of the protocol choices would be ideal for different vSphere deployments.
>
> **Solution** iSCSI would be a good choice for a customer with no existing Fibre Channel SAN and getting started with vSphere. Fibre Channel would be a good choice for a customer with an existing Fibre Channel infrastructure or for those that have VMs with high-bandwidth (200 MBps+) requirements (not in aggregate but individually). NFS would be a good choice where there are many VMs with a low-bandwidth requirement individually (and in aggregate) that is less than a single link's worth of bandwidth.
>
> **Master It** Identify the three storage performance parameters and the primary determinant of storage performance and how to quickly estimate it for a given storage configuration.
>
> **Solution** The three factors to consider are bandwidth (MBps), throughput (IOps), and latency (ms). The maximum bandwidth for a single datastore (or RDM) for Fibre Channel is the HBA speed times the number of HBAs in the system (check the fan-in ratio and number of Fibre Channel ports on the array). The maximum bandwidth for a single datastore (or RDM) for iSCSI is the NIC speed times the number of NICs in the system up to about 9 Gbps (check the fan-in ratio and number of Ethernet ports on the array). The maximum bandwidth for a single NFS datastore for NFS is the NIC link speed (across multiple datastores, the bandwidth can be balanced across multiple NIC). In all cases, the throughput (IOps) is primarily a function of the number of spindles (assuming no cache benefit and no RAID loss). A quick rule of thumb is that the total number of IOps = IOps × the number of that type of spindle. Latency is in milliseconds, though can get to tens of milliseconds in cases where the storage array is overtaxed.

Understand vSphere storage options. vSphere has three fundamental storage presentation models: VMFS on block, RDM, and NFS. The most flexible configurations use all three, predominantly via a shared-container model and selective use of RDMs.

> **Master It** Characterize use cases for VMFS datastores, NFS datastores, and RDMs.

Solution VMFS datastores and NFS datastores are shared-container models; they store virtual disks together. VMFS is governed by the block storage stack, and NFS is governed by the network stack. NFS is generally (without use of 10 GbE LANs) best suited to large numbers of low bandwidth (any throughput) VMs. VMFS is suited for a wide range of workloads. RDMs should be used sparingly for cases where the guest must have direct access to a single LUN.

Master It If you're using VMFS and there's one performance metric to track, what would it be? Configure a monitor for that metric.

Solution The metric to measure is queue depth. Use `esxtop` to monitor. A good nonperformance metric is the datastore-availability or used-capacity managed datastore alerts.

Configure storage at the vSphere layer. After a shared storage platform is selected, vSphere needs a storage network configured. The network (whether Fibre Channel or Ethernet based) must be designed to meet availability and throughput requirements, which are influenced by protocol choice and vSphere fundamental storage stack (and in the case of NFS, the network stack) architecture. Proper network design involves physical redundancy and physical or logical isolation mechanisms (SAN zoning and network VLANs). With connectivity in place, configure LUNs and VMFS datastores and/or NFS exports/NFS datastores using the predictive or adaptive model (or a hybrid model). Use Storage vMotion to resolve hot spots and other non-optimal VM placement.

Master It What would best identify an oversubscribed VMFS datastore from a performance standpoint? How would you identify the issue? What is it most likely to be? What would be two possible corrective actions you could take?

Solution An oversubscribed VMFS datastore is best identified by evaluating the queue depth and would manifest as slow VMs. The best way to track this is with `resxtop`, using the QUED (the Queue Depth column). If the queue is full, take any or all of these courses of action: make the queue deeper and increase `Disk.SchedNumReqOutstanding` advanced parameter to match; vacate VMs (using Storage vMotion); and add more spindles to the LUN so that it can fulfill the requests more rapidly or move to a faster spindle type.

Master It A VMFS volume is filling up. What are three possible nondisruptive corrective actions you could take?

Solution The actions you could take are as follows:

◆ Use Storage vMotion to migrate some VMs to another datastore.

◆ Grow the backing LUN, and grow the VMFS volume.

◆ Add another backing LUN, and add another VMFS extent.

Master It What would best identify an oversubscribed NFS volume from a performance standpoint? How would you identify the issue? What is it most likely to be? What are two possible corrective actions you could take?

Solution The workload in the datastore is reaching the maximum bandwidth of a single link. The easiest way to identify the issue would be using the vCenter performance charts and examining the VMkernel NIC's utilization. If it is at 100 percent, the only options are to upgrade to 10 GbE or to add another NFS datastore, add another VMkernel NIC, follow the load-balancing and high-availability decision tree to determine whether NIC teaming or IP routing would work best, and finally use Storage vMotion to migrate some VMs to another datastore (remember that the NIC teaming/IP routing works for multiple data stores, not for a single datastore). Remember that using Storage vMotion adds additional work to an already busy datastore, so consider scheduling it during a low I/O period, even though it can be done live.

Configure storage at the VM layer. With datastores in place, create VMs. During the creation of the VMs, place VMs in the appropriate datastores, and employ selective use of RDMs but only where required. Leverage in-guest iSCSI where it makes sense, but understand the impact to your vSphere environment.

Master It Without turning the machine off, convert the virtual disks on a VMFS volume from thin to thick (eagerzeroedthick) and back to thin.

Solution Use Storage vMotion and select the target disk format during the Storage vMotion process.

Master It Identify where you would use a physical compatibility mode RDM, and configure that use case.

Solution One use case would be a Microsoft cluster (either W2K3 with MSCS or W2K8 with WFC). You should download the VMware Microsoft clustering guide and follow that use case. Other valid answers are a case where virtual-to-physical mobility of the LUNs is required or one where a Solutions Enabler VM is needed.

Leverage best practices for SAN and NAS storage with vSphere. Read, follow, and leverage key VMware and storage vendors' best practices/solutions guide documentation. Don't oversize up front, but instead learn to leverage VMware and storage array features to monitor performance, queues, and backend load — and then nondisruptively adapt. Plan for performance first and capacity second. (Usually capacity is a given for performance requirements to be met.) Spend design time on availability design and on the large, heavy I/O VMs, and use flexible pool design for the general-purpose VMFS and NFS datastores.

Master It Quickly estimate the minimum usable capacity needed for 200 VMs with an average VM size of 40 GB. Make some assumptions about vSphere snapshots. What would be the raw capacity needed in the array if you used RAID 10? RAID 5 (4+1)? RAID 6 (10+2)? What would you do to nondisruptively cope if you ran out of capacity?

Solution Using rule-of-thumb math, 200 × 40 GB = 8 TB × 25 percent extra space (snapshots, other VMware files) = 10 TB. Using RAID 10, you would need at least 20 TB raw. Using RAID 5 (4+1), you would need 12.5 TB. Using RAID 6 (10+2), you would need 12 TB. If you ran out of capacity, you could add capacity to your array and then add datastores and use Storage vMotion. If your array supports dynamic growth of LUNs, you could grow the VMFS or NFS datastores, and if it doesn't, you could add more VMFS extents.

Master It Using the configurations in the previous question, what would the minimum amount of raw capacity need to be if the VMs are actually only 20 GB of data in each VM, even though they are provisioning 40 GB and you used thick on an array that didn't support thin provisioning? What if the array *did* support thin provisioning? What if you used Storage vMotion to convert from thick to thin (both in the case where the array supports thin provisioning and in the case where it doesn't)?

Solution   If you use thick virtual disks on an array that doesn't support thin provisioning, the answers are the same as for the previous question. If you use an array that *does* support thin provisioning, the answers are cut down by 50 percent: 20 TB for RAID 10, 6.25 TB for RAID 5 (4+1), and 6 TB for RAID 6 (10+2). If you use Storage vMotion to convert to thin on the array that doesn't support thin provisioning, the result is the same, just as it is if you do thin on thin.

Master It   Estimate the number of spindles needed for 100 VMs that drive 200 IOps each and are 40 GB in size. Assume no RAID loss or cache gain. How many if you use 500 GB SATA 7,200 RPM? 300 GB 10K Fibre Channel/SAS? 300 GB 15K Fibre Channel/SAS? 160 GB consumer-grade SSD? 200 GB Enterprise Flash?

Solution   This exercise highlights the foolishness of looking just at capacity in the server use case. 100×40 GB = 4 TB usable $\times$ 200 IOps = 20,000 IOps. With 500 GB 7200 RPM, that's 250 drives, which have 125 TB raw (ergo non-optimal). With 300 GB 10K RPM, that's 167 drives, which have 50 TB raw (ergo non-optimal). With 15K RPM, that's 111 drives with 16 TB raw (getting closer). With consumer-grade SSD, that's 20 spindles and 3.2 TB raw (too little). With EFD, that's 4 spindles and 800 GB raw (too little). The moral of the story is that the 15K RPM 146 GB drive is the sweet spot for this workload. Note that the extra space can't be used unless you can find a workload that doesn't need any performance at all; the spindles are working as hard as they can. Also note that the 4 TB requirement was usable, and we were calculating the raw storage capacity. Therefore, in this case, RAID 5, RAID 6, and RAID 10 would all have extra usable capacity in the end. It's unusual to have all VMs with a common workload, and 200 IOps (as an average) is relatively high. This exercise also shows why it's efficient to have several tiers and several datastores for different classes of VMs (put some on SATA, some on Fibre Channel, some on EFD or SSD), because you can be more efficient.

Chapter 7: Ensuring High Availability and Business Continuity

Understand Windows clustering and the types of clusters.   Windows clustering plays a central role in the design of any high-availability solution for both virtual and physical servers. Microsoft Windows clustering gives us the ability to have application failover to the secondary server when the primary server fails.

Master It   Specifically with regard to Windows clustering in a virtual environment, what are three different types of cluster configurations that you can have?

Solution   The first is a cluster in a box, which is mainly used for testing or in a development environment where both nodes of a Windows cluster run on the same ESXi host. The second is the cluster across boxes, which is the most common form of clustering in a virtual environment. In this configuration, you have the ability to use Windows clustering on VMs that are running on different physical hosts. The third is the physical-to-virtual configuration where you have the best of both the physical and virtual worlds by having a Windows clustering node on both a physical server and a virtual server.

Master It What is the key difference between NLB clusters and Windows Failover clusters?

Solution Network Load Balancing (NLB) clusters are used primarily for scaling performance. Windows Failover clusters are primarily used for high availability and redundancy.

Use VMware vSphere's built-in high-availability functionality. VMware Virtual Infrastructure has high-availability options built in and available to you out of the box: vSphere High Availability (HA) and vSphere Fault Tolerance (FT). These options help you provide better uptime for your critical applications.

Master It What are the two types of high-availability options that VMware provides in vSphere, and how are they different?

Solution VMware provides two forms of high availability in vSphere. vSphere HA provides a form of high availability by having the ability to restart any VMs that were running on a host that crashes. vSphere Fault Tolerance (FT) uses vLockstep technology to record and replay a running VM on another host in the cluster. Failover from the primary VM to the secondary VM is without any downtime. vSphere HA restarts the VM in the event of failure; vSphere FT does not need to restart the VM because the secondary VM is kept in lockstep with the primary and can take over immediately in the event of a failure.

Recognize differences between different high-availability solutions. A high-availability solution that operates at the Application layer, like Oracle Real Application Cluster (RAC), is different in architecture and operation from an OS-level clustering solution like Windows Failover clustering. Similarly, OS-level clustering solutions are very different from hypervisor-based solutions such as vSphere HA or vSphere FT. Each approach has advantages and disadvantages, and today's administrators will likely need to use multiple approaches in their datacenter.

Master It Name one advantage of a hypervisor-based high-availability solution over an OS-level solution.

Solution Because it would operate beneath the guest OS level, it would operate independent of the guest OS and could therefore potentially support any number of different guest OSes. Depending on the implementation, hypervisor-based solutions might be simpler than OS-level solutions. For example, vSphere HA is generally less complex and easier to set up or configure than Windows Failover clustering.

Understand additional components of business continuity. There are other components of ensuring business continuity for your organization. Data protection (backups) and replication of your data to a secondary location are two areas that can help ensure business continuity needs are satisfied, even in the event of a disaster.

Master It What are three methods to replicate your data to a secondary location and what is the golden rule for any continuity plan?

Solution   First, you have the backup and restore method from tape. It is a best practice to send out backup tapes off site and, when they are needed for a disaster, have them shipped to the secondary site. Second, you have the ability to replicate your data by using block-level replication at the SAN level. This gives you the ability to replicate data over both short and long distances. Third, you can use a disk-to-disk backup appliance that also offers off-site replication to another location. This method offers shorter backup windows as well as the benefits of off-site backups. Finally, the golden rule for any successful continuity design is to test, test, and test again.

Chapter 8: Securing VMware vSphere

Configure and control authentication to vSphere.   Both ESXi and vCenter Server have authentication mechanisms, and both products have the ability to utilize local users and groups or users and groups defined in Active Directory. Authentication is a basic tenet of security; it's important to verify that users are who they claim to be. You can manage local users and groups on your ESXi hosts using either the vSphere Client or the command-line interface (such as the vSphere Management Assistant). Both the Windows-based and the Linux-based virtual appliance versions of vCenter Server can leverage Active Directory for authentication as well.

Master It   You've asked an administrator on your team to create some accounts on an ESXi host. The administrator is uncomfortable with the command line and is having a problem figuring out how to create the users. Is there another way for this administrator to perform this task?

Solution   Yes, the administrator can use the vSphere Client and connect directly to the ESXi hosts on which the accounts need to be created.

Manage roles and access controls.   Both ESXi and vCenter Server possess a role-based access control system that combines users, groups, privileges, roles, and permissions. vSphere administrators can use this role-based access control system to define very granular permissions that define what users are allowed to do with the vSphere Client against an ESXi host or a vCenter Server instance. For example, vSphere administrators can limit users to specific actions on specific types of objects within the vSphere Client. vCenter Server ships with some sample roles that help provide an example of how you can use the role-based access control system.

Master It   Describe the differences between a role, a privilege, and a permission in the ESXi/vCenter Server security model.

Solution   A role is a combination of privileges; a role is assigned to a user or group. Privileges are specific actions (like power on a VM, power off a VM, configure a VM's CD/DVD drive, or take a snapshot) that a role is allowed to perform. You combine privileges together into a role. Permissions are created when you assign a role (with its associated privileges) to an inventory object within ESXi or vCenter Server.

Control network access to services on ESXi hosts.   ESXi provides a network firewall that you can use to control network access to services on your ESXi hosts. This firewall can control both inbound and outbound traffic, and you have the ability to further limit traffic to specific source IP addresses or subnets.

Master It Describe how you can use the ESXi firewall to limit traffic to a specific source IP address.

Solution Within the Firewall Properties dialog box, the Firewall button allows you to specify a specific source IP address or source IP subnet.

Master It List a limitation of the built-in ESXi firewall.

Solution One limitation of the ESXi firewall is that you cannot define your own custom firewall rules. You are limited to enabling or disabling inbound and outbound traffic for only the traffic types that are already defined.

Integrate with Active Directory. All the major components of vSphere — the ESXi hosts, vCenter Server (both the Windows Server–based version and the Linux-based virtual appliance), as well as the vSphere Management Assistant — all support integration into Microsoft Active Directory. This gives vSphere administrators the option of using Active Directory as their centralized directory service for all major components of vSphere 5.

Master It You've just installed a new ESXi host into your vSphere environment and you are trying to configure the host to enable integration with your Active Directory environment. For some reason, though, it doesn't seem to work. What could be the problem?

Solution There could be a couple different issues at work here. First, the ESXi host needs to be able to resolve the domain name of the Active Directory domain via DNS. The ESXi host also needs to be able to locate the Active Directory domain controllers via DNS. This usually involves configuring the ESXi host to use the same DNS servers as the domain controllers. Second, there could be network connectivity issues; verify that the ESXi host has connectivity to the Active Directory domain controllers. If there are any firewalls between the ESXi host and the domain controllers, verify that the correct ports are open between the ESXi host and the domain controllers.

Chapter 9: Creating and Managing Virtual Machines

Create a virtual machine. A VM is a collection of virtual hardware pieces, like a physical system — one or more virtual CPUs, RAM, video card, SCSI devices, IDE devices, floppy drives, parallel and serial ports, and network adapters. This virtual hardware is virtualized and abstracted from the underlying physical hardware, providing portability to the VM.

Master It Create two VMs, one intended to run Windows Server 2008 R2 and a second intended to run SLES 11 (64-bit). Make a list of the differences in the configuration that are suggested by the Create New Virtual Machine wizard.

Solution vCenter Server suggests 1 GB of RAM, an LSI Logic parallel SCSI controller, and a 16 GB virtual disk for 64-bit SLES 11; for Windows Server 2008 R2, the recommendations are 4 GB of RAM, an LSI Logic SAS controller, and a 40 GB virtual disk.

Install a guest operating system. Just as a physical machine needs an operating system, a VM also needs an operating system. vSphere supports a broad range of 32-bit and

64-bit operating systems, including all major versions of Windows Server, Windows Vista, Windows XP, and Windows 2000, as well as various flavors of Linux, FreeBSD, Novell NetWare, and Solaris.

Master It What are the three ways in which a guest OS can access data on a CD/DVD, and what are the advantages of each approach?

Solution The three ways to access a CD/DVD are as follows:

◆ Client device: This has the advantage of being very easy to use; VMware administrators can put a CD/DVD into their local workstation and map it into the VM.

◆ Host device: The CD/DVD is physically placed into the optical drive of the ESXi host. This keeps the CD/DVD traffic off the network, which may be advantageous in some situations.

◆ An ISO image on a shared datastore: This is the fastest method and has the advantage of being able to have multiple VMs access the same ISO image at the same time. A bit more work may be required up front to create the ISO image.

Install VMware Tools For maximum performance of the guest OS, it needs to have virtualization-optimized drivers that are specially written for and designed to work with the ESXi hypervisor. VMware Tools provides these optimized drivers as well as other utilities focused on better operation in virtual environments.

Master It A fellow administrator contacts you and is having a problem installing VMware Tools. This administrator has selected the Install/Upgrade VMware Tools command, but nothing seems to be happening inside the VM. What could be the cause of the problem?

Solution There could be any number of potential issues. First, a guest OS must be installed before VMware Tools can be installed. Second, if the VM is running Windows, AutoPlay may have been disabled. Finally, it's possible — although unlikely — that the source ISO images for VMware Tools installation have been damaged or deleted and need to be replaced on the host.

Manage virtual machines. Once a VM has been created, the vSphere Client makes it easy to manage the VM. Virtual floppy images and CD/DVD drives can be mounted or unmounted as necessary. vSphere provides support for initiating an orderly shutdown of the guest OS in a VM, although this requires that VMware Tools be installed. VM snapshots allow you to take a point-in-time "picture" of a VM so that administrators can roll back changes if needed.

Master It What are the three different ways an administrator can bring the contents of a CD/DVD into a VM?

Solution The administrator can insert the CD/DVD into the system running the vSphere Client and use the Client Device option in the Virtual Machine Properties dialog box to mount that CD/DVD into the VM. The administrator can also attach the physical CD/DVD drive in the host to the VM and mount the drive, or the administrator can convert the CD/DVD into an ISO image. Once converted, the ISO image can be uploaded into a datastore and mounted into a VM.

Master It What is the difference between the Shut Down Guest command and the Power Off command?

Solution The Shut Down Guest command uses VMware Tools to initiate an orderly shutdown of the guest OS. This ensures that the guest OS filesystem is consistent and that applications running in the guest OS are properly terminated. The Power Off command simply "yanks" the power from the VM, much like pulling the power cord out of the back of a physical system.

Modify virtual machines. vSphere offers a number of features to make it easy to modify VMs after they have been created. Administrators can hot-add certain types of hardware, like virtual hard disks and network adapters, and some guest OSes also support hot-adding virtual CPUs or memory, although this feature must be enabled first.

Master It Which method is preferred for modifying the configuration of a VM — editing the VMX file or using the vSphere Client?

Solution Although it is possible to edit the VMX file to make changes, that method is error prone and is not recommended. Using the vSphere Client is the recommended method.

Master It Name the types of hardware that cannot be added while a VM is running.

Solution The following types of virtual hardware cannot be added while a VM is running: serial port, parallel port, floppy drive, CD/DVD drive, or PCI device.

Chapter 10: Using Templates and vApps

Clone a VM. The ability to clone a VM is a powerful feature that dramatically reduces the amount of time to get a fully functional VM with a guest OS installed and running. vCenter Server provides the ability not only to clone VMs but also to customize VMs, ensuring that each VM is unique. You can save the information to customize a VM as a customization specification and then reuse that information over and over again. vCenter Server can even clone running VMs.

Master It Where and when can customization specifications be created in the vSphere Client?

Solution Administrators can create customization specifications using the Customization Specifications Manager, available from the vSphere Client home screen. Administrators can also create customization specifications while cloning VMs or deploying from templates by supplying answers to the Guest Customization Wizard and saving those answers as a customization specification.

Master It A fellow administrator comes to you and wants you to help streamline the process of deploying Solaris x86 VMs in your VMware vSphere environment. What do you tell him?

Solution You can use cloning inside vCenter Server to help clone VMs that are running Solaris x86, and that will help speed up the process of deploying new VMs. However, the Solaris administrator(s) will be responsible for customizing the configuration of the cloned VMs, because vCenter Server is unable to customize a Solaris guest OS installation as part of the cloning process.

Create a VM template. vCenter Server's templates feature is an excellent complement to the cloning functionality. With options to clone or convert an existing VM to a template, vCenter Server makes it easy to create templates. By creating templates, you ensure that your VM master image doesn't get accidentally changed or modified. Then, once a template has been created, vCenter Server can clone VMs from that template, customizing them in the process to ensure that each one is unique.

Master It Of the following tasks, which are appropriate to be performed on a VM running Windows Server 2008 that will eventually be turned into a template?

A. Align the guest OS's file system to a 64 KB boundary.

B. Join the VM to Active Directory.

C. Perform some application-specific configurations and tweaks.

D. Install all patches from the operating system vendor.

Solution

A. Yes. This is an appropriate task but unnecessary because Windows Server 2008 installs already aligned to a 64 KB boundary. Ensuring alignment ensures that all VMs then cloned from this template will also have their filesystems properly aligned.

B. No. This should be done by the vSphere Client Windows Guest Customization Wizard or a customization specification.

C. No. Templates shouldn't have any application-specific files, tweaks, or configurations unless you are planning on creating multiple application-specific templates.

D. Yes. This helps reduce the amount of patching and updating required on any VMs cloned from this template.

Deploy new VMs from a template. By combining templates and cloning, VMware vSphere administrators have a powerful way to standardize the configuration of VMs being deployed, protect the master images from accidental change, and reduce the amount of time it takes to stand up new guest OS instances.

Master It Another VMware vSphere administrator in your environment starts the wizard for deploying a new VM from a template. He has a customization specification he'd like to use, but there is one setting in the specification he wants to change. Does he have to create an all-new customization specification?

Solution No. He can select the customization specification he wants to use and then select Use The Customization Wizard To Customize This Specification to supply the alternate values he wants to use for this particular VM deployment.

Deploy a VM from an OVF template. Open Virtualization Format (OVF, formerly Open Virtual Machine Format) templates provide a mechanism for moving templates or VMs between different instances of vCenter Server or even entirely different and separate installations of VMware vSphere. OVF templates combine the structural definition of a VM along with the data in the VM's virtual hard disk and can either exist as a folder of files or as a single file. Because OVF templates include the VM's virtual hard disk, OVF templates can contain an installation of a guest OS and are often used by software developers as a way of delivering their software preinstalled into a guest OS inside a VM.

Master It A vendor has given you a zip file that contains a VM they are calling a *virtual appliance*. Upon looking inside the zip file, you see several VMDK files and a VMX file. Will you be able to use vCenter Server's Deploy OVF Template functionality to import this VM? If not, how can you get this VM into your infrastructure?

Solution You will not be able to use vCenter Server's Deploy OVF Template feature; this requires that the virtual appliance be provided with an OVF file that supplies the information that vCenter Server is expecting to find. However, you can use vCenter Converter to perform a V2V conversion to bring this VM into the VMware vSphere environment, assuming it is coming from a compatible source environment.

Export a VM as an OVF template. To assist in the transport of VMs between VMware vSphere installations, you can use vCenter Server to export a VM as an OVF template. The OVF template will include both the configuration of the VM as well as the data found in the VM.

Master It You are preparing to export a VM to an OVF template. You want to ensure that the OVF template is easy and simple to transport via a USB key or portable hard drive. Which format is most appropriate, OVF or OVA? Why?

Solution The OVA format is probably a better option here. OVA distributes the entire OVF template as a single file, making it easy to copy to a USB key or portable hard drive for transport. Using OVF would mean keeping several files together instead of working with only a single file.

Work with vApps. vSphere vApps leverage OVF as a way to combine multiple VMs into a single administrative unit. When the vApp is powered on, all VMs in it are powered on, in a sequence specified by the administrator. The same goes for shutting down a vApp. vApps also act a bit like resource pools for the VMs contained within them.

Master It Name two ways to add VMs to a vApp.

Solution There are four ways to add VMs to a vApp: create a new VM in the vApp; clone an existing VM into a new VM in the vApp; deploy a VM into the vApp from a template; and drag and drop an existing VM into the vApp.

Chapter 11: Managing Resource Allocation

Manage virtual machine memory allocation. In almost every virtualized datacenter, memory is the resource that typically comes under contention first. Most organizations run out of memory on their VMware ESXi hosts before other resources become constrained. Fortunately, VMware vSphere offers both advanced memory-management technologies as well as extensive controls for managing the allocation of memory and utilization of memory by VMs.

Master It   To guarantee certain levels of performance, your IT director believes that all VMs must be configured with at least 8 GB of RAM. However, you know that many of your applications rarely use this much memory. What might be an acceptable compromise to help ensure performance?

Solution   One way would be to configure the VMs with 8 GB of RAM and specify a reservation of only 2 GB. VMware ESXi will guarantee that every VM will get 2 GB of RAM, including preventing additional VMs from being powered on if there isn't enough RAM to guarantee 2 GB of RAM to that new VM. However, the RAM greater than 2 GB is not guaranteed and, if it is not being used, will be reclaimed by the host for use elsewhere. If plenty of memory is available to the host, the ESXi host will grant what is requested; otherwise, it will arbitrate the allocation of that memory according to the shares values of the VMs.

Manage CPU utilization.   In a VMware vSphere environment, the ESXi hosts control VM access to physical CPUs. To effectively manage and scale VMware vSphere, administrators must understand how to allocate CPU resources to VMs, including how to use reservations, limits, and shares. Reservations provide guarantees to resources, limits provide a cap on resource usage, and shares help adjust the allocation of resources in a constrained environment.

Master It   A fellow VMware administrator is a bit concerned about the use of CPU reservations. She is worried that using CPU reservations will "strand" CPU resources, preventing those reserved but unused resources from being used by other VMs. Are this administrator's concerns well founded?

Solution   For CPU reservations, no. While it is true that VMware must have enough unreserved CPU capacity to satisfy a CPU reservation when a VM is powered on, reserved CPU capacity is not "locked" to a VM. If a VM has reserved but unused capacity, that capacity can and will be used by other VMs on the same host. The other administrator's concerns could be valid, however, for memory reservations.

Create and manage resource pools.   Managing resource allocation and usage for large numbers of VMs creates too much administrative overhead. Resource pools provide a mechanism for administrators to apply resource allocation policies to groups of VMs all at the same time. Resource pools use reservations, limits, and shares to control and modify resource allocation behavior, but only for memory and CPU.

Master It   Your company runs both test/development workloads and production workloads on the same hardware. How can you help ensure that test/development workloads do not consume too many resources and impact the performance of production workloads?

Solution   Create a resource pool and place all the test/development VMs in that resource pool. Configure the resource pool to have a CPU limit and a lower CPU shares value. This ensures that the test/development will never consume more CPU time than specified in the limit and that, in times of CPU contention, the test/development environment will have a lower priority on the CPU than production workloads.

Control network and storage I/O utilization. Along with memory and CPU, network I/O and storage I/O make up the four major resource types that VMware vSphere administrators must effectively manage in order to have an efficient virtualized datacenter. By applying controls to network I/O and storage I/O, administrators can help ensure consistent performance, meet service-level objectives, and prevent one workload from unnecessarily consuming resources at the expense of other workloads.

Master It Name two limitations of Network I/O Control.

Solution Potential limitations of Network I/O Control include the fact that it works only with vSphere Distributed Switches, the ability to only control outbound network traffic, the fact that it requires vCenter Server in order to operate, or the fact that system network resource pools cannot be assigned to user-created port groups.

Master It What are the requirements for using Storage I/O Control?

Solution All datastores and ESXi hosts that will participate in Storage I/O Control must be managed by the same vCenter Server instance. In addition, Raw Device Mappings (RDMs) are not supported. Datastores must have only a single extent; datastores with multiple extents are not supported.

Chapter 12: Balancing Resource Utilization

Configure and execute vMotion. vMotion is a feature that allows running VMs to be migrated from one physical ESXi host to another physical ESXi host with no downtime to end users. To execute vMotion, both the ESXi hosts and the VMs must meet specific configuration requirements. In addition, vCenter Server performs validation checks to ensure that vMotion compatibility rules are observed.

Master It A certain vendor has just released a series of patches for some of the guest OSes in your virtualized infrastructure. You request an outage window from your supervisor, but your supervisor says to just use vMotion to prevent downtime. Is your supervisor correct? Why or why not?

Solution Your supervisor is incorrect. vMotion can be used to move running VMs from one physical host to another, but it does not address outages within a guest OS because of reboots or other malfunctions. If you had been requesting an outage window to apply updates to the host, the supervisor would have been correct — you could use vMotion to move all the VMs to other hosts within the environment and then patch the first host. There would be no end-user downtime in that situation.

Master It Is vMotion a solution to prevent unplanned downtime?

Solution No. vMotion is a solution to address planned downtime of the ESXi hosts on which VMs are running, as well as to manually load balance CPU and memory utilization across multiple ESXi hosts. Both the source and destination ESXi hosts must be up and running and accessible across the network in order for vMotion to succeed.

Ensure vMotion compatibility across processor families. vMotion requires compatible CPU families on the source and destination ESXi hosts in order to be successful. To help alleviate any potential problems resulting from changes in processor families over time, vSphere offers Enhanced vMotion Compatibility (EVC), which can mask differences between CPU families in order to maintain vMotion compatibility.

Master It Can you change the EVC level for a cluster while there are VMs running on hosts in the cluster?

Solution No, you cannot. Changing the EVC level means that new CPU masks must be calculated and applied. CPU masks can be applied only when VMs are powered off, so you can't change the EVC level on a cluster when there are powered-on VMs in that cluster.

Configure and manage vSphere Distributed Resource Scheduler. vSphere Distributed Resource Scheduler enables vCenter Server to automate the process of conducting vMotion migrations to help balance the load across ESXi hosts within a cluster. DRS can be as automated as desired, and vCenter Server has flexible controls for affecting the behavior of DRS as well as the behavior of specific VMs within a DRS-enabled cluster.

Master It You want to take advantage of vSphere DRS to provide some load balancing of virtual workloads within your environment. However, because of business constraints, you have a few workloads that should not be automatically moved to other hosts using vMotion. Can you use DRS? If so, how can you prevent these specific workloads from being affected by DRS?

Solution Yes, you can use DRS. Enable DRS on the cluster, and set the DRS automation level appropriately. For those VMs that should not be automatically migrated by DRS, configure the DRS automation level on a per-VM basis to Manual. This will allow DRS to make recommendations on migrations for these workloads but will not actually perform the migrations.

Use Storage vMotion. Just as vMotion is used to migrate running VMs from one ESXi host to another, Storage vMotion is used to migrate the virtual disks of a running VM from one datastore to another. You can also use Storage vMotion to convert between thick and thin virtual disk types.

Master It A fellow administrator is trying to migrate a VM to a different datastore and a different host, but the option is disabled (grayed out). Why?

Solution Storage vMotion, like vMotion, can operate while a VM is running. However, in order to migrate a VM to both a new datastore and a new host, the VM must be powered off. VMs that are powered on can only be migrated using Storage vMotion or vMotion, but not both.

Master It Name two features of Storage vMotion that would help administrators cope with storage-related changes in their vSphere environment.

Solution Storage vMotion can be used to facilitate no-downtime storage migrations from one storage array to a new storage array, greatly simplifying the migration process. Storage vMotion can also migrate between different types of storage (FC to NFS, iSCSI to FC or FCoE), which helps vSphere administrators cope with changes in how the ESXi hosts access the storage. Finally, Storage vMotion allows administrators to convert VMDKs between thick and thin, to give them the flexibility to use whichever VMDK format is most effective for them.

Configure and manage Storage DRS.   Building on Storage vMotion just as vSphere DRS builds on vMotion, Storage DRS brings automation to the process of balancing storage capacity and I/O utilization. Storage DRS uses datastore clusters and can operate in manual or Fully Automated mode. Numerous customizations exist — such as custom schedules, VM and VMDK anti-affinity rules, and threshold settings — to allow administrators to fine-tune the behavior of Storage DRS for their specific environments.

Master It   Name the two ways in which an administrator is notified that a Storage DRS recommendation has been generated.

Solution   On the Storage DRS tab of a datastore cluster, the recommendation(s) will be listed with an option to apply the recommendations. In addition, on the Alarms tab of the datastore cluster, an alarm will be triggered to indicate that a Storage DRS recommendation exists.

Master It   What is a potential disadvantage of using drag and drop to add a datastore to a datastore cluster?

Solution   When using drag and drop to add a datastore to a datastore cluster, the user is not notified if the datastore isn't accessible to all the hosts that are currently connected to the datastore cluster. This introduces the possibility that one or more ESXi hosts could be "stranded" from a VM's virtual disks if Storage DRS migrates them onto a datastore that is not accessible from that host.

Chapter 13: Monitoring VMware vSphere Performance

Use alarms for proactive monitoring.   vCenter Server offers extensive alarms for alerting vSphere administrators to excessive resource consumption or potentially negative events. You can create alarms on virtually any type of object found within vCenter Server, including datacenters, clusters, ESXi hosts, and VMs. Alarms can monitor for resource consumption or for the occurrence of specific events. Alarms can also trigger actions, such as running a script, migrating a VM, or sending a notification email.

Master It   What are the questions a vSphere administrator should ask before creating a custom alarm?

Solution   You should ask yourself several questions before you create a custom alarm:

◆ Does an existing alarm meet my needs?

◆ What is the proper scope for this alarm? Do I need to create it at the datacenter level so that it affects all objects of a particular type within the datacenter or at some lower point?

◆ What are the values this alarm needs to use?

◆ What actions, if any, should this alarm take when it is triggered? Does it need to send an email or trigger an SNMP trap?

Work with performance graphs.   vCenter Server's detailed performance graphs are the key to unlocking the information necessary to determine why an ESXi host or VM is performing poorly. The performance graphs expose a large number of performance counters across a variety of resource types, and vCenter Server offers functionality to save customized chart settings, export performance graphs as graphic figures or Excel workbooks, or view performance graphs in a separate window.

Master It   You find yourself using the Chart Options link in the Advanced view of the Performance tab to set up the same graph over and over again. Is there a way to save yourself some time and effort so that you don't have to keep re-creating the custom graph?

Solution   Yes. After using the Customize Performance Chart dialog box to configure the performance graph to show the desired counters, use the Save Chart Settings button to save these settings for future use. The next time you need to access these same settings, they will be available from the Switch To drop-down list on the Advanced view of the Performance tab.

Gather performance information using command-line tools.   VMware supplies a few command-line tools that are useful in gathering performance information. For VMware ESXi hosts, `resxtop` provides real-time information about CPU, memory, network, or disk utilization. You should run `resxtop` from the VMware vMA. Finally, the `vm-support` tool can gather performance information that can be played back later using `resxtop`.

Master It   Know how to run `resxtop` from the VMware vMA command line.

Solution   Enter the command **vm-support -p -i 10 -d 180**. This creates a `resxtop` snapshot, capturing data every 10 seconds, for the duration of 180 seconds.

Monitor CPU, memory, network, and disk usage by ESXi hosts and VMs.   Monitoring usage of the four key resources — CPU, memory, network, and disk — can be difficult at times. Fortunately, the various tools supplied by VMware within vCenter Server can lead the vSphere administrator to the right solution. In particular, using customized performance graphs can expose the right information that will help a vSphere administrator uncover the source of performance problems.

Master It   A junior vSphere administrator is trying to resolve a performance problem with a VM. You've asked this administrator to see whether it is a CPU problem, and the junior administrator keeps telling you that the VM needs more CPU capacity because the CPU utilization is high within the VM. Is the junior administrator correct, based on the information available to you?

Solution   Based on the available information, not necessarily. A VM may be using all of the cycles being given to it, but because the overall ESXi host is CPU constrained, the VM isn't getting enough cycles to perform acceptably. In this case, adding CPU capacity to the VM wouldn't necessarily fix the problem. If the host is indeed constrained, then migrating VMs to other hosts or changing the shares or the CPU limits for the VMs on this host may help alleviate the problem.

Chapter 14: Automating VMware vSphere

Identify some of the tools available for automating vSphere.   VMware offers a number of different solutions for automating your vSphere environment, including vCenter Orchestrator, PowerCLI, an SDK for Perl, an SDK for web service developers, and shell scripts in VMware ESXi. Each of these tools has its own advantages and disadvantages.

Master It   VMware offers a number of different automation tools. What are some guidelines for choosing which automation tool to use?

Solution   One key factor is prior experience. If you have experience with creating scripts using Perl, then you will likely be most effective in using the vSphere SDK for Perl to create automation tools. Similarly, having prior experience or knowledge of PowerShell will mean you will likely be most effective using PowerCLI.

Configure vCenter Orchestrator.   vCenter Orchestrator is installed silently with vCenter Server, but before you can use vCenter Orchestrator, you must configure it properly. The web-based vCenter Orchestrator Configuration interface allows you to configure various portions of vCenter Orchestrator.

Master It   How can you tell whether some portion of the vCenter Orchestrator configuration is incomplete or incorrect?

Solution   The status indicators in the vCenter Orchestrator Configuration interface will be a red triangle for any configuration item that is incorrect or incomplete and will be a green circle for items that have been successfully configured.

Use a vCenter Orchestrator workflow.   After vCenter Orchestrator is configured and is running, you can use the vCenter Orchestrator Client to run a vCenter Orchestrator workflow. vCenter Orchestrator comes with a number of preinstalled workflows to help automate tasks.

Master It   An administrator in your environment configured vCenter Orchestrator and has now asked you to run a couple of workflows. However, when you log into the vCenter Server where vCenter Orchestrator is also installed, you don't see the icons for vCenter Orchestrator. Why?

Solution   The vCenter Server installer creates the vCenter Orchestrator Start menu icons in the user-specific side of the Start menu, so they are visible only to the user who was logged on when vCenter Server was installed. Other users will not see the icons on the Start menu unless they are moved to the All Users portion of the Start menu.

Create a PowerCLI script for automation.   VMware vSphere PowerCLI builds on the object-oriented PowerShell scripting language to provide administrators with a simple yet powerful way to automate tasks within the vSphere environment.

Master It If you are familiar with other scripting languages, what would be the biggest hurdle in learning to use PowerShell and PowerCLI, other than syntax?

Solution Everything in PowerShell and PowerCLI is object based. Thus, when a command outputs results, those results are objects. This means you have to be careful to properly match object types between the output of one command and the input of the next command.

Use rCLI to manage ESXi hosts from the command line. VMware's remote command-line interface, or rCLI, is the new way of managing an ESXi host using the familiar `esxcfg-*` command set. By combining the features of fastpass with rCLI, you can seamlessly manage multiple hosts using the same command set from a single login.

Master It Have you migrated management and configuration operations for which you currently use the ESXi command-line interface to vMA?

Solution Migrating to vMA and the rCLI is extremely simple and can be done quickly using vMA's fastpass technology. Once a host has been configured for fastpass, you can execute the same scripts that were previously used by setting the fastpass target to transparently pass the commands to the host.

Use vCenter in combination with vMA to manage all your hosts. The new version of vMA can use vCenter as a target. This means that you can manage all of your hosts using rCLI without having to manually add each host to the fastpass target list.

Master It Use a combination of shell scripting with rCLI commands to execute commands against a number of hosts.

Solution Bash, the default shell for the vi-admin user, has a full-featured scripting environment capable of using functions, arrays, loops, and other control logic structures. Using these capabilities, in combination with the rCLI command set and fastpass, hosts in clusters can be efficiently configured to match.

Employ the Perl toolkit and VMware SDK for virtual server operations from the command line. The rCLI is designed for host management and consequentially lacks tools for manipulating virtual servers. With the Perl toolkit, leveraged against the VMware SDK, any task that can be accomplished in the Virtual Infrastructure client can be done from the command line.

Master It Browse the sample scripts and SDK documentation to discover the world of possibilities that are unlocked by using Perl, or any of the other supported languages, to accomplish management tasks.

Solution Sample scripts are provided with the Perl toolkit on vMA at `/usr/share/doc/vmware-viperl/samples`. Additional utility scripts for assisting development of Perl applications can be found at `/usr/lib/vmware-viperl/apps` in the vMA's file structure. Refer to the documentation for their location when you install the Perl toolkit on a Windows server or desktop. SDK documentation can be found at `http://www.vmware.com/sdk`.

Index

Note to the Reader: Throughout this index **boldfaced** page numbers indicate primary discussions of a topic. *Italicized* page numbers indicate illustrations.